– VOLUME I –

THE
HONOURABLE
LADIES

— VOLUME I —

THE
HONOURABLE
LADIES

PROFILES OF WOMEN MPs 1918–1996

EDITED BY

IAIN DALE & JACQUI SMITH

Biteback Publishing

First published in Great Britain in 2018 by
Biteback Publishing Ltd
Westminster Tower
3 Albert Embankment
London SE1 7SP
Selection and editorial apparatus copyright © Iain Dale and Jacqui Smith 2018

ISBN 978-1-78590-244-4

10 9 8 7 6 5 4 3 2 1

A CIP catalogue record for this book is available from the British Library.

Set in Adobe Garamond Pro and Bodoni

Printed and bound in Great Britain by
CPI Group (UK) Ltd, Croydon CR0 4YY

CONTENTS

FOREWORD

THE RT HON. THERESA MAY MP, PRIME MINISTER

This year, in which we mark the centenary of the first women winning the right to cast their vote in the United Kingdom, has been an important opportunity to pay tribute to all those who drove progress towards that important milestone, to celebrate those who led the march for further advances in the century since, and to take stock of the work that still remains to be done.

A century ago women were forbidden the franchise, could not sit on a jury and could not be admitted into the professions. Today, the United Kingdom's most senior judge is a woman. The Commissioner of the Metropolitan Police is a woman. Women are at the helm of the National Crime Agency and the London Fire Brigade. The current Chief Medical Officer is a woman. The Confederation of British Industry, the National Farmers' Union and the Trades Union Congress are all headed by women. At Holyrood, a female First Minister debates against a female opposition leader. In the National Assembly for Wales, a woman leads the third party and another is Presiding Officer. The two largest parties in Northern Ireland are led by women. And at Westminster, where suffragettes chained themselves to statues and one among their number hid in a broom cupboard on census night, the leaders of the House of Commons and the House of Lords are women. Black Rod, whose early predecessor ejected suffragettes from the palace precincts, is also a woman.

So, in this year of commemoration and celebration, I am delighted that Iain Dale and Jacqui Smith – our first female Home Secretary – have compiled this fascinating collective biography of the 491 women who have been elected as Members of Parliament. To read their stories and achievements is by turns humbling, inspiring and uplifting – showing how the efforts of those first women to enter the House of Commons have each made it that little bit easier for those who have followed. I am sure that all of us who have had the privilege of serving in Parliament have been conscious of the extra responsibility we have to encourage other women to take their full and rightful place in our democracy.

That was one of the things that inspired me to set up Women2Win with Anne (now Baroness) Jenkin. I was first elected to Parliament in 1997. The general election of that year marked a watershed in female representation, bringing seventy-one new women into the House of Commons and doubling the number of female MPs. It is no accident that this book's two volumes hinge around that date – a great testament to the work of passionate advocates such as Harriet Harman, now the Mother of the House of Commons. But my own party's poor result meant that I was one of just thirteen female Conservative MPs. Indeed, I told the story in my maiden speech of how a Labour MP rushed up to me in the Members' Lobby during my first days in Westminster and encouraged me to put my name on the list for the ballot for Private Members' Bills. I was a little surprised at this generous display of nonpartisanship – but not as surprised as he was when he realised that he had mistaken me for one of the ladies on the Labour benches.

So I am very proud of the role that Women2Win has played in bringing talented Conservative women into Parliament – doubling the number of female Conservative MPs in its first decade, and making sure the Conservative Party fielded its highest-ever proportion of female candidates at the last election – though there is still much further to go.

Until December 2016, the number of women *ever* elected was still smaller than the number of men currently in Parliament. I am delighted that we have now broken that barrier with the elections of Caroline Johnson, who equalled that number, and Trudy Harrison, who surpassed it for the first time.

Last year's general election saw 208 women elected – a record high, and the highest proportion of women elected in any UK election so far. I am proud to serve as the UK's second female Prime Minister in a Parliament with more female MPs than ever before. But I want that number to continue to climb – so that marking future anniversaries of women's suffrage with a book like this is soon too daunting a task for even the most intrepid of historians.

Prime Minister Theresa May
10 Downing Street, July 2018

PREFACE

IAIN DALE

It is incredible to think that in the century since women were first allowed to stand for Parliament, only 491 have been elected. Given that there are 650 MPs in the House of Commons at any one time – that is an astounding statistic. I suspect that there have been more than 491 MPs called David or John over the last 100 years.

Jacqui Smith and I had the idea for this book in 2016, and have spent the last two years commissioning 168 essays on the women elected to the House of Commons between 1918 and 1996. Volume II, which will be published in the autumn of 2019, will contain biographies of the 323 women elected since 1997.

We decided to commission only women to write the biographies. I am the token male in the production of the book! Its editor and publicist at Biteback are also both women.

Jacqui and I would like to thank the 120 women who have contributed the essays to this book. Most have written a single entry, but I'd especially like to thank Oonagh Gay, Mary Honeyball, Julia Langdon, Linda McDougall, Sarah MacKinlay and Elizabeth Vallance for their efforts in writing several entries each.

We would also like to thank Bernadette Marron at Biteback for tackling the herculean task of putting the book together and editing it so well. Having said that I am the token male involved in bringing this book to press, I do have a fellow traveller: Namkwan Cho has done a fantastic job in designing the cover and typesetting the text.

Naturally, every contributor has a different writing style, and we make no apology for that, and we hope you enjoy the variety. Some of our authors know or knew their subjects and were encouraged to include personal reminiscences and judgements. We didn't want this to be an academic exercise, we hoped to bring some of these remarkable characters to life. As we went through the proofing process, it was clear that we have uncovered some absolute gems – women whose achievements have been hidden for decades. Who knew that Patricia Ford, an Ulster Unionist MP for two years in the 1950s, had a stepson who was to become a minister in the Blair government, and whose son-in-law went on to be a Tory MP. Not only that, but that Tory MP had a son called Bear – Bear Grylls. Well done to Sarah MacKinlay for unearthing that particular nugget. And there are plenty more.

At the time of writing, we are busy commissioning essays for Volume II. So far we have found authors for around half of the 323 MP profiles. Should this volume inspire you to want to contribute to the next one, please contact me via email at iain@iaindale.com.

Given the length of the book and the subject matter, it is inevitable that there will be a few errors. We take full responsibility for mistakes and hope you will point them out to us so they can be corrected in any reprint. If you spot anything please email me.

We very much hope you enjoy the book.

Iain Dale
Tunbridge Wells, August 2018

PREFACE

JACQUI SMITH

The day of 8 December 2016 was a momentous one for women's representation in the House of Commons. Nearly 100 years after the first woman was elected to Parliament, Dr Caroline Johnson's victory in the Sleaford and North Hykeham by-election meant that she became the 455th woman elected to the House of Commons. On that same day, there were 455 male MPs sitting in the House. It had taken ninety-eight years for the number of women who had ever been elected to equal that of the number of men sitting in the Commons on a single day.

At the time of my first successful election in 1997, 120 women were elected to Parliament. The fact that Labour had more than 100 women MPs for the first time was celebrated with the famous Blair's Babes photo. The reality, however, was that women still constituted just 18 per cent of all MPs. This was still some progress.

So, why has progress in women's parliamentary representation been so slow in the House of Commons? And what factors led to the quickening of progress in recent years?

The first woman elected to Parliament was Constance Markievicz, who was a Sinn Féin candidate for Dublin St Patrick's. At the time of the election, Markievicz was in Holloway Prison and, like other Sinn Féin representatives, refused to take up her seat in the Commons. This was a mere three weeks after the passing of the Parliament (Qualification of Women) Act 1918 on 21 November 1918. Seventeen women stood in that 1918 election, including suffragette Christabel Pankhurst, who contested Smethwick and polled over 8,000 votes.

The first woman MP to actually take up her seat was Nancy Astor in December 1919. Like several of the women featured in this book, she had a close family link to her Plymouth Sutton constituency, effectively inheriting the seat when her husband had to give it up to succeed his father's peerage.

In 1921, Liberal Margaret Wintringham became the second sitting female MP when she was elected in a by-election in Louth. The first female Labour MPs were elected in the 1923 general election with one of them, Margaret Bondfield, going on to become the first female Cabinet minister and a member of the Privy Council in 1929 when she became Minister of Labour.

Election	Conservative	Labour	Liberal/Lib Dem	SNP	Others	Total	% of total MPs elected
1918	0	0	0	0	1	1	0.1
1922	1	0	1	0	0	2	0.3
1923	3	3	2	0	0	8	1.3
1924	3	1	0	0	0	4	0.7
1929	3	9	1	0	1	14	2.3
1931	13	0	1	0	1	15	2.4
1935	6	1	1	0	1	9	1.5
1945	1	21	1	0	1	24	3.8
1950	6	14	1	0	0	21	3.4
1951	6	11	0	0	0	17	2.7
1955	10	14	0	0	0	24	3.8
1959	12	13	0	0	0	25	4
1964	11	18	0	0	0	29	4.6
1966	7	19	0	0	1	27	4.1
1970	15	10	0	0	0	25	4.1
1974 Feb	9	13	0	1	0	23	3.6
1974 Oct	7	18	0	2	0	27	4.3
1979	8	11	0	0	0	19	3
1983	13	10	0	0	0	23	3.5
1987	17	21	2	1	0	41	6.3
1992	20	37	2	1	0	60	9.2
1997	13	101	3	2	1	120	18.2
2001	14	95	5	0	4	118	17.9
2005	17	98	10	0	3	128	19.8
2010	49	81	7	1	5	143	22
2015	68	99	0	20	1	188	29
2017	67	119	4	12	7	208	32

This table shows the number of women MPs elected across all parties since 1918.

Just as the end of the First World War brought major reform to women's parliamentary representation, so the 1945 election, at the end of the Second World War, saw a significant jump in the number of women elected. The high point for Conservative women MPs up until then had been the thirteen elected in 1931. In 1945, Labour welcomed a new generation of women MPs with twenty-one elected, including those who would make major contributions in government and the Labour movement – women such as Alice Bacon, Barbara Castle and Bessie Braddock.

In 1948, Florence Paton became the first woman nominated to the Chairman's Panel and thus able to preside over committees. In this capacity, she was the first woman to serve as chair in the Chamber of the House of Commons in a committee session of the whole House. However, as it was a committee session, she sat at the Table rather than in the Speaker's Chair. It was not until after 1970, when Betty Harvie Anderson became Deputy Speaker, that a woman presided over the Chamber. In 1992, the redoubtable Betty Boothroyd became the first female Speaker of the House of Commons.

The Whips' Office is often seen as an aggressively male operation, but the job of a whip involves persuasion, pastoral support and 'encouragement' to vote in the right direction – things that women are more than capable of. Harriet Slater became the first female whip in 1964 and Ann Taylor was made the first female Chief Whip in 1998, having served during the turbulent days of tiny and non-existent majorities during the 1970s.

In 1975, Margaret Thatcher took over the leadership of the Conservative Party and became the UK's first female Prime Minister in 1979.

Despite these notable steps, it is remarkable how little progress was made in increasing women's representation in Parliament during the first seventy years after women won the right to stand for election. They remained in a tiny minority. It was not until 1987 that the proportion of female MPs rose above 5 per cent – one in twenty. The women in this volume of *The Honourable Ladies* are the pioneers of women's representation. They had to endure the isolation, inadequate facilities and discrimination of a Parliament dominated by men. How they overcame these challenges is a fascinating theme throughout the following profiles.

Election	Conservative	Labour	Liberal/Lib Dems	SNP	Others	Total	% of total parliamentary candidates
1918	1	4	4	0	8	17	1
1922	5	10	16	0	2	33	2.3
1923	7	14	12	0	1	34	2.4
1924	12	22	6	0	1	41	2.9
1929	10	30	25	0	4	69	4

1931	16	36	5	1	4	62	4.8
1935	19	33	11	0	4	67	5
1945	14	41	20	0	12	87	5.2
1950	29	42	45	0	2	118	6.8
1951	25	41	11	0	1	78	5.6
1955	33	43	14	0	2	92	6.5
1959	28	36	16	0	1	81	5.3
1964	24	33	24	0	9	90	5.1
1966	21	30	20	0	10	81	4.7
1970	26	29	23	10	11	99	5.4
1974 Feb	33	40	40	8	22	143	6.7
1974 Oct	30	50	49	8	24	161	7.1
1979	31	52	52	6	64	205	8.4
1983	40	78	75	9	78	280	10.9
1987	46	92	106	6	79	329	14.2
1992	63	138	143	15	214	573	19.3
1997	69	157	140	15	291	672	18
2001	92	149	139	16	240	636	19.2
2005	122	166	144	13	275	720	20.3
2010	153	191	134	17	379	874	21.1
2015	169	214	166	20	464	1033	24.7
2017	186	256	191	20	310	973	29.4

This table shows the number of women who have stood for election to Parliament in every general election since 1918, the year that women were first permitted to stand.

It was not until after the mid-1990s that any real breakthrough in representation happened. For Labour, this came in 1997 when the party implemented a quota policy with all-women shortlists for 50 per cent of their winnable seats. More than 100 Labour women were elected to Parliament and the proportion of female MPs increased from 9.2 per cent at the previous election to 18.2 per cent. Interestingly, the ruling of the all-women shortlists policy as illegal saw a fall in the proportion of women MPs elected in 2001. It was not until 2005, when the government had legislated to allow this type of positive action, that the numbers increased again. Other parties rejected this type of approach, but the Conservatives made considerable progress in 2010 when the number of Conservative women MPs rose from seventeen to forty-nine.

A programme of support, and the leadership shown by David Cameron and Theresa May, seems to have been at the heart of the increase.

While the Conservatives can boast the first sitting woman MP and two female Prime Ministers, Labour easily outstrips them in terms of representation, with 45 per cent of their MPs being women in 2017 against 21 per cent for the Conservatives and 33 per cent and 34 per cent respectively for the Liberal Democrats and SNP. With 32 per cent of all MPs now women, the UK Parliament ranks fortieth in the world league table of women's representation. With many of our European neighbours ranked above us – as well as countries such as Rwanda, Namibia and Senegal – there is no room for complacency. Single-member, first-past-the-post elections make methods such as equal lists and 'zipping', where women and men are alternated on candidate lists, impossible, but surely we can't be satisfied with our lowly international position.

While you will learn about many strong and influential women in this volume, you will also discover that their contributions have often gone unreported, or that credit for their efforts has gone to the men they worked with. Women MPs have helped shape all areas of public policy and served their constituents with distinction. And from the very start they were arguing for many of the issues – equal rights and pay, childcare and protection from male violence – that would only be properly addressed when there was a critical mass of women in Parliament and government. Whichever party they belonged to, these MPs were crucial in representing the voices and interests of all women. Those of us who came later should be proud to be standing on their shoulders.

Jacqui Smith
Malvern, August 2018

PARLIAMENTARY FIRSTS FOR WOMEN

This timeline charts a number of 'firsts' and significant events over the last century for women in Parliament and political life.

1907	Qualification of Women (County and Borough Councils) Act permitting women to become county and borough councillors – many women stood in 1 November elections
1908	Elected mayor in England (Elizabeth Garrett Anderson)
1918	Women were able to stand for Parliament and those over thirty, who met minimum property qualifications, were given the right to vote
1918	MP elected (Countess Constance Markievicz)
1919	Member of Parliament to take her seat (Nancy Astor)
1924	Minister (Margaret Bondfield)
1928	Vote given to women on the same terms as men
1929	Cabinet minister and privy counsellor (Margaret Bondfield)
1948	Chair of Committee of Whole House (Florence Paton)
1958	Life Peerages Act, which allowed the first women life peers to take their seats (Lady Reading and Baroness Wootton)
1964	Parliamentary whip (Commons) (Harriet Slater)
1965	Parliamentary whip (Lords) (Baroness Phillips)
1967	Deputy Speaker (Lords) (Baroness Wootton)

1970	Deputy Speaker (Commons) (Betty Harvie Anderson)
1975	Leader of the Opposition (Margaret Thatcher)
1979	Prime Minister (Margaret Thatcher)
1981	Leader of the House of Lords (Baroness Young)
1992	Speaker of the House of Commons (Betty Boothroyd)
1997	Secretary of State for Northern Ireland (Mo Mowlam)
1997	Leader of the House of Commons (Ann Taylor)
1997	Full-time Minister for Women (Joan Ruddock)
1998	Chief Whip (Ann Taylor)
2001	Secretary of State for Scotland (Helen Liddell)
2006	Secretary of State for Foreign and Commonwealth Affairs (Margaret Beckett)
2006	House of Lords Lord Speaker (Baroness Hayman)
2007	Secretary of State for Home Affairs (Jacqui Smith)
2007	Attorney-General (Baroness Scotland)
2009	EU High Representative for Foreign Affairs & Security Policy (Baroness Ashton)
2010	Secretary of State for Wales (Cheryl Gillan)
2014	First Minister of Scotland (Nicola Sturgeon)
2016	Lord Chancellor (Liz Truss)
2017	Black Rod (Sarah Clarke)

WOMEN IN PARLIAMENT

The 1918 general election was the first in which women were permitted to stand for Parliament. Out of 1,631 parliamentary candidates, seventeen were women – one Conservative, four Labour, four Liberals and eight others. And it wasn't until 1997 that women as a proportion of all candidates would rise above 10 per cent – even up until the late 1980s the proportion had always been below 5 per cent. The 1997 general election saw female representation increase to 18 per cent, following the election of 120 women MPs. Before the 1997 general election, women MPs had never made up more than 10 per cent of the total number of MPs. The 2017 general election brought the highest-ever proportion (32 per cent) of women to the Commons.

Since 1918, 491 women have been elected as Members of the House of Commons. Four were elected as Sinn Féin MPs and did not take their seats: Countess Constance Markievicz (1918), Michelle Gildernew (2001), Elisha McCallion (2017) and Órfhlaith Begley (2018). Of the 491 women, 284 (58 per cent) were first elected as Labour MPs and 140 (29 per cent) as Conservatives. Forty-five of these 491 women MPs have gone on to serve as Cabinet ministers.

*　　*　　*

There were many triumphs for women in the 2017 general election; Preet Gill became the first female Sikh MP to join the Commons after her election in Birmingham Edgbaston, while Marsha de Cordova, a disability rights campaigner who is registered as blind, took the safe Conservative seat of Battersea for Labour. Lib Dem Layla Moran's election in Oxford & West Abingdon made her the first female Lib Dem MP to come from a minority background and the first UK MP of Palestinian descent.

A total of 973 women candidates across all parties stood in the 2017 general election – 29 per cent of the total number of 3,304 candidates. Although this marked a numeric fall in the number of female parliamentary candidates from the 1,033 that had stood at the 2015 election, there was still a percentage increase in the proportion of women standing.

This was a landmark election for Labour, who fielded the highest number

(256) of women candidates of any party at any general election. The proportion of Labour female parliamentary candidates rose from 34 per cent in 2015 to 41 per cent in 2017. There were 184 female Conservative candidates – 29 per cent of the party's total – marking the highest number in the party's history and a 9 per cent increase on 2015. There were also 184 women candidates (29 per cent) representing the Liberal Democrats. Thirty-four per cent of the Scottish National Party's candidates were women, 35 per cent of the Green Party's, 28 per cent of Plaid Cymru's and 13 per cent of UKIP's.

A higher proportion of women candidates contested Labour's safer seats (those with a 20 to 30 per cent majority), at 51 per cent, compared with 26 per cent for the Conservatives. However, 43 per cent of Conservative candidates in the most winnable seats (those with a 0 to 10 per cent majority held by another party) were women, compared with 33 per cent of Labour candidates. This indicated a rise for the Conservatives and a fall for Labour; in 2015, the opposite held true. Labour also fielded a higher proportion of women candidates in marginal seats. In seats with a 0 to 10 per cent marginality, 47 per cent of Labour candidates were women, as opposed to 20 per cent of Conservative candidates. Fifty-six per cent of female Lib Dem candidates stood in marginal seats.

There are currently 119 women Labour MPs (45 per cent of all Labour MPs), more than every other party combined. The Conservatives have sixty-seven women MPs, three fewer than before the 2017 election, and the SNP twelve. The Lib Dems, who had no female MPs in 2015, now have four, while a further seven women represent smaller parties and independents. These women make up 32 per cent of all the MPs in Parliament.

In the Scottish Parliament, 36 per cent of the members are women, compared to 42 per cent of the members of the National Assembly for Wales and 30 per cent of the members of the Northern Ireland Assembly. Following the 2014 European Parliament elections, 41 per cent of UK MEPs are women.

However, despite significant progress, according to the Inter-Parliamentary Union's global league table, the UK ranks only thirty-eighth in the world in terms of female representation in Parliament – falling behind several European nations. Rwanda tops the list, followed by Bolivia, Cuba and Iceland. Five countries in the rankings have no women in their lower or single house, while thirty have fewer than 10 per cent. There are currently female Presidents or Prime Ministers in only sixteen countries – 9 per cent of the 193 countries who are currently members of the UN.

CONSTANCE MARKIEVICZ, COUNTESS MARKIEVICZ

JULIA LANGDON

- FULL NAME: Constance Georgine Markievicz (née Gore-Booth), Countess Markievicz
- DATE OF BIRTH: 4 February 1868
- PLACE OF BIRTH: London
- DATE OF DEATH: 15 July 1927
- MARRIED TO: Count Casimir Dunin-Markievicz (m. 1900)
- CHILDREN: Maeve Alys and Stanislaus (stepson)
- UNSUCCESSFUL ELECTIONS FOUGHT: None
- CONSTITUENCY: Dublin St Patrick's
- DATE OF FIRST ELECTION: 28 December 1918
- DATE LEFT PARLIAMENT: As a member for Sinn Féin, Markievicz never took her seat in Parliament
- PARTY ROLES: None
- MINISTERIAL POSITIONS & DATES: None in the UK government. In the First Dáil Éireann: Minister for Labour 1919–22
- MOST FAMOUS QUOTATION: 'Dress suitably in short skirts and strong boots, leave your jewels in the bank and buy a revolver.'

Constance Markievicz was in Holloway, serving her second spell in jail, when she made history and was elected to the House of Commons, so she couldn't have taken her seat in Parliament, even if she had wanted to. All seventy-three Sinn Féin MPs elected to Westminster in 1918 were committed abstentionists, who wanted independence from Britain, not a seat in its Parliament. 'I would never take an oath of allegiance to the power that I meant to overthrow,' she wrote in her election address, which was smuggled out of her cell.

Markievicz was a serious revolutionary, albeit an unlikely one. Born into

1

Anglo-Irish Protestant privilege, she was one of five children of Sir Henry Gore-Booth, a land-owning fifth baronet. Despite their acres, the Gore-Booths possessed nonetheless a social conscience. Markievicz's political inspiration was the 'dispossessed people' in her 'desolate home county' of Sligo, and as a young woman she had encouraged her father's tenants not to pay their rents. They needed the money more than he did, she said.

Perhaps her parents thought it was just youthful idealism, but they would soon learn otherwise. Markievicz was presented at Court and trained as an artist in Paris, where she met her Polish-Ukrainian husband, Casimir. However, the early bohemian grew into something much more bolshie. She was a passionate, articulate woman who wanted to do something for the people of Ireland – so she picked up the gun.

Markievicz met with revolutionary patriots and joined groups campaigning for independence from British rule, nationalism and women's suffrage. She was also an active member of Sinn Féin and the Daughters of Erin, which she affectionately referred to as 'the women's rebel society'. She went to her first meeting of the women's group straight from a society event, wearing a blue velvet ball gown with a train and a diamond tiara – she even offered to sell the diamonds to fund a rebel newspaper. Although some may have been suspicious of her at first due to her privileged upbringing, Markievicz won people over easily. She was beautiful, vivacious, witty and kind, and even inspired W. B. Yeats to compare her to a gazelle in a poem. But Markievicz wasn't just a pretty face: she meant business, too.

As Irish unrest rumbled and political discontent grew, Markievicz founded Fianna Éireann, a sort of paramilitary boy scouts where teenagers were taught how to use firearms. In 1908, when Winston Churchill, then a Liberal, was standing in a parliamentary by-election, she went to support her suffragist sister, Eva Gore-Booth, who was campaigning against Churchill because he wouldn't support the rights of women workers. A superb equestrian, Markievicz drove a carriage pulled by four white horses along the streets of Manchester all day long and half the night to promote the women's cause. Churchill lost his seat.

Back in Dublin, Markievicz joined the Irish Citizen Army, burned the British flag and was arrested. She ran soup kitchens in troubled times and she used her wealth to help people and to fund their politics.

None of this went down well with her family in Sligo. While Mama got on with being a revolutionary, Maeve Alys, Markievicz's daughter, was raised by her Gore-Booth grandparents. The 'Count' – it seems to have been an assumed title – left Ireland for the Balkans, where he was a war reporter, before returning home for good to Eastern Europe, although the couple remained friendly. In revolutionary circles, Markievicz became known as 'Madame Markievicz', applauded for her daring and her physical courage. When the Easter Rising erupted in 1916, 'Year One of Irish History', Markievicz was equivalent to second in command. She should have been shot with the rebellion's other leaders, but her death sentence was commuted to life imprisonment on the grounds of her sex. 'I do wish your lot had the decency to shoot me,' she observed plangently. She kissed her revolver before handing it over when she was arrested. This would be her first jail sentence and she served fourteen months, mostly in Aylesbury prison, before being released under an amnesty. She used the time wisely, as she always did during her several spells behind bars. 'I have my health,' she reassured her sister, 'and I can always find a way to give my dreams a living form.' She would paint, if they gave her materials, or she would do gardening, or she would study political systems.

Upon returning home to Ireland, Markievicz was greeted with a heroine's welcome and received into the Roman Catholic church – but it wouldn't be long before she was back behind bars. Interestingly, she was not unaware that her imprisonment and the publicity it provoked did as much for the cause as the power of her rhetoric in her speeches. When Sinn Féin proposed that she stand as a parliamentary candidate in the 1918 general election, she agreed to do so for 'sport', even though she was in prison. 'You will have to fight without me,' she wrote. It was, of course, the first general election that allowed women to stand as candidates and there were a total of sixteen in Britain and Ireland. Upon learning that she had won – the only woman to do so – having defeated William Field, the sitting MP for twenty-six years, by more than twice his vote, she was 'yelling and dancing all over the place'. She got out of jail three months later, in March 1919, by which time she was already an absentee member of the First Dáil – the Parliament of the revolutionary Irish republic set up by Sinn Féin. For the next three years, she was Minister for Labour and the first woman Cabinet minister in western Europe, but this did not keep her out of jail. Markievicz served several more spells inside, during the continuing difficulties of the founding of the Irish state, and was elected for the last time, in 1927, to what became the Fifth Dáil. She died within weeks of the election as a result of complications from appendicitis.

Markievicz never submitted. But as the country's first woman MP, she did go once to the House of Commons. When she got out of prison after her election, she went to the Commons to inspect her name on the coat peg in the Members' cloakroom – before returning home to fight again for Ireland.

NANCY ASTOR, VISCOUNTESS ASTOR

NAN SLOANE

- FULL NAME: Nancy Witcher Astor (formerly Shaw, née Langhorne), Viscountess Astor
- DATE OF BIRTH: 19 May 1879
- PLACE OF BIRTH: Danville, Virginia, USA
- DATE OF DEATH: 2 May 1964
- MARRIED TO: Robert Gould Shaw (m. 1897; div. 1903); Waldorf Astor (m. 1906; d. 1952)
- CHILDREN: Robert (Bobbie) Gould Shaw; William Waldorf Astor; Nancy Phyllis Louise Astor; Francis David Langhorne Astor; Michael Langhorne Astor; and John Jacob (Jakie) Astor
- UNSUCCESSFUL ELECTIONS FOUGHT: None
- CONSTITUENCY: Plymouth Sutton
- DATE OF FIRST ELECTION: 28 November 1919
- DATE LEFT PARLIAMENT: 5 July 1945
- PARTY ROLES: None
- MINISTERIAL POSITIONS & DATES: None
- MOST FAMOUS QUOTATIONS: 'I married beneath me. All women do.' | 'One reason why I don't drink is because I wish to know when I am having a good time.' | 'Women have got to make the world safe for men since men have made it so darned unsafe for women.' | 'The main dangers in this life are people who want to change everything… or nothing.' | 'If you are never to speak because you are afraid to cause offence, you will never say anything. I am not in the least afraid of causing offence.' | 'I would like to say that the first time Adam had a chance he laid the blame on a woman.' | 'Pioneers may be picturesque figures, but they are often rather lonely ones.'

At about twenty minutes past nine on the evening of Tuesday 24 February 1920, a soberly dressed woman of thirty-nine got to her feet in a room full of men. She began speaking with a few observations about courage, adventure and the city of Plymouth, before moving on to the subject of temperance and the sale of alcohol. The men heckled enthusiastically, but the woman kept going. At about nine thirty-five she sat down again.

As maiden parliamentary speeches went, Nancy Astor's was not particularly remarkable, but it was historic. She was the first woman to take her seat in the House of Commons, and the first to speak from the green benches. But she was also an outsider; born and raised in America, she spoke, not with the cut-glass accent of the upper classes, but with the soft drawl of the American South.

Astor was born in Danville, Virginia, on 19 May 1879. She was the eighth child born to railway millionaire Chiswell Dabney Langhorne and his wife, Nancy. The young Astor received a rudimentary but adequate education before being packed off to a New York finishing school. There she met Robert Gould Shaw, whom she married in 1897, when she was just eighteen. The couple had a son, Bobbie, but Shaw was abusive and the marriage was miserable. Astor first attempted to leave Shaw while still on their honeymoon, but was only successful in 1901. Her divorce was finalised following her mother's death in 1903.

By 1905 Astor had decided to emigrate to England, where many an American heiress had already found happiness, or at least a titled husband and a country house. Given Astor's unhappy marriage, she may not have been actively looking for a husband so soon after her divorce, but she met Waldorf Astor on the ship over from New York and they were married in May 1906.

Waldorf's family had made their money in hotels and his father, William, had settled in England, becoming a newspaper owner and making massive donations to charity. Ostensibly in recognition of this, he was later awarded a peerage. In 1893 he had bought a house and estate at Cliveden in Buckinghamshire from the Duke of Westminster, and this was his wedding present to Waldorf and Nancy. It became their country home and the scene of Nancy's famous house parties. Later, in the 1930s, it became synonymous with the couple's controversial support for appeasement.

Nancy and Waldorf Astor had five children, and Nancy adopted the life of a rich socialite. Waldorf harboured political aspirations and, in the second election of 1910, he was elected one of two MPs for Plymouth. Nancy had entered into the campaigning with enthusiasm, particularly enjoying contact with the electorate. However, she fell easily into the traditional role of political wife, and most of her energies were spent organising their social life. Even here, however, she showed an early taste for controversy, inviting political opponents as well as allies to both dinners and house parties. Both Sylvia Pankhurst and Winston Churchill graced her table at one time or another; the former was a suffragette and noted feminist while the latter was firmly opposed to women's political rights. Neither declined their invitations.

Astor had always been of a religious turn of mind, and in 1914 she suddenly announced her conversion to Christian Science. As with many things, she took to it with rather more enthusiasm than wisdom; her attempt to convert Stalin to the religion, when she visited Russia in 1931, stands out as one of the more unlikely of her enterprises. Astor remained committed to her faith for the rest of her life and clearly found much comfort in it.

When war broke out in 1914, Waldorf Astor joined the army, rising to the rank of major. He remained an MP, however, and, in 1916, he became Lloyd George's parliamentary private secretary, acting as the Prime Minister's link to the Conservative back benches. He and Nancy held political views that ranged across party lines, and Waldorf had supported Lloyd George's pre-war People's Budget in defiance of his own party whip. By the end of the war it was clear that Waldorf had a promising political career before him, therefore the death of his father in 1919 came as a political as well as a personal blow.

Although he tried to get out of it, Waldorf's elevation to his father's peerage was unavoidable. With Waldorf joining the Lords, the question then arose of who should be the candidate in the resulting by-election in Plymouth Sutton, the constituency that he had represented since 1918. Nancy was the obvious answer, and she was happy to step into the breach. She loved campaigning and was good at talking to people as well as speaking in public and dealing with hecklers. She positioned herself as a good wife who was not ambitious on her own account, and voters were taken with the idea of a rich American society lady becoming their MP. She was elected with 51 per cent of the vote and a healthy majority.

Having taken her seat, however, Nancy found herself in a new world in which she had to learn very quickly. For one thing, as the first woman MP in Parliament, people had massive expectations of her, as much in terms of failure as success. These came not least from women, who viewed her as their representative, regardless of where they lived. She was instantly inundated with letters from women seeking advice, help or support; some simply wanted to congratulate her and, at one stage, she was getting over 2,000 a week. Astor had had little involvement with the women's movement, and she now found politically experienced and influential women viewing her with open suspicion and hostility. In her maiden speech she said that 'women have got a vote now and we mean to use it, and use it wisely', but she began with almost no support from the women's leaders themselves. Sensibly, she made it her business to build bridges and did so by asking women's organisations to advise her, and engaging with a variety of groups and individuals.

Predictably, and not for the last time, the press obsessed over what the newly elected woman MP would wear. The fashion industry, too, viewed Astor as a marketing opportunity; when she arrived at the House of Commons, she found that the small room she had been allocated was full of hats that had been sent to her by hopeful milliners. Prior to her election she had dressed to impress, spending a fortune on gowns and jewellery. Astor, however, seems to have understood immediately the need to avoid her wardrobe becoming a point of endless discussion, so she originated what became, for many years, the female politician's uniform: dark suit, white blouse, plain hat and discreet jewellery.

In other respects she was more flamboyant. Her speaking style was not the most inspirational, but she was spectacularly good at dealing with hecklers, and revelled in the challenges of debate. She pursued an eclectic collection of issues, ranging across the political spectrum. She supported universal suffrage (achieved finally in 1928), women's employment rights, improved maternity care and better nursery provisions. She tried to get a Bill through to eliminate the phrase 'common prostitute' from the law and to prosecute men as well as women for prostitution offences. But, despite her own experience, she also opposed making divorce easier, and she was distinctly squeamish when it came to the debate about birth control.

One of her main concerns was temperance, and it was in this field that she had her biggest legislative success, banning the sale of alcohol to people under the age of eighteen in 1923. The powerful brewing industry took exception to this and ran a candidate against her in the 1922 election. He did not win, but her majority was significantly reduced.

Nancy Astor never became popular in the House of Commons, partly due to her refusal to conform to the norms that would have put the institution more at ease. She was a Conservative who, as Waldorf had done, was prepared to oppose her own party when she disagreed with it. She was combative and opinionated, and would not comply with the softer, more acquiescent model of womanhood that her male colleagues found acceptable.

On the other hand, although she frequently attacked the Labour Party, she tried to draw the tiny number of women MPs together to act as a group, even after 1929, when a Labour government brought in nine Labour women MPs who were trying to find their own identity and disliked as well as distrusted Astor.

By the 1930s it had become clear that she was not going to be offered a ministerial post, and, like many other people, she began to take an interest in foreign affairs, in particular Britain's relations with Germany. She and Waldorf continued to invite a wide range of people to dinner and to Cliveden, including many of those who believed that appeasing Hitler could avoid another war, and some who had forged close connections with the Nazi regime. Many of this group were influential and well connected in government and in the press. The Astor family owned both *The Observer* and *The Times*, and when Neville Chamberlain became Prime Minister in 1937, there was every reason to believe that appeasement could work. Astor herself was not a Nazi; in fact, when she met the German ambassador, Joachim von Ribbentrop, she allegedly irritated him so much that she ended up on a list of people to be arrested after a Nazi invasion. However, she undoubtedly facilitated the coming together of a circle of people who engaged in secret diplomacy and encouraged sympathy, at the very least, for Hitler's government. Like many other people at the time, Nancy was both anti-communist and anti-Semitic but, as so often, she tended to extremes and took no trouble to conceal her prejudices. The exposing of the so-called Cliveden set in the non-Astor media irretrievably damaged her reputation, and the declaration of war in 1939 finally and completely discredited appeasement.

Astor and Waldorf spent most of the Second World War in Plymouth, where he was mayor for five years. Their house was bombed, and Astor immersed herself in war work, supporting the navy and citizens in the city she represented. She remained a Member of Parliament, but was far removed from the spheres of influence and was regarded with suspicion in many quarters. Her family were adamant that she should not stand for re-election in 1945, warning her she risked defeat if she did. She did not want to retire, but in the end Waldorf simply informed her constituency association that she would be standing down. Labour's Lucy Middleton duly won the seat, although Astor's son John regained it for the Conservatives in 1951.

After 1945 Astor settled into an unhappy retirement. She and Waldorf separated for a time, but were reconciled before his death in 1952. She received very little recognition during her lifetime for her achievements, and new generations of women politicians did not come to regard her as their role model or matriarch. She died at her daughter's house in Lincolnshire in May 1964, a few days before her eighty-fifth birthday.

As with many women who are firsts in their field, Nancy Astor was an outsider who took an independent and individual line. She had courage, flair and intelligence, but unfortunately these qualities were marred by a tendency towards extreme opinions and a combative approach which some people found off-putting. She was not a feminist, but she supported many women's rights issues and was, until the election of Margaret Wintringham in 1921, the only female voice available to raise them. Although, now as then, some of Astor's views and actions make her a controversial and sometimes unsympathetic figure, she remains a powerful, remarkable and significant parliamentary pioneer.

MARGARET WINTRINGHAM

MARY HONEYBALL

- FULL NAME: Margaret Wintringham (née Longbottom)
- DATE OF BIRTH: 4 August 1879
- PLACE OF BIRTH: Oldfield, West Yorkshire
- DATE OF DEATH: 10 March 1955
- MARRIED TO: Thomas Wintringham (m. 1903; d. 1921)
- CHILDREN: None
- UNSUCCESSFUL ELECTIONS FOUGHT: Louth 1929 and Aylesbury 1935
- CONSTITUENCY: Louth
- DATE OF FIRST ELECTION: 22 September 1921
- DATE LEFT PARLIAMENT: 29 October 1924
- PARTY ROLES: Member of the National Executive of the National Liberal Federation, elected 1927; president of the Women's National Liberal Federation 1925–26; president of the Louth Women's Liberal Association
- MINISTERIAL POSITIONS & DATES: None
- MOST FAMOUS QUOTATION: 'I have found the judgement of the average woman clearer than the average man.' – Presidential address to Women's National Liberal Federation on 22 June 1926.

It is a shame that the first UK-born woman to be elected and take her seat in the House of Commons, Margaret Wintringham, is virtually unknown today. Although Wintringham took over the seat of Louth in Lincolnshire when it became vacant due to the sudden death of her husband, Thomas, in August 1921, she was much more than a widow continuing her husband's work.

Wintringham described herself as a feminist, stating in her address as president of the Women's National Liberal Federation in 1926 that 'the vital thing is to understand the issues which are the greatest moment to the happiness and welfare of the people'.

Born in Oldfield, West Yorkshire, in 1879, Margaret Longbottom attended

Keighley Grammar School before training to be a teacher, eventually becoming headmistress of a school in Grimsby. In 1903, she married timber merchant Thomas Wintringham and they settled in Louth, Lincolnshire.

Margaret was involved in the local community, even founding a branch of the Women's Institute. During the First World War, she was a member of the Lincolnshire Agriculture Committee and chaired the Woman's War Agriculture Committee. Wintringham's local prominence may well have contributed to her husband's success in winning the Louth parliamentary seat in a by-election in June 1920.

First elected in September 1921, Wintringham held the seat in both the 1922 and 1923 general elections but lost in 1924. Her parliamentary career, though brief, broke new ground to such an extent that the *New York Times* covered her maiden speech, which savaged the public expenditure cuts made by the Lloyd George coalition as a 'false economy'.

On the left of the Liberal Party, issues affecting women and children were Wintringham's main concern. She introduced a Private Members' Bill to make the provision of child support more egalitarian. She also asked parliamentary questions about women's pay and employment conditions; the Hong Kong authorities' inability to tackle child slavery and prostitution; the dismissal on economic grounds of Fiji's only woman maternity doctor; and the Canadian authorities' failure to extract maintenance payments from former World War One soldiers who had fathered illegitimate children in the UK.

Her emphasis on social issues, together with her contempt for the male boorishness of the House of Commons, made Wintringham appear as a wild radical to many. However, there is little evidence that this affected her electability, since she increased her majority in the 1922 and 1923 general elections. Her defeat in 1924 was undoubtedly due to national anti-Liberal feeling.

Wintringham seems never to have recovered from losing her seat and failing to be re-elected to the House of Commons. By the 1930s, she had disappeared from the upper echelons of the Liberal Party. She died in 1955, aged seventy-five, in a nursing home in London.

MABEL PHILIPSON

ANNE-MARIE TREVELYAN

- FULL NAME: Mabel Philipson (née Russell)
- DATE OF BIRTH: 1 January 1887
- PLACE OF BIRTH: Peckham
- DATE OF DEATH: 8 January 1951
- MARRIED TO: Thomas Rhodes (m. 1911; d. 1911); Hilton Philipson (m. 1917; d. 1941)
- CHILDREN: Peter and Anne Rosemary
- UNSUCCESSFUL ELECTIONS FOUGHT: None
- CONSTITUENCY: Berwick-upon-Tweed
- DATE OF FIRST ELECTION: 31 May 1923
- DATE LEFT PARLIAMENT: 29 May 1929
- PARTY ROLES: None
- MINISTERIAL POSITIONS & DATES: None
- MOST FAMOUS QUOTATION: 'The reason why I have held the seat has ceased to exist.' – Philipson had hoped to remain in Parliament until her husband, who had previously held the seat, was able to return.

Mabel Philipson had never planned to go into politics. Following a career as a music hall actress, she married Thomas Rhodes, whose family were cotton manufacturers, in 1911. Sadly, the couple were involved in a car crash only months after their wedding; he was killed and she was severely injured, leading to the loss of sight in one of her eyes.

After her husband's death, Philipson returned to the theatre, turning her focus to more serious roles in plays. She appeared at the Haymarket Theatre in 1913 and was cast as the leading lady in the 1916 production of *London Pride* at Wyndham's Theatre.

In 1917 she married Hilton Philipson, a serving officer in the Scots Guards. Hilton was a director of the North East Railway Company after the war, and stood as the Liberal candidate for Berwick-upon-Tweed in the 1922 election, which he subsequently won. However, due his agent committing election fraud, his election resulted in a petition and he was forced to stand down; Mabel stood in his stead in the by-election in May 1923.

Philipson was only the third female MP to take up her seat in the House of Commons. Not only was she an advocate for women and children in need of better protections under the law, but she also acted as a voice for her constituency.

She supported farmers who were facing insolvency and local fishermen in need of support: 'I would like to ask the right hon. Gentleman whether he will shortly consider a scheme to help the English fishermen when there is a real need, and a real need can be shown just the same [as for the Scottish].' Words that could just as likely be directed by me to the incumbent Secretary of State for Environment, Food and Rural Affairs today.

Philipson challenged the problems faced by Alnwick Council, such as the slow progress of the sale of council land for housing, and the eternal question put forward to ministers: 'whether he will consider the allocation of further grants from the Road Fund towards the maintenance of roads in rural areas?' Perhaps the only change is that, in 2018, the Roads and Transport minister might be actually be a woman.

Philipson stood up for the rights of those groups of rural dwellers who, pre-social-security support, had no recourse to financial assistance from the government, like Berwick's salmon fishermen. As a constituency that includes one of the longest coastal stretches in England, it is perhaps unsurprising that Philipson spoke up on matters of coastguard duties as well as fisheries. A debate to approve the number of armed forces personnel for 1928 sparked a discussion about the use of real sailors and Her Majesty's fleet in films, which some viewed as abhorrent. Philipson responded by saying, 'I want to see things properly acted on the films.' Liberal MP Joseph Kenworthy's reply was scathing: 'I should have thought out-of-work actors and actresses might have done that better than the navy.' The debate highlights the dismissive attitude that the first women in the debating chamber were often subjected to.

Philipson's commitment to improving the lives of women and children is beautifully highlighted in one of her contributions to the Adoption Bill in 1926, and her role in leading the Nursing Homes (registration) Bill through the House. She highlighted the challenges that 'the premises of many nursing homes are structurally defective and unsuitable for the purpose ... there is an urgent need for registration and supervision, and ...in many nursing homes the accommodation for the nursing staff was seriously defective'. These challenges may still sometimes remain, but her leadership in starting oversight for the benefit of those in need of protection should not be underestimated.

In the last century we have made much progress in many areas of social policy across party divides; I am proud that my predecessor Mabel Philipson was one of the first female MPs to stand up for the welfare of those in need. She returned to the stage after standing down before the 1929 general election.

KATHARINE STEWART-MURRAY, DUCHESS OF ATHOLL

ANNE MCGUIRE

- FULL NAME: Katharine Marjory Stewart-Murray (née Ramsay), Duchess of Atholl
- DATE OF BIRTH: 6 November 1874
- PLACE OF BIRTH: Edinburgh
- DATE OF DEATH: 21 October 1960
- MARRIED TO: John Stewart-Murray, Marquess of Tullibardine (later Duke of Atholl) (m. 1899; d. 1942)
- CHILDREN: None
- UNSUCCESSFUL ELECTIONS FOUGHT: None
- CONSTITUENCY: Kinross & West Perthshire
- DATE OF FIRST ELECTION: 6 December 1923
- DATE LEFT PARLIAMENT: 28 November 1938
- PARTY ROLES: None
- MINISTERIAL POSITIONS & DATES: First Conservative woman to hold ministerial office as a Parliamentary Secretary to the Board of Education 1924–29

How can the first woman MP to be elected to the Commons from Scotland after the 1918 Act – the first woman in a Conservative government – who bravely challenged the mainstream of her party on the issue of appeasement be so little known? That was the question I asked myself as I found out more about the Duchess of Atholl, who was an MP in a constituency that seventy-four years later I was elected to represent.

The Duchess of Atholl had no ordinary political career, which makes it all the more amazing that she has such a low profile in Scottish and UK political history. The wife of a marquess who subsequently became a duke, she was never content to sit back and play the role of the duchess. Some of her views were politically uncomfortable even by standards of her day. However, in other respects she was a brave and committed champion of causes she believed in, whatever the personal political sacrifice.

In 1923, local Unionists invited her to stand for Kinross & West Perthshire, a Liberal seat that had previously been held by her husband until 1917, when he took his father's seat in the Lords. Her decision to stand must have astonished many suffragettes, as she was well known for her opposition to votes for women. The King himself tried to dissuade her from standing as he thought her role at Blair Castle more important.

A tireless campaigner, she ultimately managed to take the seat with a majority of 150, which she increased in subsequent elections. The local paper put her victory down to her own personal popularity. Prominent Conservative MP Lady Astor, however, never forgot the duchess's opposition to women's suffrage and, in 1935, she reminded the House that, 'If the Noble Lady had her way, we [women] would still be in that class [of criminal lunatics].'

In 1923, the Labour government had appointed Margaret Bondfield as the first ever woman minister. The incoming 1924 Conservative government now needed a female minister of their own. Lady Astor was the obvious choice, but she was seen as uncontrollable. The duchess, on the other hand, was viewed as loyal and, as she was experienced in education from her previous work in Scotland, was named Parliamentary Secretary to the Board of Education – the UK's first Conservative woman minister.

Her political boss, Lord Eustace Percy, never really took to the idea of having a woman in his ministerial team. The duchess was given little space to make decisions and, by all accounts, she was not a great performer in the Commons. Although undermined by Percy, she challenged him on issues important to her. When he voiced a desire to raise the school starting age to seven and to end free elementary school education in order to balance the Budget, she dug in her heels and pleaded directly with the Prime Minister. The plans were dropped.

As can often be the case, the transfer from government to the back benches gave the duchess the freedom to pursue new causes she believed in. She campaigned against oppression in the Soviet Union, publishing *The Conscription of a People* in 1931. After hearing of the barbaric practice of female genital mutilation from the Church of Scotland Mission, she raised the issue in the Commons, heckled by affronted male MPs, with Red Clydesider hero James Maxton shouting, 'Is this relevant?' Independent MP Eleanor Rathbone rallied to support the duchess, but in spite of the women's efforts, no interest was shown by male MPs, many of whom did not believe such a practice was even possible.

If the Conservative Party thought they were getting a compliant back-bench MP, they were soon to be disabused. As the 1930s progressed, the duchess became more out of step with the party leadership, to the increasing annoyance of some loyalists in her constituency association. Along with a few notables such as Winston Churchill, she was strongly opposed to the 1935 Government of India Bill.

During the Spanish Civil War, not content with second-hand reports, she visited Spain with MPs Eleanor Rathbone and Ellen Wilkinson. After General Franco's forces bombarded Guernica, she was instrumental in arranging for the transportation of 4,000 children to Britain. Praise from Communist Party MP Willie Gallacher only reinforced the views of those who thought she had gone over to the dark side, and she was referred to as the Red Duchess.

To her great credit, the plight of the children overcame narrow partisan-ship. Her views on Spain were undoubtedly linked to her deep fear of the rise of fascism. While the political elite were being courted by the Nazis, she was so convinced of the evil danger posed by Hitler that she had *Mein Kampf* translated into English and a copy sent to the Prime Minister.

It is hard to imagine how difficult it must have been to swim against the appeasement tide during the 1930s. She was one of a handful of MPs who were prepared to take a stand. She was called a 'warmonger' and the worthies in her local association finally lost patience and started to move against her.

In 1938, she called their bluff by resigning her seat, to stand as an inde-pendent on an anti-appeasement platform. The campaign was brutal. The full force of the Conservative and Unionist Party was mobilised against her, with more than fifty MPs, including Alec Douglas-Home who would go on to become Prime Minister and coincidentally MP for the same constituency, travelling to support the new Tory candidate.

On her side, although Churchill did not offer public support, he sent a private letter that was widely circulated. Ironically, suffragette Sylvia Pankhurst urged every woman who 'values their vote' to vote for her. The duchess's own base in rural Perthshire turned its back on her and, on 21 December, she lost by 1,313 votes. With regards to Hitler, I'm sure she did not take pleasure in being proved right in her judgement. The duchess never again stood for election to Parliament. Instead she nursed her ailing husband until his death in 1943. She died in Edinburgh in 1960.

MARGARET BONDFIELD

SALLY KEEBLE

- FULL NAME: Margaret Grace Bondfield
- DATE OF BIRTH: 17 March 1873
- PLACE OF BIRTH: Chard, Somerset
- DATE OF DEATH: 16 June 1953
- MARRIED TO: Unmarried
- CHILDREN: None
- UNSUCCESSFUL ELECTIONS FOUGHT: Northampton 1920 (by-election), 1922, 1924; Wallsend 1931 and 1935
- CONSTITUENCY: Northampton & Wallsend
- DATE OF FIRST ELECTION: 6 December 1923
- DATE LEFT PARLIAMENT: 27 October 1931
- PARTY ROLES: none
- MINISTERIAL POSITIONS & DATES: Parliamentary Secretary to the Minister of Labour 1924, Minister of Labour and Privy Counsellor 1929–31
- MOST FAMOUS QUOTATIONS: 'I am a socialist of thirty years' standing and today am a more convinced socialist than ever I was.' – In her maiden speech in January 1924. | 'Since I have been able to vote at all, I have never felt the same enthusiasm because the vote was the consequence of possessing property rather than the consequence of being a human being ... At last we are established on that equitable footing, because we are human beings and part of society as a whole.' – Upon passage of the Equal Franchise Act 1928.

If Margaret Bondfield had been a man, she might well have ended up leader of the Labour Party, in which case her particular blend of principle and pragmatism may have spared the party some of the setbacks of the 1920s and '30s.

As it was, she achieved a string of Labour movement firsts: first woman delegate to the TUC; part of the first intake of Labour women MPs; first woman on the TUC General Council, and its first woman chair; first woman Privy Counsellor; and Cabinet member.

These were huge achievements for a woman who was the tenth child in a West Country family of eleven children. Although her family were poor, Bondfield's childhood seems to have been happy, and the family were much influenced by the religious and social teachings of Methodism's founding father, John Wesley. Bondfield's father lost his job in a textile factory when she was barely in her teens, and that spelled the end of her limited formal education.

After a brief spell working as a school monitor, she became apprenticed, aged fourteen, to a woman in Brighton, who ran a business making fine garments to send to colonial families in India – a kind of early mail order house. However, before Bondfield was able to finish her apprenticeship, the business folded and she went into the retail trade, first in Brighton, then, encouraged by her brother Frank, in London.

The experience was searing. 'For the next three months I was nearer to starvation than at any time since. I learned the bitterness of a hopeless search for work,' she later wrote. It triggered her lifelong activism in the Labour movement, first in trade unions, and then in the socialist groupings that eventually gave rise to the Labour Party.

It was by chance that Bondfield first learned about trade unions. While on her lunch break one day, she bought fish and chips that were wrapped up with a piece of newspaper containing a letter from the Secretary of the National Union of Shop Assistants, Warehousemen and Clerks, encouraging shop workers to join the union – which is exactly what she did.

With her typical exuberance, she threw herself into trade union activism and was soon commissioned by the Women's Industrial Council to investigate employment conditions for women shop workers. Bondfield went undercover and travelled the country to document the exploitation: long hours, poverty pay and living conditions that bordered on imprisonment. Her findings led to a second commission to report on the position of married women workers in the Yorkshire wool industry. Both studies are classics that highlighted the dire position of working-class women. Already trapped in horrifyingly low-paid jobs, marriage forced women into yet more marginal employment. Bondfield's landmark reports paved the way for legislative changes.

In 1898, Bondfield became the assistant secretary of her trade union and the following year she was sent as the first and only woman delegate to the

Annual Trades Union Congress in Plymouth. She was deeply influenced by calls for unity between the industrial and political wings of the working-class movement, and voted for the establishment of the Labour Representation Council – a precursor to the Labour Party. Her commitment to the relationship between trade unions and the party was to be lifelong; although she later wrote that 'the methods and temper of the two movements were different, and as time went on some of the differences grew to be emphasised'.

The following decades saw Bondfield work her way up through the trade union movement, and the network of groupings from which the Labour Party was ultimately born. Her friends and colleagues included leading lights from both wings of the movement – suffragist Mary Macarthur, Margaret McDonald, founders of the Fabian Society Beatrice and Sidney Webb, and playwright George Bernard Shaw. Bondfield campaigned for a minimum wage, improved maternity benefits and universal suffrage. She aligned herself with the Adult Suffrage Society, which called for the franchise to be extended to all people, including the many men who were excluded from voting due to their lack of property. She travelled widely at home and abroad – including a three-month tour of the USA – but during the First World War, Bondfield was refused a passport to travel by the UK government because of her pacifist sympathies.

Her post-war visit to the Soviet Union, as part of a Labour movement delegation, had more profound consequences for Labour's position as a democratic socialist party. She recognised the achievements of the new regime, and remarked that had she been Russian she would have supported the Bolsheviks out of necessity. But Bondfield drew a line between the particularities of the Soviet Union and the generalities of communism. When the UK Communist Party subsequently applied to be affiliated to the Labour Party, Bondfield was on the negotiating committee that ultimately concluded the Communist Party's objects did not accord with Labour's constitution, principles and programme.

Early on, Bondfield had rejected the Social Democratic Federation and its call for 'bloody class war' in favour of the evolutionary politics of the Independent Labour Party. Later in life, her position was more trenchant: 'It was inherent to the Labour position that we rejected the use of force as part of politics. We were essentially constitutional – we aimed at change by legal and peaceful methods. Fascism and communism had common ground in the use of violence, and thus were anti-democratic.'

Bondfield's breakthrough into national politics came when she was invited by the Northampton Labour Party to stand as their candidate in the 1920 by-election. Despite receiving political celebrity endorsements from George Bernard Shaw and Sidney Webb, she was unsuccessful at the by-election and the subsequent 1922 general election.

Success, however, came in the 1923 general election, when Bondfield became one of the three new women Labour MPs. Her maiden speech made it clear that labour-market exploitation of women and young people was a key area of interest to her, while she also called for public ownership of key industries and declared herself to be a 'socialist of thirty years standing'. She was offered a Cabinet position, but turned it down, asking instead for a more junior government position of parliamentary secretary.

In 1924, Bondfield was asked to lead a UK delegation to Canada to examine, among other things, child migration. While she was away the Labour government collapsed – a calamity that Bondfield blamed entirely on Ramsay MacDonald's poor judgement and temerity. She was forced to make a hasty return to the UK for the doomed fight to keep her Northampton seat.

Two years later came a red herring that had even more serious personal consequences. Bondfield was asked by Conservative Prime Minister Stanley Baldwin to join a commission of inquiry into unemployment benefit, chaired by Lord Blanesburgh. It was an area where Bondfield had real practical expertise, but where the politics were toxic. The Conservative government was trying to reform the system, and a more cautious politician might have spotted the risks that came with being involved in such a project.

Instead Bondfield approached the task in her usual forthright fashion. She argued for the best deal possible for the unemployed and supported the contributory principle, which has remained a constant in the welfare system, before signing off on the commission's report. It caused uproar. She was subjected to a TUC motion of censure and was furiously criticised by colleagues in the Labour Party. She had meanwhile been returned to Parliament through a by-election in Wallsend, but her political opponents there tried to get her deselected. Ultimately she won out, with the support of Labour's male hierarchy. However, the row left her politically bruised, and with a reputation for high-handed political compromise that persisted.

Her greatest success came after the 1929 general election in which she held Wallsend and became the first woman Privy Counsellor and Cabinet member in Ramsay MacDonald's minority Labour government. It brought Bondfield international recognition, and she recalled later how congratulatory messages flooded in from around the world.

She was appointed Minister of Labour, but the position proved to be a poisoned chalice. With the global economy weakening and trade with Europe faltering, UK unemployment soared. Bondfield first reformed the unemployment benefit system with some hastily implemented and much criticised changes. She then repeatedly had to go to Parliament to get approval for budget increases – it was a punishing treadmill.

First there were the arguments about entitlement, as visceral then as now. 'Does anyone ... really think it is right,' argued Conservative Cyril Atkinson,

> That even if it be proved up to the hilt that a man has deliberately not tried to get work ... has stopped in bed for a whole week doing nothing ... has been drunk every day and making no endeavour to do anything – do you really say that that man ought to have benefit?

Then there were the arguments, made by Winston Churchill no less, about Labour being soft on benefits: 'By every device and by every dodge, by every shift and, almost, by every turpitude, they [the Labour government] have managed to keep on paying for the longest time in the loosest fashion the largest doles to the largest number. They have something to show for being socialists.'

And then there were the arguments about the impact of the Welfare Bill on the national deficit, with Conservative Herwald Ramsbotham slating Labour for believing in 'some utopia where it does not matter whether a nation exceeds its income or not'.

Bondfield fought back and won every vote on the Welfare Bill. But the worsening financial position, in which the Welfare Bill played only a minor part, finally produced the crisis which brought the Labour government down.

Although a Labour loyalist, Bondfield could not support Ramsay Mac-Donald's introduction of a government of national unity. She saw the split between him and the Labour Party as being the inevitable result of his lack of sympathy for the trade union movement. She said he regarded trade unionists as being 'so much raw material', who needed educating in 'doctrinal socialism'. Along with most of the Labour front bench, she stood aside and then lost her parliamentary seat at the 1931 general election.

Her final years were, by all accounts, happy. After Parliament she went back to work in the trade union movement, travelling, lecturing and warning of the risks to skilled labour of the mechanisation of industry. In 1935, she stood again for election in Wallsend, but although she reduced the Tory majority, she still lost the seat. Bondfield accepted an invitation from Reading Labour Party to be their parliamentary candidate, but decided to pull out when it became clear that the general election would be delayed until she would be over seventy.

In 1938, Bondfield retired from the National Union of General and Municipal Workers. During the Second World War she toured the United States, lecturing on the UK's position for the British Information Service. More far-reaching, though, was her investigation for the Women's Group on Public Welfare into the impact of wartime evacuation on children. It paved the way for some of the reforms of the 1945 Labour government with recommendations for nursery education, child benefit, a national health service and a minimum wage.

Why then should such a formative figure disappear so completely from Labour's collective memory? Bondfield was certainly criticised during her life, and excoriated by Barbara Castle after her death, but by any standards she was one of the founders of women's trade unionism, the Labour Party and a pioneer of universal suffrage.

Bondfield was among the most vocal politicians in exposing the suffering of working-class women in early twentieth-century Britain. Her work on poverty, welfare and children were formative for Labour thinking and many of her practical recommendations became central tenets of Labour policy. Yet few roll calls of Labour's heroes and heroines include Margaret Bondfield's name. My path crossed her career twice. The first was while working at the GMB union, the successor to the GMWU, where she was celebrated for establishing the women's department. The second was in Northampton North, where for many years it fell to me as one of her successors to organise the annual Bondfield dinner in her memory. A short cul-de-sac in the constituency, Bondfield Avenue, is named after her, as is a soon to be demolished university hall of residence.

If Margaret Bondfield had been a man, her name would have been up in lights.

DOROTHY JEWSON

ANNABELLE DICKSON

- FULL NAME: Dorothea (Dorothy) Jewson
- DATE OF BIRTH: 17 August 1884
- PLACE OF BIRTH: Thorpe Hamlet, Norfolk
- DATE OF DEATH: 29 February 1964
- MARRIED TO: Richard Tanner-Smith (m. 1936; d. 1939);
  Campbell Stephen (m. 1945; d. 1947)
- CHILDREN: None
- UNSUCCESSFUL ELECTIONS FOUGHT: Norwich 1929 and 1931
- CONSTITUENCY: Norwich
- DATE OF FIRST ELECTION: 6 December 1923
- DATE LEFT PARLIAMENT: 28 October 1924
- PARTY ROLES: Independent Labour Party eastern division representative
  on the national administrative council 1925–34
- MINISTERIAL POSITIONS & DATES: None
- MOST FAMOUS QUOTATION: 'There is a large body of young women and
  mothers who feel, very naturally, that if they are capable of bringing
  children into the world, and of being responsible to the state for
  those children, it is only right that they should have the privilege and
  protection of the vote in helping to mould the laws which will govern
  themselves and their children.'

Dorothy Jewson was a visionary. A conviction politician before the phrase became fashionable in a modern era of personality politics. In interwar Britain it was her strength and her undoing.

Her parliamentary career was short-lived and she is often overlooked in the history books. Yet some of what she advocated – from providing information about birth control, to equal voting rights for women and compassion for the poorest in society – entered the mainstream within a few decades.

Jewson was an unyielding socialist, militant suffragist and passionate pacifist throughout her political career. Her quest for a more equal society was not motivated by personal gain; her worldview was shaped by her learning. Her wealthy liberal parents provided her with an expensive education; she studied at Norwich High School for Girls before attending Cheltenham Ladies' College and Girton College, Cambridge, where her political beliefs crystallised.

Her beloved brother Harry was a kindred spirit, sharing her socialist and feminist aims, but he was killed in active service at the Battle of Gaza in 1917. The carnage of the early twentieth century proved difficult terrain for a political voice that advocated pacifism.

Her selection as one of the two Labour candidates for her home city of Norwich, and subsequent election to Parliament as she neared the age of forty, was the culmination of years of local campaigning and involvement in the trade union movement. Jewson was a prominent supporter of striking munitions workers.

She had a loyal following among the poorest and the working classes of Norwich, whose plight she studied and documented as part of her campaign for change. One of the self-appointed 'investigators' of Norwich, she was among those who set about highlighting social deprivation in a pamphlet entitled 'The Destitute of Norwich and How they Live', in an effort to make the case for change.

She argued – reasonably – that the poor should be helped with five shillings a week to keep them in their own homes, because the cost of keeping a person in the workhouse would be considerably more than this.

As a parliamentarian she had little time to make her mark, and like many revolutionaries she had little love for the Parliament she saw as 'overloaded with a tradition of heritage, habit and ancient customs'. Writing in an Austrian radical feminist publication, *Die Frau*, she also described it as a terrible waste of time with a lack of any sense of importance.

The first ever Labour government fell after just ten months. In Norwich, the Liberals and Conservatives joined forces to defeat socialism by only fielding a single candidate each in the two-seat constituency – a move which deprived Jewson of a second term.

Some political commentators also attribute a backlash from local clergy, who opposed her attempts to provide information about birth control in her defeat at the ballot box. Later attempts to return to Westminster in both 1929 and 1931 were marred by age-old Labour splits. Her loyalty to the radical Independent Labour Party proved incompatible with the strictures of party discipline demanded by the party of its parliamentarians.

Yet while her tenure on the national parliamentary stage was limited, she continued to be very actively involved in Labour Party politics, and as a popular city councillor in Norwich, during the thirteen years before she married.

At Norwich City Hall she was a raucous voice in the council chamber, and was part of the effort to create employment through a massive road and park building programme – the fruits of which are still in evidence in the city today.

She departed elected office when she married at the age of fifty-two, which meant that her extraordinary energy, radicalism and conviction were a distant memory for many in Norwich when she died thirty years later.

But Jewson's political legacy is perhaps of an immense but unfulfilled talent on the national parliamentary stage.

SUSAN LAWRENCE

LYN BROWN

- FULL NAME: Arabella Susan Lawrence
- DATE OF BIRTH: 12 August 1871
- PLACE OF BIRTH: London
- DATE OF DEATH: 25 October 1947
- MARRIED TO: Unmarried
- CHILDREN: None
- UNSUCCESSFUL ELECTIONS FOUGHT: Camberwell 1920
- CONSTITUENCY: East Ham North
- DATE OF FIRST ELECTION: 6 December 1923
- DATE LEFT PARLIAMENT: 27 October 1931
- PARTY ROLES: National Executive Committee 1925–41 and chair of Labour Party conference 1930
- MINISTERIAL POSITIONS & DATES: Parliamentary private secretary to the President of the Board of Education 1923–24 and Parliamentary Secretary to the Ministry of Health 1929–31

Arabella 'Susan' Lawrence MP was a passionate and determined campaigner, who made it her mission to increase state support for working-class families. She was persistent and single-minded, and pursued her goals in a straightforward, logical manner; a contemporary *Punch* cartoon depicts her as the Red Queen from *Alice Through the Looking Glass*, berating the House of Commons for being 'no good at sums'.

Lawrence was one of the first woman MPs to be elected, but seemed to take no pleasure from self-congratulation. Instead, she emphasised the needs and the agency of poor families, whom she described as 'working women with whom I am associated'. Her political home was the radical grouping of inter-war campaigners who understood that the Victorian-era welfare system needed drastic reform. She worked to pave the way for the introduction of the modern welfare state.

In 1918, Lawrence co-authored a prophetic report with William Beveridge, calling for national insurance 'to avoid the disastrous chaos of unorganised and improvised methods of relieving distress' from the anticipated rise in unemployment at the end of the war. Unfortunately, the government didn't listen, and as a result, Poplar Council, on which she served, was unable to raise sufficient rates to meet local need. Lawrence took direct action, and was one of thirty councillors jailed for refusing to collect rates on the grounds that they were regressive. With good humour, she informed the *Manchester Guardian* that she would spend her time in prison reading Tolstoy and writing a pamphlet on tax reform.

Lawrence did not have long; the Poplar councillors caught the public mood, and were soon released. They had achieved the emergency passage of legislation to increase the size of the London-wide poor fund and allow councils to borrow generously for schemes designed to provide employment. Although it was initially introduced as a temporary measure, as an MP Susan Lawrence later worked to put pan-London support for poorer areas on a permanent and sustainable footing, drawing on the policy experience she obtained during her time on the London County Council.

For Lawrence, Parliament was just another vehicle to pursue change. She was first mentioned in Parliament a full twelve years before she became an MP, when the future Labour leader George Lansbury informed the House that she was 'by far and away one of the ablest county councillors'. Keir Hardie followed suit in 1915, highlighting in the Chamber an influential paper Lawrence had presented to the Board of Education, which proposed reforms of child labour laws. Later, as an MP herself, Lawrence campaigned for maintenance grants that would allow children to stay in education for longer.

Susan Lawrence's forthright character and focus on the needs of her poor constituents was exemplified in her maiden speech in 1924, where, rather than indulging formality and apologising to the House for speaking inappropriately early, she used it to draw attention to a cut in funding for free school meals. She put it simply: 'I desired to raise this matter at the earliest possible moment, because I think it is one of prime importance.' She wasn't wrong.

LADY VERA TERRINGTON

LIZ BARKER

- FULL NAME: Vera Florence Annie Woodhouse (née Bousher), Lady Terrington
- DATE OF BIRTH: 11 January 1889
- PLACE OF BIRTH: Kensington, London
- DATE OF DEATH: 19 May 1973
- MARRIED TO: Guy Ivo Sebright (m. 1907; d. 1912); Harold Woodhouse, 2nd Baron Terrington (m. 1918; div. 1926); Max Lensveld (m. 1949)
- CHILDREN: None
- UNSUCCESSFUL ELECTIONS FOUGHT: Wycombe 1922 and 1924
- CONSTITUENCY: Wycombe
- DATE OF FIRST ELECTION: 6 December 1923
- DATE LEFT PARLIAMENT: 29 October 1924
- PARTY ROLES: Leader within Women's Liberal Federation
- MINISTERIAL POSITIONS & DATES: None
- MOST FAMOUS QUOTATION: 'It is a question of women, women, women! We have got to a certain phase in our national life, but we have not got all that we want.'

L ady Terrington used her brief parliamentary career to promote progressive Liberal causes, notably housing, women's rights and animal welfare, earning her the nickname 'the Member for homes and animals'. She was a member of the Grand Council of Our Dumb Friends League – an animal welfare charity founded during the First World War.

Widowed in 1912, Vera married Harold Woodhouse in 1918. Upon the death of his father, a former Liberal MP, in 1921, Woodhouse became the second Lord Terrington.

In 1922, Lady Terrington fought her first parliamentary contest at Wycombe, and came within 4,500 votes of Conservative William Baring du Pré, an opponent of women's rights. The stage was set for a controversial contest at the next election.

Lady Terrington suffered some harsh press. She was quoted in the *Daily Express* saying: 'If I am elected to Westminster … I shall put on my ospreys and my fur coat and my pearls. Everyone here knows I live in a large house and keep men servants, and can afford a motor-car. Every woman would do the same if she could.' Objecting particularly to the headline AIM IF ELECTED – FURS AND PEARLS, Terrington sued the *Express* for making her look 'vain, frivolous, and extravagant'; the court, however, ruled that Terrington had not suffered 'a farthing's worth of damage'.

It seemed that, technically, the court was right, and Lady Terrington was elected as MP for Wycombe with a majority of 1,682. She was one of only twelve Liberal women candidates and two Liberal women MPs in 1923. Her defeat of the avowed anti-feminist delighted women's societies such as the Six Point Group.

Her Commons interventions were rare but forthright. She supported the minority Labour government because it was committed to free trade, but challenged Health minister John Wheatley to go further on housing subsidy and construction. Lady Terrington started her own housing scheme of sorts by constructing a number of quick-build concrete houses in Wycombe, as well as accommodating six ex-servicemen in her own home. She also spoke up in Parliament for evicted tenants in London and the rights of rural smallholders.

Lady Terrington supported Margaret Wintringham's Guardianship of Infants Bill to equalise women's rights of access to their children with men's. She demanded greater protection for animals, including legislation to control traps, harsher sentences for cruelty and opposing steer wrestling at the British Empire Exhibition. When it came to animal welfare, Lady Terrington was ahead of her time; she campaigned against the export of live animals and stag hunting, declaring that 'It is a wicked thing that in a civilised country we should allow such hunting.'

In 1924, Lady Terrington lost her seat by nearly 8,300 votes to a new Conservative candidate, Sir Alfred Knox. Two years later, Lord and Lady Terrington divorced, amid scandal regarding his finances and fidelity. Following the loss of her former husband's financial support and the negative reaction in the local press and Liberal Association, Lady Terrington abandoned her nomination as Liberal candidate for Wycombe.

One of only six Liberal Women MPs between 1921 and 1951, at only thirty-five years old Lady Terrington's political career was over. And although her career was brief, she remains an early example of a good woman backbencher.

ELLEN WILKINSON

ESTELLE MORRIS

- FULL NAME: Ellen Cicely Wilkinson
- DATE OF BIRTH: 8 October 1891
- PLACE OF BIRTH: Manchester
- DATE OF DEATH: 6 February 1947
- MARRIED TO: Unmarried
- CHILDREN: None
- UNSUCCESSFUL ELECTIONS FOUGHT: Ashton-under-Lyne 1923; Middlesbrough East 1923, 1924 and 1931
- CONSTITUENCY: Middlesbrough East 1924–31 and Jarrow 1935–47
- DATE OF FIRST ELECTION: 30 October 1924
- DATE LEFT PARLIAMENT: 6 February 1947
- PARTY ROLES: None
- MINISTERIAL POSITIONS & DATES: Parliamentary Secretary to the Minister for Pensions 1940; Parliamentary Secretary to the Minister of Home Security 1940–45; Minister for Education 1945–47
- MOST FAMOUS QUOTATION: 'I felt when I came into this House, and I think the other women Members must have felt too, that we had entered it as the result of the labours of some of the best women that this country or the world has known. Women have worked very hard. They have starved in prison, they have given their lives, or have given all their time, in order that women might sit in this House and take part in the legislation of the country. I need only mention honoured names like Josephine Butler, Lydia Becker, Emmeline Pethick-Lawrence, and Mrs. Fawcett to realise that that band of women, though they may never sit here, have made possible what we are doing to-day.' – Thursday 29 March 1928, House of Commons, Second Reading of the Representation of the People's Act (Equal Franchise) Bill.

During my time at the Department for Education, one of the meeting rooms was home to a series of photographs of former Secretaries of State. Some names are still familiar, others less so; however, I suspect that most visitors to Sanctuary Buildings would recognise the name below the photograph of Attlee's first Minister of Education – and the first woman to hold the post – Ellen Cecily Wilkinson, perhaps better known as 'Red Ellen'.

Ellen Wilkinson is so closely associated with the Jarrow March that many might think her a child of the north-east, learning her politics from the shipbuilders and miners of those tight-knit communities. Without doubt, they helped shape Wilkinson's views as an adult, but she was born, raised and underwent her political baptism on the other side of the country.

Wilkinson was born in the Chorlton-upon-Medlock district of Manchester in 1891. She was the third of four children born to Richard, a cotton worker and later insurance agent, and his wife, Ellen Wood. Although they knew poverty, they were relatively secure and lived in a respectable street of terraced houses. Like most women of that era, Wilkinson's mother ran the household; however, she suffered from ill health and Wilkinson recalls a childhood dominated by her mother's sickness. Mrs Wilkinson died in 1916, before she could see her youngest daughter's political success, but she was remembered by her daughter as a woman who never complained and retained her love of life.

Richard Wilkinson came from an Irish family and was a committed Methodist. The chapel was a focal point for all the family and laid the foundations for Wilkinson's values and beliefs. She wasn't made to attend chapel and perhaps this was why it remained a force throughout her life. Her Methodism underpinned her socialism and she told a Left Book Club meeting in 1939, 'I am still a Methodist, you can never get … its special glow out of your blood.'

If the chapel was remembered fondly by Wilkinson, the same can't be said of school. She began her education at the local school when she was five years old, but bouts of illness – which she put down to the state of the school building – meant she barely attended for the following three years. However, what she missed at school was more than compensated for at home. The Wilkinsons valued education for both their daughters and their sons. These days, we might call the family economically stretched but rich in social capital. She was taught to read and debate, and her father took her to lectures on theology and evolution. By the time she was fourteen, Wilkinson said that she 'was reading Haeckel, Huxley and Darwin with my father'.

The early death of her mother was a great loss to the family but the home that Ellen and Richard had provided for their children, and the love of learning that they passed on, were key to Wilkinson's success – and she readily acknowledged it.

Wilkinson returned to school, winning a scholarship to Ardwick Elementary Grade School at the age of eleven and at fifteen was awarded a £25 pupil teaching bursary, which meant that she could attend college for half the week and teach for the other half.

She was, I suspect, too much of a rebel to ever really enjoy school, but despite her antagonism to the institution, her commitment to learning flourished and in 1910 she entered the University of Manchester, having been awarded the Jones Scholarship for history.

If Wilkinson's family helped shape the person she became, then so did the city of her birth – I, too, was born in Manchester. Indeed, the school where she taught, Oswald Road, was one attended by many of my childhood friends. I don't think it is just pride in my native city that leads me to think that Wilkinson grew up in a place that was synonymous with radical politics and progressive thought. The years of Wilkinson's young adulthood were years of debate and dissent, of ideas and possibilities, of the emergence of socialism and fascism, communism and feminism. People across the world searched and fought for better ways to build the future – and Manchester was a place where Ellen Wilkinson could be part of those debates.

Wilkinson was an inveterate 'joiner'. When she arrived at university, she joined the University Socialist Federation (USF), the Independent Labour Party (ILP), ran the local branch of the Fabian Society and in 1912 she joined the National Union of Women's Suffrage Society, becoming one of its district organisers.

When war broke out, she supported the pacifist No-Conscription Fellowship and the Women's International League for Peace and Freedom, and for all these causes she marched, campaigned and organised.

If these were formative years in Wilkinson's political career, she certainly mixed with and learned from some of the leading thinkers and campaigners – Katharine Bruce Glasier in the ILP, Beatrice Webb from the Fabian Society as well as Emmeline Pankhurst. Through the USF she listened to and took part in discussions with Ramsay MacDonald, Margaret Bondfield, economist G. D. H. Cole and anti-war activist Fenner Brockway.

Wilkinson was not exclusive in her political interests, which ranged far and wide but possessed one common thread: the fight against poverty and inequality. Women's suffrage was important to her because it was a sign of inequality, but she was just as concerned by the impact poverty, poor housing and education was having on working-class women, men and children.

She was a pacifist, a socialist and a suffragist – ideologies she shared with her elder sister, Annie. Both women joined the Women's International League (WIL) and travelled extensively overseas. They were supporters of the League of Nations and believed in the pursuit of international peace.

Annie Wilkinson was not only a political ally but a source of great personal support to her sister. She was as bright and committed as Wilkinson, though more measured in temperament. It had been Annie, as the eldest daughter, who had taken on the role of looking after the family after their mother's death and we can only speculate whether, without the family responsibility, she would have had a political career of her own.

Wilkinson graduated just before the outbreak of the First World War and in 1915 was appointed as the first woman organiser of the Amalgamated Union of Co-operative Employees (AUCE), later the National Union of Distributive and Allied Workers (NUDAW).

Her socialism and her feminism combined to make her a force for change. She led the campaign for better conditions, spoke at factory gates, recruited women into the union and fought for equal pay. If the passionate, fiery side of Wilkinson's personality served her well in these tasks, she had to learn subtlety and patience to achieve similar success in the trade boards on which she also sat.

Her time as a trade union organiser gave her every opportunity to test her political ideas against the reality of real people in the real world; it strengthened both her commitment to fighting for change and her belief that politics was the route to achieving it.

Wilkinson was strong-willed and elicited equally strong responses from others. Some of her political opponents often saw her as self-serving and opportunist, but throughout her life she had supporters who guided and promoted her political interests and who were undoubtedly critical to her success. One such figure was John Jagger, the president of the NUDAW.

It was with the support of Jagger and the union that Wilkinson entered elected politics. She had been active in the formation of the Communist Party of Great Britain in 1920 and was still a member when she fought the 1923 general election as the Labour Party candidate for Ashton–under-Lyne. Although she lost, in the same year she was elected to represent the Gorton ward on the Manchester City Council.

With the continued support of the AUCE she was selected as the candidate for Middlesbrough East. By now she had left the Communist Party and in the 1924 general election she won the seat for Labour. Wilkinson became one of only four women in the House of Commons – and the only one on the Labour benches. She was the tenth woman to ever have been elected to the United Kingdom Parliament.

Her election was greeted with acclaim by the Labour movement and the suffragists, and with interest by the media and her fellow parliamentarians. At less than five feet tall, with striking looks and at thirty-three, the youngest member of the House, she wasn't going to go unnoticed.

She had all the skills to make her a good parliamentarian. She was articulate and passionate, fearless and determined and she knew what she wanted to achieve. She stayed true to her feminist beliefs and built alliances where they were needed, including with Lady Nancy Astor. She campaigned for widows' pensions, economic equality for women, for the extension of maternity and child welfare centres and for equal job opportunities.

She lost her seat in the election of 1931 but was returned to Westminster as the Member of Parliament for Jarrow in 1935. There can be few MPs who are so closely associated with the name of their constituency, but history has written the names of Ellen Wilkinson and Jarrow on the same page.

The town had been devastated by the closure of the steel works. It wasn't just the abject poverty that led to the march, but the failure of anyone in power to take responsibility and do something about it. In 1936 200 men set off to deliver a petition to Westminster. If the marchers are remembered for their dignity and courage, the parliamentary response is remembered for its cowardice and inadequacy. However, the Jarrow crusade and the role Wilkinson played raised the conscience of the nation in a way that little else had done.

Wilkinson's work on behalf of her constituents didn't diminish her international commitment. At the same time that she was bringing the plight of her constituents to Westminster, she was actively involved in working with Jewish refugee groups, raising money to smuggle people out of Germany, campaigning for the recognition of the Republican government in Spain and working with Nehru to argue the case for Indian independence.

Today's politicians tend to become specialists, not so Ellen Wilkinson. Her breadth of activity and the energy it must have required is quite remarkable. She saw the dangers of fascism in Europe before many others and deserves greater recognition as an internationalist than she perhaps receives.

By the outbreak of the Second World War, she was no longer a pacifist and accepted a post as a junior minister in Churchill's wartime government. She served as Parliamentary Secretary in the Department of Pensions and then in the Ministry of Home Security.

After the Labour Party victory in 1945, Ellen Wilkinson was appointed to the Cabinet post of Minister of Education. She served for seventeen months, too short a time for her to have had the impact that she otherwise might have had. Her time in office saw her implementing the 1944 Education Act – which is far more closely associated with R. A. Butler – and introducing free school milk and lunches. She fought a battle inside the Cabinet to protect Labour's pledge to raise the school leaving age to fifteen and introduced scholarships for university entrance.

Her death on 6 February 1947, from an overdose of drugs taken while she was suffering from bronchitis and exhaustion, ended a life that had been lived to the full. Her idealism never faded, her commitment never weakened and her doggedness in fighting for social justice was never diminished.

The world she left may not have realised all her hopes but she had seen the defeat of fascism in Europe, the fulfilment of equal votes for women and men, and the introduction of the welfare state.

All these bore her mark and she bequeathed to the next generation of politicians, both men and women, a firm foundation on which to build. Ellen Wilkinson is part of political folklore, not because she was a great philosopher but because she believed in a cause, stayed true to it and showed what could be achieved through passion, energy and determination.

GWENDOLEN GUINNESS, COUNTESS OF IVEAGH

THERESE COFFEY

- FULL NAME: Gwendolen Florence Mary Guinness (née Onslow)
- DATE OF BIRTH: 22 July 1881
- PLACE OF BIRTH: London
- DATE OF DEATH: 16 February 1966
- MARRIED TO: Rupert Guinness, 2nd Earl of Iveagh (m. 1903)
- CHILDREN: Hon. Richard Guinness; Honor, Lady Channon; Arthur Guinness, Viscount Elveden; Patricia Lennox-Boyd, Viscountess Boyd of Merton; Brigid, Princess Frederick of Prussia
- UNSUCCESSFUL ELECTIONS FOUGHT: None
- CONSTITUENCY: Southend
- DATE OF FIRST ELECTION: 19 November 1927
- DATE LEFT PARLIAMENT: 13 November 1935
- PARTY ROLES: Chair of the National Union of Conservative Associations 1930
- MINISTERIAL POSITIONS & DATES: None
- MOST FAMOUS QUOTATION: 'I think you have done right by backing a colt when you know the stable he was trained in.'

The Guinness dynasty was the role model for political families in securing representation in Parliament, but no other family has achieved that by being the elected Member of Parliament for one constituency for eighty-five continuous years, from 1912 to 1997, with close relatives being MPs elsewhere. A Southend Conservative Club is still named the Iveagh Club.

Gwendolen Guinness, Countess of Iveagh, was married to Rupert Guinness, who was first elected for Southend in 1912. After the death of his father, the first Earl of Iveagh, Rupert ascended to the Lords in 1927. Gwendolen was selected and won the by-election comprehensively, serving until 1935.

Gwendolen Florence Mary was born in 1881 in Whitehall, the elder daughter of the Earl and Countess of Onslow. Her father served as Governor

General of New Zealand, which led to her living there for three years as a young child. She developed an interest in his work and is considered to have inherited his strong social conscience. She did, though, enjoy an aristocratic upbringing, including being a debutante, and was presented to Queen Victoria. In 1903, she married Rupert Guinness (Viscount Elveden) of the distinguished brewery family. They had five children (the first of whom died shortly after birth). With her husband, she was involved in the Guinness Trust provision of social housing in London, which still exists today.

Gwendolen took part in much philanthropic work and also organised relief efforts for prisoners of war during the First World War, for which she was awarded the CBE in 1920. In 1925, she became chair of the Conservative Women's Advisory Committee for eight years. During her time, the female membership grew to a million. In 1930, while an MP, she became chair of the National Union of Conservative Associations.

Her husband was first elected for Haggerston, east London, in a by-election in 1908 but lost his seat in 1910. He was then adopted as the candidate for Southend; Gwendolen helped her husband through nine elections there. Following the death of his father, Rupert joined the Lords, while Gwendolen was selected to contest the by-election and won the seat with 54.6 per cent of the vote. Surprisingly, there was an independent Conservative who had been an MP in Manchester from 1918 to '22, who opposed Stanley Baldwin, while Gwendolen strongly supported him.

Her majority fell in the next general election in 1929, when opposed only by the Liberals, although her share of the vote increased. In 1931, it shot up to over 85 per cent and she was returned with a majority of 38,823. Gwendolen Guinness did not contest the 1935 election, choosing instead to retire from politics. Instead, her son-in-law Henry 'Chips' Channon, who had married her eldest daughter, Honor, was elected to the seat; he served from 1935 to '58. In 1950, boundary changes led to the Guinness dynasty representing Southend West. Paul Channon, Gwendolen's grandson, was the last of the Guinness MPs; he left the Commons in 1997.

Gwendolen's parliamentary career coincided with that of her son-in-law Alan Lennox-Boyd, who was elected MP for Mid-Bedfordshire in 1931 before leaving the Commons to join the Lords in 1960. Gwendolen's grandson Mark Lennox-Boyd was an MP in Morecambe & Lunesdale from 1979 to 1997.

Gwendolen was the eleventh woman MP to be elected to the House and the tenth to take her seat. She made just nine speeches in her time as an MP. Her maiden speech was on the Church of England Book of Common Prayer reform, and she did not refer to Southend at all. She was a strong defender of the 1928 Equal Franchise Act, which extended the rights of women to vote to be in line with all electors. She vociferously challenged the opposition to women under the age of thirty not being allowed to vote, as lacking a sense of logic and justice. She also cited the challenges of women being elected, saying to the House: 'I think the statement cannot be challenged that though women are politically better organised than men and politically much more active than men, it is extremely difficult to get a woman candidate adopted in a constituency.' Later in her career, she addressed the subject of women's health, raising the issue of cervical cancer and focusing particularly on maternal mortality and support for midwives.

Gwendolen was a knowledgeable horticulturalist and spent considerable time with her husband reviving the Elveden estate (part of the Guinness empire). They also built a new home and estate near her childhood home of Clandon Park. Eventually, she purchased her childhood home, as it was falling into disrepair, and presented it, along with shares in Guinness, to the National Trust.

While expectations of politicians may be quite different today, Gwendolen Guinness, Countess of Iveagh, was clearly well regarded in Southend and commanded a huge share of the vote in 1931. A year later, she was awarded the freedom of Southend.

HILDA RUNCIMAN

JULIA GOLDSWORTHY

- FULL NAME: Hilda Runciman (née Stevenson), Viscountess Runciman of Doxford
- DATE OF BIRTH: 28 September 1869
- PLACE OF BIRTH: –
- DATE OF DEATH: 28 October 1956
- MARRIED TO: Walter Runciman (m. 1898)
- CHILDREN: Walter, Margaret, James, Ruth and Katharine (Kitty)
- UNSUCCESSFUL ELECTIONS FOUGHT: Tavistock 1929
- CONSTITUENCY: St Ives
- DATE OF FIRST ELECTION: 6 March 1928
- DATE LEFT PARLIAMENT: 30 May 1929
- PARTY ROLES: None
- MINISTERIAL POSITIONS & DATES: None
- MOST FAMOUS QUOTATION: 'The duty of every Liberal was to concern himself with the welfare and betterment of the people of this country.'

At first glance, one could be forgiven for considering the parliamentary career of Hilda Runciman little more than a footnote to that of her husband and prominent Liberal politician, Walter Runciman.

Elected for the Liberals to the constituency of St Ives in a by-election on 6 March 1928, Runciman held the seat for just over a year. She ran on a ticket of 'vote for me, get my husband', delivering safe passage to him from a precarious seat in Swansea West at the general election a year later. It would be an improbable electoral strategy today, but was one of two 'warming pan' by-elections in the 1924 to 1929 parliament.

Hilda Runciman was unanimously adopted as the Liberal by-election candidate on the same night her husband's candidacy for the general election was confirmed. She converted a Tory majority of 1,247 into a Liberal victory, by 763 votes. In doing so, she became one half of the first married couple to serve in the Commons at the same time.

This double act proved potent on the campaign trail, where she was accompanied by her husband who had pledged 'to fight it [the election] just as if I were the candidate'. Drawing large audiences both in their own right and jointly, they were a campaigning force to be reckoned with. Local newspapers report many engagements that ranged from fetes and fundraisers to debates and dances – a relentless regime that is wearily familiar to the modern battle-hardened candidate.

It was an approach that worked for the run-in to the general election as well as the by-election. Their ability to cover the many small towns and villages in the constituency drew objection from political opponents, who complained that the Runciman family had spent a year travelling all over the constituency, while their candidate had only three weeks to nurse the seat. It was not the last time Cornish Liberals would hear protests of unfair play in response to their electioneering.

A self-declared Gladstonian Liberal, in her adoption speech Runciman spoke powerfully that '… the duty of every Liberal was to concern himself with the welfare and betterment of the people of this country'. She held true to this in her parliamentary contributions: her maiden speech pointed to a housing crisis that left tens of thousands living in conditions 'positively destructive to family life', a cause she also championed as a founder of the Westminster Housing Trust. A former president of the Women's National Liberal Federation, it must have been a great source of pride to cast her vote in Parliament to support the Equal Franchise Bill of 1928, which granted women the same voting rights as men.

At the 1929 election, Walter's gain was Parliament's loss. Although Hilda Runciman stood down in St Ives, she contested the Tavistock seat, but lost by only 152 votes. She furthered the progress of women not just as an MP, but also as one of Northumberland's first woman JPs and through her work for the Women's National Liberal Federation. She has a richly deserved place in the Cornish and Liberal pantheon – an inspirational lady, I just wish I had known more about her sooner.

RUTH DALTON

MARY BEARD

- FULL NAME: Florence Ruth Hamilton Dalton (née Fox)
- DATE OF BIRTH: 9 March 1890
- PLACE OF BIRTH: Farnborough
- DATE OF DEATH: 15 March 1966
- MARRIED TO: Hugh Dalton (m. 1914; d. 1962)
- CHILDREN: Helen
- UNSUCCESSFUL ELECTIONS FOUGHT: None
- CONSTITUENCY: Bishop Auckland
- DATE OF FIRST ELECTION: 7 February 1929 (Parliament was dissolved twenty days before the election)
- DATE LEFT PARLIAMENT: 30 May 1929
- PARTY ROLES: None
- MINISTERIAL POSITIONS & DATES: None

Florence 'Ruth' Dalton shares the record, with Margo MacDonald, for being the shortest-serving female Member of Parliament, holding her seat for a mere ninety-two days. She was elected as the Labour member for Bishop Auckland in a by-election on 7 February 1929, explicitly to keep the seat warm for her husband, Hugh Dalton – who stood for it successfully in the next election, which was called on 10 May. Mrs Dalton did not consider pursuing her parliamentary career any further. She preferred her work on the London County Council (LCC), where she felt there was more action and less talk.

Born Florence Ruth Hamilton Fox (although always known as Ruth) in 1890, Dalton turned down a place to read classics at Cambridge, in favour of going to the London School of Economics, where she studied sociology. It was here that she met Hugh Dalton, later Chancellor of the Exchequer, whom she married in 1914. It appears to have been very much a working partnership in political activism, overshadowed by a personal tragedy for which the Daltons held themselves responsible. For reasons that have always been mysterious (the couple were wealthy enough to have afforded a nanny), their only child, Helen, was largely cared for in a residential home while her parents launched their careers. Helen died of a kidney condition aged just four in 1922.

Ruth Dalton was elected to the LCC in 1925, a few years before taking her seat in Bishop Auckland. Hugh (already MP for Peckham, but at odds with his agent and local constituency party) had been adopted as Labour candidate there, and was to replace the sitting MP, who inconveniently died just a few months before the general election was expected. Rather than triggering the series of by-elections that would have been caused by Hugh resigning his Peckham seat immediately, Ruth stood in his place, winning the seat with a majority of more than 7,000 over the Liberals (up from less than 3,000 in the previous election). On 13 March, she gave her maiden speech, decrying the pit closures, unemployment and poverty of her constituency – before standing aside for Hugh, as agreed, a couple of months later.

Their marriage became increasingly distant, though she made a good show of being the 'wife of the Chancellor' in the 1945 Attlee government. During the Second World War, Ruth worked with the Ministry of Supply and later the United Nations. After the war, she returned to the LCC (active on the crucial Housing committee) and became an influential figure in any number of good causes, from the National Trust to the Royal Ballet and the Arts Council. She died in 1966, four years after her husband, leaving most of her estate to fund the purchase of English books for Israeli libraries. Her life, as she would have seen it, was testament to the obvious fact that it is possible to make a political impact in local government and outside the Palace of Westminster.

JENNIE LEE

ELIZABETH VALLANCE

- FULL NAME: Janet (Jennie) Lee, Baroness Lee of Asheridge
- DATE OF BIRTH: 3 November 1904
- PLACE OF BIRTH: Lochgelly, Fife
- DATE OF DEATH: 16 November 1988
- MARRIED TO: Aneurin (Nye) Bevan (m. 1934; d. 1960)
- CHILDREN: None
- UNSUCCESSFUL ELECTIONS FOUGHT: North Lanarkshire 1931 and 1935; Bristol Central 1943 (by-election)
- CONSTITUENCY: North Lanarkshire 1929–31 and Cannock 1945–70
- DATE OF FIRST ELECTION: 21 March 1929
- DATE LEFT PARLIAMENT: 18 June 1970. Sat as Baroness Lee in the Lords until her death in 1988.
- PARTY ROLES: Chair of the Labour Party 1967–68
- MINISTERIAL POSITIONS & DATES: Minister for the Arts 1964–70
- MOST FAMOUS QUOTATION: 'There [the Open University] is, a great independent university which does not insult any man or any woman, whatever their background, by offering them second best; only the best is good enough.' – Jennie Lee, on laying the foundation stone of the Open University Library, April 1973.

Beautiful, vivacious, passionate and opinionated, 24-year-old Jennie Lee, the youngest MP in the House at the time of her election, was still too young to vote herself when she joined the Commons, taking it by storm. She was to remain a political force at Westminster and beyond for the next fifty years.

Born in the mining community of Lochgelly in Fife, she was steeped in the tradition of the Independent Labour Party (ILP) of which both her father and grandfather were scions. The family was not, as is sometimes suggested, 'the poorest of the poor'. Her father was generally in work and Jennie was encouraged by both her parents to educate herself, being seen as both clever and ambitious; she was not expected to conform to the typical domestic up-bringing of a girl at the time. For the rest of her life she cheerfully admitted, indeed with some pride, that she could neither sew nor cook and was looked after first by her parents and then by her cousin Bettina. Released from such mundane concerns, she could concentrate on changing the world. Jennie Lee was brought up to have the expectations and self-confidence of a man. She never had to overcome the normal reticence of young women of the time; she lived her life, personal as well as political, largely on her own terms and this may later have contributed both to her unwavering (and some would say tragic) commitment to the ILP, as well as her denial of the significance of women's causes. Indeed, when I interviewed her for a book I was writing on women in politics, she pointed out, somewhat irascibly, that she was not 'a woman MP' but simply a politician who happened to be a woman.

She grew up listening to the political debate between her father and ILP speakers – often family friends – who came to visit them, including James Maxton, John Wheatley and my grandfather David Kirkwood, all of whom would become Labour MPs. Maxton was to be one of Lee's sponsors when she entered the House and she later fondly recalled how my grandfather, seiz-ing the soapbox at a pacifist ILP rally, offered personally to take on any of the opposition. 'My friend Davie was the hero of the hour,' she said, 'I loved his form of "pacifism"!' She went on to follow her mentors, touring ILP branches and cutting her teeth on the public speaking circuit while still a teenager.

Jennie received a rigorous Scottish education and in her final year grad-uated as dux, the top pupil, of her school. Edinburgh University beckoned, but her parents were unable to support her financially; however, Jennie was able to pursue a degree after the Carnegie Trust agreed to pay half of her fees. Five years later, Jennie emerged with an MA, a law degree and the teaching certificate that was expected to allow her to earn her living from then on. But, although she taught for some years, her sights were always on West-minster and in September 1928, she became the prospective parliamentary candidate for the mining constituency of North Lanarkshire. Her political chance came rather sooner than she expected when, in February 1929, the sitting Conservative MP died, triggering a by-election which Jennie won with a respectable majority of 6,578. In May of the same year, there was a general election and again she was returned to the House.

For the next two years, Jennie spoke passionately in favour of what she regarded as the socialist position, which she increasingly believed was being denied and undermined by the leadership of the minority Labour government with its positions on family allowances, unemployment benefits and the hated means test. When the National Government was formed in 1931, Jennie refused to support Ramsay MacDonald and, like most of the Labour MPs who did so, she was defeated at North Lanarkshire in the general election of that year. It was to be another fourteen years before she regained a seat in the House.

While at Westminster, she fell in love with Frank Wise, MP for Leicester East and a prominent figure in the ILP. He was twenty years older than her, urbane, intellectually sophisticated, well educated (Cambridge and Middle Temple) and with a distinguished war record in the civil service which had won him a CB. He was also married with children and, although he contemplated leaving his wife, Jennie was convinced the political repercussions for both of them (and especially for her as a woman, in a conventional Scottish constituency) would be disastrous. Another of Lee's admirers at the time was Aneurin (Nye) Bevan, who became a close friend. They had similar backgrounds, both hailing from mining communities, and shared a vision of democratic socialism to which they both felt they had to hold the erring Labour Party. After losing her seat in 1931, Jennie was bereft; but she knew that she had to earn a living so she turned to journalism and to lecturing (largely in the United States and Canada) to do so.

From the late 1920s there had been constant discussion within the ILP about how far its members should go in supporting a Labour Party that seemed unwilling to pursue true socialist policies. At the 1930 ILP Easter conference a motion demanding that MPs remained loyal to ILP, rather than Labour, was put forward and among those in favour was Jennie Lee. It was perhaps not surprising, therefore, that in 1932, when they made the decision to disaffiliate from the Labour Party, Jennie chose to stay with the ILP. In retrospect, this was a disastrous decision and Jennie acted against the strong advice of her friends and political allies, including Frank Wise, Nye Bevan and my grandfather. It was a decision that would shape her life for years to come. Had she remained with Labour, she would have undoubtedly found another constituency within a year or two. She was a name, she was respected and she had the experience of Westminster behind her. But her decision left her, if not in the wilderness, then no longer in the mainstream. Writing years later, she calls the ILP decision to disaffiliate 'madness' but, she says, she was a child of her upbringing and her political and personal friends were very largely ILP. Yet, as Patricia Hollis points out in her excellent biography *Jennie Lee: A Life*, there is a certain amount of rewriting of history here.

As her record shows, Jennie was politically committed to the ILP brand of socialism, particularly in relation to economic policy, and she was simply not prepared to compromise her principles.

After losing her seat and her party affiliation in 1931 and 1932 respectively, Jennie was dealt a further blow in 1933, when Frank Wise, undoubtedly the love of her life, died suddenly and unexpectedly. Jennie, who was always prone to depression, was devastated. Her friends, and Nye Bevan in particular, took care of her, with Bevan moving into her flat. Without wanting to put pressure on her, Bevan made it clear to Jennie that he thought they should marry and when she returned from her American lecture tour in the spring of 1934, he persuaded her to get engaged. They were married in October; there was no wedding dress or wedding ring and the bride kept her own name and her own party. She was not in love with her new husband in the way he was with her, but she grew to love and admire him enormously and it became a remarkable and highly successful political marriage.

As a journalist and commentator, Jennie continued throughout the '30s to support the ILP and to persuade those in politics, particularly her husband, not to sell the pass on what she thought of as true socialism. When, in 1936, civil war broke out in Spain, Jennie worked hard to try to get the British government to support the Popular Front and, in 1937, even made a trip to Spain herself to report for *New Leader*. As war in Europe seemed increasingly inevitable, however, the focus of politics moved to Germany and Russia, and with its ultimate declaration in 1939, Jennie found herself in two minds. Was this just a Capitalist fight, 'a black-hearted game of power politics with ordinary men's lives and aspirations counting for nothing?' However, she was drawn into the war effort by Lord Beaverbrook, who had become Minister for Aircraft Production and seconded Jennie to help keep aircraft factories running regardless of the Blitz. It was a job she relished, but by 1940, she longed to be back in journalism and joined the *Daily Mirror* as political correspondent. She went on her usual lecture tours in the US, and argued for American involvement in the war, which eventually happened only after Pearl Harbor.

In 1943 Jennie stood unsuccessfully as an independent in Bristol. But in 1945 she was finally returned to the House, becoming MP for Cannock in the Labour landslide following the war. She was never a committed constituency member, complaining that she got little satisfaction from the social-worker element of the job. She was essentially a street-fighter; she needed a cause and found being in government, where she was expected to be supportive of the front bench, frustrating. Moreover, she was married to Bevan whose own star was in the ascendant. He came to be seen as the true conscience of the left and for much of their married life Jennie was supportive and protective of him. She admired him for his style as much as for his politics: 'Nye's socialism,' she said, 'had the radiant, elegant quality of his own personality.' It was therefore a huge shock when, in 1960, he died. Once again Jennie felt that she had lost everything, not just her beloved partner but her political lodestar who could have become the leader of a truly socialist party. It looked as if her own political life was all but over.

In 1964, however, Labour, led by Harold Wilson, came back into government. Wilson had a job for Jennie; he appointed her the first-ever Minister for the Arts. She relished the challenge and truly believed that the arts were life-enhancing and the poor should have access to them just as the rich did. She was instrumental in revitalising the Arts Council – trebling its budget – settling the ENO at the Coliseum and beginning the construction of the National Theatre on the South Bank. But she also supported the development of the arts outside of London, as well as arts education for the young – truly democratising what had been largely the preserve of the cosmopolitan elite. Jennie was in her element; she had, she felt, the best job in government.

The University of the Air was Harold Wilson's brainchild, but it was nurtured and coaxed into life as the Open University by Jennie, who firmly believed that education was the key to a better life for everyone. It was her determination and vision that made the Open University a reality. She fought the educational establishment, which dismissed the idea as a dilution of academic quality. To avoid that becoming a reality, she riposted, would simply require good teaching staff and rigorous standards in the curriculum and examinations. Jennie also faced up to the broadcasting lobby, which was reluctant to give up the air time to education, and confronted the Treasury, which was unwilling to fund what was seen as a dangerously open-ended project. Ultimately, Jennie won, and in 1973, when the first Open University students graduated, she was given an honorary degree.

She went to the Lords in 1970, but her real work was already done and the Open University remains a testament to her tireless efforts. She could be cantankerous and difficult, yet throughout her life her courage was formidable. She fought endlessly for what she believed in, dealt with her depression, carried on when she lost the men she loved, and came to terms with being voted out of her seat in Cannock. Jennie Lee could have given up at any point, but she did not. And she died still committed to her socialist faith.

ETHEL BENTHAM

CAT SMITH

- FULL NAME: Dr Ethel Bentham JP
- DATE OF BIRTH: 5 January 1861
- PLACE OF BIRTH: London
- DATE OF DEATH: 19 January 1931
- MARRIED TO: Unmarried
- CHILDREN: None
- UNSUCCESSFUL ELECTIONS FOUGHT: Islington East 1922 and 1923
- CONSTITUENCY: Islington East
- DATE OF FIRST ELECTION: 30 May 1929
- DATE LEFT PARLIAMENT: 19 January 1931
- PARTY ROLES: Labour Party National Executive Committee 1918–20, 1921–26 and 1928–31. She also served on the Standing Joint Committee of Industrial Women's Organisations, of which she was vice-chair for a time.
- MINISTERIAL POSITIONS & DATES: None

Dr Ethel Bentham was sixty-eight years old when she was elected to serve as the Member of Parliament for Islington East. She was in office for just twenty months, which makes her one of the shortest-serving women MPs, although that's not to say she didn't play a significant role in politics albeit mostly outside the arena of parliamentary politics. Bentham was the first woman doctor and first woman Quaker MP to be elected to Parliament, but her life before arriving in the Commons was just as pioneering as her election in 1929.

Ethel Bentham was born in London to William Bentham, a general manager of Standard Life Assurance Company, and Mary Ann Hammond, but raised in Dublin. As a young girl, Bentham would often accompany her mother on visits to local slums, where she witnessed unimaginable poverty at first-hand. These early experiences shaped Bentham's outlook and sparked in her a desire to become a doctor. These formative memories would also come to influence Bentham's politics; she took a great interest in the health and lives of the poorest, be that in Dublin, London or Newcastle upon Tyne, where she became the first female doctor in the city.

Bentham studied at the London School of Medicine for Women from 1890–93, before training a year later to be a midwife at the Rotunda Hospital in Dublin. She furthered her medical education in Paris and Brussels, qualifying as a fully fledged doctor in 1895. It is a remarkable feat that a single woman in her mid-thirties was able to study and travel so much. Bentham must have clearly been determined to achieve her own goals, despite having so few role models to aspire to at the time.

Back in the UK and practising as a doctor, it seems that Bentham found the freedom to become more politically active. In 1900, she was a member of the executive committee of the Newcastle branch of the National Union of Women's Suffrage Societies. She joined the Labour Party in 1902, first standing for election in the 1907 by-election for Westgate South ward in Newcastle.

By 1909, Bentham had moved to London, where she shared a house with Marion Phillips, who would also be elected a Labour MP in the 1929 general election. In London, Ethel started her own medical practice in north Kensington and became the driving force behind the establishment of a mother and baby clinic there, which was in memory of Margaret MacDonald, wife of Ramsay MacDonald, who died of blood poisoning in 1911.

Bentham continued to stand in local council by-elections unsuccessfully in 1909 and 1910, before being elected to Kensington Borough Council in 1912, representing the ward of Golborne. She was also one of the first women magistrates in the country to work in the children's courts and serve on the Metropolitan Asylums Board – this experience would later influence one of her longest Commons speeches during the Mental Treatment Bill.

On her third attempt to enter Parliament in 1929, she was elected to serve as MP for Islington East, becoming the fifteenth woman MP and at sixty-eight the oldest too. Sadly she passed away on 19 January 1931, after coming down with the flu, and was replaced in Parliament by Leah Manning after the subsequent by-election. It was fitting that after seven decades of fighting for women's voices to be heard, Bentham was succeeded by another woman MP.

MARY AGNES HAMILTON

ELIZABETH VALLANCE

- FULL NAME: Mary Agnes (Molly) Hamilton (née Adamson)
- DATE OF BIRTH: 8 July 1882
- PLACE OF BIRTH: Withington, Manchester
- DATE OF DEATH: 10 February 1966
- MARRIED TO: Charles Hamilton
- CHILDREN: None
- UNSUCCESSFUL ELECTIONS FOUGHT: Chatham 1923 and Blackburn 1924
- CONSTITUENCY: Blackburn
- DATE OF FIRST ELECTION: 30 May 1929
- DATE LEFT PARLIAMENT: 26 October 1931
- PARTY ROLES: Great Britain's representative at the League of Nations
- MINISTERIAL POSITIONS & DATES: Parliamentary private secretary to Clement Attlee
- MOST FAMOUS QUOTATION: 'What takes courage is ... to resist the opinion of the group to which one happens to belong and in which one lives.'

Mary Agnes Adamson, who was always known as Molly, seemed destined from birth for a career in public service. She was the eldest of the six children of Robert Adamson and his wife Margaret Duncan, both of whom had a passionate commitment to women's rights and progressive political causes. Hamilton's father became Professor of Logic and Metaphysics at Glasgow University, while her mother, a Quaker, was one of the first students at Newnham College, Cambridge. It seemed natural that their eldest daughter would follow in her mother's footsteps, and, in 1901, Hamilton arrived at Newnham on a scholarship. Although she initially read classics, Hamilton's interest soon turned to economics and she was awarded a first for her studies in 1904. Her academic prowess would influence her subsequent career, where she was always seen as a formidable intellect and a forensic questioner of the political orthodoxies, even those of her own party. But perhaps more important in her political development was her friendship with Margery Corbett Ashby and their involvement in the National Union of Women's Suffrage Societies, which was pressing for votes for women. It was a political baptism that would pave the way for both women to enter national politics.

Following university, Hamilton taught briefly at the University College of South Wales and, in 1905, made a disastrous marriage to a colleague, Charles Hamilton. Having been required to resign from her job upon her marriage, Hamilton was forced to find other ways of supporting herself when she decided to leave her husband. She turned to journalism, writing for *The Economist*, the *New Labour Leader*, *Time and Tide*, and published novels (her 1916 *Dead Yesterday* created a stir with its pacifist message) and biographies. Her writing brought her into contact with the intellectual anti-war group, including the Woolfs, Lytton Strachey and the Huxleys, reinforcing her pacifism.

Throughout this period, Hamilton was an active member of the ILP and stood unsuccessfully for Labour in Rochester in 1923 and in Blackburn in 1924. In the 1929 election, she finally became MP for Blackburn and, in her short time in the House, gave some notable speeches (always wearing her signature red shoes); became parliamentary private secretary to Clement Attlee (who called her 'one of the ablest women to enter the House'); presented the first *The Week in Westminster* for the BBC; and became a delegate to the League of Nations in Geneva.

Hamilton grew increasingly critical of Labour's employment policies and did not join the National Government in 1931, but was elected instead to the parliamentary executive and sat on the front bench, winding up for the opposition on the Budget debate. She was defeated in the 1931 general election and never returned to Parliament. Instead, she continued to make her mark as a governor of the BBC, a London alderman and by becoming head of the United States section of the Ministry of Information. It was for this rather than her specifically political work that she was made a CBE in 1949.

LADY MEGAN LLOYD GEORGE

KIRSTY WILLIAMS

- FULL NAME: Lady Megan Arfon Lloyd George, CH
- DATE OF BIRTH: 22 April 1902
- PLACE OF BIRTH: Criccieth
- DATE OF DEATH: 14 May 1966
- MARRIED TO: Unmarried
- CHILDREN: None
- UNSUCCESSFUL ELECTIONS FOUGHT: Anglesey 1951
- CONSTITUENCY: Anglesey 1929–51 and Carmarthen 1957–66
- DATE OF FIRST ELECTION: 30 May 1929
- DATE LEFT PARLIAMENT: 14 May 1966
- PARTY ROLES: Deputy leader of the Liberal Party
- MINISTERIAL POSITIONS & DATES: None
- MOST FAMOUS QUOTATION: '*Nos da. Hunan LLywodraeth I Gymru.*' (Goodnight. Self-government for Wales.)

Megan Lloyd George was a radical Welsh Liberal, who accelerated progress on issues we take for granted today. Upon reading the name Lloyd George, the mind may leap to David, but his daughter Megan was an equally formidable political force.

All too often in British political history women have been ignored and overshadowed and for Megan Lloyd George this danger is all too present. The Lloyd George surname is quite rightly revered among Liberal Democrats and David is widely regarded as one of the greatest Prime Ministers the United Kingdom has had, yet it seems that Megan Lloyd George has been overlooked. There is only one full-length biography of her, *A Radical Life* by Mervyn Jones.

It is impossible to escape the name and it would be remiss not to mention the effect her father had on Megan Lloyd George. But I do not want to define Megan by David, to sweep her achievements under the table, or relegate her to the footnotes of her father's history.

For what she accomplished is truly remarkable; she was a woman campaigning on issues well ahead of her time. She was the first female Member of Parliament in Wales – elected as a Liberal MP in 1929 to the constituency of Anglesey. She was also an outspoken campaigner for a Welsh Parliament and a consistent champion of Welsh issues.

*　　*　　*

Aside from her earliest years in Criccieth in north Wales, Megan Lloyd George was a child who grew up in Downing Street. She was not yet six when her father became Chancellor and moved into 11 Downing Street. In 1916, he made the move next door to No. 10. These circumstances meant that Megan Lloyd George's upbringing was a deeply political one.

In 1908, a suffrage rally called on women to rush the House of Commons and David Lloyd George – eager to project a sense that everything was under control – walked the streets of London with a six-year-old Megan, explaining the issues among the vocal crowds. Megan described herself as a 'marked child' in reference to her father's 1909/10 People's Budget, which challenged the privilege of many of her contemporaries at school. Her father would often hold meetings at the Downing Street family home, which Megan would sit in on. Before a 1910 meeting with Tory leader Arthur Balfour, Lloyd George said his 'little daughter of eight summers' would be attending.

By the time she had entered her teenage years, the First World War had broken out and like many children Megan grew up quickly. She recalls a day in 1915, after having just turned thirteen years old, as the end of her childhood. In 1919, at the age of sixteen, she found herself in Paris as the world came together to discuss the terms of peace after the war.

As well as the circumstances she found herself in as the daughter of a Chancellor and a Prime Minister, there can be little doubt that Megan was heavily influenced by her father's political views. Some of Megan's earliest memories would have been witnessing her father's battles to establish medical and unemployment insurance, as well as old age pensions for the first time in British history. David was a radical liberal, keenly aware of the problems caused by class distinctions, poverty and entrenched privilege, who was in favour of women's suffrage and laid the early foundations for the modern welfare state. David was Megan's political inspiration, and Megan was David's political heir.

Despite Megan's political precociousness, children can still be children and as a ten-year-old she sparked fears of a kidnapping when she went missing, along with Prime Minister Herbert Asquith's youngest son, Anthony. Search parties were despatched in the nearby area and a major diplomatic incident was only avoided when the pair were found trapped in a broken lift in 10 Downing Street.

It was undoubtedly an intensely political upbringing and in 1928 Megan said, 'I've had politics for breakfast, lunch, tea and dinner all my life.' The effects this had on her can be seen in her later life.

* * *

Megan frequently devoted her parliamentary time to speaking about matters affecting Wales and pushed forward the principle of Welsh identity in political life. On 17 October 1944, the House of Commons saw its first ever 'Welsh Day', devoted to Welsh issues – a historic milestone. Megan and other Welsh MPs had been instrumental in securing this and she was given the honour of leading the debate. In her opening remarks, she said:

> We welcome this debate as a recognition of the distinctive problems and needs of Wales, not as an area, not as a part of England, but as a nation with a living language of its own, with hundreds of years of history behind it, and with its own culture. We speak a different language in more senses than one. I hope this is the beginning of a fuller and more adequate recognition of these cardinal facts.

Despite the debate being sparsely attended and little action being taken over the demands made, she must have been extremely proud of ensuring Welsh issues were heard at Westminster.

Megan Lloyd George was also president of the Parliament for Wales Campaign. It was launched in June 1950 in Llandrindod Wells, a town in mid-Wales which I have the honour of representing today. The campaign got off to something of a slow start (she was still an MP at its launch) but between 1951 and 1957 she was not in the House of Commons and in 1955 a bill was moved in Westminster to give Wales a Parliament. It received little support and failed to get a second reading, but remains an extremely significant piece of Welsh history.

Megan's political life also saw the creation of a Secretary of State for Wales. As far back as 1945 she had called for this role, saying, 'we in Wales want things done our way and not how the English want them done', and she saw this role realised following the 1964 general election. It came with a Cabinet rank and a staffed office in Cardiff. Megan congratulated Harold Wilson on being 'the second Prime Minister to recognise the nationhood of Wales'.

Fittingly, her last full contribution in the House of Commons was promoting her country on the annual 'Welsh day', saying, 'I believe that Wales has a great deal to gain from the National Plan, because if her resources are properly developed not only will Wales make an even greater contribution to the prosperity of her own people but also to the prosperity of Britain as a whole.'

*   *   *

When Megan was first elected she was one of just thirteen women in the House of Commons, and throughout her political career she championed women's issues as well as Welsh issues.

The social changes during World War Two, where around 7.5 million women worked in industry, led to numerous campaigns on women's working conditions which Megan played an active role in.

In a *Parliamentary Studies* article called *Women in Legislatures*, written in 1948, she wrote: 'During the war women Members concerned themselves as a united body in all questions relating to the most effective use of woman power.'

She added: 'In this united front women have shown a credible independence of judgement and have not feared to criticise their own Parties.'

Her biggest victory was her role in the successful campaign for equal compensation for injuries sustained during the Second World War. The Personal Injuries Bill allocated money to people seriously injured in air raids – thirty-five shillings to men, twenty-eighty to women. In 1941 a vote to equalise this was defeated, but by 1943 the government relented and introduced a single scale.

The campaign extended to focus on equal pay. In 1944 an amendment calling for equal pay for teachers was passed by 117 votes to 116. It was the only time Churchill's coalition government lost a vote. However, in a parliamentary manoeuvre Churchill turned the issue into a vote of confidence, which he won 394–28. The Equal Pay Act was only introduced in 1970.

In truth the success of these wartime campaigns for equal treatment was mixed, but this should not be a surprise. As with so much of what she cared about, Megan was campaigning for issues that were not yet in the mainstream of public consciousness. It was the early stages of a movement that would continue in the decades to come.

In her 1948 *Parliamentary Affairs* article, Megan wrote,

> What is the conclusion to be drawn from this brief record of Women in Legislatures? It is, I think, that in a comparatively short period of time remarkable progress has been made. It is true that they have not yet produced a figure of world renown, a Cromwell, a Pitt, or an Elizabeth, but then the ration even of great men in every century is restricted. But their quality and the contribution they have hitherto made has, however, been recognized in the increased responsibilities that have been placed upon them in every country, proof that they are coming ever more into their own as equals and partners in the work of Government.

*   *   *

Change was also afoot in broadcast technology. The 1929 election was the first 'radio election', and with the BBC allocating special broadcasts by and for women, Megan spoke for the Liberals. In 1937 television broadcasts were introduced, with Megan again taking part. She was widely regarded as a powerful and inspirational speaker.

Radio and television was another opportunity for her Welshness to shine through. In a 1949 election broadcast, to a UK audience, she signed off with the line '*Nos da. Hunan LLywodraeth I Gymru.*' Only a minority would have realised she said, 'Goodnight. Self-government for Wales,' but she felt it important to say regardless. Megan also secured recognition that Wales had a national identity and should not be regarded as a region of the BBC, and in 1960 joined an outcry when the new chairman of the Broadcasting Council for Wales was not a Welsh speaker.

As well as participating in it, Megan played an active role in shaping the culture of broadcasting. She sometimes drew criticism from broadcasters for what she said – Megan conducted a long-running campaign for freedom and spontaneity on the air. While we would take it for granted today, she had to argue passionately for unscripted discussions of important political issues.

*   *   *

Megan Lloyd George's later political career saw an interesting turn as she left the Liberal Party and defected to Labour. She would explain this by saying, 'The Liberal Party left me, not the other way around.'

Megan was a big supporter of the Beveridge Report, which in many ways advanced the structures created by her father in 1911, and was a vocal advocate of the 'Radical' tradition in the Liberal Party. However, she saw her party gradually but decisively shift to the right. In a bid for unity Megan was appointed deputy leader of the party in 1949, but in speaking of 'shedding our right wing' she perhaps undermined that somewhat! On women's rights and self-government for Wales the Liberals were far more radical than Labour, and Megan focused on these issues perhaps in an attempt to keep herself anchored in the party.

In 1951 the Liberals were reduced to six MPs, with Megan losing her seat in Anglesey and all the other left-wing Liberal MPs also rejected by voters. Her battle to uphold the radical Liberal tradition was a defining point in her political career, but it was ultimately unsuccessful and Megan drifted away.

It was widely expected that radical Liberal MPs would move to Labour, and eventually Megan did, although the fact it took until 1955 suggests it was a difficult decision for her. In a letter announcing her decision she said, 'the official Liberal Party seems to me to have lost all touch with the radical tradition that inspired it'. In the 1955 general election she undertook a nationwide speaking tour for the Labour Party. One of her visits was in my constituency of Brecon and Radnorshire, for the Labour candidate Tudor Watkins. In 1957 Megan was elected as the Labour MP for Carmarthen in a by-election, a role she held until her death in 1966.

*   *   *

Despite being a high-profile politician, Megan never held governmental office. She was offered the role of parliamentary secretary in the Ministry for Pensions during the Second World War, but declined as she was campaigning with other female MPs against unequal treatment administered by the department. As part of a governing Labour Party from 1964 she may well have hoped for a junior role under the newly established Secretary of State for Wales, but this did not happen.

Her reputation as an independent-minded backbencher may have counted against her when it came to securing a job in government. Indeed when she lost her seat in 1951, the *Holyhead Mail* reported that 'she fell because of her independence'.

There have also been suggestions that personal characteristics held her back. A journalist said she had a 'bright intelligence but an untrained mind'.

She has been described as lazy, forgetful and always late, as well as someone who took weeks to write letters to constituents.

It could be said that most of Megan Lloyd George's political career was spent fighting losing battles. Certainly, I'm sure she would have liked certain issues to have progressed much further. In championing women's causes there were few outright wins, with securing equal compensation in the Personal Injuries Bill a rare success. The Liberal Party of which she was a part saw its fortunes dwindle and collapse, and her radical part of the Liberal Party was pushed aside. The Welsh Parliament campaign had its flaws and was a long way off from securing its objective.

However, it would be exceedingly harsh to lay the blame for all this at Megan's feet; indeed she deserves a huge amount of credit for pushing these issues towards the mainstream. The subsequent progress, particularly on women's rights and devolution in Wales, suggests she was campaigning on issues well ahead of her time. It is this – ahead of her time – that in so many ways is the best way to describe Megan Lloyd George.

* * *

In 1962 Megan received treatment for breast cancer, but by 1965 the remission period was coming to an end. On 4 November she made her final contribution in the House of Commons, and later that month was taken into Hammersmith Hospital. By the time the 1966 general election came around ill health meant she was unable to campaign in her constituency, but she stood (and won) regardless. Six weeks later, on 14 May 1966, she passed away.

In one last dramatic twist for Megan, the subsequent by-election proved a hugely significant event in Welsh political history, with the election of the first ever Plaid Cymru Member of Parliament.

* * *

I would like to end with some personal reflections on what Megan Lloyd George means to me. I like to think we share some characteristics. She was a Welsh Liberal female politician, first elected at twenty-seven, and an active campaigner for a Welsh Parliament. As a Welsh Liberal female politician, first elected at twenty-eight, and an active campaigner for a Welsh Parliament, I owe her a huge debt of gratitude.

My election came sixty-eight years after hers and I cannot help but reflect that life has become so much easier for women in politics and indeed women in general. There is still much to be done, but the work of Megan and her fellow female MPs at the time was trailblazing and paved the way for much of what followed.

I was struck reading about the cross-party solidarity that existed between Megan and her fellow female MPs. They were so few in number and had to work together to get things done. In 1999 I was one of twenty-four women (out of sixty members in total) elected to the National Assembly for Wales, and in 2003 was one of thirty – a 50/50 split. We have enjoyed some of the best rates of gender equality in the world and I remember a real sense of solidarity between so many of the women elected. Again, it was so much easier for us than for Megan and her colleagues.

The very fact there have been elections to the National Assembly for Wales is also a huge testament to Megan's work. We were not ready for a Welsh Parliament when Megan Lloyd George was alive; indeed we were not ready in 1979 when Wales voted against it in a referendum. But in 1997 Wales voted to have its own Parliament. It has been said many a time in Wales that devolution is a process and not an event. As someone who campaigned for Wales to have its own Parliament, one of my proudest political moments was seeing my country vote in favour of devolution in the 1997 referendum. It was part of a process that Megan Lloyd George had helped advance in her political life.

I would not be where I am today without the work of people like Megan Lloyd George. As the first Welsh female MP she symbolised progress, and as a campaigner she helped achieve it. She was not perfect, no one is. Many of her campaigns did not get as far as she would have liked during her lifetime. But she truly was ahead of her time; while neither Wales nor the United Kingdom were ready for what she believed, she helped lay the foundations for social and national progress that I and many others have been fortunate enough to benefit from.

Reading and writing about Megan Lloyd George's life has been a welcome reminder that progress is always possible.

LADY CYNTHIA MOSLEY

RUTH SMEETH

- FULL NAME: Lady Cynthia Blanche Mosley (née Curzon)
- DATE OF BIRTH: 13 August 1898
- DATE OF DEATH: 16 May 1933
- PLACE OF BIRTH: Keddlestone Hall, Derbyshire
- MARRIED TO: Sir Oswald Mosley (m. 1920)
- CHILDREN: Vivien Elizabeth Mosley, Nicholas Mosley (3rd Baron Ravensdale) and Michael Mosley
- UNSUCCESSFUL ELECTIONS FOUGHT: None
- CONSTITUENCY: Stoke-on-Trent
- DATE OF FIRST ELECTION: 30 May 1929
- DATE LEFT PARLIAMENT: 27 October 1931
- PARTY ROLES: None
- MINISTERIAL POSITIONS & DATES: None
- MOST FAMOUS QUOTATION: 'All my life I have got something for nothing. Why? Have I earned it? Not a bit. I have just got it through luck.'

To say that Lady Cynthia Mosley was an incongruous Member of Parliament for the industrial heartlands of Stoke-on-Trent would be an understatement. But then there was nothing ordinary about the life of Cynthia Mosley, who was a mass of political and class-based contradictions and just so happened to have a ringside view of inter-war British political history.

Born Cynthia 'Cimmie' Curzon, she was the second daughter of Lord Curzon, the Viceroy of India and future Foreign Secretary. Her mother was Mary Victoria Curzon (née Leiter), an American heiress with a family fortune estimated at between $25 and $30 million.

Being a society girl didn't prevent the realities of war impacting Cynthia's life, however. During the First World War she worked as a War Office clerk, and later as a land girl, but it was a chance meeting after the war in Plymouth that was to define her life.

During Nancy Astor's by-election campaign in 1919, Cynthia Curzon met a man called Oswald. Within a year, the society marriage of 1920 had been organised and the King and Queen were among the glamorous attendees. Although her marriage may have been a society affair, Cynthia Curzon would not be content with life as a socialite – she was about to take a different path.

Cynthia Oswald's selection by the Labour Party in 1925 to contest Stoke-on-Trent would be the start of a brief, but tumultuous political career, and in many ways the first chapter of a story about one family's conflicted relationship with a city and its values.

In 1929, she was elected to Parliament with a majority of 7,850, the largest swing to Labour that year and one of the largest majorities of any inter-war female MP.

Cynthia delivered her maiden speech in a debate on the introduction of the Widows, Orphans and Old Age Contributory Pensions Bill. In a well-received speech, she welcomed the measures as a step along the 'road towards the abolition of poverty and destitution'. And she used her own privilege to highlight that of those Conservative members opposing relief for the poor:

> All my life I have got something for nothing. Why? Have I earned it? Not a bit. I have just got it through luck. Of course, some people might say I showed great intelligence in the choice of my parents, but I put it all down to luck. And not only I, but if I may be allowed to say so, a great many people on the opposite side of the House are in the same position – they also have always got something for nothing.

Cynthia Mosley was, by all accounts, well liked within the Labour Party, and certainly more trusted than her husband, whose political dissatisfaction and battles with the Labour government of Ramsay MacDonald would trigger his departure and have consequences far beyond the Labour movement. Cynthia was, it seems, a conscientious MP who worked hard for her constituents. She was often seen out in the area – an unusual act for an MP in the 1920s.

She was also a popular figure on the Labour Party circuit; one reporter described her speaking voice as 'like that of Cordelia – soft, gentle and low', and her appearances often drew a crowd.

She lacked the abrasiveness and self-regard that led Oswald Mosley to make so many political enemies. But she shared his irritation for what they both saw as the stale, uninspiring and incrementalist politics of the Labour government at the time. She craved a bolder and more socialist programme, and even met briefly with Leon Trotsky in Russia. Trotsky, for his part, seemed less impressed, describing their conversation as 'banal in the extreme'.

If history had been different, it is easy to believe that a woman of Cynthia Mosley's abilities could have made a long and serious contribution to British politics. In the event, it is ultimately impossible to see her own contribution except through the prism of her husband's turbulent, opportunistic, populist, hate-filled and ultimately self-destructive political journey.

They were, from the very beginning, a political partnership, joining the Labour Party together in 1924. But Oswald Mosley's own travails within the party, his fallout with MacDonald and his eventual resignation to set up the New Party (a precursor to the British Union of Fascists which was formed by Mosley in 1932) would set both of them on a different, darker course.

Throughout this period Cynthia did not merely support Mosley as his wife, she was also one of his few consistent champions within the Parliamentary Labour Party. And when he walked away from the party, she left with him.

The years that followed would see Cynthia facing a physical and emotional decline that mirrored in many ways the moral decline of her husband, who neglected her in his pursuit for political and personal self-gratification.

After undergoing surgery for appendicitis, she contracted peritonitis and died on 16 May 1933. The leaders of all parties supported the construction of a day nursery in Kennington to honour her memory.

In the years that have followed, Cynthia Mosley's contributions have been lost beneath the legacy of her husband's fascism – today the Mosley name is synonymous with Oswald's abhorrent political ideology.

Maybe there is some irony in the fact that, despite Cynthia stepping aside in Stoke-on-Trent for Oswald, who was standing as a New Party candidate, he was roundly beaten in the election. Perhaps it is more ironic still that our great city should now be represented by a Jewish daughter of immigrants, whose family faced down Mosley at Cable Street.

MARION PHILLIPS

MARY HONEYBALL

- FULL NAME: Dr Marion Phillips
- DATE OF BIRTH: 28 October 1881
- PLACE OF BIRTH: Melbourne, Australia
- DATE OF DEATH: 23 January 1932
- MARRIED TO: Unmarried
- CHILDREN: None
- UNSUCCESSFUL ELECTIONS FOUGHT: None
- CONSTITUENCY: Sunderland
- DATE OF FIRST ELECTION: 30 May 1929
- DATE LEFT PARLIAMENT: 27 October 1931
- PARTY ROLES: Chief women's officer; secretary of the Standing Joint Committee of Working Women's Organisations; editor of *Labour Women*; member of the Labour Party War Emergency National Committee; and Labour councillor on the Kensington London Borough Council
- MINISTERIAL POSITIONS & DATES: None
- MOST FAMOUS QUOTATION: 'If Labour councillors will not support us on this demand [the need for adequate washing and bathing facilities in new municipal housing projects], we shall have to cry a halt on all municipal housing until we have replaced all Labour men with Labour women.'

An MP for a mere two years between 1929 and 1931, Dr Marion Phillips is better known for her work as the Labour Party's first chief women's officer. Appointed in 1918, following the radical overhaul of the Labour Party constitution to allow individual as well as affiliate membership, Phillips's leadership enabled the women's sections to become a vibrant component of the rapidly expanding Labour Party. Her credentials for the chief women's officer post were strong. Since 1911, she had been secretary of the Women's Labour League, whose branches became the foundation of the new Labour Party women's sections.

Marion Phillips was born in Australia, arriving in Britain in 1904 to begin a research scholarship at the London School of Economics. Following her doctorate, she became an assistant to Sidney and Beatrice Webb, and made the advancement of women her life's work.

In 1912, at the age of thirty, Phillips became both a councillor on Kensington Borough Council and the secretary of the Women's Labour League. As a Labour councillor she pressed for public provision of baby clinics, school meals, improved council housing, employment schemes and the prohibition of sweated labour. In 1913, she established *The Labour Woman* as the journal of the Women's Labour League, editing it until her death in 1932.

In 1914, Phillips was elected to the Labour Party's War Emergency Workers' National Committee to organise the working-class response to the war. From 1917 to 1919 she served on both the government's Reconstruction committee and the Consumers' Council at the Ministry of Food. She was appointed secretary of the Standing Joint Committee of Working Women's Organisations in 1917, and saw her role as keeping the Labour Party informed of the needs of women and educating women in political matters.

Phillips's prominence in the Labour Party, especially the women's organisation, led to her nomination by the Durham Women's Advisory Council and the Monkwearmouth miners as a prospective parliamentary candidate for the multi-member constituency of Sunderland in 1926. She was subsequently returned in the 1929 'flapper election'.

Marion Phillips was noted both for her prodigious appetite for work and her abrasive personality, making her unpopular with some leading women in the Labour movement. She further upset activists by opposing birth control in the 1920s, on the grounds that it would turn Catholic working-class voters away from Labour.

During her brief time in Parliament, coinciding with Ramsay MacDonald's second minority Labour government, Phillips took a strong interest in employment and social issues, supporting, among other things, amendments to the Children and Young Persons Employment and Protection Bill and the Unemployment Insurance Act. She, moreover, invented a convenient House of Commons uniform for women MPs – a well-cut overall of thick crêpe de chine lined with bright silk which buttoned over the Member's dress.

All nine Labour women elected to Parliament in 1929 were defeated in the general election of 1931, called after Ramsay MacDonald had established a National Government following the advent of the Great Depression. Tragically, Marion Phillips died a year later from stomach cancer.

EDITH PICTON-TURBERVILL

JANE MERRICK

- FULL NAME: Edith Picton-Turbervill, OBE
- DATE OF BIRTH: 13 June 1872
- PLACE OF BIRTH: Fownhope, Herefordshire
- DATE OF DEATH: 31 August 1960
- MARRIED TO: Unmarried
- CHILDREN: None
- UNSUCCESSFUL ELECTIONS FOUGHT: Islington North 1922 and Stroud 1924
- CONSTITUENCY: The Wrekin
- DATE OF FIRST ELECTION: 30 May 1929
- DATE LEFT PARLIAMENT: 26 October 1931
- PARTY ROLES: None
- MINISTERIAL POSITIONS & DATES: None
- MOST FAMOUS QUOTATION: 'Never have women as a whole held the power they hold today. Much of this power, very much, is latent, an unexpressed, unused force; it is, however, there, and is likely to become the greatest power of the world in the coming generation.'

Edith Picton-Turbervill's background did not, on the face of it, suggest a lifetime of campaigning for socialism and women's equality. She was the daughter of John Picton Warlow, a Conservative JP and army captain from mine-owning stock. Her father inherited the 3,000-acre Turbervill estate in Glamorgan when she was nineteen, and the family changed its name. As she wrote in her 1939 autobiography, *Life Is Good*, her upbringing encouraged her to live an active life. Picton-Turbervill did not become involved in party politics within the Labour movement until her forties, but her life before then was one committed to helping others, firstly through social work in her local community, and then as a missionary in India, through the Young Women's Christian Association (YWCA). During the First World War she continued to work with the YWCA, providing hostels for women in the munitions corps, and became active in the suffragist movement, alongside Millicent Fawcett. Her burning passion was for equality in the Church of England, campaigning for women to be ordained as priests, and after the war she became the first woman to preach at a C of E statutory service, as a lay reader, in North Somercotes, Lincolnshire. She was awarded an OBE for her wartime work in 1918.

In 1919, at the age of forty-seven, she joined the Labour Party. In 1921 she helped Lady Astor form the Consultative Committee of Women's Organisations, and the two women issued this joint appeal to women: 'You did your bit in the war. Are you free to do your bit in the peace? There is plenty of work to be done.' But her desire for gender equality was tempered by political reality, believing that women's progress was being held back by militancy. Writing in the suffragist newspaper *The Vote* in 1924, she warned against 'grinding the Feminist axe too freely'.

Picton-Turbervill stood unsuccessfully as a Labour candidate for Islington North in 1922. She helped campaign for Labour leader Ramsay MacDonald in Port Talbot at the 1923 election, and in 1924 was a Labour candidate in Stroud, where she did not win but finished ahead of the Liberals. Despite a friendship with MacDonald, she criticised his failure to comment on the infamous Zinoviev letter, which she said had a 'devastating effect' on Labour candidates and helped the Tories win a landslide.

In 1925 she was selected to fight the swing seat of The Wrekin, which she won in 1929 with a near 3,000 majority, and arrived in Parliament as one of just fourteen women. While her period in Parliament was short-lived – losing her seat in 1931 – it was not wasted, aided by half a lifetime spent campaigning on social and women's issues. She successfully introduced a law to stop pregnant women convicted of crimes being given the death penalty, through the Sentence of Death (Expectant Mothers) Bill, and called for women to be able to serve in the police force, arguing that it would create 'a better social order in our cities'. She was nominated as the first woman to serve on the Ecclesiastical Committee of Parliament because of her background in the Church. After leaving Parliament, she continued to be a social justice campaigner, including on the issue of Chinese refugee girls being sold into slavery in Hong Kong. Her family remembered her as an imposing figure, at over 6ft tall, with a 'rather loud voice', lack of 'domestic skills', a dislike of small talk and a love of reading.

ELEANOR RATHBONE

RACHEL REEVES AND MARY READER

- FULL NAME: Eleanor Florence Rathbone
- DATE OF BIRTH: 12 May 1872
- PLACE OF BIRTH: London
- DATE OF DEATH: 2 January 1946
- MARRIED TO: Unmarried
- CHILDREN: None
- UNSUCCESSFUL ELECTIONS FOUGHT: Liverpool East Toxteth 1922
- CONSTITUENCY: Combined English Universities
- DATE OF FIRST ELECTION: 30 May 1929
- DATE LEFT PARLIAMENT: 2 January 1946
- PARTY ROLES: None
- MINISTERIAL POSITIONS & DATES: None
- MOST FAMOUS QUOTATION: 'The struggle for the right to become politicians in itself made women into politicians.'

'It is very difficult,' Nancy Astor said, 'when we look at the hon. Lady the Member of the English Universities [Miss Rathbone], to think of her as a revolutionary, but she is, and it is her work, and her vision and courage, that have really brought us where we are today.' Astor spoke these words during a parliamentary debate on family allowances – weekly payments to mothers to help with the costs of having children – a policy which was the defining achievement of Rathbone's career. Eleanor Rathbone almost single-handedly translated family allowances from a noble idea into words on the statute book within twenty-five years. Eleanor's quiet diligence and perseverance combined with a viscerally rooted life mission to champion the rights of the vulnerable.

Eleanor Rathbone was born in 1872 to a wealthy Liverpudlian family steeped in the Liberal tradition; the family motto was 'What ought to be done, can be done.' It was a maxim she carried with her throughout her political life. From a young age, Eleanor demonstrated the qualities that would later come to define her: intellectual curiosity and drive for social change. Despite the protestations of her mother, she accepted her offer at Oxford to study Greats, a remarkable achievement for a woman at the time. Her supportive father, William Rathbone, was a Liberal MP from 1868 to 1895 and worked with Eleanor on a social investigation into Liverpool's system of dock labour. When he died in 1902, Eleanor was left bereft. Yet his death and legacy – not least in the form of a sizeable inheritance – gave her the opportunity to pursue her political dreams. She continued her investigation and social work, before becoming the first female Justice of the Peace in Lancashire and the first woman to sit on the Liverpool City Council. She also became the leader of the Liverpool Women's Suffrage Society and emerged as a prominent figure within the women's movement nationally. In 1919, Eleanor was elected as president of the National Union of Women's Suffrage Societies (NUWSS), formerly led by Millicent Fawcett. Under Rathbone's leadership, the NUWSS transformed into a broader campaign for equal rights for women, fulfilling its new name: the National Union of Societies for Equal Citizenship (NUSEC). She led the organisation as part of the big four of prominent new feminists alongside Elizabeth Macadam, Eva Hubback and Eleanor's biographer Mary Stocks. Eleanor had met Elizabeth Macadam the year after her father died, and she came to be the single most important person in her life. A Scottish social worker, Macadam supported Eleanor's political career and the two lived together for most of their lives. There is a deep affection that pours out of their letters to one another. However, after Eleanor's death almost all of their correspondence was burned, making it difficult to ascertain the true nature of their relationship.

In 1928, one of the defining aims of NUSEC – equal franchise – became a reality. A year later, having stood unsuccessfully for Liverpool East Toxteth in 1922, Eleanor was elected as a Member of Parliament. Her election could not have come at a more appropriate time. It was the first time that young, working-class women could vote, so the 1929 general election was dubbed the 'flapper election'. Eleanor rode into Parliament on the wave of those young women's votes, representing the Combined English Universities as an independent MP.

Eleanor packed in an astounding range of political campaigns, on which she collaborated with everyone from the anti-feminist Winston Churchill to the radical socialist feminist Ellen Wilkinson. In the 1930s, her campaigns for women's suffrage and against child marriage in India and female genital mutilation in Africa proved controversial. Indian women's organisations viewed her campaign as moralising and a patrician continuation of colonialism. But her fight against appeasement was perhaps her most important international campaign. Engaging in cross-party cooperation with the Conservatives' Duchess of Atholl and Labour's Ellen Wilkinson, Eleanor vociferously opposed Chamberlain's policy of appeasement towards Nazi Germany and non-intervention in the Spanish Civil War. She was deeply moved, both emotionally and politically, by the refugee crisis. She lobbied for relaxing visa requirements for temporary refuge and tried desperately to prevent the French government from sending trains of refugees to forced labour and death camps. In 1942, on hearing the first reports of mass extermination of the Jewish people, she stepped up her campaigns further, founding the National Committee for Rescue from Nazi Terror in 1943 and leading numerous deputations to the Home Office, much to the irritation and disdain of British ministers and officials.

A refugee survivor from a camp she visited recalls her saying to him, 'You are not forgotten.' This was no poetic embellishment: the plight of the refugees animated her every living thought and action. As she wrote in an article for the *Manchester Guardian* in 1939, she felt responsible for 'every bit of evil in the world'.

The arrival of family allowances in 1945 was a testament to Eleanor's perseverance, political nous and deep sense of purpose. The logic behind family allowances for her was clear: women's domestic work in the home should be valued just as much as men's work outside of it. The cooking, the cleaning and the childcare performed without fanfare by women made an essential contribution to the family's ability to earn wages and so to our national economy and civic life. Yet their lack of remuneration for this work meant that they were 'disinherited' from the family income, as her seminal book, *The Disinherited Family*, argued. Family allowances were therefore a way of remunerating women's domestic work and according it social value. She had begun her campaign towards the end of the First World War, when she created the Family Endowment committee and later the Family Endowment Society. By the late 1920s, she had gained the endorsement of William Beveridge, who would go on to write the era-defining blueprint of the post-war welfare state – the Beveridge Report.

Eleanor's lobbying abilities were second to none, and a crucial reason for the success of family allowances. Harold Nicolson recalls that government spokesmen used to dive into doorways to avoid being caught and interrogated by her about the government's position. A fellow woman MP, Edith Picton-Turbervill, described Eleanor as 'driving her points home like a sledgehammer'. Parliamentary questions were the Rathbone trademark. By the 1930s, she was asking two or more every week on a range of topics. In the final parliamentary debate on family allowances, the government proposed that they should be paid to the father rather than the mother. Rathbone was incensed. The whole point of family allowances was to empower women by paying the allowance directly to them. She threatened to vote against the Bill unless ministers accepted her amendment, despite, in her words, '[having] worked for this thing for over twenty-five years'. She attended these debates in a wheelchair, having injured her leg and not being in the best of health. In the end, the government caved to the parliamentary pressure she had instigated, and family allowances were made with payment to the mother enshrined in law.

At the 1945 general election, Eleanor considered stepping down due to her ill health, but she decided that she had to push further on women's equality and refugee issues. Having defended her seat amid a Labour landslide, in January 1946 she tragically died of a stroke – but her legacy in Parliament lived on. During her memorial service, a fellow independent MP paid a poignant tribute to Eleanor's work in Parliament:

> There must be many of us who ... looked at that second bench below the gangway and realised with a pang that we should not again see that small, gallant figure, clutching the big black bag with bulging papers, in recent months frail and stooping, but never for an instant flagging in courage or persistency, watching for every chance of pressing her case by supplementing question or intervention in debate.

Eleanor Rathbone should be remembered today as she was then: an impassioned, hard-working fighter for political change and, in the words of her biographer Susan Pedersen, as 'the most effective woman politician of the first half of the twentieth century'.

LADY LUCY NOEL-BUXTON

OONAGH GAY

- FULL NAME: Lady Lucy Edith Noel-Buxton (née Pelham Burn)
- DATE OF BIRTH: 14 December 1888
- PLACE OF BIRTH: Winchester
- DATE OF DEATH: 9 December 1960
- MARRIED TO: Noel Noel-Buxton (m. 1914; d. 1948)
- CHILDREN: Noel Alexander; Christopher Arthur Noel; Michael Barnett Noel; Lydia Victoria Noel; Jane Elizabeth Noel; and Sarah Edith Noel
- UNSUCCESSFUL ELECTIONS FOUGHT: Norfolk North 1931 and 1935
- CONSTITUENCY: North Norfolk and Cromer Norwich
- DATE OF FIRST ELECTION: 9 July 1930
- DATE LEFT PARLIAMENT: 7 October 1931 and 3 February 1950
- PARTY ROLES: None
- MINISTERIAL POSITIONS & DATES: None
- MOST FAMOUS QUOTATION: 'There is nothing between the agricultural labourer this winter and destitution but the Poor Law. In the villages, the fact that the agricultural labourer is debarred from insurance causes a certain amount of jealousy. He is working side by side, for instance, with the carpenter, who is fully insured. A father may be in the position of having to depend more or less on charity, while his son is fully insured … We must take in time Goldsmith's warning given very many years ago in the "Deserted Village".' From her maiden speech in the Commons.

Lucy Edith Pelham Burn was born on 14 December 1888 in Winchester, the eldest daughter of Major Henry Pelham Burn and his wife, Janet Edith (née Orr-Ewing). She studied at Westfield College in London, and then in 1914 married Noel Buxton, the MP for Norfolk North and a rising Liberal Party star, who was nearly twenty years her senior. The pair had met during the 1910 election campaign when, as a Conservative, she campaigned against his election. Subsequently, she changed her mind! The marriage produced six children (three boys, three girls). Initially they lived at Paycockes, in Coggeshall, Essex, an old timbered house that Buxton restored, and which he later donated to the National Trust.

Lucy was foundation trustee of the Noel Buxton Trust, established in 1919, which oversaw the spending of part of the family income on charitable purposes, in particular on child welfare, international peace and the future development of Britain's African colonies. One of her particular interests was in gardening, and she was active in the London Gardens Guild, founded by her husband when the family lived in Spitalfields, which she saw as a way of improving the quality of life for working-class city dwellers.

Noel Buxton joined the Labour Party in 1919 and served in the Labour Cabinets of 1924 and 1929. Lucy Buxton became part of the 'Half Circle Club', which was designed to equip Labour women for public office and was organised by Beatrice Webb. In 1930, suffering ill health, her husband accepted a peerage to go to the Lords, and in the subsequent by-election on 9 July, Lady Noel-Buxton won the Labour nomination against the opposition of the National Union of Agricultural Workers. She went on to win the seat, with a majority of just 179 votes in a closely fought campaign that attracted a 75 per cent turnout. Lucy used her maiden speech on 19 November 1930 to focus on widening the unemployment insurance scheme to include agricultural workers, asking the Minister for Labour, Margaret Bondfield, to act, as opinion in rural trade unions began to move towards contributory payments for farm workers.

Lucy did not speak often in the House, but she did participate in the Joint Select Committee on the Wills and Intestacies (Family Maintenance) Bill 1931, as did Eleanor Rathbone. This Bill aimed to protect surviving spouses or children who were left without means of support following the deceased spouse's will or intestacy.

Lucy was unable to hold on to her seat in 1931 and she was beaten by Conservative Thomas Cook, the owner of the *Norfolk Chronicle*, whom she had stood against in the 1930 by-election. Lucy contested the seat again in 1935, but remained unsuccessful. During the Second World War, she worked for the Soldiers, Sailors, Airmen and Families Association, but her political career revived when she won one of the double seats at Norwich in 1945. As an MP, she focused primarily on colonial matters, agriculture, land rights, democracy and education.

During the Second World War, her son Christopher was killed; her husband died in September 1948. Her son Noel Alexander succeeded to the title, taking the Liberal whip. She decided not to stand for re-election in 1950, after double constituencies were abolished in the Representation of the People Act 1948. She made her announcement in December 1948, citing bronchial trouble.

She died in Frinton on 9 December 1960.

DAME LEAH MANNING

EMILY THORNBERRY

- FULL NAME: Dame Elizabeth Leah Manning (née Perrett) DBE
- DATE OF BIRTH: 14 April 1886
- PLACE OF BIRTH: Droitwich, Worcestershire
- DATE OF DEATH: 15 September 1977
- MARRIED TO: Will Manning (m. 1914; d. 1952)
- CHILDREN: One daughter
- UNSUCCESSFUL ELECTIONS FOUGHT: Sunderland 1935; Epping 1951 and 1955
- CONSTITUENCY: Islington East 1931 and Epping 1945–50
- DATE OF FIRST ELECTION: 19 February 1931
- DATE LEFT PARLIAMENT: 23 February 1950
- PARTY ROLES: President of the National Union of Teachers 1930–31 and member of the NEC 1931–32
- MINISTERIAL POSITIONS & DATES: None
- MOST FAMOUS QUOTATION: 'Head to tail the senoritas laid out our precious cargo – on the bulkheads, in the swimming pool, in the state rooms and along the alleyways … for all the world like the little sardinas about which they were always singing.'

L eah Manning began the final chapter of her 1970 autobiography with a strikingly pessimistic statement: 'I have been able to achieve nothing of what I had in mind; things are worse in the world today than when I was eighteen.'

Eighty-four years old at the time, she had lived through two world wars and – as a staunch socialist and pacifist – it must have been hard to stay optimistic in an era of broken hopes and worsening conflict.

Yet she had achieved so much. A career in education led her to become the National Union of Teachers' fourth female president in 1930, and its first married one, at a time when most female teachers had to quit the profession after marriage.

She was elected in Islington East in February 1931, but lost her seat with the collapse of the National Government eight months later, and had a long wait to return to Parliament, succeeding Winston Churchill as the MP for Epping in 1945.

In the interim, she remained a passionate advocate for the teaching and welfare of children, never more significantly than in her hugely courageous and dramatic intervention in the Spanish Civil War, when she helped evacuate 4,000 Basque children from Bilbao to safety in Britain.

One of many staunch socialists who rushed to help in the fight against fascism, she saw comrades die and witnessed the destruction of Guernica, but bravely stayed to save the lives of thousands of children, and is today commemorated with a square in Bilbao. It was one of many times she was willing to 'stick her neck out' for the causes she believed in – a critical media label in which she revelled.

She was a passionate backbencher in the post-war Attlee government, walking through the Commons voting lobbies singing 'The Red Flag'. When Churchill heard she had lost her seat in the 1950 election, he did not celebrate the Tory victory, but called the result a 'great pity' – explaining that 'she was a good Member, and a good Commons woman'.

And for Manning, part of being a 'good Commons woman' meant supporting other female MPs. She loved her colleagues Lucy Middleton, Ellen Wilkinson and Barbara Castle, but despised Jean Mann for the way she undermined them. Once, when Mann asked why the Speaker called her (Manning) to speak so often, Manning responded, 'Because he knows I am not malicious to other lady members.'

Never one to give up a fight, she stood again for election in Epping in 1951 and 1955, and continued to campaign passionately for education and equality in the local area, including securing the first contraception clinic for unmarried women in Harlow.

Manning was made a dame in 1966, but honours never meant as much to her as making a difference. She ended her autobiography by quoting her favourite prayer, referring to herself as a brick buried at the base of a foundation, standing faithfully in her place so that the building might stand.

But she was wrong. No brick sticks its neck out the way she did.

THELMA CAZALET-KEIR

SHAZIA AWAN-SCULLY

- FULL NAME: Thelma Cazalet-Keir CBE (née Cazalet)
- DATE OF BIRTH: 28 May 1899
- PLACE OF BIRTH: London
- DATE OF DEATH: 13 January 1989
- MARRIED TO: David Keir (m. 1939)
- CHILDREN: None
- UNSUCCESSFUL ELECTIONS FOUGHT: Islington East 1931 (by-election) and 1945
- CONSTITUENCY: Islington East
- DATE OF FIRST ELECTION: 27 October 1931
- DATE LEFT PARLIAMENT: 4 July 1945
- PARTY ROLES: None
- MINISTERIAL POSITIONS & DATES: Parliamentary Under-Secretary for Education 1945
- MOST FAMOUS QUOTATION: 'Christian Science teaches that right thinking can heal, and numberless people, including myself, have been privileged to prove in a small way the sayings of Jesus that all power belongeth unto God.'

At first glance, the parliamentary career of Thelma Cazalet-Keir looks an unremarkable one. She fought only three general elections (preceded by one by-election), she had lost her parliamentary seat by her mid-forties and she never subsequently returned to Parliament. Cazalet-Keir held junior ministerial office only very briefly. Yet she is a much more interesting figure than this summary might make her initially appear.

Thelma Cazalet came from a prominent and wealthy family; the Cazalets were well connected in late nineteenth- and early twentieth-century English society, but there was much more to them than simply money and social standing. Thelma's mother was both a Christian Scientist and a strong early feminist – two influences that persisted throughout Thelma's parliamentary career and broader life. Like many families, the Cazalets were touched by tragedy in war: Thelma's oldest brother was killed in the First World War and, later, her middle brother suffered the same fate in the Second World War. (Her youngest brother, Peter, happily survived to eventually become a famous racing trainer, training horses for the Queen Mother.)

Thelma first entered electoral politics by becoming a local councillor in Kent, and then from 1924 served as an elected member of the London County Council. She stood unsuccessfully for the Conservatives in the 1931 Islington East by-election. But when the Labour government broke up later that year, and the new National Government asked for its 'Doctor's Mandate' from the people, Cazalet won Islington East in the ensuing landslide general election victory. She went on to retain the seat in the subsequent election four years later.

Cazalet always stood as a Conservative candidate, but she was not a party hardliner. For much of her life, she was close friends with Megan Lloyd George, while her parliamentary and subsequent career showed her to be far from a traditional Conservative, notably on the role of women.

Cazalet's 1931 election victory was a historic first: her triumph over the Labour incumbent Leah Manning was the first time (alongside the victory of Irene Ward over Margaret Bondfield in Wallsend) that a woman had won a seat at a general election from a female incumbent MP. Actually, Cazalet might well have preferred to have won from a male MP, to increase female representation, as feminism was a consistent strand in her life.

This feminism manifested itself in various ways, from the personal to the more obviously political. When Cazalet married the *News Chronicle*'s parliamentary lobby correspondent David Keir in 1939, she changed her name – but she didn't take her husband's name, opting instead for the double-barrelled Cazalet-Keir.

Cazalet-Keir's most significant parliamentary activity was the amendment that she advanced to the 1944 Education Bill which later became famous as the 'Butler Education Act'. The amendment would have required that female teachers receive equal pay. Despite opposition to the amendment by the government, it was passed in the House of Commons – by a single vote! This was the only defeat in a Commons' vote that was ever suffered by Churchill's coalition government. Yet even though it had been advanced by a fellow Conservative, the amendment was far too radical for the Prime Minister and some of his fellow Tories. Churchill demanded the overturning of the amendment – even to the extent of wielding the ultimate parliamentary weapon, by making the vote on overturning the Cazalet-Keir amendment a matter of confidence in the entire government. Denying women in the teaching profession equal pay with their male colleagues was apparently so important to Churchill that, to achieve this goal, he was willing to threaten the prospect of the UK being left without a functioning government even as war still raged in Europe, Asia and the Pacific. The amendment was thrown out – with Cazalet-Keir herself pressured into now voting against it.

Education had long been an interest of Cazalet-Keir's – she had served as parliamentary private secretary to an Education minister from 1937 to '40. When Prime Minister Churchill formed a caretaker government in late May 1945 (after Labour and Liberal ministers withdrew from office in preparation for the forthcoming general election), Cazalet-Keir was Parliamentary Under-Secretary for Education for the following two months. But the subsequent general election saw a huge swing to Labour and Cazalet-Keir was one of many Conservative casualties in the Labour landslide, ultimately losing her seat. She never attempted to return to the Commons.

Following her defeat, though no longer an MP, Cazalet-Keir remained active in public life. She was a member of the Arts Council for many years, and also served one term as a governor of the BBC. Her public service was recognised by the award of a CBE in 1952. But Thelma Cazalet-Keir was no staid establishment figure: she remained an active and campaigning feminist. She was made president of the Fawcett Society in the 1960s, and was also a strong advocate for the Women's Engineering Society, which sought to secure more opportunities for women in a traditionally male-dominated sector.

Feminism is about the advancement of women and their role in society – Thelma Cazalet-Keir is one of the many, now largely forgotten, people whose life and work contributed significantly to advancing that cause.

IDA COPELAND

SARAH MACKINLAY

- FULL NAME: Ida Copeland (née Fenzi)
- DATE OF BIRTH: 15 April 1881
- PLACE OF BIRTH: Florence, Italy
- DATE OF DEATH: 29 June 1964
- MARRIED TO: Richard Ronald John Copeland (m. 1915; d. 1958)
- CHILDREN: None
- UNSUCCESSFUL ELECTIONS FOUGHT: None
- CONSTITUENCY: Stoke-on-Trent
- DATE OF FIRST ELECTION: 27 October 1931
- DATE LEFT PARLIAMENT: 13 November 1935
- PARTY ROLES: None
- MINISTERIAL POSITIONS & DATES: None
- MOST FAMOUS QUOTATION: 'Every man and every woman to exercise their great privilege of voting.'

Conducting her correspondence from a George III mahogany writing desk inside her sprawling estate, Trelissick House, Ida Copeland was the twenty-fifth woman to be elected to Parliament. The grand desk was just one piece in an extensive and fine collection of antiques, wines and paintings owned by the Copeland dynasty. With its own peninsula and views of lush woodland winding down into the town of Falmouth, Trelissick House, sitting in 376 acres of land, provided a place of sanctuary and reflection for Copeland.

Copeland's upbringing was, unquestionably, privileged. The daughter of an Italian Count, Camillo Fenzi, she lived in Italy until the death of her father. Her mother, Evelyne Isabella (a first cousin of Florence Nightingale), was English so the family returned to England.

Ida's mother married the deputy governor of the Bank of England, Leonard Daneham Cunliffe, who was also a major investor in Harrods. It was

Cunliffe who left Copeland Trelissick. She in turn bequeathed it to the National Trust, on the understanding that future generations of the Copeland family would be allowed to continue to reside in the home.

She successfully fought and won the seat of Stoke against Oswald Mosley's movement, the New Party, in the 1931 election, defeating the incumbent Cynthia Mosley, Oswald's wife. Taking to the streets of Stoke to campaign, Copeland urged, 'Every man... every woman to exercise their great privilege of voting.'

Meanwhile, Mosley spent less than a week campaigning in his wife's constituency. Perhaps he was overconfident and felt that he could afford to divert attention to his national fight. This afforded Copeland an opportunity; she used her family interest and expertise in potteries and china, as well as her husband's work as a china manufacturer in the Potteries, to her huge advantage for the duration of the campaign. Copeland defeated Cynthia Mosley with a respectable 6,654-vote majority.

The Copelands had both a personal and professional interest in china, ceramics, porcelain and other collectables. Her political life was dominated by the protection of the industry; a sensible pursuit considering her Staffordshire constituency encompassed the Potteries heartland.

Copeland's maiden speech concerned the need for import duties on the pottery industry. She observed that international manufacturers often paid their workers starvation wages to produce the goods. She supported the use of tariffs, insisting they offered some protection to the industry in the UK. 'Can we allow goods manufactured under those conditions to come into this country and lower the standard of living of our own people? I say, "No." And I firmly believe that, if we raise these tariffs, the time will come when our industry will be on its feet again,' she said on the floor of the Chamber.

She warned again, in 1933, of the impact that cheap Japanese goods, some of which were imitations of British pieces, were having on the industry in both Australia and New Zealand. She urged the government to act by insisting on similar tariffs to the ones used in Britain. The government's response was said to be sympathetic, but it did not take specific action.

Copeland was often charitable and a willing advocate; she was very supportive of the Polish community, of which a sizeable number worked in the mining industry in Stoke before it closed. In 1943, she was made chair of the Staffordshire Anglo-Polish Society, and was awarded the Polish Gold Cross of Merit in 1952, the highest order of Polish state civil decoration.

Throughout her life she showed generosity and compassion. On one occasion, Copeland invited a Polish resistance fighter and prisoner of war, Julian Kulski, who was suffering from malnutrition and PTSD following the war, to stay at Trelissick to convalesce.

One of her greatest achievements is her involvement in the Girl Guides. The Copelands were great friends of the Baden-Powells, founders of the organisation, and Copeland was instrumental in helping develop the Girl Guides. Trelissick was used to host many Guides and Scouts events.

In 2013, Ida Copeland's family invited auctioneers Bonhams to Trelissick to carry out a £1.5 million sale of its contents. Some of the collection was bequeathed to the Fitzwilliam Museum in Cambridge, but other items from the extensive collection, including silverware, wine, books and paintings, went on sale without reserve.

MARJORIE GRAVES

SARAH MACKINLAY

- FULL NAME: Frances Marjorie Graves
- DATE OF BIRTH: 17 September 1884
- PLACE OF BIRTH: Allerton, Liverpool
- DATE OF DEATH: 17 November 1961
- MARRIED TO: Unmarried
- CHILDREN: None
- UNSUCCESSFUL ELECTIONS FOUGHT: Hackney South 1935
- CONSTITUENCY: Hackney South
- DATE OF FIRST ELECTION: 27 October 1931
- DATE LEFT PARLIAMENT: 13 November 1935
- PARTY ROLES: None
- MINISTERIAL POSITIONS & DATES: None

Before entering Parliament, Frances (Marjorie) Graves worked for the intelligence service and was part of the UK delegation present at the League of Nations. An impressive early career laid the foundations for a working life which promised to be extraordinary. However, as a woman, there were inevitably some constraints imposed on her and her parliamentary career lasted just one mandate.

Nevertheless, Graves's political interests challenged the traditional role women MPs played in the 1920s and '30s, where it was often expected they would participate in debates concerning the housing crisis and domestic service problems. Graves was a refreshing figure, because she was primarily concerned with international affairs.

Her maiden speech, by way of example, was compelling. She discussed the Consolidated Fund Appropriation Bill, which revealed how well informed she was on international politics.

Convention dictates that a member's maiden speech is profusely and warmly congratulated, and Labour MP Colonel Wedgewood gave glowing praise:

I have heard a great many maiden speeches, but never before a maiden speech of a lady Member, and I must say that the speech to which we have just listened is a speech for which the House has been waiting for twenty-five years … I hope that we shall hear more of the hon. Lady in this House, and that she will not confine herself to a maiden speech.

But despite this early promise, Graves was to make just nine further contributions to Commons debates during her four years in Parliament.

Graves was born in Allerton, Liverpool (famous for featuring in the Beatles song 'Penny Lane'), where the young Graves's father was a successful ship owner. There was some history of political activity within the family. Her paternal grandfather had been a Conservative MP for Liverpool. The family moved while Graves was in infancy to Newells in Horsham. It was a financially comfortable childhood, with the family maintaining property in Brompton Square, London, in addition to the family home in Horsham.

Graves was educated privately and completed her education in northern France at the Château de Dieudonne in Bornel. She was skilled enough in French to study at La Bibliothèque nationale de France and at the Archives Nationales in Paris, where three of her academic papers were published.

At the outbreak of the First World War, Graves, who was thirty years old, was working for the Foreign Office, but by the end of the war she had moved to the Home Office Intelligence department. She attended the Paris Peace Conference, which gave her the ability to contribute knowledgably to parliamentary debate on foreign affairs.

Before entering Parliament, Graves served as a Conservative councillor for Holborn Borough Council from 1928 to 1934. In 1931, aged forty-seven, she was selected as the Conservative parliamentary candidate for the constituency of Hackney South, a seat held by Labour Cabinet minister Herbert Morrison. Although she won the seat, defeating Morrison, her success was short-lived and in the following election, in 1935, Morrison stood against her, winning back his former seat.

She clearly harboured a desire to return to Parliament, and in 1937 she was selected as the Conservative candidate to contest Barnstaple in north Devon. Ultimately, however, she didn't contest the seat. It's not clear why, but the postponement of elections due to the Second World War may well have been a contributing factor.

Graves never married and retired to Wareham, Dorset, and ended her career as a county councillor. She remained there until her death in November 1961.

DAME FLORENCE HORSBRUGH

RUTH DAVIDSON

- FULL NAME: Rt Hon. Dame Florence Gertrude Horsbrugh
- DATE OF BIRTH: 31 October 1889
- PLACE OF BIRTH: Edinburgh
- DATE OF DEATH: 6 December 1969
- MARRIED TO: Unmarried
- CHILDREN: None
- UNSUCCESSFUL ELECTIONS FOUGHT: Dundee 1945
- CONSTITUENCY: Dundee 1931–45 and Manchester Moss Side 1950–59
- DATE OF FIRST ELECTION: 27 October 1931
- DATE LEFT PARLIAMENT: 7 October 1959. She sat in the House of Lords from 1959 to her death.
- PARTY ROLES: Delegate to the League of Nations 1933–36 and delegate to the Council of Europe and Western European Union 1955–60
- MINISTERIAL POSITIONS & DATES: Parliamentary Secretary to the Ministry of Health 1939–45; Minister of Education 1951–54
- MOST FAMOUS QUOTATION: 'I never run away from boos.' – *The Courier & Advertiser*, 6 November 1936.

Florence Horsbrugh is one of the great unsung heroes of the twentieth century. Her lack of recognition is baffling.

Neville Chamberlain stated: 'She always puts her case so well the sympathies of the House are inclined to be with her in the arguments which she puts forward.' The *Daily Mail* was more direct: 'She is a feminine Churchill. She goes after facts, and is not afraid to attack her own party chiefs when necessary.'

Horsbrugh's career, which took place against a backdrop of war, the emergence of women into the political sphere and the profound social changes they propelled, was one of thought, action and courage.

Although Horsbrugh started her education in Edinburgh, she finished her studies in Mills College, California, just before the First World War broke out.

During the war she worked in the Ministry of Munitions canteen, where she devised a network of 'travelling kitchens', which operated after the National Kitchens shut. Her kitchens were widely known for helping the starving as well as for quality food. As a result, she was invited to Buckingham Palace where Queen Mary is said to have particularly approved of the sweets.

After the war, she worked with Lady Haig for the British Legion, and in the 1920s she became a prolific speaker for the Scottish Unionist Association. It was in this capacity that she gave a speech to the Dundee Association, upon which they asked her to be their candidate.

Surprising herself as much as anyone, Horsbrugh won the election. Having focused a relentless campaign on the future of the Dundee jute industry, she entered Parliament in 1931, the first female MP for Dundee and the first Conservative to be elected since the city gained its own constituency, ninety-nine years earlier. She would go on to become the first Conservative woman Cabinet minister and first woman Privy Counsellor.

In the House of Commons, Horsbrugh championed the jute industry and successfully brought forward two Private Members' Bills, one designed to regulate adoption and the other to curb the drinking of methylated spirits in Scotland.

As a result of her performances in the House of Commons, she was chosen to move the address to the King's Speech in 1936. The importance of the occasion demonstrates no mere tokenism. She performed admirably, and when interviewed about the experience on television, she became the first MP to appear on the new medium.

Horsbrugh herself stated, 'I want to forget that I am a woman doing my job. It doesn't help for people to emphasise that somebody doing a certain job is a woman.'

In 1939, she was appointed Parliamentary Secretary to the Ministry of Health and reappointed by Churchill in 1940. His concern for Horsbrugh's well-being was as well intentioned as it was unnecessary: 'Can you bear it? Can you stand up to it?' he asked.

During the Second World War, Horsbrugh organised the evacuation of 1.5 million women and children from major cities. Alongside this massive logistical challenge, Horsbrugh created casualty clearing stations in London, set up hostels for the temporarily homeless and managed the rest centres. Along with fellow MP Ellen Wilkinson, Horsbrugh was responsible for health and sanitation in London's Underground shelters and Horsbrugh herself completely restructured the British Civil Nursing reserve.

After the destruction of Coventry in 1940, Horsbrugh drove into the city as it burned. She worked tirelessly, evacuating women and children and finding beds for the thousands who had been made homeless. The *Daily Mirror* described her as 'mothering the city' and even years later she was introduced to the press as 'one of the heroines of Coventry'.

In early 1944, she began the preparatory work on the NHS. In the debate on the coalition government's White Paper on health, she stated, 'At a time of an increase of suffering, of wounds and maiming and crippling, we in this House launched a scheme to allay suffering … to do something constructive for the people of this country.'

Horsbrugh travelled to San Francisco with Deputy Prime Minister Clement Attlee in 1945 to participate in the conference that would create the United Nations.

Later that year, Horsbrugh, along with many others, lost her seat; but with the help of Churchill she returned to the House as MP for Manchester Moss Side in 1950. She swiftly became the Conservatives' first female Cabinet member, when she was appointed Minister of Education. However, her previous successes were not to be repeated. The government's priority at the time was to rebuild what had been destroyed during the war and housing was first on the agenda. While a competent manager, Horsbrugh was hamstrung by the money available for education, which had been cut to help fund house building. The shortage of funds was compounded by the raising of the school leaving age, resulting in many school buildings becoming overcrowded.

Horsbrugh resigned from Cabinet in 1954, and left Parliament in 1959, aged seventy. She was made a life peer and continued to make articulate contributions to debates until age and infirmity prevented her. She died in 1969, at the age of eighty.

It is telling that Florence Horsbrugh's greatest achievements were those of a practical nature – the National Kitchens, the evacuation of women and children during the war, and the help she gave to Coventry after its annihilation. Her work on the beginnings of the NHS and the formation of the United Nations were also of tremendous importance. Her courage and resilience are inspiring. Her life story reads like the quintessential 'roll-your-sleeves-up-and-get-stuck-in' schoolmarm type of tale.

To be the first female MP in Dundee – a city that had never even elected a female councillor – must have been, at times, daunting. To overturn a 14,000 majority and serve as the first Conservative since the constituency was created, nearly a century before, is remarkable. To stand up in the House of Commons and speak to the braying male majority, pass two Private Members' Bills and make it into the Cabinet, despite prejudice and through sheer merit, is gutsy as hell.

Florence Horsbrugh proved that women had great public contributions to make beyond child-rearing or care giving. She never married and was referred to in the papers as the 'Spinster MP' or 'Maiden Aunt'. But writer and journalist Roger Hermiston described her as 'Tall, smiling and invariably unflustered, with a "humorous twinkle in her eye"'.

She ran towards argument, she helped, she organised; she never used her gender as a shield or a weapon. And although history may have largely forgotten about Horsbrugh, those who seek out her story will not.

Those of us who stand for public office seek one thing above all – the opportunity to make a difference. Florence Horsbrugh used her life to materially improve the lives of others and to bring countries together to better lives across the globe. She is a genuine political heroine.

MARY PICKFORD

KEMI BADENOCH

- FULL NAME: Mary Ada Pickford CBE
- DATE OF BIRTH: 5 July 1884
- PLACE OF BIRTH: Liverpool
- DATE OF DEATH: 6 March 1934
- MARRIED TO: Unmarried
- CHILDREN: None
- UNSUCCESSFUL ELECTIONS FOUGHT: Farnworth 1929
- CONSTITUENCY: Hammersmith North
- DATE OF FIRST ELECTION: 27 October 1931
- DATE LEFT PARLIAMENT: 6 March 1934
- PARTY ROLES: None
- MINISTERIAL POSITIONS & DATES: None
- MOST FAMOUS QUOTATION: 'There is no doubt that, on the whole, women are far better shoppers than men, because, unlike men, they do not take the first thing that is offered to them without asking the price so as to get out of the shop as quickly as possible.'

It is regrettable that Mary Pickford does not command the same profile as other first-generation female MPs. A forgotten light of blue-collar Conservatism, she saw for herself the poor working conditions experienced by women and children in Britain, and channelled all her efforts into changing them. Pickford was deeply concerned by the restrictions placed upon the people of India and strove for their autonomy.

Born in 1884, Mary Ada Pickford was the youngest daughter of Alice (née Brooke) and William Pickford QC, later Baron Sterndale. Alice died just two months after giving birth to Mary, leaving her and her sister, Dorothy, to rely on their father as he climbed the ranks as a barrister and judge.

Despite the early loss of her mother, Pickford had other inspirational female figures to look up to. Studying at Wycombe Abbey School, renowned women's rights campaigner Dame Frances Dove was her headmistress.

In her youth, Pickford escorted her father to the judiciary's social events and was presented at Court as a debutante. She studied at Oxford before joining the Home Office as an inspector in the factory department during the First World War.

Pickford worked predominantly in industry prior to becoming an MP, but other notable positions included stints as an assistant for Sir Julian Corbett from 1917 to 1921, while he was writing the British Official History of the First War from 1917 to 1921, acting on the government's committee on Education and Industry in 1926 and then as an adviser to the government's delegation at the tenth International Labour Conference.

Her passion for politics appears to have been nurtured during this time. Pickford also had a very glamorous namesake in American film star Mary Pickford. In 1928, she took part in a meeting in Burnley aimed at newly enfranchised female voters. The local paper noted: 'There was no doubt that some ... were under the impression they were to have a close-up view of the celebrated film star.' The meeting was followed by a dance, and 'many had to put on their dancing slippers prior to arrival'.

She first stood for Parliament in Farnworth in 1929 – a seat that Labour held with a near 3,000-vote majority. Following the election, the Labour majority increased to just over 11,200, but Pickford was considered to be (alongside Margaret Beaven, later first female Lord Mayor of Liverpool) a candidate 'of outstanding personality'. She sat on a party committee that considered the reasons for the 1929 electoral defeat.

Pickford did not remain disappointed for long; two years after her defeat at Farnworth she was elected as Member of Parliament for Hammersmith North. In her maiden speech, she drew on her own experiences to argue for reforms to the Factories and Workshops Act, which would provide a more humane and economic system of working hours for women and young people. From thereon in, she used her time in Parliament to focus on employment policy, improving the lot of women in the world, and on the topic of the day: India.

Her passion for social justice, women's rights and international development were ahead of her time and could easily fit into 21st-century politics. As a member of the Indian Franchise Committee in 1932, Pickford toured India, exploring how more men and women could be given the vote, and stood up for the committee's findings to increase the franchise against objections from

Winston Churchill. She clearly made a commendable impact as, ninety years on, she is warmly remembered by Indian academic Sutanuka Ghosh, who credits her for ensuring greater rights for Indian women.

Although Pickford supported Stanley Baldwin's controversial and protectionist tariffs policy, she was also a fiscal conservative, declaring that the government could have avoided cuts in unemployment benefit if they had cut down on previous abuses. Independent-minded, supportive of welfare, but not at the cost of damaging public finances, and prioritising the immediate needs of the disadvantaged in public policy over business and trade – Mary Pickford would, despite her middle-class background, today most accurately be described as a blue-collar Conservative.

NORAH RUNGE

OONAGH GAY

- FULL NAME: Norah Cecil Runge (née Hasluck) OBE
- DATE OF BIRTH: 29 September 1884
- PLACE OF BIRTH: London
- DATE OF DEATH: 6 June 1978
- MARRIED TO: John Julius Runge (m. 1906; d. 1935); Dr Thomas Arthur Ross (m. 1939; d. 1941)
- CHILDREN: Peter, John, Robert (Bob) and Margaret (Peggy)
- UNSUCCESSFUL ELECTIONS FOUGHT: Rotherhithe 1945
- CONSTITUENCY: Rotherhithe
- DATE OF FIRST ELECTION: 27 October 1931
- DATE LEFT PARLIAMENT: 25 October 1935
- PARTY ROLES: President of the London Women's Advisory Committee and vice-chair of the London Conservative Union Council 1940–47
- MINISTERIAL POSITIONS & DATES: None
- MOST FAMOUS QUOTATIONS: 'Because I am a woman I suppose I shall be expected to support this amendment, but I am not going to do anything of the sort. I expect I shall be called a traitor to my sex.' Said while opposing an amendment to the India Bill, 15 May 1935. | 'This is a burning subject and I can hardly expect to escape without being scorched. I might have decided to abstain from voting, but, speaking generally, I conceive it to be the duty of a Member of Parliament to have the courage of his or her convictions, and, if necessary, to give expression to them.' – From her maiden speech, made on 13 April 1932.

Norah Cecil Runge was born Norah Hasluck in 1884. Her grandfather was a jeweller from Birmingham who built up a large Hatton Garden-based business, before opening an additional branch in Gibraltar, where Runge's father, Lawrence Hasluck, was born. Hasluck then moved to

England to work as a chartered accountant. His early death initially left the family financially insecure, and Norah played violin in an orchestra with her sister, Phylis, who played the cello. It was the beginning of a lifelong concern for her sister, who never married.

Norah married John Julius Runge, a sugar broker of German-Jewish heritage, in 1906. He became business manager of the Royal Commission on Sugar Supplies, which was established during the First World War, and subsequently became a director of the Tate and Lyle Company. Their marriage produced four children. Their son, Sir Peter Runge (1909–70), was vice-president of the Confederation of British Industry and joint vice-chair of Tate & Lyle Ltd.

Norah threw herself into war work and was awarded an OBE in March 1918 for her service as the superintendent of the Soldiers' and Sailors' Free Buffet at Paddington Station. Her organisational flair drew her into Conservative women's groups both nationally and in Rotherhithe, where her husband's business interests were based.

The 1931 general election was a breakthrough moment for eleven Conservative women candidates who became MPs, joining Lady Astor, the Duchess of Atholl and the Countess of Iveagh in the House. The unusual political circumstances of an economic crisis, followed by the formation of the National Government and Labour's electoral collapse, enabled Tory women to win in normally rock-solid Labour seats. Norah had only been adopted as a candidate for Rotherhithe at the last moment, replacing a male Conservative Party member who unexpectedly decided not to stand. She beat the sitting Labour MP Ben Smith by just 130 votes, following some energetic local campaigning.

Of her cohort, Norah was one of the most engaged in the parliamentary process. She led a privileged life as the wife of a wealthy man, with homes in Kippington, Kent, and in St John's House, Smith Square. Her concern for her immediate family and for her friends was considerable, yet she also found time to represent the poorest constituents in Rotherhithe. She called for slum clearance and supported a Bill on Sunday cinema attendance, the subject of her maiden speech on 13 April 1932. One of her passions, as an owner of greyhounds, was greyhound racing, and she supported the extension of the sport, indicating her socially liberal beliefs (religious groups disliked associated betting and sport on Sundays). She accepted the controversial means test for unemployed households, but was sufficiently independent-minded to protest against including the income of younger household members within the test. In 1935, she opposed an amendment to the India Bill, speaking against the inclusion of more women within the franchise.

She took an active role in trying to resolve the Thames lightermen strike of 1932, a major issue in Rotherhithe. She also assisted individual constituents in weekly surgeries, decades before this became common practice for MPs. Her children helped assiduously in organising fetes and offering free legal advice. Despite her husband's terminal illness, she was not excused from three-line whips. John Julius Runge died just after his wife was defeated by Ben Smith at the 1935 general election, as Labour recovered its normally solid working-class votes. She was remembered for some decades in the area, especially with the opening of Runge Hall in Culling Road (since demolished), which was used as a community hall and Conservative Party HQ.

After leaving Parliament, Norah Runge was appointed an alderman of the London County Council in 1937 and served until 1961. She made a final unsuccessful attempt to win Rotherhithe back in 1945. She worked for the Red Cross during the Second World War and was president of the Conservative London Area's Women's Advisory Committee. She was also vice-chair of the London Conservative Union Council 1940–47. She married Dr Ross, a psychologist, in 1939, who died in 1941.

Norah Runge died in 1978, aged ninety-three, but parliamentary connections remained in the family. Her son Peter married Fiona, daughter of Lord Strathcarron, formerly Ian McPherson MP, who had sat in the Commons at the same time as Runge.

HELEN SHAW

ELAINE GIBB

- FULL NAME: Helen Brown Shaw (née Graham) MBE
- DATE OF BIRTH: 2 June 1879
- PLACE OF BIRTH: Dennistoun, Glasgow
- DATE OF DEATH: 20 April 1964
- MARRIED TO: David Shaw (m. 1902; d. 1915)
- CHILDREN: Anne (b. 1904) and Gavin (b. 1907)
- UNSUCCESSFUL ELECTIONS FOUGHT: Bothwell 1924 and 1929
- CONSTITUENCY: Bothwell
- DATE OF FIRST ELECTION: 27 October 1931
- DATE LEFT PARLIAMENT: 25 October 1935
- PARTY ROLES: None
- MINISTERIAL POSITIONS & DATES: None
- MOST FAMOUS QUOTATION: 'I am not going to talk politics – I am fed up with politics, but I am going to thank you for your cup of tea.'

The daughter of wine merchant David Graham and his wife, Annie Gillespie, Helen Shaw was privately educated in Glasgow. She married David Shaw, also a wine merchant, in 1902. Shaw was active in local causes during the First World War, sitting on committees for war pensions, prisoner of war relief and food control. Shaw's activism and commitment was all the more remarkable given the personal tragedy she faced: her husband David, a major in the 6th Cameronians, was killed in action in France in 1915. In 1920, Shaw was awarded an MBE for 'patriotic services in Lanarkshire'.

After the war, she continued to be active in public life, becoming a member of the Lanarkshire Education Authority in 1920. In 1930, she was the first woman elected to Lanark County Council. By then, she had also stood as the Scottish Unionist (Conservative) candidate in Bothwell in two general elections, coming second to Labour in each. The *Motherwell Times* noted that Shaw was 'one of the ablest Scotswomen taking part in public life today [and] her appearance locally is always welcome'. Shaw's commitment to the seat and the area was rewarded in 1931, when she stood again and was elected as part of the Conservative landslide.

As an MP, Shaw lobbied for new industries and infrastructure for her mining constituency and focused on helping her constituents, especially ex-servicemen, cope with the effects of unemployment and economic depression.

Shaw took every chance she could to champion her constituency, wearing a gown made by her regular, local dressmaker when she was presented at Court. This was at a time when it was generally supposed – at least by one journalist – that 'garments of that sort can be made only in London'.

Shaw was kept busy in her constituency opening fetes, speaking to miners' clubs and welcoming the Prince of Wales when he visited Motherwell in 1933. But she did manage to escape sometimes; in 1934, the local paper, seeking a comment from their MP on the future of the steelworks site at Mossend, reported that 'the lady MP was away on a cruise'.

Shaw still found time for hobbies, too, including botany and camping. She was reportedly also a keen airwoman, and a supporter of the proposal to allow Scottish MPs to fly between London and their constituencies, a method of commuting unheard of in the 1930s.

Shaw stood for re-election in 1935, but Bothwell was reclaimed by Labour. Her career in representative politics was over, but she continued to work and play an active role in public life, and, in 1938, she became the district administrator for air raid precautions in the West of Scotland Women's Voluntary Service. Tragedy struck once more when her son Gavin, who had followed in her footsteps politically as chairman of the Bothwell Unionist Association, was killed in 1943. Her daughter, Anne, became a successful production engineer. Shaw died in 1964, aged eighty-four.

MAVIS TATE

JANET SEATON

- FULL NAME: Mavis Maybird Constance Tate (née Hogg)
- DATE OF BIRTH: 17 August 1893
- PLACE OF BIRTH: St Helena
- DATE OF DEATH: 5 June 1947
- MARRIED TO: Captain Gerald Ewart Gott (m. 1915; div. 1925); Henry Burton Tate (m. 1925; div. 1944)
- CHILDREN: None
- UNSUCCESSFUL ELECTIONS FOUGHT: None
- CONSTITUENCY: Willesden West 1931–35 and Frome 1935–45
- DATE OF FIRST ELECTION: 27 October 1931
- DATE LEFT PARLIAMENT: 5 July 1945
- PARTY ROLES: None
- MINISTERIAL POSITIONS & DATES: None

Mavis Tate was one of the most influential women MPs in the 1930s and 40s, at a time when there were very few in the House of Commons. She was hard-working, determined and resourceful, and passionate about women's rights and equal pay.

She was born Maybird Constance Hogg on 17 August 1893 on St Helena, where her father was sheriff, and was educated privately. Most of the men in the Hogg family were either civil servants or MPs, and she was probably inspired to go into politics through helping her cousin Douglas Hogg (later 1st Viscount Hailsham) in his elections at St Marylebone. Already divorced by the age of thirty-two, in 1925 Mavis married Henry Tate, of the sugar family. Thus it was as Mavis Tate that she won the Willesden West seat from Labour at the 1931 general election. Despite her majority of over 8,000, she sought a safer seat, and at the 1935 general election she was elected for Frome, but with only a small majority of less than 1,000.

The Bystander, a society gossip magazine, gave this pen portrait of her in 1935: 'Purposeful nose, cleft chin and curly hair. Dresses in vivid colours which startle the House. Extremely feminine in every way, temperamental, delicate, enthusiastic.' Her speaking style was as forceful as her personality, and a fellow MP called her 'one of the most rude women in the House'.

Her maiden speech on 12 February 1932, on the subject of juvenile courts, demonstrated her thoughtful approach to serious subjects. She later told her Frome adoption meeting that women MPs should not only represent 'women's interests', as she did not believe there were such things as 'women's questions'.

Described as 'air-minded', she was the first woman MP who was a qualified pilot. In May 1936, she participated in a bizarre race against 166 racing pigeons, during which she flew by plane between Castle Bromwich and Frome. In Parliament, she supported increasing the country's air defences and favoured the call-up of women to help with the war effort. Characteristically, she backed up her views with evidence – in 1941, she spent a day in an aircraft factory disguised as a man, an experience that convinced her women would do a better job.

Tate fought relentlessly for gender equality, and her two main wartime campaigns were for equal compensation for injured female civilians and for equal pay. On the former, she persuaded ninety-five MPs to vote for her amendment in the King's Speech debate in November 1942, highly unusual during the wartime party truce. This led to a select committee, which supported her, and the government was forced to accept its recommendations in full.

She was just as tenacious on equal pay, founding and becoming the first chair of the Equal Pay Campaign committee in January 1944. A few months later she forced a vote on teachers' pay, inflicting the wartime coalition government's only defeat. Churchill was so enraged that he forced a vote of confidence the next day which overturned the vote, but a Royal Commission was set up to reconsider the whole question.

In the final days of the war, Tate was the only woman in the ten-person parliamentary delegation that briefly visited the notorious Buchenwald concentration camp. Strangely, she had seen a camp in 1934, when she arranged for the rescue of a German woman and her child, but nothing could have prepared her for the horrors at Buchenwald, and shortly after she was taken ill, as were most of her fellow delegates. In her case, however, this was the latest in a long series of illnesses and misfortunes that sapped her strength. In 1940, she suffered a breakdown through overwork. It was reported that she attended every sitting of the House and answered fifty letters a day. She was also keeping an eye on the nearby constituency of Bath while its incumbent was on active service. Nevertheless, she returned to work after only a short rest.

She lost her seat at Frome in the 1945 general election, but despite this blow, she agreed in the following year to be readopted as prospective candidate for Frome, and was politically active in the ensuing months. However, her troubled personal life (including two divorces) and persistent ill health led to a tragic end and she was found dead in her London home on 5 June 1947, aged only fifty-three. She left a note to her brother: 'As I have no one dependent on me it seems to me the wiser thing to do to end my life. An invalid is only a national liability today, and I cannot endure the extensive and constant pain in my head and practically no sleep at all week after week.' The coroner's verdict was that she died of coal gas poisoning, self-administered, at a time when the balance of her mind was disturbed by ill health.

Mavis Tate's colourful career and her lasting achievements in promoting the equality of women deserve to be better known. A heartfelt local tribute stated, 'In her was found a very unusual combination of qualities – a brilliant brain, a charming personality, tenacity and a sense of humour.' She is remembered in Frome by two trophies – Frome Agricultural Show's Mavis Tate Cup awarded after the war for the best local dairy cow, and the Mavis Tate Inter League Cup for adult male football leagues in Somerset. A more national, and more appropriate, commemoration is long overdue.

DAME IRENE WARD

EDWINA CURRIE

- FULL NAME: Dame Irene Mary Bewick Ward CH DBE, Baroness Ward of North Tyneside
- DATE OF BIRTH: 23 February 1895
- PLACE OF BIRTH: Tyneside
- DATE OF DEATH: 26 April 1980
- MARRIED TO: Unmarried
- CHILDREN: None
- UNSUCCESSFUL ELECTIONS FOUGHT: Morpeth 1924 and 1929
- CONSTITUENCY: Wallsend 1931–45 and Tynemouth 1950–74
- DATE OF FIRST ELECTION: 27 October 1931
- DATE LEFT PARLIAMENT: 28 February 1974
- PARTY ROLES: None
- MINISTERIAL POSITIONS & DATES: None
- MOST FAMOUS QUOTATION: She is remembered for an incident which caused amusement on both sides of the House when she threatened to 'poke' the then Labour Prime Minister Harold Wilson. Having received an evasive answer to a parliamentary question, she responded with the words: 'I will poke the Prime Minister. I will poke him until I get a response.'

Irene Ward was a large, jolly woman with a broad smile, always neatly dressed but with fly-away hair escaping from under her hat and capacious handbags. Remarkably, she still holds the record for the longest-serving Tory woman MP (thirty-eight years). During her political career, she campaigned alongside higher-profile figures such as Barbara Castle, Edith Summerskill and Megan Lloyd George for equal pay and employment rights for women.

Ward also holds the record for the largest number of Private Members' Bills ending up as legislation – four – including one to pay a pension of two shillings a week to elderly people living in Poor Law institutions. Her papers are in the Bodleian Library in Oxford; box B6 includes her rosette, her purse, good-luck horseshoe and lucky heather. She merits only a few lines on Wikipedia, there is no portrait of her in the Commons, and she is largely forgotten now. Yet she was dearly loved by all colleagues.

Irene Ward was never the Mother of the House, despite her decades of service, due to her gap as MP between 1945 and 1950. However, only Gwyneth Dunwoody and Margaret Beckett have served longer.

During the 1960s and 1970s, when I was a politics student, Dame Irene (she was made DBE in 1955) was one of a tiny band of formidable Conservative women who, through persistence and personality, had made their name in the House. What was all the more remarkable about her feat was that she represented Tynesiders – hardly natural Tories, one might think – from the depths of the pre-war Depression through Macmillan's 'never had it so good' days to the miseries of Ted Heath's Three-Day Week. She might have been forgiven for thinking when she retired from the Commons in 1974 that perhaps nothing much had changed since her first political contests in the 1920s.

Ward knew all about poverty, and campaigned for widows, ex-serviceman and single parents throughout her lifetime. Her father had died when she was only five years old, leaving her widowed mother to rely heavily on his somewhat mean-spirited four brothers for money. The sixteen-year-old Irene threatened to take one of them to court for non-payment of a £5 bill. By then she was working as secretary to the local vicar; during the First World War she also volunteered as a nursing aid, and made her first speech to a group of stretcher bearers as they left for the front. By all accounts she was a natural-born speaker, vivid and inspiring, and always willing to take on the challenge.

The partial enfranchisement of women in 1918 led Conservative Central Office to seek women candidates, in order to wean the women's vote away from Lloyd George. Irene attracted attention in 1923, when she spoke at the party conference; Conservative Central Office agreed to pay her election expenses if she would fight a seat, which she did in 1924 when actually too young to vote (and was described by the *Daily Express* as 'the girl with the pretty face' to distinguish her from other Tory women candidates!). After two attempts at being elected in Morpeth, she was made CBE in 1929 for 'political and public services' – quite a public accolade – and then moved to Wallsend to take on Labour minister Margaret Bondfield. During the election campaign, Bondfield spent most of her time giving speeches outside of the constituency, a lesson not lost on Ward, who won the trust of the miners and romped home.

From that moment onwards, Ward made a name for herself by speaking out on what were regarded as 'masculine' subjects: mining, heavy industry including shipbuilding and employment law. On 30 May 1932, in her maiden speech on the Coal Mines Bill, she urged support for 'a Bill which is regarded in the country as a socialist measure'. To reduce the mountains of unwanted coal and to avoid closing mines, Ramsay MacDonald's government proposed quotas for production.

> I am ... opposed, on principle, to parliamentary control of wages in indus-
> try generally, but the mining industry is in a very peculiar position ... and
> I wonder whether, if it had been possible to guarantee wages for a period,
> that would have been too high a price to pay for harmony and peace in the
> industry.

Germany, she noted, had closed pits and put many men out of work. Soon after, she joined a delegation to Germany, where Hitler had recently become Chancellor. To give the flavour of the time, however, the speaker who followed her, Labour MP Joseph Batey, told her, 'I thought when the honourable lady was speaking that it was a good thing from my point of view that we did not live in the same house, because our views are so very far apart that we should never agree.' Imagine the howls today if any honourable gent tried saying that to any honourable lady.

Advances in female equality had to be fought for, and Irene Ward was often in the vanguard of advancements. She was also alert to the smallest of injustices. In 1955, it was discovered that in 1946 Special Operations Executive (SOE) heroine Diana Rowden had been posthumously awarded the Croix de Guerre, but her family had never received it; like most such awards, it had been returned by the Attlee government, who wanted all references to SOE to disappear. Irene Ward called that 'a miserable, squalid' affair, and soon ensured that the heroine should be justly recognised.

Ward championed Mrs Jean Winder, the first woman Hansard reporter, who in the early 1950s was refused equal pay (her request was granted in 1953). Ward demanded that women be allowed to work in the Commons library, and when it was argued that women wouldn't be able to carry the ladders required to reach the higher shelves, Irene marched through the corridors carrying a ladder (and made sure the photos appeared in the press). She won that one, too. Then there was the first woman reporter in the Parliamentary Press Gallery, Pat Newton (whose story was relayed to researcher Helen Langley by Mrs Newton's daughter). When Mrs Newton became pregnant with her first child in 1956, she was fired on the grounds that her place should now be at home, looking after her child and husband. Outraged by this treatment of Mrs Newton, Irene Ward and Barbara Castle brought up her case while appearing at question time. The Married Women's Association and the National Union of Journalists also fought hard and soon Pat had her job back – only to lose it again when she became pregnant with her son in 1961. But again she was reinstated within months. It was easier to do that than to cope with remonstrations from the formidable duo of Irene Ward and Barbara Castle.

In a long career it's impossible to give many details. Ward described herself as 'obsessed with fighting the north's case in Parliament'. But a sense of the warmth and respect in which Irene Ward was held comes from the general election in 1964, which saw off the Tory government. As Conservative seats fell all round her, in Tyneside 'that most formidable Tory lady', Irene Ward, romped home. She won 33,342 votes while Albert Booth, chairman of the local trades' council, managed only 25,894 for Labour. But his performance was regarded as such a creditable one that he was handed a Labour stronghold for his next contest. He went on to become Secretary of State for Employment in the winter of discontent – a somewhat poisoned chalice.

In May 1968, aged seventy-two, Ward staged a Commons protest against the Labour government's guillotining of the Finance Bill before she could raise issues to do with shipbuilding, standing in front of the Mace so that tellers could not report a division (when Michael Heseltine seized the Mace and waved it about some years later, he was 'doing an Irene Ward'). It led to her being suspended for five days. Press photos afterwards of her emerging from her flat, grinning widely, suggest she thoroughly enjoyed this moment; she even bought the newspaper cartoon of the event and kept it for the rest of her life. It can only have enhanced her reputation in the Commons, for in 1972, it was Ward who nominated Tory grandee Selwyn Lloyd for the office of Speaker.

Ward was made a Companion of Honour in 1973 and stood down from the Commons in February 1974. She joined the Lords as Baroness Ward of North Tyneside in January 1975.

The papers she deposited in Oxford give us some insight into her personal life: they include her Bible and English hymnal, the rule books of the New-castle Ladies Luncheon Club, the Gosforth Women's Tea Club, the Cram-lington & District Football League and the rules of golf. She never had a family of her own; instead she chose to serve the nation and her beloved Tynesiders well into her seventies.

Irene Ward is destined to disappear from history, which is a tragedy. *The Independent*, which ought to know better, even placed her in the wrong port, calling Ward

> that splendid woman from Liverpool ... the redoubtable Dame Irene Ward of blessed memory ... a doughty and inelegant Liverpudlian built like the dock-ers she represented. She and Dame Joan Vickers both shared the distinction of representing what should have been traditional Labour seats – and keeping them solely because of their personal popularity.

As a Scouser, I grieve. But otherwise it's an accurate judgement on a fine, decent, kind-hearted woman who deserves to be remembered with affection and admiration.

SARAH WARD

OONAGH GAY

- FULL NAME: Sarah Adelaide Ward (née Ainsworth)
- DATE OF BIRTH: 25 December 1895
- PLACE OF BIRTH: Stone, Staffordshire
- DATE OF DEATH: 9 April 1965
- MARRIED TO: William J. Ward (m. 1921)
- CHILDREN: Margaret
- UNSUCCESSFUL ELECTIONS FOUGHT: Lichfield & Tamworth 1950 and Birmingham Perry Barr 1951
- CONSTITUENCY: Cannock
- DATE OF FIRST ELECTION: 27 October 1931
- DATE LEFT PARLIAMENT: 25 October 1935
- PARTY ROLES: None
- MINISTERIAL POSITIONS & DATES: None
- MOST FAMOUS QUOTATION: 'The wives of the unemployed have to bear the biggest brunt of the burden of unemployment; they have to eke out the meagre money and to cheer up the despondent husbands and sons who are unemployed.'

Sarah (Sally) Ainsworth was born at Meaford Farm, Stone, Staffordshire, the daughter of John and Harriet Ainsworth. She attended Orme Girls School Newcastle and taught for several years at Christ Church School, Stone.

Like so many women, she was a Voluntary Aid Detachment (VAD) nurse during the First World War, serving with the 90th Staffordshire VADs. She married a local tenant farmer, William Ward, in 1921 and moved south of Cannock to Grange Farm, Walsall Wood. Thus she could point to her local roots when standing for election at Cannock in 1931 as the Conservative candidate against William Adamson, who had held the seat for Labour since

1922. Ward won with a comfortable majority of 4,665, as the Labour vote share fell sharply following the formation of the National Government.

As an MP she focused on rural issues. Her maiden speech on 30 November 1931 concerned the problems facing agriculture, including death duties on estates, lack of investment and the threat of cheap food imports. She supported the levying of emergency duties on luxury food. The aim of her Private Members' Bill, the Home and Empire Settlement Bill, was to get people back to working on agricultural land, as a way of developing their skills, whether in the UK or abroad in the Dominions. Ward introduced its second reading on 24 February 1933, as part of a group of Conservatives who believed that UK agriculture desperately needed investment. The Bill received a second reading but did not progress, as it lacked government support for the necessary cost.

She was not the most active of the cohort of Conservative women MPs elected in 1931. In May 1934, she welcomed the extension of unemployment insurance and harmonisation of treatment of agricultural labourers, and paid tribute to the wives of the unemployed who bore the 'biggest brunt' of the burden of unemployment.

She stood for re-election in 1935. Her election address in the *Staffordshire Advertiser* in November 1935 noted that she had spent almost every weekend in the constituency, making herself available to the constituents. Nevertheless, she lost to William Adamson, by 1,046 votes. The seat was held again by a woman, Jennie Lee, in 1945.

After losing her seat, Ward remained active in politics as a member of Staffordshire County Council from 1950 to 1969 and chaired its welfare services committee. She stood unsuccessfully for Parliament at Lichfield and Tamworth (1950) and Birmingham Perry Barr (1951). In the Second World War she served as a junior commander in the Auxiliary Territorial Service, and was appointed OBE in 1952 and CBE in 1961.

FRANCES DAVIDSON, VISCOUNTESS DAVIDSON

ANNE JENKIN

- FULL NAME: Frances Joan Davidson (née Dickinson), Viscountess Davidson, Baroness Northchurch DBE
- DATE OF BIRTH: 29 May 1894
- PLACE OF BIRTH: London
- DATE OF DEATH: 25 November 1985
- MARRIED TO: Sir J. C. C. Davidson, 1st Viscount Davidson (m. 1919; d. 1970)
- CHILDREN: Two sons and two daughters
- UNSUCCESSFUL ELECTIONS FOUGHT: None
- CONSTITUENCY: Hemel Hempstead
- DATE OF FIRST ELECTION: 22 June 1937
- DATE LEFT PARLIAMENT: 8 October 1959. Viscountess Davidson joined the Lords as Baroness Northchurch on 13 January 1964.
- PARTY ROLES: None
- MINISTERIAL POSITIONS & DATES: None

My grandmother, known by those close to her as Mimi, was elected MP for Hemel Hempstead in 1937. She stood down in 1959, when I was four years old, but she lived on until I was in my thirties, so I knew her well. My own mother, now ninety-four, has vivid childhood memories of growing up in a politically engaged household in Westminster. Stanley Baldwin came to breakfast most days and walked with my grandmother across St James's Park with one detective in tow. Discreet meetings took place frequently in the family's London home, and she remembers some that discussed the abdication crisis of 1935.

My grandparents' marriage was one of political harmony and partnership; my grandfather, known as J. C. C. D., had been MP for Hemel Hempstead from 1920. He became parliamentary private secretary to Andrew Bonar Law and Stanley Baldwin, whose daughter introduced him to Joan Dickinson. The meeting led to marriage in April 1919.

My grandfather held high office in the Admiralty and in Parliament, where he served as Chancellor of the Duchy of Lancaster. For a time, he was also chairman of the Conservative Party, where he founded the Research Department before retiring, ennobled to the House of Lords in 1937.

My grandmother was unanimously invited to stand at the by-election and was elected with a substantial majority, serving Hemel Hempstead until her retirement in 1959. My grandparents served for more than forty years between them, during which period the voting population had risen from 26,000 to around 80,000.

Soon after their wedding, J. C. C. D. became an integral part of the Downing Street machine so my grandmother also found herself at the heart of politics. In some ways she was a more effective and natural public speaker than my grandfather. She could win over any audience with her presence, charm and technique. Her retiring address as president of the somewhat difficult Conservative Party conference in 1965 is remembered to this day. Her successor Peter Thorneycroft said, 'I do not think that any presidential speech has been, or ever will be, better made.'

She usually spoke in public without notes. These were the pre-television days when a quick high tea was followed by a long, often foggy, car ride to some distant village hall where election meetings were held and the candidates spoke. Rather than debating on the floor of the House of Commons, she preferred to use her expertise working directly for the constituency she represented, or actively behind the scenes on various parliamentary committees.

During the wartime coalition, there were only ten women Members, six of whom were Conservatives. This was soon to change.

When the 1945 post-war election swung violently to Labour, my grandmother found herself isolated as the only Conservative Member in the Ladies' Room, surrounded by twenty-one aggressive, new Labour women (now 3.8 per cent), who tended not to speak to her. She made it her task to explain how the system worked and, gradually, under her guidance, they set aside their wish to burn the place down like Guy Fawkes and she felt she had won the battle when the formidable Liverpool heavyweight, Bessie Braddock, offered her a chocolate!

In 1947 Hemel Hempstead became a 'new town', with a large influx of new residents from London's bombed East End. However, in 1951, my grandmother's majority remained virtually unchanged and it became clear that these former Labour voters, now homeowners, had changed allegiance. Her active participation in and concern for her constituents' lives was clearly part of the reason. She used to go through the local papers and personally write to everyone who had lost a relative, or she would deal quietly and efficiently with planning problems and other local matters. This all added to a daily post bag of over sixty letters a day.

When war broke out, my family moved out of London to the edge of the constituency. She used to drive up to London on Mondays, picking up Miss Doult, her secretary, at Apsley to whom she would dictate her letters. This left her time to play an active role in the party and parliamentary machine, as she was also the only woman sitting on the national expenditure committee, as well as the estimates committee until just before her retirement. More interestingly, I note that she was the first woman Member of the executive of the influential 1922 committee, to which she was re-elected in 1955. As early as 1925, she had been a member of the National Union and was on the national executive from 1933 to 1968.

It does look as if she slipped easily into politics when she took over her husband's seat; however, the selection committee's choice was unanimous.

She spoke good German and during the Great War worked for the Red Cross Prisoners of War department, for which she was awarded an OBE. As one of those who had experienced war work, she felt a sense of public duty, no doubt strengthened by her own family background. She was to become the fifth successive family member to be elected to Parliament. Her father, Sir Willoughby (later Lord) Dickinson, elected in 1906, was also a working barrister. He had two sisters, one of whom was a doctor, and Sir Willoughby couldn't understand why he had the right to vote in elections and they did not. In 1907, he used a private ballot motion to bring in one of the very earliest (although unsuccessful) Bills to introduce women's suffrage. Though by no means a rich man, he refused members' pay when it was first introduced in 1911, as he believed that it was a Member's duty to utilise experience and knowledge to facilitate the smooth running of the government. He lived long enough to see his daughter win the right to vote – and to see her take her seat in the Commons.

In 1952, Lady Davidson was appointed a Dame of the British Empire; this was followed, in 1963, by a life peerage as Baroness Northchurch. My grandparents were, therefore, the first husband and wife team to sit in the House of Lords together in their own right.

AGNES HARDIE

ANNE MCGUIRE

- FULL NAME: Agnes Agnew Hardie (née Pettigrew)
- DATE OF BIRTH: 6 September 1874
- PLACE OF BIRTH: —
- DATE OF DEATH: 24 March 1951
- MARRIED TO: George Hardie MP
- CHILDREN: One son
- UNSUCCESSFUL ELECTIONS FOUGHT: None
- CONSTITUENCY: Glasgow Springburn
- DATE OF FIRST ELECTION: 7 September 1937
- DATE LEFT PARLIAMENT: 4 July 1945
- PARTY ROLES: None
- MINISTERIAL POSITIONS & DATES: None

The name Hardie is synonymous with the Labour Party, with Keir Hardie elected as its first MP and his stepbrothers David and George both being elected to the Commons during the early days of the party.

The fourth in this quartet of Hardie parliamentarians was Agnes, who became the first woman MP returned to a Glasgow constituency in 1937, and only the second Scottish Labour woman MP, nineteen years after the introduction of the 1918 Act allowing women to sit in Parliament.

Although elected at the age of sixty-three to a seat that had fallen vacant following her husband's death, it would be too easy to dismiss Hardie as a widow inheriting her spouse's seat. She was an activist all of her life and had a considerable history of political and trade union activity in her own right, starting as an organiser for the shop assistants' union in the 1890s. She was the first woman to be elected to Glasgow Trades Council and was the Scottish Women's Organiser of the Labour Party from 1919 until she moved to London upon her husband's election to Parliament in 1923.

Hardie's politics were forged in the poverty of her native city and of the

Independent Labour Party, the latter explaining her lifelong commitment to pacifism. Her maiden speech on the Annual Holiday Bill in November 1937 showed that she was not intimidated by the Commons. She delivered a confident speech that served as a statement of her views on class issues. 'Even the employer himself can go away for a holiday ... and nothing very much happens in consequence. There is always somebody there, generally somebody belonging to our class, to see that the workers go on producing wealth while the employer is on holiday.'

An intervention in the Public Education Scotland Bill debate showed she was more than capable of using a sharp, succinct rhetoric to get her point across. 'Members may take it from me that if the schools turn out intelligent girls, they will be able to cook a dinner all right, although they have not been taught cookery at school.'

Her pacifism was as strong while the country prepared for the Second World War as it had been when she joined the Women's Peace Crusade during the First World War. She was fundamentally opposed to conscription and, in May 1939, she told the Commons during the Military Training Bill that she would take no part in recruiting as she could never ask anyone to go to fight.

Hardie earned the moniker 'The Housewives' MP' because of her focus on issues that she felt were of greatest importance to women. Her speeches highlighted the appalling poverty, the exploitation of low-paid workers and awful housing conditions of the time, drawing on her personal experiences of working in a shop and as a trade unionist. She deserves to be remembered as a champion of the voiceless. She stood down in 1945, serving nearly eight years without ever fighting a general election.

EDITH SUMMERSKILL

YVETTE COOPER

- FULL NAME: Dr Edith Clara Summerskill, Baroness Summerskill CH PC
- DATE OF BIRTH: 19 April 1901
- PLACE OF BIRTH: London
- DATE OF DEATH: 4 February 1980
- MARRIED TO: Dr Jeffrey Samuel (m. 1925; d. 1983)
- CHILDREN: Dr Shirley Summerskill and a son
- UNSUCCESSFUL ELECTIONS FOUGHT: Putney 1934 (by-election) and Bury 1935
- CONSTITUENCY: Fulham West 1938–55 and Warrington 1955–61
- DATE OF FIRST ELECTION: 6 April 1938
- DATE LEFT PARLIAMENT: 4 February 1961
- PARTY ROLES: Member of Labour's NEC 1944–58 and chair of the Labour Party 1954–55
- MINISTERIAL POSITIONS & DATES: Parliamentary Secretary to the Ministry of Food 1945–50; Minister of National Insurance 1950–51. Following Labour's election defeat, she served in the shadow Cabinet over the next eight years.
- MOST FAMOUS QUOTATION: In response to the persistent anti-feminist question, 'Why have not more women achieved eminence in the arts and sciences?' Summerskill stated, 'Personally I am astounded that so many have distinguished themselves despite the conditions which society has imposed upon them.'

I wish I had known Dr Edith Summerskill. One of a few women to qualify as a doctor in the 1920s, one of just a handful of women elected to Parliament in the 1930s, one of the first women appointed to the Privy Council, and one of the first women to be made a life peer – she spent her whole life overturning conventions, smashing glass ceilings and fighting for change.

Watching Pathé News footage of her during the war, she looks fabulously formidable. Both a feminist and a socialist, the films show her as a determined woman with a no-nonsense and frankly intimidating manner visiting patients, making speeches in Trafalgar Square and talking to journalists.

Her politics were highly principled, but deeply rooted in the practical. She argued for reforms to tackle inequality and injustice in the family just as strongly as she did for reforms in the workplace or in communities. She kept her own name when she married, had two children and still managed to work both as a doctor and as an MP at the same time. Through her life, as well as her politics, she changed laws and changed minds. Eighty years on, with our current campaigns and policies as women MPs in mind, it is remarkable to think how far ahead of her time Edith Summerskill was.

From her family came her feminism, from her work her socialism. Remarkably for a woman born in 1901, Summerskill's parents were clearly ambitious for her from the start. Her father was a doctor and took her on his rounds across London from an early age. Her mother was a housewife, but refused to teach Summerskill to cook, sending her off to her room to study instead. Visiting patients suffering not just from illness but from poverty, hunger, cold, damp and exploitation clearly had a powerful effect on her. As she wrote in her autobiography:

> Those visits with my father were undoubtedly the strongest single influence in my life. They made me wish to take up medicine to give immediate help to the sick. And they made me wish to help in the long term – removing by political action some of the causes of malnutrition and consequent ill health. In other words they made me a socialist as well as a doctor.

Encouraged by her parents, Summerskill studied medicine at London University and Charing Cross Hospital – benefiting from a brief window where medical schools accepted women as a result of the First World War. There she met her husband, Jeffrey Samuel, also a doctor who had grown up in the Welsh mining valleys, and with whom Edith and a group of other medical friends set up the Socialist Health Association to argue for national health service.

She was quickly drawn into politics. In the early '30s, Summerskill used to join the defeated former Labour MP for Tottenham, Fred Messer, on his soapbox opposite the Salisbury pub on Green Lane to campaign for his re-election. On an evening, or a Saturday morning, Summerskill and Messer would take it in turns to regale the crowd and answer questions for hours.

Asked by the local Labour Party if she would put her name forward for an apparently unwinnable council ward, she gathered a band of women and set off door-knocking her way through the suburban streets, insisting on talking to housewives and not just to the men who answered the door. It worked. Unexpectedly she won.

Westminster candidacies in Bury, Putney and Fulham all followed – and each time she put a rocket up the traditional style of political campaign. Putney was a by-election – again a seat Labour thought they had no chance of winning. Edith took music with her – gave each street a blast of 'Little Old Lady Just Passing By', and a short speech through the megaphone before hitting the knockers. She cut the winning Tory banker's majority by 18,000 – in her own words 'proving to the party hierarchy that women candidates had a vote catching potential at least equal to men if not in some cases superior'. Finally in 1938 she won the West Fulham by-election, joining Ellen Wilkinson, Agnes Hardie and Jennie Adamson as the only Labour women in Parliament through the war years.

None of it can have been easy. Often her political breaks came because none of the men thought the seats were winnable, so none of them were willing to stand. She proved them wrong in so many ways.

Often she faced additional harassment and hurdles. In the 1935 election, Summerskill stood in Bury – a seat Labour hoped to win. But she was challenged by local Catholic priests to abandon her public support for birth control and never to teach it to women again. She refused. The male Tory and Liberal candidates complied (even though, as Summerskill points out in her autobiography, they were doubtless using birth control themselves to maintain their small families). The result was that she was personally condemned from pulpits across Bury the weekend before polling day and she lost.

Writing her memoirs, she makes most of it sound so straightforward and matter of fact. Yet it just can't have been. The experience with the Catholic Church in Bury clearly shook her. While she and her husband could afford childcare, the juggling of work and family life clearly caused her all the same pangs and guilt as it does most of us today. Appointed to her first ministerial job in the Ministry of Food, she insisted on a private phone line so she could call her husband and kids without civil servants listening in. I did exactly the same when arriving at my first ministerial job in the Department of Health in 1999 – probably the last generation of juggling mothers to do so before mobile phones made those private lines redundant.

She must also have faced some unenviable abuse as well as the predictable patronising attempts to undermine her. Not just the Bury denunciations from the pulpit, but the soapbox speech sessions outside the Salisbury pub must have had their moments as the men poured out at closing time. At public meetings she was denounced as a revolutionary. And the Tory MP who backed her Private Members' Bill on married women's rights in 1952 began his contribution by complimenting Summerskill's husband on being able to listen to her passionate speech.

When she launched a campaign to ban boxing for its damage to the brain and encouragement of male violence (one of her few unsuccessful campaigns – who knows what she would have made of role models like Olympic medal winner Nicola Adams today?), a not untypical letter she received said, 'If I could have ten minutes with you I would bash your brains in.' Twitter and social media may have put it on steroids, but misogyny and abuse aimed at women politicians is clearly nothing new.

Unsurprisingly, health was a central part of many of the causes she took up over the years. In 1938, she lambasted the lack of ambition in the National Government's Cancer Bill, arguing that 'The poorer you are, the more likely you are to die from cancer.' Much of Summerskill's speech was devoted to the need for a publicly funded health service – 'It is a kind of utopia but we know that utopia will probably come in the next ten years.' Nine years and seven months later, under a Labour government, the NHS was born.

But Summerskill went further than many of the other early health campaigners, arguing as strongly for improvements in public health as in health services. As a National Insurance minister in the early '50s, she brought in new support for miners struck down by pneumoconiosis. And her calls for action on poverty, nutrition, food safety and child health were not so very different from those I put forward as Public Health minister fifty years later, as we brought in free fruit in primary schools, the health inequalities action plan and the new Food Standards Agency.

Women and children's health were a particular passion. She championed better and safer maternity services, and pain relief in childbirth. From the very beginning of her training Summerskill was angered by the thousands of children dying of preventable diseases each year. So I suspect it was one of her proudest moments when, after being appointed by Attlee as junior Minister of Food, she was able to drive through Parliament her Clean Milk Bill, which promised to bring in pasteurisation, saving thousands of children's lives each year.

For Summerskill, feminism and socialism were clearly intertwined. Like Harriet Harman many years later, Summerskill refused to accept that family issues should be kept out of politics or separate from socialism. Instead she argued for women's empowerment within the family and home just as strongly as she argued for working-class empowerment within the workplace, communities or public life.

With Vera Brittain and others she co-founded the Married Women's Association to campaign for legal rights for married women. This was to be an important cause for her throughout her life, pushing Private Members' Bills in both the Commons and the Lords and speaking in Parliament to support Eleanor Rathbone's campaign for the new family allowance to be paid to women rather than men in 1945 to tackle poverty and give women more financial independence. Over half a century later, I and a group of newly elected Labour women used many of the same arguments when we intervened to stop the Treasury paying the new child tax credit to the main earner in the household, and redirected it to the main carer instead.

In 1964, Summerskill's Bill on married women's property rights was passed into law, giving women rights over family savings for the first time. And her campaigns set the stage for further reforms that followed.

She called for childcare too. Interviewed by *Everywoman* magazine at the end of the war, Summerskill was asked whether it was possible for women to combine work and family life. She said, 'Certainly, but only of course if the community helps them. We must have day nurseries. I'm hoping that these war nurseries that have served such a useful purpose will carry on into peace days.'

Summerskill's childcare hopes sadly did not materialise. It would be another fifty years before women ministers, led by Margaret Hodge in the 1997 Labour government, drew up the first national childcare strategy, including a massive expansion of both nursery and childcare places, and before Tessa Jowell and I rolled out the Sure Start scheme, which provided families with support during their child's infancy. Seventy years on, Labour women are still demanding an expansion of childcare – this time alongside effective paternity as well as maternity leave, so that women and men can combine work and family life.

Summerskill's politics were principled but also hugely practical. At one point, haunted by the doubt that she didn't know what she was talking about because she hadn't read the erudite texts or philosophies the men seemed to be quoting from, she borrowed treatises by Karl Marx and books on economics from the library. She wasn't impressed, finding them boring and full of contradictions. She was also refreshingly scathing about the arrogance of the civil service, and its faith in the superiority of Oxbridge arts graduates rather than rigorous scientists from any background.

That determination to be rigorous rather than driven by fashion or ideology made her unusual. Her writing and her arguments were radical but also empirical rather than ideological. It made her both a resolute pioneer and also a no-nonsense sceptic. She was an uncompromising advocate of birth control to prevent the poverty and exhaustion of large families and to give women control over their bodies. However, she criticised what she saw as the premature distribution of the contraceptive pill before enough tests on its safety had been carried out. And while she was one of the most powerful and effective politicians strengthening women's rights within marriage and divorce, she warned of the potential risks that liberalising divorce laws might bring, leaving more women in poverty as men walked away taking all the money with them.

Looking back on her dedicated campaigns, her talent, her forensic arguments, it seems ridiculous she was never appointed to Cabinet. Less talented and less experienced men were. But her years of campaigning, her willingness to challenge outdated orthodoxy with up-to-date evidence and her readiness to speak out on the most controversial issues left a legacy for other women to build on for years to come.

But perhaps Summerskill's most important legacy, and that of many of the women of her generation, was her encouragement to other women to feel able to speak out, to argue for change, to make a difference with confidence. True to those values, after Summerskill entered the House of Lords in 1961, her daughter, Shirley Summerskill, was elected to Parliament as MP for Halifax in 1964. Together they became Parliament's first (and so far only) mother–daughter duo.

As she wrote to Shirley in her book *Letters to My Daughter*:

> The shades of the women who blazed the trail that you and I might be free to fulfil ourselves seemed to sit with me on the green benches of Westminster last night. I feel now that you in your turn will go forward to destroy finally those monstrous customs and prejudices which have haunted the lives of generations of women.

It could be a letter to us all.

JENNIE ADAMSON

LINDA GILROY

- FULL NAME: Janet Laurel Adamson (née Johnston)
- DATE OF BIRTH: 9 May 1882
- PLACE OF BIRTH: Kirkcudbright
- DATE OF DEATH: 25 April 1962
- MARRIED TO: William Murdoch Adamson (m. 1902; d. 1945)
- CHILDREN: Two daughters and two sons
- UNSUCCESSFUL ELECTIONS FOUGHT: Dartford 1935
- CONSTITUENCY: Dartford 1938–45 and Bexley 1945–46
- DATE OF FIRST ELECTION: 7 November 1938
- DATE LEFT PARLIAMENT: 12 July 1946
- PARTY ROLES: None
- MINISTERIAL POSITIONS & DATES: Parliamentary private secretary 1940–45; Parliamentary Secretary to the Ministry of Pensions 1945–46
- MOST FAMOUS QUOTATION: 'As we have not many housewives in the House of Commons I feel it to be my duty to champion the cause of securing fair play for women in the homes.' – Ministry of Pensions debate, 25 June 1940.

Jennie Adamson was the daughter of Thomas Johnston, a railway porter and coachman, and Elizabeth Denton. In a debate in the House of Commons in 1942, she spoke of her mother, a widow with six young children, and how 'the impressions left on me by my young life have never been removed by the passage of time'. This, alongside her experiences working as a low-paid dressmaker, a factory worker and as a teacher, was the formative background to her life in politics. In 1902, she married union organiser William Murdoch Adamson, who hailed from a Fife family steeped in politics. His father, William Adamson Sr, became Labour MP for West Fife in 1910 and remained in Parliament until 1931; he became chair of the Labour Party and Secretary of State for Scotland.

Jennie joined the Labour Party in 1908. She and William shared a life fighting for equality and suffrage for women. His work saw them living in Manchester and Jennie was active in support of the 1915 Black Country strike. They went to Northern Ireland, where she became involved in the Co-operative movement. The year 1921 found them in Lincoln, where she became a member of the Co-operative Management Committee and was on the board of guardians administering the Poor Law. During these years the couple raised a family – two sons and two daughters. William was MP for Cannock from 1922 to 1931. This brought the couple to London and Jennie represented Lambeth North on London County Council from 1928 to 1931. She became involved in national trade union and party bodies and, in 1926, was a member of the Women's National Strike Committee. She served on the NEC of the Labour Party for twenty years from 1927, chairing it from 1935 to 1936. She also chaired the party's national women's committee, and in the 1930s represented Labour women at socialist international conferences across Europe.

Jennie stood as a candidate for Dartford at the 1935 general election but it was later that parliament, in a by-election, following the death of the incumbent, that she was elected as the constituency's MP. With her husband having been re-elected in 1935, they were the only husband and wife team in the Commons at the time. At the age of fifty-six, she brought with her a depth and breadth of experience, which she set about deploying with vigour. Almost every speech she made reflected the interests of working men and women – from the cost of living, benefits for widows, orphans and dependents of service personnel, to childcare for women who were working for the war effort and as conscripts. In a 1940 debate, she spoke as 'a practical housewife and as one who knows what it is to bring up a family on a working man's wage'. The 'gallant male honourable member' of thirty years' experience who spoke next questioned whether she was justified in describing dependents' allowances for the families of naval personnel as 'niggardly and totally inadequate'.

'Could the honourable and gallant gentleman keep a wife and four children on £106 a year?' she asked. He did not answer the question.

Jennie was a parliamentary private secretary from 1940 to 1945 and spoke in support of women in the civil service and equal pay. She raised issues relating to war damage and the production of utility furniture, clothing and perambulators as a means of tackling supply shortages and inflation in such goods. She campaigned for the 1945 Family Allowances Bill – a measure inspired by Eleanor Rathbone.

In Clement Attlee's 1945 government, she was one of three women appointed to ministerial posts, serving as Parliamentary Secretary to the Ministry of Pensions. She resigned her seat following her appointment as deputy chair of the Unemployment Assistance (later National Assistance) Board, a post she held from 1946 to 1953.

Jennie Adamson was a woman whose early political activity included being active in the suffrage movement and who showed through her deeds, as well as her words, what a difference the enfranchisement of women could make.

BEATRICE WRIGHT

SARAH NEWTON

- FULL NAME: Beatrice Frederika Wright, Lady Wright MBE (née Clough)
- DATE OF BIRTH: 17 June 1910
- PLACE OF BIRTH: New Haven, Connecticut, USA
- DATE OF DEATH: 17 March 2003
- MARRIED TO: John Rathbone (m. 1933; d. 1940); Paul Wright (m. 1942)
- CHILDREN: Tim Rathbone (MP for Lewes 1974–97); Faith Wright
- UNSUCCESSFUL ELECTIONS FOUGHT: None
- CONSTITUENCY: Bodmin
- DATE OF FIRST ELECTION: 11 March 1941
- DATE LEFT PARLIAMENT: 4 July 1945
- PARTY ROLES: None
- MINISTERIAL POSITIONS & DATES: None

Seventy-five years on from the creation of the modern welfare state, it is important to remember all those who played a role in this totemic social change, not just William Beveridge. Reading the Family Guide to the National Insurance Scheme that was sent to every household in 1948, setting out details of contributions and benefits, enables us to appreciate the role played by Beatrice Rathbone, Cornwall's first female MP.

Beatrice's arrival in Parliament in 1941 followed the death of her husband, John Rathbone, in the Battle of Britain. A highly effective constituency organiser, Beatrice had played an important role in securing his election as Conservative MP for the Cornish constituency of Bodmin in the 1935 general election, defeating the incumbent Liberal Member of Parliament.

A career in politics was not something she had planned and it is to her great credit that she was asked by all political parties to take her husband's seat and was subsequently elected unopposed. She was the second American-born woman to enter Parliament, and as a result of swearing allegiance to the King, she gave up her American citizenship.

She did not seek re-election at the general election in 1945, but during her four years in Parliament she was an active and effective MP, increasing the acceptance of women in politics.

Beatrice defied convention even in her maiden speech, which made an immediate impact. The *Cornish Times* reported that, in spite of 'the greatness of the occasion – for it was one of those full dress debates that occur only occasionally in each Session, [it] did not overawe her and those who were her listeners will not leave the House when she catches the Speaker's eye on future occasions.'

She went on to make seventy speeches in her four years in Parliament, many more than her husband had made during a longer period. Working with her neighbouring MP, Nancy Astor, and her husband's aunt, Eleanor Rathbone, she was an active parliamentarian, speaking on a range of issues, from the war effort to women's rights and improving welfare provision.

She also proved a useful transatlantic envoy, visiting the United States to make speeches and give broadcast interviews that urged America to join the war. Despite the fact that the Japanese attacked Pearl Harbor while she was in America, she managed to visit her two children who had been evacuated to her family in Boston, and also had tea with the President's wife, Eleanor Roosevelt.

In 1942, she married British diplomat Paul Wright and the following year gave birth to Faith Wright, the first child born to a serving female MP. Faith was brought to the House just two weeks after her birth and left in the care of a policeman while her mother voted. Fortunately, today we have a nursery and Members carrying babies through the voting lobbies is not unusual.

Beatrice's life of public service continued throughout her retirement, most notably as vice-president of the Royal National Institute for the Deaf and as founder of Hearing Dogs for the Deaf. The teaching centre for the charity's dogs is named in memory of her contribution. She was awarded an MBE in 1996.

Her passion for politics was imparted to her son, Tim Rathbone, who represented Lewes as an MP from 1974 until 1997. Described as a 'zealous reformer' and sometimes as a 'wet', Tim Rathbone was a relation of, and godfather to, the former Prime Minister David Cameron.

LADY VIOLET APSLEY

PAM CHESTERS

- FULL NAME: Violet Emily Mildred Bathurst (née Meeking) CBE Lady Apsley
- DATE OF BIRTH: 29 April 1895
- PLACE OF BIRTH: London
- DATE OF DEATH: 19 January 1966
- MARRIED TO: Lord Apsley DSO, MC, TD, DL
- CHILDREN: Henry Allen John and George Bertram
- UNSUCCESSFUL ELECTIONS FOUGHT: Bristol North East 1950
- CONSTITUENCY: Bristol Central
- DATE OF FIRST ELECTION: 18 February 1943
- DATE LEFT PARLIAMENT: 4 July 1945
- PARTY ROLES: None
- MINISTERIAL POSITIONS & DATES: None
- MOST FAMOUS QUOTATION: 'Yield not thy neck to Fortune's Yoke but let thy dauntless mind still ride in triumph over all mischance.' – Quoting Shakespeare when describing how to deal with sudden disability.

Lady Apsley's maiden speech, on the subject of war pensions, in many ways summed up both her approach to life and the contribution she would make during her brief term in Parliament.

She spoke from personal experience about coming to terms with sudden disability. In her case, this was not from active service, but due to an earlier riding accident that left her permanently wheelchair-bound. Her view was that one could either accept the sheltered life of an invalid, or fight back and seek to live life to the full. She opted for the latter, and during her time as an MP used her passion for life to promote the needs of the war disabled so that they too could live as good a life as possible.

Although long active in the Conservative Party Women's Section, and briefly a member of Sodbury Rural District Council, her entry into

Parliament was only brought about by the untimely death, on active service, of her husband, the sitting Bristol Central MP. The convention of the day dictated that the three political parties in the wartime coalition did not contest by-elections, effectively giving the incumbent's party a free pass. While the official Labour Party observed the electoral truce, the ILP fielded its general secretary, John McNair, and Jennie Lee (wife of Aneurin Bevan) stood as an Independent Labour candidate. But Lady Apsley took 52 per cent of the vote and became Bristol's first female MP.

Electoral success was bittersweet, arising as it had from her husband's death. Since the early days of their marriage they had worked together, most notably when travelling incognito to Australia to investigate the plight of 'assisted' emigrants. There as Mr and Mrs James they experienced the settlers' life in the Northern Territory, where Lady Aspley demonstrated an early interest in the general welfare of the population and the role of women in society. With her husband, she co-authored *The Amateur Settlers*, which related their experiences.

She took her commitment to seeing things from the woman's perspective into the House. She highlighted the need for female architects to be involved in design, particularly of kitchens, in the rural housing programme and the need for a female assistant inspector of constabulary at the Home Office to advise on the selection and training of women. She drew on her experience as a former commissioned officer in the Auxiliary Territorial Service to speak on issues facing women in the services. However, she also recognised that most of these women aspired to marriage, family and a home of their own and felt that post-war education should explicitly help prepare them to carry out these roles effectively.

Lady Apsley lost her seat in the 1945 general election and unsuccessfully contested the new seat of Bristol North East in 1950.

Outside of public life she retained a passion for hunting (publishing on the subject), fishing, flying and motor car time trials, and supported her son who became the 8th Earl of Bathurst while still at school.

She was awarded a CBE in 1952 for public and social services, the citation noting she had been lately national chair for the Women's Section of the British Legion.

ALICE BACON

RACHEL REEVES

- FULL NAME: Alice Martha Bacon CBE, Baroness Bacon
- DATE OF BIRTH: 10 September 1909
- PLACE OF BIRTH: Normanton, West Yorkshire
- DATE OF DEATH: 24 March 1993
- MARRIED TO: Unmarried
- CHILDREN: None
- UNSUCCESSFUL ELECTIONS FOUGHT: None
- CONSTITUENCY: Leeds North East 1945–55 and Leeds South East 1955–70
- DATE OF FIRST ELECTION: 26 July 1945
- DATE LEFT PARLIAMENT: 17 June 1970
- PARTY ROLES: Member of the Labour Party's NEC 1941–70 and chair of the Labour NEC and Labour Party 1950–51
- MINISTERIAL POSITIONS & DATES: Minister of State for the Home Office 1964–67 and Minister of State for the Department for Education and Science 1967–70
- MOST FAMOUS QUOTATION: 'A woman MP has to do everything a man MP does. And a little bit more!'

Alice Bacon was the first woman MP in Leeds and joint first in Yorkshire. She is the longest-serving female MP in Yorkshire, and truly one of the great unsung heroes of post-war British politics.

Elected in the great Labour landslide of 1945, Bacon was part of a new generation of women in Parliament, which included Bessie Braddock and Barbara Castle. Over twenty-five years in the House of Commons, before entering the Lords in 1970, she was a champion of comprehensive education, an unusually committed constituency MP, a streetfighter for her wing of the Labour Party and, ultimately, a minister with a pivotal role to play in some of Labour's greatest achievements of the 1960s: the decriminalisation of homosexuality and abortion, the abolition of the death penalty and the development of comprehensive education.

Bacon was never an intellectual and was not part of the revisionist Campaign for Democratic Socialism (CDS), around which many of Labour's moderates, like Hugh Gaitskell, Roy Jenkins and Anthony Crosland, congregated in the 1960s. However, politically and personally, she was extremely close to its figurehead, Gaitskell, Labour's lost leader who died in 1962, just two years before the party's return to power. The two were next-door neighbour MPs in Leeds, and in her role on Labour's National Executive Committee throughout the period, Bacon did all she could to further Gaitskell's chances of becoming Prime Minister. In many ways, her life's mission was to bring about a Gaitskell premiership, and a bit of her zeal died with him. She spoke in the Commons about 'curtains [being] drawn in the small houses in the streets of south Leeds, not just for a Member of Parliament but for a very dear friend whom they knew and loved'.

Alice Bacon's politics did not come from books but from personal experience. It was her upbringing and experience of life before she ever entered politics that shaped her actions as an MP. While the left railed against consumerism and 'a hell of TV sets and homeownership', she noted the possibilities that new consumer technologies brought for working people, noting that:

> One of the good things in the post-war years has been the fact that ordinary working women have been able to take advantage of electrical appliances which were once considered to be luxuries. Only those who live among working people know the difference which it makes on washing days when the woman of the house can use an electric washing machine instead of having to do a big weekly wash in the old-fashioned way.

Bacon's father Benjamin was a coal miner, local councillor and a major figure in the Miners' Federation of Great Britain. Meanwhile, her mother, Lottie, would lay on sandwiches and help out at working men's clubs in the area. The young Alice Bacon spent much of her time in those clubs, the hub of the community in many mining towns. Growing up with a sense of responsibility to her community, in the politically charged atmosphere of a mining town a year before the general strike, Bacon joined the Labour Party in 1925, aged sixteen, and made her first political speech soon after at Normanton Railwaymen's Club. For Bacon, to join Labour was 'as natural as breathing'.

While her political allegiance was shaped by her upbringing, the cause that she would champion for most of her political career owed to her experience of the education system as both a student and teacher. Bacon was one of the few working-class girls to make it to grammar school in the interwar period, and she was acutely conscious of the advantage that this had bestowed on her. As she remarked more than half a century later, in 1976:

> We were the lucky few, the few who got through, and I know that in my small mining town ... there were a great many boys and girls of my age who ought to have gone to the grammar school and received a grammar school education, but there was not the opportunity for them to do so.

After attending teacher training college, Bacon went on to work at an interwar secondary modern school and witnessed the impact of educational segregation on those who had been denied the educational opportunities that she herself had been given. Her opposition to selective education, she said, 'had nothing whatever to do with my politics. It was due to the fact that ... I was a teacher in a secondary modern school, and saw the unfairness of the 11-plus system and the separation of children between secondary modern and grammar schools.' In the Commons Chamber in 1954, she said that she doubted 'whether many of them ever have been in a council school except to speak at general election meetings'. By contrast, she said, 'I know what it is like to try to concentrate on arithmetic when the class next door, which is separated by a thin partition, is having a lesson in music.'

The cause of comprehensive education was Alice's political *raison d'être*, long before it became official Labour Party policy, and between 1950 and 1969 she spoke about the issue in the House of Commons significantly more than any other MP. Similarly, she spoke frequently on the issue at the Labour Party conference and had a long-standing association with the National Association of Labour Teachers, later to become the Socialist Education Association, which included her serving as the association's vice-president at the same time as she was a government minister.

But despite comprehensive education being her passion, Bacon's first ministerial experience after Harold Wilson led Labour back into office in 1964 was at the Home Office, where she served as deputy to Frank Soskice and then to Roy Jenkins. She was never personally close to Jenkins. While he deemed her to have become too used to the ways of his 'remarkably bad' predecessor Soskice, she felt (according to Tam Dalyell) that Jenkins 'liked duchesses too much'. However, they worked together well enough to drive through some of the most groundbreaking social reforms of the post-war period: the abolition of the death penalty and the legalisation of homosexuality and abortion. While glory went to high-profile men – like Jenkins, Sidney Silverman, David Steel and Leo Abse – Bacon worked behind the scenes to steer the Bills through the committees and, ultimately, to transform people's lives.

In 1967, Alice was rewarded for her service in the Home Office with the opportunity to steer through the reform that she identified with most closely. Two years earlier, Anthony Crosland as Secretary of State for Education had issued Circular 10/65, which specified that only those local authorities moving towards comprehensive education would receive funding for new buildings and new schools.

Therefore, when Bacon arrived at the Department for Education and Science, change was already underway. Moreover, she was initially made responsible for higher education and science, while Shirley Williams was appointed to oversee schools – and crucially, comprehensive education policy. However, while her departmental colleague was away on holiday, Bacon successfully argued that their briefs should be swapped, on the basis that Williams had been a university lecturer, while she herself had been a schoolteacher. While Williams was apparently horrified when she found out, it meant that Bacon had the opportunity to pursue her lifelong political passion. Often, this meant using the opportunity presented by Circular 10/65 to channel further investment for building to those schools that cooperated with the policy, and seeking to incentivise change from the bottom up.

Bacon did not like to regard herself as 'a woman MP', even though she was in many ways a pioneer. The 1945 general election saw a surge in the number of women in Parliament, as the scale of Labour's victory swept in fifteen completely new female MPs and brought the party's total up to twenty-one – a total no party would better until Labour returned thirty-seven women to the Commons in 1992. As with many of her female colleagues, it is unlikely Bacon would even have been selected as a parliamentary candidate if the party had seriously believed it could win what had been, before 1945, a safe Conservative seat with a majority of more than 10,000. In many ways, the progress made in 1945 was accidental rather than evidence of party engineering to get more women into Parliament.

Alice Bacon was also one of just three women from the 1945 intake to make it to ministerial office, alongside Barbara Castle and Peggy Herbison.

Like so many of her peers, she faced practical difficulties in carrying out her job. The Lady Members' Room was cramped with just seven desks squeezed inside, and women MPs were often found working sprawled across benches or even on the floor. Her fraught relationships with senior Labour men from Richard Crossman to Jenkins, and the patronising tone that even an ally like Gaitskell took when addressing her (he described Bacon as a 'clever girl' on their first meeting) gives a sense of how unwelcome an independent-minded, working-class woman might have been made to feel even in the ranks of the Labour Party.

However, she did not see being a woman as especially relevant to her politics, she certainly never identified as a feminist, and her closest friendships in politics were with men. The historian Martin Pugh identified Bacon as an example of the 'defeminised woman' in British politics: a group who he saw as having offered 'little challenge ... to the dominant masculine culture of the labour movement'. In Bacon's own words, 'a woman MP would be a failure if she just regarded herself as a women's MP. She has got to be prepared to do all the jobs that a man does.' In many ways, class, community and equal opportunities featured more prominently in Bacon's politics than specific questions of gender.

After retiring from the Commons in 1970, Bacon entered the House of Lords, where she served as Baroness Bacon of the City of Leeds and Normanton in the West Riding of the County of York. On 24 March 1993, she died of bronchopneumonia and was buried in Normanton Parish Church, alongside her parents, who she had lived with for almost her entire life in the same house on Castleford Road, in Normanton. Like so many women throughout history, Alice Bacon was to a large extent forgotten for many years after her death, and the achievements in which she played so important a part were attributed to the individual actions of 'great men'. She remained single for her entire life and, as one colleague put it, she was 'as good as married to the Labour Party'. For a lifetime of service in Parliament and for her commitment to those communities in Leeds and in Normanton, Alice Bacon deserves to be remembered.

BESSIE BRADDOCK

MARIA EAGLE

- FULL NAME: Elizabeth Margaret Braddock (née Bamber)
- DATE OF BIRTH: 24 September 1899
- PLACE OF BIRTH: Liverpool
- DATE OF DEATH: 13 November 1970
- MARRIED TO: John 'Jack' Braddock (m. 1922; d. 1963)
- CHILDREN: None
- UNSUCCESSFUL ELECTIONS FOUGHT: None
- CONSTITUENCY: Liverpool Exchange
- DATE OF FIRST ELECTION: 26 July 1945
- DATE LEFT PARLIAMENT: 29 May 1970
- PARTY ROLES: Member of Liverpool City Council St Anne's ward (final six years as an alderman) 1930–61; member of the Labour Party NEC 1947–69; vice-chair of the Labour Party NEC 1968–69
- MINISTERIAL POSITIONS & DATES: Refused a ministerial position in 1964 on the grounds of ill health and age
- MOST FAMOUS QUOTATIONS: To her constituents after her election in 1945: 'I cannot promise you that the hellholes we have in this division will come down immediately, but exactly the same tactics as I have conducted in the council will be conducted in the House of Commons, and they will get no peace until they do something about it.' | 'I'm not a feminist. I believe I'm as good as any man in this country.'

When 'Battling Bessie' Braddock was elected to Parliament in 1945, she became the first Labour woman to sit in the House of Commons for a Liverpool constituency. A larger than life working-class Scouser, she fearlessly blasted her way through conventions, local and parliamentary. She always said what she thought, always did what she believed to be right and always called a spade a spade.

She was stereotyped as a crude, mouthy, gargantuan and humourless socialist woman by the Tory newspapers and she frequently, though often unsuccessfully, sued to protect her reputation. Braddock was never intimidated and was totally uncompromising in her views.

Even though her political position within the Labour Party went from far-left to right wing during her political lifetime, she always judged everything in terms of whether it would help her working-class constituents.

She took a seat that had never been held by Labour – the moneyed bastion of the rich cotton traders that gave the Liverpool Exchange constituency its name – and turned it into a safe Labour seat; it remains Labour today. She was only interested in getting things done, especially for the women and poorer people who lived in appalling housing. Consequently, her constituents loved her and repeatedly elected her as a councillor and MP at every available opportunity until she retired in 1970.

However, not everyone in her local Labour Party always thought so highly of her. She was narrowly 'deselected' by the party in 1952 for publicly and stridently opposing the Bevanite left, though the eligibility of some of those present who voted was disputed and the NEC reinstated her following an investigation. For her entire time on the NEC, from 1947 through to her resignation on health grounds in 1969, she was an uncompromising opponent of communist and Trotskyist infiltrators into the party. She even published the Labour Party's proscribed list of organisations, whose members were ineligible for party membership, as an appendix to her joint autobiography, *The Braddocks*, in 1963.

When I worked as a Liverpool housing solicitor, I was frequently compared to her by older women from the north end of the city, or by their younger daughters: 'Me ma says you're just like our Bessie' – especially when I had got their housing problems solved. It was always meant as a massive compliment, and I always took it as such.

I never met Braddock. She died on 13 November 1970, when I was only nine years old, but she left an indelible mark on Liverpool politics, on the House of Commons and on the lives of those working-class people in Liverpool whom she dedicated her whole life to helping.

* * *

Elizabeth Margaret Braddock was born in Zante Street, Liverpool, on 24 September 1899. Her mother, Mary Bamber, a native of Edinburgh, was brought to Liverpool as a child after Mary's father deserted the family and her mother was left to bring up her children alone. Little Mary Bamber knew about poverty; she lived it and determined to do something to try and end it.

'Ma Bamber', as she became known, was a hugely well-regarded Liverpool socialist who Sylvia Pankhurst referred to as 'the finest fighting platform speaker in the country' for her work arguing for women's suffrage. A pioneer of women's trades union organisation, Mary took her daughter to her first political meeting, leaving three-week-old Bessie kicking vigorously at the side of the stage while she made her speech. Bessie Braddock carried on kicking vigorously for her whole life and it's clear that her mother was her main inspiration.

Braddock said that it was her experience, aged just seven, of helping dole out soup made by her mother on the 'Clarion van' that made her a socialist. 'I remember the faces of the unemployed when the soup ran out and their thin, blue lips … It was the unemployed workers of Liverpool in 1906 to 1907 who made me a rebel.'

Her mother sent her to the Labour Socialist Sunday School in Edge Hill, got her stewarding meetings for the Warehouse Workers' Union, or 'Ma Bamber's sack and bag women' as they were known, and told her not to come home from her job at Walton Road Co-op without being able to prove she'd joined the union. She even signed Bessie up as a member of the Communist Party of Great Britain (CPGB), of which Mary was a founder member in 1920.

Bessie married John 'Jack' Braddock in 1922. Jack hailed from Hanley in the Potteries, but resided in Garston, where he worked as a railway wagon-builder who was more often blacklisted for his political activities than in work. Jack had met Bessie through the Independent Labour Party in Liverpool, but they eventually got involved with the CPGB – running the Lancashire, Cheshire and north Wales District – just one step ahead of the police. They both left the CPGB in 1924 because they didn't like the democratic centralism that developed, and because it had also become clear that Labour would not allow membership of both organisations.

The Braddocks were a real political partnership and they eventually dominated Labour politics in Liverpool by utilising the very techniques they learned in the Communist Party. I know of people who were told that they couldn't join the Liverpool Labour Party because it was 'full' in the 1950s and '60s – Jack and Bessie preferred to operate with very small groups of trusted people.

Jack was also known as 'Boss Braddock', which was hardly meant as a compliment; Bessie and Jack liked to be in control of the organisations they ran. Elected first in 1929 in the Everton ward, Jack ran the Labour group on the city council from 1946 until his sudden death in 1963. By the '60s, both Braddocks were behaving in a way that could lay them open to criticism for having too iron a grip on the party and for using it mainly to exert internal control.

Bessie Braddock was first elected to Liverpool City Council in 1930, in the St Anne's Ward. An atheist in a Roman Catholic ward, Braddock won because she wanted to sort out slum housing and people knew that she would. This would remain a main concern for her throughout her political life.

Selected as a parliamentary candidate for Liverpool Exchange in 1936, it was nine years before she fought a general election. Braddock spent the war as a full-time ambulance driver on the docks during the Liverpool blitz. She didn't miss a single shift during any of the sixty-eight major raids on Liverpool and became a section leader and divisional assistant. It was dangerous work; 51,000 homes in Liverpool were destroyed by the bombing.

In the 1945 general election, she beat sitting Tory MP John Shute, who had a reputation for being aloof and not replying to letters, on a slogan of 'A Woman for Westminster'. Nobody really believed she would win because of the extra business votes in the seat, but she confounded the doubters by securing a majority of 665 – the first Labour woman elected for a Liverpool constituency.

In her maiden speech in the House of Commons in 1945, Braddock said:

> All my life, I have been an agitator against the conditions, housing and every other sort, in which my class has been compelled to live and I shall continue to agitate with every means and power I have until the people whom I represent and to whom I belong are taken out of the miserable conditions in which they live.

She called the houses in her constituency 'flea-ridden, bug-ridden, rat-ridden, lousy hellholes'. She knew the truth – because she visited workers' homes regularly. Never one to rely solely on reports, she investigated conditions herself. Whether improving the situation in hospitals or old folks' homes run by the council, the actual experience of the people affected was what mattered.

For years, Bessie and Jack spent 9 a.m. to 5 p.m. on Christmas Day visiting all of the old folks' homes and hospitals she was responsible for in Liverpool.

It was this approach that made her a suitable member of the Royal Commission on Mental Health from 1953 to 1957, which eventually led to the

Mental Health Act 1959. This was the first modern piece of legislation on mental health; it aimed to deinstitutionalise mental health patients and put a focus on community care. It made treatment voluntary and informal where possible, distinguished between learning disability and mental illness, and removed sexist assumptions such as defining mothers of illegitimate children as 'moral imbeciles', which made them liable to compulsory institutionalisation. It was probably her finest parliamentary achievement.

Braddock was an early and vigorous exponent of the MP's advice surgery. Taken for granted now as a part of the job, it was far from the norm in her day. She was assiduous and opened her office every Saturday, applying herself to every case that came through the door. One of her volunteers, Sarah Phippard (now deceased), was among the first of my volunteers when I was elected MP for Liverpool Garston in 1997.

Braddock remained a councillor through most of her time as an MP, seeing the roles as complementary, until her reappointment as an alderman was blocked by the Conservatives after they took control of the city council in 1961.

Rules were never a constraint for Braddock; she would stop at nothing to achieve success for her people. She became the first woman to be thrown out of the House of Commons, for defying a ruling of the Deputy Speaker in 1952. After an all-night sitting on the Textiles Bill, in which she had a clear constituency interest, Braddock wasn't called to speak, although she thought she had been promised the opportunity to do so. Enraged, she refused to be silenced and was eventually expelled. Braddock had also been the first woman to be thrown out of the Liverpool City Council Chamber, for calling the chair of Housing a 'liar', while trying to highlight a Tory housing scandal. The police had to be called. She was an early exponent of the 'publicity stunt', though she wouldn't have put it in those words.

'If you didn't do something outrageous,' she said, 'nobody would take any notice of you.'

On another occasion, Braddock snuck two air pistols into the House of Commons Chamber and plonked them down on the table in front of the Home Secretary, in order to make a point about increasing injuries caused by these easily obtainable, unlicensed weapons.

'This caused quite a stir,' as she put it with great understatement, 'as there was no machinery for getting these forbidden objects out of the Chamber again.'

Braddock was as active on council committees as she was in the House of Commons. Her work on Liverpool's Port Sanitary and Hospitals Committee saw her oversee standardising nurses' uniforms, improve the drab, depressing surroundings of many institutions and ensure that the elderly in the council's old folks' homes could wear their own clothes rather than uniforms that identified and stigmatised them as poor. She fought to improve maternity and child welfare services too.

In Parliament, Braddock championed the needs of larger women, demanding more clothing coupons for those who were plus-sized and persuading manufacturers to provide more styles – a real practical achievement. She often focused on consumer issues, insisting that British eggs should have a lion mark to distinguish them from imported eggs. She once produced a small Danish egg in the Commons and protested against its issue as a ration. Her statue in Liverpool has her holding up an egg – with the lion mark printed on it.

There's an enduring image of Bessie Braddock, cruising around the docks in her black Rover 90 with a loudspeaker always fitted to the roof – small boxing gloves given to her by world heavyweight champion Jack Dempsey dangling from the rear-view mirror – telling striking dockers what she thought about industrial relations. They usually listened to her, too.

A perennial backbencher, she turned down a ministerial job in 1964 on the grounds of illness and old age. She eventually left Parliament in May 1970, and spent the last months of her life living with dementia. She died in Rathbone Hospital in Liverpool, a place which she had done much to improve, in November of that year.

BARBARA CASTLE

ANNE PERKINS

- FULL NAME: Barbara Anne Castle (née Betts), Baroness Castle of Blackburn
- DATE OF BIRTH: 6 October 1910
- PLACE OF BIRTH: Chesterfield
- DATE OF DEATH: 3 May 2002
- MARRIED TO: Edward 'Ted' Cyril Castle (m. 1944; d. 1979)
- CHILDREN: None
- UNSUCCESSFUL ELECTIONS FOUGHT: None
- CONSTITUENCY: Blackburn
- DATE OF FIRST ELECTION: 26 July 1945
- DATE LEFT PARLIAMENT: 3 May 1979. Sat as Baroness Castle in the House of Lords from 1990 until her death.
- MEP: Greater Manchester North 1979–84 and Greater Manchester West 1984–89
- PARTY ROLES: Chair of the Labour Party 1958–59 and member of the NEC 1950–79
- MINISTERIAL POSITIONS & DATES: Minister for Overseas Development 1964–66; Minister for Transport 1965–68; First Secretary of State and Secretary for Employment and Productivity 1968–70; shadow Secretary of State for Employment 1970–71; shadow Secretary of State for Health and Social Services 1971–72; Secretary of State for Health and Social Services 1974–76
- MOST FAMOUS QUOTATION: 'I will fight for what I believe in until I die. That's what keeps you alive.'

The word feminism does not appear in the index of any of Barbara Castle's published works of autobiography. In volume one of her diaries, where it should sit between Fekete, a banker she met on an official visit to Hungary in 1967, and Ernie Fernyhough, the MP for Jarrow and a junior minister at the Department for Employment, there is nothing. Nor does the word feminism appear in volume two, where it should fall between Anthony Fell, a Tory MP who moved a no-confidence motion against the new Wilson government in March 1974, and Ferranti, a major defence contractor.

Invited in 1968 to celebrate the fiftieth anniversary of women winning the vote, Castle wrote, 'Preparing my speech was agony because I am too busy exercising my emancipation to have time to think about it ... Talking to that crowded room full of elderly or ageing earnest women was like trying to talk to a room full of cotton wool.'

Yet the list of her achievements for women stretches from the small and practical to the structural and transformative. On the back benches at the end of the 1950s, she won a campaign against penny-in-the-slot turnstiles for women's public lavatories. In the 1960s, Castle's backing for women machinists at the Ford car plant in Dagenham heralded her introduction of equal pay legislation. In the 1970s, her reforms of the benefits system recognised for the first time that household incomes failed to reflect the economic contribution of women as carers, and she fought for child benefit, the first benefit that directly transferred cash from men's pay packets to women's purses.

If she had thought about it at all, Castle would have thought feminism too limiting a description of the purposes of political power. She was a soldier in the battle to change society, to redress its gigantic imbalances that had long been weighted in favour of the well-to-do and the well connected. It is no surprise that of the Pankhurst sisters, there was never any doubt in her mind that the real heroine was not Christabel, but the radical Sylvia. If pressed, Castle would probably have described herself as a socialist who was in politics to fight injustice, wherever it was found.

Yet she was also a politician with a keen sense of where power lay and where it could be exploited to her advantage. It was a recognition of the advance of feminism as a political force that her first and almost only use of the language of 1970s feminism came in 1976, after she had been sacked by Jim Callaghan, her old enemy and (unfortunately for her) the new Prime Minister. She called him 'a bit of a male chauvinist'. What matters most in politics is power, and Castle recognised that feminism was a growing force.

Men were singularly important in her life, particularly in her formation as a politician. Her childhood and early youth were spent in thrall to her clever, duplicitous father, Frank Betts. He lived an imperial life at home, his needs invariably coming before any of his family's, even while he betrayed them all with a long affair that only ended with his death. Only then did Castle discover he had not been alone on the foreign holidays he had taken while the rest of the family went to the seaside. She may not have recognised it, but something of the imperial – occasionally cruel – attitude lingered in her own approach to the people around her.

Her father was replaced in her life by her lover, William Mellor. Mellor in turn cheated on his own wife with Castle for years, stringing both women along for a decade.

These two men were formative influences. But by the time Mellor died, Castle had the self-reliance and contacts that she needed to launch her career on the national stage. The romantic and ideological socialism that she had learned from her family, and which had been honed into more disciplined and practical radicalism by Mellor, provided the core of conviction that she needed to keep going, even when her own self-confidence faltered, bolstering her courage despite the wall of male prejudice and political opposition that she often encountered.

When Barbara Anne Betts was born in 1910, the youngest of three children, industrial Britain was in an unprecedented state of militancy. Inflation was eating away at living standards. But the twenty-nine Labour MPs elected in 1906, after a secret electoral pact with the Liberals, had chosen to support the Liberals' reformist ideas rather than agitate for radical change. The 'Great Unrest' of 1910–14, which contributed to the structural fault line in the left, envisioned revolution, not wishy-washy parliamentary socialism.

Barbara's father, Frank Betts, was a tax inspector and a natural intellectual who been denied the chance of university by a parsimonious father. Betts was a lover of poetry and a student of Greek and Latin. Although his work as a government employee limited his public activities, the household took a close interest in radical politics. After they moved to Bradford – the cradle of the Independent Labour Party – when Castle was twelve, Betts surreptitiously became editor of the *Bradford Pioneer*, the ILP newspaper. The Betts family's politics became even more firmly rooted in the world of the left, coloured by the romanticism of William Morris.

From Bradford Girls Grammar School, Castle swotted her way to a place at St Hugh's College, Oxford, with a scholarship. It was barely a decade since the university had first admitted female students; it was a world that profoundly limited the opportunities available to women. Castle found every door to formal political engagement at university level closed against her. (The ban on women becoming members of the Union wasn't lifted until 1963, the year before she became a Cabinet minister.) Only the university's Labour Society allowed women to participate on equal terms. She was a grammar school girl from the north of England in a world of well-heeled southern snobbery and privilege, and it confirmed everything that her instincts and political education had already shown her: life – as she titled her autobiography – was going to be a fight, all the way.

The first fight would be for the soul of her party. Castle's time at Oxford coincided with the existential catastrophe that nearly finished Labour as a political force. As a minority government between 1929 and 1931, the Wall Street Crash and the onset of global depression split the party between radicalism and Ramsay MacDonald's economic orthodoxy. Winifred Holtby, the radical Yorkshire writer ten years older than Castle, described MacDonald's party as lost in a tragic embrace 'of a hierarchy of wealth ... with its leisured ladies, conspicuous consumption, social superiorities and all'. It was not only that Labour at Westminster seemed to have come untethered from its voters, many of whom were unemployed, and almost all hurt by falling real wages and insecurity. Labour's ambition to establish 'an entirely new standard of human values' appeared to have been squandered, too.

No young woman who aspired to succeed in Labour politics at the time would take up the cause of women. The political contest remained framed as a fight between capital and labour. Yet there was another revolution underway in the labour force, one that was undermining domestic servitude – paid and unpaid – and laying the foundations for a culture of female independence that flowered as second-wave feminism forty years later. The rise of light industrial work and the huge expansion of the number of working women barely impinged, however, on mainstream politics of the time.

Labour was the party of trade unions who abhorred equally Eleanor Rathbone's campaign for family allowances that would undermine patriarchy, and the 'educated middle-class women' who argued in favour. It was the Labour MP Margaret Bondfield, the first woman Cabinet minister, who singled out married women as 'welfare scroungers'. The married women who made up a tenth of the workforce, and a considerable share of the two-thirds of women aged fifteen to twenty-four who went out to work in these years, turned to the Conservatives, not Labour.

The 'new standard of human values' was more easily expressed privately, in attitudes to sexual relationships. Castle had tried to spread sexual enlightenment by bringing a sex educator to talk to her fellow students at Oxford, and her affair with Mellor was framed as an equal relationship between independent individuals, and recognised as such by family and friends.

Castle's political apprenticeship began in a depression-stricken Manchester, working dead-end jobs by day, campaigning by night. But her affair with Mellor, whom she met soon after graduating, gave her both new intellectual ideas – he was an apostle of guild socialism and then chairman of the radical-left Socialist League – and access to some of Labour's leading left-wing figures. Stafford Cripps, Aneurin Bevan and later Michael Foot all became part of a circle of political activists who, as the threat of fascism escalated, fought to build a united front that extended beyond Labour.

Mellor became the founding editor of *Tribune* when it was set up in January 1937, the same year that Castle became a councillor in St Pancras. But Mellor soon fell out with Cripps over the inclusion of communists in a popular front. In a nervous and patriotic capital of empire, the taint of communism was more dangerous even than the threat of fascism – and Mellor wanted to get into Parliament.

Mellor's wife continued to refuse him a divorce; he died in 1942, suddenly, after surgery for a duodenal ulcer. Castle always felt that in death he was finally hers. She attended his funeral. Mellor's wife did not.

In December 1942, the Beveridge Report into social insurance and allied services was published. It became Labour's blueprint for a radical domestic agenda. It also provided Castle with a natural platform for her politics.

Beveridge had a gift for sloganising: his report aimed to slay the 'five giants' of idleness, poverty, ignorance, sickness and squalor. But it also prompted difficult questions for future generations – the 'wicked questions' of how to pay for cradle to the grave security, of how to manage the power that a pledge of full employment gave to trade unions, and how to reinvigorate the institutional inertia of a nationalised health service. Two of these problems would later fall to Castle to tackle.

A nervous Labour leadership was reluctantly persuaded to adopt the whole Beveridge agenda by a rank-and-file revolt in which Castle starred at the party conference of 1943. 'Jam tomorrow, but never jam today. We want jam today,' she demanded, rebuffing the cautious approach of the party line. The quote featured on the front page of the *Daily Mirror*. The paper's night editor was Ted Castle. The news coverage led to a meeting, and the meeting to a marriage that lasted until his death thirty-five years later.

By the time of her wedding, in July 1944, Castle had been selected to fight the mill town of Blackburn in the coming general election. She had just had her appendix removed and had been warned by her doctor not to undertake the journey, made unusually arduous by wartime conditions: 'I want you to forget two things,' she told the packed and smoke-filled selection meeting.

'The first is that I am just out of hospital. The second is that I am a woman. I'm no feminist. Just judge me as a socialist.'

Castle began life as an MP with good contacts from her years of political activism: Aneurin Bevan and Jennie Lee had attended her wedding, and Stafford Cripps was an old associate from *Tribune*. Cripps made her his parliamentary private secretary, the entry-level job for aspiring ministers, and when Harold Wilson replaced Cripps at the Board of Trade she made the most important political friendship of her career. Like her, Wilson had made the journey from northern grammar school to Oxford, and though both younger (he was born in 1916) and cleverer than Castle, they shared a political outlook that bound them together for the next thirty years.

It may also have been a sexual friendship. Castle's male critics invariably assumed that Wilson only promoted her because she had some kind of hold over him. But less biased observers could see that he valued Castle's astonishing capacity for detail, her ability to frame an argument and her refusal to compromise on core left values, a quality that sometimes even her closest friends found infuriating.

At the same time, Castle did exploit her femininity. She liked men; she dressed for impact, wore eye-catching hats, flirted relentlessly and worked long hours largely in male company. Particularly in the 1950s, she was dogged by questions about her childlessness and rumours about her sex life. All of these were the normal fare for women in politics at that time. The politics of class not gender interested Castle.

Promotion at Westminster was only ever partly related to merit. But Westminster prizes a certain skill set and a style of politics – theatrical and confrontational – that though suiting Castle's personality, was hostile territory for someone neither large nor booming.

And though power was exercised in Westminster and Whitehall, it was derived from beyond. For the left, in the 1950s, that meant individual party members. Castle worked on *Keeping Left*, the second of the pamphlets produced by Michael Foot, Richard Crossman and Ian Mikardo. In 1950, after Labour had squeaked back to power, she had enough support in the wider party to be elected to the national executive's women's section. But the trade unions controlled the women's section, so the following year she switched her candidacy to the constituency section, the power base of individual members, and became the first woman to be elected to it.

Castle became a star of the touring Brains Trust, organised to promote the counter-narrative that the left was developing in opposition to the party's right, as the battle over who was to succeed Attlee and shape the party began. The battle lines are still familiar: the right argued for fiscal caution, policy pragmatism and the careful nurturing of Britain's role in the world by staunch support for NATO, the Atlantic alliance and the UN. The left wanted a multi-polar world order, the expansion of state investment and nationalisation, and redistributive taxation. In the 1950s, that meant opposing the introduction of some health charges, challenging the cost of rearmament to fight in Korea and, later, the flat rejection of the bomb.

Perhaps the only policy issue uniquely of its time was the end of empire. A Labour government had already granted Indian independence, but Africa was projected to proceed at a much more gradual pace. The demand for colonial liberation deepened the left–right fault line, not least because it became bound up with the global race between Soviet Russia and the West. Castle became one of the movement's most prominent campaigners and also – on the domestic front at least – one of the most courageous.

Castle wrote about the early days of apartheid in South Africa; in 1958 she attended the preliminary hearings of the treason trial, where she first met Nelson Mandela. She was vilified in Parliament for drawing attention to the abusive treatment of Kenyans accused of belonging to the Mau Mau insurgency and nearly destroyed her standing in her own party – and Blackburn constituency – by her criticism of the extreme use of force by British troops trying to keep the peace in Cyprus amid a Greek Cypriot insurgency.

Her criticism was well founded, but (a trait that often weakened her position) she went too far. British soldiers and their families were being murdered on an almost daily basis. For most Britons, retaliation seemed entirely justified; even fellow Labour MPs attacked her. Hugh Gaitskell, who had won the fight for the leadership in 1955, gave her a public dressing-down and told friends that nothing would induce him to make her a minister. Within five years, Castle was in the Cabinet and Gaitskell was dead.

By the early 1960s, Castle had found a way to perform that made her a politician worth watching. A *Daily Herald* sketch writer described her breathlessly:

> Pale and vivid and watchful ... in attack she provides one of the most awesome sights the House of Commons has to offer. She crouches forward, her glowing head lowered, gathering herself for the assault ... sometimes she makes a kill; sometimes she misses her spring and suffers for it.

But the aggression that parliamentary performance demanded of her was not how women were supposed to be. In her diary she wrote, 'I suppose that I have a domineering manner. At times it makes me look as if I am a bully. People think that I am bitter and aggressive ... I am very self-absorbed.' There is a suggestion in her comments that the quiet and the self-effacing were somehow lesser people. She asked rhetorically, 'What can it have been like for those Victorian women? – fancy having to pretend all the time you were a fool.'

When Harold Wilson, both a unifying figure and the repository of the hopes and ambitions of the left, became Labour leader in 1963 Castle's prospects were transformed. He promised her the job of Minister for Overseas Development, a new post in a new department, as soon as Labour was in power. Castle fought, hard and ultimately successfully, for the department's minister to be in the Cabinet, a symbol of the party's belief in global economic development. In October 1964, with almost no power base in Parliament beyond the backing of the Prime Minister, Castle, the crusading left-winger, was transformed into Mrs Castle, minister and pragmatic administrator.

Castle found her metier. She allied clear political priorities with an exceptional capacity for detail, a bottomless appetite for work and usually, although not infallibly, considerable political acumen. Labour came to power, after thirteen years in opposition, with a plan to reform government: Castle, who had never served in government, brought all her skills to bear on creating a new department from bits of the foreign and colonial offices and the newly formed department for technical cooperation.

She was working against the grain – of Whitehall, but also of many of her Cabinet colleagues – but managed to produce a White Paper setting out her programme. However, she lost her fight to persuade the Treasury to honour the manifesto commitment to spending 1 per cent of GDP on aid. In addition, Castle was making a lone stand in Cabinet demanding aggressive action against Ian Smith, the white minority leader in Rhodesia/Zimbabwe who threatened to make a unilateral declaration of independence rather than accept majority rule. There were times when Wilson found Castle's principles too uncompromising for comfort. At a reshuffle just before Christmas 1965, he decided to move her.

The department was downgraded, a kind of proof that Castle's tenure had been a success. Certainly, her promotion to Minister for Transport was much less of a surprise than the original decision to include her in the Cabinet line-up.

Transport was a big brief: it included the docks, some responsibility for road haulage, British Rail, and most of all responsibility for a policy to accommodate the explosion in car ownership which had led to a terrifying increase in death and serious injury on the roads. This was a world of big trade unions, nationalised industry and above all, men. Men did all the driving, whether it was in the family car or in a lorry; they also drove the trains and they, literally, manned the docks. Castle was not just a woman; she had never taken her driving test. Yet her forceful, largely effective and highly political leadership of this small department with a slender budget left her as the favourite outsider for the party leadership.

She used the department to construct a public identity as a strikingly good-looking woman with a grasp of big ideas and an unwavering commitment to them. Her achievements were less than she might have hoped. She aimed to introduce an ambitious integrated transport policy, but was moved on before her enormous Bill could get through Parliament, and her successor lopped off the difficult bits.

But Castle could claim to have achieved more for ordinary people than almost anyone else in government. She brought in the breathalyser, perpetuated the 70 mph speed limit and by requiring all new cars to be fitted with seatbelts, she began the process of making them compulsory. Castle also saved a substantial part of the UK's canal network and gave the go-ahead for the Humber Bridge, a move that secured the local seat of Hull North for Labour in a by-election and precipitated the 1966 general election, which Labour won by a landslide. The bridge was known thereafter as Mrs Castle's pork barrel.

All politicians need luck, and this proved to be her lucky moment. The government was in trouble. A second election victory in 1966 had been followed by devaluation, a fierce squeeze on domestic spending and the start of a series of attempts to hold down pay rises as inflation began to bite. Wilson decided that, in order to demonstrate energy and direction, he should remake his government. Castle fought her way into the heart of it: she became First Secretary of State and Secretary of State for Employment and Productivity. The new role was confirmed on 5 April 1968. It was to be the high-water mark of her success.

Over the next two years, Castle went from being the most successful woman politician Britain had ever seen, spoken of as a future Chancellor or perhaps even Prime Minister, to a defeated, derided shadow. Her attempts to reform trade union law destroyed her standing on the party's left and very nearly brought down the government.

The tale of 'In Place of Strife', the title Castle chose for her White Paper, a conscious echo of Bevan's 'In Place of Fear' pamphlet written fifteen years earlier, is too long and complex to be rehearsed here. The important points are these: Castle completely miscalculated the trade union response because she failed to comprehend how her proposals would destroy union power. She failed to try to secure support for her plans, particularly among Wilson's rivals and especially with Jim Callaghan, former Chancellor and now Home Secretary.

It was not only the politics of right and left, his trade union background and hers as a party activist that put Callaghan and Castle on opposite sides of every political argument. Callaghan found everything about Castle offensive. He refused to talk to me when I approached him for an interview while I was writing her biography, leaving me in no doubt that even thirty years later, he could not bring himself to be generous about her. He was the only surviving colleague not invited to her ninetieth birthday party.

Castle persuaded herself that she was trying to advance a common-sense plan to balance free collective bargaining with the power that the commitment to full employment gave the unions – thus making a prices and incomes policy, loathed by the unions, unnecessary. She refused to recognise the fact that the trade unions saw only an attack on their ability to fight for better pay and conditions. Perhaps she could not see beyond her objectives; she did not think that ending trade union 'strife' in order to achieve a political objective amounted to the destruction of the careful balance between union and political interests that Labour in government has to manage.

The tragedy is that her ambition, if not the details of her policy, was on the right track. Had she been able to put her proposals into practice, it is possible that Thatcher would never have been elected, or at least not with a mandate to hammer the unions in the aftermath of the Winter of Discontent that came a decade after Castle's failure. It is hardly the first time that the right policy has foundered on bad politics, but the consequences are not often quite so devastating.

Yet those two years culminated in the legislation for which she will always be remembered. When she became Employment Secretary in 1968, progress on implementing the party's manifesto commitment to legislating for equal pay was stalled. There had been a bit of action and an agreement that in an era of pay restraint, it was too difficult to pay women more, as introducing equal pay would unquestionably require.

Castle, exposed to the lengths that union negotiators would go in order to maintain differentials between sectors of their membership, soon realised how badly action was needed. The now famous sewing machinists strike at Ford's Dagenham plant in the summer of 1968 confirmed her belief. But the opposition was entrenched among employers, some trade unionists, and many of her Cabinet colleagues.

Partly because her almost invariable response to defeat was to return with a bigger and bolder plan, in the wake of the humiliation over 'In Place of Strife', in the summer of 1969, she revived the issue. It was a shrewd move: the demand for equal pay for equal work was being taken up widely beyond Parliament. Yet she still had to fight tooth and nail in the final parliamentary session to get space for the Bill that finally reached the statute books just before the 1970 general election. Its introduction was delayed for five years, and it turned out not to be the magic solution that people had hoped for. But it marked a new political frontier: it gave women their own political identity.

But it did not seem like that in June 1970, when Labour lost the election and Castle found herself the object of vilification, not only by the right of the party but by a radical left that angrily cried betrayal. Six years of Labour government had left barely a memorial. Roy Jenkins's liberal reforms in the Home Office and Castle's breathalyser and equal pay were high on the slim list of achievements. The party entered a crisis of confidence, increasingly divided over what its purpose should be. Castle herself, in her sixtieth year, was determined to re-establish herself on the left. She even toyed with the idea of running for the deputy leadership. But she was out of favour with her oldest ally Harold Wilson; she had never had a power base in the parliamentary party and her standing with the rank and file had been badly damaged by 'In Place of Strife'.

Yet less than four years later, Labour, now a minority government, was back in power. Castle returned to the Cabinet with responsibility for running the huge and complex Department of Health and Social Security. Once again she plunged in with a challenging political agenda, some of it forced on her by circumstances, others more planned. She inherited a tense contract negotiation with consultants that became dangerously conflated with an attempt to impose tight limits on the growth of private medicine. Although the BMA would later accept some responsibility for what was the lowest point in relations with the government since the foundation of the NHS, at the time the cost seemed borne mostly by Castle.

But doctors were only part of her brief. She also oversaw the introduction of a programme of reallocation of funds in an attempt to increase spending in less-favoured regions, and tried to introduce a system of generous pay awards to senior doctors who worked in them. Social security reforms were also in train when she inherited the department from the proto-Thatcherite Conservative, Sir Keith Joseph. Many were more or less bipartisan, in particular the introduction of a state earnings related pension that was intended to end pensioner poverty. But even here, Castle's innovation of counting only the twenty best years of a pensioner's working life allowed women who had taken time out for motherhood, independence in retirement.

The introduction of child benefit, to be paid direct to mothers, was also bipartisan. Yet the plan would almost certainly have been shelved by any other minister because it replaced tax allowances paid to married men. That meant an apparent tax rise. Castle was sacked before the reform was introduced, and Callaghan tried to drop it. From the back benches, she defeated him.

Castle stood down as an MP in 1979 and spent another ten years leading the Labour group in Europe. In 1990, she took a seat in the House of Lords from where she launched forensic criticisms of New Labour's pension reforms.

Few have achieved as much. This extract from her old friend Richard Crossman's diaries, written as she answered a critical debate in defence of the government's climbdown on 'In Place of Strife', does as much as anything to explain why she deserves her place in history:

> I arrived just as Barbara was getting up to boos and cheers and for the first seven minutes she was on her feet, she only got out half a dozen sentences. I was sitting right at the end below the Speaker's chair and I saw her trembling as she got up, nervous, tense and tiny and somehow pathetic. If you are little and can only just see over the top of the dispatch box, if you have a high-pitched woman's voice and if you are trying to still the postprandial, alcoholic clouds of noise you are at a terrible disadvantage, especially if you are a bit schoolmistressy and try to hector and lecture them at the same time. Barbara did her best and the angrier she got the more effective she got.

GRACE COLMAN

JAGRUTI DAVE

- FULL NAME: Grace Mary Colman
- DATE OF BIRTH: 30 April 1892
- PLACE OF BIRTH: Wandsworth, London
- DATE OF DEATH: 7 July 1971
- MARRIED TO: Unmarried
- CHILDREN: None
- UNSUCCESSFUL ELECTIONS FOUGHT: Hythe 1929 and 1931, and Sheffield Hallam 1935
- CONSTITUENCY: Tynemouth
- DATE OF FIRST ELECTION: 26 July 1945
- DATE LEFT PARLIAMENT: 3 February 1950
- PARTY ROLES: None
- MINISTERIAL POSITIONS & DATES: None

Grace Mary Colman was born in April 1892, the daughter of Frederick Selincourt Colman, a vicar in Earlsfield who later became a canon of Worcester Cathedral, and Constance Mary Hawkings. She was home schooled, as many upper–middle-class young women were, and went on to attend Newnham College, Cambridge, under a scholarship in 1914, emerging with a First in history and economics. Despite her Conservative upbringing, she joined the Labour Party while at Cambridge and remarkably ended up persuading the rest of her family to do the same.

Prior to entering politics, she worked briefly as a civil servant before settling in education and tutoring at Oxford and the University of London. Her connection with the north of England was forged by teaching at Labour Party summer schools for women and becoming increasingly involved with trade union movements – she even took on the role of assistant secretary to a Nottingham Trades Council committee.

Given her activism and extraordinary success at converting her family from blue to red, it was really only a matter of time before she set her sights on Parliament. After three unsuccessful attempts at obtaining a seat, Colman finally became MP for Tynemouth in the north-east of England in 1945.

This was at the time an incredible achievement. Women were allowed to stand as MPs from 1918, but the first woman to take her seat as an MP was Viscountess Nancy Astor in 1919. By the 1931 elections, the number of women MPs had reached the giddy heights of fifteen, but fell back to nine at the next election in 1935. In 1945, when Colman took her seat, she was one of twenty-four women MPs.

The constituency of Tynemouth was created in 1885 under the Redistribution of Seats Act and was a Conservative-leaning seat in the otherwise Labour heartland of the north-east. Grace Colman took the seat from Alexander West Russell, who had been MP for the Conservatives since 1922; however, at the next election, Dame Irene Ward regained the seat for the Conservatives and became the only woman to ever have unseated two female MPs: Margaret Bondfield in Wallsend in 1931, and Grace Colman in Tynemouth.

Colman was an MP dedicated to local causes; she notably declined when asked by Prime Minister Clement Attlee to go to India as part of a parliamentary commission preparing for its independence, choosing instead to focus on her constituents. Unlike her predecessor, Russell, who apparently rarely uttered a word in Parliament, Colman spoke on issues such as coastal erosion and the fishing industry. Most of all, she was passionate about women's education and, in recognition of her contributions, the Northumberland Women's Advisory Council set up the Grace Colman Summer School, which provided free tuition for Labour summer schools.

Colman's first love was her dogs. She was known to take long walks in the countryside and supported Bills in Parliament to ban hunting with dogs and reform the trade in pets. She was unmarried and died in North Shields in 1971.

FREDA CORBET

ELIZABETH VALLANCE

- FULL NAME: Freda Corbet (née Künzlen, later Mansell)
- DATE OF BIRTH: 15 November 1900
- PLACE OF BIRTH: Tooting, London
- DATE OF DEATH: 1 November 1993
- MARRIED TO: William Corbet (d. 1957) and Ian McIvor Campbell
- CHILDREN: None
- UNSUCCESSFUL ELECTIONS FOUGHT: Lewisham East 1935
- CONSTITUENCY: Camberwell North West 1945–50 and Peckham 1950–74
- DATE OF FIRST ELECTION: 26 July 1945
- DATE LEFT PARLIAMENT: 28 February 1974
- PARTY ROLES: Chief Whip for the Labour-held London County Council
- MINISTERIAL POSITIONS & DATES: None
- MOST FAMOUS QUOTATION: 'May one Honourable lady say to another Honourable lady [Miss Fookes], how much she enjoyed her maiden speech? I recall the maiden speech of the Rt Hon. lady on the government front bench [Mrs Thatcher] which was of equally good calibre.'

Freda Corbet was a Londoner through and through, by birth and commitment. She never left the capital in her long political career, representing the same part of south London both as councillor and MP. She was more interested in local rather than national politics and it was at the London County Council (LCC) that she had the greatest influence and impact. Encouraged by Labour Cabinet minister Herbert Morrison to go into local politics, Corbet believed, in common with many women politicians before and since, that real power resided in having a key role in a big, metropolitan council as opposed to the shadow-boxing and posturing of Parliament. She would have agreed with Ruth Dalton, who represented Bishop Auckland for only ninety-two days in 1929, when she decided to leave national politics and return to her work on the LCC arguing that: 'There we *do* things; here it seems to be all talk.' Corbet was a power in the Labour Party at a national level as well as at a parliamentary level, largely due to her reputation for toughness and the uncompromising style she had forged at the LCC.

She was born in London in 1900, the eldest child of Adolf Frederic Hermann Künzlen and his wife, Nellie, who had a great interest in politics and tried to foster the same enthusiasm in her children. Her father changed the family name to Mansell during the First World War and it was as Freda Mansell that she attended first Wimbledon County School and then University College London, both on scholarships. She read history and, graduating with a First, began a career as a teacher.

In 1925, she married William Corbet, taking his name and helping for many years in his newsagent's shop in Putney (which she always referred to as a 'confectionary business'). Throughout this period she retained her intellectual curiosity and, in the late 1920s, Corbet began to read law and was called to the Bar in 1932. There might have been no political career if she had had children but, as both she and her husband were active members of the ILP (which she had joined in 1919 while still a student), she channelled much of her energy into the Labour Party locally and she and William both contested several elections. In 1934, Corbet was elected to the Camberwell North West council, thus beginning her long association with the constituency, which she would go on to represent at Westminster.

Corbet stood unsuccessfully as the Labour candidate in Lewisham East in 1935, the last general election before the Second World War, after which elections were suspended until 1945. During this period, she became a magistrate, working predominantly with young offenders, while maintaining her role on the LCC's Education Committee, where the comprehensive schools initiative started. But it was her war work, assisting victims of the Blitz in Camberwell, that ensured she would win the local parliamentary seat in the Labour landslide of 1945. She was to remain the MP for nearly thirty years.

For almost the whole of her parliamentary career, Corbet maintained the 'dual mandate' in the House of Commons and on the LCC, where, in 1947, she became Chief Whip, ruling the council for the next thirteen years with a rod of iron. In spite of her size – she was less than five feet tall – 'the Tiny Tyrant' enforced solidarity by denying members the right to any public dissent from the party line, leading Clement Attlee to suggest disapprovingly that there was more than a hint of totalitarianism in the Corbet leadership style. Although this may have been something of an exaggeration, there is no doubt that the Labour group regime maintained by Corbet was authoritarian, dirigiste and, in some party circles, increasingly unpopular. There were attempts to topple her and, indeed, to deselect her from her safe Peckham parliamentary seat, all of which were unsuccessful until the 1958 elections brought in a new set of councillors, who were markedly more liberal and demanded a more democratic approach to local government.

In 1960, having fought off further abortive challenges, Corbet was eventually replaced as Chief Whip and made chair of the General Services Committee. There she was able to facilitate the expansion of London's South Bank to include the Queen Elizabeth Hall, the Purcell Room and the Hayward Gallery. Her influence, however, was on the wane. She had no power base among, and little sympathy with, the new councillors and she opposed the transition from the LCC to the Greater London Council (GLC). And as her sway in Parliament was largely based on the political nous and connections she had acquired at the LCC, when she lost these connections, she had less to offer the parliamentary scene.

She left the GLC in 1965 but remained an MP. In 1972, she abstained on a Labour three-line whip, allowing the Conservative government to take forward legislation to join the European common market; ironic, perhaps, given that she had upheld party discipline so staunchly at the LCC. Corbet left the political stage in 1974, when she resigned from the House to spend more time with her second husband, who was unwell (William Corbet having died in 1957). In the year she left Parliament, she was given the Freedom of the Borough of Southwark. She died in November 1993, a fortnight before her ninety-third birthday.

CAROLINE GANLEY

JULIA LANGDON

- FULL NAME: Caroline Selina Ganley (née Blumfield) CBE, JP
- DATE OF BIRTH: 16 September 1879
- PLACE OF BIRTH: Stonehouse, Plymouth
- DATE OF DEATH: 3 August 1966
- MARRIED TO: James William Henry Ganley
- CHILDREN: Ada, Charles and John
- UNSUCCESSFUL ELECTIONS FOUGHT: Paddington North 1935
- CONSTITUENCY: Battersea South
- DATE OF FIRST ELECTION: 26 July 1945
- DATE LEFT PARLIAMENT: 24 October 1951
- PARTY ROLES: None
- MINISTERIAL POSITIONS & DATES: None
- MOST FAMOUS QUOTATION: 'Serve because you want to serve and not because of what you want to get out of it.'

It was public opposition to the Second Boer War, as the century turned and the old Queen died, which made a radical out of Caroline Ganley. She was twenty-one, only just married and living in lodgings without a bathroom, in the gloomy shadow of the railway in Battersea, when the protests started about the war. Ganley immediately went out and joined the Social Democratic Federation, the grouping of Marxists, trade unionists and Fabians that would, in time, evolve into the Labour Party. Ganley declared herself a pacifist and had no time for anyone who suggested that this stance was anti-patriotic. She soon became an advocate for women's suffrage, too.

Ganley had three children in as many years, but this didn't stop her attending political meetings – she would simply take her children with her. They went to meetings of the Garment Workers' Union – her husband was a tailor's cutter – and she heard people talking about things in a way that captured how she felt. She went to listen to the socialists on Clapham Common and it wasn't too long before she was speaking in public herself. On a Sunday, she could get through three meetings – Bethnal Green, Hyde Park and then home to Battersea Park – speaking for an hour at each and still not losing her voice. James, her husband, put her forward to speak at a demonstration against the Tsar of Russia in Trafalgar Square. She was the only woman speaker.

By the time she was ward secretary of the Bolingbroke Labour Party branch, running the Battersea Women's Socialist Circle and writing letters to the newspapers, she knew she could make things happen. One letter she wrote to the *Sunday Chronicle*, during the First World War, led to servicemen's wives getting their allowances paid through the post office. She stood for Battersea Council in 1919 and she and two other women were elected. Ganley chaired the Health and Child Welfare Committee and organised for a maternity home to be built in Bolingbroke Grove; generations of women would be grateful for that and it would become her legacy.

In 1920, the year the Sex Disqualification Removal Act came into force, Ganley gained the right to be a magistrate. She was among the first batch of women appointed as JPs and sat in the juvenile court for decades. She also served for six years in the town hall and then for another seven on the old London County Council. 'Vote for your working-class candidate,' she declared on her election leaflet. The picture shows a determined young woman with a strong brow and kind eyes. The image elicits trust; you know she will be fair. She served on the London County Education Committee, too, and still found time to become the first woman president of the London Co-operative Society, the largest retail society in the country with nearly one million members. The Co-op backed her to stand against Brendan Bracken in 1935, and two years later she was the candidate for Battersea South.

Ganley was sixty-five when she entered Parliament; one of the oldest elected MPs and one of the very few with little formal education. She spent six years helping to get the NHS Bill on the statute book, a 'glorious service to humanity' she called it in one speech. And when it was all over and she lost her seat by 494 votes because of boundary changes, well, they gave her a CBE and she just went right back and did another twelve years on the council.

BARBARA AYRTON-GOULD

KATHRYN PERERA

- FULL NAME: Barbara Ayrton-Gould (née Ayrton)
- DATE OF BIRTH: 1 June 1886
- PLACE OF BIRTH: Kensington, London
- DATE OF DEATH: 14 October 1950
- MARRIED TO: Gerald Gould (m. 1910)
- CHILDREN: Michael Ayrton
- UNSUCCESSFUL ELECTIONS FOUGHT: Lambeth North 1922; Northwich 1924, 1929 and 1931; Norwood 1935; Manchester Hulme 1935
- CONSTITUENCY: Hendon North
- DATE OF FIRST ELECTION: 26 July 1945
- DATE LEFT PARLIAMENT: 22 February 1950
- PARTY ROLES: Member of the National Executive Committee of the Labour Party (first elected in 1929); vice-chair of the Labour Party (elected in 1938); chair of the Labour Party 1939–40
- MINISTERIAL POSITIONS & DATES: None
- MOST FAMOUS QUOTATION: 'The government, largely responsible, both by what it has done and by what it has failed to do, for the magnitude and the duration of this social disaster, is sunk in lethargy.' – On the blight of mass unemployment.

Scientist, writer, professional suffragette, skilled administrator and an elected representative – Barbara Ayrton-Gould led an extraordinary life. Her dramatic early years spanned the most important political movements of her day, while her later attempts to achieve representative office neatly demonstrate the barriers women faced within the early Labour movement.

Ayrton-Gould's upbringing helps to explain the breadth of her achievements. Both her parents were professional scientists and active in the women's rights movement. Her mother, Hertha Ayrton, was a scientist of such distinction that, in 1902, she became the first woman to be nominated a fellow of the Royal Society of London. Hertha's status as a married woman meant that, despite her nomination, she was ineligible for election. Yet a 2010 panel of female fellows of the Royal Society voted her one of the ten most influential British women in the history of science.

Following in her mother's footsteps, Ayrton-Gould excelled academically and won a place at University College London to read chemistry and physiology. Her studies were to be short-lived. Though a diligent student, Ayrton-Gould found herself increasingly drawn to activism.

This was an explosive time in the fight for women's suffrage. Along with her mother, Ayrton-Gould became a member of the Women's Social and Political Union (WSPU) at a time when the organisation was trialling more militant tactics in the face of government intransigence. Hertha Ayrton-Gould focused her resources on bankrolling the WSPU (papers from 1912 suggest that she helped to 'launder' WSPU funds through her personal bank account to frustrate government attempts to seize WSPU assets). Meanwhile her daughter, full of fire in the belly, became a full-time WSPU organiser in 1909.

Growing government pressure on the WSPU led Ayrton-Gould and other suffragettes to forge close links with a web of sympathetic organisations. These included the Men's League for Women's Suffrage, one of whose founders was the charming Oxford academic Gerald Gould. Barbara and Gerald's shared commitment to feminism and socialism drew them closer together, and they married in July 1910.

Gerald actively encouraged Barbara in her work, even as the government used increasingly draconian measures to punish WSPU activists. In March 1912, Barbara was one of some 200 suffragettes arrested and jailed following a window-breaking demonstration in central London. When she was refused bail, the prospect of a lengthy and unpleasant prison sentence loomed. In a daring move (the precise details of which remain unclear), she fled to France disguised as a schoolgirl. Only when an amnesty was granted to suffrage campaigners, following the outbreak of war in 1914, did Ayrton-Gould return to London.

By that time she had become deeply disillusioned with WSPU militancy. Like many, she felt that the strategic use of arson campaigns was a step too far. In 1914, Barbara left the WSPU and became a founding member of the non-violent United Suffragists.

The horrors of the Great War brought a new direction to Barbara's activism. From 1915 onwards, much of her energy was focused on establishing peace organisations, such as the Women's International League for Peace and Freedom. She joined the Labour Party to push for the establishment of peace-focused initiatives within the party's internal structures.

As ever, Ayrton-Gould's rise through the ranks was fast. By 1922, she was the Labour Party's Chief Officer for Women, as well as a contributor to the magazine *Labour Women*. Yet her ambition to achieve representative office was thwarted time and again. Like most women of her generation, she was selected for 'unwinnable' seats rather than being offered the opportunity to contest the target constituencies. She would stand for Parliament six times in thirteen years without success, watching as a generation of male colleagues entered the Commons ahead of her.

Barbara's consolation was a seat on the Labour Party's National Executive Committee, leading to her election as vice-chair and eventually chair. In these roles she pushed the Labour Party to speak more forcefully on long-term unemployment, co-authoring (with Hugh Dalton and George Dallas) a special commission report, 'Labour and the Distressed Areas', in 1937. The report caused a national stir. And the strength of its content owed a great deal to Barbara Ayrton-Gould.

Only with Labour's 1945 landslide victory did she finally realise her dream of becoming an MP. She devoted her brief time in Parliament to highlighting the scandal of child poverty. Narrowly defeated in 1950, and in failing health, Barbara retired from public life. She died only eight months later.

PEGGY HERBISON

ELIZABETH VALLANCE

- FULL NAME: Margaret (Peggy) McCrorie Herbison
- DATE OF BIRTH: 11 March 1907
- PLACE OF BIRTH: Shotts, Lanarkshire
- DATE OF DEATH: 29 December 1996
- MARRIED TO: Unmarried
- CHILDREN: None
- UNSUCCESSFUL ELECTIONS FOUGHT: None
- CONSTITUENCY: North Lanarkshire
- DATE OF FIRST ELECTION: 26 July 1945
- DATE LEFT PARLIAMENT: 18 June 1970
- PARTY ROLES: Member of the National Executive Committee of the Labour Party; chair of the Labour Party 1957; delegate to the Council of Europe
- MINISTERIAL POSITIONS & DATES: Parliamentary Under–Secretary of State for Scotland 1950–51; Minister of Pensions and National Insurance 1964–66; Minister of Social Security 1966–67; opposition spokesman on Scotland 1951–56 and 1959–62, on Education 1956–59, and on Pensions 1958–59 and 1962–64
- MOST FAMOUS QUOTATION: 'My people, for a long time, have been suffering deplorable conditions ... living, eating, sleeping, bearing and rearing children in one room ... In many parts of my constituency there are people surviving in houses in which ... the Minister of Agriculture would not allow cattle to live.'

Peggy Herbison was, in some ways, an unlikely politician. Not that she was unengaged politically, or lacked a social conscience, but she did not seek office and seemed set and content to make her contribution in another profession. She was born, the fourth of six children, into the Scottish mining community of Shotts, where her father was a coalminer; her mother, Maria (née McCrorie), hailed from Northern Ireland.

After attending the local primary school, she went to Bellshill Academy and then, in the best Scots tradition of the time, where clever, working-class children were encouraged and supported to go on to further studies, went to Glasgow University. Here she chaired the Labour club, took a degree in English and, after teacher training, became a schoolteacher. She was highly successful and loved her work, first in a primary school and then, during the war, at Allan Glen's boys' secondary school, where the diminutive but authoritative Peggy was affectionately known as 'wee Herbie' and one pupil referred to her as 'a right proper bantamweight!'

Although she had always been active in local Labour politics and had lectured at the National Council of Labour Colleges, she was taken entirely by surprise when, after the death of her father in a mining accident, his union nominated her for the North Lanarkshire constituency. She was duly selected and won the seat in the Labour landslide of 1945, taking it from the sitting Conservative MP, Sir William Anstruther-Grey. Peggy had not planned this career change but, at the age of thirty-eight, she saw it as another way of repaying society for her privileged university education.

In the House, she immediately made her position as 'the miners' little sister' clear, announcing in her maiden speech on 17 October 1945, 'My people, for a long time, have been suffering deplorable conditions' and going on to insist what had to be done about this. This moral outrage, the sense of social injustice and the desire to redress the balance in favour of those who had nothing, was common to many of the Scottish MPs at the time and, as my grandfather, David Kirkwood, MP for Dumbarton Burghs, used to say, Peggy was a 'bonnie fighter' in their righteous cause.

In 1947, she seconded the address in reply to the King's Speech, an honour accorded to a woman only once before, when Florence Horsbrugh moved the address in 1935, attired in full evening dress, with train and long white gloves. Peggy was mercifully spared the theatrics and allowed to address the House in her day wear, which in those days often still involved hats. Baroness (Helen) Liddell remembers Miss Herbison's penchant for 'little pill-box (ones) with net and flowers' well.

When Clement Attlee retained power in early 1950, Peggy was made joint Under-Secretary of State for Scotland and launched a successful drive to build new primary schools. But this ended with Labour's defeat in the 1951 general election. In opposition, she sat on the front bench, shadowing Scotland, education and pensions. Having been elected to Labour's National Executive Committee in 1948, she chaired the 1957 Labour Party conference in Brighton, using to great effect her 'deep, clarion bell-like voice' (Tam Dalyell), which another commentator likened to the tones of 'a torch singer'. In any case, it could equally command attention in both a rumbustious classroom and the House of Commons.

When, in 1964, Harold Wilson's Labour Party was returned to power, she was made Minister of Pensions and National Insurance (later Minister of Social Security). She fought long and hard to get the government to raise pensions and markedly increase child benefits, and it was generally believed that it was her failure to get these measures through that led her to quit the front bench in 1967. However, the true position was more complicated and difficult to determine, as Peggy would never publicly speak about her reasons for quitting. Harold Wilson claimed that she had told him she was going in the autumn of 1966, but, through loyalty to the party, stayed on until the next summer.

Peggy had found it impossible to accept the expenditure estimates for 1967/68, which allowed for a much smaller increase in benefits than she believed Labour was committed to. However, she accepted that she could not make public her objections to policies that had yet to be announced and would therefore stay in her job for the time being.

Whether this was due to Peggy's weakness in failing to stand up to her colleagues or simply a commendable desire not to allow other parties to make political capital out of the situation is debatable. What is certain, though, is that she had been put in an extremely difficult position, without a proper Cabinet appointment and with political heavyweights like James Callaghan and Douglas Houghton (as Richard Crossman asserts in his diaries) intent on wrecking her proposals. What is also clear is that she was instrumental in the abolition of the National Assistance scheme – much hated because it left proud poor people facing the indignity of publicly claiming 'assistance', which many simply refused to do. When this was replaced by the more discreet supplementary benefit, hundreds of thousands of people were willing to claim their rights.

For Peggy, politics was never about power or self-aggrandisement (she resolutely refused any honour from Wilson), but about improving the lives of her people. Baroness Liddell, who would sit in Peggy's seat in the 1990s, remembers meeting her predecessor marching into Glasgow Exhibition Centre, followed by at least twenty Shotts miners, whom she had brought to hear Pavarotti sing. Her people deserved the best. After she retired, the one honour she proudly accepted was to become Lord High Commissioner to the General Assembly of the Church of Scotland in 1970; she was the first woman to hold the post. In the same year, she was appropriately chosen as Scotswoman of the Year.

JEAN MANN

AYESHA HAZARIKA

- FULL NAME: Jean Mann (née Stewart)
- DATE OF BIRTH: 1889
- PLACE OF BIRTH: Glasgow
- DATE OF DEATH: 21 March 1964
- MARRIED TO: William Lawrence Mann (m. 1908)
- CHILDREN: Six
- UNSUCCESSFUL ELECTIONS FOUGHT: West Renfrewshire 1931 and 1935
- CONSTITUENCY: Coatbridge 1945–50 and Coatbridge & Airdrie 1950–59
- DATE OF FIRST ELECTION: 26 July 1945
- DATE LEFT PARLIAMENT: 8 October 1959
- PARTY ROLES: Member of the Labour Party National Executive Committee 1953–58
- MINISTERIAL POSITIONS & DATES: None

Jean Mann was an exceptional politician for many reasons. She was elected to Parliament in 1945 to represent the seat of Coatbridge near Glasgow, which included the Lanarkshire steel-producing community of the Monklands, at a time when there were very few female politicians. She was also a mother to five children.

Mann became politically active in the early 1920s and stood unsuccessfully as a councillor in Rothesay and then as a Member of Parliament for West Renfrewshire in 1931 and 1935. But these setbacks did not deter her. Mann built up a reputation as an impressive, inspiring public speaker and was particularly active during the interwar years, when her five children were very young. Prominent far-left politician and leader of the Independent Labour Party James Maxton teased her that she was known all over Scotland as 'haud the wean Jean' and that comrades would have to decide who would take the chair, lift the collection and 'hold her bairn'.

Mann worked long and hard to fulfil her political ambitions. She became a councillor in Glasgow from 1931 to 1938 and was fifty-six years old when she became an MP. She made much of her ability to combine family commitments with an active public life and cultivated the image and mantle of being 'the Housewife's MP'. As one of Scotland's early female MPs, Mann was proud to be associated with issues including social welfare, austerity and food shortages. In her autobiography, *Woman in Parliament*, she wrote about her post-war work of challenging inconsistencies in rationing policies, which affected every housewife in the land, and of combatting the notorious activities of black marketeers who sought to profit from the hardships that families were enduring.

Passionate about improving the quality of housing, Mann had served as Labour's housing convener in 1933, when the party won control of Glasgow City Council. She became vice-president of the Scottish branch of the Housing and Town Planning Association, and was a senior magistrate in Glasgow. Mann supported a shift from building tenements to constructing low-rise, cottage-style accommodation, which she believed would enhance family and community well-being. Inspired by municipal developments in Manchester Wythenshawe Garden City, she tried to raise the standards of new housing estates being built on the outskirts of Glasgow. Mann was implacably opposed to high-rise but more cost-effective housing when she worked for the corporation, but financial restrictions were against her and she quit her post in 1938. However, by this time, she had already become well known for her strong views on housing. She also campaigned to raise public awareness of fire safety, an issue close to her heart as one of her children had died as a result of a fire.

Mann's keen expertise and strong opinions resulted in Thomas Johnston, the wartime Secretary of State for Scotland, appointing her to the Scottish Housing Advisory Committee and, in 1940, she edited a book titled *Replanning Scotland*. Her passion for housing caused, however, a scandal that almost lost Mann her seat. After she had taken the oath, it came to light that her position on the Rent Tribunals (under the Rent of Furnished Houses Control Scotland Act 1943) was a paid one, suggesting a possible conflict of interest as she held an 'office of profit under the Crown'. A select committee was set up to investigate Mann and concluded that her election was invalid. Such was the drama that Prime Minister Clement Attlee ordered special legislation to be rushed through Parliament in October 1945 in order to validate Mann's election and she was able to retain her seat.

Although Mann enjoyed her time in Parliament, in her autobiography she revealed that she had experienced some male chauvinism there. This had encouraged bonds to develop between female MPs who tried to support one another. Mann was known for being an accomplished, confident orator and, in 1953, she brought up the subject of bare legs and hosiery with humour in the Chamber. She asked,

> Is the honourable gentleman aware that there has been a great reluctance on the part of British manufacturers to enter the fishnet, non-ladder stocking trade in spite of the fact the women of this country want that type of stocking? And would he, while attending to the long leg, short leg of the female stocking, also direct his attention to the same thing along the front bench in male socks – short leg, long leg, visible bare leg?

Mann witnessed many fierce internal battles within the Labour Party over her career. When she started out, she was very much part of the more left-wing, radical and socialist ILP, which was affiliated to the main Labour Party, but in time Mann became more aligned with the main party. When the ILP disaffiliated from the Labour Party in 1932, she described the decision as 'an honest but foolish one'. In the 1950s, the Labour Party became very divided again with the left and the right bitterly railing against each other. Mann's declared opposition to the left-wing Bevanites helped win her a seat on the NEC in 1953 as she secured the support of some of the more right-wing trade unions. Two years later, though, when the NEC had to decide whether to expel Nye Bevan from the party for disloyalty, Mann voted in his favour. Even though she had little time for the Bevanites, whom she considered too extreme and influenced by communism, she respected Bevan's achievements, which included establishing the NHS, so she saved him with her vote. This attracted a huge amount of criticism from the right of the party who decried her for losing her nerve, but she was clear that she made her decision based on the future interests of the party and unity. She was a strong, fair and independent-minded politician and would not be pushed around by men on the right or the left of the party. She never shied away from controversy or speaking her mind and ultimately resigned from the NEC in 1958 after a row about a staff appointment in Scotland. She stood down in 1959.

Jean Mann was a pugnacious, tough, determined working-class woman. With five children and a long-term unemployed husband, she understood the brutal realities of grinding poverty and squalid living conditions, which shaped her passion for better housing and a decent welfare state. That was her political mission. She embraced a Christian socialism that reflected the values of the west of Scotland at the time, which were socially conservative, and placed a moral emphasis on motherhood and traditional family values. She was hostile to decriminalising homosexuality, and even though she was keen to get more women into Parliament, she was dead set against George Bernard Shaw's rather radical idea of doubling the number of MPs, so that each constituency would pick a male and female member. By today's standards, it's unlikely that Mann would be labelled a progressive.

However, Jean Mann fought and spoke up for issues that affected the everyday lives of low-paid women, housewives and their families at a time when such matters were rarely given the time of day. Her down-to-earth, persuasive Glaswegian style made her a formidable force for good, and she deserves to be celebrated as an important pioneering woman in Scottish and British politics.

LUCY MIDDLETON

LINDA GILROY

- FULL NAME: Lucy Annie Middleton (née Cox)
- DATE OF BIRTH: 9 May 1894
- PLACE OF BIRTH: Keynsham, Somerset
- DATE OF DEATH: 20 November 1983
- MARRIED TO: Jim Middleton (m. 1936; d. 1962)
- CHILDREN: None
- UNSUCCESSFUL ELECTIONS FOUGHT: Paddington South 1931, Pudsey & Otley 1935 and Plymouth Sutton 1955
- CONSTITUENCY: Plymouth Sutton
- DATE OF FIRST ELECTION: 26 July 1945
- DATE LEFT PARLIAMENT: 24 October 1951
- PARTY ROLES: None
- MINISTERIAL POSITIONS & DATES: None
- MOST FAMOUS QUOTATION: 'We too are engaged on a voyage of discovery for a new world for ourselves, a world where justice, liberty and opportunity shall be opened not only to a few and not only to a class but to the citizens of the entire world.' – Referencing the Mayflower Pilgrims in her maiden speech, 20 August 1945.

Middleton's parents, Sidney and Ada Cox, came from rural, working-class backgrounds. She trained to be a teacher at Bristol University and worked in West Country schools for ten years. Although her father was a radical Liberal, Middleton was attracted to Labour. In 1916 she joined the Independent Labour Party, before becoming secretary of its Keynsham branch in 1919. In the 1920s, she worked with Bristol socialists on a programme of municipal reforms. With a strong interest in the peace movement, from 1924 to '34 Middleton was secretary of the No More War movement. During the 1931 Round Table Conference to discuss granting self-government to India, Middleton acted as an adviser to the colonial Hindu minorities.

In 1934, she joined the staff at Labour Party headquarters. She began a secret relationship with the assistant party secretary, Jim Middleton, who was a married man. In 1935, Jim became general secretary of the Labour Party. Following the death of his wife, he married Lucy on 1 May 1936. He later remarked: 'Everything about us seems to chime. We have the same interests; we share in mind and thought, openly and frankly. There is never a jot of misunderstanding.'

Lucy Middleton was adopted as the Labour candidate for Plymouth Sutton, where Nancy Astor was the sitting MP, in 1936. Labour's success in Plymouth had been limited. The city's first Labour MP, Jimmy Moses, won Plymouth Drake in 1929 but lost the seat in 1931. Labour had never been in control of Plymouth Council, and an election victory for Middleton seemed unlikely.

After Jim Middleton retired from his role as the party's general secretary, he became his wife's election agent. Lady Astor did not contest the July 1945 election and the Labour landslide saw Middleton capture Plymouth Sutton with a majority of 4,679.

Speaking of how few women members had been elected in her maiden speech, she shared

> the incredulity of the bright and unbelieving young lady I met last Wednesday morning when, on the strength of the fact that I was a Member of the House, I was trying to gain access to the House through the crowds outside. She looked at me half mockingly, and altogether unbelievingly replied, 'Sez you.'

Rebuilding Plymouth and housing were Middleton's main political priorities. Lucy persuaded the Chief Whip to establish a Blitzed Areas Committee, which she chaired for six years. The War Damages Commission was refusing many of the applications that were made to them. Middleton and the committee urged that late claims be accepted where accuracy was confirmed by local authority records. This became government policy.

In 1950, Middleton was nominated to be chair of the Parliamentary Labour Party. She was the only woman on the list of nominees, but the male-dominated PLP ultimately elected a male nominee to the post.

Service on the executive of the British section of the Inter-Parliamentary Union took Middleton to various conferences in western Europe. She prepared a report assessing international social welfare provision and legal protection for women and children. In 1949, she was invited to talk to German

Social Democrats, and she made a second visit to Germany that year when the Foreign Office invited her to speak to political and community activists.

Plymouth Sutton's Conservative candidate in the 1950 general election was Jakie Astor, Lady Astor's youngest son. The Astor family remained an important political force in Plymouth, and with boundary changes Middleton's majority fell to 924.

Prompted by its involvement in Korea, the Labour government adopted a rearmament programme. The tensions caused by this and health service charges in Gaitskell's 1951 Budget prompted ministerial resignations and aided the growth of the left-wing, 'Bevanite' movement, of which Devonport MP Michael Foot was a prominent supporter, that was critical of the party leadership's policies.

Middleton described United Nations troops fighting in Korea 'as pioneers in the field of world government'. She saw the government's rearmament programme as a deterrent and the best way of preventing military conflict. Plymouth Conservatives attempted to exploit policy differences between her and Foot. Aware that political disunity could have damaging electoral consequences, Middleton tried to minimise Labour's internal divisions. The differences, she said, 'did not affect the essential unity of the party, in fact it made the party stronger'.

At the October 1951 general election, Jakie Astor was again the Conservative candidate in Plymouth Sutton. Jim Middleton was ill and unable to act as his wife's agent, and turnout was exceptionally high. Middleton lost by 710 votes. The Conservatives secured a small parliamentary majority.

In 1952, Plymouth Sutton's Labour Party unanimously reselected Middleton as their prospective candidate. In the run-up to the May 1955 election, she remained worried that the Tories would exploit policy differences between herself and the outspoken Bevanite, Michael Foot. The two maintained a public show of unity by jointly addressing shopping crowds in Plymouth's city centre and campaigning together across the two constituencies.

Although Middleton fought a feisty campaign, contrasting Jakie Astor's background with her own humble origins, she was unable to defend her seat. 'Those who had rank, wealth and privilege would do right to vote for him, for he comes from that class. But I am far better able to represent those who work by hand and brain, and I make that same claim for my party.'

At national level, and in Plymouth, the Tories substantially increased their majorities. In Devonport, Conservative Joan Vickers narrowly defeated Michael Foot.

For the 1959 election, the Plymouth Sutton Labour Party shortlisted, but did not adopt Middleton as their candidate. Lucy and Jim Middleton remained active in Labour politics. She became foundation chair and a director of War on Want from 1958 to 1968. After her husband's death in 1962, Lucy Middleton's work continued through Wimbledon Labour Party and other party organisations. As vice-president of the Trade Union, Labour and Co-operative Democratic History Society, she edited the 1977 book *Women and the Labour Movement*. In October 1983, ill health saw Middleton in hospital and she died on 20 November 1983.

Lucy Middleton was a Plymouth MP for six years during a seminal period in the city's reconstruction. Her work on war damage claims was important, not only to Plymouth, but to other heavily bombed British communities. A woman from working-class origins, she was an example of the social change Labour sought to achieve.

MURIEL NICHOL

LINDA MCDOUGALL

- FULL NAME: Muriel Edith Nichol (née Wallhead)
- DATE OF BIRTH: 2 February 1893
- PLACE OF BIRTH: Wilmslow, Cheshire
- DATE OF DEATH: 28 May 1983
- MARRIED TO: James Nichol (m. 1920; d. 1962)
- CHILDREN: –
- UNSUCCESSFUL ELECTIONS FOUGHT: Bradford North 1935; Stockport North 1955
- CONSTITUENCY: Bradford North
- DATE OF FIRST ELECTION: 26 July 1945
- DATE LEFT PARLIAMENT: 22 February 1950
- PARTY ROLES: None
- MINISTERIAL POSITIONS & DATES: None

Muriel Nichol came from a political family. Her father, Richard Wallhead, was a painter and decorator who became an activist in the Independent Labour Party. He opposed the First World War and was detained until it ended under the Defence Against the Realm Act.

After she finished secondary school, Muriel Wallhead became an active member of the ILP and an organiser and speaker for the National Union of Women's Suffrage Societies. While her father was in prison, she took over his campaigning role and travelled around Britain as a successful public speaker for women's suffrage as well as peace. When the war ended, her father was released from prison and became an ILP MP for Merthyr from 1922 to 1934.

Muriel earned her living as a welfare supervisor. She married James Nichol, a Bradford school teacher, in 1920. Katharine Bruce Glasier, founder of the Women's Labour League, was a witness at their wedding.

The Nichols moved to Welwyn Garden City, where they continued teaching and became pioneers in the new town. James Nichol became headmaster of the local grammar school, while Muriel became a local councillor. Following the birth of her son, she became chair of the council in 1937 and continued speaking out about women's suffrage and peace. In the 1935 election, she contested Bradford North for the Labour Party. She improved Labour's vote share but was over 7,000 votes behind her Conservative opponent. There wasn't another election for a decade because of the Second World War.

In 1945, Muriel was again selected as the Labour candidate for Bradford North. She fought hard and gave impassioned speeches warning people of the dangers of re-electing a Conservative government. Her speeches on the hustings were reported in the local paper, the *Telegraph and Argus*. She argued that, 'It may well be that if the Tories were returned because of a wave of gratitude for Mr Churchill, they would, before the next election, bring the country to the very depths and make things so terrible that a later Labour government would have difficulty in altering them.'

For good measure, she also dismissed the Liberal Party, accusing them of looking to indulge in political blackmail in the House of Commons. 'The Liberals,' she said firmly, 'were a corpse of a party.'

Strong and tough, Muriel Nichol won Bradford North with a 12 per cent swing to Labour. She was the fiftieth female MP in Britain and, along with Alice Bacon, the first to be elected to a Yorkshire seat. In her maiden speech she talked authoritatively about education in her own constituency:

In 1919, Bradford undertook something which was at that time almost revolutionary – free secondary education – and the results were as good as those who promoted it expected them to be. It fulfilled the highest hopes of those educationists who believed that free secondary education was the right policy for Bradford, and, indeed, for the rest of the country.

She went on to argue that the 1944 Education Act did not satisfy socialist aspirations. She spoke often in Parliament about the welfare of children and the lack of suitable housing for all.

Muriel believed that the world was her oyster and was delighted to be chosen for a parliamentary delegation to India. When she returned, she spoke out in support of the nation:

India is sick to death of British imperialism. She wants independence. Indians rightly stress their dissimilarity from the Australians, New Zealanders, Canadians and South Africans ... There is, believe me, no shortage of political leadership in India. There is political leadership of very high moral and intellectual integrity. In the past, we have underestimated this.

She urged the government to grant India its independence immediately.

Boundary changes saw to Muriel Nichol serving only one term in the House of Commons for Bradford North. In 1955, she unsuccessfully contested Stockport North. She had been appointed a Justice of the Peace in 1944 and remained on the bench for twenty-four years.

Muriel died of pneumonia in 1983 in Welwyn. There was a special commemoration of her life and work in the council chamber, which James Callaghan, former Prime Minister attended.

FLORENCE PATON

NAN SLOANE

- FULL NAME: Florence Beatrice Paton (née Widdowson)
- DATE OF BIRTH: 1 June 1891
- PLACE OF BIRTH: Taunton, Somerset
- DATE OF DEATH: 12 October 1976
- MARRIED TO: John Paton MP (m. 1930)
- CHILDREN: None
- UNSUCCESSFUL ELECTIONS FOUGHT: Cheltenham 1928 and 1929; Rushcliffe 1931, 1935 and 1950; Carlton 1951 and 1955
- CONSTITUENCY: Rushcliffe
- DATE OF FIRST ELECTION: 26 July 1945
- DATE LEFT PARLIAMENT: 22 February 1950
- PARTY ROLES: None
- MINISTERIAL POSITIONS & DATES: None

Florence Paton was the MP for Rushcliffe between 1945 and 1950, and was the first woman to preside over a debate in the House of Commons.

She was born in 1891 into a working-class family in Taunton. When she was four she moved to Wolverhampton, where she received a good education and became a teacher, a Methodist lay-preacher and, like many young people of her generation, a Liberal at a time when the Asquith government was bringing in radical redistributive legislation. She particularly supported Lloyd George's land reform proposals, retaining an interest in the issue throughout her life.

The First World War made Paton rethink her liberalism, and in 1917 she joined both the Independent Labour Party (ILP) and the Quakers. After the war, she travelled abroad and undertook work for the ILP's research department. In 1928, she stood as the Labour candidate in a by-election in Cheltenham. She was not elected, but the experience clearly gave her a keen desire to get into Parliament and she stood in every subsequent general election for nearly thirty years.

In 1929 and 1931, she was unsuccessful in Rushcliffe in Nottinghamshire, and, in 1930, she married John Paton, the ILP's general secretary. In the troubles that followed Labour's 1931 electoral collapse, the couple saw themselves as peacemakers, but, unfortunately, agreement proved impossible and the ILP separated from the Labour Party in 1932.

In 1933, Paton and her husband left the ILP over its increasingly close relations with the Communist Party. She was defeated in Rushcliffe again in 1935, but the advent of the Second World War in 1939 meant that she had to wait until 1945 for another chance at election. In 1945, however, she was at last successful. In the same election her husband gained the much safer seat of Norwich.

Although she had a reputation for being anti-authoritarian, Paton seems to have taken to Parliament with enthusiasm and, in 1946, she became the first woman to be appointed to the Speaker's Panel of Chairmen. In 1947, she was a delegate to the United Nations. On 31 May 1948, she became the first woman to preside over a debate in the Chamber of the House of Commons, although since the House was sitting in Committee on Scottish civil aviation estimates, she did not actually occupy the Speaker's chair.

Florence Paton opposed the retention of conscription beyond the end of the war and, although she detested communism, she also had reservations about Britain's relations with the United States. On the whole, however, she was a conscientious and hard-working backbencher with a useful eye for detail and the ability to take people with her.

Constituency boundaries changed in 1950, and she was defeated in the successor seat of Carlton. In 1955, she was the only woman member of the Royal Commission on Common Land, the recommendations of which laid the foundations for modern public access rights.

In 1976, Paton and her husband, who remained an MP until 1964, died within two months of each other.

MABEL RIDEALGH

LINDA PERHAM

- FULL NAME: Mabel Ridealgh (née Jewitt)
- DATE OF BIRTH: 11 August 1898
- PLACE OF BIRTH: Wallsend on Tyne, Northumberland
- DATE OF DEATH: 20 June 1989
- MARRIED TO: Leonard Ridealgh
- CHILDREN: One daughter and one son
- UNSUCCESSFUL ELECTIONS FOUGHT: Ilford North 1950 and 1951
- CONSTITUENCY: Ilford North
- DATE OF FIRST ELECTION: 26 July 1945
- DATE LEFT PARLIAMENT: 23 February 1950
- PARTY ROLES: National president of the Women's Co-operative Guild 1941–42 and general secretary of the Women's Co-operative Guild 1953–63
- MINISTERIAL POSITIONS & DATES: None
- MOST FAMOUS QUOTATION: 'The health of the people is the nation's greatest asset and health is the concern of the whole nation.'

With only an elementary school education and a London University certificate from evening-class study, in 1945, Mabel Ridealgh, the Labour and Co-operative candidate, was elected as the first MP for the new Ilford North constituency. Her Second World War service involved being honorary regional organiser for the Board of Trade's 'Make Do and Mend' initiative; member of the Ministry of Labour's National Committee for the Welfare of Workers; the National Council of Social Service; and the London area committee of the Citizens Advice Bureau.

In Parliament, her maiden speech focused on the National Insurance Bill, and her contributions in the Chamber reflected her determination to fight for her constituents, especially women, who were suffering in the aftermath of the devastation of the Second World War. She spoke in strong support of the National Health Service Bill in 1946, urging the inclusion of compulsory health prevention and aftercare measures. In a debate on the care and education of young children, she stressed the importance of training nursery school teachers.

In 1949, Ridealgh secured an adjournment debate on overcrowding and the lack of housing in Ilford. There were 10,000 people on the waiting list – all married with children. She also wanted action on local employment, education and transport problems. She pressed the government on compensation for war damage. The debate on the Sterling Exchange Rate saw her concerned about the effect of devaluation particularly on widows and pensioners, and she called for a minimum wage for every adult worker – fifty years before it was actually introduced by another Labour government.

On the international stage, Ridealgh served as deputy delegate to the Council of Europe in 1949 and travelled to Belgium and Luxembourg as a member of parliamentary delegations.

Ridealgh had a long and distinguished history of commitment to the co-operative movement, joining the Women's Co-operative Guild (WCG) in 1920 and serving as general secretary for ten years after losing her seat in Parliament, where she was successful in modernising the organisation. She led WCG campaigns on peace and nuclear disarmament, including international protests, and headed the presentation of an anti-nuclear petition to MPs in 1962. Twenty years after her retirement from office, she was guest of honour at the guild's centenary, and continued active membership for many years. Ridealgh's final days were spent in a residential home in Ilford, where she died aged ninety in 1989.

As a newly elected borough councillor in May 1989, I was honoured to be asked to speak at her funeral on 27 June and to find out more about her work and service to the causes of peace, women's rights and co-operative values.

CLARICE SHAW

MEG MUNN

- FULL NAME: Clarice Marion McNab Shaw (née McNab)
- DATE OF BIRTH: 22 October 1883
- PLACE OF BIRTH: Leith
- DATE OF DEATH: 27 October 1946
- MARRIED TO: Benjamin Howard Shaw (m. 1918; d. 1942)
- CHILDREN: Marjorie (stepdaughter)
- UNSUCCESSFUL ELECTIONS FOUGHT: Ayr Burghs 1929 and 1931
- CONSTITUENCY: Kilmarnock
- DATE OF FIRST ELECTION: 26 July 1945
- DATE LEFT PARLIAMENT: 2 October 1946
- PARTY ROLES: Representative of the Women's Labour League to the Scottish Executive Committee; vice-chair of the Scottish Advisory Council; chair of the Scottish Labour Party 1939; founder member of the Scottish Co-operative Committee, Labour and Trade Union Women
- MINISTERIAL POSITIONS & DATES: None

Clarice Shaw's story is one of accomplishment coupled with misfortune. Failing to be elected for the seat of Ayr Burghs in the 1929 and 1931 general elections, she was successful in 1945 for the constituency of Kilmarnock and became the first female MP in Ayrshire. Elected on the post-war wave of support for Labour, she was one of twenty-one Labour women, fifteen of them first-time MPs.

She took the oath but never spoke in Parliament, as she was struck down with serious illness and unable to attend Westminster. There is little doubt that had she been able to engage in the House of Commons, she would have pursued with vigour the causes she fought for throughout her life.

Born in Leith, she was the eldest child of Thomas and Mary McNab. Her father, a one-time shoemaker and cloth weaver, was a Leith councillor and director of Leith Co-operative Association. His beliefs influenced his daughter, who became a founder member of the Glasgow Socialist Sunday School and was national president for twenty-five years. By profession a music teacher, she joined the Labour Party in 1913, becoming the first female Labour councillor in Scotland. In 1914, she was appointed convener of the public health committee for the alleviation of disease among children; she also served on the Leith School Board.

Shaw was very active in the Women's Labour League and, in 1916, became the representative to the Scottish Executive Committee of the Labour Party. Here she met Benjamin Shaw, a recent widow twenty years her senior. They worked together on issues of female employment and building up the organisation of the Labour Party, and two years later they married in Edinburgh. They were both staunch teetotallers, Shaw having supported her husband's campaign for temperance reform during the First World War.

After marriage, Shaw resigned from Leith Town Council but, following a move to Troon in 1921, was elected to Troon Town Council and Ayrshire County Council, also serving as a magistrate. As convenor of the Ayrshire Public Health Committee, she campaigned for state provision of hospitals, maternity services, school milk and meals. Shaw also pioneered the opening of the first nursery school.

Clarice and Ben Shaw were one of the most successful and popular partnerships in the Scottish Labour Party. Clarice was a gifted speaker while Ben was more introverted. He was active in the Scottish TUC and was a long-serving secretary of the Scottish Labour Party. He supported her efforts to be elected to Parliament but sadly died in 1942. Three years later, Clarice finally achieved her goal of being elected an MP; her own death deprived Parliament of a strong and talented advocate.

Clarice Shaw may not have been able to fulfil her potential in Parliament, but her dedication and achievements have not been forgotten. In 2014, Cathy Jamieson MP for Kilmarnock & Loudoun (2010–15) organised the 'Clarice Shaw Art Competition' with East Ayrshire Schools to commemorate and celebrate the achievements of this local female pioneer.

EDITH WILLS

KATHRYN STANCZYSZYN

- FULL NAME: Edith Agnes Wills (formerly Burnett, née Hook)
- DATE OF BIRTH: 21 November 1891
- PLACE OF BIRTH: Newent, Gloucestershire
- DATE OF DEATH: 7 April 1970
- MARRIED TO: David Burnett (d. 1917) and Frank Wills (m. 1921)
- CHILDREN: Ronald Frank Wills
- UNSUCCESSFUL ELECTIONS FOUGHT: None
- CONSTITUENCY: Birmingham Duddeston
- DATE OF FIRST ELECTION: 26 July 1945
- DATE LEFT PARLIAMENT: 22 February 1950
- PARTY ROLES: Secretary of the West Midlands Labour MPs Group
- MINISTERIAL POSITIONS & DATES: None
- MOST FAMOUS QUOTATION: 'So I say, let us alter our propaganda, if we can call it that, and urge the women to come forward. Let us tell them how good they are, and how much they can do, and I am sure they will not disappoint us.'

The first two things I read about Birmingham's first ever female MP, Edith Wills, were that she was an 'enthusiastic worker in progressive causes', and that she was the 'hardest working housewife in Birmingham'. A sign of a different time in British democracy maybe, where female MPs were seen within the context of their familial relationships, but I'm not sure it isn't true. Edith Wills was a campaigner and activist in the city at a time of huge societal change – a councillor, educator, union organiser, board director and company president, magistrate and MP over the course of a lifetime dedicated to her ideals of social reform and civic improvement within her beloved Co-operative movement and the Labour Party. She represented the views of the 'ordinary' housewife, a pioneer at a time when the male grip on parliamentary seats was tight, but the class grip for both men and women even tighter.

Edith Agnes Wood was born in 1891 in rural Gloucestershire to a working-class family, but moved to inner-city Birmingham at some point before her tenth birthday. What a shock to the system that would have been at the turn of the twentieth century, and it's hard not to assume this played a part in shaping what came next. In 1911, aged twenty, she started work as a tailor in the city, and just a year later formed her own Birmingham union branch of the Amalgamated Society of Tailors and Tailoresses. Thus began her interest in the rights of workers, an interest that would diversify into different forms throughout her life.

Throughout the years of the First World War (in which she lost her first husband David) and the 1920s, Edith continued her union interests, becoming the worker's representative on the Tailoring Trade Board in 1913. She married Frank Wills in 1921 aged thirty; they had their only child, Ronald, when she was thirty-five. And as a rather admiring *Evening Despatch* profile of Edith in 1939 pointed out, she also dedicated 'much of her leisure' to causes; becoming Secretary of the Nechells Women's Co-operative Guild in 1921, the President of Duddeston Labour Party in 1924, as well as serving on the Education Committee of the Birmingham Co-op Society and its management board for many years. Despite the titles, it's clear she was the essence of what we would now call grassroots, personally teaching youth classes for the Co-op movement, and frequently providing individual help and advice to her community.

It was during the 1930s, though, that her political career and gravitas in the city really took off. Having been the only female director of Birmingham Printers Ltd from 1933, she was elected president of those directors in 1939, an unprecedented move. By this stage she was also a member of Birmingham City Council, having been elected in 1930, and served on the education and public assistance committees, which were her specialisms.

And so to Parliament. In the 1945 general election, Edith Wills stood for the Co-op and Labour Party in the inner-city Birmingham Duddeston constituency, against Conservative incumbent Sir Oliver Simmonds. She won in the Attlee Labour landslide with a majority of just under 5,000, one of only twenty-four female MPs in that Parliament. She made her maiden speech during the 1945 Rent Control Bill, calling for families living in other people's homes to be protected from paying high rents. She argued that her Labour government should be going even further with fixed rent tenures; starting as she meant to go on, this was an indication of the general tone of what was to come during her single term in Parliament.

She urged the post-war continuance of seventy-six day nurseries in Birmingham, which were invaluable for working women, and pointed out the shortage of nurses in the city, as well as the need for cheap, easily obtainable public meals for workers. In 1946, she spoke in defence of the (by now fairly unpopular) bread rationing bill. 'In the Co-operative movement we are willing to share our crust with the rest of the community,' she said. 'This is the only way in which you can guarantee to safeguard our housewives.'

Edith Wills appears to have been a fearless campaigner, and also seems never to have been intimidated in the Commons – as demonstrated in one of her most important speeches, on the Consumer Goods Bill of 1947. She made an impassioned argument for tapping into the skills of part-time female workers, stating: 'If they are duly encouraged, I think it is possible to get more out of women than out of men.' Wills advocated a more positive relationship between employers and employees, even suggesting the Board of Trade needed a psychologist to help convey the message of productivity that benefited everyone and to encourage people into jobs seen as less attractive in the post-war era. At the end of this speech, Wills referred to Conservative peer and wartime Minister of Food Lord Woolton's 'good housekeeping'. She pointed out that it was easy to be a good housekeeper with a full pantry – 'and Lord Woolton had a very full pantry'. Asked immediately afterwards by one of her right honourable colleagues to take back her criticism – she refused.

Edith Wills became a displaced MP when boundary changes meant her Duddeston constituency was merged with areas of Small Heath and Aston. She was asked to contest several other areas in 1950 but chose to retire. However, Edith wasn't one for sitting around. She returned to Birmingham City Council in 1956 and remained a councillor for another eight years. She also served on the official government-appointed and spectacularly named Tomato and Cucumber Marketing Board from 1950 to 1962, as well as on several charity boards. She was awarded an OBE in 1966.

A profile of Edith as the second city's first female MP in the *Sunday Mercury* in 1948 has a series of photos showing her two lives – as a Birmingham housewife chatting to people on the inner-city streets where she lived for the majority of her life, and as an MP striding across Westminster Bridge with three of her male Midlands counterparts, gesturing strongly as she makes a point now frozen in history. The profile ends with the sentence: 'Above all she is Edith Wills, of Rupert Street Duddeston, the voice of the city's housewives and champion of Birmingham's underdogs'. This seems a fitting testament to her devotion to the people of the city, but it might be even more fitting to let Edith Wills have the last word. 'So I say, let us alter our propaganda, if we can call it that, and urge the women to come forward. Let us tell them how good they are, and how much they can do, and I am sure they will not disappoint us.'

PRISCILLA BUCHAN, LADY TWEEDSMUIR

DAME ANNE BEGG

- FULL NAME: Priscilla Jean Fortescue Buchan (née Thomson), Baroness Tweedsmuir of Belhelvie
- DATE OF BIRTH: 25 January 1915
- PLACE OF BIRTH: Kensington, London
- DATE OF DEATH: 11 March 1978
- MARRIED TO: Sir Arthur Grant, 11th Baronet of Monymusk (m. 1934; d. 1944) and Lord John Norman Stuart Buchan, 2nd Baron of Tweedsmuir (m. 1948)
- CHILDREN: Joanna Grant, Anne Grant and Susan Buchan
- UNSUCCESSFUL ELECTIONS FOUGHT: North Aberdeen 1945
- CONSTITUENCY: Aberdeen South
- DATE OF FIRST ELECTION: 26 November 1946
- DATE LEFT PARLIAMENT: 30 March 1966. She was made a life peer in July 1970.
- PARTY ROLES: Executive member of 1922 Committee; delegate to the Consultative Assembly of the Council of Europe 1950–53; British delegate to the United Nations 1961–62
- MINISTERIAL POSITIONS & DATES: Joint Parliamentary Under-Secretary of State at the Scottish Office 1962–64; Minister of State at the Scottish Office 1970–72; Minister of State at the Foreign and Commonwealth Office 1972–74
- MOST FAMOUS QUOTATION: 'There is no halfway house between capitalism and communism.'

Indomitable is the word that springs to mind whenever my predecessor Lady Priscilla Tweedsmuir, the Conservative and Unionist MP for South Aberdeen from 1946 to '66, is mentioned. She was irrepressible and a prominent character in Aberdeen's political history.

Born Priscilla Jean Fortescue Thomson in 1915 in Kensington, she married

Sir Arthur Grant, the 11th Baronet of Monymusk in Aberdeenshire, in May 1934. Tragically, he was killed in action in 1944, leaving Lady Grant a war widow with two small daughters.

It was as Lady Grant that she first stood for Parliament, losing in the safe Labour seat of North Aberdeen in the 1945 general election. However, in November 1946, she stood and won a by-election for the more prosperous and naturally Conservative seat of South Aberdeen. She was to remain the MP for South Aberdeen for the next twenty years, making her the longest-serving MP for the constituency.

At only thirty-one, she was the youngest woman in the Commons when elected. She was tall, slim, young and pretty, with fair hair and blue eyes. So it was inevitable, given the times, that her appearance was often remarked upon and the press dubbed her the 'glamour girl'. Even in later life, she was called 'Parliament's most glamorous granny'.

However, she is best known by the title Lady Tweedsmuir, which she obtained by virtue of marrying, in 1948, the 2nd Baron of Tweedsmuir, Johnnie Buchan, son of the author John Buchan. After the war, Lord Tweedsmuir took his seat in the Lords. The couple had one daughter.

In 1954, Lady Tweedsmuir and her husband carried out a remarkable feat when she in the Commons and he in the Lords, successfully piloted the Protection of Birds Act through Parliament. This Act was to become the model for all future conservation laws.

Her good looks and gender were put to use in a short film made in 1949 – an early form of a party political broadcast – entitled 'Lady Tweedsmuir, Unionist MP for Aberdeen, addresses the housewives of Britain on the dangers of socialism'. It was clearly aimed at a female audience, with a vase of flowers on the desk beside her. Despite her cut-glass accent, Lady Tweedsmuir comes over as much more natural than the male politicians of her generation. In the film, she is emphatic that there is 'no halfway house between capitalism and communism' and that socialism is really a form of communism.

In 1957, she was the first female MP to move the Loyal Address to the Queen's Speech. At the end of her speech, she welcomed the proposed legislation to allow the creation of life peers of either sex, thus opening the House of Lords up to women, something from which she was to benefit in 1970.

Unlike many MPs of her time, Lady Tweedsmuir kept constantly in touch with her constituency. The family home was at Balmedie in Aberdeenshire, and her youngest daughter went to school in Aberdeen. She took up causes that were important to her constituency, such as becoming a champion of deep-sea fishermen, and even made a virtue of dealing with individual constituency problems in her 1966 election address.

Lady Tweedsmuir also made sure she kept the local Aberdeen daily newspaper, the *Press and Journal*, on her side. While the local Labour Party paid the price for criticising the *P&J* for alleged bias, Lady Tweedsmuir got excellent coverage.

She possessed a long-term interest in foreign affairs, especially Europe, and was at various times involved with the Assembly and Council for Europe. She was the British delegate to the United Nations General Assembly in both 1961 and '62.

Despite her obvious talents, Lady Tweedsmuir had to wait until 1962 for her first ministerial appointment as the very junior Joint Under-Secretary of State at the Scottish Office. She was one of only three women with ministerial positions at that time, Mrs Thatcher being another. Mrs Thatcher wrote to her on her appointment saying, 'At last the powers that be have done what they should have done as far back as 1951.'

In her party communications at election time, Lady Tweedsmuir railed against socialism and its failures. However, she was also admired across the political divide. At her farewell party in the Beach Ballroom, after losing the 1966 election to Donald Dewar, the Labour Lord Provost, Norman Hogg, who was to become Labour MP for Cumbernauld and Kilsyth said, 'I have always had a great admiration for Lady Tweedsmuir. She has a very shrewd political mind.' And in 1983, Labour stalwart Manny Shinwell said that Lady Tweedsmuir was the 'best' female MP Britain had ever had. Clearly her charm captivated many, despite their differing political affiliations.

When she said she wouldn't fight the Aberdeen South seat again after losing, because 'to begin and end with South Aberdeen is good enough for me', many thought that this was the end of her political career. It wasn't. Lady Tweedsmuir was made a life peer in her own right in the 1970 dissolution honours list and so began her second political career as Baroness Tweedsmuir of Belhelvie of Potterton in the County of Aberdeen.

She was immediately appointed a Minister of State in the Scottish Office and then, from 1972 until 1974, she was the first woman to serve as a Minister at the Foreign and Commonwealth Office. In 1974, she was also elevated to the Privy Council.

However, her lasting achievement was in her role as chair of the European Communities Select Committee in the House of Lords from 1974. She was a firm European but realised the importance of detailed scrutiny. She attracted about eighty peers from all backgrounds to examine in detail the proposed legislation from the European Community. This they did with the thoroughness missing from the equivalent committee in the Commons.

Lady Tweedsmuir lost her battle with cancer at the age of sixty-three in 1978. A memorial service was held in St Machar's Cathedral, attended by almost 200 people from all walks of life.

ALICE CULLEN

SARAH MACKINLAY

- FULL NAME: Alice Cullen JP (née McLaughlin)
- DATE OF BIRTH: 18 March 1891
- PLACE OF BIRTH: Scotland
- DATE OF DEATH: 31 May 1969
- MARRIED TO: Three marriages; widowed twice
- CHILDREN: Three daughters
- UNSUCCESSFUL ELECTIONS FOUGHT: None
- CONSTITUENCY: Glasgow Gorbals
- DATE OF FIRST ELECTION: 30 September 1948
- DATE LEFT PARLIAMENT: 31 May 1969
- PARTY ROLES: None
- MINISTERIAL POSITIONS & DATES: None

Alice Cullen's political career was dedicated to improving living standards for the people of Gorbals – especially the woefully inadequate housing in which many lived. The Gorbals was notorious as one of the most deprived parts of the UK, home to Britain's worst slums. Although midway through the twentieth century, life in Gorbals was still reminiscent of the Victorian era.

Unsurprisingly, Cullen's maiden speech detailed some of the dreadful conditions that families had to contend with; large families, often in excess of eight or more individuals, would live in a single room. Many buildings were at the point of collapse and rat-infested, and two districts in her constituency contained properties which, although deemed uninhabitable, were filled with families living in them. Tuberculosis was rife.

Eventually, the overcrowded, dilapidated and insanitary tenement buildings were replaced with high-rise flats – a change largely brought about by Cullen's tireless campaigning. At the time, high-rise buildings were seen as groundbreaking feats of architecture, but have since been demolished as part of a regeneration programme.

Due to Cullen's work, more than 60 acres of slums were demolished and, by the 1960s, were replaced with modern housing and flats.

The *Sunday Express* referred to Cullen as the 'champion of the slum dweller'; a nod to her tireless campaigning to improve housing for thousands of residents in and around Gorbals. It was a well-deserved and fitting description of the woman who had done so much to improve the poor living conditions in the area.

Cullen wasn't born into a particularly politically active family. Educated at Lochwinnoch Elementary School, Cullen joined the Independent Labour Party aged twenty-five, in 1916, and became politically active at a local level. She started out as the secretary of the local war committee, and was a member of Glasgow Corporation (now Glasgow City Council) from 1935 to 1945, during which time she was named a Justice of the Peace, before being elected to Parliament.

Cullen's predecessor, George Buchanan, had stood down from the seat to become chairman of the National Assistance Board. In her bid to be adopted as the ILP's prospective parliamentary candidate, Cullen defeated three other men who were also vying for the candidacy. Once Cullen was selected, Prime Minister Clement Attlee encouraged voters to support her, stating, 'Don't be distracted by "red herrings" issued by the other two candidates, Mr Kerrigan [Communist] and Mr Roxburgh [Conservative Unionist].'

However, it should be remembered that not only were women MPs rare during Cullen's time in office, they were more transient too. In the 1950 election, just twenty-one women MPs were elected, fourteen Labour.

Significantly, Cullen was the first female Roman Catholic to be elected to Parliament. The importance of this should not be underestimated. Anti-Catholic feeling took hold during the 1930s in Glasgow, fuelled by deep sectarianism. It was not uncommon, if you were a Catholic, to find it difficult to secure work in central Glasgow.

However, some years into her parliamentary career there was something of a resurgence of Catholicism, aided by extensive post-war Irish immigration. A major growth in the building of Catholic churches and schools throughout the central belt of Scotland took place. If the start of her office had been difficult for Cullen as a Catholic, the years following may have presented significantly fewer challenges in this respect.

Although Cullen's constituency, Glasgow Gorbals, no longer exists, over the years it achieved some notoriety. Cullen, alongside other Glasgow MPs, supported legislation that prevented the sale of American horror comics to minors, following an unpleasant turn of events in the Gorbals area in the 1950s. The Gorbals vampire incident occurred in 1954, when hundreds of schoolchildren searched a cemetery armed with stakes after they claimed 'a vampire with iron teeth' had murdered two children.

In total, Cullen fought and won seven general elections, representing Glasgow Gorbals from 1948 until her death in 1969. Throughout her parliamentary career she strove to better the lives of her constituents and succeeded in effecting lasting change.

ELAINE BURTON

COLLEEN FLETCHER

- FULL NAME: Elaine Frances Burton
- DATE OF BIRTH: 2 March 1904
- PLACE OF BIRTH: Scarborough, Yorkshire
- DATE OF DEATH: 6 October 1991
- MARRIED TO: Unmarried
- CHILDREN: None
- UNSUCCESSFUL ELECTIONS FOUGHT: Hartlepool 1943, Hendon South 1945 and Coventry South 1959
- CONSTITUENCY: Coventry South
- DATE OF FIRST ELECTION: 23 February 1950
- DATE LEFT PARLIAMENT: 7 October 1959
- PARTY ROLES: None
- MINISTERIAL POSITIONS & DATES: Spokesperson on Civil Aviation and Consumer Affairs (SDP, House of Lords)
- MOST FAMOUS QUOTATION: 'I suggest that the test of a good government, and I use the word 'good' in the sense that one speaks of a good man or a good woman or a good scheme, is not whether we add more to the abundance of those who have plenty, but whether we provide enough for those who have too little.' – In her maiden speech, 8 March 1950.

Elaine Burton was elected to the House of Commons in 1950 for the newly created consituency of Coventry South, and joined Maurice Edelman and Richard Crossman in representing the city. She became an MP during a time of great change for Coventry. The post-war reconstruction was moving apace and this had a major impact on the demographics and politics of both the city and Burton's constituency. During this period, it was the development of new private housing estates that changed the make-up of Coventry South most significantly, and it was those changes that Burton felt contributed towards her defeat by Conservative Philip Hocking in the 1959 general election.

Burton was particularly concerned by the significant private residential development on the Allesley Hall and Mount Nod estates, coupled with slum clearance in the city centre, which meant that Labour voters were relocated to the neighbouring constituency of Coventry East, while more Conservative-leaning voters moved into Coventry South. In addition, she felt that local party activists were ignoring the new residential estates and that campaigning in Coventry South was not as good or as comprehensive as it should have been. This led to a number of disagreements between Burton and the local party over her political decision-making, but she was keen to lead by example and, sensing the political changes in her constituency, spent entire days canvassing these new estates with teams of activists that she and her agent had organised, convinced that this was the only way to retain her seat.

But Burton never neglected parliamentary duties at the expense of her constituency work. She utilised her platform in the Commons to campaign on issues as diverse as Coventry's employment needs, women's opportunities in business, improved funding for amateur sports and consumer affairs. She even became the unofficial housewives' voice in Parliament as she fought numerous battles on their behalf to secure greater consumer protections and better value for money for households.

Burton also found the time to successfully sponsor the Disposal of Uncollected Goods Bill, which authorised the disposal of goods left with shopkeepers for repair but that were not subsequently collected. The motivation to introduce such a Bill arose following a conversation with the secretary of the Coventry Boot Trade Association, who told her that cobblers had at least 450,000 pairs of uncollected repairs on their shelves, which they estimated were worth some £166,000 in labour and materials. Burton felt her Bill could remedy unfairness by allowing tradesmen to sell on these repaired items and recoup their costs. Burton was also proud of and relished her role as the first woman chair of the Sub-Committee of the Commons Select Committee on Estimates.

As a senior female MP in Coventry and Warwickshire, Burton was active in women's groups across the region including the Young Women's Christian Association and the Warwickshire Labour Women's Advisory Council. She spent a significant amount of time challenging sex discrimination, most notably winning concessions from the government to prevent building societies from discriminating against women applying for mortgages. She also believed that her focus on consumer affairs would be of most benefit to women and extolled her parliamentary successes in her campaign literature under the heading 'A Fair Deal for Housewives'.

During the 1950s, a split emerged in the Labour Party between supporters of Hugh Gaitskell and Aneurin Bevan. The Bevanite wing of the Labour Party had become organised in Coventry – no doubt aided by key Bevan supporter and Coventry East MP Richard Crossman – and there was an active Bevanite 'Brains Trust' in the city. Burton was faced with local pressure to support the Bevanite line. However, it is far from clear whether Burton could be considered a Bevan supporter. Indeed, prior to the general election in 1955, she was threatened with deselection after she voted to deny Bevan the parliamentary whip, in defiance of instructions from her local party. Equally, Burton was hesitant to attend meetings that the local party were organising to discuss a Bevanite foreign policy. Given her apparent scepticism of Bevanism, it could be argued that Elaine Burton's political views were more attuned with the right of the Labour Party rather than the left. Indeed, she would eventually leave the Labour Party to join the Social Democratic Party (SDP) as a result of the rise of the hard-left in the late 1970s and early 1980s.

In April 1962 – just three years after losing her parliamentary seat, but almost two decades before her switch to the SDP – Burton returned to Parliament after being made Baroness Burton of Coventry. Her elevation to the House of Lords as a life peer was enabled by the Life Peerages Act 1958, which Burton had, ironically, opposed as an MP, as she sought a far more fundamental reform of the Second Chamber than that legislation was proposing. Nevertheless, Burton made a substantial contribution to the work of the Lords, using her time there to continue to campaign on and progress many of the issues she had championed as an MP. She even became the SDP's spokesperson on civil aviation and consumer affairs in the 1980s.

Elaine Burton remained an active parliamentarian well into her eighties and died on 6 October 1991.

EVELINE HILL

NATALIE BENNETT

- FULL NAME: Eveline Hill (née Ridyard)
- DATE OF BIRTH: 16 April 1898
- PLACE OF BIRTH: Manchester
- DATE OF DEATH: 22 September 1973
- MARRIED TO: John Stanley Hill (m. 1922; d. 1947)
- CHILDREN: John, Betty and Faye
- UNSUCCESSFUL ELECTIONS FOUGHT: None
- CONSTITUENCY: Manchester Wythenshawe
- DATE OF FIRST ELECTION: 23 February 1950
- DATE LEFT PARLIAMENT: 14 October 1964
- PARTY ROLES: None
- MINISTERIAL POSITIONS & DATES: None
- MOST FAMOUS QUOTATION: 'I think that a woman will feel much happier if she knows that she is the tenant of the house and is not merely there on sufferance because her husband is the tenant. There is rather more security in feeling that one's name is in the rent book.' – 26 January 1951.

Reading between the lines of the *Guardian* account of the 1964 general election in Manchester Wythenshawe, Eveline Hill was having a tough time. With thousands of new council tenants moving into the constituency that she had won three times, the demographics were now against her as a Tory. Even though Harold Wilson was not to secure the expected Labour majority in this election, with the Liberal vote rising, Hill's majority was to drop by nearly 5,000 votes.

But at the age of sixty-six, with fourteen years in Parliament and nearly three decades on Manchester City Council behind her, it seems likely that she only fought in this election because a new Conservative candidate would have had no chance at all of winning it. She'd unexpectedly held the seat in 1959, postponing hospital treatment for what seems to have been a serious condition in order to fight the election. Colleagues told *The Guardian* it was 'a great personal triumph' that she'd held on. In 1966, two years after the Westminster defeat, she would stand down from the council.

When she left state-funded secondary school, she joined the modest family catering business, which she left, in 1922, upon marrying, becoming a housewife – which at the time would have been an unimaginably stellar future. Much that came next might have been predicted: the respectable charity and public service work of the comfortably middle-class wife. Hill was elected to the council in 1936, where she specialised in health issues, while service during the war with the Women's Voluntary Service saw her rise to county borough organiser, as well as having a role in running the family business with her brother.

It seems likely that had she not been widowed in 1947, Hill would never have stepped beyond the Manchester political stage. When she stood for election to Parliament in 1950, she was one of only twenty-eight Tory women candidates. Despite massive Conservative gains – Labour's 146-seat majority was cut to just five – only six of these seats were won by women.

As an MP, Hill's service, perhaps unsurprisingly, was solid rather than standout. She worked mostly on 'female' issues of health, education and social services. Her maiden speech was on housing, but from the perspective of how important it was to health. That, following her, Conservative MP Derek Walker-Smith suggested that she'd demonstrated 'by her very concise and logical marshalling of her facts what a slander it is to say that women are not logical' is a demonstration of the barriers still facing a woman in Parliament. Hill seems to have made relatively little of her business experience – perhaps because it wasn't sufficiently 'womanly'. And she laboured away on such unglamorous issues as the Heating Appliances (Fireguards) Bill and the House of Commons Kitchen's Committee.

Perhaps her bravest step was to join three other Tory women backbenchers in writing to *The Times* in 1952. They called for more women candidates to be selected in winnable seats, and argued that the lack of such candidates was primarily the fault of local constituency organisations. Hill and her colleagues noted that the problem applied in all parties, with a total of just seventeen women MPs in Parliament. Sounding very Conservative, they commented, 'We write this letter, not as feminists, but because we believe there are many able and distinguished women who could serve their party and the country if given the chance.'

Hill's most prominent individual effort was the Private Members' Deserted

Wives Bill, which would have given women left by their husbands the right to remain in the family home, and not be made homeless by their husband's actions, while also protecting their household possessions. Although the Bill failed narrowly at its second reading, chiefly for complex legal reasons it seems, it had an impact on the terms of reference of the Royal Commission on Marriage and Divorce. Tellingly, all of the women in the chamber at the time, three Labour and three Tory, backed it.

Hill also was prominent in the 1952 debate on equal pay for women in the civil service, although she was following Irene Ward rather than leading. She also added into the debate the issue of deeply unequal pay for women in the Health Service, returning to what was clearly her favourite subject, one that was grounded in a long and close engagement with South Manchester Hospital. One issue on which she worked again and again was hospital staffing. Her suggestion of a sherry party to woo former midwives back into employment seems to have met with some success, with one of the outcomes, suggested by attendees, being a day nursery for the midwives' children.

Born during the reign of Queen Victoria, Eveline Hill was, in a quiet, respectable way, a pioneer. And she served her community in traditional, but hard-working, ways. She deserved more than the scant four-paragraph obituary *The Guardian* afforded her in 1973, even as it described her as 'for more than thirty years ... one of the leading figures in Manchester public life'. I've not been able to find any memorial to her in Manchester, something that really should be corrected.

DAME PATRICIA
HORNSBY-SMITH

ANGELA BROWNING

- FULL NAME: Dame Margaret Patricia Hornsby-Smith DBE, Baroness Hornsby-Smith
- DATE OF BIRTH: 17 March 1914
- PLACE OF BIRTH: East Sheen, Richmond
- DATE OF DEATH: 3 July 1985
- MARRIED TO: Unmarried
- CHILDREN: None
- UNSUCCESSFUL ELECTIONS FOUGHT: Aldridge-Brownhills 1974
- CONSTITUENCY: Chislehurst
- DATE OF FIRST ELECTION: 23 February 1950
- DATE LEFT PARLIAMENT: 27 February 1974. She joined the Lords on 13 May 1974.
- PARTY ROLES: Chair of the Surrey Young Conservatives and South-East Area Young Conservatives
- MINISTERIAL POSITIONS & DATES: Parliamentary Secretary to the Department of Health 1951–57; Under-Secretary of State Home Office 1957–59; Parliamentary Secretary to the Department of Pensions and National Insurance 1959–61
- MOST FAMOUS QUOTATION: 'The most potent citadel of prejudice – selection committees.'

A doughty fighter, Pat Hornsby-Smith became a Member of Parliament in the post-war years. As a woman from a working-class background she blazed a trail for those who came after her, battling successfully against the prejudices of the Conservative Party's selection process.

Her modest beginnings – the daughter of a saddler, growing up in East Sheen – added to the challenges of a woman who, at an early age, was determined to play her part in national life.

Attending what was considered to be a good school (Richmond County School) undoubtedly contributed to her intelligence, tenacity and self-confidence. Joining the Junior Imperial League, the forerunner of the Young Conservatives, at the age of sixteen, her debating skills were quickly recognised and a year later, in 1931, she was included in a team of speakers to help fight the general election. Hornsby-Smith remained staunchly loyal to the Conservative Party for the rest of her life, although she did not hesitate to make her views known, even if they did not always find favour. She opposed capital punishment, not a policy to endear her to some selection committees. An active party member, she chaired her local Young Conservative branch and represented it on national committees.

After leaving school, she worked as a secretary at engineering, electrical and textile firms, and also worked for the Employers Federation. Industry and manufacturing was to be her choice of subject when she made her maiden speech years later in the House of Commons.

Hornsby-Smith's experience as a private secretary stood her in good stead during the Second World War. Her wartime service was impressive. She became principal private secretary to Lord Selborne, Minister of Economic Warfare. Here the Special Operations Executive (SOE) would have given her an insight into some of the highest level secret operations of the war. She joined the Special Forces Club after the war but, according to her god-daughter Jacqui Lait (later to become MP for Hastings & Rye 1992 and Beckenham 1997), she never discussed her work for the ministry. Apart from this important work, Hornsby-Smith was also active in several wartime voluntary organisations. Friends and colleagues credited her wartime activities – which required Hornsby-Smith driving numerous vehicles – with forming her habit of always starting her car while it was in second gear.

After the war she was elected to Barnes Borough Council, where she served as a councillor for four years, and began her quest to find a parliamentary seat. It is worth mentioning that the cost of nursing and fighting a parliamentary seat is expensive. For a single woman the vagaries of a parliamentary career, particularly having to fund it out of earned income, is a challenge. Hornsby-Smith had no family income, and after her father died she supported her mother. She was raised with a strong work ethic and throughout her life did numerous jobs, building a reputation as a good businesswoman.

Repeatedly rejected by constituency selection committees, she formed the opinion that prejudice existed against women. This led her to observe that the 'most potent citadel of prejudice' was a selection committee, a view that has been endorsed by many women parliamentary candidates down the generations.

Her tenacity finally paid off, though, and at the 1950 general election she was selected to contest the Labour-held seat of Chislehurst. She duly over-turned Labour's majority of 6,279, winning the seat with a majority of 167. She quickly gained a reputation as a hard-working local MP, and went on to increase her majority at each election until she finally lost the seat in 1966.

For her maiden speech on 1 May 1950, she chose the subject of Anglo-Canadian trade; Pat Hornsby-Smith was never going to settle for one of the domestic topics that were considered 'women's subjects'. Her fifteen-minute well-researched speech was packed with economic analysis and policy suggestions. As is parliamentary custom, the next speaker, Joseph Percival William Mallalieu, Labour MP for Huddersfield East, responded. He said:

> The Honourable Lady, the Member for Chislehurst, who has just addressed the committee most effectively for the first time, was preceded into this House by a lively political reputation. Certainly we on this side of the committee, and, I should think Honourable Members in all quarters, have been waiting for her maiden speech with expectant anticipation. Not one of us has been disappointed this afternoon. If she will allow me to say so, her speech sounded every bit as attractive as she herself looks.

Pat was certainly a good-looking woman; her auburn hair was always well ar-ranged and she often wore a hat, as was the fashion in the 1950s. She possessed a good sense of dress and colour. Her career in the Commons blossomed, and within a year of her election, she was asked to make a Conservative Party Political Broadcast to woo women voters at the 1951 election.

As the salary for a Member of Parliament was low, Hornsby-Smith could not afford to employ a secretary; so fifty-four businesses in her Chislehurst constituency formed a supper club, 'The 54 Club', to help her out. A year after her election she became Parliamentary Secretary at the Ministry of Health, a post she held for six years. The Hansard records of her ministerial offices depict her as the 'doughty fighter' she always was. Never afraid to defend herself robustly, she thought on her feet, and was always ready with a strong riposte for those who challenged her. Asked by John Mendelson MP: 'When did the Right Honourable Lady last live on £21 a week?' she retorted, 'When I was Under-Secretary of State at the Home Office.' She went on to hold min-isterial office at the Home Office and then Pensions & National Insurance.

Even though she herself was clearly at home at the despatch box, the gentleman's club culture of the House of Commons impacted on women Members of Parliament. It was not until Pat became a minister that she ventured into the Smoking Room. This is a bar, only frequented by MPs, that is situated off the library corridor. Furnished with deep leather arm-chairs and sofas, it would have been a familiar environment for those men who belonged to the established clubs at the other side of St James' Park. After a sterling performance at the despatch box, Hornsby-Smith's boss at the Department of Health, Harry Crookshank, said she deserved a drink and escorted her to the Smoking Room. Thereafter Pat felt entitled, as she cer-tainly was, to enter the bar on her own. But the gentlemen's club ambiance of the Smoking Room persisted for several more decades.

Ministerial office dominated Pat's time in the Commons, but a place in the Cabinet eluded her. She was well regarded by the government, though, and in 1959 became the youngest woman to be appointed to the Privy Coun-cil. When her ministerial career ended, in 1961, she was made a Dame.

Despite never becoming a member of the Cabinet, Pat Hornsby-Smith enjoyed a national profile. She was deployed by the Conservative Party to promote Tory policies, taking part in media interviews and guesting on pro-grammes such as *Any Questions?*

Appearing on a Radio 4 programme in 1972, which focused on the twenty-six female MPs in the House of Commons, Hornsby-Smith described them as 'among the top bracket of hard workers', but regretted the tendency to expect them to focus only on 'women's subjects'.

She lost her seat at Chislehurst in the 1966 general election, but regained it in 1970, although the new Prime Minister Edward Heath failed to offer her a ministerial position. Because of boundary changes to her seat, and out of loyalty to her party, she gave way to Heath, her neighbour from Bexley, and went to the Midlands to fight the Labour seat of Aldridge-Brownhills. She lost by 366 votes and was elevated to the House of Lords. Despite declining health, she led several delegations abroad and continued her business career, holding several directorships.

It would be wrong to mention Pat Hornsby-Smith without also mention-ing Margaret Thatcher. There is no evidence that they were ever close friends, but they were colleagues in the House. In 1950, the year Hornsby-Smith won Chislehurst, Mrs Thatcher secured the nomination for nearby Dartford. The future Prime Minister was asked by Conservative Central Office to put up a good fight, to ensure that Labour activists stayed in Dartford rather than undermining Pat Hornsby-Smith's chances in Chislehurst. A film about Margaret Thatcher's fight to become Prime Minister, *The Long Walk to Finchley*, featured Pat. She was played by actress Sylvestra Le Touzel.

Pat Hornsby-Smith died in July 1985. At her memorial service held at St Margaret's Church, Westminster, Prime Minister Margaret Thatcher read one of the lessons.

DOROTHY REES

JULIE MORGAN

- FULL NAME: Dame Dorothy Mary Rees (née Jones)
- DATE OF BIRTH: 29 July 1898
- PLACE OF BIRTH: Barry, Wales
- DATE OF DEATH: 20 August 1987
- MARRIED TO: David George Rees
- CHILDREN: None
- UNSUCCESSFUL ELECTIONS FOUGHT: Barry 1951
- CONSTITUENCY: Barry
- DATE OF FIRST ELECTION: 23 February 1950
- DATE LEFT PARLIAMENT: 5 October 1951
- PARTY ROLES: None
- MINISTERIAL POSITIONS & DATES: Parliamentary private secretary to Shirley Summerskill, Minister of National Insurance

Dorothy Rees was the first female Labour MP to be elected in industrial South Wales – it was a short-lived honour but hard won. She was elected in 1950 to the newly redrawn constituency of Barry, now in the Vale of Glamorgan, winning by just 1,025 votes.

Her election meant that for a short time Wales had three female MPs. Sadly, she lost her seat in the 1951 general election – again by a small margin, this time of 1,649 votes – to her Conservative opponent. And after the death of Lady Megan Lloyd George in 1966, Wales was back to having only one woman MP.

Although Dorothy Rees was only an MP for a very short period of time, it is reported that she did valuable work as PPS to the Labour MP Dr Edith Summerskill at the Ministry of National Insurance. She was also a great advocate of the education of girls – coming from humble beginnings, she understood the power of education.

Dorothy was not cut from the same cloth as many of the female MPs of the day. Unlike MPs Megan Lloyd George and Eirene White, she was not born into a family with political connections – which makes her achievement in becoming an MP all the more remarkable. A docker's daughter, she won a scholarship to Barry County School and then trained as a teacher at the local training college.

In her short time in Parliament, Dorothy spoke out on Welsh affairs, championing the creation of more educational facilities for children with disabilities – citing the Llandrindod School for Deaf Children as an example.

She spoke in favour of more technical education for children of industrial communities like those in her own constituency, as well as in rural Wales. She also paid tribute to the work of the government for its industrial strategy and the building of factories in towns like Barry, which had helped to create job opportunities and introduced a more diverse range of jobs.

Dorothy's contribution to politics was predominantly in local government and, in 1934, she was elected to Glamorgan County Council – becoming the second female county councillor in Glamorgan. Like many politicians, she earned her stripes in local politics – I, too, began my political career as a county councillor for South Glamorgan, a smaller geographical area than the old Glamorgan where Dorothy had served and eventually became its chair in 1964. Dorothy's interests lay predominantly in girls' education, health and housing.

My husband, Rhodri's interest in politics was stimulated by a meeting he attended in Radyr in 1951, where Dorothy was fighting to save her seat after having been MP for eighteen months. Rhodri was twelve years old but still remembers the merciless heckling of the Radyr Tory crowd, calling out, 'What about rising prices?' Dorothy could not make herself heard and after ten minutes she left the stage in tears, having never experienced such crowd hostility. Rhodri couldn't believe that these seemingly respectable business types were just short of baying for blood. Sadly, Dorothy lost the seat in the subsequent general election and returned to local government.

EIRENE WHITE

JANE MERRICK

- FULL NAME: Eirene Lloyd White (née Jones), Baroness White of Rhymney
- DATE OF BIRTH: 7 November 1909
- PLACE OF BIRTH: Belfast
- DATE OF DEATH: 23 December 1999
- MARRIED TO: John Cameron White (m. 1948; d. 1968)
- CHILDREN: None
- UNSUCCESSFUL ELECTIONS FOUGHT: Flintshire 1945
- CONSTITUENCY: East Flintshire
- DATE OF FIRST ELECTION: 23 February 1950
- DATE LEFT PARLIAMENT: 17 June 1970. She sat in the Lords as Baroness White of Rhymney until her death in 1999.
- PARTY ROLES: Member of Labour's NEC 1947–53 and 1959–72; chair of the Labour Party 1968–69
- MINISTERIAL POSITIONS & DATES: Under-Secretary of State for the Colonies 1964–65; Minister for Foreign Affairs 1966–67; Minister for Wales 1967–70
- MOST FAMOUS QUOTATION: 'I can see no reason whatever for what seems to me to be a completely outmoded social distinction by which certain young ladies have the privilege of being presented at Court for no virtue of their own.'

Eirene White, who held senior positions in the Labour Party and was Britain's first female minister in the Foreign Office, should have been a Cabinet minister alongside her contemporary Barbara Castle. Educated at St Paul's and Oxford, she possessed a fierce intellect and strident ambition. George Bernard Shaw, whom she met when she was younger, once told her: 'Women of your qualifications and antecedents do not grow on gooseberry bushes.'

Despite never making it to the Cabinet, White nevertheless achieved many firsts in her career both as an MP and as a political journalist. As well as being appointed the first female Foreign Affairs minister, she was the first woman to be a minister at the old Colonial Office. White also became the first ever female lobby correspondent, in 1945, writing for the *Manchester Evening News*.

White was the daughter of Tom Jones, deputy Cabinet Secretary to four Prime Ministers: David Lloyd George, Bonar Law, Ramsay MacDonald and Stanley Baldwin. In the 1930s, after studying at Oxford, White travelled to the United States and worked as readers' adviser at the New York Public Library. It was in the city that she was prevented from going to a restaurant with Paul Robeson, the singer and civil rights activist, due to racial segregation. This episode led to White being an opponent of racial discrimination in her later career.

Back home, at the outbreak of the Second World War, White joined the Women's Voluntary Service, later becoming its Welsh regional secretary. She also took up a post as an officer in the Ministry of Labour, overseeing workers in Wales as part of the war effort.

At the 1945 election, White stood as the Labour candidate in Conservative-held Flintshire, but failed to win despite the Attlee landslide. Instead, she took up a post as political correspondent for the *Manchester Evening News*. It was while in the lobby, attending Downing Street press briefings, that she met John Cameron White, a fellow journalist. They married in 1948.

In 1947, White won a seat on Labour's ruling NEC in the women's section, establishing herself as a key figure in Labour Party politics. At the 1950 election, she won the seat of East Flintshire with a majority of just seventy. Her maiden speech, on the iron industry, gave a hint of her desire not to be pigeonholed as a female MP.

Early on in her parliamentary career White tried to reform divorce law, tabling a Matrimonial Causes Bill to allow divorce after seven years' desertion. Although her own Private Members' Bill did not become law, the government set up a royal commission on marriage and divorce, carrying forward her proposed reforms.

During the 1950s, Labour's executive was riven by battles between left and right, between which White found herself caught. She stood down from the NEC in 1953, letting rip at the 'bludgeons of the right and poisoned arrows of the left', but returned in 1959. She was also chair of the Fabian Society in 1958–59.

When Harold Wilson became Prime Minister in 1964, he appointed White Under-Secretary of State for the Colonies, while Castle became Minister for

Overseas Development. Given women had previously held 'domestic' ministerial jobs in education and labour, this was a great progressive step.

In 1964, the journalist Mary Stott described White in *The Guardian* as a 'fairly plump but elegant, well-dressed woman, with a really beautiful smile, who sits behind the huge red leather-topped desk in the rather forbidding, hospital-like Colonial Office in Great Smith Street'. In this job, White raised the problem of education in Commonwealth territories, as well as promoting the work of the United Nations, something she continued to do in her ministerial job in the Foreign Office, to which she was appointed in 1966. She committed what was seen in the Foreign Office as a diplomatic gaffe when, in 1966, she declared she would not want to go on holiday to Spain because she said it was 'determined to bully' the people of Gibraltar. The incident highlighted what observers saw as characteristic of someone intellectually rigorous and earnest yet who lacked political skills of persuasion and was not the smoothest talker.

White's husband died from lung cancer in 1968, leading her to campaign against the tobacco industry. While she retired from the Commons in 1970, White did not quit her political career, taking a peerage as Baroness White of Rhymney and holding various appointments including chair of the Land Authority for Wales, deputy chair of the Metrication Board, as well as Deputy Speaker of the House of Lords between 1979 and 1989.

HARRIET SLATER

RUTH SMEETH

- FULL NAME: Harriet Slater (née Evans) CBE
- DATE OF BIRTH: 3 July 1903
- PLACE OF BIRTH: Tunstall, Staffordshire
- DATE OF DEATH: 12 October 1976
- MARRIED TO: Frederick Slater
- CHILDREN: None
- UNSUCESSFUL ELECTIONS FOUGHT: None
- CONSTITUENCY: Stoke-on-Trent North
- DATE OF FIRST ELECTION: 31 March 1953
- DATE LEFT PARLIAMENT: 31 March 1966
- PARTY ROLES: Government whip and Co-operative Party national organiser
- MINISTERIAL POSITIONS & DATES: None

It is a sad truth that history does not always remember those who make it. Harriet Slater was born into obscurity, and in the years since her passing she seems, unjustly, to have returned to it. But during her lifetime, Harriet Slater was a pioneer.

Not only was she the first woman to represent the seat of Stoke-on-Trent North, she was also the first woman to serve as a government whip, and did so at a time of intense political turbulence, helping to steer a government with a majority of just three through the choppy waters of Westminster.

Slater was a teacher, a co-operator, an organiser, a councillor and a parliamentarian – and her work reveals a woman of courage, kindness and fortitude.

A potter's daughter, Slater was born in Tunstall in 1903, in a terraced street just around the corner from where my office stands today. Educated at Hanley High School and Dudley Teacher Training College, she grew up in Burslem, the mother town of the Potteries, among the bustling factories and smoke-blackened bottle kilns that distinguished Stoke-on-Trent during its industrial peak.

A teacher by trade and a socialist by conviction, she taught at local girls' schools before her appointment, in 1943, as a national coordinator for the Co-operative Party. Responsible for the north-west of England, her work took her throughout the region lecturing on the work of the Co-operative Party and its place in the wider labour movement, as well as running its summer schools, a role she continued until 1953.

It was a natural fit for a woman who had been a dedicated mutualist her whole life. Slater had served as the president of the Milton guild in Burslem and as a member of the Burslem co-operative management committee, and even met her husband, Frederick, through their shared work for the Co-operative Party.

Slater's first foray into elected politics came in 1933, when she was voted in as a councillor for Stoke-on-Trent City Council, a role that she maintained until 1965. She used her experience as a teacher and her commitment to education to good effect, serving as chair of the Stoke-on-Trent education committee from 1953 to 1966.

First elected to Parliament in a by-election in 1953, Slater became the first woman to represent the seat and the only woman MP to represent the Co-operative Party. She would go on to comfortably hold the seat in the 1955, 1959 and 1964 general elections and served until her retirement at the 1966 general election.

Her grounding in mutualism and local government was reflected in her approach to Parliament. Slater was not one for lofty, abstract ideas or niche constitutional matters. Instead, she focused her attention on the bread-and-butter issues affecting her constituents, including in one instance the actual price of bread and butter (not to mention tinned peaches!).

Harriet Slater viewed her role in Westminster as being a practical advocate for the working class, especially working-class women. Throughout her time in the Commons her primary interest was in securing better standards of education and healthcare, as well as achieving tougher consumer protection. She fought for improvements in educational opportunities for working-class children – including the provision of playing fields and school dental care – and spoke out against price increases that would impact tight household budgets.

During her time in Parliament, she was a pragmatic and determined advocate for the people of Stoke-on-Trent. As her parliamentary colleague

Laurie Pavitt MP once wrote of her, 'Harriet *was* Stoke-on-Trent'. She knew what mattered to the people she represented, because she was one of them. She had attended and taught in the schools that she now urged the government to invest in, and she had lived among the housewives who were finding it harder and harder to make ends meet. She was a parliamentarian who was rooted in her community and her class.

But Slater was also a courageous and outspoken advocate for racial justice, another deed for which I hold her in the highest regard.

The first speech a newly elected MP makes in the House is their maiden speech. It is our first chance to rise from the famous green benches and make an impression. My own maiden speech in Parliament was a source of frayed nerves and frantic preparation, and I am sure I am not alone in that regard.

But Harriet Slater didn't fret about her parliamentary oratorical debut, in fact she delivered her maiden speech by accident. During a debate on the abolition of the colour bar, Slater was so incensed by those who were advocating to retain the bar that she leapt angrily to her feet, delivering a powerful speech on the injustice of segregation and the rights of all people to be treated with dignity and respect.

Casting aside all thoughts of convention or personal advancement, she threw herself into the proceedings in support of the values that had brought her to Parliament. Equality and social justice were to shape Slater's life as her father's hands had once shaped the clay. And throughout her years of political activism she remained an exemplary advocate for them.

The story of Harriet Slater may well serve as a reminder that history can be fickle. But it is also a reminder that one does not have to be a 'great name' to do great things, or to make a great contribution.

Perhaps the most encouraging moral to draw from her story is that for every well-known figure there are a thousand Harriet Slaters: the unsung men and women of our movement who work tirelessly, day in and day out, driven not by glory or recognition but by the values and the people they hold dear.

Slater dedicated her life to lifting up our movement. And the movement, in turn, raised her from potter's daughter to alderman and finally to a Lord of the Treasury and a CBE.

Harriet Slater deserves to be remembered. She remains an inspiration for many and an enviable example of a life well lived.

PATRICIA FORD

SARAH MACKINLAY

- FULL NAME: Patricia Ford, Lady Fisher (née Smiles)
- DATE OF BIRTH: 5 April 1921
- PLACE OF BIRTH: Donaghadee, County Down, Northern Ireland
- DATE OF DEATH: 23 May 1995
- MARRIED TO: Neville Ford (m. 1941; div. 1956); Sir Nigel Fisher (m. 1956)
- CHILDREN: Sally and Mary Rose Ford
- UNSUCCESSFUL ELECTIONS FOUGHT: None
- CONSTITUENCY: North Down
- DATE OF FIRST ELECTION: 15 April 1953
- DATE LEFT PARLIAMENT: 25 May 1955
- PARTY ROLES: None
- MINISTERIAL POSITIONS & DATES: None
- MOST FAMOUS QUOTATION: 'It is sometimes difficult to see in the dark.'

Sitting in the Commons for just two years, Patricia Ford's parliamentary career was brief. Most significantly she is the first ever Northern Irish woman to be elected to the House of Commons.

Her move to Westminster would today be extraordinary in that there was no by-election, as her election was unopposed. She inherited the seat of North Down from her father, after he drowned in the 1953 sinking of the *Princess Victoria* in the Irish Sea. The car ferry sank just off the coast with Portavo Point, the large family home that Patricia's father built, within sight.

Patricia Ford was responsible for some significant political errors. Even before she had given her maiden speech, she upset formidable Labour MPs Bessie Braddock and Dr Edith Summerskill. Ford had made ill-judged comments that appeared in the *Sunday Express* on 26 April 1953 about life as a newly elected MP. She claimed to have witnessed both Braddock and Summerskill snoring during an all-night sitting in Parliament.

Both women were indignant and angry. The following day, Hansard recorded a point of order by Bessie Braddock in which she vociferously denied Ford's claims. Ford was reprimanded by the Speaker and the matter was referred to the Privileges committee. She made a profuse apology and said of her indiscretion: 'If I have offended the Honourable Lady the Member for Liverpool Exchange [Braddock] in any possible way, I apologise most wholeheartedly. I can only add that it is sometimes difficult to see in the dark.'

Her poor judgement landed her in hot water again when she was photographed attending the Brompton Oratory, a Catholic church. There was some dispute over whether she was merely attending a wedding, or was in fact 'participating' in a Mass. Suffice to say, she was expelled from the women's branch of the Orange Order.

Though her opportunity to make a significant impact in Parliament was limited, some of her political achievements can be described as truly pioneering. Her most important parliamentary campaign concerned equal pay for women. Standing at an impressive six foot, Ford is sure to have made an impact, striding through London to deliver a petition of 8,000 signatures, which in those days was considered a large number.

There were no slick spin doctors on hand to deliver the perfectly executed campaign. Despite this, Ford and her doughty female colleagues including Barbara Castle and Edith Summerskill received significant media coverage. On 8 March 1954, they arrived in Parliament with the petition on horse-drawn carriages adorned with white and green rosettes, in homage to the suffragette movement.

Life in Parliament was set to get even more complicated for Ford after she embarked on a torrid affair with the Conservative MP for Hitchin, Nigel Fisher. Following her divorce from Neville Ford, she quickly married the dashing Fisher. He subsequently moved to the newly formed constituency of Surbiton and served as its MP from 1955 until 1983.

Nigel Fisher served as a junior minister for the Commonwealth and Colonies Office in the Macmillan government. Their marriage created a new political generation. Ford's stepson, Mark Fisher, was a Labour MP and minister in the Blair government, while her son-in-law Sir Michael Grylls was Conservative MP for Chertsey. Choosing not to pursue a job in Westminster, despite hailing from a veritable political dynasty, Michael's son instead emerged as a TV personality and is the spider-eating Chief Scout Bear Grylls.

There was an entrepreneurial streak in Ford – the great-niece of the domestic and household management guru Mrs Beeton, Ford launched a business that produced preserves and other produce under the Beeton name.

It was, however, in her charitable work that she seemed to flourish. She founded the Women Caring Trust in 1972, later renamed Hope for Youth, which combatted sectarian issues in Northern Ireland among young people. She remained its president for twenty-three years.

DAME EDITH PITT

GISELA STUART

- FULL NAME: Dame Edith Maud Pitt DBE, OBE
- DATE OF BIRTH: 14 October 1906
- PLACE OF BIRTH: Birmingham
- DATE OF DEATH: 27 January 1966
- MARRIED TO: Unmarried
- CHILDREN: None
- UNSUCCESSFUL ELECTIONS FOUGHT: Birmingham Stechford 1950 and 1951; Birmingham Small Heath 1952 (by-election)
- CONSTITUENCY: Birmingham Edgbaston
- DATE OF FIRST ELECTION: 2 July 1953
- DATE LEFT PARLIAMENT: 27 January 1966
- PARTY ROLES: Member of 1922 Committee
- MINISTERIAL POSITIONS & DATES: Parliamentary Secretary at the Ministry of Pensions and National Insurance 1955–59; Parliamentary Secretary at the Ministry of Health 1959–62
- MOST FAMOUS QUOTATION: 'Birmingham is not just a city of machines, although there are plenty of them, but of hard-working, warm-hearted men and women. I know, because all my life I have been one of the thousands of weekly wage earners in the city.'

The Conservative and Unionist Party was confident of holding Birmingham Edgbaston in the 1953 by-election, triggered by the sitting MP, Sir Peter Bennett, joining the House of Lords, and invited Colonel Douglas Glover from Nantwich to stand as the candidate. This sparked some robust exchanges in the *Birmingham Post*. People wrote in to argue that there was a perfectly good local candidate for the seat, 'albeit a woman'. But *The Times* reported that for some people, local councillor Edith Pitt 'was too little of a patrician to represent Birmingham's richest suburb'. This sentiment was not shared by the voters.

The colonel, who went on to win Ormskirk in a by-election later that year, graciously conceded his nomination and, on 2 July 1953, Edith Pitt was elected. The sixty-fourth woman to be sworn in as an MP, Pitt was also the first female MP to be elected to Birmingham Edgbaston.

Edgbaston had something of a history of firsts for women. The first woman city councillor represented the Edgbaston ward, the Girl Guides started in Harborne and to this day the constituency can boast the longest unbroken line of women MPs.

In 1953, officials at Conservative Central Office thought they saw signs of changing attitudes at constituency level towards women candidates. But they were wrong. It wasn't until Labour's all-women shortlists for the 1997 general election that Parliament finally had more women MPs than male MPs called John. Even then I was only the 193rd woman MP to take my seat in 1997.

Edith Pitt was a true Brummie. After leaving school at fourteen, she worked as an industrial welfare officer before representing Small Heath as a councillor from 1941 to 1945 and again from 1947 to 1954. In addition, she chaired various local committees including the Birmingham Women Conservatives and was by all accounts a popular and sought-after speaker. It seems that she was more at ease at a personal level; her style of delivery from the despatch box was not always well received.

Politics was in Pitt's blood and she never thought of herself as anything other than a Unionist. MPs gave her a warm welcome when she arrived in the Commons. She was asked to second the Address in Reply to the Gracious Speech, which was also her maiden speech. For most MPs, the maiden speech is nerve-wracking enough, but to deliver it to a packed House as part of the choreography of the Queen's Speech takes courage. Pitt clearly possessed the potent combination of guts, determination and persistence, as well as a clear ability to deduce right from wrong. She reminded the House that until her election, she had been one of Birmingham's thousands of weekly wage earners and described housing as social services' main priority.

Pitt was angered when a fellow MP used the term working class, responding that 'we do not like it. We think that it is used in a derogatory sense.' She much preferred to talk about wage earners, and for her there wasn't a scintilla of doubt that they were better served by Conservatives rather than socialists.

She was quickly promoted, first to the Ministry of Pensions and National Insurance and later to the Ministry of Health, developing a reputation for single-mindedness and exceptionally hard work. Meticulous attention to detail, mastering her brief and always focusing on the individual, rather than espousing sophisticated ideologies, were her hallmarks. Pitt was a member of the first Western delegation to the Soviet Union. She also visited the United States to examine the social security system and industrial working conditions. She signed the Anglo-Turkish convention on social security in Ankara and represented the UK at the independence celebrations in Cyprus in 1960 – but Pitt always returned to her Birmingham roots and her family. It was her constituency work, as well as helping her sister care for their father, that always came first.

In the brutal Macmillan Cabinet reshuffle of July 1962, Pitt was sacked and returned to the back benches. It is said that she never quite got over the abrupt manner of her dismissal. She was offered a top-level public appointment, but she declined as it would have forced her to stand down from Parliament. In May 1965, she presided over the AGM of the local Women's Association, whose speaker was a fellow MP named Margaret Thatcher. In January 1966, Pitt suffered a brain haemorrhage and died in the Queen Elizabeth Hospital, located in her constituency and her hometown.

LENA JEGER

SARAH HAYWARD

- FULL NAME: Lena Jeger (née Chivers), Baroness Jeger
- DATE OF BIRTH: 19 November 1915
- PLACE OF BIRTH: Yorkley, Gloucestershire
- DATE OF DEATH: 26 February 2007
- MARRIED TO: Santo Jeger (m. 1948; d. 1953)
- CHILDREN: None
- UNSUCCESSFUL ELECTIONS FOUGHT: Holborn & St Pancras South 1959
- CONSTITUENCY: Holborn & St Pancras South
- DATE OF FIRST ELECTION: 19 November 1953
- DATE LEFT PARLIAMENT: 3 May 1979. She sat in the Lords as Baroness Jeger from 1980 until her death in 2007.
- PARTY ROLES: Labour Party chair 1979–80
- MINISTERIAL POSITIONS & DATES: None
- MOST FAMOUS QUOTATION: 'An MP cannot win by being all things to all men and women. Constituents want more shops open on Sunday, or all shops closed on Sunday; they want more abortion or no abortion; hanging or no hanging. This is where you cannot be arithmetically answerable to your constituency. I believe, without any mandarin pretensions, that the House of Commons often has to give a lead to public opinion and not always follow it.'

Lena Jeger is one of a long line of pioneering political women that history seems to have forgotten. Her legacy is frequently overlooked even by the Labour Party that she served for decades, and barely mentioned in our national political history. And yet her contributions were groundbreaking, radical and frequently brave. In a long career, in both the House of Commons and the Lords, Jeger was an effective activist politician – both for her Holborn & St Pancras South constituency and the causes that she championed.

Her passion, compassion and intellect were evident from her maiden speech. Speaking in a debate about German rearmament after the Second World War, she made an impassioned plea for Britain to fight as hard for peace as it did during the war, and to monitor the growth of nuclear weapons. From this first speech, it was possible to spot what would become some of the enduring themes of her parliamentary career.

Lena Jeger became MP for Holborn & St Pancras South following the death of her husband and previous incumbent, Santo Jeger. She had already been active in local and London politics as a councillor and made a name for herself on many local issues.

Her political passions were equality, particularly women's equality, and foreign affairs, particularly the plight of Cyprus. Jeger would return to issues time and again and ministers must have known that any line of questioning was likely to be repeated to monitor progress and push for more. Equal pay, particularly from the government, was a key cause. From the House of Commons porters to Hong Kong-based civil servants, no corner of the government's operations was too remote or obscure for her to compare pay rates and campaign for equality. In 1968, she discovered that female porters and bar staff in the Commons refreshment department were paid thirty shillings a week less than the men, so Jeger pressed for change. Her work made a real difference. Barbara Castle credits Jeger's efforts with strengthening the 1970 Equal Pay Act – Jeger threatened to lead a backbench revolt against what she viewed as weakened provisions, which ultimately strengthened Castle's negotiating hand around the Cabinet table.

The Equal Pay Act was one of a number of groundbreaking bills that came before Parliament during her term. Others were the 1967 Sexual Offences and Abortion Acts that decriminalised homosexuality and abortion respectively. A representative of what was, at the time, a solidly Catholic constituency – and for a time a marginal one (the Tories captured the seat in 1959 but Jeger regained it in 1964) – her support for these causes was considered politically risky. Jeger never relented, however, and later, as attempts to restrict the provisions of the 1967 Abortion Act came before Parliament, she defended it determinedly.

After her induction into the Lords, Jeger continued to push the boundaries. She was the first person in Parliament to use the term 'mutilation' instead of 'circumcision' to refer to what is now commonly known as female genital mutilation. Her speech arguing for the linguistic change was graphic, but understated. She spelled out just how barbaric the practice is. Most years, following Royal Assent of the Prohibition of Female Circumcision Act (1985), she would ask for an update on how many prosecutions had taken place under the Act. The answers she received are a stark reminder that despite the determination with which she acted and the progress that she and her sisters made, much of her work remains unfinished business.

Her other passion was foreign policy. Having worked as a civil servant for the Foreign Office before entering Parliament, she was well travelled and had an extraordinary depth of knowledge about foreign affairs. While her primary passion was Cyprus, her interests covered a huge range of foreign policy issues, from relations with the Soviet Union after Stalin to the anti-landmine campaigns of the '80s and '90s. It is worth pointing out that there has still been no female Defence Secretary and only one female Foreign Secretary, Labour's Margaret Beckett. At the outset of Lena Jeger's parliamentary career, foreign policy was firmly in the hands of the men. Jeger's riposte set the tone for her career – these were just as much women's issues as anything else.

Cyprus was Jeger's vocation. She made hundreds of contributions on the issue over her decades in Parliament. She opposed the Macmillan government's position on partition and was credited by many with persuading the Labour Party to adopt her stance by giving a passionate conference speech during the years between her two stints in Parliament.

Jeger's parliamentary interests were informed first and foremost by being rooted in Holborn & St Pancras South. She was loved in the constituency and had a reputation across Parliament for being one its most effective constituency representatives.

Above all, Lena Jeger embodied what it was to be a great activist politician. Passionate, caring and determined, she showed that change involves hard work and can be slow to effect, but that lives are improved by dogged work over months, years and decades.

Friends and colleagues remember her as good company with a warm sense of humour, but also for her sharp mind and determination that was not easily matched. This can be seen in her speeches and other parliamentary contributions. Many of her insights would be as relevant today as they were when she made them, decades ago.

JOYCE BUTLER

LYNNE FEATHERSTONE

- FULL NAME: Joyce Shore Butler (née Wells)
- DATE OF BIRTH: 13 December 1910
- PLACE OF BIRTH: Birmingham
- DATE OF DEATH: 2 January 1992
- MARRIED TO: Abraham Victor (Vic) Butler
- CHILDREN: One daughter and one son
- UNSUCCESSFUL ELECTIONS FOUGHT: None
- CONSTITUENCY: Wood Green
- DATE OF FIRST ELECTION: 26 May 1955
- DATE LEFT PARLIAMENT: 2 May 1979
- PARTY ROLES: Labour Party councillor, Wood Green Borough Council 1947; leader of Wood Green Borough Council 1954–55; first chair of Haringey Council 1964–68 (after reorganisation of London boroughs); deputy mayor 1961–62; chair of council's housing, planning and development committees during the 1950s; vice-chair of the Parliamentary Labour Party 1968–70 (first woman to hold the position)
- MINISTERIAL POSITIONS & DATES: None

I visited the archives at the Bishopsgate Institute to find out more about Joyce Butler, who was Labour MP for Wood Green fifty years before my election to the same seat as a Liberal Democrat.

I discovered that Butler, like me, was an uber-feminist. Hurrah! – a clear female continuum of fighting the good fight in this north London seat which, following boundary changes, later became Hornsey & Wood Green.

Butler was the first woman to hold the position of vice-chair of the Parliamentary Labour Party. She fought ferociously in Parliament for a number of Bills to improve the lot of women; she introduced the first Bill to outlaw discrimination against women in education, employment, social and public life and this became the basis of the Labour Party's landmark 1975

Sex Discrimination Act. She championed research into cervical cancer and when, in 1945, the National Cancer Control Campaign was founded, Butler became its first president.

When I stumbled across a letter Butler wrote to Prime Minister Harold Wilson about his failure to promote her to a ministerial position, I could have hugged her. On 23 March 1967, Butler wrote:

> *Dear Harold*
>
> *When Jennie Lee was promoted to Minister of State last week, it was reported in the Press that she had made known her dissatisfaction at being the only woman Parliamentary Secretary in the Government.*
>
> *Because I have not published the fact in any way, you may perhaps not have realised that I myself have not been happy at being excluded from the Government, despite considerable experience in administration. I am, I believe, the only Parliamentarily active woman from the pre-1964 Parliament in this position.*
>
> *I am writing this, not in any carping sense, but in order that there may be no misunderstanding of my feelings in the matter.*
>
> *Yours sincerely*

Go, Joyce Butler! You have to let them know what you want. I took the same approach with Nick Clegg when a reshuffle was imminent and I wanted to move from the Home Office. I told him directly, and through various gatekeepers, that I wanted to move to international work as a minister. I got what I wanted on that score, but I was left to moan publicly (unlike Butler) about Clegg's failure to put me (or any woman) in the Cabinet.

Butler was passionate about many things: the environment, protecting women against violence, resisting any attempts to curb the grounds on which abortion was legally available, the force-feeding of geese, trying to get the advertising of sweets banned from children's television programmes, nuclear disarmament, local government, unleaded petrol and many consumer issues. These are well documented.

But for me, the *pièce de résistance* is Butler's resignation over the vote on joining the common market in 1967 – particularly in light of today's Brexit situation. Perhaps Butler would have been a Brexiteer if she were alive today or perhaps not – her constituents are clearly Remainers, with 75.4 per cent of Haringey voting to stay in the EU.

In 1967, we launched our second attempt to join the European Economic Community (EEC). French President Charles de Gaulle had vetoed the

UK's first application in 1963, arguing that '*L'Angleterre, ce n'est plus grand chose*' ('England is not much any more'). He had not revised his opinion of the UK in 1967 – and vetoed our second bid.

Judging from the letters Butler was receiving from committed members of the Labour Party at the time of the 1967 vote, there was a great deal of anger directed at Wilson's push to join the common market. Ron Yates, the chairman of Brecon & District Co-operative Party, wrote to Butler,

> Wilson's policies have already lost the Peace movement to us and the Trade Unions will soon be joining them. This Government can no longer be regarded as Socialist in any manner or form, that at least is my view and I have been on the Constituency Executive for over twenty years.

Harold Wilson brought the issue of joining the EEC to the Commons for a vote on 10 May 1967. All parliamentary private secretaries who abstained from this vote were sacked – except Joyce Butler. In defence of her own position, Butler always stated that she had actually intended to abstain from voting, but was struck down by a nasty cold and ended up going home before the vote.

When Butler returned to the Commons the next day her boss, Housing and Local Government minister Frederick Willey, asked what had happened the previous night. Butler explained that she had intended to abstain from the vote, but because of her cold had gone home. Willey told her he would let the Chief Whip know that she had been ill, and Butler thought no more about it.

That was until she was asked by a correspondent in the Members Lobby what it felt like to be sacked. Confused, she asked the journalist what he meant. He informed Butler that she, together with other PPSs who had abstained from the vote, had been dismissed. Butler rushed to check the list of those who had been sacked and saw her name. Realising the significance of Willey's earlier question, she sought him out in order to urge him to say nothing to the Chief Whip about her being unwell, as it would look like she was attempting to secure preferential treatment.

However, she could not locate Willey in time. When she did manage to speak to him, she discovered that he had already met with the Chief Whip. Butler then went in search of the Chief Whip, who told her she was no longer on the list of those who had been sacked. She implored him not to remove her name, but it was too late.

EDITED BY IAIN DALE & JACQUI SMITH

Butler felt she was just as committed to abstention as the other PPSs who had been sacked. She wrote: 'It was in these circumstances that I felt I had no alternative but to resign, and I handed my resignation to my minister at the conclusion of the committee stage of the Leasehold Bill.'

Joyce Butler: a woman of principle.

EVELYN EMMET

NUSRAT GHANI

- FULL NAME: Evelyn Violet Elizabeth Emmet (née Rodd), Baroness Emmet of Amberley
- DATE OF BIRTH: 18 March 1899
- PLACE OF BIRTH: Qasr al-Dubara, Cairo, Egypt
- DATE OF DEATH: 10 October 1980
- MARRIED TO: Thomas Addis Emmet (m. 1923; d. 1934)
- CHILDREN: Two boys and two girls
- UNSUCCESSFUL ELECTIONS FOUGHT: None
- CONSTITUENCY: East Grinstead
- DATE OF FIRST ELECTION: 26 May 1955
- DATE LEFT PARLIAMENT: 3 February 1965. She then joined the Lords, where she served until her death.
- PARTY ROLES: London county councillor for North Hackney 1925–34; West Sussex county councillor 1946–67; chair of Conservative Women's National Advisory Committee 1951–54; chair of National Union of Conservative and Constitutional Associations 1955
- MINISTERIAL POSITIONS & DATES: None
- MOST FAMOUS QUOTATION: 'One of the principal reasons I am offering you my services is that I am a woman. I know this may sound a strange reason to those who still object to women Members of Parliament … On the socialist side there are nineteen women, on our side two only. These two gallant ladies are being killed by the work that is being put upon them and it is no secret that the leaders of the party are very seriously concerned and desperately anxious to get a few more well-qualified women in the House to relieve the pressure.'

Long before I was proud to become the first female MP for the constituency of Wealden in East Sussex, Evelyn Emmet, under slightly different constituency boundaries, was elected as Member of Parliament for East

Grinstead in 1955. While being a female MP was unusual enough at the time, Emmet stood out more than most of the women in the House in the 1950s as she was selected with no external influence from family members, and it was the first seat that she had contested.

Her career up to 1955 had been varied and extensive, and perfectly equipped her to become one of the best-qualified women in the House of Commons. She served as a London councillor in Hackney, as a West Sussex councillor and as a Justice of the Peace. In 1952, she was appointed United Kingdom delegate to the United Nations General Assembly, joining a small number of non-MP women who were also delegates.

Perhaps most notably within the Conservative Party, she chaired the Women's National Advisory Committee from 1951 to 1954, before chairing the Conservatives' national union and the annual party conference at Bournemouth in 1955.

Evelyn Emmet was all too aware, not only of the lack of women in the parliamentary Conservative Party, but also of the need to do something about it. In a letter to a constituency committee, when canvassing for selection, she pressed that, 'One of the principal reasons I am offering you my services is that I am a woman.' With only two female Conservatives in the Commons, she argued that she would be able to lighten their load and help carry the torch for Tory women.

As a long-time member of the Conservative Party, and in her role as an MP, Emmet campaigned tirelessly for women's issues. She supported equal pay, as well as an increase in widows' pensions, separate taxation of married women and the admission of female peers to the House of Lords.

Emmet became the first woman to be elected as vice-chair of the Foreign Affairs committee, despite not being a particularly strong orator. I've done my own time fighting the testosterone-fuelled arrogance of the Foreign Affairs committee, and I can assure you that Emmet's achievement is not one that should be lightly dismissed.

Her time in the House of Commons would be brief, and she retired in 1964. But Emmet's influence in British politics would not end there, as upon dissolution in 1964 she was granted a life peerage, to become only the tenth woman – and fourth female Conservative – member of the House of Lords as Baroness Emmet of Amberley. It was an impressive achievement, and one that her perseverance in pushing for female life peers no doubt contributed to.

As a baroness she made waves in the Lords, serving on various committees and eventually becoming a Deputy Speaker and deputy chair of committees.

In another first, therefore, Emmet became the first Conservative woman to sit on the woolsack.

By the time of her death in 1980, at Amberley Castle in West Sussex, Evelyn Emmet had left a considerable mark on British politics. The Conservative Party she joined was vastly different to the Conservative Party in 1980. The foundations she laid as a member of the national committee, and as an MP, undoubtedly enabled people like me to become candidates and MPs.

PATRICIA MCLAUGHLIN

ANNABELLE DICKSON

- **FULL NAME:** Florence Patricia Alice McLaughlin (née Aldwell)
- **DATE OF BIRTH:** 23 June 1916
- **PLACE OF BIRTH:** Downpatrick, County Down
- **DATE OF DEATH:** 7 January 1997
- **MARRIED TO:** William (Henry) Wood McLaughlin
- **CHILDREN:** One son and two daughters
- **UNSUCCESSFUL ELECTIONS FOUGHT:** Wandsworth Central 1970
- **CONSTITUENCY:** Belfast West
- **DATE OF FIRST ELECTION:** 26 May 1955
- **DATE LEFT PARLIAMENT:** 14 October 1964
- **PARTY ROLES:** None
- **MINISTERIAL POSITIONS & DATES:** None

On the face of it Patricia McLaughlin was an archetypal tribal Northern Irish politician. She wore her Unionism with pride, often dazzling in outfits of red, white and blue. However, dig a little deeper and you find a liberal pragmatist who was not always defined by her political allegiances.

True, her contributions in the debating chamber were often of a parochial nature. Unemployment ran high in her industrial West Belfast constituency, meaning much of her effort was devoted to a (largely unsuccessful) mission to save the Northern Irish linen industry from cheap Eastern European imports. Those red, white and blue outfits were, of course, made from Northern Ireland's most famous fabric.

That said, McLaughlin was more outward-looking than many of her fellow countrymen and displayed a strong interest in Europe and the wider world during almost a decade on the front line of politics. She was a delegate to the assemblies of the Council of Europe and the Western European Union, for example, from 1959 to 1964. Her time at Westminster also coincided with a period of great foreign policy soul-searching for Britain. The

Suez Crisis of 1956, sparked by the British and French invasion of Egypt over the nationalisation of the Suez Canal, occurred just a year after she became an MP. Like many Conservatives at the time, she was frustrated by the UK's failed attempts to join the European common market.

While championing women's rights was not McLaughlin's *raison d'être* in Westminster, as a female MP she naturally brought a fresh approach to policymaking in a largely male-dominated House of Commons.

Most notable was her campaign to stop local authorities putting turnstiles into public conveniences. It was supported by other female MPs across the house, among them the Labour feminist hero, Barbara Castle.

In an angry House of Commons speech, McLaughlin claimed turnstiles 'could only have been designed by a man with no idea of the needs and number of women who would use' them. 'Women were being treated as pennyworths in the country,' she added.

In the later part of her parliamentary career, and in her life beyond Westminster, McLaughlin was a consumer champion, backing, among many campaigns, protections against dangerous fireworks and flammable materials. She served as the vice-president of the Royal Society for the Prevention of Accidents from 1962 to 1985.

McLaughlin's liberal Unionism, shaped by an active association with the moderate Unionist Society think tank in the early 1950s, was also evident in her sympathy for the unemployed. This was not born out of personal experience – she was the daughter of a Church of Ireland clergyman and married Henry Wood, a director of the well-known and successful Ulster building firm McLaughlin and Harvey Ltd – but from a middle- and upper-class tradition of public service.

Her departure from Parliament in 1964 marked the beginning of the end of an era of Northern Irish rule by the old Unionist 'elite'. James Kilfedder, the lawyer who succeeded her in the West Belfast seat, courted a more hardline Unionism which emerged in the mid to late 1960s. Four years after McLaughlin left Parliament, the Northern Irish Troubles began in earnest. Ironically, boundary and demographic changes later turned West Belfast into one of the most secure nationalist seats in Northern Ireland.

Despite taking the Tory whip, Patricia's support for the Conservatives was not unqualified. Harold Wilson, the then opposition leader and future Prime Minister, recalled how she had sat on the opposition front bench to register her distaste for a payroll tax, before marching through the opposition lobbies with him.

Like many political careers, McLaughlin's departure from the Commons was not without controversy. She retired citing ill health, but there were suspicions that the scandal surrounding the zip manufacturer Seenozip, of which she had been a director, may have played a part in her decision.

The company defrauded the Northern Ireland Ministry of Commerce of £30,000 before going bankrupt in 1964. Although McLaughlin had resigned from the board two years earlier, her reputation was inevitably tarnished by the scandal.

Even then, her political ambitions remained strong. A charismatic parliamentarian who relished the debating chamber, Patricia McLaughlin stood unsuccessfully as a Conservative candidate for the marginal London seat of Wandsworth Central in 1970.

DAME JOAN VICKERS

JANET FOOKES

- FULL NAME: Dame Joan Helen Vickers DBE, Baroness Vickers
- DATE OF BIRTH: 3 June 1907
- PLACE OF BIRTH: London
- DATE OF DEATH: 23 May 1994
- MARRIED TO: Unmarried
- CHILDREN: None
- UNSUCCESSFUL ELECTIONS FOUGHT: Poplar 1945; Plymouth Devonport October 1974
- CONSTITUENCY: Plymouth Devonport
- DATE OF FIRST ELECTION: 26 May 1955
- DATE LEFT PARLIAMENT: 28 February 1974
- PARTY ROLES: None
- MINISTERIAL POSITIONS & DATES: None
- MOST FAMOUS QUOTATION: 'Anti-feminism is just as serious a problem as racialism or any other prejudice.'

I nearly fell into the Thames when I first beheld Dame Joan Vickers on the Terrace of the House of Commons in the late '60s. She was elegantly dressed in navy blue, with a massive choker of pearls around her neck, but sporting hair an amazing shade of deep blue! She subsequently gave me the name of the salon that she patronised. I did go there myself, but only discovered years later that they had very reluctantly used the blue rinse at Joan's specific request – or more likely command! The colour became a subject of comment in France, where she was known as '*la truite au bleu*' (the blue trout).

Her early life did not immediately suggest she would become a formidable politician. She was born into a well-connected family and her stockbroker father was a friend and financial adviser to Winston Churchill. Vickers's mother having passed away, it was Churchill's wife, Clementine, who presented the young girl at Court. Vickers was resplendent in the debutante's traditional white dress with a train and ostrich feathers in her hair. She then trained as a Norland Nurse, before working in a hospital in Notting Hill.

Her political aspirations led her to meet Churchill for lunch at Chartwell in 1936. Churchill disapproved of women in the House of Commons and poured cold water on the idea, suggesting that Vickers join the London County Council instead.

He recommended her to Sir George Hennessy, later Lord Windlesham, as 'a very clever young lady who has done a good many years' political work in Islington. She is a brilliant horsewoman and an independent and attractive spinster. She wishes to devote herself seriously to municipal politics. She could pay her own expenses at a County Council election.' Joan Vickers was duly elected as a councillor for Norwood in 1937 and served in that role for nine years.

During the war she worked with the Red Cross, but never gave up on her political ambitions and was in no way daunted by the difficulties women faced in getting elected. Vickers fought the 1945 general election in the solidly Labour seat of Poplar, where she adopted an old sweet shop with a leaky roof as her campaign headquarters – at times she would work sitting under an umbrella.

When the Poplar electoral venture predictably failed, she set off with the Red Cross to the Far East where she served as an area welfare officer, spending the majority of her time in Indonesia and Malaya. Indeed, her work with returned prisoners of war earned her a well-deserved MBE in 1946.

Her quest for a parliamentary seat led her to contest Plymouth Devonport, which appeared to be another impregnable Labour stronghold held by Michael Foot, one of several distinguished brothers from a well-known Devon family. Even Randolph Churchill had failed to unseat him. However, Vickers's determined canvassing led to an unexpected victory by 100 votes in the general election of 1955. It was said that she had knocked on every door in the constituency! She held the seat until February 1974, but boundary changes ultimately made it untenable and she lost narrowly to David Owen, the Plymouth Sutton incumbent who wanted a safer seat. Joan was rightly known as a good constituency MP. She made her home in Devonport, held regular surgeries and dealt with thousands of letters – at a time when she would have had to pay for most postage out of her own pocket as only restricted forms of communication were paid for. It was not until 1969 that prepaid envelopes were allowed for all parliamentary work.

Joan Vickers cared deeply about issues affecting her constituents, including the Naval Dockyard, housing, the care of the aged and the disabled. Voters, in turn, supported her in several hard-fought general elections. She fought fiercely for them, and for the issues she made her own at Westminster. Ministers were said to dread her onslaughts and even I felt her displeasure when, despite being her protégé, I decided to plough my own furrow rather than take Joan's advice.

She astonished fellow MPs and ministers by her deep understanding of defence issues at a time when defence was definitely not regarded as a woman's subject. But Vickers never became a minister. Perhaps this owed to the fact that she occasionally voted against the government. In any case, it was not an era especially noted for promoting women. I suspect that the 'prickly' side of Joan's character made people think she would not be a team player – charm was never part of her armoury. She remained single, though she claimed that she had been engaged on two separate occasions. With her temperament and determination to do things her own way, any marriage would doubtless have proved to be a tempestuous union.

As a backbencher Vickers was extremely active, introducing, in 1957, the second reading of the Orders (Attachment of Income) Bill which allowed defaults in maintenance payments to be deducted from earnings. She was also responsible for introducing the Young Persons (Employment) Bill in 1964. However, as she trenchantly observed many years later when making her maiden speech in the House of Lords:

> When making my maiden speech in the other House, I was interrupted. When I brought in my first Bill three Conservatives and three Labour members sat in the corridor so that I should not get a quorum. When I brought in my second Bill I got it through committee stage but it was then beaten by forty amendments being put down at Report Stage and it was talked out!

She was prepared to fight for controversial causes, notably the interests of prostitutes. Her research on the subject took her to Shepherd's Market and when the girls told her, 'You won't want to see the rooms where we operate,' she retorted that she certainly did want to see them and up the stairs she went.

This led Lord Hailsham to describe her as 'their non-batting Captain!'

She was an early advocate of the ordination of women, and I can imagine how pleased she would have been by recent developments in the Church of

England, including the arrival of the first woman bishop on the benches of the House of Lords.

Always a great fighter for the rights of women, a highlight of her career was presiding in 1968 over the Golden Jubilee celebrations of Votes for Women in her role as chair of the Status of Women Committee. She shared a platform with Harold Wilson and Edward Heath at the meeting in the Central Hall, Westminster.

Vickers made a rousing speech calling for equal pay, equal guardianship of children and a 50 per cent share of the marital home in the event of divorce. Memorably, she said that 'anti-feminism is just as serious a problem as racialism or any other prejudice!'

After her shattering defeat in February 1974 at Devonport, as well as in the October election that same year, she embarked on virtually a second political career in 1975 when she took her seat in the House of Lords as Baroness Vickers. She attended assiduously, sitting bolt upright on the red benches and still elegantly attired in her trademark blue with pearls. If I remember correctly, though, by the end of her career she did allow her hair to be more white than blue.

In 1982 she steered the Falklands Nationality Bill through the House of Lords, and after the Falklands War was over the islanders invited her to visit them. She accepted and was accorded a great welcome.

Increasing frailty led her to withdraw from the House of Lords and Joan spent her final years in her much loved home in Wiltshire, though these were years of frustration. She needed nursing attention and her brother quipped 'one nurse for Joan and the other to look after the first one!' When she died, aged eighty-six in May 1994, she left her body for medical research – typical of Joan's determination to help beyond the grave. It is a great sadness to me that she did not want either a funeral or a Memorial Service. It would have been an opportunity to point out that she could have lived an idle, privileged life and been what we now call a socialite. Instead, Joan Vickers chose a political career in a world which did not favour women in such roles and did so with a steely resolve, ceaseless hard work and sheer guts.

I hope this essay helps to remind us all of her invaluable contribution as we welcome the centenary of women being given the vote in 1918 – albeit only if they were over thirty years of age!

MERVYN PIKE

EDWINA CURRIE

- FULL NAME: Irene Mervyn Parnicott Pike, Baroness Pike of Melton
- DATE OF BIRTH: 15 September 1918
- PLACE OF BIRTH: Castleford, East Riding of Yorkshire
- DATE OF DEATH: 11 January 2004
- MARRIED TO: Unmarried
- Children: None
- UNSUCCESSFUL ELECTIONS FOUGHT: Pontefract 1951 and Leek 1955
- CONSTITUENCY: Melton
- DATE OF FIRST ELECTION: 19 December 1956
- DATE LEFT PARLIAMENT: 27 February 1974. She was elevated to the Lords on 15 May 1974, where she sat as Baroness Pike of Melton.
- PARTY ROLES: Yorkshire representative on the Conservative Party's National Executive 1953–61 and Women's National Advisory Committee 1955–57
- MINISTERIAL POSITIONS & DATES: Assistant Postmaster-General 1959–63 and joint Under-Secretary of State for the Home Office 1963–64

Mervyn Pike was one of those formidable Tory women MPs who were in the Commons during the 1960s, when I was a student. A solid Yorkshire woman who had to fight two unsuccessful general elections before entering the House at a by-election soon after Suez, she (and others like Dame Irene Ward and Joan Quennell) seemed to suggest that it was virtually impossible for women to get anywhere in politics unless they were single and childless, and thus able to devote themselves entirely to the job. That was why Margaret Thatcher's election in 1959 piqued my interest; by contrast she was young and married with two small children when she arrived at Westminster.

Mervyn Pike could easily have gone by her first name, Irene, but instead she was known all her life by a man's name. Mervyn had been the name of Pike's father's best friend, who would have been her godfather had he not died in action a few days before she was born in 1918. Pike's father decided that he would name his baby after his dear friend.

Pike's family were pottery manufacturers in Castleford. She was educated at Hunmanby Hall in Yorkshire and at Reading University, where she read economics and social psychology. She was also commissioned into the Women's Auxiliary Air Force (WAAF) during the Second World War. One of the roles of the WAAF was to fly newly built fighter planes to their destination airfields, a dangerous and lonely activity. Pike's job was to organise the selection and training of air crews.

Once demobbed, she took over Clokie & Co, the family firm and one of the oldest pottery manufacturers in the country, running it as managing director for thirteen years. This practical role was unusual in itself for a woman, but perhaps especially so in Yorkshire. Her no-nonsense demeanour combined with a shrewd business sense and a kind heart would, however, stand her in good stead.

Pike was ambitious. After serving on local councils, at the age of thirty-three she contested hopeless seat Pontefract in 1951, before standing for the more marginal Leek in 1955. She then made it to the final stage of the selection process for a by-election in Leeds North East in the spring of 1956, despite local grumbles that the constituency executive faced a choice between a Jew and a woman (they picked Sir Keith Joseph). But when Anthony Nutting resigned over Suez in December 1956, a by-election in Melton ensued. Mervyn Pike proved a competent and likeable candidate at a difficult time for the Tories. She arrived at the Commons as the eleventh Tory woman MP and one of only twenty-five in total in the House.

As the *Telegraph* has pointed out, Mervyn Pike was in fact a new type of female Conservative politician. Not only a woman of charisma and strong character, she entered the House with a professional career behind her, instead as the widow or wife of a well-known man (like Lady Astor or the Duchess of Atholl). She was also knowledgeable and liberal-minded on industrial relations, with which successive governments wrestled, but despite this she was never given the opportunity to put this experience into action.

In her maiden speech, instead of the usual platitudes, she launched into a solid argument for change. She pointed out that all the effort since the war had been to improve productive capacity, but now it was time to focus on

> flexibility, adaptability and reliability. These are qualities that only come from good human relations ... The medical profession is now increasingly

recognising the influence of emotional stress on mental health, physical health and the great problem of absenteeism. If we can do something to build the integrated personalities of our people, to help them have a feeling of oneness with their work and with society, we shall be going a long way towards building those good, mature human relations which can do much to solve some of the problems in our industrial life.

Sentiments that ring true today.

Once in the House, it was easier for women to progress, at least onto the lowest rung of the ministerial ladder, although the Whips' Office remained barred to Conservative women MPs until decades later. Pike soon became PPS to Pat Hornsby-Smith at the Home Office, and then moved to a junior ministerial post as Assistant Postmaster-General from 1959 to 1963 under Harold Macmillan. She attracted comment for her campaign to brighten up Post Offices, which then boasted a uniformly sombre brown and cream decor. Her reasoning – that redecoration would have 'a beneficial psychological effect on staff and public alike' – seemed almost revolutionary at the time. After four long years – why wasn't she promoted? – she was reshuffled to become Under-Secretary of State for the Home Office, from 1963 until the Douglas-Home government lost office the following year.

Thereafter, Pike became shadow front bench spokesman on social services, often giving the Wilson government a hard time when it did not live up to its promises, and urging better support for widows, abandoned mothers and the elderly. Quite suddenly, however, she stood down from the front bench after a year, citing ill health (she lived to be eighty-five). Perhaps she grew tired of being sidelined, as she had been in the years of junior minister slog. But Mervyn Pike was not the type to complain. Instead, she chaired the Conservative backbench Health committee, working with her old rival Sir Keith Joseph. Her 1967 pamphlet, 'Needs Must', is credited with shifting Tory attitudes away from assuming all claimants were feckless and undeserving; poverty, she pointed out, was often caused by circumstances beyond a person's control.

To a young MP in a neighbouring constituency, Ken Clarke, Mervyn Pike seemed 'a woman of formidable aspect, who belied her appearance by being perfectly approachable, very nice and very sensible'. He added that she was 'very popular in her own constituency'. She was herself very kind to younger people and she was often present at 'agreeable gatherings' arranged to encourage younger members of the party in their political careers.

It was expected that Ted Heath would give her a ministerial job on his success in 1970, but he ultimately did not, to general surprise. Perhaps, as Mrs Thatcher made her first appearance in the Cabinet, he felt he had appointed enough women – such was the thought process back then. Not a natural backbencher, she decided not to stand again and left the Commons at the next election in February 1974.

She thought highly of Ted Heath, paradoxically, and the *Telegraph* on her death recalled a kind gesture of Heath's. As an MP, Mervyn Pike had visited Canada for Expo 67. On arrival in Quebec, Pike found a cable from Heath saying, 'Your hotel not up to scratch. Have booked you into Ritz-Carlton.' When she went to check out, she discovered that Heath had also footed the bill for the room. 'Sweet, thoughtful, generous,' Mervyn Pike commented later.

Heath appointed Pike a life peer in his resignation honours (she put a teapot on her coat of arms), but she rarely voted in the Lords. Instead, she chaired the Women's Royal Voluntary Service from 1974 to 1981, which involved drawing up plans for civil defence in the event of nuclear war. On retirement from that position, she was made a dame. Then – there really was no stopping her – Pike became the first chair of the new Broadcasting Complaints Commission from 1981 to 1985. She then chaired Michael Spicer's think tank, Economic Models.

In the judgement of a much younger colleague in her last Parliament, she was 'a very capable woman who suffered undoubtedly from the discrimination that was then prevalent'. No less than *The Guardian* said, she 'combined the social conscience of an enlightened, small manufacturer with the keen eye of a voluntary social worker', and named Pike 'the most socially conscious Conservative of her time'.

LADY MURIEL GAMMANS

OONAGH GAY

- FULL NAME: Annie Muriel Gammans (née Paul)
- DATE OF BIRTH: 6 March 1898
- PLACE OF BIRTH: Portsea, Hampshire
- DATE OF DEATH: 6 June 1978
- MARRIED TO: Leonard David Gammans (m. 1917; d. 1957)
- CHILDREN: None
- UNSUCCESSFUL ELECTIONS FOUGHT: None
- CONSTITUENCY: Hornsey
- DATE OF FIRST ELECTION: 30 May 1957
- DATE LEFT PARLIAMENT: 10 March 1966
- PARTY ROLES: Chair of Essex and Middlesex Area Women's Advisory Committee and chair of political section of Ladies Carlton Club
- MINISTERIAL POSITIONS & DATES: None
- MOST FAMOUS QUOTATION: 'In Hornsey there has always been a great deal of civic pride, and quite rightly, because it is a borough with a long and honourable history. The letters I have received show a great fear that the good local government which Hornsey has always had will disappear, for the three main reasons which I have mentioned – wrong communications, wrong density, and lack of community of interests.' – February 1963.

Annie Muriel Paul was born in Portsea Island, Hampshire in 1898. She married Leonard David Gammans, also a member of a Hampshire county family, in 1917; she was nineteen and he was twenty-two. David Gammans's father had been a local councillor, while Gammans himself had served as an artillery captain during the First World War, and then as a colonial civil servant in the Far East. Muriel accompanied her husband abroad, and then around England when he became president of the Land Settlement Association.

Muriel undertook war work in the hospital supply service from 1939 onwards, but life changed when her husband stood as the Conservative candidate in the Hornsey by-election in 1941. His opponent was the eccentric former MP Noel Pemberton Billing, who campaigned for a tougher approach to bombing Germany, and who later launched an unsuccessful libel suit against Gammans, citing comments the captain made during the election campaign. Gammans was ultimately successful in winning the seat and went on to achieve modest ministerial office, serving as Assistant Post-master General from 1951 to '55; while in the post he was responsible for speeding up telephone connections.

He was perhaps more famous for being the only MP to speak Japanese, having served in Japan during his colonial career. In January 1956 he was made a baronet, but only a year later he passed away, aged sixty-one. Muriel Gammans was nominated to contest the seat in the upcoming by-election, with the hope that her active local presence would see off a strong Labour challenge. Gammans duly won the seat with a majority of 3,131 votes, and held it through two subsequent general elections until her retirement in 1966.

Her priority remained nursing the constituency rather than making a name for herself in Parliament. Gammans's maiden speech, on 8 November 1957, concerned the independence of Malaya, and this indicated her main interest in parliamentary debates. Gammans was active in the Inter-Parliamentary Union. Her domestic concerns were primarily local, including traffic problems, the rent acts and the well-being of pensioners; she rebelled against the government on the Resale Prices Bill. She fought hard, but un-successfully, against government proposals in the London Government Bill in 1963 to create Haringey Council as an amalgam of Hornsey, Wood Green and Tottenham, instead of a north-south entity of Hornsey, Wood Green and Southgate. Local feeling in Hornsey still runs strong on this issue.

Lady Gammans preferred attending teas – the local press referred to her 'Maginot Line of tea cups' – to addressing meetings and, at election time, she liked to campaign face to face rather than make speeches at public meetings. Eventually this approach came to be seen as outdated, and after her 12,000-vote majority was cut to just 4,000 in the 1964 general election, she stood down in favour of Hugh Rossi. In his maiden speech, Rossi paid tribute to the Gammans' constituency work: 'In twenty-five years the names of Gammans and Hornsey have become virtually synonymous.'

MARY MCALISTER

ANN MCKECHIN

- FULL NAME: Mary Agnes McAlister CBE (née McMackin)
- DATE OF BIRTH: 26 April 1896
- PLACE OF BIRTH: Rathmullan, County Donegal
- DATE OF DEATH: 26 February 1976
- MARRIED TO: J. Alexander McAlister
- CHILDREN: Winifred, Molly, Elinor and Sheila
- UNSUCCESSFUL ELECTIONS FOUGHT: None
- CONSTITUENCY: Glasgow Kelvingrove
- DATE OF FIRST ELECTION: 13 March 1958
- DATE LEFT PARLIAMENT: 7 October 1959
- PARTY ROLES: None
- MINISTERIAL POSITIONS & DATES: None

Mary McAlister, an Irish-born nurse, became Glasgow's third female Member of Parliament when, in 1958, she unexpectedly won a previously Conservative-held seat. In a period of 100 years, the city has elected just a dozen women, with five serving for periods of less than two years. McAlister's experience of a brief period at Westminster is not unusual, as women were rarely elected in Glasgow under 'normal circumstances'.

Her constituency spanned two very diverse areas of the city: the prosperous houses surrounding the University of Glasgow and Kelvingrove Park, which gave the seat its name, and the soon to be demolished slum tenement housing in Anderston, adjoining the Glasgow dock area.

The by-election in March 1958 arose from the death of the sitting Tory MP, Walter Elliot, who had first been elected to the seat in 1924. The Conservatives chose to select his widow, Kay Elliot, as their candidate (who later in 1958 became one of the first women to be appointed a life peer). The national controversy at the time concerning the Rent Acts, and the lack of effective rent controls, provided the perfect political conditions to allow the

Labour Party to land a rare blow on the Conservative government. Undoubtedly McAlister's experience as a local councillor for Anderston, where she had served since 1945, and her knowledge of the suffering caused by unscrupulous private landlords gave her the upper hand.

Glasgow's historic rent strikes during the First World War, led by another formidable Labour woman Mary Barbour, who also held office in the City's council, led directly to the first rent control legislation to be passed in Europe – it was an issue which resonated with working-class voters in the 1950s and continues to resonate today.

A two-horse race with both main candidates being women was unusual, not least in a heavily industrialised city such as Glasgow, but the election was also notable for being one of the first political campaigns to include a TV debate between the candidates. It was certainly the very first in which female candidates had participated. The new independent channel, Granada Television, had introduced this novel approach to UK viewers at the Rochdale by-election, which had been held earlier that year, and it had proved popular – the TV political age had truly begun.

On her first day in Parliament, the *Glasgow Herald* reported that 'Mrs McAlister was given the honour of being the first member to enter the lobby to record her vote in favour of ... a Ten Minute Rule Bill seeking to amend the Rent Act'. It was an appropriate way to launch her parliamentary career and an issue that she spoke about in her maiden speech, and continued to focus on during her short term in Westminster.

Despite increasing her vote in the 1959 general election, Mary lost to the Conservative Frank Lilley, who held the seat until 1964 after which it returned to Labour control. It was an era when former parliamentarians were often offered opportunities to perform public service in non-electable positions. McAlister was appointed to a position in the National Assistance Board and was awarded a CBE for her services in 1968. She died in 1976.

BETTY HARVIE ANDERSON

ELEANOR LAING

- FULL NAME: Margaret (Betty) Harvie Anderson OBE, TD
- DATE OF BIRTH: 12 August 1913
- PLACE OF BIRTH: Glasgow
- DATE OF DEATH: 7 November 1979
- MARRIED TO: John Francis Penrose Skrimshire (m. 1960)
- CHILDREN: None
- UNSUCCESSFUL ELECTIONS FOUGHT: West Stirlingshire 1950 and 1951; Sowerby 1955
- CONSTITUENCY: East Renfrewshire
- DATE OF FIRST ELECTION: 8 October 1959
- DATE LEFT PARLIAMENT: 2 May 1979
- PARTY ROLES: Executive of the 1922 Committee 1962–70 and 1974–79
- MINISTERIAL POSITIONS & DATES: First Deputy Chairman of Ways and Means and Deputy Speaker 1970–73
- MOST FAMOUS QUOTATION: 'We are one nation. We divide at peril to ourselves and to the delight only of our enemies.' – House of Commons debate on devolution, January 1977.

Betty Harvie Anderson was the first woman to sit in the Speaker's Chair. It was the pinnacle of a successful political career, during which she loyally and energetically represented East Renfrewshire for twenty years and ably stood her ground as a defender of the Union.

Having been a senior officer in the Auxiliary Territorial Service during the war (1938–46), she was well prepared both for leadership roles and for her determined pursuit of the principles and causes in which she believed. As a commissioned officer she saw active service on the home front during the German air raids on the River Forth and became the chief commander of a mixed anti-aircraft brigade. Having held this senior post until 1946, she then became the first woman to join the Glasgow Territorial Association.

Harvie Anderson's early life was spent at her family's estate, Quarter, in Stirlingshire and she remained attached to that part of the country throughout her life. She was educated at St Leonard's School, a leading girls' boarding school in St Andrews.

Unusually for a young woman in Scotland in the 1940s, she clearly took delight in following in the footsteps of her father, Colonel Thomas Alexander Harvie Anderson CB TD DL, a solicitor and magistrate. Her letters to friends following his death, many years later, illustrate how very close she was to him and how alike they were. It is perhaps fortunate that this remarkable lady did not have a brother and was, therefore, the heir to her father in many ways, affording her the confidence to play the difficult role of a woman in a man's world.

Her first venture in the democratic process was to stand for election to Denny District Council at the age of only twenty-five. She then went on, in 1945, to be elected to Stirlingshire County Council, taking over the very seat that her father had held up until then. Here she developed her interests in agriculture, housing, welfare and particularly education, serving on the Secretary of State for Scotland's Education Advisory Committee. Her local government experience, for which she was recognised with an OBE in 1956, stood her in good stead during her time in Parliament. As an MP she served, from 1966 to '69, on the Royal Commission on local government in Scotland, which resulted in the controversial Wheatley Report.

It was even harder in those days than it is now for a woman to be elected as a Member of Parliament, and Harvie Anderson was defeated when she stood in West Stirlingshire in 1950 and 1951 and in Sowerby in Yorkshire in 1955. She was finally elected as MP for East Renfrewshire, a Conservative stronghold, in 1959.

I met Harvie Anderson only once, when I was ten years old, and she came to a meeting with my father who was chairman of the district council in her constituency. I was rather overwhelmed by her presence, her dignity and her authority.

I owe this great lady, however, an enormous personal debt of gratitude for the beneficial effect that she had on my life and I vividly remember that one meeting. My father, a typical Scotsman of his generation, who had entrenched ideas about the different roles of men and women, had seen Harvie Anderson address a crowd of some 26,000 people, gathered to see Sir Winston Churchill speak at Ibrox Stadium in Glasgow in 1950. He had developed an enormous admiration for her that grew during the twenty years that he served as a district councillor while she was our MP. I still have a letter she sent to him about their successful joint efforts to have a new primary school built in our village of Elderslie, the birthplace of Sir William Wallace.

Although my father assumed that most women should be at home looking after children, he had the firm and revolutionary belief that I should be like Betty Harvie Anderson. So he supported and encouraged me to pursue my ideals in politics at a time when most Scottish fathers would have forbidden such an absurd notion in their daughters.

I cannot claim that Harvie Anderson was a mentor to me, just an inspiration. She was, however, a successful mentor to some of my friends, notably Jacqui Lait and James Gray. Jacqui was an MP from 1992 to 2010 and served as an excellent shadow Secretary of State for Scotland. James Gray has been MP for North Wiltshire since 1997. His father, the Reverend John Gray, was a lifelong friend of Harvie Anderson's from their student days. James kindly gave me copies of some of their correspondence, which shows Harvie Anderson to be witty, amusing, caring, compassionate, appreciative of the efforts of others and grounded in her Christian faith.

In her maiden speech, in 1960, she called for action in education, 'so that we achieve a better percentage of our young people reaching their potential ability'. I said something similar in my own maiden speech thirty-seven years later. She went on, 'I believe that the knowledge of equal opportunity, irrespective of means and on a gauge of ability alone, would lift a great burden of anxiety from parents and children alike.' We are still trying!

Harvie Anderson's most enduring political legacy was her staunch opposition to the potential break-up of the United Kingdom. On more than one occasion she put her Unionist principles before her personal political advancement, stood her ground and encouraged others to do likewise. Thus she was instrumental in turning Conservative Party policy against devolution.

She spoke vehemently against the Scotland and Wales Bill in the House of Commons in 1977. 'It seeks to divide the authority of this sovereign Parliament in a way which makes conflict between Westminster and Edinburgh inevitable.' I wonder whether she would have been pleased or disappointed, forty years later, to find that she had been proved right.

It is a unique achievement to have been the first woman to occupy the Speaker's Chair. Although she was addressed, rather absurdly, as 'Mr Deputy Speaker', Harvie Anderson decided not to try to emulate the traditional dress or style of the Chair's other occupants. Instead, she had carefully tailored business dresses made in colours that complemented the greens of the

Commons Chamber. Thus she exerted quiet authority based on profession-alism, a sound grasp of parliamentary procedure and instinctive political nous.

She served as Deputy Speaker from 1970 to 1973, but, as the debate on Scottish devolution began to gather pace, she could no longer accept the restraints of impartiality and silence, telling friends that she 'had to get out of that Chair' in order to speak up for the principles of Unionism in which she so passionately believed.

She retired from the Commons in 1979 and was elevated shortly thereafter to the Lords. Having kept her maiden name, for the simple reason that she was well known by it, when she married Dr John Skrimshire in 1960, she took her husband's name on her elevation, becoming Baroness Skrimshire of Quarter.

Betty Harvie Anderson combined steely determination, intelligent rhet-oric, caring compassion and elegant femininity. What a tragedy that her life was cut short by an asthma attack, just a few days after her introduction to the House of Lords, at the age of only sixty-six.

It was meeting her as a child that gave me the confidence to challenge the people who said that a woman could not expect to succeed as an MP. When I went into my new office, having just been elected Deputy Speaker in 2013, her portrait, along with those of my other predecessors, was looking down at me. It brought tears to my eyes. My father would have been so pleased.

DAME JUDITH HART

MARGARET BECKETT

- FULL NAME: Dame Constance Mary Hart (née Ridehalgh) DBE, Baroness Hart of South Lanark
- DATE OF BIRTH: 18 September 1924
- PLACE OF BIRTH: Burnley, Lancashire
- DATE OF DEATH: 7 December 1991
- MARRIED TO: Dr Anthony Bernard (Tony) Hart (m. 1946)
- CHILDREN: Richard and Steven
- UNSUCCESSFUL ELECTIONS FOUGHT: Bournemouth West 1951 and Aberdeen South 1955
- CONSTITUENCY: Lanark 1959–83 and Clydesdale 1983–87
- DATE OF FIRST ELECTION: 8 October 1959
- DATE LEFT PARLIAMENT: 11 June 1987. From February 1988 until her death, she sat in the Lords as Baroness Hart of South Lanark.
- PARTY ROLES: NEC 1969–83; vice-chair 1980–81; chair 1981–82
- MINISTERIAL POSITIONS & DATES: Under-Secretary of State for Scotland 1964–66; Minister for Commonwealth Affairs 1966–67; Minister for Social Security 1967–68; Paymaster General 1968–69; Minister for Overseas Development 1969–70, 1974–75 and 1977–79; shadow Minister for Overseas Development 1970–74 and 1979–80

Judith Hart was a major player in Labour politics and in the Labour governments of the 1960s and 1970s. As many colleagues testify, she was even better known and certainly admired, respected – even loved – on the international stage than at home. She not only fought consistently for the most vulnerable, she was effective in delivering for them. Hart was both striking and flamboyant. She and her husband, Tony, a senior scientist, opened the doors to their stylish home in Kew (to which she devoted much thought and energy in creating a wonderful garden), offering refuge to the widow of Chilean President Salvador Allende and others, following the Pinochet coup in Chile.

Judith was born and brought up in the north-west. It was witnessing the mass unemployment of the 1930s that led her to join the Labour Party at eighteen. (It may be evidence of her lifelong independence of spirit that – named Constance – she chose, at twelve, to call herself Judith). She studied at the LSE, where she obtained a First in sociology.

Judith's late mother had been a pacifist and Judith herself served on the Campaign for Nuclear Disarmament's national committee, taking part in the first Aldermaston march. She met her future husband, Tony Hart, when he gave a speech against nuclear weapons. Married in 1946, she and Tony formed a formidable team, with both becoming involved in the World Disarmament Campaign.

When her husband's work took the family to Dorset, Judith worked as a researcher for the Ministry of Health and was an unsuccessful candidate in the local council elections. She stood for Parliament in 1951.

The family moved to Scotland where Judith campaigned against corporal punishment, which was still prevalent even in Scottish primary schools, and contested Aberdeen South against Lady Tweedsmuir – dubbed by the media as the 'Battle of the Housewives'!

Tony was already a prospective parliamentary candidate for Glasgow Hillhead when Judith was selected for Lanark. He withdrew his candidacy in order to work on her campaign. It was in the old mining region of Lanark that she won – and held – her Scottish parliamentary seat. She was one of only nine Labour gains at the 1959 election and one of only twenty-five women MPs.

Judith was immensely proud of Lanark's history, and of her constituents. In her maiden speech, she largely focused, as she did throughout her political life, on employment and economic opportunities in her constituency, in the mining villages and the new town, stressing the consequences not just for individuals, but for whole communities. She called for industrial expansion and bringing new industry to the area, with government intervention where private enterprise was 'unable or unwilling to move rapidly enough to those places where it is needed'.

After Labour's election victory in 1964, she was appointed as Parliamentary Secretary dealing with health, children and education in Scotland. Though she declared it vital to have responsibilities beyond 'women's issues', Hart vigorously pursued school building and the interests of children with disabilities.

As a Minister of State in the Commonwealth Office she fought for decolonisation in Rhodesia and became friendly with liberation movement activists across Africa. In addition she advertised UK government scholarships for study in Britain – training the aspirant generation.

After a period at Social Security, Hart reached the Cabinet as Paymaster General in 1968 – only the fifth woman to hold a Cabinet post. She was highly regarded and was close enough to Prime Minister Harold Wilson to be given his old office in No. 10.

However, they became politically estranged – not least when she attacked 'In Place of Strife'. Though elected to the NEC of the Labour Party in 1969 (a much more powerful and independent body then than it is today) and made Minister for Overseas Development, Hart was not reappointed to Cabinet. NEC members had hitherto felt free in that capacity to criticise government policy (e.g. over arms sales to Chile) while remaining in office. To Hart's chagrin, Wilson insisted on observance of collective responsibility.

She did, though, become the first co-chair of the Women's National Commission, and, when Labour once again found itself in opposition after losing the 1970 general election, she worked closely on industrial policy with Tony Benn.

Judith chaired the Public Sector Working Group (of which I was secretary), which controversially proposed the creation of a National Enterprise Board (NEB) – a state holding company – to stimulate innovation. These proposals, which envisaged working with twenty-five major British companies, were unpopular with many, including the Prime Minister. However, when set up in 1975, the NEB had its successes. One of its early investments was in Inmos, which later grew and prospered in Silicon Valley.

Judith never lost sight of the importance of wealth creation. I well recall her fury and frustration at our failure to get Rover to expand the production line for Land Rovers. The massive demand across the Third World led to a long waiting list for delivery – an opportunity for export expansion to which the then management were completely indifferent.

Overseas aid was one of Judith Hart's great passions. She quite literally wrote the book on it with *Aid and Liberation: A Socialist Study of Aid Politics*, which stressed the importance of debt relief long before it was widely understood.

In Judith's self-authored White Paper, the chief purpose of official development assistance was defined as support for the poorest people in the poorest countries. She worked to replace traditional loans with, at first, interest-free loans and then with grants. She considered this change one of her main achievements.

She set a development target of spending 0.7 per cent of GNP on aid. When she finally left office in 1979, it had reached 0.52 per cent. (After the Tories won the 1979 election we slid backwards.)

Following Labour's election victory in February 1974, MI5 queried her re-appointment as Minister for Overseas Development. Judith had been tasked by the NEC, with Harold Wilson's consent, to keep abreast of the situation in Chile (an interest she maintained throughout her life). The Communist Party were one of the best sources outside government on events in Chile. There was also said to be a photograph of Judith at a Communist Party event, which turned out to be of a completely different woman also called Mrs J. Hart. Ultimately, Judith was reappointed Minister for Overseas Development.

More than once, Judith's ability to influence her colleagues seemed to take officials by surprise. In February 1974, she was determined to seek from the new Chancellor, Denis Healey, a substantial increase to the budget for overseas aid. She was strongly advised by the department's finance team not to waste her time. This would, they insisted – on the basis of their own conversations with Treasury officials – be a hopeless cause. Needless to say, Judith wrote a strong letter to Denis regardless, making just such a demand. To the astonishment of both sets of officials, Denis agreed.

As her then special adviser, I naively assumed the department would be delighted. The finance team were, in fact, furious, complaining that their relationship with Treasury civil servants had been wrecked!

Later, as the UK's lead negotiator for the Lomé Convention, Judith wanted to make a radical proposal on trade in sugar – of huge importance, especially to many in the Commonwealth – but wanted agreement from Peter Shore, president of the Board of Trade.

Obstacles were put in her way by Foreign and Commonwealth Office (FCO) civil servants, who disapproved. Again Judith persisted, and again her judgement was validated. Peter Shore agreed at once.

Barbara Castle, among many others, thought one of Judith's greatest achievements to be her role in securing the Lomé Convention – a trade and aid agreement between the EU (then EEC) and seventy-one African, Caribbean and Pacific countries where she won concessions for associated developing countries.

It was testament to her international reputation at that time that, when the Mozambique Liberation Front, FRELIMO, sought a 'safe house' where they could pursue the talks with the Portuguese, which ultimately lead to independence for Mozambique, it was not the then Foreign Secretary, Jim Callaghan, or the FCO they approached, but Judith Hart.

Judith's interest in and involvement with Chile continued. After the overthrow of Salvador Allende in 1973, it became quickly and horribly apparent, not only that many opponents of the new military dictatorship were being tortured and slaughtered out of hand, but that hundreds more were at risk of the same treatment.

With the full cooperation of Home Office ministers, it was agreed to offer a way out, funded from the overseas aid budget and run on the ground by the World University Service. This prevented many people from falling into the clutches of General Pinochet's thugs and murderers.

Judith and Tony were very much a political, as well as a personal partnership, as – not insignificantly – were a number of other major players of the day, who, like Tony and Judith, were on the left of the Labour Party.

Harold Wilson deeply disliked anything that smacked of plotting but, despite this, a group including Judith decided, in 1974, to have regular husbands and wives dinners (which as Judith's special adviser I organised) where Judith and Tony could chat privately and convivially about matters of the day with Michael and Jill Foot, Ted and Barbara Castle, Tony and Caroline Benn, Liz and Peter Shore, and Pen and Tommy Balogh. Among the issues on which there was common ground was the thorny matter of the common market, which all were opposed to and chose to campaign against in the 1975 referendum on the UK's continued membership.

It was after that referendum, during which dissenting ministers had been promised they would suffer no recriminations, that Wilson proposed to move Judith – the only one so to suffer – to Transport, which she regarded as a demotion. What was worse was that Wilson also proposed putting her former department back into the Foreign Office, which had long been a matter of contention.

There was a considerable row from Cabinet allies, but despite a great deal of pressure, especially from Michael Foot and Tony Benn (all meeting in, as I recall, Tony's room in the House of Commons), Wilson refused to change his mind.

Judith resigned from the government and made a statement in the House saying that she did so without bitterness, but with the intention of supporting the government in pursuing socialist policies, though she objected strongly to putting her department back into the Foreign Office. I'm afraid, however, that it was not true that she resigned without bitterness. She felt extremely bitter, though many colleagues thought that such feelings were justified.

When James Callaghan became Prime Minister in 1976, he reappointed Judith to overseas aid where she remained until Margaret Thatcher's election in 1979.

As part of the dissolution honours list, she was made a DBE, accepting the honour in the name of 'the Third World'.

Characteristically, Judith sought to combine her commitment to overseas aid with the interests of her constituents. Abercrombie House, the Department for International Development's joint headquarters with Whitehall, is in East Kilbride where Judith fought to create new jobs. Although it opened in 1981, the initial plan was Judith Hart's.

Judith left the NEC in 1983. During the Thatcher years, she continued to pursue her interests, including opposition to military action in the Falklands. She stood down from Parliament at the 1987 general election and entered the House of Lords in 1988 as Baroness Hart of South Lanark. Her maiden speech in the Lords was on the security services and raised the issues of tension between security and privacy that are prevalent today. She felt they would be eased by a Freedom of Information Act, which was eventually passed in 2000.

Unfortunately, Judith became ill shortly after entering the Lords and did not play an active role, something that some of her colleagues regretted, as they felt she could have made a major contribution. She died on 8 December 1991.

The then leader of the Labour Party, Neil Kinnock, said of Judith, 'She was a woman of high abilities who will long be remembered and admired for her distinguished work to advance human rights and her tireless courage campaigning for the defeat of world poverty.'

Throughout her twenty-eight years in Westminster (and beyond), Judith Hart strove to take action to protect those suffering from injustice both at home and abroad.

A final word: the longer I worked for Judith Hart, the more I both liked and admired her – something that cannot be said of every politician.

MARGARET THATCHER

VIRGINIA BOTTOMLEY

- FULL NAME: Margaret Hilda Thatcher (née Roberts), Baroness Thatcher LG, OM, DStJ, PC, FRS, HonFRSC
- DATE OF BIRTH: 13 October 1925
- PLACE OF BIRTH: Grantham, Lincolnshire
- DATE OF DEATH: 8 April 2013
- MARRIED TO: Denis Thatcher (m. 1951; d. 2003)
- CHILDREN: Carol and Mark (twins, b. 1953)
- UNSUCCESSFUL ELECTIONS FOUGHT: Dartford 1950 and 1951
- CONSTITUENCY: Finchley
- DATE OF FIRST ELECTION: 8 October 1959
- DATE LEFT PARLIAMENT: 9 April 1992. Sat in the Lords as Baroness Thatcher from 30 June 1992.
- PARTY ROLES: Leader of the Conservative Party
- MINISTERIAL POSITIONS & DATES: Parliamentary Secretary to the Ministry of Pensions and Insurance 1961–64; shadow Minister for Fuel and Power 1967–68; shadow Secretary of State for Transport 1968–69; shadow Minister for Education 1969–70; Secretary of State for Education and Science 1970–74; shadow Secretary of State for Environment 1974–75; Leader of the Opposition 1975–79; Prime Minister 1979–90

A s our first female Prime Minister, Margaret Thatcher transcended the perceived limitations of a woman; she also launched a revolution in economic thinking that continues to shape our world almost forty years later.

Through her ability, drive and tenacity, this remarkable woman defied the odds by progressing from a Grantham corner shop to a grammar school and Oxford; and then from a successful career as an industrial chemist and tax barrister, to a parliamentary seat in north London and ministerial office by her mid-thirties. In a House of Commons dominated by men, she demonstrated an energy, thoroughness and grasp of her brief that few of her contemporaries could match.

In later years, there was authentic and legitimate ideological opposition to what became known as 'Thatcherism'. From her earliest days as an MP, Mrs T also had to endure patronising snobbery from those within the Conservative Party and beyond, who sneered at her as a lower-middle-class arriviste.

At the height of her powers, she displayed an ability to connect, directly and electrifyingly, with the decent and hard-working people of this country that remains unparalleled in my experience. Mrs T had an intuitive ability to connect with the C2s – the so-called skilled working class – with a political hotline to their aspirations, hopes and fears. She was also a more practical, consensus-minded politician than most of her detractors or admirers would have us believe. She could be shrewd and opportunistic. She was contemptuous of the 'middle ground', but she could always detect the common ground. Inevitably, some people were envious, but the spiteful asides, the arrogant, privileged social one-upmanship (and it was almost invariably one-up*man*ship) directed against her was deplorable.

How did Mrs T achieve so much, in defiance of the undermining and unjustly low expectations of others? How was it that the unkind prejudices she encountered never filled her head with doubts or caused her to falter, but simply served to make her stronger and more determined? Whence did she derive her supreme self-confidence?

Much has been made of her family background. Her inherited Methodist attitude helped her to maintain impressive resolve under pressure. Her training as a scientist and barrister seems crucial in any attempt to make sense of this complicated woman. She had a capacity to see through bluff and bluster. She devoured briefings and she liked facts: hard, clear, empirical facts. Her early economic policies were founded less in political theory, but more in sophisticated econometric analysis of the apparent connections between interest rates, the money supply and inflation. She was no intellectual as such, but she did greatly admire intellectuals, such as Keith Joseph, Milton Friedman, Alfred Sherman and Alan Walters.

When she was dubbed the 'Milk Snatcher', she was attacked not only as a politician, but also as a woman, as a mother. This made her stronger. She could exploit her femininity – she had her hair attended to on a daily basis and never looked less than immaculate – but she never for one moment considered this to be a weakness. When the time came for her to appoint a Cabinet, there were no berths reserved for women. The 'distaff side' would be appointed 100 per cent on merit – or not at all. Her one-time close ally Janet Young made it into her first Cabinet, but there was no sense of 'sisterhood' and Young's services were dispensed with at the first opportunity, brutally in the eyes of many.

Margaret Thatcher so dominated political life in this country – and still does, in many ways. Every aspect of her life – professional, political and personal – has been relentlessly pored over and written about, sometimes in formidable detail, most recently in an excellent short study by Sir David Cannadine. The archive of the Margaret Thatcher Foundation is comprehensive. It is daunting to contribute this essay on the subject of such a remarkable woman, whose inner personality always remained curiously elusive, but whose unique approach to decision-making – and also her many acts of personal kindness – made an indelible impression on my life and also on the lives of countless others.

The challenge is to provide fresh insights on someone about whom everyone still has an opinion. I spent a certain amount of time with Mrs T when she was leader of the Conservative Party. It was, after all, as a result of her telling Gordon Reece that 'we need more female MPs, get Virginia Bottomley' that I embarked on a parliamentary career in my own right. As one of a relatively few female ministers to have worked closely with her as Prime Minister, I focus attention less on her early life or on her ministerial career, both of which have been widely scrutinised, but on Margaret Thatcher the Member of Parliament for Finchley.

Various notable parliamentary figures of the past – Ted Heath, Tony Benn, Julian Amery and Quintin Hogg – are still spoken of as 'true House of Commons men'. In my view, although she could dominate the House when required (never more so than in her final, exhilirating speech as Prime Minister), Mrs T was never, in an equivalent sense, a true 'House of Commons woman'. She became a minister in October 1961, two years almost to the day after becoming an MP, and she did not leave the front bench until November 1990. It was principally her meticulously prepared performances as an opposition frontbencher – her coruscating, well-informed attacks on the likes of Jim Callaghan, Roy Jenkins and Denis Healey – that caught the eye, marked her out as one to watch and demonstrated her remarkable ability to master parliamentary debate.

Characteristically, Mrs T dispensed with the usual formalities of a maiden speech, preferring to break her silence in the Commons on 5 February 1960 not with the traditional canter around the course of her constituency, but by introducing a Private Members' Bill requiring local councils to allow the press to report upon their proceedings. Already freedom was her watchword and it is easy, when reading her opening lines today, to hear the authentic timbre we came to know. 'This is a maiden speech,' she began, 'but I know that the constituency of Finchley which I have the honour to represent, would not wish me to do other than come straight to the point and address myself to the matter before the House.' That Private Members' Bill duly became law – a noteable achievement for a supposedly callow new Member of the House. Mrs T became one of the first of her intake to achieve ministerial office and she rapidly earned a reputation for mastering her brief and, in government, for fiercely defending her record and those of her colleagues. In opposition, she proved no less fierce when in attack mode.

Her early voting record on matters of conscience makes surprising reading for those who have been weaned on the myth, not on the woman and her genuine record. On 29 June 1960, she was one of a tiny handful of Conservative MPs who voted with Labour and Liberal MPs in favour of the partial decriminalisation of homosexual acts, as had been recommended in the Wolfenden Report three years earlier. Among the others was Enoch Powell. The proposition was defeated by 213 votes to ninety-nine. Its time would come, but joining the thin ranks of its early advocates was by any token a courageous act by a newly elected MP. In June 1967, Mrs T voted through the night with other reformers in support of David Steel's Abortion Bill, resisting a series of attempts to dilute its provisions or to make a total nonsense of it. Again, she was in unlikely company, but on this occasion she was in the majority. She later claimed, in her memoir *The Path to Power*, that the 'permissive society' had gone too far and that it could be argued the reforms she herself had supported in the 1960s 'have paved the way towards a more callous, selfish and irresponsible society'.

Mrs T decisively developed her reputation as a significant frontline politician during her time as an economic spokesman for the Conservative opposition in the late 1960s. The nation was limping from crisis to crisis, but the debating skills on the Labour side were never open to question: Jim Callaghan and Jack Diamond were formidable figures in the House of Commons and taking them on was a major task. Mrs T never wavered. Her command of facts, figures and arguments was relentless. A powerful example is her performance in a debate on Labour's Finance Bill on 2 May 1967. It must have been intimidating to be on the receiving end of her torrents of precisely informed, withering criticism. Her scathing attacks on the Inland Revenue are as persuasive today as they must have been half a century ago, as she called for 'redrafting and redesigning some of those arrogant, dictatorial form letters' and mused how 'most of us know that it takes far longer to get money out of the Inland Revenue which has been overpaid to it than it takes the Inland Revenue to get money out of a taxpayer on which the taxpayer has been under-assessed'. Already she was the champion of the hard-pressed, tax-paying citizen, against an overconfident, arrogant and inefficient state.

When she challenged Ted Heath for the party leadership in 1975, Mrs T had been on the front bench for almost fifteen years. She used that position cannily. She was in demand for engagements out and about in the country, where she developed a reputation for candour, loyalty and personal kindness. Choosing the party leader was now a decision made by Conservative MPs. She was generally at her scintillating best when dealing with economic matters and, as the nation struggled time and again to free itself from the baneful influence of over-powerful trade unions and ancient industrial practices, it was economic matters that mattered most.

Quite possibly, Ted Heath signed his own political death warrant when he appointed Mrs T as deputy to Robert Carr, shadow Chancellor, after the general election of October 1974. She was already receiving considerable support as a potential challenger to Heath before she took up the cudgels against Labour's proposed Budget.

On 14 November 1974 she gave one of her most important performances to date in the House of Commons, responding to Labour's Harold Lever, a dyed-in-the-wool moderate whom she both liked and respected. Reading her speech today, one senses how her growing interest in free-market economics and her increasingly close association with Keith Joseph and the Centre for Policy Studies were emboldening her to strike out in her own, distinctive direction. Her combination of praise and barbs reveal not only complete mastery of her brief – but also of the Commons itself. 'The Right Honourable Gentleman spoke warmly about private enterprise ... I only wish that some of his colleagues would speak as warmly about it as he does ... Some of us feel that just as I have been a statutory woman in the Cabinet, he is perhaps a statutory moderate in the Cabinet now.' Just days earlier, Ted Heath's response to the Queen's Speech had evoked scarcely any enthusiasm from Tory backbenchers.

A week later, she confirmed she would challenge Heath for the leadership; and, at the height of the contest that ensued, she spoke time and time again during Finance Bill committee debates, often at unearthly hours, but always to good effect, rallying vital support around her. As Charles Moore puts it in his magisterial account of her life, *Not For Turning*, 'She combined an astonishing mastery of the technical facts with a sure sense of the emotions aroused among voters by tax, inflation and economic mismanagement.'

My first encounter with Margaret Thatcher came when I was the dutiful wife of the Conservative candidate in the Woolwich West by-election, which took place on 26 June 1975. I shall always remember the political nous she showed. She had been leader only since February and this was a serious – and rather precipitate – test of the party's popularity, just eight months into a still-new Parliament, whose increasingly precarious arithmetic has become the stuff of legend. The sitting Labour MP, Bill Hamling, had died on 20 March and, even before a by-election was called, Mrs T was brought down to open the new Conservative Party office in Eltham. She was briefed that, upon entering the local Conservative club afterwards, she should turn left, 'because that's what women do'. Not for the first time, she ignored the advice and turned right instead, not for the first time nor the last, finding herself in a room full of men playing billiards. They cheered her to the echo.

My husband Peter had fought the seat twice in 1974, and Labour's majority in October was just 3,541 votes. If Peter were to win, Mrs T naturally wanted to be associated with his victory, but it was only after we had assured her office team – on two separate occasions – that local bookies had Peter at 4–1 on, with just days to go, that it was decided she would make an appearance. Peter won by 2,382 votes, reducing Harold Wilson's working majority to just one seat. On a trip to the British Army in the Rhineland, Mrs T declared herself 'over the moon' and gave a Churchill-style 'V for Victory' sign (it was her first victory and she learned later to hold her palm outwards). Peter's win settled nerves in the parliamentary party and also among the rank and file, many of whom retained great loyalty towards Ted Heath. It was a timely and welcome boost for an inexperienced leader. The tale demonstrates Mrs T's shrewd political judgement.

I was the Conservative candidate for the Isle of Wight at the 1983 general election. The highlight of the final day of my campaign consisted of Margaret Thatcher arriving by helicopter at Cowes, where she boarded a hovercraft to make a symbolic and extremely theatrical landing on the magnificent BAE East Cowes airstrip, with a great Union Flag serving as a potent backdrop. The metaphor was to reflect her retaking the Falklands. We had a cheerful day in East Cowes and she wished me well.

I received almost 35,000 votes, but, sadly, that was not enough. The Labour vote had been squeezed down to a mere 2.4 per cent and Stephen Ross, who had first won the seat in February 1974, was returned for the fourth time as Liberal MP. Having had my campaign featured on *Woman's Hour* on BBC Radio 4 throughout, I then had to be a graceful loser on the programme. Returning home, I received a call from Leon Brittan and then, to my astonishment, from the Prime Minister herself, now triumphantly re-elected. Not only was she celebrating her great victory and forming her Cabinet, she also had found enough time to call me. I had kept a stiff upper lip throughout the bitter disappointment of missing out on election, but her sympathy now dissolved me into tears.

In contrast to her Iron Lady image – which she did little to discourage or undermine – Mrs T frequently showed acts of remarkable kindness to those around her. I recall, for instance, Kirsty Lang, now a prominent BBC journalist, who worked for my husband and me in 1984. Kirsty thought Mrs T was 'Public Enemy Number One'. Then, when Kirsty was pushed over by a crowd at Lockerbie, Mrs T refused to start her press conference until she had stepped forward to help Kirsty to her feet and brought her to the front. Everyone was struck and impressed by this, not least Kirsty herself.

Reaching Westminster in 1984, after a by-election, I soon became the first woman MP to be invited to join the One Nation dining club, which suited my style of conservatism. In those early days, Mrs T regarded me as rather 'wet' and probably too much like my husband Peter for comfort. A single event changed her perception fundamentally and that did not happen by chance, but at the behest of a shrewd colleague. It was said in the mid-1980s that in order to become a minister you first had to be an 'MOT', a 'Mate of Tristan' (Garel-Jones); and so it turned out for me.

Sir Keith Joseph had played a significant role in Mrs T becoming leader of the Conservative Party and also in the development of what came to be known as 'Thatcherism'. Keith stepped down in May 1986 from his final ministerial job, as Secretary of State for Education, and then, at the 1987 general election, as a Leeds MP. Sometime later, Tristan Garel-Jones hosted a small dinner party for Keith – now Baron Joseph – and some of his close associates, at which the Prime Minister was the guest of honour. I was included, having been a PPS to Chris Patten at the Department for Education. When I was working at the Child Poverty Action Group in the early 1970s, Keith and I had a discussion about a pamphlet I had written on poverty. Keith had congratulated me, but also advised me always to bear in mind that it's much easier to divide the cake up than it is to bake it in the first place. This was a key reason why I became a committed Conservative. Mrs T was surprised to find me at the dinner party and, during the course of the proceedings, I sensed that she had begun to see me in a new light and almost as 'one of us'. Sure enough, at the next reshuffle I was invited to become a junior minister at the Department of the Environment. Only in hindsight did I make the connection.

It was traditional for reshuffles to take place in the early autumn, with the inevitable consequence that all but the most confident ministers would spend the summer fretting about their prospects. In 1988, Mrs T wisely – being compassionate and practical-minded – opted for a July reshuffle, giving new ministers the opportunity to master their briefs before the party conference and giving sacked ministers time to take a holiday and regain their dignity and composure. The PM said, upon appointing me: 'Never turn down the opportunity to explain the government's case. No one else will.' Throughout my ministerial career, I tried to emulate her quality of marching towards the guns and speaking up for our policies.

I was surprised to be invited to become a minister. I had made my maiden speech on defence, going on to address subjects such as pesticides and transport, because I was determined to avoid stereotypically 'female' subjects. I felt thoroughly vindicated when the PM asked me to go to the Department of the Environment, rather than education or health. My husband Peter was a junior Transport minister and Willie Whitelaw was reputed to have said, 'You can't have the two of them in government.' When Mrs T asked whether I had any comment to make, I was tempted to ask, 'Is it all right with Willie?' She then asked what I thought about my new brief. 'I know nothing about it,' was my response. She replied, 'In that case you will just have to read it up, Virginia.' Off I went, happily, to deal with heritage, toxic waste, seals and much else besides. It struck me subsequently that a man would have answered, 'Prime Minister, I will bring a clear mind to the problem.'

Peter and I did both serve as ministers, for around eighteen months. This was 1988 and Mrs T, ever eager to be combative on as many fronts as possible, needed a new campaign. She had sorted out the miners and the trade unions; and she had retaken the Falkland Islands. She needed a new adversary. This one was much more quixotic: human-caused damage to the environment. She was strongly influenced by Crispin Tickell *inter alia* and I took a lowly role in her 'Saving the Ozone Layer' conference at the QE2 Centre in March 1989 – the first major international conference on the subject. I was with her during the preparations and her approach somewhat alarmed me at first, until I learned to adopt it for myself. Every kind of question and challenge was hurled at her advisers, until all possible questions and attacks had been addressed.

Confident there was no possible angle she had not thought through in advance, Mrs T then went out to address the conference in magnificent style. As an accomplished scientist herself, she had no illusions about the scale of the challenge the planet was facing and she was not in the least bit bothered about being dubbed a scaremonger: 'Even if all the chemicals which damage the ozone layer were banned tomorrow, ozone depletion would continue for more than a decade and it would take our planet something like one hundred years to replenish the ozone already lost. Such is the extent of the damage we have already done.'

This destroys another myth about Mrs T – that she was all for letting the free market rip, whatever the consequences. She was so much more than that; and the scientist in her was always wont to shine through. Her genuine environmental concerns were politically escalated just three months later, by the extraordinary high polling of the Greens in the European elections of June 1989; they received almost 15 per cent of the vote.

Mrs T had strikingly few close female relationships, but she did greatly admire Dorothy Hodgkin, her science tutor at Somerville, her Oxford College. She also maintained a close relationship with Cynthia Crawford, her personal assistant. She must also have been strongly influenced by the two impressive women who served as the Principal of Somerville: first, the literary scholar Helen Darbishire, who had been a tutor at the college since before the First World War; and, secondly, the eminent haematologist Dr (later Dame) Janet Vaughan. It was a rarity for a female scientist to become head of house at an Oxford college in those days (for a time she was the only one) and she would have been a self-recommending role model for the fiercely ambitious young Margaret Roberts.

In her early years, Mrs T was, if not exactly a champion of the European ideal, a strong and consistent supporter of vigorous and active UK membership of the European Community. Read her notable speech on 16 April 1975 to the Conservative Group for Europe, opening the Conservative referendum campaign under the chairmanship of Ted Heath.

But as the unpalatable political aspects of European integration began to outweigh, in her mind, the very considerable economic advantages of membership, her opinion began to sour. After around 1983 or 1984, if anyone ever made the mistake of informing her there was pressure from the European Community or Brussels to do or change anything, a pained expression of distaste would spread across her features. She was on the road to her Bruges speech, which has been lauded and reviled in equal measure for three decades.

Thatcher was in no sense a Little Englander. She distrusted the political leaders of Germany while greatly admiring the industry and creativity of the German people; she admired the United States as a beacon of freedom. She was, perhaps less obviously, a great champion of Japan, which she regarded almost as a kindred spirit: a proud island nation with a monarchy, which had turned itself round economically in the most striking and admirable fashion. As a minister I was directed on a number of occasions to Japan to exchange views on numerous aspects of public policy.

Holidaying in Switzerland, Mrs T was struck by its cleanliness and tidiness and she duly became obsessed with litter. Richard Branson was appointed to lead a campaign, but he disappointed and, as the junior environment minister, I was summoned to a meeting at No. 10 to produce an action plan. Home Secretary Douglas Hurd was instructed to raise penalties for offenders and so on. Keep Britain Tidy was given a boost. I was sent to Paris to examine the way streets were kept clean with two water systems. The highlight was observing a number of motor scooters (scooter-poopers) which drove up on the pavement to squirt water at high pressure on dog mess. This extraordinary demonstration continued at length in spite of my growing levity. I did not succeed in reporting back to Mrs T in a sufficiently persuasive and favourable way.

In 1985 the Church of England veered dramatically into matters temporal and political with its inner-city report 'Faith in the City', commissioned by the then Archbishop of Canterbury, Robert Runcie and widely perceived to be highly critical of the government's social policies. Most recommendations were to the church and to local government. This came close to home for me. During Mrs T's early years as leader and Prime Minister, I had worked with the Child Poverty Action Group and in Brixton and Peckham for a child guidance unit.

The Thatcher view that the vast majority of the population have common aspirations rang true with me. Remember the maxim of 'an Englishman's home is his castle': the wish to own your own home and play a part in creating a property-owning democracy is about the social fabric we want to build. Parents of the most impoverished West Indian immigrant children, with whom I worked closely, had the same aspirations for their children as everyone else, if anything to an even more intense degree: to read and write, to know their tables, to stand up for the national anthem and to look clean and tidy. Too often they were patronised by well-intentioned 'do-gooder' teachers, inclined to exculpate indiscipline and shrug off academic under-achievement, whereas the children's parents sought a more traditional education, with homework and achievement.

Denis Thatcher was extraordinarily important in Mrs T's life. Contrary to the caricature promulgated in *Private Eye*, he was in fact an enlightened and modern man who willingly sacrificed his own privacy and, in some degree, his own professional ambitions, in furtherance of her career. He provided the necessary emotional, financial and public support that a female Prime Minister needed. Denis was phenomenal.

Thatcher was a lucky general and especially lucky in her opponents: Michael Foot and General Galtieri, Arthur Scargill and Neil Kinnock. But, by the end, she had lost her once unerring capacity to subject both policies and personalities to focused, rigorous examination. Appointing Ian Gow as her parliamentary private secretary was an inspired choice. Choosing Peter Morrison as PPS in her later years as PM was less astute.

In the early days she had many in her shadow Cabinet, and later in her Cabinet, who were older and more experienced than she was. She had the wisdom to treat them with respect and to listen thoughtfully and courteously, even though many (indeed most) of them she had inherited directly from her predecessor Ted Heath. There was not only Peter Carrington and Willie Whitelaw, but also the likes of Jim Prior and Patrick Jenkin. The early permanent secretaries, Cabinet Secretary Robert Armstrong, and many others, carried real weight with Mrs T, even when she was in full flow. By the end, though, her arteries had hardened. She stopped taking dissent seriously and believed her own propaganda too much. The Iron Lady's reputation would be different today if she had retired after ten years as Prime Minister.

She had a profound affection for Finchley. In each post I held, I was constantly addressed from the Finchley perspective. Any discussion about the GP contract involved hearing what GPs in Finchley thought of the situation. This connectivity with a constituency is deeply ingrained in Britain, but Margaret Thatcher possessed an extreme version of it. Finchley was also a constituency with strong Jewish participation, and I used to think that as a woman, Mrs T probably had a particular affinity with the Jewish community. Women were still excluded from many clubs, and from being a Church of England priest and so forth. We had few women in public life. She was on her own, celebrated and excluded at the same time. I felt this was a situation many people disgracefully still faced.

Women frequently underestimate themselves and can feel doubts more than men. For instance, upon reading that I might be promoted to the Cabinet, I called the Chief Whip, to ask whether it was true and suggested that a sideways move might be better at this stage in my political career. Mrs T never seemed to suffer from 'impostor syndrome'. She possessed an apparently unswerving confidence in her own ability; perhaps this stemmed from being a scientist, or the fact that she was a Methodist. Maybe it was because she was the favoured daughter of a former Mayor of Grantham. It is strikingly unusual. In Sheryl Sandberg's words, Mrs T was always someone to 'lean in' throughout her career. She dressed in a particularly striking, feminine style, which made an impact. Every day she dressed to kill. She was a power-dresser before it was fashionable.

When I worked for Geoffrey Howe as his PPS, I learned the system within No. 10 for dealing with appointments and disappointments was pretty deplorable. It was argued by some that Mrs T hated to sack colleagues. This is not unusual, but there are no compromise agreements in politics. Being sacked means returning to the back benches with a grudge and a cause to fight.

For a long time, I was the only female minister with school-age children. Mrs T used to say, 'It's not the time you spend with your children, but the quality of the time you spend with your children.' I certainly sensed a degree of hostility and suspicion towards her, and indeed to myself, particularly from educated women who had felt obliged to dedicate their lives to their family, when in many ways they would have loved to have had a career. Mrs T must have had tough emotional skin to tolerate the comments about her becoming an MP while the mother of young twins. This was all before being a working woman and mother became more common. Just as Ted Heath had, Mrs T endured patronising, socially insulting comments. But what she possessed – and what Heath had lacked – was a great ability to connect with the C2s. This has long been the key to political success, as John Major demonstrated in 1992 and Tony Blair proved in 1997, 2001 and even 2005. It may be a failure of mainstream politics today.

Mrs T intuitively understood the aspirations of the British people, and her political opponents always resented – even hated – her for this. The patronising attitudes of some in the Labour Party – 'we send our children to an elite school and own our homes in Hampstead, but they live in council houses and send their children to comprehensives' – she regarded with visceral contempt. She was no paternalist, but nor was she indifferent to other people's fates. If anything, she was a very particular type of egalitarian. More paternalism perhaps might have helped her to show greater sensitivity to those who fell on the wrong side of her policies, but she would have made a fine leader writer for *The Sun* newspaper. This is a secret of political success – taking the whole country, or at least a good half of it, along with you.

Testing arguments, policies and ministers to destruction was a feature of Margaret Thatcher's decision-making process. In 1990, the NHS reforms had to be finally approved. Ken Clarke, Tony Newton and Sir Duncan Nichol, the resilient and talented NHS chief executive, were summoned to Downing Street. I joined the team. The debate opened with the Prime Minister asking her adviser, the successful businessman David Wolfson, to comment on the plans. An intense, almost hostile, critique ensued and we all knew that the onus was very much on us to persuade the Prime Minister to abandon the status quo. We survived and the NHS reforms proceeded.

I admired Mrs T in numerous ways, even though she was not a 'woman's woman' in my judgement and was not a kindred spirit. What did she do for women? You might ask what David Blunkett did for blind people. Blunkett demonstrated that there was no job, however complex, that a blind person of sufficient ability cannot undertake. Thatcher did the same for women. She also displayed innate pragmatism and caution in her early years in power. This has been consistently underestimated by many commentators.

If more politicians thought through the implications of their initiatives with the same focus, preparation and attention to detail as Margaret Thatcher did, we might achieve more. I feel privileged to have worked for a woman who profoundly altered Britain and our place in the world. She transformed opportunities for women through her personal example, splendidly undertaking a hugely demanding role that no female had previously secured in this country. We should recognise too that, as well as being courageous and tenacious, she consistently demonstrated generosity, profound loyalty and genuine human kindness.

JOAN QUENNELL

CLAIRE PERRY

- FULL NAME: Joan Mary Quennell MBE
- DATE OF BIRTH: 23 December 1923
- PLACE OF BIRTH: −
- DATE OF DEATH: 2 July 2006
- MARRIED TO: Unmarried
- CHILDREN: None
- UNSUCCESSFUL ELECTIONS FOUGHT: None
- CONSTITUENCY: Petersfield
- DATE OF FIRST ELECTION: 17 September 1960
- DATE LEFT PARLIAMENT: 9 October 1974
- PARTY ROLES: None
- MINISTERIAL POSITIONS & DATES: None

Looking back from today's political world, which is so dominated by headlines and influenced by imagery, it is quite refreshing to see that there is so little in the public domain about Joan Quennell, the MP for Petersfield from 1960 to 1974. The basic facts are these: she was born in 1923; educated at Bedales School in Hampshire; volunteered as a Land Girl during the Second World War; managed a mixed arable and dairy farm in West Sussex; served as a county councillor for ten years; was a Justice of the Peace and a governor of Crawley College of Further Education. She won a three-way contest in the 1960 Petersfield by-election, seeing off two male challengers by taking 55 per cent of the vote, and served the constituency for fourteen years, rising only to the ranks of a Transport PPS for two years, but speaking out often and confidently across a wide range of subjects.

But what kind of woman was she? There are no in-depth interviews or photoshoots; in fact I have only been able to find one good photo of her, striding confidently across a ploughed field in a zippered, covetable country suit and natty low-top wellies, her perfectly coiffed hair in a bun.

Quennell looks no-nonsense and purposeful, someone whose experiences and words you would trust. And her written and spoken words – recorded in over a thousand entries in Hansard – show a long, productive and efficient parliamentary career, with a strong interest in education and training and farming matters, but neatly bookended by her first and last questions in the House which are concerned entirely with local matters – gliding clubs and district council rates.

While she led no high-profile campaigns – the most notable appears to be an animal welfare petition – Quennell's long experiences outside Westminster added weight to her work.

Despite never marrying or having children, she used her experience as a governor of the local further education college to great effect, making numerous compelling interventions on the need for proper post-education training and useful careers guidance, and on the job-limiting effects of limited public transport in rural areas – issues that are as relevant and fresh today as when Quennell raised them half a century ago.

Was Joan Quennell a feminist? It is hard to tell when viewing her career through the prism of stilted speeches and the language of the time, but there are several themes that give me reasons to hope – a series of questions on what the government was doing to make it easier for married women to return to work, for example, and helpful suggestions on National Insurance contributions adjustments for part-time workers. She supported a move towards individual taxation, and urged the government to get more women involved in return-to-work training schemes.

She was unafraid to bring her thumping common sense to bear on tricky issues. When the then Health Secretary Kenneth Robinson pompously asserted that the root cause of venereal disease among teenagers was promiscuity, Quennell responded by pointing out that 'the spread of these diseases is caused largely by ignorance'.

She kept up with current affairs too, asking in 1964 for clarification on whether the Beatles had been manhandled at the British Embassy in Washington. She was informed that, on the contrary, John, Paul, George and Ringo had enjoyed a charming evening. But the truth was that drunken diplomats and gate-crashing fans had made it a far from fabulous time for the 'Fab Four'. Drummer Ringo even lost some of his locks!

And then, in the aftermath of the disastrous February election of 1974, something seemed to go sour for Quennell. She was openly vehement in her criticism of the party's campaign and wrote a 'trenchant' letter to *The Times*, saying that she 'received not a single scrap of paper from Central Office, a call to Smith Square took six hours to be answered and she agreed that the Party's message [did] not get through to the country and certainly not to this candidate'.

She was vocal in relaying her disgust with the reappointment of those responsible for the Conservative Party's electoral disaster, and at the age of fifty-one, decided to stand down at the autumn election that year. She retired to a life in the country, living on the beautiful estate she had inherited from her father and bequeathing it, with 'much improved gardens', to the National Trust when she died in 2006, only for it to be sold in a mini cash-raising controversy.

Joan Quennell died in 2006, the year I first went to work for the then shadow Chancellor George Osborne and started my own journey into the world of Conservative Party politics. Although our paths never crossed, I admire Joan for her many years of service, her common-sense approach to politics, her strong sense of duty – and her stylish country suits.

ANNE KERR

NATALIE BENNETT

- FULL NAME: Anne Patricia Kerr (formely Clark; née Bersey)
- DATE OF BIRTH: 24 March 1925
- PLACE OF BIRTH: Putney, London
- DATE OF DEATH: 29 July 1973
- MARRIED TO: Russell Whiston Kerr MP
- CHILDREN: Patrick Clark
- UNSUCCESSFUL ELECTIONS FOUGHT: Twickenham 1959
- CONSTITUENCY: Rochester and Chatham
- DATE OF FIRST ELECTION: 15 October 1964
- DATE LEFT PARLIAMENT: 17 June 1970
- PARTY ROLES: Member of Tribune Group
- MINISTERIAL POSITIONS & DATES: None
- MOST FAMOUS QUOTATION: 'It is time for Britain to take a fresh look at its policies on federal Nigeria and Biafra and its policies on Vietnam … War is a disease and we must talk to people in these terms and stop sending arms to Nigeria and the Middle East. We should stop having an arms salesman, and until we do the people of this country will not believe in us. They will not believe in Socialism – and we are here, on this side of the House, as Socialists.' – Queen's Speech, 30 October 1969

In May 1970, local campaigner Kathleen Swan penned a note to Anne Kerr, apologising for the fact that ill health would unfortunately prevent her from assisting with Kerr's third campaign for Rochester and Chatham. It's one of a few such letters that Kerr preserved. Swan wrote: 'People who think will remember that you have always had the courage of your convictions at all times and your great compassion for the suffering of people everywhere.'

That might serve as a fitting epitaph for a woman who was a peace campaigner from Biafra to Vietnam, a founder of the Campaign for Nuclear Disarmament and a champion of the fight to abolish the death penalty. Kerr was also a leader of those opposed to Britain joining Europe's common market, and was a committed Socialist (she always wrote it with a capital letter) often deeply frustrated with her own party.

The depth and passion of her work is recorded in the Hull History Centre, which dedicates II metres of shelving to Kerr's papers. Reading these files, all of them neatly sorted by subject, Kerr's passion and her refusal to suffer fools gladly shines through. A pamphlet promoting the case for keeping the death penalty as a religious duty has a note written at the top: 'File – wicked rubbish'.

Educated privately at St Paul's Girls' School in London, she served in the Women's Royal Naval Service for two years from the age of eighteen, before enjoying a short career in television. Kerr's political career began when she was elected to London County Council in 1958. In her second attempt at entering Parliament, in 1964, she overturned Conservative Julian Critchley's majority of 1,023 and was elected as MP for Rochester and Chatham.

Her key election meeting featured an audience of 500 people, most of them dockworkers, who heard Michael Foot shout over the noise of hecklers that 'you can't defend this country with nuclear weapons'. Foot added that Sir Alec Douglas-Home's policy of buying nukes from America was 'criminal', and not truly independent.

Kerr won the seat with a 1,013 majority, and proved a popular local MP, more than doubling her majority in 1966, with a bold election address in a local paper headed 'AN MP WITH GUTS'. She demonstrated her tenacity later that year, with a question to Prime Minister Harold Wilson: 'Does not my Right Honourable Friend agree that the ships that are really required for keeping peace throughout Asia are probably grain-carrying ships rather than nuclear, Polaris or any other kind of military ships?' (Wilson came back swinging, suggesting that she should 'on her next visit to China … make that point in Peking'.)

In 1968, at the Democratic Party's convention in Chicago, an incident occurred that profoundly shook the doughty campaigner. In a letter to the Foreign Secretary, Kerr writes that she was speaking to some Vietnam War protestors in the street when she was arrested and thrown into a police van, and then

> at close range, squirted full in the face with a chemical which I now learn was 'Mace'… I was in custody for about four hours before being released on a bond of $25.00. During this time all requests for access to a lawyer, to the British Consul, or for my husband to be notified were ignored.

A photo caption notes that she also recorded bruises to her arms and legs. In the file of the case a note, written in Kerr's own shaky hand, states: '[I] have firmly decided to proceed my case against [Chicago Mayor Richard] Daley and police'. However, the police concerned could not be identified (in a 1970 letter Rusell Kerr writes that they were 'by no means surprised') so no one was held accountable for the attack.

As the international legal wrangles rumbled on in the '70s, it became clear that Kerr's seat was in danger and that the peace campaigner was becoming compromised. Her election leaflets contained a large section about Chatham dockyard, boasting that Labour had provided new buildings and equipment 'so that Chatham can become a refitting port for the nuclear-powered hunter-killer submarines, postponed by the Tories but now being built'. Kerr was running against Peggy Fenner – a publican's daughter who played to the hilt the role of respectable housewife.

The result was a stinging defeat for Kerr. Fenner's victory may have particularly grated on Anne, as Fenner was a fervent supporter of the death penalty. During her London County Council days, Kerr had grown close to the family of Derek Bentley, a young man unjustly executed for the death of a police officer in a now notorious case. Kerr's 1970 election file, together with the standard notes about expenses, contains her rosette. Hand stitched, with a cheerful orange 'Anne Kerr Labour' sticker clinging to its centre, these days it evokes an atmosphere of crushing disappointment.

Yet only a year later, Kerr was on the B-list for selection to run again, and being courted by constituency parties from South Dorset to North Norfolk, particularly by women's wings and women ward secretaries. She must have been torn between choices, but ended up sending out a standard, characteristic note:

> I have responsibilities as chairman of 'Women Against the Common Market' which I feel I must pursue. Should Britain be trapped into joining one part of Western Europe our chances of real Socialism at home, and of being able to convey something of truth elsewhere, might be lost forever. Our Party and the Labour Movement must become Socialist – not only in local government as it sometimes tries to do, but at parliamentary level. I hope [seat name] selects a Socialist of calibre and sincerity – and the latter is not the least of these.

Three years later, aged just forty-eight, Anne Kerr died of acute alcohol poisoning at the Twickenham home she had long shared with her husband.

Kerr's papers suggest that her death was not entirely surprising. They reveal there was a wrangle about a bar bill at one Labour conference in Blackpool, and imply there was massive wine and vodka consumption. Occasional letters hint at periods of Anne's incapacity, although regular references to chiropractors suggest this might have been a form of self-medication. But in a hard-drinking environment, and as a woman operating in a man's world, perhaps Kerr was drawn into dangerous territory.

Alcohol perhaps played a role in a disastrous 1970 election meeting, which might have sealed Kerr's electoral fate in Rochester & Chatham. A hostile local paper, the *Chatham News*, reported that at the meeting 'she produced America's veteran anti-Vietnam war campaigner [Dr Benjamin Spock] as her main supporting speaker. Repeatedly faltering and almost breaking down in tears when she started to speak about "social cruelties", she ended up by telling *Chatham News* readers "to stick their questions up their jumper".' The newspaper added: 'By normal British election standards the meeting can only be described as "extraordinary". As entertainment it veered between melodrama and farce.'

Those events must have been hard to recover from, and the surprise 1970 general election victory of Edward Heath's Conservative Party may have proved too much for a woman with a passionate, visceral hatred of Tory policies.

Peggy Fenner, the Conservative who defeated Kerr, went on to have an unremarkable parliamentary career that was only ended by the 1997 Labour landslide. But Kerr would hardly have celebrated Labour's overwhelming victory, given the 'New' direction that her party had taken under Tony Blair.

MARGARET MCKAY

ZOE WILLIAMS

- **FULL NAME:** Margaret McKay (née McCarthy)
- **DATE OF BIRTH:** 22 January 1907
- **PLACE OF BIRTH:** Oswaldtwistle, Lancashire
- **DATE OF DEATH:** 1 March 1996
- **MARRIED TO:** William McKay (for four years)
- **CHILDREN:** One daughter, Morag
- **UNSUCCESSFUL ELECTIONS FOUGHT:** Walthamstow East 1959
- **CONSTITUENCY:** Clapham
- **DATE OF FIRST ELECTION:** 15 October 1964
- **DATE LEFT PARLIAMENT:** 17 June 1970
- **PARTY ROLES:** General secretary of the Socialist League and women's officer for the TUC
- **MINISTERIAL POSITIONS & DATES:** None
- **MOST FAMOUS QUOTATION:** 'I was possessed by a frenzy for change; and since a change, any change, could hardly be for the worse, it must inevitably be for the better.'

Margaret McKay, née McCarthy, saw herself as a natural rebel, the daughter to a rebel mother, Betsy-Ann, whose principal subversion was to marry outside her Lancashire family, the Catlows. When Betsy-Ann chose a luckless Irish Catholic, Joseph McCarthy, over her nobler roots, she became a socialist, as did her daughter.

McKay's first affiliation, to the Labour Party's Guild of Youth, ended when they proved insufficiently supportive of the 1926 general strike, and she joined the Young Communist League (of which my grandfather always claimed to have been leader, yet there is literally no record of him; just another blowhard Williams). This was the locus of both her boldest adventures and most brutal disillusionment.

She was part of a youth delegation to Russia to celebrate the tenth anniversary of the revolution; she met Lenin's widow and imbibed a pretty rare, foreigners-only communist cocktail of culture, beauty and stardust. The revolutionary roadmap pointed the way to a better future and showed 'how, by revolutionising the economic pattern of society, we could solve the remainder of our problems and cure all the ills to which humanity, and particularly the workers, were subjected'. Twenty years old, with the smart, up-in-your-grill features of Charlotte Coleman circa Marmalade, McKay had found her people.

But in 1931 she quit the Communist Party of Great Britain, showing a moral clarity and independence of spirit for which the communists were not, let's face it, known. From then until the 1960s, she devoted herself full time to the underdog of the United Kingdom (and, she once memorably corrected Tam Dalyell, 'the under-bitch').

The first union she joined was the enchantingly named, but actually quite radical, Accrington Weavers Winders and Warpers Association. She took part in the Bradford hunger march of textile workers, and contributed to the war effort via the Civil Service Clerical Association, and the National Unemployed Workers Movement, a fascinating experiment in solidarity separated from labour. Her first senior position was with the National Union of Domestic Workers in 1939, and it was around this time she married, leading her to observe that most women would benefit more from a union card than a wedding ring (William McKay left the family in 1943).

Her greatest mark on the union movement was made as women's officer for the TUC, and she is remembered in general Labour history mainly for her flamboyant rows. Indeed were it not for her book, *Women in Trade Union History*, she would be refracted entirely through the vexations of Arthur Deacon and later George Woodcock – and all this before she became an MP and started irritating the hell out of the Foreign Secretary.

Many of her causes stand out as both timeless and ahead of her time. Her efforts within the Transport and General Workers Union on behalf of Polish and German refugees after the war inscribed this humanitarian priority into the union's soul, where it endures.

Her time as the MP for Clapham was rather short-lived – she won the seat in 1964, defended it successfully in 1966 then stood down before the 1970 election – and marked by a set of priorities one could recognise in a Momentum meeting today. While a passionate advocate of workers' rights, using her maiden speech to highlight the days lost to injury, her attention was otherwise occupied in seeking justice for Palestine. She seemed to find that bridging area of socialist politics, where one's attention turns from the local but before it reaches the international, rather grubby and careerist. Known by the press as the 'woman on the Abu Dhabi omnibus', she was held to have alienated her constituents with what became full-throated campaigning across a range of Middle Eastern issues. She herself blamed the press for her declining constituency popularity, though she was heard to speculate that it had also been infiltrated by a Trotskyist-Zionist cell.

Perhaps the stand-out quality of Margaret McKay, not as a female MP but as any MP, was to know when to stand her ground and when to revise her opinion. The normal range is to be good at one of those things. She had an insatiable appetite for justice and the fearlessness to feed it, but lacked the self-interest for advancement; she'll be known to history as defender-in-chief of the 'under-bitch'.

RENÉE SHORT

EMMA REYNOLDS

- FULL NAME: Renée Short (née Gill)
- DATE OF BIRTH: 26 April 1919
- PLACE OF BIRTH: Leamington Spa, UK
- DATE OF DEATH: 18 January 2003
- MARRIED TO: Dr Andrew Short (m. 1940)
- CHILDREN: Ginette (b. 1941) and Jennie (b. 1945)
- UNSUCCESSFUL ELECTIONS FOUGHT: St Albans 1955 and Watford 1959
- CONSTITUENCY: Wolverhampton North East
- DATE OF FIRST ELECTION: 15 October 1964
- DATE LEFT PARLIAMENT: 10 June 1987
- PARTY ROLES: Member of the Labour Party National Executive Committee 1983–88
- MINISTERIAL POSITIONS & DATES: None
- MOST FAMOUS QUOTATION: 'The House should accept it as a basic fact that if a woman is so desperate that she believes that she must terminate her pregnancy, she will go to all lengths to do so and that whatever the House decides today, abortions will continue.'

Renée Short MP first entered Parliament in the nail-biting general election of 1964, when Labour returned to power with a four-seat majority after thirteen years of Tory government. Short became the first woman MP to represent a constituency in Wolverhampton. Her parliamentary career would span the next twenty-three years and she would continue to have a great impact even decades after her retirement. She was a fearless and passionate campaigner for a number of different causes including women's rights, legalising abortion, sexual health, penal reform, decent housing and nursery education.

Born in 1919 in Leamington Spa, Short was the daughter of a Romanian-Hungarian engineer and Jewish mother. She was brought up by her Church of England grandparents and educated at Nottingham County Grammar

School and Manchester University. After her graduation, she worked as a freelance journalist and then ran her own stage design business. She met her husband, Dr Andrew Short, at university; the couple married in 1940 and had two daughters.

Renée Short served as a councillor on Watford Rural District Council (1952–64) and Hertfordshire County Council (1952–67). Before winning her Wolverhampton North East seat, she stood unsuccessfully for election in St Albans in 1955 and Watford in 1959.

Short successfully balanced the demands of family life and her career. She once said of Andrew, 'I couldn't have done it without the best possible husband.' Born André Schwartz, he too was Jewish and his family originated from Romania. He fled to the UK to escape persecution prior to the Second World War. His brother and sister suffered the horrors of the Nazi's concentration camps, though both of them managed to survive. Andrew Short was a successful and renowned structural engineer, who worked at the Building Research Centre and took a keen interest in politics. The couple's daughter, Ginette, confirms that her dad was a great support to his wife, often helping her with drafting speeches and talking through political issues. People regularly came to the family home to engage in lively discussions about politics.

The marriage was a partnership of equals. Both were good cooks and instilled an appreciation of delicious and adventurous cuisine in their daughters. The Shorts enjoyed family holidays to Scandinavia, Italy and France. Renée Short's time in Sweden was particularly influential in her political thinking, and she was fluent in both Swedish and French. Her great personal interest was in breeding Standard Poodles, which she exhibited at Cruft's.

Local party members in Wolverhampton describe Short as charismatic and fearless, and as someone who had a great presence, something that was enhanced by her stature and height. Short was a tall, red-headed woman with larger than average feet. She claimed she had bigger feet than any other woman MP and campaigned for the shoe industry to cater for women with very small or very large feet.

A fearless campaigner for many different causes, Short was often one of the first people to voice support for important issues that were unpopular and controversial. She was a vocal advocate of women's rights and described the lack of women's representation in Parliament as 'scandalous'. An early proponent of family-friendly working hours for MPs, she frequently spoke about how the unsociable hours had a detrimental effect on family life, arguing that this would deter many women from entering politics. Short was well ahead of her time and we should be grateful to her for starting an important discussion about working hours. It was only in 2002–03 (Short died in 2003) that some parliamentary improvements were made to curtail late-night sittings.

One of Short's most notable contributions to women's rights was her support for amending the law on abortion. In 1965, she tried to introduce her own Private Members' Bill on the subject and described illegal abortions as 'a terrible pool of human misery and unhappiness'. Her own Bill proved unsuccessful, but a year later she co-sponsored David Steel's groundbreaking Abortion Act, which granted women the legal right to have an abortion carried out by a medical practitioner, and the ability to access this service on the NHS.

In a powerful speech during the passage of the Bill, Short described the existing law as 'unenforceable', adding that 'it is one law for the rich and one for the poor. Those who know where to go and those who have the money with which to do it are able to have their terminations carried out in suitable circumstances by a gynaecologist.' In subsequent years, she opposed several attempts in Parliament to weaken the Act's provisions.

Short also cared deeply about other elements of women's sexual health. She fiercely denounced the practice of female circumcision and advocated for teen mothers to be given more education and access to contraception. Her knowledge of backstreet abortions was impressive and her work in this area was recognised years later, when she was appointed as a lay member of the Medical Research Council.

Passionate about improving housing, Short focused on the issue in her maiden speech. Touching on her experiences as a local councillor, she highlighted the difficulties she had faced as a member of a local authority housing committee. She said: 'The most difficult and often the most heartrending part of my job ... was the allocation of the few housing units which came along from time to time between the hundreds of families on the housing list, all of which had equal and good claims.' After outlining these difficulties, she called for her constituents and fellow British citizens to be housed in 'good, well-designed, well-built homes at a reasonable cost'. She firmly believed that happiness and family life were largely dependent on the security of having a good home. Short argued that prefabricated housing, which had become popular in Sweden and socialist countries in Europe, should be used to help resolve the UK's housing shortage problems.

Penal reform was another of her passions and she pushed for the reform of prisoner rights, the introduction of conjugal visits and for the greater provision of education for prisoners. Short maintained that such measures would help rehabilitate prisoners into society when they had served their sentences, as well as supporting inmates' family units and their mental well-being while they were in prison. Short frequently met with prison officers and governors and visited prisons in many different countries. She used her expertise to write a seminal book, *The Care of Long-Term Prisoners*, which was said to have influenced the thinking of the Labour government of the mid-1970s.

A pioneer of good nursery education, Short served as president of both the Campaign for Nursery Education and the Nursery Schools Association. She argued that 'a child's life must be given the right foundation' and was passionate about improving the life chances of children from deprived backgrounds. Short was inspired by her visits to Scandinavian countries, particularly Sweden, where nursery provision was way ahead of its time. It is important to note that in the 1960s and 1970s, this was not a cause that many politicians focused on. Short campaigned for greater funding for nursery education, improved pay and conditions for nursery nurses, and was an early advocate for nurseries in work places.

She campaigned against the UK's membership of the European Economic Community in the 1975 referendum, regarding the EEC as a capitalist club that served the vested interests of big corporations and media tycoons. She argued that American free-market thinking would exploit the opportunities of the EEC to influence the political direction of Europe.

Britain's membership of the EEC, Short claimed, would mean higher food prices and living costs for working-class people. Small- and medium-sized businesses would struggle to compete with large corporations and British producers would suffer due to increased competition when European goods entered British markets. Short preferred a closer trading relationship with Eastern European countries, which she claimed would prove more beneficial in the long run.

During the HIV/AIDS crisis of the 1980s, Short repeatedly spoke out on this taboo subject and challenged minsters to address the issue. She asked the Secretary of State for Social Services to explain what plans the government had to increase medical facilities and how they were going to improve counselling services in hospitals and provide better information for at-risk groups.

Short understood how to campaign, how to communicate and how to grab attention for a particular cause. Her background in journalism and theatre clearly helped her in this regard. She was a straight-talker who was not afraid to shock her audiences in order to make a point. During a Commons debate about drug addiction, seeking to demonstrate how easy it was to acquire illegal drugs, Short threw a piece of silver paper onto the floor and claimed that it was a wrap of heroin.

From the 1960s to the 1980s, Short made a political journey from the hard left to the soft left. It is important to remember that the jury remained out in the 1960s as to whether capitalism or communism was the best system. Although she never described herself as a communist, Short was enthusiastic about the East German regime and chaired the British-GDR Parliamentary Group for fifteen years. She was also secretary to the Anglo-Soviet Parliamentary group, treasurer of the British-Romanian Friendship Association and frequently visited socialist countries.

Various theories exist as to why Short was never promoted to a ministerial role. Some commentators argue that she was restricted by rigid adherence to the far-left socialist principles that earned her the nickname the 'matriarch of the left'. While many in the Labour Party admired her she was out of step ideologically with the then Prime Minister, Harold Wilson. In 1974, she stated on the BBC election results programme that she would like to be promoted and added that 'if Harold has any sense, he will know what to do'. Wilson chose not to make her a minister and she subsequently described his appointments as 'offensive'.

Prior to Short's election, only three women MPs had held Cabinet positions, and during her twenty-three years as an MP, only five more women became Cabinet ministers. This reality demonstrated a gender bias within the parliamentary system, and it was clear that the glass ceiling remained unbroken. Short's gender certainly seemed to act against her and probably restricted her political career.

Although Short never achieved ministerial office, she was a powerful parliamentarian and senior MP. She served as chair of the Commons' Select Committee for Social Services for ten years and was the first woman to chair the Commons' Scientific committee. In 1970, she became an influential member of the Labour Party's NEC and served on it for almost two decades.

Her political journey became most apparent during this time. She supported many hard-left causes on the NEC, including voting down measures to deal with the Militant Tenancy, and consistently opposing membership of the EEC. But her political views began to mellow after Labour's defeat to Margaret Thatcher in 1979. Two years later, Short opposed Tony Benn when he challenged Denis Healey for the party's deputy leadership, and she nominated Neil Kinnock for Labour's leader in 1983. Much to the dismay of her former supporters, Short backed Kinnock's one member, one vote proposals for the selection of Labour MPs.

Short faced selection problems of her own within her Constituency Labour Party in Wolverhampton North East, seeing off a challenge by only four votes ahead of the 1983 general election. She then faced her toughest general election battle, holding the seat with a majority of 214; it seems that she lost 10 per cent of her vote share to the SDP–Liberal Alliance candidate. At the following general election in 1987, Short decided to retire after a distinguished parliamentary career.

Renée Short was a fearless and visionary campaigner who fought to support a range of controversial issues decades before they became part of the mainstream. During her career, she pursued many different causes, such as equal representation of women in politics, improved nursery education and better rehabilitation of offenders. These might be mainstream concerns today, but they were not popular at the time. We need visionaries like Renée Short. People who have the foresight and imagination to push for the unimaginable, so that one day the unimaginable finally becomes our reality.

SHIRLEY SUMMERSKILL

LINDA MCDOUGALL

- **FULL NAME:** Dr Shirley Catherine Wynne Summerskill
- **DATE OF BIRTH:** 9 September 1931
- **PLACE OF BIRTH:** London
- **DATE OF DEATH:** –
- **MARRIED TO:** John Ryman (m. 1957; div. 1971)
- **CHILDREN:** None
- **UNSUCCESSFUL ELECTIONS FOUGHT:** Blackpool North 1962
- **CONSTITUENCY:** Halifax
- **DATE OF FIRST ELECTION:** 15 October 1964
- **DATE LEFT PARLIAMENT:** 8 June 1983
- **PARTY ROLES:** None
- **MINISTERIAL POSITIONS & DATES:** Shadow Health Minister 1970–74; shadow Home Affairs minister 1979–84; Parliamentary Under-Secretary for the Home Office 1974–79
- **MOST FAMOUS QUOTATION:** 'While the passage in the gracious speech concerning the government's productivity, prices and incomes policy is a most welcome one, the exclusion of any mention of equal pay for women will not pass unnoticed. I would respectfully remind right hon. Gentlemen in the government that the railings around the Palace of Westminster can be used again.' – Loyal address, seconding the reply, 21 April 1966.

They don't make Labour women MPs like Shirley Summerskill any more. Brimming with confidence, well educated at what is still regarded by many as the best girls' school in England, St Paul's, and with a feminist mother who argued publicly that in every way women were smarter, fitter and better at pretty much everything than men.

As a young London doctor and former Secretary of the Oxford University Labour Club, Shirley Summerskill wrote to the Blackpool North constituency in the early 1960s, after hearing they were looking for a candidate for a by-election. She was then invited to a selection meeting. There were three male hopefuls and Shirley.

Despite being a woman and a feminist, Summerskill was selected. 'I won the selection conference because it was a safe Tory seat, and they knew no Labour candidate could win the by-election'. She came third after the Conservatives and Liberals, but she did a good job and increased the Labour vote by 5 per cent. Regarded as a promising prospect, she was recommended to Halifax, who were looking for someone who would do a good job in another unwinnable seat. They too chose Summerskill. In a major upset, she beat Maurice Macmillan, the sitting Conservative MP and son of former Prime Minister Harold, in the 1964 election by a thousand votes. And there she stayed for nearly twenty years until the Conservatives took the seat back in the 1983 rout of the Michael Foot-led Labour Party.

> I thought I wouldn't hold Halifax more than one election. I got in by a miracle. So I decided to continue my medical career. I had surgery in the morning and then visits to patients in their homes. They don't do visits now like we used to. Sometimes on a winter's day I would do about eight visits walking through the snow, and then go down to the House of Commons.

She was following in the footsteps of her mother, Baroness Edith Summerskill, who was also a physician and a feminist. She had been a Labour MP, a government minister and then chair of the Labour Party for most of Shirley's childhood.

> Both my parents were doctors in Wood Green when I was born. I was four years younger than my only brother. My mother was an MP in the war. My father [Dr Jeffrey Samuels] was in the Royal Army Medical Corps. I had a full-time nanny from birth. Me and my brother and Nanna were evacuated out of London. We kept moving about and I went to six different schools. When the war got better, we moved to Camberley and I went to St Paul's Girls School.
>
> My political feminist urge was there when I was thirteen. I remember in Berkshire I was waiting at the bus stop with the girls, and a girl said to me 'What do you want to be when you grow up?' and I said an MP, and I was thirteen. They all roared with laughter and said I was very stupid and silly and what a ridiculous thing to say, and I always remember that I went home and told my nanna this and she said not to worry, they were only jealous.

After St Paul's, Summerskill went to Somerville College Oxford to study medicine.

> I saw a film about surgeons during the war, a sort of M*A*S*H-type film. I thought I would like to be a surgeon and do something in that field.
>
> It was very hard work. At Oxford, everyone else was sitting round for three years doing nothing until the last minute when they did the exam, whereas medical students had weekly anatomy vivas. There were five girls out of forty-five. They were all very clever. They all went into practice, became consultants or very active in one field or another.'

At Oxford, Summerskill became secretary of the Labour Club and met lawyer John Ryman. The couple married when she was twenty-seven, but divorced in 1971. Ryman became a maverick Labour MP for Blythe in Northumberland. I asked Summerskill what her mother thought of Ryman to which she replied she had no idea. She had never asked her. But in 1957, Edith had written a book, *Letters to my Daughter,* in which she gave advice to Shirley, firmly advancing the argument that in almost every way women were superior to men. Edith Summerskill was in the Lords when her daughter arrived in the Commons.

> The first day I went to the House my mother showed me the Women's Room by the terrace, which was full of Tory women, but I didn't mind because it was the nicest room by the river, and then she showed me the lavatory. I had already been in the House several times to see her when she was an MP, and when she was a minister she had a room there, so I knew the building. I knew so much about the life that they lived that it was very easy to adapt when I became a member and I didn't suffer. A lot of the women who come in here, they say 'the men are sometimes so awful to us, they imitate us when we speak and they make signs about bosoms and some of them are very sexist'. That's how a lot of them talk, those present women. Now I don't want to say this isn't happening, but I can only say it didn't happen to me.

In her maiden speech, Shirley Summerskill spoke proudly of her new constituency: 'My constituency of Halifax is probably best known as a textile town. In fact, the town weaves one-seventh of the world's worsted yarn.'

Over fifty years on, it is as hard to see the Halifax of today of as a once proud wool town, as it is to imagine the relaxed and confident Dr Summerskill in the modern House of Commons.

Winding up her maiden speech she moved on, controversially, to equality for women. It would become the focus of her career at Westminster.

> May I express, too, the hope that in the spring Budget help will be given to single women with dependants? These women are a vast unsung army with no trade union to represent them. Many of them have one parent or two elderly parents to look after, sometimes sick parents, and at the same time they go out and do a full-time job of work. A fallacious argument often put against the case for equal pay is that women have no dependants. These women definitely do. I hope that the government will not forget them in the spring.

Shirley was thirty-two when she became MP for Halifax. Was there any discrimination against her because she was a woman?

> One journalist said to me, 'How do you think you can represent Halifax as a woman, when the factories and industries are the main business in the town?' And I said, 'Don't you think that there are any women working in those factories?' It never occurred to him that those factories were full of working women, that the town was full of working women. That was the sort of discrimination. I once sat next to the editor of the *Yorkshire Post* at a dinner and he said 'We follow your activities very closely, Dr Summerskill.' And I said, 'Yes, but you don't write about them.'

Labour improved its majority in the 1966 election and Shirley won Halifax by 5,702. 'I thought maybe I am going to stay here for a while, so I gave up the medicine because I couldn't do both.' She was chosen to second the Loyal Address and used the opportunity to taunt the House gently about the low number of female MPs:

> At this point I wish to pay tribute to another small group in this Parliament – the women Members. The psephologists, all of whom seem to be male, have decreed that the swing to female candidates at the election was greater than that to male candidates. Whatever the reasons for this may be, no hon. Member would deny that in the government women are playing a successful part. We have come a long way from the time when militant suffragettes accosted ministers in Downing Street and demanded the vote.

She went on to issue a warning about the danger of ignoring the issue of equal pay for women.

While the passage in the Gracious Speech concerning the government's productivity, prices and incomes policy is a most welcome one, the exclusion of any mention of equal pay for women will not pass unnoticed. I would respectfully remind right hon. Gentlemen in the government that the railings around the Palace of Westminster can be used again.

Harold Wilson made Shirley Summerskill a shadow Health minister from 1970 to 1974, and when Labour regained power in 1974 she became a Home Office minister and got her chance to try to implement equal pay for women.

I was put in charge of the Sex Discrimination Act, which went through under Roy Jenkins, but we still haven't got it properly. The reason is they are not comparing like with like and giving exactly equal pay for equal work. They are comparing the overall wages of women with the overall wages of men. That's not equal pay for the same job.

Shirley's own position is an excellent example of why women so often fail to break through the glass ceiling.

I am told, which I don't really care about, that I should have made sure I was a Minister of State and not do five long years as the lowest possible minister.

If I had been a man, I would definitely have said to Merlyn Rees 'I should be the Minister of State'. It simply didn't occur to me at the time. It is only that a few people have mentioned it. Jim Callaghan, when he became PM in '76, took over from Wilson. He phoned me and he mentioned Northern Ireland. I didn't want to go to Northern Ireland and he said, 'What about the Home Office?' And I said 'I am very happy at the Home Office, Jim, and I would like to stay there.' And I did. He left me there, but he didn't put me up. I was so pleased that I was going to carry on working there that I didn't care what rank I was; it wasn't that important.

Dr Summerskill sees now that, like so many women before and after her, she let her delight in doing well at a job she loved overwhelm her personal chance to have equal rights and opportunities with her male colleagues.

In the 1979 election, which brought Margaret Thatcher to power, Shirley Summerskill clung on by a whisper-thin majority of 198 in Halifax. She became a shadow Home Office minister. In 1983, Labour under Michael Foot suffered a disastrous loss, and Shirley Summerskill was defeated in Halifax.

At fifty-two she had to look for another job. 'I didn't want to go back to general practice again, so I went to work as a medical officer in the Blood Transfusion Service until I retired at sixty.'

I asked Shirley Summerskill if she is still politically active.

'I am eighty-five and a half. I would go on a march if there was anything to march about.'

So I mentioned Jeremy Corbyn. Did she have any advice for him?

My advice to him is to resign. He is not intelligent, he is not very well educated and he is not a leader. It is amazing that he is there at all. They have never been very good, Labour, in selecting leaders.

Heaven knows what the future is. I don't think anyone knows. I find it depressing. Terribly depressing. I don't know what the future is. I won't leave the Labour Party whatever. I haven't left so far and I don't see in my remaining years me leaving it. I feel I have done my bit.

SHIRLEY WILLIAMS

JACQUI SMITH & ELIZABETH VALLANCE

- FULL NAME: Shirley Vivian Teresa Brittain Williams (née Catlin), Baroness Williams of Crosby CH, PC
- DATE OF BIRTH: 27 July 1930
- PLACE OF BIRTH: Chelsea, London
- DATE OF DEATH: –
- MARRIED TO: Bernard Williams (m. 1955; div. 1974); Richard Neustadt (m. 1987; d. 2003)
- CHILDREN: Rebecca Williams and a stepdaughter
- UNSUCCESSFUL ELECTIONS FOUGHT: Harwich 1954 (by-election) and 1955; Southampton Test 1959; Cambridge 1987
- CONSTITUENCY: Hitchin 1964–74, Hertford & Stevenage 1974–79 and Crosby 1981–83
- DATE OF FIRST ELECTION: 9 June 1983
- DATE LEFT PARLIAMENT: 28 February 1974. Shirley Williams was made a life peer on 1 February 1993 and retired from the Lords in 2016.
- PARTY ROLES: Member of the Labour Party NEC, president of the Social Democratic Party 1982–87 and leader of the Liberal Democrats in the House of Lords 2001–04
- MINISTERIAL POSITIONS & DATES: Parliamentary Secretary at the Ministry of Labour 1966–67; Minister for Education and Science 1967–69; Minister for Home Affairs 1969–70; shadow Secretary of State for Health and Social Services 1970–71; shadow Home Secretary 1971–73; shadow Secretary of State for Prices and Consumer Protection 1973–74; Secretary of State for Prices and Consumer Protection 1974–76; Paymaster General 1976–79; Secretary of State for Education and Science 1976–79
- MOST FAMOUS QUOTATIONS: 'I am not as much a passionate European as a passionate internationalist ... with a deep sense of the special and unique nature of Britain.' | 'People like me because I look as crummy as they do.'

Shirley Vivian Teresa Brittain Catlin was born to be a politician. Daughter of the political scientist, Sir George Catlin, and Vera Brittain, the feminist and pacifist writer and activist, the young Shirley, named after the feisty, eponymous Charlotte Brontë heroine, grew up in a home where writers and politicians were family friends and the talk was constantly of political and social issues. She was born in London in 1930 at a time when the city, only just recovering from a great depression, faced the rise of both communism and fascism and, once again, the possibility of world war.

When war broke out, Shirley, aged barely ten, and her brother John, who was two years older, were sent to Minnesota and didn't see their mother again for three years. This undoubtedly encouraged her independence and self-confidence and instilled in her a love of America, a country she has returned to throughout her life. Her precocious intelligence was clear to her parents – even when she was on the other side of the Atlantic – her mother recording, 'another letter from Shirley ... turned into a thesis on England'.

On her return to the UK, Shirley attended St Paul's Girls' School but was bored and nearly turned down her Oxford scholarship (to Somerville), wanting instead to go to the LSE. However, the scholarship meant she could leave school immediately, which she did with joy. She spent the intervening months before university working in the north of England, on a farm and as a waitress, discovering a world far removed from her Chelsea home.

When she arrived at Oxford, she was immediately a star. Small and pretty, with strong opinions and an intellectual self-confidence born of her parents' belief in equal opportunities, she admitted that it simply did not occur to her until later that 'it would be tricky going into politics as a woman'. But it had also never occurred to her to do anything else. Her university career – acting with OUDS (Cordelia to Peter Parker's Lear); becoming, in 1950, the first women chair of the University Labour Club; and after graduation (with what she was to call 'an undistinguished Second Class degree') winning a Fulbright Scholarship to study at Columbia – was, for her, largely a preparation for her future as a politician.

The only things that might have militated against her political ambitions were a rather disorganised approach to life and her almost total disregard for her appearance. She tells the story of her father introducing her to Nancy Astor, saying that his daughter wanted to become an MP, to which the acerbic viscountess responded, 'Not with that hair!' Co-author of this profile, Elizabeth Vallance, recalls that the first time, as a young academic, she interviewed Shirley, she arrived twenty minutes late, apologising for her timekeeping and her cold hands as she had just lost her gloves. These foibles, however, became part of her appeal and as she rightly claimed later, 'People like me because I look as crummy as they do.'

Shirley had joined the Labour Party at sixteen, the minimum age required for membership, and had been Labour's agent in Chelsea while still in her teens. She was known as a party stalwart and a possible future candidate, but even someone with her commitment and experience would have to win her spurs by standing not once, but four times, before she finally made it to Westminster. In late 1952, having been asked to attend a selection conference for a by-election in Harwich, she abandoned her research on American trades unions and returned to England, where she was chosen as the Labour parliamentary candidate to contest the safe Conservative seat. She lost in the by-election of 1954, and was again unsuccessful when she stood for the same seat in the general election of 1955, having been dubbed, at the age of twenty-four, 'the schoolgirl candidate'. In 1959, she failed to win Southampton Test and it was not until 1964 that she was finally re-turned as MP for Hitchin. Like many aspiring women politicians, she had learned the hard way that the first rule of political success is to stand for a winnable seat!

She had many romances at Oxford and thereafter, for example with Peter Parker and Roger Bannister, but it was the philosopher Bernard Williams whom she married in 1955, taking his name. She had known him since Oxford, where she credited him with explaining logical positivism to her, and their friendship had deepened as postgraduates in America. They had one daughter, born in 1961, but although a marriage of two brilliant minds, it was not always an easy relationship. Two-career families were unusual at the time and Shirley's Catholicism sat rather uneasily with Bernard's critical ag-nosticism. They separated in 1970, although they did not divorce until 1974.

In the 1950s, while she waited for the chance of a seat, Shirley taught brief-ly in Africa, worked as a journalist on the *Daily Mail* and *Financial Times* and, in 1960, became general secretary of the Fabian Society. In this role she was much admired by members of the Labour leadership, so that as soon as she entered the House, her ascent was swift and assured.

Elected at the age of thirty-four, she was one of only twenty-nine women MPs. She had role models in older women like Edith Summerskill, whom she admired for combining life as a public figure and feminist with being a successful wife and mother. Shirley was frank that the challenge of combin-ing Parliament with a family life and caring for her daughter, Rebecca, was only made possible by a 'helpful husband, sharing a home with devoted and tolerant friends and being able to rely on my daily household help'.

Admiring other women like Jennie Lee and Barbara Castle, she says that she didn't feel isolated or alone, enjoying the camaraderie of women MPs from across the parties. This sisterhood was put to good effect when several women complained of being pinched in the crowded division lobbies. Retaliation was planned, and with the aid of stiletto heels and a swift stamp, the assailant was permanently discouraged from this behaviour. Shirley had her own role models, but she also served as a role model to profile co-author Jacqui Smith, who lived in her constituency until the age of nine. Jacqui's parents campaigned for Shirley Williams, with her mother actually acting as Shirley's election agent. One of Jacqui's earliest political memories is of taking part in a car cavalcade through Hitchin with loudspeakers and posters. Being a contrary eight-year-old, Jacqui declared that she thought she'd be a Liberal when she grew up – ironic, given Shirley Williams's final political destination.

Shirley also formed strong friendships with male MPs – including with Bill Rodgers and Roy Hattersley – which provided support throughout her political life. She recognised the value of finding a mentor and was lucky to be encouraged by former Labour Home Secretary, Herbert Morrison.

Very soon after her election, Shirley Williams became parliamentary private secretary to Kenneth Robinson, Minister of Health. While many PPSs are little more than bag carriers, Robinson enabled her to attend departmental meetings and help develop policy. This was good preparation for her first 'proper' ministerial job as Parliamentary Secretary in the Ministry of Labour which followed soon after.

This was the era of direct government involvement in resolving industrial disputes, and when the National Union of Seamen called an official strike in May 1966 and the senior minister in the department was taken ill, Shirley found herself at the heart of the negotiations to end the strike. Also during this short tenure, she steered the contentious Prices and Incomes Bill through Parliament.

Shirley's view is that this close but stormy relationship with the trade unions, coupled with the loss of faith in Labour's ability to manage the economy following the 1967 devaluation of the pound, sowed the seeds for the Labour government's defeat in 1970. These issues would also be central to Labour's defeat in 1979 and to the subsequent splits and conflicts that led to Shirley's alienation from the Labour Party.

She had impressed in her early government roles so it was not surprising that after just nine months, she was promoted to be the Minister of State at the Department for Education and Science in charge of schools. In this role, she made progress on the policy of comprehensive schooling and on developing nursery education. However, as you can read in Rachel Reeves's excellent profile in this book, she was usurped while away on holiday by Alice Bacon, who took the lead in driving through comprehensive education. Shirley was moved to the Higher Education and Science portfolio. Once again, she experienced tempestuous times with the eruption of student protests throughout the UK. She remembers escaping from protesting students in Birmingham with the vice-chancellor, making her way to safety through central heating ducts.

Her final ministerial role in the 1966 Wilson government came at the Home Office, where she was given responsibility for Northern Ireland – a canny choice by Harold Wilson to give the enthusiastic Catholic, Shirley, a role alongside the Protestant Home Secretary Jim Callaghan. Her affinity with the US aided her when she was sent on a visit to Boston to try to dissuade Irish-Americans from collecting funds for the Provisional IRA. Her Home Office responsibilities further encompassed what she called the three 'Ps' – prisons, probation and pornography. Her weekend ministerial box contained pornographic material in brown packages, which she had to review to decide whether it should be banned.

Despite enormous bureaucratic opposition, she also managed to spend twenty-four hours 'undercover' in Holloway Prison. While she was shocked at the conditions of the cells, she admits to making little progress with her officials on this, managing to convert just a couple of cells in each wing into toilets and washrooms.

When Edward Heath's Conservatives won the 1970 general election, Shirley's ministerial career was put on hold. The new Conservative government had an overriding objective: to take the UK into Europe's common market. Labour's Harold Wilson had already proposed membership in 1967, with support from his Cabinet. But he had faced a veto from French President Charles de Gaulle, which had prevented progress at that time. However, in opposition, Labour moved away from support for the European project and towards rejection of the EEC, with strong motions passed at the party's annual conference in 1971. Labour imposed a three-line whip to oppose entry when the legislation came before the House of Commons, but Shirley was one of sixty-nine Labour MPs who voted with the government to endorse entry.

Her period in opposition saw Shirley elected to the shadow Cabinet and to Labour's National Executive Committee, but it also marked a period of intense personal sorrow with the death of her beloved mother and estrangement from her first husband, Bernard Williams.

She became shadow Home Secretary in October 1971. But with characteristic female humility, she argued that this was only because Roy Jenkins and other senior figures had resigned from the shadow Cabinet to vote against the Labour position to support a Conservative backbench call for a referendum on joining the common market. She was undoubtedly worthy of the role, but perhaps realistic in her assessment as, when Roy Jenkins returned to the shadow Cabinet in 1973, he became shadow Home Secretary and Shirley was moved to Social Security.

When Labour returned to government in 1974, Shirley entered the Cabinet in the fiendishly difficult role of Secretary of State for Prices and Consumer Protection – a new department. The month she took on the role, annual inflation stood at 13.5 per cent. This government took a more interventionist position on the economy than any since and she worked closely with Chancellor Denis Healey and Secretary of State for Employment Michael Foot. Crafting a careful path between the trade unions arguing for tighter price controls and business representatives who wanted more flexibility required all her intellect and political skills. But her gender still played a role, with senior business leaders eager to embrace her in the lift or to invite her out for dinner. 'These were tactics reserved for women ministers, but they told me something about the vanity of the men involved,' she said.

She found female friends on both sides of the political divide and recounts a gruelling parliamentary question time where the Tory opposition worked hard to lay blame for inflation at her feet. She noticed Margaret Thatcher watching her from behind the Speaker's Chair and then encountered her again after questions, when she retreated to the Lady Members' Room. 'You did well,' Thatcher said. 'After all, we can't let them get the better of us.'

In September 1976, after Jim Callaghan had taken over from Harold Wilson as Prime Minister, Shirley was appointed Secretary of State for Education and Science. She also stood against Michael Foot for the deputy leadership of the Labour Party – losing by 166 votes to 128 – a closer contest than many had predicted.

Callaghan had a strong commitment to education but distrusted progressive methods. He worried that a variation of subjects and teaching methods would make the curriculum a 'secret garden' that few could fully understand

and which lacked consistency and support. As his Education Secretary, Shirley started work on a consultation which proposed a core curriculum of fundamental subjects. And worrying about the status of teachers, she also proposed a professional body to be consulted about training, entry and professional standards. Facing opposition from teachers' unions, and with only a small government majority, she was forced to back off. However, these were clearly the policy forerunners of the national curriculum and of Labour's General Teaching Council, which Jacqui Smith worked on as an education minister.

Alongside her role as Education Secretary, Shirley served as Paymaster General. She jokes that neither she nor her predecessor Judith Hart could come up with a suitably non-gendered title without running into potential difficulties, so they left the title alone. In practice, the role involved chairing Cabinet committees and the Prime Minister nominated her to chair committees on industrial democracy and Scottish devolution – perhaps recognising her considerable skill in addressing some of the most contentious issues of the day.

A vote of no confidence in the government following the 'winter of discontent' brought Margaret Thatcher to power in 1979. Labour's election defeat marked the end of Shirley's ministerial career, but it also signalled the start of her role as a key player in a major realignment of British politics.

A combination of boundary changes and the swing to the Conservatives in the election saw Shirley lose Hertford and Stevenage to Conservative Bowen Wells by 1,295 votes. She claims never to have fallen in love with the 'clubby and exclusive' House of Commons, but nevertheless felt numbed and humiliated by the defeat. She was the only Cabinet minister to lose her seat. However, she was quickly invited to the John F. Kennedy Institute of Politics at Harvard to act as a fellow for a term, which gave her the opportunity to think about her own life and about the future of the Labour Party.

She returned to the UK and her place on the National Executive Committee of the Labour Party with a deep pessimism regarding the party's future. Labour's special conference in May 1980, where Jim Callaghan and Denis Healey were heckled and booed, the rubbishing of the record of the Labour government and the entryism of the hard left led Shirley and others to contemplate their futures in the party. In August 1980, with David Owen and Bill Rodgers, she published a lengthy statement suggesting that the Labour Party faced 'the gravest crisis in its history' and going on to speculate about the conditions necessary for the formation of a new party. When Michael

Foot won the leadership, others on the right of the party were also willing to contemplate leaving Labour. However, as Shirley says, it was a painful process. 'For me, leaving the Labour Party was like pulling out my own teeth, one by one.' Many begged her not to quit, and Harold Wilson told her that if she stayed he could see her as a potential future leader. Despite her loyalty and pressure from others, she felt unable to argue publicly for the Labour programme as it was developing and, on 24 January 1981, alongside Roy Jenkins, Bill Rodgers and David Owen, she made the Limehouse Declaration and two months later launched the Social Democratic Party.

She turned down the chance to fight the Warrington by-election in July that year, which she calls the biggest mistake of her political life. Roy Jenkins fought the seat and, despite losing, cut Labour's majority from 10,000 to 1,759. Shirley was probably even better placed to win it, but in rejecting the opportunity she says that her 'reputation for boldness, acquired in the long fight within the Labour Party, never wholly recovered'. She also damaged her chances to become the leader of the SDP.

She returned to Parliament as an SDP MP in November 1981, when she took Crosby – then the eighth-safest Tory seat in the country – with a majority of 5,289. She clearly had the profile, the intellect and the experience to lead the SDP, but when the party decided to elect a leader in 1982, she didn't stand. In her autobiography, she claims to have lacked the self-confidence to take this on – and she faced considerable negative briefing from the supporters of Roy Jenkins. In the end, Jenkins became leader, having defeated David Owen. Owen went on to become leader himself when Jenkins resigned. By this time, Shirley could not stand for the leadership as she had lost her Crosby seat in the 1983 general election, and although she became the SDP's president, this was clearly a missed opportunity. This is a cautionary tale for women politicians of the need to seize the moment and to believe in yourself.

Shirley fought one more election, representing the Alliance in Cambridge in 1987, but was beaten by the Conservative Robert Rhodes James. With the SDP forming the Alliance with the Liberal Party, many SDP members had to eventually decide whether to move on with the Liberal Party or to return to Labour. Shirley continued her political journey with the Liberal Democrats, whom she represented in the House of Lords until her retirement in 2016. In her autobiography, she talks of having been approached by Peter Mandelson to rejoin New Labour but, ultimately, she declined.

She was made a life peer in 1993 and led the Liberal Democrats in the House of Lords from 2001 to 2004. Having spurned Peter Mandelson, she claims that she was not approached again by Labour until Gordon Brown became Prime Minister in 2007. Jacqui can remember meeting Shirley Williams in Foreign Secretary David Miliband's office in 2008; she was advising the Labour government on nuclear proliferation. She remained active in the House of Lords until her retirement, playing a particularly important role in delaying the Health and Care Act in 2011 and 2012.

In her distinguished ministerial career, and in her role in setting up the SDP, Shirley Williams was one of the most important politicians of her generation. Harold Wilson is probably right about her being a contender for the Labour Party leadership had she stayed. Having chosen the SDP, her experience of ministerial life coupled with her ongoing profile and contacts within the Labour Party would have made her a stronger and more attractive leader of the SDP than the more aloof Roy Jenkins. Who knows where the realignment of British politics in the early '80s would have gone if Shirley Williams had believed in herself as much as many lesser men have throughout the years.

GWYNETH DUNWOODY

LAURA SANDYS

- FULL NAME: Gwyneth Patricia Dunwoody (née Phillips)
- DATE OF BIRTH: 12 December 1930
- PLACE OF BIRTH: Fulham, London
- DATE OF DEATH: 17 April 2008
- MARRIED TO: John Dunwoody MP (m. 1954; div. 1975)
- CHILDREN: Two sons and a daughter
- UNSUCCESSFUL ELECTIONS FOUGHT: None
- CONSTITUENCY: Exeter 1966–70, Crewe 1974–83 and Crewe & Nantwich 1983–2008
- DATE OF FIRST ELECTION: 31 March 1966
- DATE LEFT PARLIAMENT: 17 April 2008
- PARTY ROLES: Member of the Labour Party NEC 1981–88
- MINISTERIAL POSITION & DATES: Parliamentary Secretary at the Board of Trade 1967–70; shadow Secretary of State for Health 1980–83; shadow Secretary of State for Transport 1984–85

Gwyneth Dunwoody, like many politicians, had a rollercoaster of a career. She had high expectations upon arriving in Parliament, moderate success as MP for Exeter, defeat at the ballot box, films and furs – and even near bankruptcy. She was then re-elected as MP for Crewe & Nantwich; became a backbencher thorn in the government's side; was fired as chair of the Transport Select Committee, only to be reinstated a few days later, following a parliamentary rebellion; she was nicknamed 'Gunboats Gwyneth', and received the totally enviable award from *The Oldie* – Battleaxe of the Year.

As a friend, colleague or to the wider world, Gwyneth presented many different 'faces'. Described as a 'dragon with merriment never far away', 'a fierce façade but greatly generous', 'down to earth, yet with the style and presence of a "mink-clad" Duchess' all politicians, not least from her own party, experienced the full spectrum of the faces of Gunboats Gwyneth.

Gwyneth was born into the Labour movement and worked throughout her life to support and protect the Labour Party she grew up with – she was often at odds with both Militant Tendency and New Labour. In addition, and what grew stronger as she got older, was her dedication to the role of Parliament. Her commitment to both, however, never held her back from strong and determined criticism of how Parliament and the Labour Party performed. With an independence of mind and with memorable fallings out, her dedication to both the Labour Party and Parliament drove her to hold them to the highest standards.

Born Gwyneth Phillips, she came from a Labour-supporting family – and more than a few strong women. No shrinking violets as female role models for Gwyneth! Her mother was a leading politician at the London County Council, who was appointed a peer and was the first female whip in the House of Lords. Her two grandmothers were suffragettes. There could have been few perceived 'political' ceilings for Gwyneth, as she grew up watching the women in her family flourish.

Her father, Morgan Phillips, also must have shaped the debate at home. There must be few, if any, Labour activists who held the post of general secretary of the Labour Party for eighteen years as Phillips did from 1944 to 1962. A former coalminer from Wales, he identified strongly with the working people in the trade union movement and across nationalised industries up and down the country.

Gwyneth left school at sixteen to join the local Fulham paper, where she was responsible for writing up any births, marriages or deaths – the bottom rung of the journalistic pecking order. In her early working days, she was also a repertory actress – never a bad training for politics – and spent time learning Dutch in the Netherlands.

Like her parents, Gwyneth met her husband through the Labour Party. John Dunwoody and Gwyneth became one of a handful of husband and wife parliamentary teams when they moved to the West Country. In 1966, she was elected as MP for Exeter, while her husband represented Falmouth & Camborne. In their one term as MPs together, they were both promoted to junior ministerial positions – Gwyneth at the Board of Trade and John at the Health Department. They must have been perceived as quite the young power couple, with expectations of further promotion – however, politics is never quite as predictable as that.

It was amusing to read her maiden speech, which praised my father for introducing the Civic Amenities Bill. Gwyneth supported his Bill with a strong personal caveat: 'With great respect [the best political put down], I welcome [this Bill] also since I rather feel that I might not always find myself in such wholehearted agreement with the Rt Hon. Gentleman, the Member for Streatham.' I have no record if they ever found themselves on the same side of any argument again, but I somehow doubt it. She extolled the beauty of Exeter saying, rather politically incorrectly, 'I always feel that beautiful cities, rather like beautiful women, require a certain amount of judicious preservation.' She was never inhibited by the 'norms' of the day.

She no doubt knew that a political life would involve uncertainty and, in 1970, both Dunwoodys lost their seats. Picking herself up, Dunwoody threw herself into a new role as director of the Film Producers Association and as a consultant to the Association of Independent Cinemas.

During this period, Gwyneth's relationship with her husband deteriorated and they divorced amicably in 1975.

It wasn't until Gwyneth was elected as MP for Crewe that her parliamentary career really took off. Crewe was a safe Labour seat and this afforded Gwyneth the security needed to get her feet well and truly under the table in Parliament.

While not a prominent figure in the media, Gwyneth was a very active parliamentarian, as well as an MEP. Her time spent in the European Parliament led her to become a strong Eurosceptic. She voted against the Maastricht Treaty seven times and no doubt would have campaigned to leave the EU in the 2016 referendum.

She was dedicated to eradicating Militant Tendency's insidious influence on the Labour Party and was very much the Labour loyalist under the leadership of Neil Kinnock. Betty Boothroyd include a wonderful description of Gwyneth during those dark days, in her obituary of her friend: 'I remember her sitting in meetings for hours and hours on end with her tapestry, like Madam Defarge at the guillotine, not a smile on her face, just raising her hand to vote each member out.'

During this period, Gwyneth found herself in quite serious financial trouble, and she began to fear the knock of the bailiffs on her door. Friends blamed Gwyneth's financial problems on her overly generous nature; she would overspend, taking friends on holidays and to restaurants. To try and turn the financial tide, Gwyneth became a consultant to a Canadian fur company. Despite previously having said, 'I am not employed for my dress sense', in the '80s and '90s, she was remembered as going into Labour headquarters draped in her marvellous minks.

While a strong supporter of women, she never signed up to the sister-hood. She opposed all-women shortlists and disliked anything she deemed to be a sense of female entitlement. She said that Harriet Harman 'was one of certain, particular women who are of the opinion that they have a God-given right to be among the chosen'. Gwyneth was less interested in whether she was chosen by others, she didn't need patronage, just her own beliefs and strength of character – she knew what she thought was right and was deter-mined to fight for it.

During the eighteen years of opposition, she was a shadow spokesperson for a wide range of portfolios and was on the NEC from 1981 to '88. When Blair was elected, she did not receive the ministerial call. No one knows if she was disappointed, but she might not have realised at the time, but this was the start of the highest point of her career. It was as a parliamentarian rather than a party politician that she has left a lasting legacy.

In 2000, she stood for Speaker of the Commons and lost out to Mi-chael Martin, but it was as chair of the Transport committee from 1997 to her death that allowed her to shake up the political, and her own party's, establishment.

As chair of the Transport committee, she was better known and feared than any of the ministers in the department. She set the agenda and geared up her committee to be the real brake on Transport decisions being made in Whitehall. Few came out of the committee without having gone through the wringer, few emerged without a long to do or not to do list. It wasn't just her drive, it was her ability to create a coherent, united committee that left party politics at the door and were clear that they were there to represent the public. She ran the best select committee of its time – and maybe ever – focusing on misgovernment and mismanagement, constantly questioning New Labour's mantra that the private sector 'knows-best'.

Her high points – and the Labour government's low points – included calling out the failings of Railtrack three years before the beleaguered Ste-phen Byers arrived at the same view. Railtrack was subsequently replaced by Network Rail and Stephen Byers was moved on. She brought ministers back down to earth when they claimed that the railways could be totally solvent within ten years. She was right.

She fought against hyperbole, political catchphrases and grandiose long-term targets. She fought for realism, clarity and substance, diving down beyond the political spin to the detail of the policy, and as importantly White-hall's ability to deliver on any given policy. While any minister promoted to Transport must have been thrilled with their new Red Box, their second thought would be, 'Oh my God – I will have to face Gunboats Gwyneth!'

The intransigence of her leadership of the committee in holding government to account did not please the leadership of her party. Blair, who felt powerful with his overwhelming majority, asked Hilary Armstrong, his Chief Whip, to remove both Gwyneth and Donald Anderson, who was the then chair of the Foreign Affairs committee and not as compliant as No. 10 had hoped. Gwyneth called the attack on their position 'pernicious' and an abuse of the government's patronage of the select committees. She added that, 'A self-confident government should not be afraid of criticism and should know that it is sometimes in its own interests to see policy scrutinised, refined and improved.'

Possibly as surprising to Gwyneth and Donald as it was to the Labour Whips' Office, parliament rejected the pair's dismissal. With even New Labour loyalists against the decision, Parliament reinstated the pair, tabling a Commons motion to overturn the executive's diktat and re-establishing the rights of Parliament to choose their select committee chairmen. It must have come as a shock to the all-powerful control central at No. 10 that Parliament would not have its committees stuffed with yes men and women. This vote still stands as a warning to all governments who wish to manipulate select committees. An important victory for Parliament.

Now reinstated, Gwyneth was as powerful as ever and had the explicit support of Parliament. Not holding back, she gave Blair a hard time at a Liaison committee hearing, asking what he thought he was doing about immigration. After a Gunboat inquisition, Blair admitted that he didn't have a robust immigration policy, leading Gwyneth to respond acerbically, 'I thought that was what you were paid for.'

Gordon Brown suffered the same Gunboats treatment, with Gwyneth criticising the Metronet contract and commenting on the debacle, 'Any reasonable person, looking at the current situation, would find scant evidence to sustain a dogma that the private sector will always deliver greater efficiency, innovation and value for money than the public sector.'

There was no love lost between Gwyneth and the New Labour movement. She was politically aligned with Labour politics under Kinnock, while she still held the politics of her father and mother close to her heart – that of working people and their needs, not fancy corporate headquarters and inflated executive pay.

Having met her once, it has been really special to understand more about

Dunwoody beyond the public face. Getting to know much more of the humanity, humour and the generosity she showed others has been a revelation. It further illustrates how politicians are given one-dimensional personalities by the media and stereotyped as difficult, rebellious or part of the awkward squad when politicians' motivations are often far more complex. Gwyneth's flamboyance hid behind a no-nonsense exterior. Her throaty laugh, her loyalty to the party that she loved, and her determination to protect Parliament from the Executive as the custodian of the citizen, was described as rebellious and intransient.

She was unusually grand in the way that only very confident people can be. She had an internal strength that meant that she didn't need others to endorse her actions, but was instead guided by clear principles that led her to do what she believed was right. As Betty Boothroyd said, 'Gwyneth never let anybody have a quiet life.'

She died very suddenly on 17 April 2008, at the age of seventy-seven, following emergency heart surgery. This was a shock to her friends and to all in politics who had witnessed a true defender of Parliament and its crucial role.

She will be remembered as a passionate parliamentarian saying, 'For me, Parliament is not only the most important forum for the British people, it also the last defender of the rights of all citizens.' She might have added that it is also should be the defender of independent-minded, dedicated and passionate parliamentarians.

JILL KNIGHT

GISELA STUART

- FULL NAME: Dame Joan Christabel Jill Knight DBE MBE, Baroness Knight of Collingtree
- DATE OF BIRTH: 9 July 1923
- PLACE OF BIRTH: Bristol
- DATE OF DEATH: –
- MARRIED TO: James 'Monty' Montague Knight (m. 1947; d. 1986)
- CHILDREN: Andrew and Roger
- UNSUCCESSFUL ELECTIONS FOUGHT: Northampton 1959 and 1964
- CONSTITUENCY: Birmingham Edgbaston
- DATE OF FIRST ELECTION: 31 March 1966
- DATE LEFT PARLIAMENT: 30 April 1997. She was made a life peer but retired from the Lords on 31 March 2016.
- PARTY ROLES: None
- MINISTERIAL POSITIONS & DATES: None
- MOST FAMOUS QUOTATION: 'You never know when your vote is going to make a colossal difference.' – Speaking with regards to the Thatcher vote of confidence on 29 March 1979.

When, in March 2016, Baroness Knight of Collingtree invited some fifty of her friends and colleagues to lunch in the Houses of Parliament, she could take some justifiable pride in having become the longest-serving woman parliamentarian. At around the same time, she announced that after thirty-one years in the Commons and nineteen years in the Lords, she was taking official leave and retiring.

Some round the table that day could recollect happy occasions when rather than singing for her supper, Knight would sing a 'Thank you'. As a keen member of the parliamentary heritage group, she once asked if she could sing to their Spanish hosts after the formal speeches had been delivered. There might have been some nervousness, but colleagues agreed, only to discover that she had an engaging singing voice and a commanding stage presence. Singing to hosts on overseas visits became something of a tradition. In later years, she recounts how in her youth she had to choose between the stage and politics. She never regretted choosing politics.

Jill Knight was elected as the Member of Parliament for Birmingham Edgbaston in the 1966 general election. Her predecessor, Edith Pitt, had died in the January of that year. Knight was forty-three years old, married to an ophthalmologist from Northampton and was the mother of two sons.

She'd been a Northampton Borough councillor for ten years, unsuccessfully fought the Northampton parliamentary seat in two previous general elections and failed to get selected in Birmingham Hall Green. However, the 1966 general election provided her with an opportunity to defy the odds. Knight beat 215 other applicants and got the nomination. It is said that one member of the selection panel thought that 'as we had a woman last time, we should now have a man'. To which Knight is reputed to have replied that she would accept that argument if the same principle was applied to seats where a man had previously sat. When later asked about how she became an MP, she singled out persistence as the most important element for her success.

Knight was never given to deeply analytical or profound statements, but she was a quick thinker and in tune with the grassroots. By ensuring her selection and subsequent election as the eighty-second woman MP in the history of Parliament, she contributed to a uniquely unbroken line of Edgbaston women MPs, which began in 1953 with Edith Pitt up until this day with incumbent Preet Gill.

Edgbaston is a leafy part of Birmingham. It covers the university, the Test cricket ground, has an Archery and Lawn Tennis club as well as several of the King Edward Grammar schools. Edgbaston High School for girls can claim Nobel Prize-winner Malala Yousafzai as an alumna. The Catholic Orotarians under the leadership of Cardinal John Newman settled on the Hagley Road and gave shelter to the young J. R. R. Tolkien. It is sandwiched between the industrial Longbridge to the east and the more deprived and ethnically diverse Ladywood constituency to the west.

In 1974, Keith Joseph visited Birmingham and discussed cycles of depravation before lamenting that 'the balance of our human stock is threatened'. This became known as the 'Edgbaston Speech' and put a stop to any Conservative Party leadership hopes he might have harboured. In the same decade militant trade unions in general and Red Robbo in particular went on to become household names in the industrial disputes of the Three-Day week and the Winter of Discontent.

There could never have been the slightest doubt that Jill Knight was a Tory, a unionist, and a loyalist. She may have led the parliamentary rebellion against the abolition of universal free eye tests, but that was more due to her ophthalmologist husband, Monty, who had died of leukaemia in 1986. She always said that she believed in arguing her case from inside the party. Knight's parents divorced when she was young, and her political outlook is perhaps best described as a deep commitment to what she regarded as traditional family values. When it came to abortion, she argued that a woman had a right to choose not to become pregnant. Journalists liked her pithy phrases, shooting straight from the hip and being immensely quotable. 'Babies are not like bad teeth to be jerked out'. In a debate on IVF, she drew parallels between freezing embryos and freezing pastry dough. In 1974, she argued that the death penalty should be available for the IRA and other terrorists. Tony Benn recalls that, in the last days of the Ted Heath government, Knight condemned strikers as enemies of the state.

When Ted Heath decided to sack Enoch Powell after his infamous Rivers of Blood speech in Birmingham, Knight attacked the Prime Minister. Warning about the consequences of uncontrolled immigration, Powell quoted the Sibyl's prophecy from *The Aeneid*. He claimed that he too was filled with foreboding and like the Romans could see 'the river Tiber foaming with much blood'. She didn't explicitly defend Powell, but believed that he 'knows the special problems of the Midlands'.

AIDS and greater openness about same-sex relationships brought the issue of what should or should not be taught in schools into the political spotlight. Jill Knight was a key player in getting Section 28 of the 1988 Local Government Act into the statute book. Section 28 prohibited the promotion of homosexuality through teaching or the publishing of material that supported homosexuality. The abolition of S28 became a totemic issue for Tory modernisers, but it was a Labour government which repealed it in 2003.

There was little about her politics, economically or socially, which could be described as liberal. And yet in the 1970s, Knight successfully introduced a Bill that enabled women to pass on their nationality to children who were born outside of the UK and supported legislation giving women the right to half of the family property. Knight never held government office nor served on the front bench in opposition, but she was reckoned to have got more Private Members' Bills through than anyone else by simply adding clauses to existing Bills. For outsiders this may not seem like much of an achievement, but fellow parliamentarians will appreciate the effectiveness of this approach.

The journalist Edward Pearce thought that there was no malice in Knight's politics but that she suffered from a 'terrible poverty of perception'. But perhaps this is an unduly harsh assessment. The Tory Party at the time was probably a difficult place for a woman MP to navigate and, on occasion, Knight may have acted out of necessity. Shortly after my own election in 1997 I was wearing red shoes and one of the doorkeepers asked, 'Is it red shoes no knickers or red hat no knickers?' I couldn't think of an appropriate response then, nor do I have one now, but I did reflect on what Jill Knight might have done. I bet she would have dismissed the incident with a throwaway, slightly flirtatious smile and a giggle, before moving on. I took comfort from the fact that less than a year later such an exchange would have been unimaginable.

During the difficult years of the Major government, she remained one of his most loyal supporters. A long-time friend, Knight had sponsored Major's application to be accepted onto the official list of Conservative Party electoral candidates in 1971. He repaid her loyalty by supporting fundraising dinners in her constituency and subsequently elevating Knight to the House of Lords.

Her local Conservative association was fond of her. After stepping down as MP, she remained president of the association's supper club. Unlike her predecessor Edith Pitt, she wasn't a Brummie, but she did stand up for Birmingham. The Schools of King Edward VI in Birmingham foundation could rely on her firm support whenever any of its schools went through a rough patch. Advice surgeries were by appointment and by all accounts she ran an efficient constituency office. Her advice for new MPs was never to accept political engagements on Sundays and to avoid sharing a platform with opponents at all costs. Although the advice encouraging Members to keep Sundays free for family seems sound, it seems unlikely that you would be able to avoid sharing a platform in a modern election campaign.

She did her fair share of public events and campaigning in support of colleagues. On one occasion, when she was mistaken for the then Speaker of the Commons, Betty Boothroyd, she did what any seasoned politician would have done: she smiled, accepted the compliment and walked on.

When the 1997 election arrived, Knight decided to stand down. It is unlikely that had she stood, she would have been able to retain the seat. The tide of the Labour landslide combined with revised constituency boundaries would have, like many a Tory MP, seen her lose her seat. The boundary review in 1983 had made Edgbaston a safer Tory seat, but the inclusion of the Bartley Green ward in 1997 changed the voter dynamic.

Her local association were said to be determined to select a pro-life candidate and they opted for a man, Andrew Marshall. Edgbaston had grown rather fond of women MPs and Marshall must have been one of the very few Tory candidates who had to endure criticism for not being a woman.

I remember inviting Knight to the Edgbaston Botanical Gardens to celebrate fifty years of women MPs in 2003. In the spirit of cross-party sisterhood, I asked her to give a speech. She got up, made no reference to the overwhelming presence of Labour supporters in the room and went on to tell us that 'coming up from London on a Thursday evening was an inconvenience, but I came because I realised that without me you poor dears wouldn't have anything to celebrate'.

I might not have quite put it like that, I thought. But then again she did have a point.

JOAN LESTOR

FIONA MACTAGGART

- FULL NAME: Joan Lestor, Baroness Lester of Eccles
- DATE OF BIRTH: 13 November 1931
- PLACE OF BIRTH: Vancouver, British Columbia
- DATE OF DEATH: 27 March 1998
- MARRIED TO: Unmarried
- CHILDREN: David (adopted in 1967) and Susan (adopted in 1969)
- UNSUCCESSFUL ELECTIONS FOUGHT: Lewisham West 1964
- CONSTITUENCY: Eton & Slough 1966–83 and Eccles 1987–97
- DATE OF FIRST ELECTION: 31 March 1966
- DATE LEFT PARLIAMENT: 1 May 1997. She sat in the Lords from 1997 until her death in 1998.
- PARTY ROLES: Member of the National Executive Committee 1967–82 and 1987–97; chair of the International Committee of the Labour Party 1978–82 and 1987–97; chair of the Labour Party in 1977/78
- MINISTERIAL POSITIONS & DATES: Under-Secretary of State for Education 1969–70; Under-Secretary of State for Foreign and Commonwealth Affairs 1974–75; Under-Secretary of State for Education and Science 1975–76; shadow Minister for Overseas Development 1994–96
- MOST FAMOUS QUOTATIONS: When asked what she had most missed about Parliament, she replied without hesitation, 'The sexual harassment.' | Or more reflective of her values: 'We must also consider the children in our society, babies and older, who fall through the net and are victims of abusers, sometimes of cruelty and also, I am afraid, of a country which has not yet made the provision for children that it should.' – Hansard, 20 December 1989.

I met Joan Lestor briefly at Labour Party conferences and on anti-Apartheid protests, but our first real conversation happened in 1982. I had just become general secretary of the Joint Council for the Welfare of Immigrants (JCWI), a daunting responsibility for a young activist. Lestor's phone call, however, was reassuring, 'Come to the House of Commons and I will show you how to work with MPs. My constituents need you to be good at what you do.'

That kind of an approach was typical of Lestor. She was concerned about how racist immigration laws affected the people of Eton and Slough. This cause was particularly unpopular in the aftermath of Margaret Thatcher's infamous assertion that 'people are really rather afraid that this country might be rather swamped by people with a different culture'. Lestor generously reached out to a young woman at an early stage of her career. She was determined to make a difference for the people she represented and knew that JCWI could help her diverse constituency. Sadly she was not to continue as MP for Slough for long after our meeting; she was defeated in the 1983 general election by just over 3,000 votes.

Lestor was brave – she didn't care what people thought, she cared about what was just and right. She was elected to Parliament in 1964, the same year that Peter Griffiths unexpectedly won Smethwick for the Conservatives on the slogan: 'If you want a n***** for a neighbour, vote Labour.' The Labour government was under pressure on the issue of immigration. When people of Asian origin from Kenya and Uganda began to arrive in Britain, fleeing the dictator Idi Amin and discrimination in Africa, the government responded with the Commonwealth Immigration Act of 1968. This shameful law divided Britishness on racial grounds; only those with a parent or grandparent who was born in, or was a citizen of, the UK were to be admitted to the country of their citizenship. In panic, the law was pushed through in three days. Lestor was among the handful of MPs, both Labour and Conservative, who defied their whips to vote against the Act. It took over three decades for the consequences of this legislation to be overcome in David Blunkett's Immigration, Nationality and Asylum Act of 2002.

Lestor was passionate about racial justice but also many other things: children, the Labour Party and Africa in particular. Throughout her career she showed how much she cared about these issues. Her commitment was a product of her political beliefs. Frank Judd, a fellow MP, friend and latterly member of the House of Lords, said, 'I remember Joan saying that on race, on gender, all these issues matter, but that she didn't see them essentially as race and gender issues. She saw them as socialist issues – we are about people.'

Lestor's parents had been members of the Socialist Party of Great Britain, which she joined as a teenager, but she departed for the Labour Party in 1955 and from that time on was consistently active. She was elected to

Wandsworth Council in 1957 where among a tiny group of women she was the only 'Miss'. It was a title she later rejected. Tam Dalyell wrote of Labour's women MPs, '[we] loved our flaming red-headed girls – the diminutive Ellen Wilkinson, Barbara Castle, Jo Richardson, and the not so diminutive Joan Lestor. Joan – no Labour MP could call her Miss Lestor'.

Lestor became chair of Wandsworth's public health committee, introducing fluoridation of water, and when the council created a children's committee, Lestor became its first chair. She was elected to the London County Council from 1962 to 1964, then the Labour Executive in 1967, before becoming chair of the party in 1977.

While she was a councillor, Lestor worked in nursery education and childcare. And although single, she successfully adopted two children, David in 1967, and Susan in 1969. She listed her hobbies in *Who's Who* as 'playing with children and animals'.

Lestor maintained her commitment to challenging racism. Active in the anti-Apartheid movement, she helped found the anti-fascist magazine *Searchlight*. In her first attempt to enter Parliament, standing for Lewisham West in 1964, Lestor reduced a Conservative majority of over 4,000 to under 1,000. It was not, however, until 1966 that she was elected MP for Eton & Slough, winning the seat from Antony Meyer, who later became a stalking horse candidate for the Tory leadership against Margaret Thatcher.

Once elected, Lestor threw herself into the issues that consumed her, introducing a Bill to tighten regulations on nursery schools and providers of child care, fighting the government's attempt to stop paying social security benefits to unwed mothers, and working to ensure that abandoned wives could obtain financial support from their husbands.

In Slough she won people over with her straightforward approach, spending time on the doorstep with constituents, getting around on a bicycle, never being grand. Lydia Simmons, who became Mayor of Slough – the first black woman to do so in any town in Britain – also fostered a son, Jason, who had been removed from the care of his mother. She recalls canvassing in Slough's Britwell estate with Lestor and Lestor's son David. Jason's birth mother caught sight of the group and reported Lydia for taking her son canvassing, after mistaking David for Jason. Lestor often took her children out with her as she worked. Baroness Jean Corston remembers seeing them together at many Labour events across the country. Most of Corston's other memories of her are not fit to print, because Lestor was never shy about telling people, in the plainest possible language, what she thought.

Lestor's first ministerial post from 1969 to '70 was Under-Secretary of State for Education, with responsibility for nursery education. She was in office for only eight months, before the general election defeat of 1970. When Labour came to power again in 1974, Lestor served as an Under-Secretary in the Foreign Office, using this role to advance the anti-Apartheid cause to such a degree that it irritated her boss Jim Callaghan and earned her the soubriquet 'the African Queen'. With the generosity to young activists which she was later to show me, she invited Peter Hain (later Labour MP and peer) to the House of Commons to discuss his campaign against apartheid sport. She wanted to stop the British Lions rugby tour to South Africa, as she felt it was in breach of the UN sports boycott of all-white South African teams. The tour went ahead, but Lestor refused British embassy receptions and facilities for the Lions and would not meet the victors on their return to Britain.

In June 1975, Lestor was moved back to education. This post did not last long either as she resigned in February 1976 over cuts to the education budget. Margaret Beckett, who was given the role following Lestor's resignation, recalls, 'I don't think Joan had any intention of resigning ... She went to lunch with what she thought was a friendly journalist and was too open about how worried she was and how she might have to consider her position, opens the paper [the] next day and she's resigning.' In fact Lestor was very angry that Beckett, a fellow left-winger, had agreed to take up her post. Her resignation letter to Harold Wilson trenchantly declared, 'I believe investment in education is as important as investment in industry,' an attitude now held by most Labour women. Beckett told me that in order to respect Lestor's commitment, she tried in office to protect nursery education from spending cuts.

But although Lestor was prepared to sacrifice her own career on an issue of principle, she was profoundly loyal to the party. She robustly condemned splits in the party, admonishing the Gang of Four who eventually left to form the SDP, by saying 'people should work within the party to change it – or leave'. Frequently finding herself in the same camp as Neil Kinnock, she supported efforts to stop Militant Tendency from infiltrating labour. Tony Blair later said, 'I will always remember her as a member of the shadow Cabinet when I first became leader of the Labour Party, whose support was always steadfast and whose advice was always welcome.'

In 1983, Labour was at a low ebb and the Slough constituency had new boundaries. Lestor lost by over 3,000 votes to Conservative John Watts. Nicholas Bosanquet, the SDP candidate, had won over 9,500 votes, and on the night Lestor claimed that 'the SDP took votes from us. Our vote did not fall dramatically.'

Following her defeat, despite no longer being an MP, Lestor carried on campaigning, becoming the head of the Lambeth Council police unit, which highlighted racism in policing, worked for the World Development Movement and led a trade union childcare project, which had a focus on child sexual abuse – an area neglected by mainstream politicians at the time.

But she was good at Parliament, and although she was sad to leave Slough, (telling me a decade later that she particularly missed her constituents' Asian food) she set out to find a new constituency. She tried Chesterfield and Brent East, but it was Eccles that adopted her and she represented the constituency from 1987 to 1997, in what she described in her last speech in the House of Commons as a 'love affair'.

Two years after her re-election, Neil Kinnock appointed her shadow spokesperson for Children and Families, and in 1994 she became shadow Minister for Overseas Development.

Robin Cook MP described Lestor as 'the darling of Labour conference'. This was because her commitment to Labour values shone through in everything she said. Speaking in Eccles in 1993, Lestor summed up her response to the Thatcher era,

> The so-called success of the last ten years is often judged by the spread of yuppie city brokers. We look nearer; we look at the worsening deprivation for thousands of ordinary people; people who have never benefited from tax cuts but who suffer from reductions in services and benefits; from increased interest rates and rising mortgages. It is a good measure of the humanity of any administration to examine how it treats those least able to care for themselves. Children born at the beginning of the Thatcher decade have suffered year after year as a result of the government's relentless support of the private sector to the detriment of decent public services.

But although she was known as a tireless campaigner, ultimately she grew tired and with the onset of motor neurone disease, she signalled her intention to step down from Parliament. On 18 March 1997, for an obscure adjournment debate, a large array of Labour MPs doughnutted Lestor. Normally those present for such a debate would include only the backbencher, one minister and a government whip. But many wanted to be present for Lestor's farewell speech. The subject was child poverty; 'the issue that has dominated my life has been that of children, both here and abroad, and I wanted to go out on a note that highlighted that interest'.

It wasn't only Labour supporters in the chamber that day. Conservative backbencher Michael Colvin, who had clashed with Lestor on South Africa, intervened to pay tribute to 'the social conscience that she has shown whenever she has spoken in the House ... and fought her corner with a robustness which sometimes has not received the recognition it deserves'.

Lestor didn't stay away from Westminster for long. In June 1997, she was admitted to the House of Lords as Baroness Lestor of Eccles. She used her new status to become an active patron of the fledgling Overseas Adoption Helpline, but only nine months later she succumbed to motor neurone disease.

WINNIE EWING

DEBORAH MATTINSON

- FULL NAME: Winifred Margaret Ewing (née Woodburn)
- DATE OF BIRTH: 10 July 1929
- PLACE OF BIRTH: Glasgow
- DATE OF DEATH: –
- MARRIED TO: Stewart Ewing (m. 1956)
- CHILDREN: Fergus (b. 1957), Annabelle (b. 1960) and Terry (b. 1964)
- UNSUCCESSFUL ELECTIONS FOUGHT: Orkney & Shetland 1983
  CONSTITUENCY: Hamilton 1967–70 and Moray & Nairn 1974–79
- DATE OF FIRST ELECTION: 2 November 1967
- DATE LEFT PARLIAMENT: 3 May 1979. She joined the Scottish Parliament
  in 1999 and stood down in 2003.
- MEP: Highlands & Islands 1975–99
- MSP: Highlands & Islands 1999–2003
- PARTY ROLES: SNP president 1987–2005 and SNP spokesperson on
  external affairs and the EEC
- MINISTERIAL POSITIONS & DATES: None
- MOST FAMOUS QUOTATION: 'Stop the world, Scotland wants to get on.'

In early 2012, and ahead of local government elections which Labour feared might cost it Glasgow Council, I was commissioned to conduct focus groups in Scotland. Though pretty used to hearing voters speak their minds about politicians, I was unprepared for the vitriol that was heaped upon Labour, especially the Scottish Labourites who, I was told, had 'betrayed' the people of Glasgow, turning their backs on Scotland to 'feather their nests' down south. I was also unprepared for the passion and optimism that the focus group members displayed when they talked about the SNP, describing the party as a 'fresh start', and seeing its politicians as uniquely able to understand their needs. These focus groups foretold the SNP's electoral triumphs, both in the Scottish Parliament and, by 2015, in Westminster. Older, long-standing Labour voters and young, first-time voters alike told me how inspired they felt by the SNP, who were politicians who 'got' them and gave them hope.

Winnie Ewing, arguably, triggered the start of this movement fifty years ago with her historic victory in the Hamilton by-election. Hamilton, a traditional Labour stronghold, epitomised the 'one-party state' that had been Scottish politics. Ewing's brief from her party was to 'come a good second to encourage the members', but second-best was not her style. The election campaign was an epic eighteen months, gifting her the time to really connect with people and rally support, and, as she did so, bring verve and vitality not seen before to Hamilton's streets.

This contrasted with Labour's apparent sense of entitlement: the sitting MP, Tom Fraser, had resigned to take on a 'cushy' job as head of the Hydro Board – as veteran Scottish Labour MP Tam Dalyell remarked, 'Parties that do that get punished.' The combination of this with Ewing's panache proved fatal for Labour, but launched Ewing's career in elected politics. Following the unexpected victory, she became a local celebrity, appearing on the front page of every Scottish newspaper and arriving in Westminster with her entourage on a new train known as the 'Tartan Express'. It also gave a massive boost to the SNP; some believe that it was the shock of the Hamilton result that led to the then Labour government establishing the Kilbrandon Commission to discuss the establishment of a devolved Scottish assembly. As Ewing herself said, 'Stop the world, Scotland wants to get on!'

Ewing's passionate nationalism began early. She describes visiting the Highlands as a young schoolgirl and being awestruck by the beauty: 'I thought, this is my country – why is it in such a hopeless state? I became a nationalist then and there and I've been one ever since.'

Born to George and Chris Woodburn, Ewing grew up in a lively and politically engaged household. Her father was a member of the ILP and Ewing would often find members debating and gossiping at the Woodburn table. Ewing studied law and arts at Glasgow University, graduating in 1952. There her nationalism was influenced by John MacCormick, lawyer and nationalist politician, who was rector of the university. She became politically active herself, despite her father's warning that being a member of the SNP would not help when she made job applications, such was the poor reputation of the party at that point.

Ewing met her husband-to-be, accountancy lecturer Stewart Ewing, in 1955. It was a whirlwind romance and he proposed to her on their second date. They married a year later and went on to have three children: Fergus, Annabelle and Terry. Stewart was to introduce her to Robert McIntyre, the SNP's first MP – and arguably the party's founding father, who encouraged Ewing to stand for Hamilton in 1966. Her husband was to be her greatest political ally and influence – and also provided invaluable practical support. 'He was always there you see – he was really my unpaid help, reading the papers and so on.' She was typically pragmatic after his death, saying, 'Well, these things, that's what you have to face up to in life, you lose people. You just have to accept it.' But the fact that she almost retired entirely from public life following the loss, suggests how dependent upon Stewart she had become.

Stewart's support was invaluable in a sometimes hostile world. When Fergus, their first child, was born in 1957, Ewing lost her job. This, according to Ewing, was simply the way things were: 'You had a baby, you lost your job.' She later started her own business to counter the threat: 'Then I was an independent person, you see. No one could tell me what to do.' When Hamilton presented itself as a possibility, even Stewart had assumed that she wouldn't be selected 'because there are two men in the short lead'. Ewing was determined to prove her husband wrong: 'I'll be in that short lead myself.' At the time, there were only twenty-six women MPs and, like many other women, she struggled with the 'boys club' of Westminster, but her perseverance was to pave the way for her many female successors. Nicola Sturgeon describes how 'Winnie started the process of shattering the glass ceiling for women in politics.' The SNP's Hannah Bardell has recently called for Ewing's portrait to be hung in Westminster as 'a fitting tribute' to celebrate the centenary of suffrage.

It was Ewing's own campaigning style that best defined her. Hamilton was described as 'a very modern campaign, with cavalcades, flyers, songs and even a celebrity endorsement from Sean Connery'. More than anything, she understood the importance of personal relationships, and it was said that she 'was shopping for independence' as she went from town to town, going into shops and chatting to the people she met.

In the 1979 European Parliament election, Stewart, in his role as 'unpaid helper', would pore over local papers in the Highlands and Islands and cut out the wedding announcements. Ewing would then write to all the newly-weds mentioned, building up a massive database of contacts and becoming that rare thing – a politician that people recognised and felt that they knew. She saw the importance of this herself, and was not afraid to blow her own trumpet. Talking about the Hamilton campaign, she observed, 'I got on really well in the factories. And I don't know if any candidate had ever done that before … I don't think anyone has ever wooed them before.' Another first was her idea of sending out videos to every village hall and community association in her constituency, showcasing her work as a European MP.

A self-proclaimed Europhile, her love affair with Europe began when she studied international law at The Hague after leaving Glasgow. As EEC spokesperson, she was chosen by the SNP to be their representative to Europe in 1975, following the positive UK referendum vote (Harold Wilson, then Prime Minister, had decided one nationalist MP should be a member of the European Parliament). That evening there was a smart Westminster reception with champagne flowing, but Ewing was escorted on to a Brussels-bound plane instead. Later that evening, fellow SNP MP Donald Stewart looked at his watch and said to colleagues, 'Any minute now, war will be breaking out on the European continent.' It was a sly reference to Ewing's fierce demeanour, but belied her own pro-European stance, which at that time was at odds with that of most of her party. As she observed, 'Everyone thought I should be against Europe for everything.'

This did not mean, however, that she was a pushover in the European Parliament. Choosing her battles, she fought hard for Scotland's national interests, earning herself the nickname 'Madame Écosse', which Ian Paisley accused her of 'milking for everything it was worth'. In particular, she campaigned passionately on EU fishing policy – successive UK governments had used fishing as a bargaining chip and she championed the fisherman's cause against bureaucrats and businessmen, arguing that 'men in offices are going to end up with blood on their hands'. She felt that joining the Common Fisheries Policy (CFP) was a huge betrayal, as, under the CFP, the Scottish fleet was cut back significantly, while the Spanish fleet was allowed access to the North Sea. 'Britain broke my heart with fishing, and broke the fishing industry into pieces, and gave it all to Spain for some reason.'

Overall, her career as an MEP was successful. She was skilful at promoting Scotland's profile on the global stage, notably bringing the Lomé convention – an international trade delegation – to Inverness. She was also effective at attracting funds to the region: 'I learned early on that there was European money for more deprived areas and the issue was to get your area to fit the legal definitions, and we worked hard at that in the Highlands.' Her efforts supported Gaelic culture as well as infrastructure projects including roads, transport facilities and ferries.

Some have argued that Ewing's achievements have been exaggerated, especially her claim to be one of the architects of the modern SNP. In a blistering critique in the *Scottish Herald* in October 2017, David Torrance said of the legacy of the Hamilton campaign, 'There had, of course, long been a gap between political promises and delivery, but both the nature of the by-election campaign and its impact on the political discourse in Scotland widened it further.' I believe this underestimates her considerable talents as a campaigner – and her own personal battle against the considerable odds that she faced, as an outsider in every political club she joined.

Ewing's determination is evidenced in her willingness to fight again, even after electoral defeat – winning Moray & Firth after losing Hamilton, going on to become both an MEP and an MSP. Had Labour listened harder after Hamilton and recognised the resilience of the SNP brand, as personified by Winnie Ewing, the extent of its humiliation almost five decades later might have been reduced. Instead, it was business as usual after winning the seat back in 1970, but as Alex Salmond said, 'This woman is irresistible and irrepressible. Every time she gets knocked down, she gets back up again.' So, as it turned out, was the party she represented.

BERNADETTE DEVLIN

JULIA LANGDON

- FULL NAME: Josephine Bernadette Devlin McAliskey (née Devlin)
- DATE OF BIRTH: 23 April 1947
- PLACE OF BIRTH: Cookstown, County Tyrone
- DATE OF DEATH: –
- MARRIED TO: Michael McAliskey (m. 1973)
- CHILDREN: Roisin, Deirdre and Fintan
- UNSUCCESSFUL ELECTIONS FOUGHT: None
- CONSTITUENCY: Mid Ulster
- DATE OF FIRST ELECTION: 17 April 1969
- DATE LEFT PARLIAMENT: 27 February 1974
- PARTY ROLES: None
- MINISTERIAL POSITIONS & DATES: None
- MOST FAMOUS QUOTATION: 'It wasn't long before people discovered the final horrors of letting an urchin into Parliament.'

Bernadette Devlin was like a firework; she exploded into the House of Commons, illuminating the political sky and showering sparks throughout the duration of her time in Parliament. It was as if her presence at Westminster was a literal evocation of the coming Troubles in Northern Ireland, which would cause much suffering and death in the last three decades of the twentieth century. Indeed, her maiden speech, which some said was the finest since Disraeli's in 1837, defined with chilling accuracy the social and economic misery of the 'have-nots' in the Six Counties, whose justifiable demand for civil rights, after fifty years of neglect by the British, had already lit the fuse for the incendiary events of the next thirty years.

Devlin was originally elected at a by-election, as the independent socialist unity candidate for the nationalist community of Mid Ulster, on a record voting turnout of 91.5 per cent. She was twenty-one years old, until recently a psychology student at Queen's University, Belfast, who had been forbidden to sit her finals because of her participation in protests staged by the newly formed People's Democracy movement of which she was one of the founders. She was the youngest MP for over 200 years, a record she would hold for another forty-six years, and her politics were an extraordinarily combustible mixture of radical, anti-clerical, feminist socialism.

That much was made evident in her first Commons speech, made within an hour of swearing the oath of allegiance, in which she summarily dismissed the convention of avoiding controversy. 'I think the situation of my people merits the flaunting of such traditions,' she told the House, before embarking upon a fluent 24-minute tirade, delineating the deprivations of her people; 'peasants', she called them, and her articulacy was such that her oratory provided its own ironic quotation marks. She explained and justified her own participation, building barricades in the course of the recent riots on the streets of Derry. This was not a Catholic uprising, she explained, but about ordinary people who had had enough and who wanted equal access to jobs and housing and the politics of the place. That was why she had already stood, unsuccessfully the previous month, for Stormont.

She warned, too, in that same first speech, about the implications of sending the army to sort out what was happening on the streets of Northern Ireland. 'If the British troops are sent in, I should not like to be either the mother or the sister of an unfortunate soldier stationed there,' she said. The troops were sent in three months later and remained stationed in Northern Ireland for thirty-eight years, during which time 3,600 people were killed, of whom 763 were in the services. Countless thousands were injured.

Years later, reflecting ruefully on what she saw as her early naiveté, Devlin would recall how she went to London to tell them that it wasn't fair, expecting them to hear her and to understand what they didn't previously know and to think that they needed to do something. 'But then I realised, the bastards, they do know and not only do they know, they don't see anything wrong with it.' It didn't cause her to compromise; she wasn't the sort. Instead she spent her first summer as an MP demonstrating her all-round radicalism. She went to the United States to raise funds and meet the Black Panthers and at home, during the prolonged Battle of the Bogside, she was arrested. She was re-elected, this time as an independent socialist MP, in the summer of 1970, before her case came to court. She was convicted for incitement to riot, obstruction and disorderly behaviour and sent to prison for six months. The stint didn't tame her.

She was there, of course, in January 1972, on 'Bloody Sunday', when thirteen unarmed civilians (another died from his injuries four months later) who had been engaged in a peaceful civil rights protest were killed in Derry by members of the Parachute Regiment. And she was also in the House of Commons when Conservative Home Secretary Reginald Maudling made a parliamentary statement concerning the situation, suggesting that the British Army had fired out of self-protection. According to parliamentary custom, an MP who has been present at an event under discussion in the chamber may expect to be called to speak. Mr Speaker Selwyn Lloyd did not call the MP for Mid Ulster, so she left her seat on the opposition benches and crossed the floor of the House and slapped Reginald Maudling across the face because he had lied about what had happened. It took two government investigations and thirty-eight years, before the whitewash of the first inquiry was followed by the Savile Inquiry conclusion – after hearing evidence over twelve years at a cost of £195 million – that the British Army action was unjustified and unjustifiable. Bernadette Devlin would say later that she didn't hit the Home Secretary half hard enough.

Devlin lost her seat in February 1974 and did not stand for the Commons again, but not because she had lost any of her socialist idealism. In any case, getting elected had never been part of her plan – she claimed once never to have fought an election with the aim of being elected. That year she helped found the Independent Republican Socialist Party and, three years later, the Independent Socialist Party, which only lasted a matter of months. Her problem was that her ideology was rooted in a somewhat simplistic belief in working-class solidity, which didn't allow for the historical, cultural and religious divide in the population of Northern Ireland, of all places. Her radicalism alienated some, while the wide spectrum of her political canvas, embracing socialism, feminism and anti-clericalism, was too mixed a message for the growing body of support then for the brutal simplicity of Irish republicanism.

In 1979, Devlin stood unsuccessfully for the European Parliament in the first round of direct elections. She had run as an independent in support of the prisoners on the 'dirty protest' in Long Kesh and, in Dublin North Central, for the two elections to the Dáil in 1982.

By this time, she had survived a horrific assassination attempt. Now known as Bernadette Devlin McAliskey, in 1973 she had married Michael McAliskey, a schoolteacher and the father of her first child, Roisin, and two younger children born after their marriage. Both parents were attacked in their home by three members of an Ulster paramilitary group, despite supposedly being under British Army protection, because Devlin had been rallying support during 1980 and 1981 for the hunger strikers in what had been Long Kesh and what was now called The Maze. The three small children watched as their mother was shot fourteen times. A helicopter to hospital saved their lives and their assailants were caught, tried and imprisoned.

She disappeared from public life after her tilt at election to the Dáil, but her ideas never really much changed. As the history of the Troubles unfolded and the long road to some sort of peace process was pursued, Devlin became occupied instead with trying to help people on the margins. She said there should be two peace processes: one from the top down and one from the bottom up and she became involved with the latter. She played no part in any of the formal talks; she didn't belong to any participating organisation and besides, she remained too radical, too socialist, too difficult because of not being someone who would ever be prepared to compromise. She described herself as being 'awkward'; she meant this in the sense of being difficult.

Her agenda was instead to bring an end to segregated schooling, to end the 11-plus exam, to help the disabled, immigrants or travellers. In 1996, this led to the South Tyrone Empowerment Programme, which she helped found and run. She said in a rare interview, as she approached her seventieth birthday, by now a grandmother of seven, the elder stateswoman of anti-establishment politics, that this was another way of slowly closing the door on war. But even as an older woman, she remained contrary. She still believed in justice and fairness and she was a woman of principle. What she was not, was someone who would play any game by the rules. 'My only interest in rules is seeing how far they can be pushed,' she said. She went on pushing. She was not going quietly into her old age. Her anger was not for public consumption, as it had been so dramatically when she was a young woman, but that didn't mean it had gone away. The worst thing that happened to her, she said once, as for so many others of her time in Northern Ireland, was the thirty years between 1969 and 1999. That was what caused the anger.

DAME PEGGY FENNER

TRACEY CROUCH

- FULL NAME: Dame Peggy Edith Fenner (née Bennett) DBE
- DATE OF BIRTH: 12 November 1922
- PLACE OF BIRTH: London
- DATE OF DEATH: 15 September 2014
- MARRIED TO: Bernard Fenner (m. 1940)
- CHILDREN: One daughter
- UNSUCCESSFUL ELECTIONS FOUGHT: Newcastle-under-Lyme 1966
- CONSTITUENCY: Rochester & Chatham 1970–74 and 1979–83; Medway 1979–97
- DATE OF FIRST ELECTION: 18 June 1970
- DATE LEFT PARLIAMENT: 1 May 1997
- PARTY ROLES: None
- MINISTERIAL POSITIONS & DATES: Parliamentary Secretary for Agriculture 1972–74 and 1981–86

I really liked Peggy Fenner. I actually only met her once, but she was spoken about so often by local people that it felt like I had known her for years. When I did meet her, it was in the basement ballroom at one of the Park Lane hotels – I forget which and what the occasion was – there she was in the middle of the room, looking stunningly film-star-like in a way that women of a certain generation just did. Her hair was perfectly curled, her shawl sparkled and her posture commanded a humble respect from all around. I nervously went over to say hello and introduce myself as the prospective candidate for Chatham & Aylesford. She grabbed my hand with a strength and energy that defied her age and with a huge smile she said, 'I am so glad they picked a woman.' I can't remember much else of the conversation and instead basked in the glory that Peggy, the actual real Dame Peggy Fenner, approved of my selection to fight the seat that she had represented for many years.

Peggy was in some respects a real champion of women. She advocated the cause for getting more women into Parliament and as the ninety-first woman to take the Oath in the House she bemoaned the fact that she beat another woman, the Labour MP Anne Kerr, in the election. There are only two MPs left in the House from Peggy's intake – Dennis Skinner and Ken Clarke; I think there was something in the water that election as all three appear to have an independent-minded streak, a quality in MPs that has been watered down after years of slavish loyalty to leaders and whips.

Peggy did two stints in Parliament. In her first election, representing Rochester & Chatham, she bettered the national swing to capture the seat. Then in the October 1974 election, she lost the seat to the Labour candidate Robert Bean, but not being one to give up and walk away, she won it back off Bean again in 1979. The seat was abolished in 1983 and reconfigured into the new constituency of Medway, which she represented until 1997, when nearing her seventy-fifth birthday, she lost to the unforgettable and colourful barrister Bob Marshall-Andrews. She is remembered very fondly by the army of local Conservatives who fought the elections with her and, as one told me, Peggy's energy was unbeatable. Just when you thought it was time for a cup of tea, she'd run off to the next street to start canvassing.

By all accounts, it seems that Peggy also had an incredible knack for re-membering faces. Recently, I met a gentleman who, knowing that I was writing this chapter, told me he had first met Peggy at an event in Parliament. Several years passed before they met again, but incredibly when they did meet, Peggy called him by his first name. I can barely remember what I have for breakfast. She had a knack and a charm that I think is of an age where things were slower, simpler and therefore much more polite than the instant response age we live in now.

Peggy was a publican's daughter born into a troubled, modest family. As a child, she was bought up by her grandmother in Brockley. Her parents divorced when she was three and she never saw her father again. At fourteen she left school in Sevenoaks to become a mother's help, before marrying at eighteen and heading into wartime factory work.

The no-nonsense housewife, as she was described in her obituaries when she died in 2014, made a strong impression early on and soon she was racking up successes in Parliament shortly after first being elected. As the MP for the naval dockyard in Chatham, at the time a thriving shipbuilding town, she saw many problems with young sailors being led astray while away from their home port. She took up the cause, supported by navy wives, and forced the Royal

Navy to scrap its 'dial a sailor' scheme which allowed the public to befriend a visiting sailor. It was no doubt an innocent invention but one that had been re-engineered into something else by entrepreneurial types in certain towns, leaving a legacy of prostitution that existed long after the ships had sailed.

And when they did sail from Chatham for the last time after her own Conservative government decided to close the dockyard, she could at least say she fought every step of the way for her constituents. I feel for Peggy on this. If anything breaks down the veneer of steel from an MP it is when your own government makes a decision that impacts negatively on your constituency. I can only imagine how many private tears she shed knowing that there was little she could do to stop the tidal force of Whitehall's decision-makers shafting an industry that employed and supported tens of thousands of workers across all three of the Medway towns. But fight it she did and cemented her reputation for standing up for her constituents.

Her stint as a Minister was no less spirited. She was quick-witted and chippy and as Minister for Food under both Heath and Thatcher used her home duties to keep her in touch with fluctuating prices, culminating in a well-known spat with the Labour MP Willie Hamilton about the price of bananas. She was the ministerial architect for legislation that obliged food producers to put sell-by dates on products and campaigned for better labelling of fat, sugar, salt and fibre content that we all take for granted now. Once the food crisis was over and prices stabilised she turned her attention to welfare standards in production, curbs on pesticides and, very importantly, residues on lemons that were polluting gin-and-tonics, a noble cause worth her appointment as a Dame alone!

She didn't sulk when she was unceremoniously returned to the back benches and instead used her energy as a delegate to the Council of Europe and Western European Union. She continued to support women in high places and supported the ordination of women and the nomination of Betty Boothroyd as Speaker.

Peggy loved her Kentish maid and housewife labels. She naturally epitomised the classless conservatism that many today still find difficult to master. She was a straight-talking no-nonsense politician who fought many a battle, some successfully, others less so. Chatham took nearly twenty years to recover from the closure of the dockyard and she knew the devastation it would cause when first proposed by John Nott in 1981. But she never let the challenge of taking on her own government cow her, locally or nationally, and it is that attitude that means all those who remember her do so with fondness and respect.

DORIS FISHER

BARONESS CHRISTINE CRAWLEY

- FULL NAME: Doris Mary Gertrude Fisher (née Satchwell)
- DATE OF BIRTH: 13 September 1919
- PLACE OF BIRTH: Birmingham
- DATE OF DEATH: 18 December 2005
- MARRIED TO: Joseph Fisher (m. 1939)
- CHILDREN: Two daughters
- UNSUCCESSFUL ELECTIONS FOUGHT: Birmingham Ladywood 1969 (by-election)
- CONSTITUENCY: Birmingham Ladywood
- DATE OF FIRST ELECTION: 18 June 1970
- DATE LEFT PARLIAMENT: 27 February 1974
- PARTY ROLES: Member of Birmingham City Council 1952–74 and delegate member of the European Parliament 1975–79
- MINISTERIAL POSITIONS & DATES: Whip and shadow spokesperson on the Environment 1983–84
- MOST FAMOUS QUOTATION: 'I never dreamed I would see the day when people would sleep rough on our city's streets but it's here and we must do something.'

Doris Fisher was the genuine article, a proud working-class achiever who, though never destined for high office, put in a high-quality shift as a parliamentarian. Today, when everyone wants politicians to be authentic above all else, Fisher would have thrived.

One story captures her hinterland. In 1939, aged twenty, she married Joseph Fisher, a sheet metal worker at the Austin plant in Longbridge, Birmingham. On one occasion, when Joseph was ill in hospital, Fisher kept the family going by selling newspapers near the gates of the Longbridge works.

Birmingham born and bred, Fisher went on to leave an indelible mark on all those who remember her in that city and in Parliament. Betty Boothroyd recalls how, as a new MP, she was in awe of Fisher – who was a real character, popular and hard-working. Anne Knowles, a prominent member of the local Labour Party branch, still remembers her magnificent laugh, her Brummie warmth and her striking presence.

Doris Fisher – ultimately elevated to the Lords as Baroness Fisher of Rednal – was born Doris Mary Gertrude Satchwell in Birmingham on 13 September 1919. Her father, Frederick, was a decorated First World War veteran. She was educated at Tinker's Farm Girls' School and Bournville Day Continuation College. She worked at Cadbury's and in wartime factories. Later, she attended Fircroft College, founded by George Cadbury.

Having joined the Labour Party in 1945, Doris was elected to Birmingham City Council in 1952. In a famous victory (hinterland again), she succeeded in getting the penny charge removed from women's lavatories in the city – men at the time were not charged.

At the council, she also became chair of housing. Decent homes for all became a lifelong passion. I met Fisher when she was in her seventies – age had not dampened her vigour. Indeed, at seventy-two, she slept rough overnight by St Philip's Cathedral in Birmingham to draw attention to the homeless.

Back in 1969, amid a turbulent time for the Wilson government, Fisher was selected to fight Birmingham Ladywood in a by-election, but she was unsuccessful. However, the following year in the general election, she won with a majority of 980 and began her four years as an MP. Her fellow councillor, Denis Minnis, remembers her on the megaphone at election time – though, from what one hears, she hardly needed one.

Boundary changes beckoned and Fisher decided not to stand again in 1974. That year, Harold Wilson needed to replenish his troops in the House of Lords and she was thus ennobled.

In her un-dilutable Brummie accent, she made her maiden speech on 6 November 1974 and, in her time in the Lords and in the European Parliament (1975–79) until her death in 2005, she continued to ensure that the voice of Birmingham people and women in particular was heard loud and clear. So often in her many speeches and questions, she spoke of the burdens placed on women: family budgets, pension provision and discrimination. She was always their natural champion.

Talking to her fellow MPs about her now is to hear the same affectionate reflection. This was a no-nonsense grafter for her causes, someone who loved a good laugh and who loved her city very much indeed.

JANET FOOKES

BRIDIE PEARSON-JONES

- FULL NAME: Janet Evelyn Fookes
- DATE OF BIRTH: 21 February 1936
- DATE OF DEATH: —
- PLACE OF BIRTH: London
- MARRIED TO: Unmarried
- CHILDREN: None
- UNSUCCESSFUL ELECTIONS FOUGHT: None
- CONSTITUENCY: Merton & Morden 1970–74 and Plymouth Drake 1974–97
- DATE OF FIRST ELECTION: 18 June 1970
- DATE LEFT PARLIAMENT: 1 May 1997. She has sat in the House of Lords since September 1997.
- PARTY ROLES: Member of the Hastings County Council 1960–61 and 1963–70
- MINISTERIAL POSITIONS & DATES: Deputy Speaker (Second Deputy Chairman of Ways and Means) 1992–97
- MOST FAMOUS QUOTATION: 'Are you starting a matrimonial agency, Mr Day?'

It is 1974 and Janet Evelyn Fookes, the newly elected Conservative MP for Merton and Morden, after a long and nervous wait, is interviewed on the BBC. She wants to talk about education reform but her interviewers, Cliff Michelmore and Robin Day, hardly discuss politics at all. Michelmore tells viewers: 'Miss Fookes is the most gorgeous redhead. Something you are missing if you're watching in black and white.'

Robin Day cuts in: 'May I talk to Mrs Fookes first?'

The new MP informs Mr Day that she is, in fact, 'Miss' Fookes.

Day insists that's only 'because no man has ever had the courage to ask', adding that this is 'a challenge to any bachelors in the House of Commons – perhaps one in particular, who knows?'

Fookes remains calm and professional; she tells Day she is particularly interested in the role of women in modern Britain and the law, and how it affects them adversely.

He asks if she is interested in music or sailing.

'Are you starting a matrimonial agency, Mr Day?' she retorts.

Today the interview seems blatantly sexist and patronising – it is cringe-worthy and has gone viral on the internet. But speaking in 2018, the now Baroness Fookes said the term sexist had not occurred to her at the time. 'I was just glad to get the interview over as it was the first national broadcast I had ever done. I was very nervous and was grateful to Robin Day for repri-manding the organisers for keeping me waiting so long.'

She says she never experienced overt sexism during her career and adds that, because of social media, women MPs have it tougher now than she did in the 1970s.

First elected in 1970, she was one of fewer than twenty female MPs in the Commons at that time. Almost fifty years later she still sits in Parliament, as a Deputy Speaker in the House of Lords.

She decided at an early age that she wanted to be an MP. Born in London, she grew up in St-Leonards-on-Sea, Sussex, and describes her childhood as happy. She recalls 'quite clearly' telling an interviewing board for Hastings High School for Girls that one day she hoped to be an MP. 'I was then aged eleven. I cannot tell you why this was so important to me, but it was.'

She was drawn to the Conservative Party as it seemed 'more practical in its approach of keeping what was good and changing only what was seen as bad'. Teachers told her not to vote Tory just because her parents told her to, but she insists this was never the case.

'My father was a trace cynical about the party – what I would call a re-luctant Conservative. My mother was more keen on the character of the individual candidate.'

Growing up, Janet Fookes had 'no idea about discrimination against women' and 'never experienced that assumption women couldn't do as much as men'. Her parents weren't particularly active in politics, but there was always political discussion in the house. She was influenced by her 'wonder-ful, very intelligent and witty' mother.

She says she was 'very lucky' in her early education thanks to 'excellent teachers' who encouraged public speaking and later a teaching career. Her biggest setback came when a headmistress advised her not to bother apply-ing to higher education because 'she did not have a university brain'. Later, though, she went to a private college and became a teacher and chair of the governors of the school.

Her long-term goal remained to become an MP, although she says 'sometimes, that seemed as remote as getting on the moon'. On the advice of 'a senior man in Conservative Central Office' she decided that local government was the best route into the Commons. In ten years she fought eight elections, won four and lost four, and came close to losing her Plymouth Drake seat in October 1974. It took five recounts before she was announced as the winner by thirty-four votes.

She recalls her first day in the House of Commons in June 1970 when she 'went in and bagged a desk in approved schoolgirl style' in an area that is now in the Strangers Bar. Back then it was for women only. Her early days in Parliament were 'excellent' and 'sexism free'. The few female MPs became friends. Women were more memorable due to their rarity. 'No one treated me nonchalantly,' she says. 'I was not the object of ridicule, nothing bad happened to me.'

She became a Deputy Speaker, only the third woman ever to take the role, and says she would have needed to be 'extraordinarily lucky' to become a minister. 'Many, many women have not made it, but I don't bewail what didn't happen.'

She introduced three significant Private Members' Bills. Her proudest piece of legislation was the Private Members' Bill that became the Sexual Offences Act, which outlawed kerb-crawling for the first time.

Introducing the Bill in the Commons in 1985, she said its overriding purpose was 'to afford far greater protection to women and girls'. She hoped to – and managed to – make men and women more equal before the law, because women were grossly under-protected by the existing legislation. In her Plymouth constituency residents were plagued 'by the activities of prostitutes on the street, with their pimps and ponces in the background, and by the development of the menace of what is usually called kerb-crawling'.

The bill, which became The Sexual Offences Act 1985, also increased the maximum sentence for attempted rape from seven years to life.

Other highlights included being the chair of sub-committees, in particular the expenditure committee dealing with prisons and education. 'We pinpointed flaws in the prison system and the education system which are still of concern to this day,' she says.

> I also enjoyed my time on the panel of chairmen chairing the committee stages of Bills and I did have one proud moment at the end of the British Nationality

Bill – later an Act – when it was customary for the minister and his opposite number to thank the chairman. Enoch Powell then rose and said he had never served under such a good chairman, which was amazing because I had at one point pointed out that he was not speaking to the amendment as he should have been.

Other highlights include her long-term work with the armed services.

'Some of my most vivid memories are of being winched up into a helicopter on Bodmin Moor, as well as coming down from one onto the deck of a moving ship, and weeks in the Arctic seeing the Royal Marines during their warfare training.'

Her proudest moment was when she became Deputy Speaker. She was only the second woman to hold the position of Second Deputy Chairman of Ways and Means, after Labour's Betty Boothroyd.

'I had certainly cherished ambitions of becoming Speaker,' she recalls, adding that 'it was a very interesting five years'.

As Deputy Speaker, she channelled her experience as a teacher; she was 'firm but fair' and dealt with some MPs like 'naughty school children'. The worst part of being Deputy Speaker was giving up her select committee work, one of her greatest passions as a parliamentarian.

In 1997, just before an influx of female MPs doubled the number of women in the Commons from sixty to 120, Janet Fookes decided not to stand for re-election. However, she was not ready for retirement, and a few months later she became a life peer. She still sits as Deputy Speaker in the Lords and has had as long-serving a parliamentary career as Ken Clarke, Father of the House of Commons.

Having worked with some of the best-known female politicians in history, Baroness Fookes says the greatest change that has happened to women in politics is that it is now accepted they can occupy top positions. Perhaps unexpectedly, she says she never experienced 'the kind of personal insults many women members now suffer, nor did I feel that male colleagues ever treated me differently because I am a woman'.

She suspects that as a chair of committees, and as a Deputy Speaker, men were more scared of her than she was of them. 'I don't recall any great change of mood in the Commons after Thatcher became leader,' she recalls, 'but she was Leader of the Opposition for several years so everyone had time to adjust before she became PM. I was personally very pleased to have a woman leader as it crashed firmly through a massive glass ceiling.'

JOAN HALL

LINDA MCDOUGALL

- FULL NAME: Joan Valerie Hall CBE
- DATE OF BIRTH: 31 August 1935
- PLACE OF BIRTH: Barnsley West Yorkshire
- DATE OF DEATH: –
- MARRIED TO: Unmarried
- CHILDREN: None
- UNSUCCESSFUL ELECTIONS FOUGHT: Barnsley 1964 and 1966
- CONSTITUENCY: Keighley
- DATE OF FIRST ELECTION: 18 June 1970
- DATE LEFT PARLIAMENT: 27 February 1974
- PARTY ROLES: Vice-chair of the London Young Conservatives
- MINISTERIAL POSITIONS & DATES: Parliamentary private secretary to the Minister of State Agriculture, Fisheries, Food 1972–74
- MOST FAMOUS QUOTATION: 'Like a great many people I am in favour of the common market economically speaking but am not at all happy about it politically speaking.'

Joan Hall made an important contribution to the advancement of women in politics, but not for anything she did in her single term as the Conservative MP for Keighley. She was a key figure along with Airey Neave and Sir Keith Joseph in Margaret Thatcher's campaign to become Tory leader.

Hall was born in Barnsley on 31 August 1935 and went as a boarder to Queen Margaret's School in York. In her further education she was already committed to the Conservative Party. She attended the Ashridge House of Citizenship, which was established in memory of Tory politician Bonar Law as a sort of right-wing equivalent to Labour's Fabian Society.

Joan's first appearance on the political stage was as the Conservative candidate for Barnsley in the 1964 general election. Labour's Roy Mason won 67 per cent of the vote. Joan Hall got 17 per cent.

In 1966 there was an important by-election in Hull North. Harvey Proctor, then a student at York University, wrote in his memoirs:

> I went to help twice at the Hull by-election. Toby Jessel who was later to become Tory MP for Twickenham was an energetic young candidate but Labour held on to the seat. I recall being fed sandwiches and bananas by Joan Hall who went on to be the MP for Keighley but then played the role of surrogate mother to the helpers who flocked to Hull almost bringing the place to a standstill. Inevitably political women have a big impact.

But in those days, not a big enough impact to be chosen for a safe seat. Harold Wilson called a general election immediately after Labour's victory in Hull, and Joan was back fighting Roy Mason in Barnsley. This time he won over 75 per cent of the vote, and she managed 24 per cent.

Like so many political women Joan's chance came when she was chosen for a marginal seat: Keighley. Elected in 1970, she beat the Labour incumbent John Binns by 616 votes. In her maiden speech she began by teaching southerners to pronounce her constituency 'keith lee' not 'Keely'. She said how proud she was to be the first ever female Conservative Member in Yorkshire but cautioned that she was not a militant suffragette.

Joan Hall was elected as the decline of the wool industry was underway. Family firms closed, the mills stood empty or were sold off and the cotton industry, which had also developed in Keighley, collapsed due in each case to competition from the Far East and from Prato in Italy. With them went textile engineering and machinery which were concentrated in Keighley.

Poverty and unemployment increased. The once bustling little town became a depressed area needing jobs, development and regional support. Joan Hall raised her concerns in Parliament not as a plea for government spending but to make ministers aware of the needs of the North and her constituency.

In a debate on the steel industry, Joan Hall spoke passionately about the situation in Keighley:

'Obviously it is not appreciated just how hard competition is in the textile industry. Yet firms in Keighley, for example, have not asked to be subsidised; they neither expect nor want to be subsidised. But such firms are no less important to the industrial and commercial life of the country than the steel industry.'

Joan Hall fought hard for Keighley and when the first election was called in 1974 it was felt she had a good chance of winning again:

'That she won at all is put down to her own personality. She worked as hard as she talks, non-stop, and did two per cent better than the national swing,' wrote *The Spectator*, who thought she would win again in 1974. But the new Labour candidate Bob Cryer just pipped her at the post with a majority of 878.

Jobless at thirty-five, Joan Hall must have wondered what she could do with the rest of her life but when Airey Neave asked her to 'help out' with Margaret Thatcher's campaign to become Tory leader, Joan, with the feisty efficiency for which she was becoming well known, became Thatcher's right-hand woman for the campaign. For just a few weeks Thatcher and Hall became the 'Thelma and Louise' of the British Conservative Party. Mrs Thatcher was driven everywhere on the campaign trail by Joan Hall in her Harvest Gold MGBGT.

On the night of her final victory when the celebrations were over Thatcher and Hall were accidentally locked in the House of Commons and had to be rescued.

In another bold move Joan Hall went off to New Zealand to work as assistant to Sir Robert Muldoon, the National Party (Conservative) Prime Minister. Just once she was the subject of a question in Parliament. In 1976 she had asked for time off to join Margaret Thatcher on a visit to Australia. Warren Freer, the Labour MP for Mt Albert, demanded to know if the New Zealand government was paying for Hall's travel and expenses. He was reassured that they were not.

Joan Hall came back to the UK after Prime Minister Muldoon was defeated and retired from politics. For many years she was a Member of the Council of the University of Buckingham.

Margaret Thatcher never forgot the key role Joan Hall had played in her career. In her 1990 resignation honours Hall was made CBE.

MARY HOLT

LINDA MCDOUGALL

- FULL NAME: Mary Holt
- DATE OF BIRTH: 31 July 1924
- PLACE OF BIRTH: Preston, Lancashire
- DATE OF DEATH: –
- MARRIED TO: Unmarried
- CHILDREN: None
- UNSUCCESSFUL ELECTIONS FOUGHT: Preston North October 1974
- CONSTITUENCY: Preston North
- DATE OF FIRST ELECTION: 18 June 1970
- DATE LEFT PARLIAMENT: 27 February 1974
- PARTY ROLES: None
- MINISTERIAL POSITIONS & DATES: None
- MOST FAMOUS QUOTATION: 'May I remind my right hon. Friend not to repeat the mistake of his predecessor in trying to give an imaginary name to the new town. The name Redrose was greeted with the utmost scorn and derision in Lancashire, the inhabitants of which are quite capable of providing their own postal address.' – On the search for a name for the new town of Preston/Leyland/Chorley.

O n 2 December 1970, Mary Holt, a 46-year-old barrister, rose to her feet in the House of Commons to make her maiden speech. She was the first female MP to be elected to Preston North.

Mary Holt, daughter of Preston solicitor Henry James Holt and his wife Sarah Holt (née Chapman), was educated at Park School in Preston and Girton College, Cambridge (MA LLB with First-class honours).

Upon her election she immediately became involved in the Courts Bill, which was to unite the County Palatine courts of Lancashire with the High Court nationwide. She was determined that this enlargement would improve the lot of women barristers like herself:

In some courts there is no separate cloakroom accommodation for women members of the Bar. I well remember going to Blackburn County Court, where the courtroom is like a stable and where there is no separate robing room for women advocates ... Now that the provision of this accommodation is to be in the hands of the Lord Chancellor, I look forward to seeing attractive robing rooms for women barristers.

In her comparatively short time in Parliament, Holt was also involved in the Domicile Bill, which fought for women to be free to have a different address from their husbands. Up until 1973, a woman's domicile had to be with her husband even if they lived apart and in different countries.

Mary Holt spoke powerfully in support of the Bill.

This bill can be described as one further step in the slow march of every woman towards obtaining equal rights with men in law ... The existing law, under which a woman automatically acquires on marriage the domicile of her husband, is a relic of the days when women were regarded as appendages of their husbands.

The Bill was passed successfully.

In a closely fought election in February 1974, Ronald Atkins, the Labour candidate, beat Holt by just 255 votes. She stood once more for the seat in the second 1974 general election in October, which again she lost narrowly.

Mary Holt returned to the bar and was made a circuit judge in Preston in 1977; she remained in the position until her retirement in 1995. Her Honour Judge Holt is still a Preston resident but has suffered ill health for several years.

DAME ELAINE
KELLETT-BOWMAN

CAT SMITH

- FULL NAME: Mary Elaine Kellett-Bowman (née Kay) DBE
- DATE OF BIRTH: 8 July 1923
- PLACE OF BIRTH: St Anne's, Lancashire
- DATE OF DEATH: 4 March 2014
- MARRIED TO: Charles Norman Kellett (d. 1959); Edward Bowman (m. 1971)
- CHILDREN: Three sons, one daughter and three stepsons and a stepdaughter
- UNSUCCESSFUL ELECTIONS FOUGHT: Nelson & Colne 1955, South West Norfolk 1959, Buckingham 1964 and 1966
- CONSTITUENCY: Lancaster 1970–97
- DATE OF FIRST ELECTION: 18 June 1970
- DATE LEFT PARLIAMENT: 11 May 1997
- MEP: Cumbria 1979–84
- PARTY ROLES: None
- MINISTERIAL POSITIONS & DATES: None
- MOST FAMOUS QUOTATION: 'I would shoot that man.' – Comment aimed at Dr Martin Cole after watching the film *Growing Up*.

Elaine Kellett-Bowman is still a name that means something to many Lancastrians, after all she was their outspoken MP for twenty-seven years and tends to divide opinion even now. I never met her myself; she retired at the 1997 election and at that point the teenage me had no interest in politics I'm ashamed to admit. Despite this I often wonder what would have happened had we met. Would we have found some common ground to agree on or are we just very different kinds of MPs?

It would be lazy to say that we would have nothing in common, and quite wrong. However, on the issues she's best known for, opposing the liberalisation of divorce laws, fierce opposition to abortion and gay rights, and generally being on the right wing of the Conservative Party, it's clear we take a different approach on these matters. Eighteen years after her retirement as Lancaster's first woman MP, they elected their second woman MP in myself, who has previously served on the national executive of Abortion Rights and is proud to be a patron of LGBT Labour. It's fair to say public opinion on these social issues shifted dramatically in the New Labour years.

So while we clearly have different political priorities, I do have respect for the woman that Elaine Kellett-Bowman was, the challenges she faced which would have defeated many others, and the work ethic she possessed which she seemed to maintain throughout her life.

Born and raised a Methodist, something which we have in common, she had a fierce work ethic which saw her study Modern Greats at St Anne's College in Oxford alongside Margaret Thatcher, although apparently at the time she did not know her classmate had an interest in politics! She stayed on at St Anne's, taking a postgraduate diploma in welfare, and went from university to practising social work in the East End of London, not a typical path of a would-be Conservative politician. She practised social work for a year before marrying her husband Charles Norman Kellett, a farmer in North Wales, where she relocated and at this point dropped the social work.

Despite moving to North Wales, starting a family and by all accounts being an active farmer's wife, she was elected as a Conservative councillor in Denbigh in 1952 and later that year, aged just twenty eight and a mother of three, was selected to fight the Nelson and Colne parliamentary constituency. This wasn't a seat the Conservatives were likely to gain at the 1955 general election but she halved the majority of the sitting Labour MP and this must have helped her gain a good reputation within her party as she was next chosen to fight the much more promising constituency of South West Norfolk, which had a Labour majority of just 193 votes.

The following set of events would at best frustrate and at worst cause despair to any aspiring politician. They say politics is as much about luck, but Elaine's luck wasn't in for the following set of events.

After the death of Sidney Dye, the Labour MP for South West Norfolk, there was a by-election in March 1959 where the heavily pregnant Kellett missed out by 1,354 votes. This must have been deeply frustrating but she had a second chance at the October 1959 general election, only to see the new Labour MP hold on by seventy-eight votes!

Then, as if 1959 hadn't been a tough enough year for Kellett, she and her husband were involved in a road accident, which resulted in his death. She was left widowed with four children and the accident affected her memory, having to learn even the basics of reading and writing again.

This would have been enough to crush most women, but not Kellett. She took over running the 149-acre farm and raising her four children single-handedly. But given advice to keep her brain active she ran the farm by day and by night read for the bar on a correspondence course, passing her finals in just nineteen months. She was called to the bar in 1964.

This was also the year she next stood for Parliament, this time losing out to Labour candidate Robert Maxwell in the Buckingham constituency by just 1,181 votes. However, always one to persist, she challenged Maxwell again in 1966, this time losing out by 2,254 votes.

Two years later she gave up the farm. Yes – remarkably she was still prac-tising law, running a farm and running for Parliament, and she moved to Hampstead to concentrate on her legal career. While in London she was also chair of the Welfare committee on Camden Council, yet despite this she was selected to be the Conservative candidate in the Lancaster constituency 233 miles to the north.

In the 1970 general election, at the sixth attempt, she was elected to serve as the Member of Parliament for Lancaster with a majority of 1,741 votes. It's hard to imagine how she must have felt after so many attempts to finally find herself on the green leather benches in Westminster, one of just fifteen women MPs on the Conservative side. She would go on to hold Lancaster for the Conservatives at every election until her retirement in 1997, with her majority peaking at 10,636 in 1983.

It is worth noting at this point that a year into being MP for Lancaster she married again, this time to Edward Bowman, and became step-mother to his three sons and one daughter. In what must have been an unusual move in 1971, both husband and wife adopted the name Kellett-Bowman.

Elaine Kellett-Bowman never held back in sharing her opinions and with the platform of being an MP started to make her mark by co-sponsoring a motion expressing concern at the liberalisation of divorce laws a month after being elected.

The incident which strikes me as most shocking, showing Kellett-Bowman's intolerance to LGBT people, happened in 1987 after the paper *Cap-ital Gay*'s offices were targeted in an arson attack. Hansard reports that Labour MP Tony Banks said, 'On a point of order, Mr Speaker. I heard the hon. Member for Lancaster say that it was quite right that *Capital Gay* should have been fired.' In reply Mrs Kellett-Bowman said, 'I am quite prepared to affirm that it is quite right that there should be an intolerance of evil.' She would oppose any liberalisation of homophobic laws throughout her time as MP.

Outside the domestic sphere, Kellett-Bowman was also elected to serve as an MEP for Cumbria (a constituency not contiguous with her Lancaster one) from 1979 until 1984, which she did alongside being an MP in Westminster. While it's highly usual for a sitting MP to contest election to another legislature while serving on one with no intention of standing down, it doesn't seem to have damaged her reputation in Lancaster, where she would enjoy her biggest majority. Although she did only serve one term as an MEP, it was alongside her husband Edward Kellett-Bowman; they were the first husband and wife duo to serve alongside one another in the European Parliament.

For a politician so obviously able and bright, it surprises me that Kellett-Bowman spent twenty-seven years on the back benches. I wonder if this was due to her being outspoken, never quite trusted for the diplomacy needed to be a frontbencher. She was clear in her own mind of her own opinions on matters, and she was a moralist in what she pursued politically. Although we would never have seen eye to eye on the 'moral issues', I respect that she would rebel against her own party when it came to cutting child benefit and she recognised the support that families needed.

Shortly after I was elected in 2015 an older gay man commented to me about the remarkable change in his MP from eighteen years previous. He'd written to Kellett-Bowman on many occasions calling on her to support liberalisation on homophobic laws and had always had letters back, disagreeing with him. He commented that Kellett-Bowman would be turning in her grave to see me as the MP for Lancaster (and Fleetwood) but I'd disagree. I doubt Kellett-Bowman would agree with my opinion on very much, although we are both Methodists, but she would probably have a grudging respect for one of my first acts as an MP, nominating the leader I wanted to see in the Labour Party even though everyone told me Jeremy Corbyn couldn't get on the ballot paper!

I too have a grudging respect for a woman who said what she believed in even though it wasn't popular at the time and looks increasingly dated in the historical context. She overcame huge personal challenges and had a work ethic which made Thatcher look like she got too much sleep every night. She had to fight time and time again to get the political platform she eventually found as MP for Lancaster and endured so many close elections it would have been enough to make weaker souls falter. Who says dogged determination can't get you there in the end? It certainly did for Elaine Kellett-Bowman.

CONSTANCE MONKS

LINDA MCDOUGALL

- FULL NAME: Constance Mary Monks (née Green) OBE
- DATE OF BIRTH: 20 May 1911
- PLACE OF BIRTH: Chorley, Lancashire
- DATE OF DEATH: 4 February 1989
- MARRIED TO: Jack Monks (m. 1937)
- CHILDREN: One son
- UNSUCCESSFUL ELECTIONS FOUGHT: Chorley 1966
- CONSTITUENCY: Chorley
- DATE OF FIRST ELECTION: 18 June 1970
- DATE LEFT PARLIAMENT: 27 February 1974
- PARTY ROLES: None
- MINISTERIAL POSITIONS & DATES: None

Connie Monks was a Chorley woman through and through. She lived in the town all her life save for her student years, which were spent studying at a teacher training college in Leeds.

Born Constance Green, Monks was the daughter of Ellis Green, an education clerk, and his wife, Bessie Burwell, whose father had been the first chairman of Chorley Rural District Council. Monks attended Wheelton County School, where she was a promising and hard-working student. She then won a scholarship to Chorley Grammar School, where she excelled at sport and became head girl. It was as a teenager that she joined the Conservative Party.

Monks began her teaching career at Coppull Moor Church of England School. She also worked hard to promote the Conservative Party. She had co-founded a branch of the Young Conservatives in Chorley and went on to become secretary of the North West Conservative Association.

On 11 May 1937, Monks married Jack Monks, a Chorley grocer. During the Second World War, Monks continued to teach while Jack joined the RAF. When Jack came home, they opened a newsagent and tobacconist's shop in Chorley and, in November 1947, Monks was elected to Chorley Borough Council. She went on to serve on every council committee and almost every public organisation in Chorley. She was a governor of ten local schools and from 1954 she was a magistrate. In 1959, she became Mayor of Chorley and from 1961 to '64, she served on Lancashire County Council. She was also the chair of the Conservative Women's Advisory Committee for Lancashire, Cheshire and Westmorland. In 1962, she was awarded an OBE for her work.

In 1965, at her second attempt, Constance Monks was selected as the Conservative parliamentary candidate for Chorley, but she failed to win the seat in the 1966 election. She would have to wait another four years for victory. In the 1970 election, with a majority of 1,677, she became Chorley's first Conservative MP since 1945 and Chorley's first-ever female MP. That year, seven new Tory women were elected to Parliament; Labour languished with just one.

Monks's strong ties to her constituency were unusual for an MP at that time. MPs across the political spectrum tended to be men who lived in London and nipped down to the constituency a couple of times a month. Constance Monks hoped that her local activities would demonstrate democracy at its best and combat public cynicism about politics. Her visits home every weekend were successfully combined with excellent parliamentary attendance, but she was a shy woman and in the brief four years she was at Westminster she spoke little. As a campaigner she preferred door-to-door canvassing rather than addressing meetings.

In the March 1974 election, Chorley was a very marginal seat, and leading figures from the major parties campaigned there. Monks was beaten by just over 400 votes. She declined to stand again, choosing instead to spend more time with her husband.

In the 1974 local government reforms, Chorley Borough Council was replaced by a new body and Constance Monks stood down from the council after 27-years membership. Her husband died not long afterwards and this, combined with the earlier loss of her son, dulled much of her spark.

Although Monks did not make a major impact during her brief time at Westminster, she was devoted to Chorley and her community. Sadly, even there her contributions faded from public memory, as the market town she knew and loved became part of the Central Lancashire new town.

After a long battle with illness, Constance Monks died of kidney failure and dementia in Chorley and South Ribble District Hospital on 4 February 1989. She was buried in Chorley cemetery.

SALLY OPPENHEIM-BARNES

JO-ANNE NADLER

- FULL NAME: Sarah (Sally) Oppenheim-Barnes (née Viner)
- DATE OF BIRTH: 26 July 1928
- PLACE OF BIRTH: Dublin
- DATE OF DEATH: —
- MARRIED TO: Henry Oppenheim (m. 1949; d. 1980); John Barnes (m. 1984; d. 2004)
- CHILDREN: One son (Philip) and two daughters
- UNSUCCESSFUL ELECTIONS FOUGHT: None
- CONSTITUENCY: Gloucester
- DATE OF FIRST ELECTION: 18 June 1970
- DATE LEFT PARLIAMENT: 18 May 1987
- PARTY ROLES: None
- MINISTERIAL POSITIONS & DATES: Minister for Consumer Affairs 1979–82
- MOST FAMOUS QUOTATION: 'The traditional figures of revolution, Rousseau, Karl Marx, Lenin and others, were no great emancipators of women and were themselves chauvinists. They left their wives slaving over a hot stove.'

If Sally Oppenheim had made no further contribution to the Conservative Party story other than appearing in the right place at the right time on a certain historic day in 1975, she would still have earned her place in Tory folklore. When Margaret Thatcher emerged from a mass meeting of her party at the Europa Hotel on 2 February 1975, she did so as its newly confirmed leader. How big a radical departure this was for the party, and indeed for Britain, would become more evident in the next few decades. At that moment, though, it already seemed to be a seismic event.

Thatcher had just become the first female leader of a British political party, a woman with a prescription for curing Britain's ills that conflicted not only with the moribund socialism of the Callaghan government, but also with the views of many of her own Tory colleagues. Not, though, with those of Sally Oppenheim, whose presence in the photo marking Thatcher's accession denoted her explicit approval of the new leader. Unlike others in the picture, with whom she was soon to be appointed (as the only other woman) to Thatcher's first shadow Cabinet, Oppenheim had actually voted for the new leader in both ballots.

The famous photograph shows the blonde Thatcher in a chic, white suit flanked by male colleagues who are garbed in regulation dark grey. Whether by accident or design Oppenheim, on the edge of the picture, is also wearing a dark suit, ensuring she takes none of the focus off the star player that day. But to be included in the picture at all, a second female Conservative Party politician, similarly immaculately dressed, was a measure of Oppenheim's own significant contribution to the cause of women in politics. As was the case with Margaret Thatcher, Oppenheim's feminism never came spelled out with a capital 'F'. Rather it rested on strong female role models, women who did not consider their gender a bar to success in what was still very much a man's world.

Sally Oppenheim (now Baroness Sally Oppenheim-Barnes) was born in Ireland in 1928 named Sarah Viner, to non-practising, Jewish parents. The threesome soon moved to Wales and then to Sheffield, where the wider Viner family's cutlery and silverware business was already well established. It was the right place for Sally's father to practise his profession of diamond cutting. Politics were not a feature of her home life, yet growing up during the war seems to have had a significant political impact on the young Sally, who considered herself a Conservative from childhood and cried when Churchill lost the general election in 1945.

Friends of Oppenheim have often referred to her glamour as being a notable feature of her character. The word 'glamour' seems to denote more than her evident sartorial panache, it infers that Oppenheim was also a compelling personality. Perhaps it is not surprising, then, that her first ambition was to become an actress. She studied for three years at London's Royal Academy of Dramatic Arts, but an early marriage to Henry Oppenheim, and then motherhood to three children while she was in her twenties, disrupted her acting plans.

An alternative passion, this one for politics, soon emerged. It proved a suitable pursuit for the gregarious Sally, whose husband had become a prominent organiser of Finchley Conservative Association, which in 1958 adopted one Margaret Thatcher as its election candidate.

Although Sally's Judaism has never been a key feature of her political identity, she and her husband would have felt perfectly at home in the Finchley Conservative milieu. Spurred on, Oppenheim sought advice from the

Conservative candidates' department, which recommended that in order to be chosen as a general election candidate, she would need to demonstrate a broad understanding of contemporary issues. Taking this message to heart, the now well-to-do Oppenheim became a social worker in Hackney, where she spent three years assisting new immigrants with health matters. It was an experience she would draw on later when she became an MP, and also in more recent years, during debates in the House of Lords.

Harold Wilson was in his second term as Prime Minister when, in 1967, Oppenheim applied to become the Conservative Party candidate for the Labour-held seat of Gloucester. Unsurprisingly, she was the only woman on the selection panel's shortlist. According to a contemporary who remembers the selection meeting, Oppenheim won because she was 'head and shoulders' above the male competition.

Oppenheim threw herself into campaigning and became a prominent local figure, establishing strong connections with groups across the constituency. She was frequently seen in the city centre with her shopping basket, a motif which affected the common touch and made her an obvious choice for the consumer affairs brief.

In the run-up to the general election of 1970, Oppenheim and her team successfully raised her profile and ensured there was a sea of blue posters across the town. Indeed, visitors from Gloucester's German twin town of Trier expressed disappointment at being greeted at a civic reception by Gloucester's MP and Treasury minister, Jack Diamond. They had wanted to meet the 'Sally' they had read so much about. At the 1970 election, Oppenheim narrowly captured Gloucester for the Tories. Her Labour opponent Jack Diamond became the only Cabinet minister to lose a seat.

The men Oppenheim had beaten at her selection meeting had found themselves challenged by the extent of her political convictions. She also proved a challenge for party whip Kenneth Clarke during the run-up to Edward Heath's critical vote on joining the common market. Despite the efforts of the young Clarke, Oppenheim was, to Heath's fury, among the minority of MPs who voted against the European Communities Act in 1972. She has since described herself as the first of Kenneth Clarke's 'difficult women'.

In spite of, or perhaps because she was 'difficult', Oppenheim graduated from shadowing the consumer affairs brief to handling the portfolio as a minister when Thatcher became Prime Minister in 1979. Regardless of her shopping basket chumminess, Oppenheim was no apologist for financial success. She once notoriously commented that she was 'relieved' by the sight of a

Rolls-Royce, as the flaunting of wealth would stimulate a 'trickling-down' into the pockets of humbler folk. What such folk could afford became a political weathervane, with Oppenheim's own formula for the cost of a family Christmas used by *The Times* as one indicator of inflation. When first calculated, in 1973, Oppenheim's average family Christmas shopping basket cost just less than £35. Thirty years later the same selection had multiplied in price tenfold.

Given their political empathy and personal acquaintance, it might seem surprising that Oppenheim never made it into Thatcher's Cabinet. While critics could seize on this as evidence of Thatcher's 'Queen Bee' syndrome, or perhaps Oppenheim's lack of ability, the determining factor was actually a family-related one.

The Thatcher premiership was still in its infancy when Sally's husband Henry died prematurely in 1980. That same year she was responsible for piloting the Competition Act through the Commons. The combined pressures of ministerial work and a busy constituency outside London caused the widowed Oppenheim to resign from her department in 1982. In the following year her son, Philip, was elected to Parliament for Amber Valley and they became the first mother and son to sit in the House at the same time until Oppenheim, who married John Barnes in 1984, stood down at the 1987 general election. She had spent seventeen years as an MP and had proved herself a redoubtable campaigner, with a style and flourish that matched the buccaneering spirit of Thatcherism.

Speaking in a BBC programme about feminism that coincided with the passage of sex-discrimination legislation of the early 1970s, Oppenheim clashed with a feminist academic who wanted fundamental change. Oppenheim argued for improving the lot of women without changing the nature of womanhood. Much as did Margaret Thatcher, Oppenheim never considered herself discriminated against by male colleagues, perhaps privately considering that in any case women are the tougher sex.

She became Baroness Oppenheim-Barnes of Gloucester in 1989. She reprised her own 'difficult woman' routine in a speech to the House of Lords during the European Withdrawal Bill of 2017. Describing herself as the only living Conservative in Parliament who had voted against joining the EU 'in the first place', Oppenheim explained that her antipathy to the institution had only increased as its scope had grown. But the self-proclaimed difficult woman, when it came to the EU at least, was not too invulnerable to admit that she will have a 'small tear in one eye' when Britain finally leaves Europe.

BETTY BOOTHROYD

NUSRAT GHANI

- FULL NAME: Betty Boothroyd, Baroness Boothroyd
- DATE OF BIRTH: 8 October 1929
- PLACE OF BIRTH: Dewsbury, Yorkshire
- DATE OF DEATH: –
- MARRIED TO: Unmarried
- CHILDREN: None
- UNSUCCESSFUL ELECTIONS FOUGHT: Leicester South East 1957, Peterborough 1959, Nelson & Colne 1968 and Rossendale 1970
- CONSTITUENCY: West Bromwich 1973–74 and West Bromwich West 1974–2000
- DATE OF FIRST ELECTION: 24 May 1973
- DATE LEFT PARLIAMENT: 23 October 2000. Since 2000, she has sat in the Lords as Baroness Boothroyd.
- MEP: 1975–77
- PARTY ROLES: Secretary to Barbara Castle MP and Geoffrey de Freitas MP; researcher in Labour HQ Research Department; member of National Executive Committee 1981–87
- MINISTERIAL POSITIONS & DATES: Assistant whip 1974–75; Deputy Speaker of the House of Commons 1987–92; Speaker of the House of Commons 1992–2000
- MOST FAMOUS QUOTATIONS: 'Call me Madam!' | 'Time's up' | 'You've got to ensure that the holders of an opinion, however unpopular, are allowed to put across their points of view.'

'Elect me for what I am, not for what I was born.' So said Betty Boothroyd during her historic and momentous campaign to become the first female Speaker of the House of Commons in 1992. Baroness Boothroyd's determination to be judged purely on ability and character, rather than on background, family or, of course, her gender, epitomises her approach to life and her political career.

As the Member of Parliament for West Bromwich and then West Bromwich West between 1973 and 2000, and as Speaker of the House of Commons from 1992 to 2000, Boothroyd's career on the green benches was remarkable, unique and exemplary but above all, inspirational.

I recall first meeting Boothroyd as a newly elected MP in the House of Commons tea room, and her gently chiding me for saying that she had been one of my inspirations growing up. Seeing her in Parliament made me realise that it was possible for a woman like me to aspire to public office, despite coming from a background where the very idea seemed a pipe dream. Boothroyd has never forgotten her roots, so the thought of being seen as an inspirational figure doesn't necessarily sit easily with her – but that only makes her even more admirable.

Boothroyd is a Labour stalwart, someone who, in her own words, 'came out of the womb of the Labour movement'. As an MP, she spent almost two decades fighting Conservative governments on every imaginable front, and prior to joining the Commons she was an activist and a researcher with the Labour Party. And yet to me, and to so many people of all political persuasions, Betty Boothroyd is an inspiration, a role model and a friend – as she once said, 'You've got to ensure that the holders of an opinion, however unpopular, are allowed to put across their points of view.'

It is difficult to find heavyweight political figures from the post-Thatcher era that genuinely changed the political weather and challenged the status quo through the politics of ideas and values, not the politics of politics. But it is Boothroyd's election as Speaker of the House of Commons that has cemented her place in history.

She was the first female Speaker in the role's 700-year history. Her predecessors were grandees and aristocrats – in other words, privileged men. Indeed, she had to fight against this centuries-old bias in her campaign for election as Speaker. Her main opponent for the role was Peter Brooke MP (now Lord Brooke), who had just left John Major's Cabinet. The son of a former Home Secretary and a descendant of Sir Robert Brooke, who coincidentally had served as Speaker in the mid-sixteenth century, to many in the Commons at the time, Peter Brooke was another typical candidate for the position.

By contrast, Boothroyd's background was altogether more humble. Born in the industrial town of Dewsbury in Yorkshire in 1929, and educated at local state schools, she was the daughter of two textile workers who both worked long hours. The depression of the late 1920s and early 1930s affected her family and Boothroyd's upbringing was tough. Not only was her mother, Mary, responsible for running the household, she also worked full time at the woollen mill. Boothroyd has recalled how her mother used to say to her, 'You know, I am not employed for my sex appeal. I'm employed because my rate of pay is lower than that of your father's. That is the only reason.'

As a child, Boothroyd dedicated much of her free time to dancing, specifically tap and ballet. It was Betty's dance teacher who first recognised that her strong, powerful voice was an asset – this discovery led to Boothroyd being given the principal male role in three school plays. As a teenager, she joined a high-kicking dance troupe known as the Tiller Girls, entertaining audiences packed full of men. Even as a young woman Boothroyd was formidable; she was in charge of her own destiny and took no flak from men. Half a century later, she would become famous for her powerful and distinctive voice and turn of phrase.

Few politicians have had such a tangible impact on life in Westminster as Betty Boothroyd. As the first female Prime Minister, Margaret Thatcher unquestionably showed that women could do the top job every bit as well as men. Yet in 1992, when Boothroyd was elected as Speaker, politics, especially within Parliament, was still very much a man's world.

When Betty was first elected to the House of Commons in a 1973 by-election in West Bromwich, she was just one of twenty-seven female MPs in the House of Commons – and one of only eleven in the Labour Party. In the 1950s, when she first considered putting herself forward for selection as a parliamentary candidate, Boothroyd was told by a party grandee that she was 'too young and needed to get some age on her shoulders'.

After some research into the demographics of the parliamentary Labour Party, Betty found it to be dominated, unsurprisingly, by old male trade union officials. By definition, most (winnable) parliamentary seats were out of the question for her, as their selections were sponsored by the unions and she, as a woman, would not be considered.

So favoured were male candidates in the early 1950s that even working as a secretary for the formidable Barbara Castle did not help Boothroyd win a selection contest. Castle failed to support Betty's bid to have her name included on the list of candidates that would be circulated to Constituency Labour Parties across the country. Castle judged that Labour's national agent, Len Williams, 'wouldn't have it and [she] didn't want to push it'. Sexism was a clear obstacle for women, but Betty Boothroyd was determined not to let it stand in her way.

Eventually, her determination and perseverance won over the Labour Party officials and she was selected to contest the 1957 by-election for Leicester South East, a seat which lay deep in the Tory heartlands. The *Leicester Evening Mail* welcomed her selection, describing her as a 'Yorkshire lass of twenty-six chosen to oppose a Tory', before going on to describe, in some detail, her figure and appearance.

Her first parliamentary contest ended in defeat. Boothroyd's relentlessness in the face of adversity would be tested over the next two decades. It is not uncommon for MPs to have fought and lost elections before finally winning a seat, in fact, it is almost expected. I stood unsuccessfully in the safe Labour seat of Birmingham Ladywood in 2010, before being elected MP for Wealden five years later – but Betty's persistence was admirable. She contested, and ultimately lost, four parliamentary elections.

It is a testament to her character and determination that she fought the West Bromwich by-election in 1973 with the same vigour, excitement and energy as she had her very first contest fifteen years earlier. She won the seat with a majority of 8,325.

Once in Parliament, it was always going to be impossible to curb Betty's infectious personality, or to dullen her campaigning spirit and robust mind. She spent just eighteen months on the back benches and then, after the October 1974 general election, she joined the Whips' Office.

As an assistant whip, I have had first-hand experience of the Whips' Office, and what I can say is that it's not a place where you can show weakness, nor was it then perceived as a place for women. Whips were the first to arrive, and the last to leave, often with votes running until the early hours of the morning. Betty's 'flock' consisted of thirty-two Birmingham and West Midlands MPs. Even after the 1974 elections she was still just one of eighteen female Labour MPs, and now she was in charge of ensuring discipline and order from a large group of men. An excellent training ground for her later career, perhaps.

Internal party strife would dominate much of the next decade and a half. In her early career, Boothroyd had worked for two Labour MPs – resolute left-winger Barbara Castle and the moderate Geoffrey de Freitas. Betty personally swayed towards the more centrist side of the Labour Party and had spent time working for the Democrats during John F. Kennedy's presidential campaign. Her hostility towards hard-left factions in Labour would, almost, come back to bite her as the party imploded while in opposition during the 1980s. Boothroyd survived a deselection attempt by left-wingers in her constituency committee, just holding on by two votes – something today's Labour crop might do well to remember.

Betty Boothroyd had been born into Labour and she was Labour through and through. While she never agreed with the Gang of Four's actions in setting up the SDP, it is easy to see why she felt it possible to distance herself from the partisan politics of the front and back benches. She was soon asked to serve as a Deputy Speaker to the venerable Bernard Weatherill in 1987. Though she could keep her party affiliation as a deputy, this marked the beginning of the end of her career as a Labour politician.

'Call me Madam,' Boothroyd told confused MPs on her first appearance as a Deputy Speaker, laying the precedence for addressing female Speakers. While politics was still very much a man's game back then, and still is now to a lesser extent, this marked a step change in addressing the historic imbalance and bias in favour of men that this most ancient of parliaments had been consumed by for hundreds of years.

Betty's election as Speaker, following the 1992 general election, was extraordinary for more than just creating the first female Speaker. Throughout the twentieth century, the Tories, as the natural party of government, had dominated the Speakership, accounting for seven of eleven twentieth-century Speakers. Just two of those eleven had come from Labour, both elected when Labour was in power. As she writes in her autobiography, 'for a Tory Parliament to put a Labour nominee in the chair was as unprecedented as electing a woman'. Betty became the first Speaker to come from the Labour Party when Labour was not in government, winning the support of 134 more MPs than her opponent – significantly larger than the majority John Major's government had just been re-elected with.

Her time as Speaker was filled with parliamentary drama, controversies and embarrassment. The 1992 Parliament would have been difficult for any Speaker to control. As Speaker, it was Boothroyd's job to protect the reputation of the House of Commons and ensure that all parties were represented fairly in the Chamber, and that the executive was properly and fairly held to account. To an outsider it may look like Parliament is a raucous bear-pit, but today's goings-on are positively civil compared with the tooth-and-claw parliamentary back and forth of Betty's period.

Early on in her time as Speaker she dealt with rebellious Scottish MPs protesting in front of the mace, and with the resignation of a government minister that came dangerously close to breaking the House's self-imposed rule of *sub-judice* that prevents the Commons from interfering with the courts.

She also faced off with Labour MP Ann Clwyd, who repeatedly parked her car in the Speaker's reserved parking space – if Clwyd parked there again, she would find she wouldn't be able to get her car out, Boothroyd warned. Publicly or privately, Betty would not allow her authority to be questioned.

Her command of the Chamber was enviable; from the infamous subtle yawns she would deploy to hint that an MP should probably wrap things up, to cutting off the microphone of Ann Widdecombe to restore quiet. Unceremoniously Boothroyd would cut Question Time short with a sharp and distinctive 'Time's up!' whether MPs had finished speaking or not. Her firm Yorkshire tones were even able to control an obstinate Dennis Skinner. The new Speaker became famous for her brutal put-downs, unwilling to take anything unparliamentary from the floor.

Outside Parliament, Boothroyd has lived a life of adventure and daring. She explored the far reaches of the globe, and even took part in paragliding. When Lembit Opik, the former Liberal Democrat MP, suffered a horrific paragliding accident, it is said that upon his return to Parliament he received a note from Betty with well wishes, informing him that she, too, enjoyed paragliding.

In his congratulatory speech after Boothroyd's election as Speaker, John Major described her election as a 'House of Commons occasion'. Betty, characteristically self-aware, knew she had been elected with large swathes of support from the party she had spent almost her entire life fighting. She has since revealed in interviews with the BBC that this was at the forefront of her mind: she could not let the House of Commons down, she could not let democracy down, and she certainly could not let womankind down.

'Having a bad woman Speaker would be disastrous. It would be a tragedy for this House, and it would be bad for the country, and it would be bad for the cause of women everywhere,' she lamented in her speech to the Commons as it voted for its next Speaker. As is the case with the rest of her life, Betty Boothroyd's time in the Chair met and exceeded all the wildest possible expectations. She furthered the cause for women not just in the House of Commons, but across the country, too.

She continues to leave her mark on Parliament from the House of Lords today. Hers is a remarkable story. When she began her political career, women were barely visible in leadership positions. We did not hold positions of power in the House of Commons or in company boardrooms; nor did we feature on the covers of glossy magazines or head up TV shows. Boothroyd defied her working-class expectations and managed one of the oldest, grandest and most peculiar legislative chambers in the world.

Her story isn't one about a woman of privilege, with a ready-made network and a high-flying mum and dad. It is one of determination and conviction, persistence and courage. She was an inspiration to so many at the time. And she continues to be an inspiration to so many of us now.

For the first time in history, Parliament Square is now adorned by a statue of a woman; Millicent Fawcett has rightly taken her place there, her statue commemorating the courage and dedication of suffragists and suffragettes a century ago. I hope that one day we will also commemorate the contribution of the first female Speaker, a woman who, together with Margaret Thatcher, showed the next generation of female leaders that a woman's place was in fact in the House of Commons.

When I suggested recently on TV that Betty Boothroyd was deserving of a statue, I received my second ticking off from her. Not I suspect this time because she doesn't appreciate why she has left her mark on me and so many of my colleagues, but because I am certain she feels she has much more to contribute before such a tribute is necessary. I have no doubt that when the right time comes, Betty will be honoured as the expectation-defying inspiration that she is.

MARGO MACDONALD

JOANNA CHERRY

- FULL NAME: Margo Symington MacDonald (née Aitken)
- DATE OF BIRTH: 19 April 1943
- PLACE OF BIRTH: Hamilton, South Lanarkshire
- DATE OF DEATH: 4 April 2014
- MARRIED TO: Peter MacDonald (m. 1965; div. 1980); Jim Sillars (m. 1981)
- CHILDREN: Petra MacDonald and Zoe MacDonald
- UNSUCCESSFUL ELECTIONS FOUGHT: Glasgow Govan October 1974; Hamilton 1978 (by-election); and Glasgow Shettleston 1979
- CONSTITUENCY: Glasgow Govan
- DATE OF FIRST ELECTION: 8 November 1973
- DATE LEFT PARLIAMENT: 28 February 1974
- MSP: Lothian 1999–2014
- PARTY ROLES: Depute leader of the SNP 1974–79
- MINISTERIAL POSITIONS & DATES: None

On the night of 8 November 1973, Margo MacDonald won the Glasgow Govan by-election in a blaze of glory. She was only thirty years old – blonde, beautiful, intelligent and very feisty. The seat had been a Labour stronghold for as long as anyone could remember and the newspapers described 'scenes of near hysteria' as her supporters celebrated. A few months later, she failed to hold the seat in the first of two 1974 general elections but she went on to become depute leader of the SNP from 1974 to 1979.

Her famous Govan victory presaged the election of eleven SNP MPs in 1974, with a third of Scottish voters choosing to support the party. This was a result which rocked the British establishment to the core, at a time when the advent of the SNP as the natural party of government in a devolved Scotland could never have been imagined,

I did not know Margo, but I remember as a child seeing her as a glamorous figure and one who indicated what women could achieve in politics.

She was a rebel who rarely toed the party line. But she was also a bit of a prophetess, as it was she who urged the SNP to move to the left to win seats in Labour's heartlands. A theory that was put into practice under the leadership of Alex Salmond in the 1990s, but only after a pretty major hiccup in the SNP's history, which led to Margo resigning from the party in 1982 after leading left-wingers, including Alex Salmond, were expelled for their membership of the socialist 79 Group.

In 1981, MacDonald married her second husband, Jim Sillars, a former Labour MP and the founder of the Scottish Labour Party (SLP). He went on to join the SNP and in 1988 won Govan in another by-election, following in the footsteps of his wife, who had won the seat fifteen years earlier. This, too, proved a turning point in nationalist history. Two years later, Alex Salmond became leader of the party and led it to a series of historic victories.

In the years before devolution, Margo forged a successful career in broadcasting and journalism, before returning as an SNP MSP for Lothian in the first elections to the devolved Scottish Parliament in 1999. Undoubtedly, she brought colour and style to the new Parliament with her lively and intelligent contributions to debate and the warmth and wit of her personality, as well as her flamboyant fashion sense.

In 2003, she announced she would stand as an independent candidate after being ranked low on the Lothian regional list, effectively deselecting her. She was subsequently expelled from the SNP. She stood as an independent and won, which was a testament to her public image and the genuine respect and affection people had for her. At that time her six-year-old diagnosis with Parkinson's became public knowledge. She continued to work hard for her constituents as an independent MSP until her death; winning an unprecedented two further elections as an independent. She will be remembered in particular for her campaign for assisted dying.

She died on 4 April 2014, aged seventy, less than six months before the independence referendum that would come to change the face of Scottish politics for ever – independence, which Margo had fought for all her adult life, had been within reach. It was a tragedy that she did not live to experience the last, heady six months of the indyref campaign, which would never have happened without her early contributions.

Margo's fortitude in the face of a debilitating illness and her steadfast determination will be an inspiration to many in the independence movement for years to come. Perhaps the best tribute to her came from her erstwhile friend and sometime adversary, Alex Salmond, who said,

Margo MacDonald was one of the great rallying figures of Scottish nationalism. From her Govan by-election victory in 1973, she had a profound role in
Scotland's home rule journey. Very few politicians are recognised and known
to the public by their first name – Margo was. Even fewer have the profile and
talent to be elected comprehensively as an independent candidate – Margo had.

In the week before her death, Alex visited her to talk tactics on the independence referendum. He said, 'Despite great physical infirmity, she dispensed
wise advice and her enthusiasm and commitment to the independence cause
was bright and undimmed.' She remains an inspiration to many in the nationalist movement, particularly women.

In the weeks after her death, she was commemorated at a special session
of the Scottish Parliament and at a moving celebration of her life at the Assembly Hall on the Mound in Edinburgh, which I was privileged to attend.

LYNDA CHALKER

ESTHER MCVEY

Growing up on Merseyside in the 1970s there were few Conservative role models, and even fewer female ones. It was a time of political uncertainty. Industrial relations between the government and the UK's trade unions soured, while the war between the Arabs and Israelis saw the price of oil rocket, damaging an already frail UK economy. Miners rejected a 13 per cent pay rise and went on strike. It felt as if the country wanted change, and Lynda Chalker was just the breath of fresh air the Wirral needed. As the first and only female Conservative MP for the area, her political career would always be one of firsts. But few predicted that this thirty-something would not only act as a role model for young girls growing up on the Wirral, but would help to change the lives of communities across the world.

Born on 29 April 1942 to the late Sidney Bates and Marjorie Randell, the then Lynda Bates was educated at Roedean School in Sussex, where she became head girl – the first early indication of her talent. She went on to study at Heidelberg University and Central London Polytechnic, and then spent time working in market research and as a statistician. She was the first female chair of Greater London's Young Conservatives before entering Parliament in 1974 as MP for Wallasey.

She was a popular and respected constituency MP from the start, but local association members were shocked that a woman had even made the candidate shortlist. The gender divide was still very real despite it being more than fifty-five years since the first female MP entered Parliament. Members of Wallasey Conservative Association told me that Lynda had been up against a strong panel of other applicants, but her refreshing view of politics and new vision won the members over. Her first hurdle behind her, she proceeded to win the seat and the rest is history. She wanted to make a difference and she knew she was now in the place to make that happen.

Any new MP will tell you that speaking in the Commons is daunting, and almost all MPs are nervous about their maiden speech, knowing that every word they say is going to be scrutinised and will be a matter of public record. There is no room for error. Perhaps Lynda had become used to public speaking during her time as head girl at school, or maybe she genuinely was not concerned about what people thought about her – whatever the reason she showed she was no shrinking violet.

It was obvious from her fourteen-minute maiden speech that this was someone who was going to be a force to be reckoned with. She was passionate about helping people, would speak her mind and was what people would call a 'glass half-full' person. She was a problem solver, not a problem maker. She made the expected reference to her predecessor before launching a series of demands, followed by suggestions. Less than a minute into her speech she was suggesting that more money was needed to help disabled people, pointing out that everyone had a duty to help. And so she continued. She wanted the tricycles that were given to disabled people, which she called 'little wobbly blue things', to be replaced with proper four-wheeled vehicles allowing people to have a quality of life. She demanded a toy library, so that parents of disabled children could see what was best for their child before spending large amounts of money on items, and she called for the Transport Minister to look at introducing slopes on the pavement to improve accessibility. Her suggestions kept flowing. It was obvious that she was talented and that she had done her homework. She knew the figures, she had the information and she had the solutions. She had exactly what would later make her a great minister – attention to detail.

Lynda's parliamentary career spanned four government departments. Entering Parliament in 1974, she was appointed as a shadow spokesperson for Health and Social Security in 1976. After the 1979 general election, when Margaret Thatcher led the Conservative Party to victory, Lynda was made Parliamentary Under-Secretary at the Department of Health and Social Security, serving from 1979 to 1982. She became Parliamentary Under-Secretary in the Department for Transport from 1982 to 1983, before being promoted to Minister for Transport, a post she remained in until 1986.

In January 1986, she became Minister for the Foreign and Commonwealth Office, concentrating for more than three years on Europe and the Commonwealth, and served as Minister for Africa all through to 1997, as well as becoming Minister for Overseas Development in July 1989.

Despite her impeccable credentials and being widely viewed as one of the most promising Conservative women of her generation, she never made it to the Cabinet. Lynda says there was only room for one handbag around the Cabinet table in the Thatcher government.

She never became bitter, but this comment to a reporter speaks volumes: 'I had a very marginal seat so I considered my first duty was to work as hard as I could for that. Yet now when I look at the younger people in the Cabinet, who were not even in Parliament when I came, I am very conscious that maybe it could have been different.'

She was one of only four ministers who served continuously throughout the Thatcher and Major governments.

As a constituency MP, even to this day, she is greatly admired by local residents and the community for always remaining a local MP, even while holding down demanding ministerial positions. She was described to me by one local member as a 'hard-working MP in every respect' – a touching tribute I thought, and a great compliment. No matter the issues of the day in London, Lynda would always be sure to travel back to the constituency and make time to meet with local people. Whether it was holding surgeries for local residents who had issues they needed help with, meeting with local businesses, or canvassing and chatting with people on the doorsteps – Lynda was always busy doing something around the community. That is what I respected. She knew who had put her in Westminster, and while she was going to use her position as an MP to help others around the world, her constituents were never going to be neglected.

A passionate advocate for small businesses, Lynda was a huge supporter of the local business community. Not only did she support them as a local resident when she lived in the constituency, but also through regularly visiting and staying in contact with them throughout her time as the Wallasey MP. She worked closely with neighbouring MP Frank Field, and despite their party differences they collaborated to get partnerships established in the area for the best interests of their constituents. One of the things that they were instrumental in laying the foundations for was the Wirral Investment Network, a precursor to the Wirral Chamber of Commerce.

Lynda lost her seat at the 1992 general election and was made a life peer, choosing the title Baroness Chalker of Wallasey, of Leigh-on-Sea in the County of Essex. This passionate believer in driving development through assistance from private sector investment was still at work, using her time in the International Development Department for the greater good. In 1997 she founded the Africa-focused commercial consultancy, Africa Matters Limited (AML).

Utilising her considerable experience and passion for Africa, AML worked to establish itself as a partner of choice for companies and organisations with interests or projects in Africa – aligning private-sector commercial goals with country-level developmental agendas. It aimed to challenge the narrative at the time of Africa as the 'Hopeless Continent'. Today, twenty years later, AML has grown to play advisory roles to some of the world's biggest organisations. Based in London, its longevity is testament to its global reach and influence.

It is this commitment and drive that has made Lynda's career, spanning over forty years as a member of both the lower and upper houses, so significant. Back in 1996, when asked to describe her role as Minister for Overseas Development, she replied, 'On a bad day this is the best job in British government; on a good day it is the best job in the world.'

MAUREEN COLQUHOUN

SALLY KEEBLE

- FULL NAME: Maureen Morfydd Colquhoun
- DATE OF BIRTH: 12 August 1928
- DATE OF DEATH: –
- PLACE OF BIRTH: –
- MARRIED TO: Keith Colquhoun (divorced); Barbara 'Babs' Todd
- CHILDREN: Andrew, Mary and Edward
- UNSUCCESSFUL ELECTIONS FOUGHT: Tonbridge 1970
- CONSTITUENCY: Northampton North
- DATE OF FIRST ELECTION: 28 February 1974
- DATE LEFT PARLIAMENT: 2 May 1979
- PARTY ROLES: Treasurer at the Tribune Group
- MINISTERIAL POSITIONS & DATES: None
- MOST FAMOUS QUOTATION: 'Two battles face women today. One is to hold on to what they have won, and the other is to get a better share of what they have not yet won.'

Maureen Colquhoun defied political conventions. A left-winger, she had an uneasy relationship with the Tribune Group for whom she was for a while treasurer. A committed anti-racist, she was criticised and forced to apologise for seeming to excuse Enoch Powell. Her radical feminism caused her to lambast the Labour government's efforts to promote gender equality.

And then there was her sexuality. Married with three children, she came out as a lesbian, the first MP ever to do so, courageously setting an example that no other MP dared follow for more than two decades.

The move defined her politically and triggered Colquhoun's deselection by her constituency party. And although this was overturned by the NEC in the run-up to the ill-fated 1979 general election, in which she lost her seat, the relationship between Colquhoun and the local party was restored only recently.

Maureen's earliest political influences were from her Irish family, especially her mother who was a member of Sinn Féin. She says she 'gave her heart' to the Labour Party at the age of eighteen and first held public office as a councillor in Shoreham by Sea where she lived with her husband Keith, a newspaper journalist.

There she showed the feistiness that was to characterise her time in Parliament. The youngest, and evidently the liveliest councillor, she fell foul of the male Conservative establishment, which tried to silence her by banning her from sitting on any council committees.

Northampton North was a new constituency, created by the division of Northampton which had been held for three decades by the eccentric right-winger Reg Paget, and briefly in the 1920s by Margaret Bondfield. Maureen captured the seat with a majority of 1,033 in February 1974, and increased this to 1,538 when she won the October election of that year.

Parliament, with its male-dominated seniority system, was not kind to Colquhoun. Her pithy interruptions brought rebukes from the Speaker, who struggled with the correct pronunciation of the title of the first MP who asked to be addressed as 'Ms'. Colquhoun objected to the sexism that kept women off public bill committees and out of debates on economic issues. An economist by training, almost all her contributions to parliamentary debates were on the social issues that are still too often perceived as the domain of women politicians.

'Whichever way one looks at it, the House of Commons is not a democracy but a maleocracy,' she concluded.

Her anger at the injustice of the exclusion of women from public life lay behind her Balance of the Sexes Private Members' Bill, which provided for public positions to be allocated to women, or to be left vacant until there was gender equality. It aimed to end the 'smug, discriminatory' establishment world in which 'decisions are made which affect the lives of everyone in the community by men from the inner circle of privilege'.

Colquhoun's Protection of Prostitutes Bill achieved notoriety because of the number of sex workers she brought to the public gallery to witness its introduction.

Media coverage of her private life started soon after her election. She met and fell in love with the editor of *Sappho*, Barbara 'Babs' Todd. During the parliamentary second reading of her Bill, Colquhoun looked up to see Babs and her husband Keith sitting a few seats apart in the public gallery.

Colquhoun and Todd decided to set up home together, but their house-warming party was infiltrated by the *Daily Mail*'s gossip columnist who threatened exposure. Courageously, Maureen decided to come out, the first British politician to do so. The media hounding of the couple was vitriolic and, shamefully, few political voices were raised in their defence.

After losing her seat in 1979 she continued to work in Parliament, as an assistant to two Labour MPs, and remained politically active as a councillor in Hackney where she and Babs lived. They moved to Cumbria, where Maureen served on the Lake District National Park Authority and as a local councillor.

They were still there, happily married although physically frail, when I visited them in the summer of 2017. Maureen remained passionate about her politics. The bitterness evident in her autobiography, *Woman in the House*, had mellowed and she displayed all her characteristic generosity of spirit and loyalty to the Labour Party.

She regretted having lost her parish council seat, at the age of eighty-six, two years previously. She also regretted not speaking enough in Parliament, although as a new woman backbencher she would have needed the patience of a saint to get speaking slots in the parliamentary seniority system. She regretted the sexism that still persisted in politics and said the 1997 influx of Labour women had not produced the breakthrough she had been hoping for.

But that, it seemed, was all she regretted.

Not the apparent apologia for Enoch Powell?

'My views were misrepresented and misunderstood – deliberately so – in what I said about Enoch Powell. The journalists aren't stupid; they knew what they were doing. But there was a problem in the inner cities then. And there's still a lot of racism in our society, an enormous amount of hidden racism. It exists and people don't like to admit it now as much as they used to.'

She also argued that she had been warning then, as she does now, that Labour was losing touch with its working-class roots. 'Labour's not communicating; they're failing to communicate with working people. One of the strengths of that dreadful man in America is that he communicates with working people. We don't do that any more, and people feel diminished by it.'

And she doesn't regret coming out, despite the personal and political price she paid for her courage in prioritising love over convenience.

'We have been together for forty-two years, Babs and I. It's a long time now and we are just as happy now as we were in the beginning. It says a great deal for a good relationship. If you fall in love with someone you fall in love with them.'

Forty years after it tried to deselect her, Northampton Labour sent a letter of appreciation to Maureen Colquhoun in recognition of her work for local people and the Labour Party. It's a long-overdue acknowledgement of a woman who spent only five years in Parliament, but whose contribution to national politics was profound.

JO RICHARDSON

JOYCE GOULD

- FULL NAME: Josephine Richardson
- DATE OF BIRTH: 28 August 1923
- PLACE OF BIRTH: Jesmond, Newcastle upon Tyne
- DATE OF DEATH: 1 February 1994
- MARRIED TO: Unmarried
- CHILDREN: None
- UNSUCCESSFUL ELECTIONS FOUGHT: Monmouth 1951 and 1955, Hornchurch 1959 and Harrow East 1964
- CONSTITUENCY: Barking
- DATE OF FIRST ELECTION: 28 February 1974
- DATE LEFT PARLIAMENT: 1 February 1994
- PARTY ROLES: Chair of the Labour Party 1989–90 and National Executive Committee Constituency Section 1980–91
- MINISTERIAL POSITIONS & DATES: Shadow spokesperson for Women's Rights and Welfare 1984–94 and shadow Minister for Business Innovation & Skills 1983–92

The fact that Jo Richardson has had a school named after her (Jo Richardson Community School in Castle Green, Dagenham) shows that she was no ordinary woman. Richardson was an initiator and a staunch feminist, paving the way for the next generation of left-wing feminists. She was ahead of her time in her abhorrence of discrimination, in whatever form, be it racism, sexism or homophobia, challenging it both in Parliament and within the Labour Party. This at a time and in an atmosphere when such views were sneered and jeered at. She was the first Member of Parliament to raise in the Commons her concerns about female genital mutilation, and the level of violence against women, and led the campaign in defence of the 1967 Abortion Act.

I first met Jo in 1975 when I became Chief Women's Officer of the Labour

Party. It was a time of great excitement for women in the party, the Labour government having introduced the Equal Pay and the Sex Discrimination Acts.

I worked closely with Jo over the next twenty years; she became a member of the National Executive Committee with responsibility for women, and the shadow spokesperson for Women's Rights and Welfare. Ten of those twenty years were spent fighting to retain the right for women to have an abortion.

So who was this remarkable woman? To her family, her nieces and nephew, she was an aunt they all adored; an aunt who was 5ft 8in. tall, with flaming red hair, and was always beautifully made up and immaculately dressed. She was an aunt who loved her gin and tonic, and who was always seen behind a screen of cigarette smoke. Most importantly, she was an aunt who bequeathed to them an understanding of the importance of having a society that is fair and equitable, and who influenced and encouraged their hopes and aspirations.

Politics ran in her blood. Her father had been a Liberal Party parliamentary candidate in Darlington, though he never managed to persuade Jo, her elder sister or her brother to become Liberals. A theatrical family, Jo's participation in amateur dramatics gave her a talent for delivering anecdotes with theatrical aplomb. Leaving school at fifteen, she studied shorthand and typing; her skill saw her become head of the typing pool at a large steelworks in Letchworth aged twenty-two. Her many conversations with men at the works influenced her political thinking and made her more keen to join the Labour Party, which she did in 1945 when the Second World War ended. Because she could type she became the Minutes Secretary for Letchworth Labour Party. She wanted to be a journalist, but was not really sure how to go about achieving her ambition. She thought that meeting some journalists might help, so after spotting an advert in *Tribune*, she successfully applied for a job as secretary for Ian Mikardo, the Labour MP who wrote for *Tribune*.

It was in the office designated in the Commons for secretaries that Jo first met Betty Boothroyd, who was then Barbara Castle's secretary. Jo and Betty struck up a friendship which lasted a lifetime. Despite some differing positions, they agreed on issues such as opposition to apartheid and on achieving equality. They holidayed together, lived next door to each other, and shared family occasions. Betty recalls making supper for Jo, and sitting giggling for hours with her while talking about old boyfriends. Jo soon became the doyenne of the fourteen secretaries in the office, alerting them to the benefits of becoming members of a trade union. It is reputed that Jo and Betty were the first secretaries to become MPs.

Richardson was not only secretary to 'Mik', she became a director of his Industrial Consultancy Trading Company. She became the company's main agent, going back and forth to negotiate business in Eastern Europe and Russia, regularly passing through Checkpoint Charlie in Berlin. The job demanded ingenuity and patience. It was also dangerous at times and there were some hairy moments.

Jo was the long-serving secretary of the Tribune Group and also joined the harder-left 'Campaign Group', but resigned in 1982 when the group supported Tony Benn standing against Neil Kinnock as the Leader of the Labour Party.

Richardson was absolute in her loyalty and commitment to the Labour Party. She was adamant that she could not belong to any other political party as only a Labour government could introduce the type of society that she craved to be part of.

She knew that at times her left-wing politics made her unpopular with some people, but even those who disagreed with her felt that she was never sectarian and she had many friends irrespective of political differences. She believed people should be brave and honest about their views, and expressed her own views forcibly. As far as she was concerned, socialism was 'not a system of economics but a way of life, it won't come tomorrow or even the day after, but we have to hasten its progress'.

She supported public ownership of major public services, as well as the nationalisation of the major industries and financial services. She was also a unilateralist and was devastated when, at the Labour Party conference in 1957, Aneurin Bevan reversed his opposition to the bomb. Richardson became a founder member and national organiser of the Campaign for Nuclear Disarmament, and was a stalwart supporter of the Greenham Common women. She enjoyed being the catering manager for the Aldermaston Marches, but got the sack when she mistakenly ordered 1,000 eggs, and when marchers complained that she had charged 6d for a 5d Lyons fruit pie, so that she didn't have to bother handing over change.

She made a substantial intervention while on the board of the National Council for Civil Liberties, assisting in writing and then taking forward legislation on civil liberties. This resulted in the setting up of the All Party Parliamentary Group on Civil Liberties.

Jo campaigned passionately for women's rights. 'I am not interested in the high-achieving women, I am concerned about all the women with expertise and women who never get to first base, they're poor, they've got kids, their lives are a drudgery,' she said. 'It is about women getting a greater share of the cake, it is not just about changing the recipe.'

Elected to Labour's National Executive Committee in 1979, Richardson became the first chair of the newly formed NEC Women's committee, having campaigned for women members of Labour to have a direct voice on the major committee of the party. While the committee condemned and publicised the iniquities of the Tory government, members also set about challenging deep-rooted chauvinism within the Labour Party, making it clear to the NEC that it could no longer just pay lip service to women members when determining policy. Jo succeeded in getting the NEC to agree that the resolutions carried at the important annual women's conference should be considered and responded to by the then ministers and subsequent shadow ministers. Scorned at the time, she raised the possibility of quotas in all units of the party, which took five years to achieve, and said all shortlists for parliamentary and local government elections should include a woman.

The NEC did, if reluctantly, agree to conduct an examination of the discrimination of women within the party structure, and to discuss why there were so few women councillors and MPs.

On becoming Labour's leader, Neil Kinnock appointed Jo as spokesperson for Women's Rights and Welfare, giving her a brief across departments. Her first act was to set up a women's rights study group to examine women's position in society, looking at areas previously ignored such as divorce, rape and sexual harassment, as well as the changing structure of the family and parental responsibilities. To get her evidence Jo and a team of volunteers toured the country and talked to women's groups. As a consequence, the NEC agreed that in government there would be a Minister for Women, not as an adjunct to some other department but a minister with a voice in the Cabinet. In 1990 Jo was named the 'Good Housekeeping Woman of the Year'. Prime Minister Margaret Thatcher, who made the presentation, said that Jo had 'won the award for keeping women's issues on the national agenda' – what irony.

A further irony was that Jo was voted off the NEC by left-wingers in the party, because she was concentrating too much on issues of women and discrimination, instead of focusing on a more traditional left-wing agenda. There had been an expectation that Jo would become Labour's first Minister for Women's Rights, but she died before the party returned to government. Although there is now a Minister for Women, it is allied to some other policy, but at least Jo's wish was partially fulfilled and issues facing women can now be discussed around the Cabinet table.

Jo had the advantage of having worked in Parliament before becoming an MP. Her parliamentary experience was recognised by the *Sunday People*, when she was a candidate in Monmouth. Under the heading 'DON'T BE ASHAMED TO VOTE FOR HER', the newspaper reported that 'Miss Josephine Richardson, Labour's 27-year-old candidate for Monmouth, has mighty good looks, plus a lot to qualify her as an MP: she has had training as an MP's secretary. At the Commons, she is so popular that even Cabinet ministers call her "Joe".'

She contested the next two general elections, but after failing to win a seat, she was unsure whether she should try again. However, in 1974, although only after some hesitation, she put her name forward for Barking. After a strenuous selection conference and five ballots, she won by one vote.

Her majority was 14,834, and she retained the seat for the next twenty years. Throughout her time as an MP, her level of activity was breathtaking. Despite advancing arthritis she stretched herself beyond her limit, uniquely publicising her private phone number to electors, which meant her being available seven days a week. She was assiduous in holding regular surgeries, and even when she was seriously ill in hospital she insisted on reading her mail.

She battled fiercely for better health services, as well as free school meals and nursery provision, and ran a long campaign to get support for women who were victims of domestic violence. She moved a Private Members' Bill in Parliament and was infuriated when it failed at the second reading due to a technicality. Eventually, she succeeded in establishing the first women's refuge in the borough.

Just four weeks before the twentieth anniversary of the day she became MP for Barking, Jo died.

Jo never shied away from controversy, even breaking with tradition during her maiden speech on 5 April 1974, by berating an opposition member who criticised the achievements of the Labour government. She also developed a great flair for using parliamentary procedures to pursue vital but often hugely unpopular issues. It is impossible to detail the many issues she raised during her years in Parliament; she spoke more than 600 times, and at a rough estimate put down 1,500 written questions. She was helped by her staff, most of them volunteers, who thoroughly enjoyed their work and were stimulated by the diversity of subjects, including the major battle to protect the 1967 Abortion Act, which Jo led.

Jo chaired the Labour Party conference in 1990, but her last contribution came at the conference that was held the following year. In great pain and suffering from bronchitis, her opening remarks were typical: 'I thought I had better come in case you thought I had died. The Labour Party is my family. Hearing Neil's great speech, I could feel how much of a family the Labour Party is and how much we want Britain to be a family caring for each other under a Labour government. So thank you all.' For the next two years she attended the conference in her wheelchair.

On Thursday, 1 February 1994, Jo died in her sleep. Two weeks later she was given a grand send-off. John Smith and Betty Boothroyd led the many tributes. Declared a wonder woman by residents in Barking, by her colleagues and friends, no issue was too great a problem. Just three weeks before she died, very frail and in great pain, she was taken on a stretcher by taxi to chair a meeting of residents concerned about the effect the widening of the A13 would have on their homes.

Jo will be remembered for her great loyalty and her friendship. People always came first for her. Betty Boothroyd, after visiting Jo in hospital for the last time, recalls what Jo told her: 'You are my best friend, don't forget me. Nor shall I ever.'

Jo Richardson was no ordinary woman.

AUDREY WISE

MARY HONEYBALL

- FULL NAME: Audrey Wise (née Brown)
- DATE OF BIRTH: 4 January 1932
- PLACE OF BIRTH: Newcastle upon Tyne
- DATE OF DEATH: 2 September 2000
- MARRIED TO: John Wise
- CHILDREN: One son and one daughter
- UNSUCCESSFUL ELECTIONS: Woolwich East 1983
- CONSTITUENCY: Coventry South West 1974–79 and Preston 1987–2000
- DATE OF FIRST ELECTION: 27 February 1974
- DATE LEFT PARLIAMENT: 2 September 2000
- PARTY ROLES: Tottenham Borough Council councillor 1953–57 and member of the Labour Party NEC 1979–87
- MINISTERIAL POSITIONS & DATES: None
- MOST FAMOUS QUOTATION: 'Pregnancy should be regarded as a normal event, not an illness.'

Audrey Wise, an outspoken and uncompromising left-winger, is best known for the amendment to the Budget she moved with fellow Labour MP Jeff Rooker in 1977. The Labour government under the premiership of James Callaghan was struggling at the time, with the inflation rate spiralling at around 15–17 per cent. This meant that if and when wage increases went up in line with inflation, people would have to pay more tax.

Wise and Rooker persuaded the Labour whips to put them both on the Finance committee scrutinising Denis Healey's Budget. The upshot was the famous Rooker-Wise amendment that introduced retrospective inflation-proofing on tax allowances. The amendment was passed by Parliament thanks to Conservative support, and was an embarrassing defeat for the Callaghan government. It resulted in £450 million being handed back to taxpayers.

Audrey Brown was born in Newcastle upon Tyne in 1932, though her date of birth is sometimes given as 1935, due to her giving her age as thirty-nine when she was nominated for the Coventry South West parliamentary seat in 1974. Her father, an optician and stalwart of the Union of Shop, Distributive and Allied Workers (USDAW), was a member of the Communist Party, but renounced his membership the day the Red Army entered Poland. He later became a Labour councillor. Audrey's maternal grandfather, Charles Crawford, was also an active socialist; left-wing politics was the life-blood of the Brown household.

Nevertheless, it was marriage that made the first claim on her time. Almost as soon as she left Rutherford High School, Audrey married optician John Wise. They had two children, a son and a daughter, both born at home as Audrey was against the medicalisation of childbirth. She was always a political activist, and at the age of twenty-one became a councillor on Labour-held Tottenham Borough Council in north London. Her daughter, Valerie, was also politically active and chaired the Greater London Council Women's Committee in the 1980s.

Audrey campaigned throughout her life for women's rights; in 1970 she spoke at the first women's liberation conference at Ruskin College, Oxford, and stayed connected to the movement. Moreover, she did not always toe the official Labour Party line on women. In the early 1970s she contributed to the Institute for Workers' Control pamphlet 'Women and Workers' Control' and promoted her own line, which diverged from the official Labour Party view. The received wisdom was that women should accept the same conditions as men, for example by working nights. A woman apparently once told Audrey that if the economy wanted women to work nights then she wanted a different economy. Audrey agreed; equal working conditions and equal pay were important but not enough.

Around the same time she wrote an article called 'Trying to Stay Human', which was published in the socialist and feminist magazine, *Red Rag*. The article was mainly about nurseries. Audrey insisted that it was not enough to demand that the state provide them; the management of nurseries should be placed under community control. As well as being heavily involved in the Institute for Workers' Control, a significant left-wing pressure group in the 1970s, Audrey was a member of the Campaign for Nuclear Disarmament. It was fitting, therefore, that she helped the workers at Lucas Aerospace, who had developed plans for saving jobs if defence spending was reduced – armaments factories would instead produce goods for sectors like medicine, the environment and transport. Audrey was an indefatigable activist on what were, in reality, the left-wing fringes of politics but given some prominence through the support of MPs and leading Labour figures such as herself. She was an old-fashioned socialist, who continued to make demands throughout her life, but was also a democrat. The extension of democracy was a constant theme of her life.

She was elected as the Labour MP for Coventry South West in February 1974, the general election which ushered in a minority Labour government that lasted until 1979. She was seemingly proud to be regarded at Westminster during the 1970s as a left-wing nuisance, considering this both necessary and desirable. Not only did she meet members of the Official IRA, she regularly attacked the teetering Labour government's economic policies. On the plus side, she visited Portugal in 1974 to report on and participate in the Carnation Revolution, which overthrew the fascist dictatorship.

Nearer to home, in 1977 Wise joined the ranks of the 500 people who were arrested on the picket line during the Grunwick strike. The dispute at Grunwick Film Processing Laboratories in Willesden, north London, concerned union recognition and lasted from 1976 to '78. Not only was it an extremely long-running dispute, but most of the workforce were Asian women recently arrived from East Africa. Wise, who took the view that Grunwick had employed these women as slave labourers, was apprehended for obstructing a policeman. She claimed in court that the officer had been pulling a woman demonstrator's hair, but despite a reference from Tony Benn, she was found guilty and fined £20.

The 1979 general election saw Margaret Thatcher become Prime Minister, while Audrey lost her seat. She did, however, receive some compensation by being elected to Labour's ruling National Executive Committee, a position she held until 1987. She was not so lucky in her attempts to return to Parliament; in the 1983 general election she lost at Woolwich East, a supposedly safe Labour seat. Nevertheless, she remained active, positioning herself as a powerful critic of Neil Kinnock's attempts to root out supporters of Militant, decrying it as a witch-hunt.

She returned to Parliament in 1987, this time as MP for Preston, a seat she held until her death. Having failed to become the chair of the Select Committee on Social Services, she became a long-standing member of the All-Party Committee on Health. Her most significant contribution was to persuade the committee to hold an inquiry into maternity services. The report, which was endorsed by the Conservative government, called for increased access to home births and water births, and for maternity services to be more women-centred. Audrey's most important work was, in fact, on behalf of women, children and families and the way in which women experience childbirth. Sadly, she gained little recognition for her energy and commitment in this all too neglected field.

From 1991 to 1997 Audrey Wise was a member of the USDAW National Executive Committee, becoming its first women president. From 1997 until her death in 2000, she continued her tradition of opposing the Labour government. She was a strong critic of the NATO action in Kosovo and of the bombing in Iraq. Although she voted against the 1997 cut in benefits for lone parents, she was, as ever, not completely predictable. She disapproved of single mothers going out to work, arguing that children needed their mothers.

The struggle for social justice always meant everything to Audrey while the pursuit of power was only a secondary objective. Her great friend, the former MP Alice Mahon, put it like this: 'She [Audrey] was simply passionate about the Labour Party. It was her life. Honest, clever and tenacious, Audrey Wise represented everything I value in the Labour movement ... she never forgot her working-class roots.'

MARGARET EWING

JO SWINSON

- FULL NAME: Margaret Anne Ewing (formerly Bain, née McAdam)
- DATE OF BIRTH: 1 September 1945
- PLACE OF BIRTH: Lanark
- DATE OF DEATH: 21 March 2006
- MARRIED TO: Donald Bain (m. 1968; div. 1980); Fergus Ewing (m. 1983)
- CHILDREN: None
- UNSUCCESSFUL ELECTIONS FOUGHT: East Dunbartonshire February 1974; Strathkelvin & Bearsden 1983
- CONSTITUENCY: East Dunbartonshire October 1974–79 and Moray 1987–2001
- DATE OF FIRST ELECTION: 10 October 1974
- DATE LEFT PARLIAMENT: 7 June 2001
- MSP: Moray 1999–2006
- PARTY ROLES: Depute leader of the SNP 1984–87 and leader of the SNP Parliamentary Group 1987–99
- MINISTERIAL POSITIONS & DATES: None
- MOST FAMOUS QUOTATION: Labour First Minister Henry McLeish was berating an SNP MSP whose conduct was apparently so appalling it could not be named in the chamber but, the First Minister thundered, the word began with an H and ended in a Y. Quick as a flash, Margaret Ewing interjected, 'Aye – Henry!' at which the entire debating chamber collapsed in laughter, including those on the First Minister's own benches.

'The county of Dunbartonshire seems rather sympathetically disposed towards women candidates...' began a *Glasgow Herald* article on 21 February 1974 about the 'attractive young SNP candidate' Margaret Bain. She came third at that general election, but in the October election of the same year she defeated the Conservative MP by twenty-two votes – the closest result in the country.

The area does seem fruitful for women candidates, in particular for young women like Margaret and me, elected aged twenty-nine and twenty-five respectively. East Dunbartonshire is one of only two constituencies to have elected two twentysomething women (Bolton West elected Ann Taylor in 1974 and Ruth Kelly in 1997 – just thirty-two women in their twenties have ever been elected as MPs).

Delving into the archives of Margaret Bain's life threw up many unexpected similarities. Like me, she was elected eight years after joining her party, won her party's first seat in west central Scotland at a general election, and became one of her party's eleven Scottish MPs. We both won our seat from one party, before losing it to a different one. As well as experiencing the sharp pain of losing – she told a friend after her 1979 defeat how 'the phone doesn't ring any more' – we both returned to Parliament, in Margaret's case by winning a different seat, Moray, in 1987.

A teacher by profession, Margaret immersed herself in politics. She met her first husband, Donald, at the 1967 Hamilton by-election. The SNP scored a stunning victory with Winnie Ewing – a towering figure in Scottish politics, who would later become Margaret's mother-in-law, after her second marriage.

The daughter of a farm labourer, Margaret combined her commitment to helping others, especially poor and disadvantaged children, with an easy manner that made her popular with the party, the media and MPs. A people person, she was known for her warmth, passion, sincerity and her ability to work constructively beyond party lines. More than three decades on, she is still fondly remembered in East Dunbartonshire for her assiduous service as a local MP.

Fiona McLeod, who later served as MSP for Strathkelvin & Bearsden, recalls her sixteen-year-old self tentatively signing up to volunteer at the SNP campaign caravan in Bearsden Cross in 1974, and being warmly welcomed by the 28-year-old Margaret. 'She always kept an eye out for me from then on. It was in the days before mentoring schemes, but she was just doing it naturally.'

Over the years Margaret quietly grafted, laying the groundwork for today's improved gender representation. She was at the first SNP women's event in the 1980s, served in high-profile roles including deputy leader, and in 1990 was the first woman to stand for the SNP leadership, when she took on Alex Salmond. Although many considered her to be the favourite, Salmond defeated her by a surprising margin of 486 to 146 votes.

Margaret's sympathies were on the left, so she found it tough when the SNP voted with the Conservatives to bring down Jim Callaghan. The subsequent general election saw Margaret and eight of her SNP colleagues lose their seats. Years later, as leader of the SNP Parliamentary Group, she was negotiating with another beleaguered Prime Minister, John Major, over Maastricht. As a committed Europhile, Margaret agreed that SNP MPs would vote with Major's government in a key division, in return for more Scottish representation on an EU committee. Responding to the controversy, she said, 'The criticism seems to be that we should not talk to the Tories and I feel that is a bit daft since it says on my membership card that I should seek to further the interests of Scotland.'

When the Scottish Parliament was created, she was one of the first MPs to say she would stand for Holyrood, and as group convener played a pivotal role in helping newly elected SNP MSPs to find their feet. Her passion for Scottish independence never diminished, and she continued to fight for her constituency interests, even as her health deteriorated after her breast cancer diagnosis in 2002.

HELENE HAYMAN

SARAH CHILDS

- FULL NAME: Helene Valerie Hayman (née Middleweek), Baroness Hayman of Dartmouth Park GBE, PC
- DATE OF BIRTH: 26 March 1949
- PLACE OF BIRTH: Wolverhampton
- DATE OF DEATH: –
- MARRIED TO: Martin Heathcote Hayman (m. 1974)
- CHILDREN: Ben, Joe, Jake and David
- UNSUCCESSFUL ELECTIONS FOUGHT: Wolverhampton South West February 1974
- CONSTITUENCY: Welwyn Hatfield
- DATE OF FIRST ELECTION: 10 October 1974
- DATE LEFT PARLIAMENT: 3 May 1979
- PARTY ROLES: None
- MINISTERIAL POSITIONS & DATES: Parliamentary Under-Secretary of State for Environment, Transport and the Regions 1997–98; Parliamentary Under-Secretary of State for Health 1998–99; Minister of State, Agriculture, Fisheries and Food 1999–2001; Lord Speaker 2006–11

Helene Hayman is best known today for being the first Lord Speaker, rather than for her time as a Member of Parliament. She spent only five years in the House of Commons, but has sat in the Lords since 1996. In her official portrait Baroness Hayman is depicted in the Speaker's black and white apparel, wearing the traditional breeches, with striking, pearlescent hair, and looking directly at the viewer.

Wolverhampton was where she was born and where she attended the local grammar school. She studied law at Newnham College, Cambridge, and became the youngest president of the Cambridge Union. Hayman's parliamentary career began in October 1974 when she was elected Labour MP for Welwyn Hatfield; her first attempt at entering the Commons had ended in failure earlier that year at the February general election. Hers was a classic case of women's political recruitment, one that remains familiar today: she was asked to stand.

Hayman was boosted by her local party's confidence in her and accepted the invitation to stand for election in Wolverhampton South West, Enoch Powell's old seat. As a young, local woman Hayman was considered to be precisely the sort of candidate who might win additional votes for Labour. Referred to by her opponent as a 'dolly bird', she garnered extensive publicity – the British media's attention to women MPs is nothing if not long-standing. Although she lost to Powell's Tory successor in February 1974, Hayman achieved the biggest swing in the UK (Conservative to Labour, 16.6 per cent).

The second of the two general elections in 1974 provided an opportunity for Hayman not only to stand for election again, but this time to do so successfully and to be 'catapulted in', as she herself put it. Her local Wolverhampton constituency party encouraged her to contest the winnable seat of Welwyn Hatfield. Elected at twenty-five, and the 'baby' of the House, she entered the Commons with a majority of just 520. There were plenty of male MPs who thought that a young woman should not be sitting alongside them on the green benches. In the October 1974 Parliament, the total number of women MPs was only twenty-seven (4.3 per cent of all MPs), with eighteen of these being Labour female MPs.

Two years later, Hayman had the audacity to have a baby. Being pregnant was not easy in the long, hot summer of 1976. There were late parliamentary votes, night after night; pairing had been suspended. Hayman recalls that this was the only time she ever spoke with Margaret Thatcher. While she was lying down in the Lady Members' room, Mrs Thatcher came in and declared: 'I've got a sore throat, you're pregnant; we are going home.' The Labour whip, Michael Cocks, exclaimed: 'And she (Mrs Thatcher) says I've got to send you home in my fucking car.' There would be no formal maternity leave, or even any informal latitude shown to the new mother. Hayman's absence from the division lobby risked a government defeat, so she was forced to bring her two-week-old baby into the House. This is the source of the myth that Hayman breastfed her baby in the Chamber. Back in 1976, the Serjeant at Arms had apparently briefed the doorkeeper on how much force he could use to stop Hayman taking her son into the Chamber.

The issues that Hayman would champion in Parliament reflected her post-university involvement in a variety of social campaigns. She worked for Shelter, the housing and homelessness charity, as well as for the National Council for One Parent Families. Hayman's main constituency concern was the aircraft industry; in an age of nationalisation, she fought a long and ultimately successful campaign to fund the civilian aircraft, the HS146. Hayman learned that politics is the art of the 'long game'. Women's issues were also a significant part of her parliamentary life. As one of the less than 5 per cent of MPs who were female, she willingly accepted the responsibility to speak up for women; if women MPs did not do this, who would?

In 1975, she became embroiled in procedural rows about select committee composition, as she and other women fought to defend the 1967 Abortion Act from the 'White Bill'. Four of the fifteen committee members for the Bill were women; one amendment suggested that all male MPs be removed from it. In her intervention, Hayman called attention to the 'male chauvinism' of the House; one MP had spoken of her 'graceful presence'. Hayman also collaborated with Labour women MPs to stop proposed changes to family allowances that would, if implemented, see money going to men's wallets when it had previously gone into women's purses. For Labour's women, this was a straightforward betrayal of mothers.

The 1979 general election saw Margaret Thatcher lead the Conservatives to overall victory, while Hayman went down to defeat at Welwyn Hatfield, losing her seat by 3,474 votes. Happenstance can make all the difference to a parliamentary career. In Hayman's case, if there had been no second 1974 general election, she would have been a young mother by 1979 and might never have stood as a Member of Parliament. As it was, she did not stand for election again after her 1979 loss. In the long interlude before she returned to Parliament as a peer, Hayman brought up her four sons, while in her professional and public life she focused on health, education, charities and medical ethics.

Appointed by Tony Blair as a Labour peer in 1996, Hayman now sits (following her Speakership) as a crossbencher. She held three ministerial positions: Agriculture, Fisheries and Food (1999–2001); Health (1998–99); Environment, Transport and the Regions (1997–98). As Animal Health Minister at the time of the foot and mouth disease, she co-chaired COBRA with the Prime Minister, Tony Blair. As a former MP, Hayman has the right to access the members' tearoom, an important advantage for a minister sitting in the Upper House, and especially so in the post-1999 era where the Lords was frequently the site of parliamentary opposition to the Labour government.

Following reform to the role of the Lord Chancellor in 2006, Hayman was elected by Members of the House of the Lords as the first Lord Speaker. In this role, one of her key goals was to embed the institution of the Lord Speaker, so that it became 'part of the furniture'. To this end, she worked to support the House's tradition of self-regulation and counter critics who thought that the new post would see the Upper House ape the Commons. She also wanted to act as an ambassador for the Lords, devoting considerable effort to representing the House of Lords beyond Westminster, setting up the 'Peers in Schools' programme, and the 'River Room seminars' for journalists and experts, for example. To her fellow peers, she sought to demonstrate that there was huge value in having someone chosen by the House (and not the government) to represent it, and to explain and defend its central role in British politics.

Over her parliamentary lifetime Baroness Hayman has witnessed considerable gendered transformation of Parliament. When she was busy sitting her 11-plus school exam, no women were allowed to sit in the House of Lords; it was not until 1958 that the Life Peerages Act allowed women life peers to sit in the Upper House. It was ten years later, in 1968, before female hereditary peers were allowed in. Today, the percentage of women in the Lords and Commons is 24 per cent and 32 per cent, respectively; much improved on the levels of the mid-1970s but still far from parity. There have been women Speakers in both Houses – two in the Lords. Baroness De Souza was elected to succeed Hayman. Women have also occupied many, though not all, the ministerial and Cabinet posts; notably we have not yet had a female Chancellor of the Exchequer. Hayman recalls the Conservative Lords' reactions to the 1997 Labour front bench which included a good number of women peers. 'They really thought it below the dignity of the House that there would be comparatively young women in positions of power.' In her view, 'I really think we put them back in their box.' Her successful Speakership shows that Parliament's women – both MPs and peers – have done precisely this.

DAME MARGARET BECKETT

GILLIAN MERRON

- FULL NAME: Margaret Mary Beckett (née Jackson) DBE
- DATE OF BIRTH: 15 January 1943
- PLACE OF BIRTH: Ashton-under-Lyne, Lancashire
- DATE OF DEATH: –
- MARRIED TO: Lionel (Leo) Beckett (m. 1979)
- CHILDREN: David and Roger Beckett (stepsons)
- UNSUCCESSFUL ELECTIONS FOUGHT: Lincoln February 1974
- CONSTITUENCY: Lincoln October 1974–79 and Derby South since 1983
- DATE OF FIRST ELECTION: 10 October 1974
- DATE LEFT PARLIAMENT: Incumbent
- PARTY ROLES: NEC member 1980–81 and 2012–15; Leader of the Opposition 1994; deputy leader of the Labour Party 1992–94
- MINISTERIAL POSITIONS & DATES: Government whip 1975–76; Parliamentary Under-Secretary of State for Education and Science 1976–79; shadow Chief Secretary to the Treasury 1989–92; shadow Leader of the House 1992–94; shadow Secretary of State for Health 1994–95; shadow Secretary of State for Trade and Industry 1995–97; President of the Board of Trade 1997–98; Leader of the House of Commons and Lord President of the Council 1998–2001; Secretary of State for Environment, Food and Rural Affairs 2001–06; Secretary of State for Foreign and Commonwealth Affairs 2006–07; Minister for Housing and Planning 2008–09
- MOST FAMOUS QUOTATION: 'To be brutally frank...'

Margaret Beckett is Labour royalty, a woman of political class whom we can take pride in counting as one of our own. Who could have been surprised, in 2013, when Margaret became the Rt Hon. Dame Margaret Beckett MP DBE? The conferment of a damehood in the New Year's honours list seemed an obvious way to celebrate our longest-serving female MP, who continues to be as assiduous as ever in carrying out her political and public duties.

In common with so many of us, Beckett's political drive was heavily influenced by her early years. It clearly touches her today to talk about her upbringing, and about the struggles her parents endured. Her father's chronic ill health was a constant for the Jackson family in Ashton-under-Lyne. Having contracted rheumatic fever as a child, Beckett's father was unable to join the army, serving instead as a Bevin boy, using his skills as a carpenter to carry out repairs on bomb-damaged buildings. He returned home when Margaret was three years old, but his health was still poor, and he died when she was only twelve. An intensely proud man, he would never allow anyone to buy him a drink if he could not return the favour, a practice he instilled in his family who were not allowed to accept hospitality if they could not reciprocate. Mrs Jackson was a trained teacher, and it resonates with Margaret that her mother did not receive equal pay until Margaret was fourteen years old.

Her father's ill health was a source of great sadness for Beckett's family, but the Jacksons were lucky that their mother earned more than most women did, which just about kept the family afloat, and that Beckett and her two sisters won scholarships to grammar school.

Beckett was acutely aware of living on a knife edge, and she also knew that if their mother had not been a teacher, she and her sisters might never have had any chance in life. Such awareness made Beckett acutely conscious that Britain needed political change.

Referring to herself and her two sisters, Lesley and Eileen, as a 'holy trinity', Beckett is entertained by the thought that they were described as the 'sublime to the ridiculous' at the time when Lesley was a nun, Eileen a psychiatrist and Margaret a politician.

Beckett's efforts to join the Labour Party in her early twenties were thwarted when, for two years, she received no replies to her repeated enquiries. Eventually, however, she managed to join and became treasurer at her inaugural ward meeting as everyone took on roles in a flurry of activity prior to the 1964 general election.

Going on to work for the Labour Party, preparing policy briefings and as joint secretary of the industrial policy committee, Beckett observed at close quarters what MPs such as Judith Hart and Tony Benn actually did. Surrounded by people who also wanted to be MPs, Beckett's attitude was, 'I can do that'. Influential figures such as Barbara Castle with her pioneering spirit also left their mark, and regularly being around Parliament meant that Beckett got to know the police officers guarding it – a sure way to feel at home.

It was the late and kindly Fred Peart, Minister for Agriculture, who paid what he thought was a great compliment to the young Beckett, telling her that as she was doing such a wonderful job for the Labour Party, she should marry a nice young Labour MP to whom she'd be a tremendous help. The well-intentioned minister was somewhat stunned when Beckett replied that she herself could be a Labour MP.

Peart's advice strengthened Beckett's resolve to stand for election, thus providing Lincoln, and subsequently Derby South, with the committed services of their first-ever woman MP. With their industrial and manufacturing bases, both of Beckett's constituencies were a natural fit. They thoroughly suited her scientific approach to life, crystallised in her engineering apprenticeship.

In 1974, Beckett fought two elections in Lincoln, both of them against the ex-Labour MP Dick Taverne, who stood as Democratic Labour, having quit Labour after disagreements over Europe. The Lincoln Labour Party decided that they wanted something different and would 'try a woman'. Fighting two elections in one year was tough, but, at only thirty-one years old, Beckett managed to win the second, making her a woman ahead of her time.

Having lost Lincoln in 1979, it was hard work to get back into Parliament. In the course of the Derby South selection process, the secretary of the women's section left the room to get Margaret. While she was gone, the chair persuaded the members to back Bruce (now Lord) Grocott, a handsome young man who regularly appeared on TV. By the time Beckett arrived, that particular nomination was all sewn up. Nevertheless, she went on to win the selection contest for Derby South.

Once back where she belonged in Parliament, after the 1983 general election, the string of firsts continued unabated. Margaret sailed on to become the first woman deputy leader and acting leader of the Labour Party, and when in government, the first woman President of the Board of Trade, Secretary of State for DEFRA, and Britain's first and only female Foreign Secretary.

Some civil servants felt that the job of Foreign Secretary was not a suitable one for a woman. They envisioned someone who had gone to the right school and university, and who had a reputation primarily as an intellectual. But no one dared express these thoughts to Beckett who, despite resistance from the Foreign and Commonwealth Office, as chair of the UN Security Council, forced through the first of the debates on climate change as a matter of peace and security. As Margaret does, she 'insisted' that this be the case – nicely and gently but with an edge of steeliness.

In her speech, in the biggest debate the Security Council had ever seen, she argued that scientific evidence exceeded the worst fears about climate change, leading to migration on an unprecedented scale because of flooding, disease and famine.

The speech found its way into a book of twenty speeches that changed the world. Beckett's words are right up there, sandwiched between those of Winston Churchill and ... Osama bin Laden. With an overwhelming number of achievements and firsts to call on, it is the national minimum wage that provides Margaret with the greatest thrill and sense of pride. Its deep and life-changing impact was put into perspective when she heard about a woman whose pay was so low that the minimum wage had transformed her family's well-being – it meant she earned an extra £100 per month.

While many claim it as their success, it was Margaret Beckett as the Secretary of State for Trade and Industry who dealt with the politics when arguments were had in Cabinet, legislative battles won in Parliament and lives improved for millions of low-paid workers.

As a member of the standing committee that examined the legislation line by line, I experienced the deliberate campaign by the Conservatives to frustrate progress, which meant sitting for an unprecedented number of hours and going through the night. Margaret appeared, unannounced and unexpected, to observe proceedings in the public gallery and show her support – a gesture that was quintessentially her. I can remember the shiver that coursed down my spine when walking through the division lobbies for the final vote on the Bill, and realising the difference our election had made to the lives of people who looked to us. It was an achievement indeed – and one based in fact and evidence in true Beckett style.

As Leader of the House, she steered reforms on the House of Lords and the ban on fox-hunting through Parliament. The sight of Margaret and an unusually large number of MPs marching down to the Lords to hear the reading out of the list of Bills that had been passed, and the unparliamentary cheer that went up when these two flagship Bills were announced, caused more than a stir on the red benches.

As Environment Secretary and lead negotiator for the UK and the EU, Margaret successfully brokered an agreement in Montreal to a follow-on to the Kyoto Protocol, now the Paris Agreement on climate change. Groundbreaking and lasting in its effect, when the negotiations were concluded they all cried – men and women alike.

As the Foreign Secretary, a post she would have liked to have held for another year, Margaret's last pitch was to go to Washington to commit to active pursuit under the Treaty on Non-Proliferation of Nuclear Weapons.

While it was little noticed in the UK, her speech received a standing ovation in Washington and was described as 'a game changer in this town'. Henry Kissinger asked if he could circulate the speech. It was the first time since the 1940s that a government with nuclear weapons had taken such a stance. Always a pragmatist, Beckett believed that the renewal of Trident was the right thing to do alongside renewed efforts for nuclear disarmament.

When faced by the weight of evidence versus the force of opinions, it is evidence and hard facts that will always win through with Margaret. With a mind that is clear and logical, there are some who make the mistake of reading that as simply coming across as cold. It's just the way of Margaret Beckett.

With Margaret as my mentor, I have also been supported by her husband, the ever loyal and present Leo. Political comrades, partners in life and politics, the dearest of friends and always with enough love, time and interest to share with the rest of us, they are a one-off. To know Margaret and Leo is to be blessed with the friendship of a remarkable couple who are as inseparable from each other as they are from politics.

In Bournemouth in 1985, as a first-time Labour conference delegate for Derby South, I sat a few rows from the front to witness the unforgettable speech by Neil Kinnock as he tore into Militant. Who could forget that moment? Margaret, however, remembers a more personal one. A complete newbie, I joined her at a TGWU reception and, shocked to find a television crew in tow, declared that I didn't know she was famous. To me, Margaret was just our MP, which was quite enough to get my respect.

Some nine years later, when I nervously confided to her that I wanted to be an MP, she slammed down the hairbrush she was using and exclaimed, 'About time too!' This gave me the support and validation I needed. Our bond continued as I was selected to win back the seat of Lincoln that had let Margaret go in 1979. It seemed so fitting.

Margaret appears to effortlessly lead by example, continually demonstrating that women don't have to be confined to particular roles. When she was first elected in the 1970s, there was an assumption that women did 'women's things' like health and education. Margaret has shown in deed and word, and by being supportive, that women don't have to do what is expected of them. For her, this is what feminism is about – that we can each do what it is that we seek to do.

She was once asked in a radio interview whether she would describe herself as a feminist. Typically and modestly she replied, 'I hope others would describe me as one.'

She has taken her fair share of knock-backs, particularly in losing a few elections along the way, including those for Leader of the Labour Party to Tony Blair and Speaker of the House to John Bercow. Her pragmatism sees her through. She acknowledges that this is the system, and that if you're putting yourself on the line you need to know the risks. And if you're not prepared to take those risks, then don't do it. Never one to say that losing doesn't hurt, Margaret instilled in me that sense of humility, service and reality.

As a new MP, she advised me to keep my constituents at the centre of everything, no matter what position I might achieve. One time, I sat in on her constituency advice surgery so that I could learn the ropes. She saw everyone and anyone, instinctively treating them all with the same respect as the heads of state with whom she was so familiar.

Some members of the media scrum have a notion that Margaret lacks strong opinions and simply does what she's told. This seems to be largely based on her principled stance: she doesn't leak information and never briefs against colleagues. The media mistakenly views her as 'a boring little person'. And it's true that Margaret isn't flashy, or always on the lookout to grab the limelight and headlines while trampling over her peers. I admire that and I think most people would find her attitude refreshing in a cynical age.

But she fights her corner, too, winning Cabinet battles over the National Minimum Wage (with the exception of the youth rate which she unsuccessfully opposed); writing a stinker of a letter to make a passionate, unbridled case in favour of government backing for the development of the Trent engine by Rolls-Royce in her constituency; co-authoring a minority report with the late Audrey Wise in the 1980s, when some wanted to expel anyone on the Left, not just those in Militant. Margaret has never sought to be fashionable, popular or noticed. She just gets on with the job and does what she believes is right.

Straightforward and authoritative, politically savvy and sharply intelligent, fallible and encouraging, there is something understated about Margaret Beckett. And yet, there's also something politically regal that cannot be ignored. It's the way she operates and the way she is. The girl from Ashton-under-Lyne done good. And she brought many of us along with her. That is the true measure of a class politician of our time. A right royal one at that.

JOAN MAYNARD

LOUISE HAIGH

- FULL NAME: Vera Joan Maynard
- DATE OF BIRTH: 5 July 1921
- PLACE OF BIRTH: Easingwold, North Yorkshire
- DATE OF DEATH: 27 March 1998
- MARRIED TO: Unmarried
- CHILDREN: None
- UNSUCCESSFUL ELECTIONS FOUGHT: None
- CONSTITUENCY: Sheffield Brightside
- DATE OF FIRST ELECTION: 10 October 1974
- DATE LEFT PARLIAMENT: 11 June 1987
- PARTY ROLES: Member of the Labour NEC 1972–82 and 1983–87; vice-chair of the Labour Party 1980–81
- MINISTERIAL POSITIONS & DATES: None
- MOST FAMOUS QUOTATION: 'Is it good for our class?'

In 1983, Jeremy Corbyn and Harry Cohen were sitting in the members' tearoom with Joan Maynard, who by then had been in Parliament for nine years. Joan insisted on pouring the tea; she liked things done properly and took tea very seriously. In one of the ritual questions that bright-eyed new members ask of their more senior colleagues, one of the young men asked Joan for advice on how to be an effective MP. Joan barely had to think about it before replying: 'If both front benches agree, the workers are losing out.'

It was this attitude that defined Joan's entire political career. From her activist days in establishing the first local Labour Party branch in Thirsk and Malton, and during her remarkable career in the trade union movement and later as an MP, she reiterated this sentiment constantly:

I have never believed in consensus politics. We must refuse to continue with the so-called mixed economy which enables the private enterprise to milk the

public sector … the Labour Party must take over the banks and end the subsi-
dies of multinational companies in Britain; the 300 largest corporations should
be nationalised right away.

I have to confess that when I was first asked to write about Joan, the first
thing that came to mind was her well-known nickname, 'Stalin's Granny'. I
spoke to people who knew of Joan, but who perhaps didn't know her very
well, who called her stubborn and uncompromising. The *Daily Telegraph*
described her as possessing 'characteristic authoritarianism'; her Wikipedia
entry barely mentions anything else. By all accounts Joan took it well, perhaps regarding her nickname as a badge of honour. But although I'm sure
many comrades intended it as a tribute to her staunch left-wing views and
uncompromising stance on any and all issues relating to workers, the more
I thought about it, the more I became uneasy that it belied an undertone
of sexism and ageism, one that Joan would undoubtedly have been wise to.

Joan Maynard was a fearless and dedicated defender of workers. She was
undeniably uncompromising at a time when the establishment viewed that
quality in a woman who had grown up in poverty with contempt and more
than a little fear. But it was this that won her the respect and admiration of
her class. Yes, she was uncompromising. How could you not be when your
communities were under ideological assault? But she was also kind, intelligent and thoughtful. When the alternative history of these islands is written,
in place of noble men from august homes there will be women like Joan, and
the qualities that her class embodied will be lionised.

Maynard was a matriarch of Sheffield, a woman who organised and rad-
icalised anyone and everyone she came across. As Dick Caborn put it, she
loved and trusted everyone, and would chat to anyone. She was 'hard in her
politics but soft on humanity', he said. 'You know he's a Tory MP, don't you?'
Dennis Skinner would remark, after he'd seen her chatting to someone across
the lobby. 'Well he wasn't when he was talking to me,' she would reply.

And I think this side of her character explains why she was so loved
and respected in her home town of Thirsk, a part of Britain that never has
been anything other than true blue. And yet it championed this left-wing
firebrand as its own. The market town of Thirsk made Joan; it informed
everything about her politics and everything she championed, even when she
represented an inner-city seat in industrial Sheffield. She served as a parish
and district councillor in Thirsk, maintained her home there while she was
an MP and moved back when she left Parliament. The residents of Thirsk

THE HONOURABLE LADIES: VOLUME I

loved her and were proud of her. She was, as Dennis Skinner said, the 'toast of the town'.

Joan's parents were tenant farmers from smallholder families. Her child-hood was marked by debt and financial hardship, but she remembered it as being a happy one and bore great loyalty and commitment to the country-side and to rural workers; her politics were shaped by the rural poverty she grew up in and she dedicated her career to tackling it.

Joan left school at fourteen to work on her parents' farm and although her parents were keenly political, correcting at home some of the colonial narratives that she was taught at school, it was Joan's enrolment at WEA classes in Thirsk and Malton that drove her into politics.

On her 29th birthday, with the support of the Labour Party and the National Union of Agricultural Workers (NUAW), she became the youngest Justice of the Peace in the North Riding of Yorkshire. She regarded it as good training for being able to stand up to landowners on behalf of the workers, and to speak her mind with confidence, which came as something of a shock to her new colleagues. 'The working-class people in Thirsk and Malton were just a bit different to me for a while,' she explained. 'And I realised that they thought that if you became a magistrate you'd joined the other side. Well, they soon found out that wasn't right.'

Sometimes she confounded other magistrates by opting to criticise the law instead of implementing it. 'And they'd be saying, but we're here to im-plement it, Joan, you'll have to go somewhere else if you want to alter it! So I got there eventually, but didn't find it easier when I got there.'

In 1952 she stood for election to the county council, where education – a passion of Joan's formed through experience of its power – was the key theme.

'If people are to live really full lives, education must not be neglected. We hear a lot about waste from the Tories. By that they always mean monetary waste. They never seem to be concerned about wasted lives.'

But time and again, Joan would return to her central and motivating passion: the plight of agricultural workers. She became well known for it in the labour movement and played a pivotal role in bringing the agri-cultural workers into the Transport and General Workers Union; she also wrote extensively for *The Landworker* magazine. In 1958, she moved a res-olution at the Labour Party conference: 'That this conference, recognising that socialism cannot be achieved as long as private ownership of the land remains, instructs the National Executive Committee to explicitly accept the nationalisation of land as party policy, without which many agricultural problems have no solution.'

When she was elected to the NEC in 1972, it was not only because of her profile in the trade union movement and the backing of the TGWU, it also owed to the powerful speech she made when once again moving a motion on land nationalisation.

After being elected to the Commons in the October 1974 election, she delivered her maiden speech.

> I come here not only to represent Brightside, but as the only sponsored member for farm workers ... As I come as a sponsored member for farm workers I speak for one of the lowest-paid groups. At the moment, farm workers are on a basic rate of £25 a week. It would be a mistake to think that the only people who live in poverty are pensioners; low-paid people and particularly those with families are often living in poverty. Although I represent an industrial seat, I have the full backing ... of my constituency to put forward the farm workers' case on an issue of vital importance ... My constituents understand the human problems brought by the tied-cottage system in agriculture. The system means that a man's home is dependent on his job.

On that point she was wrong. Tied cottages were a concept entirely alien to the good people of Brightside, but that was the beauty of Joan Maynard – she was so respected by her constituents that she could get away with focusing almost entirely on agricultural issues because she always spoke the truth to power.

But she also ably demonstrated that there are injustices in rural areas that need a Labour government, and indeed the labour movement, to respond to. The coalition government, in contrast, scrapped the Agricultural Wages Board. Cuts to local authorities from central government have depleted rural public transport and diminished access to jobs and services, and even though rural employment is often higher than it is in urban areas, wages are often low. Maynard would have been outraged by zero-hours contracts, false self-employment and the exploitation of migrant workers.

As Tam Dalyell wrote in his obituary of Joan, 'From the moment she arrived in the House of Commons, there was hardly a left-wing cause which she did not ardently espouse.' But she was also fiercely independent-minded and raised issues that few, if any, other MPs ever bothered with. Not only did she campaign tirelessly on tied cottages, but on land nationalisation in response to the threat of automation, on ecological and environmental issues, and on bringing politics out of London; she believed vehemently that politics was much too London-centric.

What troubled me about her reputation was that it masked, and perhaps deliberately distracted, from the truth about Joan – that she was well respected, knowledgeable in an area of policy that was almost unrivalled in the Labour Party, and someone who was well ahead of her time.

There's nothing wrong with being hard in your politics. Some may paint it as uncompromising, but for Joan it meant nothing more and nothing less than the unrelenting pursuit of issues that mattered to her, and to the people who she knew needed her to represent them.

So Joan was right to regard the nickname 'Stalin's Granny' as a badge of honour; staying true to your principles is hardly something to be ashamed of. But in getting to know Joan better, as I have done while writing this essay, I have discovered that what almost certainly led her to be so steadfast in her approach was the fact that she loved people. She wanted a better life for us all.

Joan's legacy can be seen in today's Labour Party: her commitment to the cause, and not to herself; her passionate defence of issues that were right but not necessarily popular in Westminster; her inexorable determination to advance the fortunes of those who had sent her to Parliament to represent them. But I hope that another part of her legacy becomes equally as lasting and powerful. I hope that, in fighting for what we truly believe in, we all endeavour to also believe in humanity. Just as Joan Maynard did, so often and so wonderfully.

MILLIE MILLER

LINDA PERHAM

- FULL NAME: Millie Miller (née Haring)
- DATE OF BIRTH: 8 April 1922
- PLACE OF BIRTH: Shoreditch, London
- DATE OF DEATH: 29 October 1977
- MARRIED TO: Montague 'Monty' Miller (m. 1940)
- CHILDREN: Bernard and Elizabeth
- UNSUCCESSFUL ELECTIONS FOUGHT: 28 February 1974
- CONSTITUENCY: Ilford North
- DATE OF FIRST ELECTION: 10 October 1974
- DATE LEFT PARLIAMENT: 29 October 1977
- PARTY ROLES: Labour councillor, Stoke Newington 1945; Mayor of Stoke Newington 1957–58; chair of Stoke Newington Housing Committee 1959; Mayor of Camden 1967–68; Leader of Camden Council 1971–73; chair of the London Labour Party's women's advisory committee
- MINISTERIAL POSITIONS & DATES: Parliamentary private secretary, Department of Prices and Consumer Protection 1976–77
- MOST FAMOUS QUOTATIONS: 'I am all in favour of the women's liberation movement. Every statistic shows that women in Britain do not get fair representation in any field.' | 'When things go wrong with the economy, governments will always intervene to save the banks.'

Despite serving for only three years as a Member of Parliament, tiny, auburn-haired Millie Miller became a local legend – adored and respected by her constituents. After her premature death from Hodgkin's disease in 1977 an annual memorial lecture was organised by the Ilford North Labour Party. When he launched his anti-poll tax campaign in 1990, Labour's Tony Benn said of Miller: 'It was a great honour to know her: a most remarkable woman.'

Millie Miller attended Dame Alice Owen's School in Hertfordshire, but left at the age of fourteen to work as a clerk in a draper's shop. During the Second World War, she held a senior position at W & T Avery Ltd and became a fire watcher. She also organised local girls' clubs.

In 1945, aged twenty-three, Miller began her distinguished service in local government after being elected to Stoke Newington's council where, as the youngest-ever mayor in 1957–58, she established a committee to support elderly and disabled people.

Moving to Camden, she was elected to St Pancras and then Camden council. As Mayor of Camden (1967–68), she planted the Hiroshima commemorative cherry tree in Tavistock Square (her ashes were scattered there).

In 1971, she became the Labour Party's first woman leader of a London borough council (Camden). In an interview with *The Times*, she said: 'The council has got too ladylike under the Tories. I am all in favour of ladies, I like to see them behave like members of the female sex, not like guests at a tea party.'

Her passions were conservation and housing. As chair of the public buildings committee, she helped to preserve local facilities such as the Roundhouse and Camden Lock. She led opposition to rent increases imposed under the Housing Finance Act 1972, and promoted innovative housing design projects, including Branch Hill, Hampstead Heath's first council estate.

While working as a social worker for the Inner London Education Authority, Miller decided to stand for Parliament. She contested both of the elections that were held in 1974. The Tory candidate for Ilford North, Thomas Iremonger, defeated her by 285 votes in February but Millie then captured the seat in the October election, securing a majority of 778. Her maiden speech on housing led the *Daily Mirror* to proclaim her the most promising new MP.

Miller campaigned in Parliament on women's rights and domestic abuse (serving on two select committees). In 1975, she voted against her own government's move to increase MPs' salaries from £4,400 to £4,500. Her son Bernard, writing in the *Camden New Journal* in 2009 about the MPs' expenses revelations, said that if his mother had not been cremated, she would have been 'spinning at high speed' in her grave.

Despite her rebellion over MPs' pay, in 1976 Millie was appointed parliamentary private secretary at the Department of Prices and Consumer Protection. In the last months of her life, she spoke in Parliament about the availability of vaccines for infectious diseases, the Common Agricultural Policy, mobility allowances for disabled people, and the problems of rent increases for London businesses. She co-sponsored the Housing (Homeless Persons) Act 1977.

Millie's care and concern for her constituents continued into her final hours. As the ambulance arrived to take her to hospital, a woman whose child was being taken into care called to ask for help. Mille phoned local resident Lord Soper and asked him to assist the young mother. That was Millie Miller: ready to serve to the end.

ANN TAYLOR

JUSTINE LANCASTER

- FULL NAME: Winifred Ann Taylor, Baroness Taylor of Bolton
- DATE OF BIRTH: 2 July 1947
- PLACE OF BIRTH: Motherwell, Lancashire
- DATE OF DEATH: –
- MARRIED TO: David Taylor (m. 1966)
- CHILDREN: Andrew and Isabelle
- UNSUCCESSFUL ELECTIONS FOUGHT: Bolton West 1974
- CONSTITUENCY: Bolton West 1974–83 and Dewsbury 1987–2005
- DATE OF FIRST ELECTION: 10 October 1974
- DATE LEFT PARLIAMENT: 11 April 2005
- PARTY ROLES: None
- MINISTERIAL POSITIONS & DATES: Opposition spokesman for Education
  & Science 1979–81; Assistant whip 1977–79; opposition spokesman
  for the Environment 1988–92; shadow Secretary of State for Education
  1992–94; shadow Chancellor of the Duchy of Lancaster 1994–95; shadow
  Leader of the House of Commons 1994–97; Leader of the House of
  Commons and Lord President of the Council 1997–98; Chief Whip
  1998–2001; Minister for Defence Procurement 2007–2008; Minister for
  International Defence and Security 2008–10

First elected as MP for the northern constituency Bolton West in October 1974, Ann Taylor became one of Labour's fastest-rising female stars. Three years after becoming one of only ten female MPs to win a seat in the 1974 general election, she was appointed assistant whip in James Callaghan's government.

She subsequently went on to become the first female leader of the House of Commons, following Tony Blair's election as Prime Minister in 1997. Just a year later, Taylor became the first female Chief Whip; in the role she pushed for House of Lords reform, devolution and the minimum wage. She stepped down from the House of Commons ahead of the 2005 general election, returning to Parliament as Baroness Taylor of Bolton.

In *This House*, James Graham's political comedy about the Wilson–Callaghan Labour government of 1974, Taylor is portrayed as an MP who wants to be one of the boys, despite her Labour colleagues assuming that she is the secretary. 'Looking for your office, love? 'Tis a bit of a maze, here,' says one Labour MP on her first day of work in the post. Taylor says her colleagues did – contrary to the script – know exactly who she was, but the play nevertheless captures the prevailing attitudes of the time: it was still unusual to be a mother and a politician.

While in office, Taylor was also raising two children with her husband, David, who she married in 1966 at the age of nineteen, after meeting him through the Labour youth wing. Their courtship was spent knocking on doors campaigning, she says.

She believed that male colleagues in the 1970s were not 'intentionally chauvinistic', but simply believed that they alone 'had the responsibility to be the bread winner'. All the same, Taylor was aware of the contradictions – that although her male colleagues were not keen on their wives going out to work, they felt differently about their daughters who they wanted to have better opportunities, much as Taylor had after growing up on a council estate and winning a place at grammar school at the age of eleven.

Ann had won a seat on the local council while studying for her PhD at Sheffield University, before being adopted as the Labour candidate to contest the Bolton West seat. The shortlist had consisted originally of five trade union sponsored males, but it was felt that a women needed to be added to the mix and Taylor was chosen, ultimately winning the selection at only twenty-four years old, and the seat at twenty-seven.

Newly elected in October 1974, Taylor joined Parliament at a febrile time, following the second general election that year. The Labour government's shoestring majority of just three was eliminated over time, forcing the party into a pact with the Liberal Party in 1977.

Taylor was appointed as a whip in Parliament, but much of her work was focused in her constituency, where she fought for years to win compensation for workers who had suffered from byssinosis – known as 'brown lung disease' – which was caused by exposure to cotton dust. There were also race issues, including an incident where the BNP paid for white parents in the area to educate their kids in a room above a pub rather than send their kids to a so-called black school.

By 1992, Taylor had been appointed to John Smith's front bench, where she was assigned the position of shadow Education Secretary. In this role, Taylor fought to establish nursery education as a right for every three- and four-year-old, pushed for more money to be spent on schools and argued against charitable status for private schools. It was not an easy ride and Taylor was often pilloried in the newspapers.

Taylor's conservatism on certain issues softened slightly over time. She had initially voted against lowering the gay age of consent, and in 1994 she abstained from voting to lower the homosexual age of consent from eighteen to sixteen, which would make the legal age equal to that for heterosexuals. This was still contrary to Tony Blair and other senior members of the shadow Cabinet who had largely voted yes.

In 1997, Taylor joined the wave of record-breaking numbers of female MPs elected to Parliament under Tony Blair's Labour government. There her loyal and disciplined manner and her strong support for the creation of NHS foundation trusts, which reorganised the health service, and for the Iraq War saw her rapidly promoted. In his autobiography, Blair described her as a member of the 'if necessary we'll take the world on and screw them all brigade'.

Taylor became Minister for International Defence and Security under Gordon Brown in 2008, and remained in the position until Labour lost the general election in 2010. Taylor chose to step down from the Commons ahead of the 2005 general election, citing the need to 'rebalance her life'. She joined the Lords as Baroness Taylor of Bolton.

OONAGH MCDONALD

POLLY BILLINGTON

- FULL NAME: Dr Oonagh Anne McDonald CBE
- DATE OF BIRTH: February 1938
- PLACE OF BIRTH: Stockton-on-Tees, Co Durham
- DATE OF DEATH: –
- MARRIED TO: Unmarried
- CHILDREN: None
- UNSUCCESSFUL ELECTIONS FOUGHT: South Gloucestershire February 1974 and October 1974
- CONSTITUENCY: Thurrock
- DATE OF FIRST ELECTION: 15 July 1976
- DATE LEFT PARLIAMENT: 11 June 1987
- PARTY ROLES: None
- MINISTERIAL POSITIONS & DATES: Parliamentary private secretary to the Chief Secretary to the Treasury

It is often said that the Labour Party owes more to Methodism than it does to Marxism, and Oonagh McDonald is a testament to that. By her own admission McDonald does not hail from a political family, but with a father who was a non-conformist minister and then a theologian, she grew up in an atmosphere where issues of social justice were important.

While a philosophy lecturer at Bristol University, McDonald became involved in the Labour Party. She contested the rock-solid Tory seat of South Gloucestershire in the general elections of February and October 1974, losing out on both occasions.

When Thurrock's MP Hugh Delargy died of a heart attack in 1976, McDonald put her name forward as a candidate for the ensuing by-election. At that time the selection process required all would-be candidates to write to the CLP secretary. As a mark of respect, Oonagh did not write her letter until after Hugh Delargy's funeral had taken place. She partly attributes winning the selection to having adopted this approach.

The British summer of 1976 was belting hot, and the Thurrock by-election was held at the height of it. As the polls closed a thunderstorm broke, bringing a dramatic end to the long campaign. Supporters of the National Front, almost always a presence in this part of the world, paraded around the grounds of the civic hall where the count was taking place. The NF polled more than 3,000 votes. Oonagh McDonald became the MP for Thurrock with a majority of 4,937 – a 10 per cent swing to the Conservatives.

With a background as a schoolteacher and a lecturer, the atmosphere of the House of Commons held little fear for the newly elected MP, and when the Tory benches got rowdy she often deployed the same tactics that she had used on fifteen-year-old schoolboys. Some Conservative MPs even admitted to behaving badly when they encountered her in the lobbies later.

McDonald's friends in Parliament included Joel Barnett, her boss when she was his parliamentary private secretary and he was Chief Secretary to the Treasury, John Silkin, Kevin McNamara and Jeff – now Lord – Rooker.

Her responsibilities included financial regulation, especially when she was in the shadow Treasury team in the 1980s. This paved the way to a life after politics.

But while she was an MP it was her ability to raise issues as an elected representative that enabled McDonald to change people's lives. She was part of the campaign to free two men wrongly convicted and jailed for the Luton Post Office murder in 1969, one of a number of cases of police corruption.

A piece of constituency casework kick-started a campaign for justice for hundreds of ex-servicemen. Second World War veteran Bertram Stevens of Chadwell St Mary came to see her after being diagnosed with the after-effects of exposure to mustard gas. Officially, the chemical weapon had not been used during the Second World War. But an American ship, the USS *John Harvey*, had been secretly carrying it when it was blown up in Bari harbour; hundreds of British and American troops had thus been exposed to the gas. Despite the US government admitting responsibility shortly afterwards, the UK documents were destroyed. It was not until 1986, partly as a result of McDonald's efforts, that the British government finally came clean. It admitted that survivors of the Bari raid had been exposed to the poison gas and amended their pension payments.

During the Labour Party's deputy leadership contest in the 1980s, Oonagh voted for her friend and ally John Silkin in the first round. In the second round, after Silkin had been eliminated, she voted for Denis Healey, and thus helped secure Healey's narrow victory over left-wing challenger Tony Benn. The vote for Healey was contrary to the wishes of her CLP, which had threatened to deselect her. This made McDonald all the more determined to vote with her conscience.

Thurrock changed during her time as an MP. McDonald's maiden speech had been about dock regulation and securing employment rights for dock workers. But by the time of the 1987 election, when she lost her seat, the number of dockers living in Thurrock had collapsed as containerisation took hold. McDonald fought hard for the creation of the Lakeside shopping centre, which helped create warehousing and retail jobs. But in terms of skills, pay and security these jobs never replaced lost manufacturing jobs in the saw mills, the paper mills, the Ford factory or the oil refinery.

As the employment situation in Thurrock changed so too did the social structure, with people starting to commute to clerical jobs in London. They bought new homes in Chafford Hundred – a private housing development built in a former chalk quarry – that is now home to thousands. Less reliant on the docks and more dependent on the financial services industry for work, Thurrock's connection with the trade unions declined. The shift leftwards of the Labour Party might have energised activists in London, but it left the voters of Thurrock cold.

The 1987 election is usually seen as a milestone on the way back to electability for Labour from the nadir of 1983. But although McDonald had managed to survive in 1983, she lost her seat in the 1987 election: the very right-wing Conservative Tim Janman beat her by just under 700 votes. The National Front candidate, whose supporters had marched around the civic hall grounds in the 1976 by-election, chose this time to stand aside, enabling Janman to eke out a narrow victory.

Oonagh McDonald chose not to stand again for election as the Labour Party's selection process had changed, putting more power into the hands of the trade unions. Instead she developed a career in financial regulation, which took her all across the globe. She now lives in Washington DC, having been awarded permanent residence there on the grounds of exceptional ability, and plans to continue her work on financial regulation.

Her book *Fannie Mae and Freddie Mac: Turning the American Dream into a Nightmare* made her a regular contributor to the BBC's *Today* programme, where she explained the causes of the financial crash.

McDonald received a CBE for her work on financial regulation in 1998. The letter came from No. 10 and a certain Tony Blair who had been one of her colleagues – and rivals – in Labour's shadow Treasury team in the 1980s.

SHEILA FAITH

SHAZIA AWAN-SCULLY

- FULL NAME: Irene Sheila Faith (née Book)
- DATE OF BIRTH: 3 June 1928
- PLACE OF BIRTH: Newcastle
- DATE OF DEATH: 28 September 2014
- MARRIED TO: Denis Faith (m. 1950)
- CHILDREN: None
- UNSUCCESSFUL ELECTIONS FOUGHT: Newcastle Central October 1974
- CONSTITUENCY: Belper
- DATE OF FIRST ELECTION: 3 May 1979
- DATE LEFT PARLIAMENT: 8 June 1983
- MEP: Cumbria and Lancashire North 1984–89
- PARTY ROLES: None
- MINISTERIAL POSITIONS & DATES: None

Sheila Faith had what was, by most standards, a fairly unremarkable four-year career as a backbench MP at Westminster. Yet her entry to Parliament was, in at least one sense, extraordinary. In the substantial Conservative intake of new MPs in 1979, Faith was the only woman.

Born Irene Sheila Book in 1928, Faith grew up in Newcastle where her family owned a fashion business (of which she was to become a director for much of her adult life). After studying dentistry at the University of Durham, she worked in this field for some years before becoming more actively involved in politics. She married Denis Faith in 1950.

Faith's first major involvement in electoral politics came in local government. She was elected to Northumberland County Council in 1970, serving until 1974 and then once again between 1975 and '78.

Having stood, unsuccessfully, for the Conservatives in Newcastle at the October 1974 election, Faith was adopted as the Conservative candidate for

Belper – a seat that had famously been won by the Tories from the then Labour deputy leader George Brown in 1970, but which was subsequently regained by Labour four years later. The seat had long been a marginal constituency, and it remained so even in the swing to Mrs Thatcher's Conservatives in 1979: Sheila Faith won the seat by a mere 882 votes.

Thatcher's election brought in a large cohort of new Conservative MPs, with new seats gained by the Tories, and the replacement of some MPs who had retired after a gruelling five-year parliament marked by extensive parliamentary trench warfare against a government that had lacked a House of Commons majority for most of the term. It is a measure of how much Parliament has changed that Sheila Faith's status as the sole new Conservative female MP would now be utterly unthinkable.

Faith served as an MP for four years. She never held ministerial office during that period. As a backbench MP she showed particular concern with health issues, serving as a founder member of the Commons Select Committee on health and social services. Faith was also concerned with issues regarding law and order, on which she tended to take a traditional Tory stance. For instance, in 1982, she drew on her previous service as a magistrate to oppose what she saw as Home Secretary Willie Whitelaw's overly liberal proposed reforms to the law on soliciting.

Boundary changes prior to the 1983 general election abolished the Belper seat. The closest thing to a successor seat was the new constituency of South Derbyshire. Faith felt that this seat was unwinnable and so decided to seek an alternative seat, but she was unable to secure the Conservative nomination in another constituency. Ironically, in the post-Falklands Thatcherite landslide victory of 1983, the South Derbyshire seat was won by the Conservatives with a majority of 8,613 votes – and by another woman, Edwina Currie. While Currie went on to become one of Parliament's most well-known MPs, Faith left Parliament.

A year later, however, Faith was back as an elected politician – this time as MEP for Cumbria and Lancashire North. She took what was then the mainstream view in the Conservative Party and was a strong supporter of British membership of the EEC. She served one, five-year term in the European Parliament – a period that saw the passage of the Single European Act, championed by Mrs Thatcher, which strengthened European integration and significantly enhanced the status of the European Parliament itself. As the 1989 European election approached, however, Faith, by now in her sixties, had little appetite for the near-continuous travel demanded of an MEP. Instead of standing for election, Faith chose to retire from the European Parliament and from elected politics.

In subsequent years, Faith's main contribution to public life was several years of service on the Parole Board for England and Wales. She died in 2014.

SHEILA WRIGHT

NATALIE BENNETT

- FULL NAME: Sheila Rosemary Rivers Wright (also Rivers-Gregory)
- DATE OF BIRTH: 22 March 1925
- PLACE OF BIRTH: Kanpur, India
- DATE OF DEATH: 5 July 2013
- MARRIED TO: Married
- CHILDREN: Children and grandchildren
- UNSUCCESSFUL ELECTIONS FOUGHT: Birmingham Handsworth 1964, 1966 and 1970
- CONSTITUENCY: Birmingham Handsworth
- DATE OF FIRST ELECTION: 3 May 1979
- DATE LEFT PARLIAMENT: 9 June 1983
- PARTY ROLES: None
- MINISTERIAL POSITIONS & DATES: None
- MOST FAMOUS QUOTATION: 'The House should remember that there is a small minority of British citizens who are both black and women who are today watching to see whether the House is prepared to treat them as equal citizens regardless of their sex and colour.'

Sheila Wright's parliamentary career was short, just one term, but her life of public service was long and distinguished. Her fate and her gender were surely crucially related: she fought long and hard to win the seat of Birmingham Handsworth, through multiple elections, but the combination of its abolition and family responsibilities meant she never returned to Westminster. Not a story you could tell about many male MPs.

And that was a great pity, for Hansard tells a story of an analytical, strong, fluent speaker who showed no fear or favour in taking on the government of Margaret Thatcher.

Wright already had plenty of experience of taking on the 'Iron Lady' directly, as chair of Birmingham's education committee, seeking to effectively end the 11-plus exam in the city in 1973, when Thatcher was education secretary. That reflected a long, deep period of service: twenty-two years on the City Council (1956–78) and eight on the West Midlands County Council.

Wright's speaking style was not at all floury, but direct and to the point. So on housing, she was saying in 1979: 'The problems of the inner cities stem straight from the inheritance of the Industrial Revolution, that heyday of untrammelled free enterprise which left a legacy of miserable housing, worse environment and considerable ill health to the descendants of those who created its wealth.'

Speaking after her constituency was hard hit by what became known as the 1981 race riots (also in Toxteth, Brixton and Chapeltown), she said, 'A spark will not ignite a tinder box if the tinder box is not there for the spark to fall into it… let us not be so preoccupied with dousing the sparks that we forget to remove the tinder box,' explaining she was referring to bad housing, poorly provided schools, cuts in social services and unemployment.

Not from an ethnic minority background herself, although foreign-born, she took her personal experience, and the nature of her constituency, as a driver to be strong and direct in defending immigration and individual immigrants. In a classic representation for a constituent threatened with deportation, she pointed out that he had applied at age fifteen, but was nineteen by the time the application was processed. He hadn't told the authorities that he was married and had a child, she said, because no one had asked.

She seems to have fitted on the 'practical left' of the often febrile Labour Party of the time, being listed by *The Guardian* as one of nineteen MPs who abstained in 1981 to allow Denis Healey victory in the leadership contest against Tony Benn. Her Constituency Labour Party seems to have often been fractious, with reports of an attempted Militant takeover during her time in Westminster, and of 'fisticuffs' at meetings. But then she did represent a constituency infamous at the time for the Reggae band Steel Pulse, which sang of a 'Handsworth Revolution', 'even if it does take ammunition'.

Yet I've not been able to find a single obituary marking Wright's death at the age of eighty-eight. It was many years after her Westminster service, yet she surely deserved more than the simple family funeral notice that appeared in the *Birmingham Mail.*

DAME ANGELA RUMBOLD

ELIZABETH PEACOCK

- FULL NAME: Dame Angela Clare Rosemary Rumbold (née Jones) DBE PC
- DATE OF BIRTH: 11 August 1932
- PLACE OF BIRTH: Bristol
- DATE OF DEATH: 19 June 2010
- MARRIED TO: John Rumbold
- CHILDREN: Two sons and one daughter
- UNSUCCESSFUL ELECTIONS FOUGHT: None
- CONSTITUENCY: Mitcham & Morden
- DATE OF FIRST ELECTION: 3 June 1982
- DATE LEFT PARLIAMENT: 30 April 1997
- PARTY ROLES: Deputy chair of Conservative Party 1992 and vice-chair Conservative Party 1995–97
- MINISTERIAL POSITIONS & DATES: Parliamentary private secretary for Transport; Under-Secretary of State Department of the Environment; Minister for Education; Minister of State at the Home Office

On the Friday after the Tory election triumph of 1983, I was telephoned by Donald Thompson, the twenty-stone MP for Calder Valley who was also a government whip. He congratulated me on my election as the new Conservative Member of Parliament for Batley and Spen. Most of the constituency had never previously had a Conservative MP; Batley and Spen had been represented by a National Liberal in 1931, and there had then been Labour MPs ever after.

Donald asked me when I was planning to come down to London. I suggested the following Wednesday; I had taken a month's leave from work to fight the election and needed to first tell Mike Clemson at York Community Council that I would not be going back there to be his assistant director. Donald had other ideas and told me to be in Central Lobby on Tuesday morning at 10 a.m., when he would meet me and then take me on a tour of the House. When

I reached Central Lobby Donald had not yet arrived, but Angela Rumbold was there. She had become the MP for Mitcham and Morden the previous year after winning a by-election. Angela introduced me to Jim Spicer and Jim Lester, and the four of us then lunched together at a restaurant somewhere near Church House. This was the start of a great friendship with Angela.

The next day when I met Angela in the Members' Lobby, she asked me if I smoked! Strange question, I thought. I told her I didn't smoke, which proved to be the right answer, as she then asked me if I would like to share her office. My whip had told me not to expect to get an office – not even a shared one – for at least a month, as there were many more important people who needed one! Angela and I enjoyed a very happy working relationship and became firm friends.

Dame Angela Rumbold CBE was a principled politician who was never afraid to speak her mind, and her fearless and powerful spirit was evident from that very first day I met her. While our friendship may have begun in Central Lobby, it long outlived the end of both our political careers in 1997.

Angela was elected for Mitcham and Morden in a by-election in 1982 (defeating former Labour MP Bruce Douglas-Mann, who had defected to the newly formed Social Democratic Party) and held the seat for fifteen years. She had served as a councillor in Kingston for nine years before becoming an MP, and it was this life-long commitment to public service and political representation that was so evident in all her decisions; she was never afraid to prioritise those who had elected her, or to put her strongly held beliefs above the mercurial nature of party politics.

Her outspoken nature, however, did not prevent her from having an illustrious ministerial career. Stepping up to be PPS to Nicholas Ridley in 1983, Angela then served as a junior minister at the Department of Education from 1985 to 1990, and subsequently as the minister of state in the same department. Indeed, even after the loss of her position she was long seen as an unequivocally straight-talking authority on educational matters, once famously remarking that Margaret Thatcher's policies on universities were 'absurd'.

Although she had been elected while Thatcherite fever was sweeping the country during the Falklands War, Angela's talent survived the transition of power to John Major and she was appointed Minister of State at the Home Office in 1990. In all her ministerial positions she proved to be both passionate and capable and I – like many others – believe the only reason she never received a Cabinet promotion was because she refused to be cowed by the conventions of party machinery.

Indeed, her prominence in the Conservative Party did not end with her exit from the ministerial ranks: in 1992 she became a deputy chair of the party, and served as a vice-chair from 1995 to 1997. Her fierce drive and commitment to political progression found another outlet here; as the first woman with responsibility for selecting parliamentary candidates she played an integral part in the drive to get more women into Parliament. It is important to remember that in the early years of both Angela's, and my, parliamentary tenure, there were only twenty-three women MPs in the Commons.

In the period before the 1997 election, she eschewed the party's principle of ambiguity on the matter, declaring that 'scrapping the pound' would be accompanied by a dramatic 'erosion of sovereignty'. This fiery statement, typical of her commitment to straight-talking, was then extremely rare in the euphemism-steeped halls of Westminster. Although her statement was used by the media as an indication of division within the Conservative Party, its real value was in highlighting Angela's willingness to set herself apart from her party; her independence was not altered by the rosette she wore on election days.

Late in 1983 one day she arrived back in the office after a meeting, threw her papers on her desk and declared loudly, 'This bloody place runs on the old boy's network, and you and I are not on it – so what do we do? Set up an old girl's network.' Over a cup of coffee, we decided on our strategy. Angela would put together a list of women in various backgrounds of work in the London area, and she would give me 'the rest of the world to sort out'.

Early in 1985, we held a dinner in the House of Commons for twenty-four women from around the UK and we invited four junior ministers to join us. The dinner was a success and marked the start of an organisation that over many years brought a huge number of women from all walks of life to the Commons to dine and meet Ministers of the Crown that they otherwise would have been unlikely to meet.

Angela lost her seat in 1997. This was, however, by no means the end of her career or endeavours in education and women's rights, and she was involved with the governing boards of a number of schools. She was appointed CBE in 1981, DBE in 1992 and died, aged seventy-seven, in June 2010. Although her time in the House was only a small part of her life in public service, she greatly enjoyed it and was, to all who knew her, a force of nature. She was the only MP then (or even I suspect now) to park a sporty white Chevrolet in the Member's car park. Angela and I remained good friends after losing our Parliamentary seats and still met in London from time to time and kept our involvement with the Westminster Dining Club.

HARRIET HARMAN

SCARLETT MCCGWIRE

- FULL NAME: Harriet Ruth Harman
- DATE OF BIRTH: 30 July 1950
- PLACE OF BIRTH: London
- DATE OF DEATH: –
- MARRIED TO: Jack Dromey (m. 1982)
- CHILDREN: Harry, Joe and Amy
- UNSUCCESSFUL ELECTIONS FOUGHT: None
- CONSTITUENCY: Peckham 1982–97; Camberwell & Peckham 1997–present
- DATE OF FIRST ELECTION: 28 October 1982
- DATE LEFT PARLIAMENT: Incumbent
- PARTY ROLES: Deputy leader of the Labour Party 2007–15; chair of the Labour Party 2007–10; acting leader of the Labour Party 2010 and 2015
- MINISTERIAL POSITIONS & DATES: Shadow Chief Secretary to the Treasury 1992–94; shadow Employment Secretary 1994–95; shadow Health Secretary 1995–96; shadow Social Security Secretary 1996–97; Secretary of State for Social Security 1997–98; Minister for Women 1997–98; Solicitor General for England and Wales 2001–05; Minister for Constitutional Affairs 2005–07; leader of the House of Commons 2007–10; Lord Privy Seal 2007–10; Minister for Women and Equality 2007–10; acting Leader of the Opposition 2010; shadow Deputy Prime Minister 2010–15; shadow International Development Secretary 2010–11; shadow Culture, Media and Sport Secretary 2011–15; acting Leader of the Opposition 2015
- MOST FAMOUS QUOTATION: 'When it comes to equality, today's heresy is tomorrow's orthodoxy.'

When Harriet Harman was first elected to the House of Commons in 1982, there were more MPs called John than there were women MPs. At Prime Minister's Questions, Harman asked about care for school-aged children during the holidays; Margaret Thatcher smirked and answered in a condescending voice that such provision was hardly the business of government. The laughing and jeering Tory MPs were joined by many on the Labour benches. The next day Keith Waterhouse called her absurd in his column in the *Daily Mirror* for asking a question which had nothing to do with government. Nearly four decades later, both parties vie with each other to promise affordable provision, understanding that childcare is a matter of public policy.

Thus, from the outset, Harman battled not only against male dominance in Parliament, but against an assumption that relegated the family agenda – a major barrier to women taking their place in public life – to the domestic sphere. For Harman, the political was indeed personal, as she was pregnant with her first child when elected to the Commons and would go on to have two more as an MP. Yet while she fought for affordable childcare for working women, she found herself torn between the demands of work and family, particularly once she became a shadow minister. The demanding hours kept her from seeing enough of her children. Added to that were the mocking comments she endured, but she never allowed herself to become a victim. While she became the first woman deputy leader of the Labour Party, and even acting leader during two interregnums, far more important is her legacy. Harman changed the rules so that women are not only better represented in Parliament and the public sphere, but their needs are part of the public policy agenda.

The third of four daughters born to a doctor father and a barrister mother who ultimately gave up her career to raise her children, Harman was brought up in middle-class north London. After attending the prestigious St Paul's School and York University, she followed her siblings into law, but realised quickly that stuffy firms did not suit her. At Brent Law Centre, she shared an office with her future husband, Jack Dromey, a trade union activist. She advised the women workers who battled successfully for equal pay at the Trico factory, which made windscreen wipers, and helped in the celebrated fight for union recognition at the Grunwick film processing factory. When she became the legal officer of the National Council for Civil Liberties (NCCL, but now known as Liberty) and challenged the government on a host of issues, she became a national figure, appearing regularly on radio and television.

As a radical and progressive woman, she joined the Labour Party after university and she pursued a feminist agenda within it. Understanding that she could effect change more radically as an MP than at the NCCL, she successfully fought to be selected for the safe Labour seat of Peckham, after the sitting MP, Harry Lamborn, announced he was retiring at the next election. With the general election thought to be two years away, Harman decided the timing was right to get pregnant and marry Jack. Holidaying in France after her marriage (refusing to call it a honeymoon), and suffering from morning sickness, Harman read a three-day-old copy of *The Times* to discover that Lamborn had suddenly died and she had to return to fight a by-election. It would have taken a political earthquake to defeat Labour in Peckham and she duly took her seat in the Commons. Looking along the rows of grey-suited men in the chamber, she realised how isolated she was: a Labour MP in a Tory-dominated parliament; a London Labour MP in Tory London; a woman in a predominantly male parliament; and to top it off she was pregnant. Inviting the ten other Labour women MPs to a meeting, she established the Parliamentary Labour Party Women's Committee, now an accepted part of life in the Commons, but when established, it was greeted with horror and opprobrium due to its explicit exclusion of men.

Her first son, Harry, arrived three months after her election, followed by Joe and Amy. Harman juggled the demands of her job with her desire to spend more time with her children, yet she knew that being an MP was a privilege and she could not complain. She was all too aware of the irony as she battled for affordable childcare to allow women to work.

This was a time when the hours of the Commons were predicated around men having second jobs in London during the day, so most evenings were filled with voting that would often go on into the early hours of the night, sometimes even all night. It resembled a nineteenth-century gentlemen's club rather than a modern workplace. Changing those hours to suit families took decades of campaigning.

Journalists poked fun at her feminism, dubbing her 'Harriet Harperson' in the tabloids. Overwhelmingly male, the lobby depicted her as humourless, priggish and stupid. For her part, while funny and open-minded, she is bad at small talk and gossiping at the expense of her colleagues. That combined with not wanting to spend time socialising when she could be getting her work done to get home, meant she did not win them round. Only when women broke into the lobby journalists' ranks did the coverage change, though many of the men clung to their old prejudices.

Harman joined the front bench in 1984, when Neil Kinnock appointed her shadow Minister for Social Services. In the 1987 election, she took five-month-old Amy on the campaign trail and afterwards moved to the Department of Health. Harman had not come into Parliament only to fight the Tories, she wanted to change the system so that women's voices could be heard. As well as cataloguing the disastrous effect the Tory government was having on the health service, she fought for more women to be elected and promoted in local and national government. On this she locked horns with many Labour men, who felt their position threatened. Yet Kinnock shared her aspirations and understood that to attract the women's vote, the party had to change. As long as the Conservatives attracted the majority of women's votes, Labour would be out of government.

At the time, the shadow Cabinet was elected, with barely a woman garnering enough votes. Harman pushed successfully for the top three women to be given a place as well as the twenty-three top men. This annoyed many Labour men who felt discriminated against. In the first elections under this system, Harman was not elected. They were determined that the architect of the reform should not benefit.

Labour women were also battling to get more of their number elected. The bias against selecting women to stand as MPs was wrong on a number of levels. Good women were being denied a chance to stand, which not only deprived Parliament – and the opposition – of their distinctive voice and expertise, it made the party appear rampantly male to the voters. A look at voting breakdown shows that if women had been denied the vote, Labour would have been in power for most of the twentieth century. Research found that many considered the party off-putting, so there were both moral and pragmatic reasons for change. All-women shortlists were implemented after years of trying persuasion; the only way to even up the numbers in Parliament would be to make sure women were selected to fight elections. The battle was vicious: many men felt they were being discriminated against and some women found it patronising. As a leading proponent in Parliament, Harman took much of the public flak and the journalistic opprobrium. In 1993, all-women shortlists became party policy. The media hated it. Winning the 1997 general election, Labour had 101 women MPs. Even when they lost power, Labour had more women MPs than all the other parties put together. The policy delivered.

After John Smith became leader of the party following the 1992 election defeat, he promoted Harman to the shadow Cabinet as shadow Chief Secretary to the Treasury, in Gordon Brown's team. She poached a young TV researcher to work as her adviser, Ed Miliband. When Tony Blair became leader, she became one of the architects of New Labour – modernising the party meant a greater role for women. Blair appointed Harman shadow Secretary of State for Employment and during her time in the role she developed the idea of the Low Pay Commission to set up a National Minimum Wage. In 1996, she became shadow Secretary of State for Social Security and set in motion a minimum guarantee for the poorest pensioners, most of whom were women who had taken years out of work to care for children or elderly relatives.

In 1997, with the election of Tony Blair as Prime Minister, Harman became Secretary of State for Social Security and Minister for Women and Equality. While full of energy and great ideas, she would soon discover that, unfortunately, she was totally unprepared for government and running a massive department. Apart from a staff of 93,000 and a completely different way of working, she had two particular problems. The first was her deputy, Frank Field, who Tony Blair had appointed to 'think the unthinkable'. This put him at odds with Harman over policy; but Field also made no secret of his belief that the job should have been his. The second was Gordon Brown's pledge to stick to Conservative spending limits, which included cutting the extra six pounds a week that lone parents received in child benefit. It seemed that a Labour government which had come into office with the theme song of 'Things Can Only Get Better' were making things much worse for one of the most vulnerable groups, who had been constantly pilloried by the Conservatives. In Cabinet, Brown demanded loyalty, but on the outside Harman was attacked for a policy she did not believe in. Her work on the New Deal for the unemployed and her particular success in helping single parents get into work was as nothing; she had been cast as a pantomime villain. Shockingly, when the House of Commons voted on the cut on lone parents' child benefit neither Blair nor Brown turned up. She had been hung out to dry. Her sacking in the summer of 1998 came as no surprise.

When I went in to see her in September 1998 to advise her on her next steps, she was probably the most unpopular person in the country. We had known each other since her days at the NCCL, when I was a radio journalist, and in the intervening years I had become a media adviser. I believed she was young enough for another career and that there was no future for her in Parliament. She shook her head: Peckham was her political lodestone and the people there kept her grounded, she would not leave them. In that case, I told her, we would prepare her for her return to government and see what happened. She had to stay out of the media and work, so that the next interview she did would be about what she was doing, not who she had been. For three years she set to work: chairing the Southwark Early Years Partnership in her constituency; chairing the Childcare Commission, which called for a children's centre in every area; publishing 'Mothers in Manufacturing', a report on making factories more family friendly; and successfully lobbying Brown into extending maternity leave. Yet it was a pretty miserable time. Having fought for years in opposition, she was again pushing for changing policies rather than implementing them, while most of her friends were on the front bench.

After the 2001 election, Blair appointed her as Solicitor General. She had proved me wrong and returned to government. It was a reward for loyalty and resilience: not once had she publicly criticised the government or Blair's role in her departure. Most sacked ministers bitterly take to the media to denounce the government or sulk; she had worked hard, mainly behind the scenes. Of course this also conveyed a message to other sacked ministers: behave and there is a way back.

Her new role put her in charge of the Crown Prosecution Service. With two women a week murdered by partners or ex-partners and hundreds more being beaten in their home, she set about changing the way the law dealt with such cases. She brought in the Domestic Violence Crime and Victims Act, working with women's groups and the CPS to make sure the law worked, establishing CPS specialist domestic violence prosecutors who understood that this was a crime not a private matter. She also brought in impact statements, which allowed victims to tell the court how the crime had affected them. She had been particularly moved by her conversations with the families of murder victims who felt that they could not express their pain.

After the 2005 election, she was made Minister for Constitutional Affairs and started working on a specific 'democratic deficit': the more dependent a person is on the state, the less likely they are to vote. She became Minister for Justice when the ministry changed its name to the Department of Justice.

While Labour won their unprecedented third term, albeit with a reduced majority, Tony Blair announced that he would retire before the next election. So the jostling around the Labour leadership began. Gordon Brown ensured that he would enjoy a coronation rather than an election, but the deputy leadership of the party was up for grabs. And it was time for a woman. Persuading Harman that she was the right person for the job proved remarkably difficult; she believed the deputy should be a woman, just that that woman was not her. Finally I went to Sunday lunch at her home and secured her agreement. Quite rightly she had been worried about the press coverage; when she declared she would be putting herself forward, the journalists were scathing and the bookies put her at 100/1, the rank outsider. For months she and her small campaign team worked to get votes. First there were the nominations from MPs – she needed forty-four even to be allowed on the ballot paper, which seemed impossibly daunting; yet in the end she managed sixty-five. Then there were hustings and meetings all over the country – for months she spent every weekend on trains. Her major problem was finance; small donations paid for her travel and a couple of staff but she had no major backers. When the Labour Party allowed all the candidates to send out a leaflet to every member, which was going to cost £40,000, she had to mortgage her house to raise the money.

At a special conference in Manchester on 27 June, Brown was anointed leader, becoming Prime Minister, and Harman won the deputy leadership by the narrowest of margins, less than 1 per cent from Alan Johnson, Secretary of State for Education. When reporters asked Johnson about losing he said, 'I was the best man, but as is so often the case, along came a better woman.' Gordon Brown was rather more curmudgeonly and refused to make her his Deputy Prime Minister – something that many believe he would not have done to a man. Less than a year later, he tried to appoint Peter Mandelson Deputy Prime Minister, ironically on the same day as Caroline Flint resigned as Housing minister after accusing Brown of using women as window dressing. Between interviews defending him on that score, Harman met with Brown three times to threaten that he would give the post to Mandelson over her dead body. In the event, he made Mandelson First Secretary of State, briefing that it was effectively Deputy Prime Minister. Harman felt betrayed but decided that party unity was more important than making a fuss.

As deputy leader, she returned to the Cabinet as Leader of the House and Brown asked her to be the Minister for Women and Equality. With her new power as a Cabinet minister she designed the 2010 Equalities Act. The thinking behind it was that 'today's unreasonable demand is tomorrow's conventional wisdom'. Consolidating all the existing equality legislation, the Act legally protected people from discrimination in their work place and wider society. It placed an equality duty on the public sector which had to consider all individuals when shaping policy, delivering services and managing its own employees. However, most radical was clause one of the Act, which put a duty on all public sector bodies to take active steps to narrow the gap between rich and poor. Opposition by ministers within the Labour

Cabinet delayed the Bill reaching the Commons, so it became the final piece of legislation before the 2010 election, opposed by the Conservative opposition. As the Act had been passed so late, it did not have the necessary commencement order to implement it. The incoming Conservative government, with Theresa May as Equalities minister, announced that they would support much of it, but not clause one. So the Harman Act became an early Tory law, with the radicalism removed. She believes that had there not been so much opposition and clause one had been enacted it would have countered the sense among white, working-class communities that the government is an elite which is never, even when it is Labour, on their side. It also would have made it harder for those who later declared that the Labour government had not cared about class inequality. However, it did bring in legislation for the gender pay gap. In 2018, firms with over 250 employees had to show the difference in hourly earnings between men and women – 80 per cent paid men more than women.

When David Cameron became Prime Minister of a coalition government in 2010, Brown resigned as Labour leader and Harman stepped up to become interim leader, while five candidates vied for election, including both Miliband brothers. For four months she kept the party's spirits up as supporters came to terms with their defeat.

After Ed Miliband's election as party leader, she became the shadow Secretary of State for International Development before moving to Culture, Media and Sport to work on the Labour response to the Leveson Inquiry into phone hacking by News International journalists. She also set up the Older Women's Commission. Travelling round the country to take evidence, she was shocked at the discrimination older women faced at work, where they were the least-valued members of staff and the first in line for redundancies – the pay gap for women between fifty and fifty-nine was twice as large as for women overall. She conducted a survey into older women in television and discovered that while a minority of the over-fifties are men, they make up the vast majority of presenters (82 per cent). The commission culminated in a series of policy proposals that were welcomed by all parties, yet not taken up.

Brown's 2010 election campaign had been almost devoid of women; in fact, even the wives of the three major party leaders garnered more coverage than women MPs. When Miliband appointed two men to run Labour's campaign in 2015, Harman decided to ensure that women would not be marginalised, instead they would have their own place in the campaign. She came up with the controversial pink bus. While it garnered metropolitan ridicule, outside London it was a stunning success, attracting both women and the media. Local newspapers would devote a whole page to its visit to their patch, while commercial radio, which was trying its best to ignore the election, would send along reporters. However, against all the polls, Labour lost the election, with the Conservatives winning an outright majority.

Once again Harman found herself the interim leader as the contenders fought it out. This time she was also stepping down from being deputy. Research showed that one of the prime causes for the election loss was that the party was seen to be on the side of benefit claimants against so-called hard-working people. When the Chancellor George Osborne moved a punitive Bill against welfare dependents including only allowing benefits for the first two children, Harman backed it, like a general fighting the last war instead of the next one, and brought the Cabinet with her. Many members of the Labour Party were outraged at this attack on the most vulnerable, which became totemic of all New Labour had stood for. Veteran left-winger Jeremy Corbyn was the only leadership contender to oppose this. With a rule change that allowed people to vote for only £3, leading to tens of thousands of new members, and MPs no longer having weighted votes, Corbyn won by a landslide.

Harman had always planned to return to the back benches; at her instigation Corbyn appointed her chair of the Joint Committee of Human Rights, one of the few joint committees of the House of Commons and House of Lords. She also wrote her autobiography, *A Woman's Work*, which charted her battles, dilemmas and achievements. It looks back on a country and Parliament very different from today. Its publication meant a host of public appearances at which the audience could enjoy the real woman – funny, self-deprecating and always a feminist.

Harman used her position in Parliament to fight for and achieve many changes to the parliamentary system that have made life easier for women. While too many battles are still to be fought, women's representation and influence at all political levels have increased, the barriers allowing mothers to blend work and family are being dismantled, women have stormed business, if not as yet the boardroom, and, above all, women's voices are heard throughout the public realm. Harman deserves, perhaps more than any single politician, her share of the credit. She has said that had she stood for leader in 2010, she could have won that election. And Labour would have had a worthy first woman Prime Minister.

HELEN MCELHONE

BRIDIE PEARSON-JONES

- FULL NAME: Helen Margaret McElhone (née Brown)
- DATE OF BIRTH: 10 April 1933
- PLACE OF BIRTH: Glasgow
- DATE OF DEATH: 5 June 2013
- MARRIED TO: Frank McElhone
- CHILDREN: Gerard (Gerry), Lorraine, John (Johnny) and Rozanne Gerry
- UNSUCCESSFUL ELECTIONS FOUGHT: None
- CONSTITUENCY: Glasgow Queen's Park
- DATE OF FIRST ELECTION: 2 December 1982
- DATE LEFT PARLIAMENT: 9 June 1983
- PARTY ROLES: Councillor on the Strathclyde Regional Council
- MINISTERIAL POSITIONS & DATES: None
- MOST FAMOUS QUOTATION: 'I don't believe in being a caretaker MP.'

Helen Margaret McElhone is best known for only serving 189 days in Parliament, but the impact she had was enduring.

McElhone was known – and campaigned as – 'a Glasgow housewife'. She was elected MP for Glasgow's Queen Park in a by-election triggered when her husband, Frank McElhone, died unexpectedly from a heart attack, aged fifty-two, while campaigning for the NHS.

In less than nine months in the Commons, McElhone proved herself to be a valiant fighter for social justice, with a particular focus on better housing conditions. The reason her short spell in Parliament made such an impression was not just her clear emotional bond with Glasgow (she was born and lived her whole life in the constituency), but the reality of her long-served work without credit.

She acted as assistant to Frank during his thirteen years as an MP. Often, she took his surgeries, and even sat on Westminster committees in his place. She was clearly a huge driving force behind her husband's career and was regarded as a natural successor following his premature death.

Her victory over the SNP with a majority of 5,694 was bittersweet. She had avoided trying to attract the sympathy vote, but nonetheless Glasgow was soon dubbed 'McElhone' county.

The comparisons to her late husband followed her. Labour MP Norman Buchan welcomed McElhone to the House on her first day in Parliament, announcing that her victory was final judgement on the ineptitudes of Thatcher's first government.

Mrs McElhone's maiden speech set the path for her short-lived parliamentary career. In an impassioned address she attacked tower blocks as 'the new slums' and criticised high levels of unemployment, speaking of childhood friends who had reached their twenties without 'a sniff of a real job' or 'any hope of a real future'.

Her affinity with her constituency and her connection to Glaswegians defined her career. She told the Commons 'that generations of electors in my part of Glasgow have lived in houses which many people further south would not dignify by calling homes'.

On economic policy McElhone was left wing, but she was socially conservative. As a Catholic, she opposed abortion. Her husband served as Tony Benn's parliamentary private secretary, but she bemoaned the term 'Bennite', and supported separate Roman Catholic schools, nationalisation and unilateral nuclear disarmament. On more than one occasion, she went toe-to-toe with Margaret Thatcher. At one Prime Minister's Questions, she implored the Prime Minister to call a general election. Thatcher heeded McElhone's words – and her decision spelled the end of McElhone's parliamentary career. The June 1983 election abolished the constituency of Glasgow Queen's Park. Helen McElhone failed to be selected for the new Glasgow Central constituency, and began to channel her energy into local government instead, ultimately winning a seat on the Strathclyde Regional Council in March 1985. By 1989 she rallied to build new sports grounds, which she regarded as life-changing for local communities. A decade later she was one of five on a panel who vetted potential Labour candidates in the first elections to the Scottish Parliament.

EDWINA CURRIE

NADINE DORRIES

- FULL NAME: Edwina Currie (née Cohen)
- DATE OF BIRTH: 13 October 1946
- PLACE OF BIRTH: Liverpool, England
- DATE OF DEATH: –
- MARRIED TO: Ray Currie (m. 1972; div. 1997); John Jones (m. 2001)
- CHILDREN: Deborah and Susannah Currie
- UNSUCCESSFUL ELECTIONS FOUGHT: None
- CONSTITUENCY: South Derbyshire
- DATE OF FIRST ELECTION: 9 June 1983
- DATE LEFT PARLIAMENT: 9 April 1997
- PARTY ROLES: None
- MINISTERIAL POSITIONS & DATES: Parliamentary Under-Secretary of State for Health 1986–88
- MOST FAMOUS QUOTATIONS: '[Northerners die of] ignorance and chips.' | 'Most of the egg production in this country sadly is now infected with Salmonella.'

Like many Jewish immigrants from Eastern Europe in the 1890s, Edwina Cohen's family found themselves in Liverpool instead of America, and decided to stay. Growing up, Edwina would pass bomb craters left by the Luftwaffe as she walked to and from school, while at home she would be told tales of family members who had perished in the gas chambers.

Because of this intense family grief, and living with the physical reminders of what happens when it goes wrong, politics never seemed to be a remote or esoteric subject. It had real influence on how people lived their lives. When done right, it brought great benefits to communities and the wider country. Sitting back and hoping to avoid the consequences of the alternative was never an option for Edwina.

413

Edwina's father was a tailor who made uniform coats for sea captains using Liverpool's docks; the family was considered middle class at the time and Edwina grew up in a semi-detached house. To the masses in the teeming terraces of the city this would have seemed like the height of luxury. Edwina noticed the difference between her family and others less fortunate. That her father could raise his family to modest prosperity through his own efforts seemed to confirm the promise of Britain, compared to the stratified, oppressive society that they had left behind.

While Edwina was growing up, it was almost unheard of for children from poorer backgrounds to attend university – for girls it was even rarer. The young Edwina knew she wanted to pursue her education; she decided to apply to Oxford and was accepted. By the time she graduated with a PPE degree, she was determined to try and enter Parliament. Like many women of the time, Edwina felt that the reality of Labour's socialism was anathema to her values of hard work and self-sufficiency. So she joined the Tories.

Edwina's political career began in local government; she was a Birmingham city councillor for eight years before moving to Westminster. From 1980, she began attending selection meetings and she was determined to find a winnable seat. She rejected advice from well-meaning Tory men, who suggested that she focus on keeping down Labour majorities in their safe seats. It took twenty-one attempts but in June 1983, Edwina Currie was finally elected MP for South Derbyshire.

Many times while looking for a constituency to represent, Edwina had been told by pompous male association chairmen that they were looking for an MP who would eventually make it to the Cabinet. That meant a man, so she had no chance. Conservative agents were more encouraging and made sure she kept looking, despite the initial setbacks.

Both major parties have sought to increase the representation of women in Parliament, with Labour opting to do so through all-women shortlists. Currie fiercely opposes this practice on the basis that preventing men from challenging women for winnable seats sends out entirely the wrong message.

In 1986, Edwina became one of the first of the huge 1983 intake of Conservative MPs to be a made junior minister. She was appointed Parliamentary Under-Secretary of State to the Department of Health. Despite Barbara Castle's term as Secretary of State in the 1970s, women's health issues had never received the attention they deserved, but Edwina resolved to tackle this.

When the UK introduced nationwide breast and cervical cancer screenings, it became the first country in the world to do so. Screenings have since been adopted by almost every advanced healthcare system in the world. As achievements in government go, this is life-saving, impressive and almost entirely unnoticed by the general public.

For all the good work Edwina was doing in office, she was also developing a habit of expressing herself carelessly and enraging certain groups along the way. Distilling the debate concerning obesity and public health to the phrase: 'northerners die of ignorance and chips' was one such case. Given the fear and misunderstanding surrounding the AIDS crisis, suggesting 'good Christian people' would avoid the disease was another.

With two minor scandals caused by a poor choice of words already under her belt, the third and ultimately final scandal was expected. The distinction between salmonella in eggs and in flocks of laying chickens might seem arcane even now, but to egg-producing farmers at the time it was crucial. In a rather dramatic ITN television interview in which 'Eggwina' blurred that distinction with the comment: 'Most of the *egg production* in this country, sadly, is now affected with salmonella.' She later admitted it had been a slip of the tongue and she had intended to say 'much'. Sales of eggs fell by 60 per cent in the UK. Four million hens were slaughtered. The farmers were calling for her head.

Edwina's was not the first ministerial career brought short because of a poor choice of words at a sensitive time. MPs in rural constituencies were demanding a ritual sacrifice in the form of her sacking. A later report which showed that Edwina had been correct on her facts, if tactless with her delivery, made little difference. Mrs Thatcher had always been a fan of Edwina and was reluctant to dispose of her colourful personality in a rather monochrome male government, but political realities dictated otherwise and Edwina returned to the back benches, never to return to ministerial office again. John Major offered her the position of Minister for Prisons at the Home Office, but she refused on the basis that she wouldn't work with Kenneth Clarke, the Home Secretary, who she felt had been less than supportive as her boss at the Department of Health.

Like any decent parliamentarian, Edwina seethed at injustices in society. Unlike most of them at the time, she wasn't afraid of challenging taboos and prejudice as well. Her campaign to equalise the age of consent for all partners, whether straight, lesbian or gay, was groundbreaking in 1994. It was predictably opposed by the social conservatives on our benches, although she did manage to reduce the age of consent for gay couples from twenty-one to eighteen. Her support for the gay community didn't dim over the next two decades.

I have been on my own journey on this subject, which makes Edwina's actions back in 1994 all the more impressive. In 2013, I voted against gay marriage, in accordance with the overwhelming majority of my constituents but against the fervent (even angry) advice of my own daughters. I now regret that vote. Treating gay people differently does not protect anyone or the institution of marriage. The UK is moving towards consensus on that score at long last – and Edwina led the way.

When Edwina arrived in Parliament in 1983, she was one of only twenty-three women. In May 1997, 121 women were elected to the Commons. Edwina wasn't one of them. She lost her South Derbyshire seat in the Blair landslide to a man. She had seen the writing on the wall and, having seen no prospect of ministerial advancement, she looked elsewhere and stood to be an MEP in the 1994 European Parliament elections. She failed to be elected.

As politics started to take a back seat, Edwina took to writing full time and published a series of bestselling novels, including *A Parliamentary Affair* and *A Woman's Place*. She went on to publish non-fiction books, too, including two volumes of diaries. After she lost her seat, Edwina became a regular media pundit and secured a long-running, weekend evening phone-in show on BBC Radio 5 Live. She also took part in various reality TV shows, including *I'm a Celebrity, Get Me Out of Here* and *Strictly Come Dancing*. As always, the opinionated woman was criticised for daring to have an opinion and finding an avenue by which to share it. Times haven't changed.

As a high-profile woman, Edwina was subject to abuse sadly still too familiar. A newspaper labelled her 'the vilest lady in Britain'. The article in question made a series of outrageous slurs against her, comparing her with a rapist and a war criminal, as well as with Myra Hindley and Rose West. This clearly misogynistic tone is all too familiar, but Edwina had the last laugh – she sued for libel and won damages.

It's hard to escape the fact that Edwina's time since leaving Parliament has been dominated by the revelation in the first volume of her diaries (published in 2002) that she had had an affair with John Major in the years before he became Prime Minister.

Edwina and her critics make less fuss about the charity work she's done since leaving Parliament. Using her profile to raise money for good causes is admirable and effective. She has pursued some of the same issues she worked on in Parliament, particularly improving healthcare for women. The charity single with Ant and Dec is best forgotten, but the money raised isn't.

There are now 209 women in Parliament. Yet there is still, in both main parties, an expectation that you must sit there quietly, toe the line and refrain from making waves. Men are entitled to voice their opinions on any issue, regardless of whether they understand it or not. If a woman does the same thing, she starts to get a reputation. Currie was referred to as a 'vile woman', while I'm 'Mad Nad'. We can only wonder what Edwina would have had to put up with if she'd been in the Commons in the social media age.

When I look across at female Labour MPs of the quality required to make it as leader, I hear the same criticisms launched at them that were directed at me and Edwina in the past. We're seen as mouthy, opinionated and even obnoxious. An opinionated MP? Who'd have thought.

Edwina Currie was a working-class northern girl, from Liverpool no less, who made it to Parliament. She did it at a time when sexism was the norm. From ministerial office she drove changes to improve women's health that have saved countless lives since and been copied around the world. On the back benches she fought against prejudice that was deeply ingrained in the psyche of the country at the time.

These are real achievements and yet they're often overlooked. Edwina perhaps made it easy for detractors to focus on her affair rather than anything of substance, but they hardly needed the excuse. Mrs Thatcher's achievements were too great to ignore. She became the exception that proved the rule. Edwina Currie's parliamentary career, against huge odds, had notable successes that have since been almost entirely forgotten.

ANNA MCCURLEY

ANNABEL GOLDIE

- FULL NAME: Anna Anderson McCurley (née Gemmell)
- DATE OF BIRTH: 18 January 1943
- PLACE OF BIRTH: –
- DATE OF DEATH: –
- MARRIED TO: Married
- CHILDREN: None
- UNSUCCESSFUL ELECTIONS FOUGHT: West Stirlingshire 1979, Glasgow Central 1980
- CONSTITUENCY: Renfrew West & Inverclyde
- DATE OF FIRST ELECTION: 9 June 1983
- DATE LEFT PARLIAMENT: 10 June 1987
- PARTY ROLES: None
- MINISTERIAL POSITIONS & DATES: None

Anna McCurley was a breath of fresh air; she differed from the archetypal, traditional Conservatives of Renfrew West & Inverclyde – whose number I counted myself among. This was a new constituency, which now included a large part of the former West Renfrewshire seat that had been represented by Labour MP Norman Buchan since 1964. Vibrant and attractive in both appearance and personality, Anna made an indelible impression on the local Conservative Association.

Her campaign for election was not born out of some superficial appeal, but was supported by the firm foundations of a Scottish upbringing, her background as a teacher and the gritty but invaluable political experience of serving as a councillor on Strathclyde Regional Council from 1978 to '82. She had also waded in to the waters of parliamentary elections, contesting West Stirlingshire in 1979 and Glasgow Central in a 1980 by-election.

Given her background and experience, she was, unsurprisingly, commended to the Conservative Association of Renfrew West & Inverclyde. The new constituency was an unwieldy mix of rural and urban communities and home to different types of economic activity. Selected as the Conservative candidate, there was a sense of excitement among activists, who believed that with Anna as a candidate, it might be possible to take what had been essentially a Labour area – and in the general election, the possibility was realised.

The result was close; Anna won with a majority of 1,322, in a tightly fought contest among the Conservatives, the SDP and Labour. I still remember the sense of elation I felt upon learning that Anna had won the seat, and I owe her a lot. She demonstrated that with commitment, hard work and passion anything was possible, sparking life into the local Conservatives.

She knew her constituency, identified what were the priorities of her constituents and wasted no time in making her mark in Parliament. She was the first MP to introduce a Bill opposing commercial surrogacy in the UK, a proposal subsequently adopted by the government. She also supported the Labour MP Clare Short in a bid to ban page-3 girls, an innovative stance at the time. She was passionate in her desire to see a steel industry retained in Scotland and shipbuilding stay on the Clyde, thereby putting herself at odds with her own government.

On the international front, pursuing her interest in defence, she was in the first group of MPs to go to the Falklands Islands after the visit by the then Prime Minister, Margaret Thatcher in 1983. She was also invited by the United States, as one of two representatives from the UK, to visit various institutions in the States related to defence, including the armed services, to study Global Defence Priorities. The visit lasted six weeks and was described by Anna as 'hectic, hard work and highly illuminating'.

Her directness of approach characterised her political and parliamentary activity. She was regarded as a formidable politician, making many significant contributions to Westminster. One of her former parliamentary colleagues commented that she was an energetic, approachable and collegiate member of the party. Anna herself was the first to admit that she was of an independent mind and not always regarded as biddable.

In 1987, the constituency remained a marginal, with Labour ultimately winning the seat. That same parliamentary colleague also confirmed there was regret that she was not returned.

In the 1990s, Anna reluctantly left the Conservatives and in 1998 joined the Scottish Liberal Democrats. Notwithstanding having been an MP for one term, it is a measure of the impact which she had that people still remember her locally.

ELIZABETH PEACOCK

LINDA MCDOUGALL

- FULL NAME: Elizabeth Joan Peacock (née Gates)
- DATE OF BIRTH: 4 September 1937
- PLACE OF BIRTH: Skipton, Yorkshire
- DATE OF DEATH: –
- MARRIED TO: Brian Peacock (m. 1963)
- CHILDREN: Jonathan and Nicholas
- UNSUCCESSFUL ELECTIONS FOUGHT: Batley & Spen 2001
- CONSTITUENCY: Batley & Spen
- DATE OF FIRST ELECTION: 9 June 1983
- DATE LEFT PARLIAMENT: 1 May 1997
- PARTY ROLES: None
- MINISTERIAL POSITIONS & DATES: Parliamentary private secretary to the Social Security and Disabled People's Unit 1992
- MOST FAMOUS QUOTATION: 'I should like to think that in the years to come, when the history of this period is written, that the Conservative government will not be seen to have abandoned the miners and this country's energy policies. I would not wish to see myself depicted as having abandoned those miners and the whole coal industry either.'

Elizabeth Peacock joined the Conservative Party in 1971 and became MP for Batley & Spen on 9 June 1983. She was one of twenty-three female MPs in the House of Commons. The Conservatives had the biggest election victory since Labour's landslide in 1945. Peacock was no ordinary Conservative newcomer; she was interviewed as a potential Conservative candidate by Richmond MP Anthony Royle, whom Margaret Thatcher had appointed party vice-chair in charge of candidate selection. Peacock, who was from Yorkshire and grew up in a working-class Catholic family, wasn't Royle's type. She was a mother to two young sons and had been very successful in the Business and Professional Women's Club, she had also been a county councillor for two years. Despite her credentials, Royle decided that she was unsuitable as a candidate and turned her down without explanation.

Royle was, Peacock explained, 'a toffee-nosed twerp'. Her sponsors and supporters, including MP Nicholas Winterton, complained to the Conservative Central Office but got nowhere.

> I knew a few people who were on the candidates list. I rang up one of them, Cecil Franks in Manchester. In those days they sent out the vacancies to people on the list by letter. I said to Franks, 'Why don't you send me the ones you don't want?' [He agreed, so] I sent him a pile of stamped addressed envelopes.

Peacock was invited to selections for three Yorkshire seats. 'I wanted a Yorkshire seat because I am a Yorkshire woman. I didn't want to go anywhere else.' Batley & Spen had been Labour for fifty years, but boundary changes had made it less of a shoo-in. Elizabeth succeeded in being selected as the Conservative candidate, and the news was published in the local paper before central office could disapprove.

> There was no office and no agent. We just blitzed it, my husband, Brian, and me. We went out from dawn to dusk, the office was the back of my car. Our son Jonathan was waiting to go to university so he became my driver and handed out leaflets. We had very little money and very few leaflets.
>
> People would come out and talk. We had a chairman who said he would take me round the constituency; we went past this huge council estate and he said we wouldn't bother with that. I didn't tell him I had lived on one. I said I wanted to canvass it, and he said he couldn't allow local people to come with me. So I went on my own. People were amazed that a Conservative candidate was appearing on their doorstep.

Peacock won Batley & Spen by just 870 votes.

> Once I got to the House I didn't have any trouble. My whip was Donald Thompson. He tried to be a bully at first. When we met he virtually got me up against the wall and said do you realise if you vote against the government you are going to ruin your career? I told him I hadn't come for a career, I had come to represent the people of Batley & Spen and if it's not right for them I won't support it.

She also spoke and voted along with her own beliefs rather than party lines. She wanted the time frame for legal abortions cut back. In the 1988 debate on the Abortion Amendment Bill, she said, 'Some 43 per cent of those seeking abortions in recent years have come from other countries. We are becoming the foetal dustbin of Europe.'

It would be the debates on pit closures that most defined Elizabeth Peacock as a tough campaigner for her constituents, rather a loyal servant of the Conservative Party. Throughout the strikes, Peacock had been very involved in negotiations with Michael Heseltine, president of the Board of Trade. She told him that she believed,

> The coal industry needed reforming, but not all at once. You can't take 3,000 jobs and get rid of them all at once. If they had done it a different way, they would have got a lot of support but they wanted to do it all in a hurry. We kept pumping money into the coal industry. In 1984, when we had the first strike, money was going in at £2 million a week – it was a lot of money to support them.

Early in 1992, Peacock became PPS to Nicholas Scott, Minister for Social Security and the Disabled. 'He was a delight to work with and it was an interesting time to be there. When I realised I was going to have to vote against the government, I told him I would have to resign, but Nick persuaded me not to do it in advance.' Elizabeth voted against the government.

> When I came out of the lobby a whip was there. 'You are fired,' he said. I said I was about to resign and I was about to talk to Nicholas. 'You don't need to talk to him,' he said. 'You are fired!'
>
> When I was phoned by the Whips' Office the next day, I thought I would get strung up. But Alastair Campbell in the *Daily Mirror* had wrongly said that I was going to do what the government told me and vote with them. My secretary said that the lines to our office were jammed with obscene and nasty phone calls. Brian called the *Mirror* and demanded that they withdraw their mistake and apologise.
>
> We were all going into the lobby for the start of questions at 14.30 and Alastair Campbell ran across to me. I said, 'Go away.' The attendants were listening and he knew they would take action if he didn't move. By the evening, he was there with a bunch of flowers. I can't tell you what I would have liked to tell him to do with them. It was the toughest part of my career. I got over 3,000 letters. People felt very strongly and human beings felt it was too much all at once.

Elizabeth continued to fight for Batley & Spen, and her own strongly held beliefs, until she lost her seat in the Labour landslide of 1997.

DAME MARION ROE

MEG MUNN

- FULL NAME: Dame Marion Audrey Roe (née Keyte) DBE
- DATE OF BIRTH: 15 July 1936
- DATE OF DEATH: –
- PLACE OF BIRTH: London
- MARRIED TO: James Kenneth Roe (m. 1958)
- CHILDREN: William, Jane and Philippa (now Baroness Couttie)
- UNSUCCESSFUL ELECTIONS FOUGHT: Barking 1979
- CONSTITUENCY: Broxbourne
- DATE OF FIRST ELECTION: 10 June 1983
- DATE LEFT PARLIAMENT: 11 April 2005
- PARTY ROLES: Vice-chair of the 1922 Committee 2001–05; President Broxbourne Conservative Association
- MINISTERIAL POSITIONS & DATES: Parliamentary Under-Secretary of State at the Department of the Environment 1987–88

Marion Roe followed the typical route of many Conservatives to Parliament: a period as a councillor, contesting an unwinnable parliamentary seat then becoming candidate for the newly drawn seat of Broxbourne in the 1983 election. Although considered marginal by Conservative Central Office, the election proved that it was one of the safest seats in the country, which Marion represented for the next twenty-two years. She chose to stand down in 2005 to support one of her daughters, who had been diagnosed with an aggressive cancer.

Marion Keyte was born in London in 1936, educated at Bromley High School, Croydon High School and the English School of Languages in Switzerland. She married James Kenneth Roe in 1958 and they went on to have one son and two daughters.

Marion describes the role of wife and mother as the most important career she could have had, moulding a future generation and teaching them the most important things in life. As the children grew older she watched with concern 'the destabilisation of our British way of life by political extremists' in the trade union and Labour Party. She felt the need to stand up for the British way of life and determined on becoming a Member of Parliament.

Active in her local Conservative Association, in 1975 she was elected to Bromley Borough Council, serving until 1978. From 1977 she was a Greater London councillor for Ilford North, until the abolition of the GLC in 1986. In 1979 she fought the constituency of Barking, losing to Labour's Jo Richardson, before securing the candidature for Broxbourne prior to the 1983 election.

Marion was described as a right-wing Conservative on social and economic issues; she was a supporter of greater curbs on abortion, the return of capital punishment and in favour of a low tax and regulation business environment.

However, her greatest achievement in Parliament received support across the political spectrum. She piloted the Prohibition of Female Circumcision Act 1985 through Parliament as a Private Members' Bill. She said at the time, 'When I did that, nobody knew what female circumcision was.' There had been two prior attempts in the House of Lords to get legislation on the statute, but this should not detract from Marion's determination to take legislation forward. Her choice was not universally welcomed in the House, such matters being deemed by some as inappropriate for parliamentary discussion. As the issue affected immigrant communities, she also received mail calling her a racist and accusing her of interfering in cultural and religious practices.

Important as it was in raising awareness of the issue of female genital mutilation (FGM), no prosecutions took place under the 1985 Act – a fact she described as gravely disappointing. A further Private Members' Bill, the Female Genital Mutilation Act 2003, presented by Ann Clwyd MP, strengthened and amended the 1985 Act. Marion Roe supported the changes and spoke in debates. The updated legislation made it an offence for UK nationals or permanent UK residents to carry out FGM abroad and increased the maximum penalty from five to fourteen years' imprisonment.

Soon after her 1983 election, Marion became a parliamentary private secretary, and joined the government herself in 1987 as an Under-Secretary of State at the Department of the Environment. Marion's husband had organised an outing to Glyndebourne as a post-election treat when she was passed a note to ring a London number urgently. Fearing a family emergency Marion found a telephone and was astonished when the No. 10 switchboard answered and she was put through to the Prime Minister. Mrs Thatcher complained about how difficult it had been to get hold of Marion, told her to enjoy the rest of the opera and be at the department first thing the next day.

As Minister for Housing, Planning and New Towns, Marion's role included persuading Labour-controlled councils to put into operation the policy allowing council house tenants to buy their property, known as the Right to Buy scheme. Marion's ministerial career lasted only a year. In 1992, she became the first female Conservative MP to chair a select committee when appointed to the Health Select Committee. Throughout the rest of her time in Parliament, she took on a number of different roles: chair of the Administration committee and, as a member of the chairs' panel, she chaired many Bill committees.

When I was elected to Parliament in 2001, I first recognised Roe as one of the Conservative women who would position herself behind the Leader of the Opposition for Prime Minister's Questions. Despite there being fewer Conservative than Labour women MPs in the House, the Conservatives understood the value of having women visible during the most-watched parliamentary session. As the TV screen rarely showed the faces of the second row, it was Marion's knees that were usually on show. She told me that her knees had even received fan mail!

The following year, I was selected by the Inter-Parliamentary Union, along with Marion, to attend a session for parliamentarians on children's rights at the UN in New York. Together we provided political balance. Marion turned out not only to be a good travelling companion, but to share my interest in child protection. I learned about her passionate advocacy for children's rights and her work to end child labour, as well as her legislation on FGM, which I had been aware of during my time in social work.

Marion took her interest in child protection into many international forums, seeking to influence policy around the world. She was successful in persuading the Inter-Parliamentary Union to establish an international committee on child protection.

Marion's approach to Parliament has much to commend it. After her short period as a minister, she returned to the back benches not disappointed, but determined to continue to make a difference to the issues she cared about. Marion Roe was a dedicated constituency MP, a doughty and successful campaigner on issues affecting women and children, as well as a friendly colleague. After our short trip to the UN together, we remained on good terms and on her occasional visits to Parliament after she stood down she would always greet me warmly.

CLARE SHORT

HOLLY LYNCH

- FULL NAME: Clare Short
- DATE OF BIRTH: 15 February 1946
- PLACE OF BIRTH: Birmingham
- DATE OF DEATH: –
- MARRIED TO: Alex Lyon (m. 1981; d. 1993)
- CHILDREN: Toby Graham
- UNSUCCESSFUL ELECTIONS FOUGHT: None
- CONSTITUENCY: Birmingham Ladywood
- DATE OF FIRST ELECTION: 10 June 1983
- DATE LEFT PARLIAMENT: 12 April 2010
- PARTY ROLES: Member of the Home Affairs Committee 1983–85
- MINISTERIAL POSITIONS & DATES: Shadow Minister for Women 1993–95; shadow Secretary of State for Transport 1995–96; shadow Minister for Overseas Development 1996–97; Secretary of State for International Development 1997–2003
- MOST FAMOUS QUOTATION: 'It is disrespectful to the House and to the office that he holds, that he should come here in this condition.' – Accusing Conservative minister Alan Clark of being drunk at the despatch box.

When I was asked to write about Clare Short, I felt that my biggest challenge would be to write a chapter, rather than a book, as I knew there would be so much to cover. Yet as Clare served as the Member of Parliament for Birmingham Ladywood from 1983 to 2010 and I was elected to the Commons in 2015, I never had the chance to serve alongside her, so I was keen to hear from those who did. I asked my colleagues in the Women's Parliamentary Labour Party for any stories or interesting facts about Clare.

While she achieved many great things during her time in office, her tenacity in getting stuck into controversial issues, her complicated relationship with the leadership over Iraq, and her subsequent decision to resign from the Labour Party in 2006, certainly meant that she was a divisive figure.

However, those I have spoken to, particularly the long-standing female powerhouses of the Labour Party, like Harriet Harman and Margaret Beckett, were keen to make sure that her achievements were front and centre of this chapter, as far too often her legacy and contributions are overshadowed by the way she left the party, and her struggle with the Iraq War.

Rosie Duffield, the recently elected MP for Canterbury, told me that Clare Short was one of her childhood heroes for the brave work she did taking on *The Sun* for its tradition of topless women on page 3. Clare twice sought to introduce legislation that would have prohibited such images from appearing in print media. Her first Ten Minute Rule Bill, Indecent Displays (Newspapers) Bill, was passed for second reading on 12 March 1986, just three years into her time in office.

In an attempt to seize the opportunity to bring a Bill before the House, she engaged in one of the oddest of Westminster practices. She slept outside the Clerk's office the night before the slots for Bills became available in order to be first in line for a chance to change the law – a tactic employed only by the most committed of MPs.

As is so often the case with Ten Minute Rule Bills, it ran out of time and the parliamentary year ended before it could receive a second reading. Clare tried again in 1988, but with the same frustrating outcome. However, she had succeeded in getting the campaign firmly on the political agenda.

While she received overwhelming support from women all over the country, *The Sun* began seeking to discredit Clare in the most baseless and morally corrupt of ways. When Clare stood down from government in 2003, page 3 of *The Sun* featured a topless woman called Keeley with a speech bubble that read: 'Keeley is over the moon that MP Clare Short is on the way out. Keeley said, "Page 3 and the fans will all be glad to see the back of her – mind you, who'd want to see the front of her!"'

It was a shameless display of ruthless undermining. The new editor of *The Sun*, Rebekah Brooks (then Wade), seemed determined to prove that, although a woman, she was certainly not going to be the paper's great reformer and had topless photos of the MP mocked up. There were times when page-3 girls and double-decker buses plastered in *Sun* posters were sent to Clare's home address, with headlines calling her 'Fat, Jealous Clare'. It was print media at its worst.

Yet looking back through Clare's career, she was no stranger to sticking to

her guns and digging deep if there was an injustice she felt needed addressing. She later admitted that the weight of that campaign had at times been a
burden. However, the way she handled not just this particular issue, but how
she conducted herself in the face of some of the nastiest tactics an MP can
square up against while trying to change something for the better, has been
a source of inspiration for women.

Clare always cited her strong Irish Catholic upbringing as providing the
foundations for her understanding of social justice and fairness which led her
to the Labour Party. That is until, as she put it, she 'gave up on the Church
because of ridiculous teachings on contraception and the rest'.

It was that sense of needing to make a difference that meant a career in
the civil service would never have been enough to satisfy her appetite to
really change things for the better. She needed to be in elected office to effect
tangible change.

She gave up her role at the Home Office, her first serious job after graduating from Leeds University, and fought the Birmingham Ladywood seat,
where she had grown up, in the 1983 general election. She was elected with 51
per cent of the vote and was appointed to the front bench soon after.

In 1993, she was appointed as the shadow Minister for Women by party
leader John Smith, a man she greatly admired. She felt he was a leader who
welcomed debate and understood collective decision-making through Cabinet, which she felt was sadly lacking throughout the New Labour years.

She went on to serve as the shadow Secretary of State for Transport,
shadow Minister for Overseas Development and Secretary of State for International Development under Tony Blair. Her time on the front bench was
interrupted by periods of resignation. When asked if she felt that she had
quit too many times, having resigned on three separate occasions, she argued
that 'gesture politics and toeing the line offended' her. She wasn't prepared
to do either.

In her book, *An Honourable Deception?*, published in 2004, Clare reflected
that 'I think it is important to have a bottom line, otherwise there is a danger
that principles are steadily eroded and you end up wanting power for power's
sake rather than to help you carry your values into practice.' She did however
recognise that 'looking back, it is perhaps surprising that I was allowed to
return to the front bench on three occasions'. It's clear that for Clare, the
back benches were not something that she feared. She enjoyed the freedom
it gave her and did some of her best work there.

Short's first resignation was over the Prevention of Terrorism Act in 1988.

The legislation didn't sit well with her as she felt it allowed for too much harassment of those with Irish heritage and risked serving as a recruiting sergeant for terrorist organisations. Her second was in 1990, having not taken Neil Kinnock's instruction to keep her views on the Gulf War out of the public domain. Despite her battles with Neil Kinnock, she always backed his leadership and they remained good friends.

Clare was elected to the NEC around 1987, at a time when Labour was being ripped apart by divisions. Factionalism was starting to become unmanageable and Militant candidates had begun standing against Labour. She was adamant that the only way for Labour to return to being an honest party was for its membership to choose between the party or their factions; a challenge that seems to have a cyclical nature for the Labour Party. She engaged in developing practical policies to that effect, inviting the factions that didn't share the core values or the mission of the party to simply leave.

She had been a member of the Socialist Campaign Group (SCG), a grouping of MPs considered to be on the very left of the party; However, she resigned from the SCG when Tony Benn, one of its founding members, took the decision to challenge Neil Kinnock for the leadership in 1988. She didn't agree that this would in any way serve the party and so resigned her membership alongside fellow MPs Margaret Beckett and Joan Ruddock.

One of her greatest achievements on the NEC, and in her capacity as the shadow Minister for Women, was her delivery of all-women shortlists, a policy from which I have personally benefited. The party introduced AWSs in 1993, having realised that the lack of women's representation in the party was partially to blame for its failure to meaningfully connect with women voters. Although we now regard AWSs as a benchmark of progress for representation in the Labour Party, sadly that was not always the case. When AWSs were first introduced, the party found itself embroiled in legal disputes and bitter contests with local parties. Clare Short, however, was a great champion of the system.

One of the first things Harriet Harman wanted me to understand about Clare was that she was absolutely 'rock solid' on AWS, and my generation of women MPs certainly owe her a debt for her stance.

Another story Harriet told me about Clare was one that really showcased her tenacity for getting a job done at all costs. Clare, as a dedicated constituency MP, had met with a grandmother who attended one of her surgery appointments with letters from her ten-year-old granddaughter. The grandmother had custody of the girl; however, the child had failed to return after visiting her father in Germany. The girl had sent letters back home distressed that her father was preventing her return, and explaining that he was making her babysit for his new family. The case went to court, confirming that the granddaughter should return, yet this was not forthcoming. That is until Clare, frustrated with the red tape, went to Germany and waited for the girl to finish school. Upon checking that the girl did indeed want to return to her grandmother and the UK, Clare took her to the airport with nothing more than her birth certificate, and flew her home to her grandmother.

That seemed to be Clare Short in a nutshell. If there was a wrong that needed putting right, she'd get it done. If it wasn't protocol, or was against due process, she'd simply make a new process in order to make it happen.

Of course, the other occasion when Clare notoriously found herself in trouble was when, still in her first year as an MP, she accused Conservative minister Alan Clark of being drunk at the despatch box. She told the chamber, 'It is disrespectful to the House and to the office that he holds, that he should come here in this condition.'

She was forced to withdraw her remarks by the Deputy Speaker for being 'unparliamentary' and the minister, who was making only his second outing to the despatch box, issued a rebuttal of the allegation immediately. It was only when Alan Clark published his diaries years later that he confessed to having been at a wine tasting prior to the debate, as well as having very little grasp of his speech or brief on that occasion. Clare had been entirely right. Clark recalled in his diary that he knew he was in trouble when the Leader of the House appeared at his side while he was still at the despatch box and even his own colleagues, who had rushed to his defence in the chamber, told him later in the voting lobby that they were struggling to support him given his performance.

It is staggering to think that suggesting someone might be drunk at the despatch box is unparliamentary behaviour, but apparently it is not unparliamentary to actually be drunk at the despatch box. I can only imagine that the fear of being called out by Clare Short came as a stark warning to any other ministers tempted to engage in such activity in the future.

Clare did some of her best work while in her role as the Secretary of State for International Development, a post she held for six years and which was to be her last on the front bench. The department was formed in 1997 under new Prime Minister Tony Blair and Clare was tasked with reforming the work of its predecessor, the Department for Overseas Development.

She was particularly proud of the work that she and her team did leading up to the Millennium Development Goals. The MDGs were agreed by world leaders through the UN, in the run-up to the new millennium, with the ambition of halving the number of people living in poverty by 2015. The world needed a new framework for delivering this ambition on the ground, as well as financing it. The new Department for International Development (DFID) headed up by Clare was at the forefront of that international work.

In the time that she held office, she transformed international development from a side issue into a measure of a nation's seriousness about its own role in the world. She was zealous about the importance of the work, sometimes to the extent of rubbing up against her colleagues if there was overlap in policy areas.

In the early years of the Blair government, although thriving in her role, Clare became increasingly uncomfortable with New Labour under his leadership. She felt that Labour's large majority after 1997 had the potential to generate executive arrogance, as governments with inflated majorities have no need to listen to dissenting voices. She had been elected to the shadow Cabinet by the Parliamentary Labour Party and although she enjoyed a degree of freedom at DFID, there was also a sense that she had been granted that freedom by No. 10 because from there, she had a limited opportunity to rock the boat.

Unlike John Smith, who Clare said preferred to put integrity first when devising policies, rather than presentation, Clare felt that New Labour was preoccupied with presentation as a starting point, and working backwards to determine policy.

Given her treatment by *The Sun* over the page-3 furore, it is no wonder that close relationships between government and the media didn't sit well with her. Reflecting in *An Honourable Deception*, Clare wrote, 'I find it very sad that the degraded *Sun* has been courted so strongly and shown so many favours by Tony Blair and the spin merchants at No 10.'

Some of her colleagues have told me that she was Alastair Campbell's worst nightmare, but that even he understood that she was popular with the electorate, which made her a Labour asset.

Clare later said that, under Blair, the Cabinet did not function as a Cabinet and that he began to confide in an increasingly small group of people. She felt that the build-up to the Iraq War was handled in much the same way and she voiced her reservations, but a 'rush' to war seemed to be gathering momentum.

With the vote approaching and being unable to support the war, she had planned to resign alongside Robin Cook and had 'put-in' to the Speaker's office to request a speaking slot to make what would have been her resignation speech in the chamber. However, following a series of eleventh-hour meetings with the leadership, her stay and her support were negotiated in exchange for DFID having an instrumental role in the rebuilding of Iraq.

She later explained that she had deduced that she could not stop the war, so the next best thing was to be involved in shaping the humanitarian effort that would be required to mitigate its impact on civilians.

She had been promised a UN mandate for reconstruction in Iraq, as well as a road map for where the conflict was going and how the recovery efforts would be managed. Clare voted for the war in March 2003, but resigned from her post on 12 May, two months later, having realised that her conditions for supporting the intervention would not be met.

Her decision to support the war, but later resign, perplexed some who felt that the time to go was surely prior to the vote. Some commentators and even colleagues suggested that it was her lack of recognition within Blair's tight group on Iraq which she ultimately couldn't tolerate.

Extracts from her resignation speech to the House of Commons offer some insight into her decision-making and how she came to the decision to resign.

> I have been attacked from many different angles for that decision [to stay] but I still think that, hard as it was, it was the right thing to do. I had throughout taken the view that it was necessary to be willing to contemplate the use of force to back up the authority of the UN. However, the problem now is that the mistakes that were made in the period leading up to the conflict are being repeated in the post-conflict situation.

She cites the draft resolution on reconstruction being driven through the UN Security Council and states that it was far from the one she had been promised.

'The draft resolution risks continuing international divisions, Iraqi resentment against the occupying powers and the possibility that the coalition will get bogged down in Iraq.'

She had no way of knowing at the time, just how much that last fear would become a reality.

Clare returned to the back benches and grew increasingly distant from the party and the leadership, to the extent that she resigned from the Labour

Party in 2006. She later confessed that she hadn't actually intended to leave the party altogether, but on having resigned the Labour whip in order to become an independent MP and stopped paying her party subs, she found that she was no longer a member and did not seek to correct this.

In her personal life, Clare has openly spoken of her joy at being reunited with the son she gave up for adoption when she was just eighteen – a decision that she said she had regretted from a very early stage. She now has a close relationship with him and his children. She married Alex Lyons in 1981, the minister she had worked for during her time as a civil servant at the Home Office, who, after losing his own seat, ran Clare's office, supporting her career with the benefit of his own experience.

While some who served with Clare told me she could at times be aloof and that her sense of moral high ground sometimes isolated her from colleagues, others have told me that with hindsight, she never once failed to make the right call.

Harriet Harman told me that Clare had on occasion been accused of not being a team player, but if the teams don't fit, then there is nothing wrong with carving out your own path. It seems to me that throughout her time in politics that is exactly what Clare Short sought to do.

ANN WINTERTON

CAROLE WALKER

- FULL NAME: Lady Jane Ann Winterton (née Hodgson)
- DATE OF BIRTH: 6 March 1941
- PLACE OF BIRTH: Sutton Coldfield, Warwickshire
- DATE OF DEATH: –
- MARRIED TO: Sir Nicholas Raymond Winterton
- CHILDREN: Robert Nicholas, Andrew James and Sarah Jane Alison
- UNSUCCESSFUL ELECTIONS FOUGHT: None
- CONSTITUENCY: Congleton
- DATE OF FIRST ELECTION: 9 June 1983
- DATE LEFT PARLIAMENT: 6 May 2010
- PARTY ROLES: None
- MINISTERIAL POSITIONS & DATES: Shadow spokesperson on Drugs 1998–2001; shadow Rural Affairs minister 2001–02
- MOST FAMOUS QUOTATION: 'Congleton's campaigner for family values.'

Ann Winterton was an outspoken, independent-minded and controversial Conservative MP whose prospects of promotion were wrecked when she told racist jokes. She married the irrepressible Nicholas in 1960 and together the Wintertons hold the record for the longest-serving couple in the history of the House of Commons, with a combined service of sixty-six years.

They were known by many of their colleagues as 'the bloody Wintertons', frequently embroiled in controversies and often refusing to toe the party line.

In person, Ann Winterton is polite, warm and much less combative than her public image would suggest. When I met her at their immaculate family home in Cheshire, she said she found it difficult to make her own mark at Westminster. When she was elected in 1983, her husband was already well established after twelve years in Parliament. 'I knew I had to make my own footprints in the sand,' she told me, but she admitted to being racked with nerves at the prospect of making political speeches.

The couple met at Pony Club when they were teenagers. Ann Winterton was the youngest ever joint master of foxhounds when she took charge of the South Staffordshire hunt at the age of seventeen. Yet for many years her role was supporting her husband's political career, running what she describes as a 'traditional household', looking after their three children. Their daughter Sarah recalls her mother's ferocious battles to persuade her father to increase the weekly housekeeping allowance.

Family life changed dramatically in 1983, when constituency boundaries were redrawn, and the new seat of Congleton was created, taking in part of Nicholas Winterton's Macclesfield constituency. Ann was approached by senior figures in the local Conservative Association who wanted her to stand. She beat a strong field to secure the nomination and won her seat in the Conservative landslide election of 1983.

Ann Winterton was one of just thirteen female Conservative MPs at the time, but she is scathing about those she accuses of 'playing the women's card'. She says she never tried to blaze a trail for women, but focused on making a difference on the issues she cared about.

At Westminster, Ann Winterton won a reputation as Congleton's campaigner for family values. She chaired the all-party parliamentary pro-life group, battling against embryo research, euthanasia and the liberalisation of abortion laws. She also took a keen interest in defence, campaigning for better vehicles and equipment for British troops in Iraq. It is an indication of the attitudes of the time that in one debate, a Labour MP asked her whether she played with toy tanks on the kitchen table.

Winterton was a Brexiteer before such a term existed. She was a Maastricht rebel, voting against John Major's government on numerous occasions in his notorious battles to get Parliament's endorsement of a new EU treaty. She opposed what she saw as the increasing power of Brussels bureaucrats and the erosion of British sovereignty. She wanted to leave the EU then and voted for Brexit in the 2016 referendum.

Ann Winterton has always been passionate about rural affairs and spent a decade on the Agriculture Select Committee. When Iain Duncan Smith became party leader in 2001, she was promoted to the job of deputy agriculture spokesperson in his shadow ministerial team.

Her frontbench career did not last long. The following year she was invited to make an after-dinner speech at the annual Congleton Rugby Union Club dinner. After a desperate search for a joke to amuse an audience not known for its politically correct views, she came up with what her own daughter described as 'a shocker'. It included a line describing Pakistanis in Britain as 'ten a penny'. The story leaked and within twenty-four hours the front page of the *Sunday Mirror* denounced 'TOP TORY'S RACIST JIBE'.

Winterton immediately issued an unconditional apology. But the Conservative leader Iain Duncan Smith saw the damage the remarks would cause, in the year of Theresa May's warning that voters saw the Tories as the 'Nasty Party'. Duncan Smith swiftly decided Winterton would have to go. He phoned her to demand her resignation from his shadow team and, when she refused, he sacked her.

Winterton insists she is not racist and says she deeply regrets her mistake. But just two years later, another joke brought more unwelcome headlines. She was at a dinner of the Denmark Parliamentary Group, which includes MPs from all parties. Mrs Winterton says she was expressing her surprise at receiving a 'joke' in an email from someone at party HQ. It was about a shark, fed up with chasing tuna, deciding to go to Morecambe Bay to get some Chinese. This was just weeks after more than twenty Chinese migrant labourers had drowned while picking cockles at Morecambe Bay in Lancashire.

Despite the inevitable outcry when her comments were made public, Ann Winterton refused to apologise, blaming what she said was 'inaccurate reporting' of what she believed was a 'private conversation at a private dinner party'.

The new Tory leader Michael Howard was furious, describing her remarks as 'completely unacceptable'. He apologised on behalf of his party and immediately withdrew the Conservative whip from the Congleton MP.

It was, she says, an 'absolutely ghastly' period in her political life. Months later, she backed down, apologised unreservedly and the party whip was restored.

At the height of the row she faced calls to stand down as an MP, and she was concerned about a possible backlash from voters. But at the general election less than a year later, her share of the vote was hardly dented and she held her seat with a healthy majority of more than 8,000.

In 2009, the Wintertons were among dozens of MPs whose expenses were exposed during an investigation by the *Telegraph*. It led to what their daughter describes as a 'public pillorying' of her parents.

They had bought a flat close to the House of Commons in the early 1990s and later paid off the mortgage. They then put the property into a family trust, controlled by their children. From 2002, the couple rented the flat from their children and paid the trust £21,600 a year. They claimed the rental and other costs on the property from the Commons allowance for running a second home, amounting to more than £120,000 over six years.

The arrangement had been cleared by the Commons authorities in 2002, but the rules were changed four years later. When the details hit the headlines, the party leader David Cameron described the Wintertons' behaviour as 'indefensible'. An inquiry by the parliamentary standards watchdog found they had unwittingly breached Commons rules and should have acted sooner to change their living arrangements.

The couple point out that they had been open with the authorities throughout and had written to the Fees Office to try to clarify the position. They both feel their names were unfairly blackened in the wider scandal that did so much damage to the reputation of Parliament.

Later that year, they announced jointly that they would be standing down at the 2010 general election. Ann Winterton insists it was not the furore over their expenses that prompted the decision. She told me she had decided that she wanted more time with her family and their growing grandchildren.

David Cameron thanked her and her husband for their 'service, energy and commitment'. But many in the party hierarchy were privately relieved at their departure.

Ann Winterton acknowledges she made mistakes and she frequently made life difficult for those trying to maintain party discipline. Throughout her twenty-seven years in Parliament, the first MP for Congleton displayed a loyalty to her constituents, rather than the party machine. Undoubtedly, she suffered from some lapses of judgement. But, unlike some of her colleagues, she was never driven by personal ambition and remained true to her own beliefs and principles.

VIRGINIA BOTTOMLEY

KITTY USSHER

- FULL NAME: Virginia Hilda Brunette Maxwell Bottomley (née Garnett), Baroness Bottomley of Nettlestone
- DATE OF BIRTH: 12 March 1948
- PLACE OF BIRTH: Dunoon, Scotland
- DATE OF DEATH: –
- MARRIED TO: Peter Bottomley MP (m. 1967)
- CHILDREN: Adela, Cecilia and Joshua
- UNSUCCESSFUL ELECTIONS FOUGHT: Isle of Wight 1983
- CONSTITUENCY: Surrey South West
- DATE OF FIRST ELECTION: 3 May 1984
- DATE LEFT PARLIAMENT: 5 May 2005
- PARTY ROLES: Member of the Conservative Women's Organisations in the 1970s and '80s.
- MINISTERIAL POSITIONS & DATES: Parliamentary Under-Secretary of State for the Environment 1988–89; Minister for Health 1989–92; Secretary of State for Health 1992–95; Secretary of State for National Heritage 1995–97
- MOST FAMOUS QUOTATION: 'Smoking is a dying habit.'

My mother's brother's wife, that is to say, my aunt, Virginia Bottomley, does not at first relish the idea of being interviewed for this book. Her neural pathways flick instinctively to previous, not-always-pleasant, experiences with the written word. When she does relent, and we sit down together over cups of instant coffee to talk about the past, I soon come to realise to my shame, that although she has long made a point of looking out for me, her Labour niece, I still had quite a lot to discover about her.

With a degree in sociology under her belt, Virginia began her working life in 1971 as a researcher at the then newly established Child Poverty Action Group (CPAG), working for its director, Frank Field. She took responsibility for a pioneering piece of longitudinal research that tracked the budgeting behaviour of low-income families over several years, with periodic updates published in *The Guardian*. The key insight from her work went beyond the truth of hard life on the breadline; it demonstrated that the instability and uncertainty of income that resulted from households' changing family circumstances was just as detrimental. The research also found that many of the poorest families were not claiming the benefits they were entitled to. Aged twenty-four, with her work published as a CPAG pamphlet, Virginia began to campaign for family allowance to be paid directly to the mother – a simple policy that would address many of the problems she had identified.

It was not at all clear at this time that she was destined to wear a Conservative rosette. Many in her family were Labour supporters. Although her mother, a teacher, had in retirement served as a Conservative member of the Inner London Education Authority, as an eighteen-year-old she had joined the Jarrow marchers. Virginia's father was the director of the Industrial Society, later to become the Work Foundation, and Virginia's own formative political experiences were obtained canvassing with her paternal aunt, Peggy Jay, who was a senior Labour member of the then London County Council. In fact, Virginia had been the Labour Party candidate in her 1966 school general election (the Liberal candidate won).

Two personal events appear to have influenced her decision to join the Conservatives. Following the publication of her CPAG pamphlet in 1972, she had the opportunity to discuss its findings with Sir Keith Joseph, then Secretary of State for Social Services. His feedback was stark, explaining to Virginia that 'it's harder to grow the cake than to decide how to cut it up'. Virginia was persuaded by his message that the call to action should therefore be the harder task of wealth creation. The second was her disappointment with how the trade unions responded to her call to have family allowance paid to mothers. Her feedback from a meeting with the Transport and General Workers' Union was that they were 'resistant to protecting the women at home when, as trade unionists, their concern was for the man at work ... the very poorest were those outside unions for whom the leaders showed little concern ... and there was a virtual closed shop for white males with ethnic minorities being as disregarded as females'. Labour's closeness to organisations who held these views was not a selling point.

The political journey of her husband, Peter, who was soon to enter Parliament as a Conservative MP, was also relevant. He had 'chosen' the Conservatives because, in her words,

Old Labour in the late 1960s and early 1970s were making a hash of housing and education in south London; tenants and parents were disregarded. At the same time while some trade unions were wrecking everyday lives and ruining Britain's economic prospects, some around Tony Benn seemed intent on 'democratic centralism', allowing a few from the centre to make major mistakes.

As a young, politically aware activist, Virginia saw her choice as between 'making the Conservatives more socially aware or battling to make Labour more economically responsible' – she chose the former.

The fact that it was a *choice* to be a Conservative does, with hindsight, explain some aspects of Virginia's later career. She never had any qualms in bringing the voices of the most vulnerable to the highest table – after all, part of her decision was to make the Conservatives 'more socially aware'. Although loyal to her team and idealistic, she was also a policy pragmatist, basing her decisions on the practicalities – this works, that won't work – rather than on an underlying belief set.

In 1973, Virginia left CPAG and went to the front line, training as a psychiatric social worker at the Maudsley Hospital and then working in practice at the Brixton and Camberwell child guidance units for the next ten years, with a one-year MSc in social policy and administration at the London School of Economics 'squeezed between Peter's October 1974 general election candidacy and his successful by-election in June 1975'.

With a strong sense of public service, she also became a magistrate in 1975, rising five years later, at the unprecedented age of thirty-two, to become chair of the Lambeth Juvenile Magistrate Court as it dealt with the fallout from the Brixton riots. The experience of the juvenile court further developed her understanding of multidimensional aspects of poverty. She explains how the young people who ended up there were not just financially disadvantaged, but also disadvantaged in terms of not having adults looking out for them: 'They lacked stakeholders, champions, opportunity and optimism. Few could even read the oath.' By her mid-thirties, Virginia was not only well connected in political circles but was also acutely socially aware, articulate and had a far greater knowledge of the lived experience of deprivation than many politicians either of her generation or the generation before her.

In terms of politics, however, she initially saw her role as supporting Peter's career. Gradually, however, that began to change. Sitting in the Strangers' Gallery when Peter was speaking, she came to the view that many of the men she was watching in the Chamber might make a lot of noise but in fact her subject knowledge was superior to theirs. She began to do more speaking engagements on the policy circuit in her own right, increasing her profile beyond that of simply the MP's wife. And so it came to pass that when Margaret Thatcher decided in 1980 that she needed more women, her adviser Gordon Reece rang Virginia and asked if she would apply to go on the selection panel.

Before committing, Virginia sensibly checked that her mother-in-law – my grandmother – was all right with this development. She got unqualified support, not just from her but from Peggy Jay and many other talented women among her social and family networks, some of whom undoubtedly felt that their own political potential had lain unfulfilled because of their gender. Peter strongly concurred. And so Virginia put herself forward: because of her sense of public duty, because she had something to say, because she had been asked and also explicitly for the hugely able women whom she knew personally and who had gone before her but been denied the ultimate prize. It was a decision based on gender as much as anything else.

At the ensuing Conservative Party selection weekend to get on the candidate list, Virginia got the highest score and was subsequently selected as the candidate in the 1983 election for the Isle of Wight constituency where she has a family base. She campaigned obsessively, but lost. The following year, along with 305 others, she threw her hat in the ring for the Surrey South West by-election, following the death of the sitting MP Maurice Macmillan. She beat out all the alternatives – including Stanley Johnson and Iain Sproat – and with a majority of 2,599 in the ensuing election entered Parliament in May 1984, one of only twenty-four female MPs.

In her early years, Virginia mainly pursued the causes of social reform and child poverty that were familiar to her, but when Mrs Thatcher asked her to join the government in 1988, it was as a junior minister at the Department for the Environment, responsible for heritage, climate change and local government. Since Peter was at the time also a junior minister in the Department of Transport and then at the Northern Ireland Office, this was the first time a husband and wife had served simultaneously as ministers in a Conservative government and only the second time in any government (John and Gwyneth Dunwoody were both Labour ministers from 1969 to '70). The next year, Virginia was back in more familiar territory, promoted to Minister of State in the Department for Health (which included social services) and was given responsibility for implementing the 1989 Children Act that importantly, and for the first time, put a legal duty on public bodies to make the welfare of the child paramount. She was promoted to Secretary of State in the same department following the 1992 general election, becoming the tenth-ever female Cabinet minister. She then moved to the culture and heritage brief in 1995, before returning to the back benches shortly after Labour's victory in 1997.

Virginia's approach to ministerial office is, I feel, summed up in three words: pragmatism, courage and tenacity. On the big decisions, she saw her role as being the person that campaigns for necessary change, being brave enough to make the tough choices that were needed based on evidence, principle and taking the technocratic advice of her team seriously, regardless of what it might mean for her own personal reputation. The industry of political strategy, 'public permission' and focus groups was anathema to her and she never engaged in the shadowy world of press briefings. This approach may not always have made her popular, but it may have made her right: Geoffrey Rivett's history of the NHS states that she took decisions many of her predecessors had avoided for fear of the effect on their reputations. Moreover, she was conscious that as a member of John Major's Cabinet, what the government needed, and by extension the country too, was people who were solid and tough enough to keep making progress on public service reform, despite the obstacles of an unaccommodating political climate.

Her achievements included pushing through a controversial hospital rationalisation which created large centres of clinical excellence in London that she considered overdue ('none of my decisions got judicially reviewed'); consolidating the shift to a commissioning/provider model within the NHS that further decentralised decision-making ('essential to ensure the right services were provided'), the introduction of a patients' charter ('patients have rights, like consumers') and the championing of a preventative approach to healthcare through the groundbreaking Health of the Nation White Paper. Shifting the debate onto healthier lifestyles led to her getting a lot of flak from her party, with accusations of being anti-free market and 'nannying', but she stuck to her view that it was no more than enlightened self-interest.

She courted controversy by bringing hitherto taboo issues around mental health into the mainstream policy debate, which included a policy shift to supporting people in their own homes where possible. She pushed boundaries by talking about suicide in her first party conference speech in 1993, because 'if as Secretary of State you do something unfashionable you can achieve a lot more impact'. She also mounted a targeted and ultimately successful campaign to get the European Medicines Agency located in London.

Around the fringes of these big strategic decisions, Virginia ran softer campaigns, picking projects that she could run with personally and which would allow her to make an impact. In her first post as Minister for the Environment, she wrote to all FTSE chairmen asking for their ideas of how to increase take-up of unleaded petrol (leaded petrol was eventually banned by Labour in 2000). As Secretary of State for Health, she used her personal convening power to hold a monthly lunch for ethnic-minority professionals working in the NHS; if necessary she would just ring the individuals up and request their attendance. Similarly, she was determined that the NHS should be a best-practice employer on gender equality, embracing the business-led *Opportunity 2000* campaign for more women in leadership positions. She was personally proud to have played a cross-party role to ensure the passage of the 'pioneering social policy' that was the 1990 Embryology and Fertilisation Act. As Secretary of State for National Heritage, she chose the location of her ministerial visits carefully, trying to counter the impression that 'arts was for toffs'.

Virginia is generous to her core, and modest, deriving her sense of self-worth from the extent of personal effort she expends to improve the world she finds herself in. She thinks of herself not as a radical window breaker, but more of a window cleaner or glazier – making clear sight possible, patching up the holes. As a parliamentarian, her strong sense of responsibility to do the job well meant pushing herself to put in the usual long hours without complaint even though they weren't conducive to a normal family life, stating starkly that 'it was only later I came out as a woman'. She is committed to the causes she chooses, for example serving for thirty-one years as a governor of the London School of Economics, where she had studied for her MSc (her great-grandfather had been involved in setting it up) until they made her an emeritus governor in 2016.

Since leaving the Commons for the Lords in 2005, the same desire to touch and improve in a very human way has found a home in her work as a senior headhunter for Odgers Berndtson, where she chairs the board practice, as well as chancellor of Hull University and the first female sheriff of the City of Kingston upon Hull, where she was a strong supporter of Hull's successful bid to be UK City of Culture 2017. She is also the longest-serving trustee of *The Economist*, has been a lay canon of Guildford Cathedral and an extremely enthusiastic grandmother.

When I was reaching political awareness in the 1980s and making my own very personal choices to improve the world through the vehicle of the

Labour Party, there were of course times when having a Conservative Cabinet minister as an aunt did not seem to be the most useful aspect to my personal backstory. But actually, the simple fact that I grew up with the knowledge that politics was something that could be done – given sufficient determination, public service ethos and drive – not just by women, but just by people I knew, means I owe her far more than I have ever previously let on.

ANN CLWYD

SARAH MACKINLAY

- FULL NAME: Rt Hon. Ann Clwyd Roberts (née Lewis)
- DATE OF BIRTH: 21 March 1937
- PLACE OF BIRTH: Denbighshire, Wales
- DATE OF DEATH: –
- MARRIED TO: Owen Roberts (m. 1963; d. 2012)
- CHILDREN: None
- UNSUCCESSFUL ELECTIONS FOUGHT: Denbigh 1970 and Gloucester 1974
- CONSTITUENCY: Cynon Valley
- DATE OF FIRST ELECTION: 3 May 1984
- DATE LEFT PARLIAMENT: Incumbent
- MEP: Mid and West Wales 1979–84
- PARTY ROLES: Member of the Labour Party NEC 1983–84, vice-chair of the Parliamentary Labour Party 2001–05 and chair of the Parliamentary Labour Party 2005–06
- MINISTERIAL POSITIONS & DATES: Shadow spokesperson for Foreign and Commonwealth Affairs 1994–95; shadow spokesperson for Work and Pensions 1993–94; shadow Minister for Culture, Media and Sport 1992–93; shadow Secretary of State for Wales 1992; shadow Secretary of State for International Development 1989–92; shadow Minister of Education 1987–88; Special Envoy on Human Rights to Iraq 2003–10
- MOST FAMOUS QUOTATION: 'So would I have still voted in Parliament in 2003 to support military action in Iraq – with the benefit of hindsight and in light of the Chilcot report? Yes. No one will ever be able to convince me that the world is not better off without Saddam Hussein and his Baathist regime in power.'

Ann Clwyd was one of the first people to be sacked by Tony Blair shortly after he became Labour leader. The dismissal was the consequence of taking an unofficial, and unauthorised, trip to Turkey and northern Iraq where she observed the Turkish invasion of Iraqi Kurdistan. The Whips' Office had given neither Clwyd nor her colleague, shadow Foreign Affairs minister Jim Cousins, permission to visit the Kurdish guerrilla territories. In addition, while away they had missed several three-line whip votes and were dismissed immediately upon their return.

A rift between Clwyd and Cousins developed. It was reported that both sought to discredit the other's strength of character and resolve in the depths of the hostile war-torn territory. Cousins complained he had been forced to stay on in Iraq to protect Clwyd from herself. Meanwhile, she took exception to such an affront, and to what she perceived to be his condescending tone. She responded with characteristic scorn, telling journalists from *The Independent*, 'The idea he went out to protect me is ludicrous. He even came home twelve hours early having taken fright.' When the two MPs were confronted by Saddam Hussein's troops she said, 'I'm afraid Mr Cousins was bleating and whimpering, and I had to hold his hand.' Before adding, 'Everybody who knows me knows I don't need protection in these circumstances. I've been into dangerous areas before without having to call for the assistance of Mr Cousins.' Regardless of the purpose of the trip it rooted her as a conviction politician, fighting human-rights abuses across war-torn territories around the globe.

The visit to the Kurds was not Clwyd's first sacking. Labour leader Neil Kinnock let her go in 1988, after she rebelled over his plans to increase spending on nuclear weapons.

Eight years on from the Iraq trip, Tony Blair appointed Clwyd his Special Envoy on Human Rights in Iraq, an unpaid post. Almost immediately after being given the role in 2003, Clwyd flew to Kuwait to discuss the 600 missing Kuwaiti prisoners of war. She then went on to Iraq to speak with Iraqi women in a hope to raise awareness of their plight.

She is described as 'awkward', but then surely that's a prerequisite for any Member of Parliament. In an interview in 2003, an unnamed Labour MP told *The Times*, 'She can be very awkward,' and warned the then Labour leader, 'Tony Blair could be in for a shock.' She was even publicly denounced by Saddam Hussein. Call her a government patsy at your peril! Clwyd has said of herself, 'If anyone thinks I can be muzzled, they've another think coming.' Her resolve was demonstrated most recently when she defied Jeremy Corbyn's three-line whip and voted against the triggering of Article 50. In 1997, she was one of forty-seven Labour rebels who opposed lone parent benefit cuts.

Before entering politics, Clwyd, who had studied at the University of Bangor, worked as a student teacher in Flintshire, where she grew up. She soon retrained in journalism, working across both print and broadcast media. She was a studio manager for BBC Wales and then Welsh correspondent for *The Guardian* and *The Observer*, a post she held for almost fifteen years.

She was persuaded to stand for Parliament by Welsh trade union leader Hugh T. Edwards. He believed Parliament needed more women and spotted an obvious talent in Clwyd. However, she was unsuccessful in both Denbigh in 1970 and again for the seat of Gloucester in 1974. Then in 1984, winning the seat of Cynon Valley, she became the first woman to represent a Welsh Valleys constituency in Parliament.

Prior to winning the Westminster seat, Clwyd was one of the first British MEPs to be directly elected to the European Parliament in the first European elections in 1979. This experience dramatically changed her view on the common market and integration with Europe. She had been a firm Euro-sceptic when she began her mandate, but sitting in Brussels as an MEP she started to believe there might be benefits to our membership. As her work gathered pace, she decided to write about her changing beliefs. In February 1982, she wrote a piece entitled, 'WHY I CHANGED MY MIND ON THE COMMON MARKET', which was published in the *New Statesman*. For an ordinary politician beginning their political career it may have appeared a bold and controversial move, considering party policy was still so overtly against any integration with Europe. In addition, her view was entirely at odds with many Welsh voters, where the majority voted in favour of not joining.

Also in this first group of British MEPs was Clwyd's Labour colleague, the doughty Barbara Castle. The two women had a cordial relationship rather than a firm friendship but there was obvious respect on both sides and perhaps some comradely competition.

She has said that the five years she served as an MEP were a 'key period of my life and it broadened my mind'. Her views on Europe were once again published in an article for the *New Statesman* on 6 June 2016, some forty years after her initial polemic and just two weeks before the EU referendum.

After returning to the UK from Brussels, Clwyd was elected to Parliament in the 1984 election. Her defiant support for the intervention in Iraq has had a significant impact on her political legacy. In 2003, she wrote an article in *The Times* alleging that Saddam Hussein and his sons fed opponents into plastic shredders, using their human remains as fish food. It was this article, claimed the then *Sun* political editor, Trevor Kavanagh, that largely swayed public opinion and encouraged voters to support Tony Blair in sending troops into Iraq.

However, some believed her principled stand may have inflicted wounds on her political career. For example, from 2001 to 2005 she was the vice-chair of the Parliamentary Labour Party, even becoming chair in 2006; however, in 2006, she was defeated in the annual election – her close links to the Prime Minister are thought to have contributed to her defeat.

Clwyd has been described as a fierce ally of the Iraqi people for decades and this earned her a place on the regime's most-wanted list. Despite this, or maybe because of it, she has won the affection of the country's citizens.

In 2010, Clwyd gave evidence to the Chilcot Inquiry, where she maintained her position on Iraq:

> So would I have still voted in Parliament in 2003 to support military action in Iraq – with the benefit of hindsight and in light of the Chilcot Report? Yes. No one will ever be able to convince me that the world is not better off without Saddam Hussein and his Baathist regime.

Meanwhile closer to home, and in a protest of an altogether different tone, she famously held a sit-in, 500 feet underground, at Tower Colliery. The pit, thought to be the oldest continuously working deep coal mine in the UK, was the last of these mines to remain in the South Wales Valleys. The 1994 sit-in was in response to the mine being threatened with closure unless 250 miners agreed to a wage cut. Just a year later, she was photographed proudly cutting red tape when it reopened, having been bought out by the miners. However, by 2008, the colliery closed for a final time. A poignant portrait shows Clwyd linking arms in solidarity with the miners and their families, leading the march away from the pit on its closure.

Clwyd is also a vocal campaigner working to improve the lives of women and girls globally. She was the driving force behind a campaign to improve the law for victims of female genital mutilation (FGM). She was successful in securing a Private Members' Bill on the issue, which led to a significant amendment to the law. Although FGM had been criminalised in the UK in 1985, under the Prohibition of Female Circumcision Act, the law was ambiguous. The Act didn't go far enough in protecting girls and women from enduring the barbaric procedure. Clwyd's Private Members' Bill, introduced in 2002, sought to address the weaknesses of the 1985 legislation. It became the Female Genital Mutilation Act 2003.

Today, she remains the MP for Cynon Valley, despite informing Ed Miliband of her intention to stand down at the 2015 general election. As a result, she had to participate in the candidate selection process, as Labour had already started looking for her successor.

Her husband, Owen Roberts, a TV director and producer whom she married in 1963, died in October 2012. Witnessing the suffering her husband endured in hospital – she likened the cramped conditions of his last days to those of a 'battery hen' – triggered Clwyd to campaign for better-quality care in the NHS.

Her memoir, *Rebel with a Cause,* was published in 2017.

ELIZABETH SHIELDS

SUSAN KRAMER

- FULL NAME: Elizabeth Lois Shields (née Teare)
- DATE OF BIRTH: 27 February 1928
- PLACE OF BIRTH: Bushy Hill Park, Middlesex
- DATE OF DEATH: –
- MARRIED TO: David Shields
- CHILDREN: None
- UNSUCCESSFUL ELECTIONS FOUGHT: Howden 1979; Ryedale 1983 and 1992
- CONSTITUENCY: Ryedale
- DATE OF FIRST ELECTION: 8 May 1986
- DATE LEFT PARLIAMENT: 11 June 1987
- PARTY ROLES: None
- MINISTERIAL POSITIONS & DATES: None
- MOST FAMOUS QUOTATION: 'The mother of Parliaments has seen many fine sons, not least those who sat on the Liberal benches, but the number of her daughters is far too few for the continuing health of the nation.' – In her maiden speech on 22 May 1986.

Following her victory in May 1986 in a hard-fought by-election, Elizabeth Shields was described in a piece in *The Times* as 'a mouse whose roar has been heard all over Britain' – and, despite the rather sexist tone of that article, boy did she roar. The Liberal Alliance which had backed her with enthusiasm proved its capacity to win a by-election in even the most unlikely of seats and women across the party were enthused. For me, the resonance was comparable with Sarah Olney's success in 2016 in the Richmond Park by-election. Elizabeth's election success was the political shock of the day.

Elizabeth Shields had been a long-time committed Liberal, persuaded to stand as an MP by Jeremy Thorpe and determined to get to Parliament to pursue the issues that most motived her. She never thought that her hopes were realistic but when she campaigned she just went flat out regardless. She was a classics teacher at the local comprehensive school and committed to education; she also served as a district councillor whose reputation was built on fighting for housing for her constituents and she was a supporter of women's rights whose maiden speech was on the Sex Discrimination Bill. In the year when we celebrate women's suffrage, she still takes rightful pride in being the first female Liberal candidate to win the coveted position of being selected as a by-election candidate. She became the first female Liberal MP in Parliament since the resignation of Lady Megan Lloyd George thirty-five years earlier, and brought the number of women in Parliament to twenty-six. As now, there was then a camaraderie among many women MPs across party lines, which Elizabeth finds both touching and warming to this day.

Her time in Parliament is covered in her own book, *A Year to Remember*. Although short, it gives a very immediate sense of the strange experience of life in Parliament with its rituals and inconveniences – especially for women of that era. But in pressing her for anecdotes I tapped into her bubbling humour as she remembered sharing an office with Clement Freud and Cyril Smith, both full of stories as well as taking up most of the space. It really is hard to imagine ever focusing on work with such office mates. Their office was at the top of a spiral staircase and Elizabeth always had to check if Cyril was on the staircase, in which case the path was effectively blocked.

Aged ninety now, and still a district councillor after thirty-eight unbroken years, Elizabeth continues fighting for her local community. Indeed, she used her time in Parliament to press local concerns ranging from transport cuts and inadequate financing for new social housing to the threatened removal of the local coastguard. The issues sound all too familiar today, which tells us how inadequately fundamental local problems have been addressed. Elizabeth is one of only four people to have been honoured by Norton-on-Derwent with the honourable freedom of the parish, in large part for spearheading and chairing the successful campaign to not only save the local library, but for turning it into a community hub. She held a county seat for four years, including two years chairing the Children's Services committee, and for a time chaired the Rydale Housing Association. Elizabeth only retired from teaching Latin at York University in the summer of 2017. She still inspires children in schools and on Radio York, persuading the girls especially to consider a life in politics. I wish I had known her earlier in my career. She certainly inspires me.

LLIN GOLDING

RUTH SMEETH

- FULL NAME: Llinos Golding (née Edwards), Baroness Golding
- DATE OF BIRTH: 21 March 1933
- PLACE OF BIRTH: Caerphilly
- DATE OF DEATH: –
- MARRIED TO: John Rowland Lewis (m. 1957; div. 1971); John Golding MP (m. 1980; d. 1999)
- CHILDREN: Caroline, Stephen and Janet
- UNSUCCESSFUL ELECTIONS FOUGHT: None
- CONSTITUENCY: Newcastle-under-Lyme
- DATE OF FIRST ELECTION: 17 July 1986
- DATE LEFT PARLIAMENT: 7 June 2001. Since 2001, she has sat in the Lords as Baroness Golding.
- PARTY ROLES: None
- MINISTERIAL POSITIONS & DATES: None

There are some people in the Labour Party whose reputations inspire awe (and a little fear) even before you meet them. In my experience, people rarely live up to their reputations and are all too often a disappointment – Llin Golding, however, is a very notable exception.

Llin was an extraordinary MP and is now a hard-working peer who has achieved so much for the Potteries. For many in our movement, though, Llin will be for ever linked to the battle against Militant. The political partner, wife and ultimate successor to the infamous John Golding (the Hammer of the Left), Llin is as hard as nails and a genuine inspiration for men and women alike across my county. And while she was a daughter of one great Labour MP, Ness Edwards, and wife to another, she is above all else her own woman, whose personal contributions to our politics and to the Labour movement are immense.

Llin began leafletting for the Labour Party at the age of six; she was campaigning for her dad's election to Parliament in the 1939 Caerphilly by-election. By-elections would prove to be incredibly important events in her life. Ness Edwards was duly elected and Llin's outlook was shaped by his experiences both as an MP, and as a proud internationalist and trade unionist.

Ness was a member of the miners group of MPs and was sent to Prague at the outbreak of the war to assist in the evacuation of trade union leaders. Exposed to the evil of the Nazis, Ness risked his life and was instrumental in helping some of those trade unionists to escape. These events had an immediate impact on Llin's childhood, with her dad demanding that she and her four siblings each donated one of their toys to the children who had fled. Llin had to choose between her two teddy bears and Mickey Mouse – she vividly remembers deciding that Mickey Mouse had to go because she couldn't separate the father and son teddies – that would be the same as what was happening to the children she was helping and was simply unacceptable. It was these memories that made the war so personal and drove her to work so tenaciously on the War Crimes Act – which finally received Royal Assent in 1991, after the Parliament Act had to be invoked.

Before her own election to Parliament, Llin was a radiographer and chose to locum across the NHS, working in twenty-three different hospitals and clinics. Wherever she found herself, she immediately became active in the local Labour Party, organising everyone she met – as is her forte. Ultimately, she and her family moved to Newcastle-under-Lyme, working at North Staffs Royal Infirmary. She quickly became active in the party and was membership secretary when Stephen Swingler MP passed away in 1969 and a by-election was called.

It was then that a young, dynamic trade unionist, John Golding, turned up to contest the seat. Although Llin didn't vote for him to be the candidate, once he was selected she was all in. She said he was fantastic and she would spend every Sunday driving him around the constituency, and she became his constituency organiser. In fact, in the 1983 general election, Llin made it clear that the candidate wasn't necessary for the election. John wrote, 'In Newcastle they operated on the basis that elections were too important to allow candidates to muck them up.'

John and Llin became one of those special things – a true partnership, both in politics and in life – marrying in 1980. She ran the constituency and ensured that the local party ran like clockwork, from fundraising to out-organising Militant in the Constituency Labour Party. And, on a night out, Llin was never without House of Commons letterheaded paper – so that anyone who approached John, and later Llin, with casework could have an immediate, handwritten letter to post to whichever organisation was causing them a problem.

Llin and John were truly loyal to the wider Labour movement and when John became general secretary of the National Communications Union in 1986, there was to be yet another by-election. John, however, didn't vote for Llin to be adopted as the Labour candidate as he had been mandated by the union to vote for someone else. As she told me, 'Of course he had to vote with the union, I'd do the same. John said he would vote for me in the second round and I said what second round?' As ever, Llin was right – there was no second round, she won on the first ballot.

> I knew everyone because I'd been organising for so long. I'd helped get all our councillors elected and I was secretary of the local Trades Council – usually the only woman there. One of the men said to me: 'Llin, I respect you but I can't vote for you. You're a woman and a woman's place is at home looking after the children – and I'm sorry about that.' I replied, 'Don't worry, I'll manage without you.'

And she did.

Llin Golding was duly elected on 17 July 1986 after a tough by-election against the Liberals, winning with a majority of 799. She was determined not to be labelled as a woman MP. In fact, her list of parliamentary interests was extensive, ranging from angling to racing and betting to boxing. Her maiden speech made it clear that she was going to be her own woman; she combined an attack on the Liberal campaign against her with jokes about her predecessor – his name had simply escaped her! And she made it clear she would not be seeking to emulate his long speeches in the Commons – because she wasn't John.

Llin became a whip almost straight away and was the only woman in the Whips' Office under Chief Whip Derek Foster. Her role was to charm the awkward squad. Her job as a whip also enabled her to work on one of her proudest achievements – a Home Office Bill that gave children the right to give evidence in court via video link, something that has changed the criminal justice system for ever. This work demonstrated the real value in working across the House to deliver change – especially in opposition.

In 1997, Llin finally got to see what a Labour government could do for the Potteries. New schools and a new hospital which would never have been delivered for her constituents by anyone other than a Labour government. 'It was just great to be in Parliament not to change the world, but just change things for the better one step at a time.'

Llin retired as an MP in 2001, and was elevated to the House of Lords as the Baroness Golding later that year. Llin remains the most active parliamentarian in North Staffordshire and is on the doorstep with the latest generation of Labour activists every week, where she has one message for her colleagues – 'organise'.

ROSIE BARNES

MIRANDA GREEN

- FULL NAME: Rosemary Susan Barnes (née Allen) OBE
- DATE OF BIRTH: 16 May 1946
- PLACE OF BIRTH: Nottingham
- DATE OF DEATH: –
- MARRIED TO: Graham Barnes (m. 1967)
- CHILDREN: Daniel, Daisy and Joseph
- UNSUCCESSFUL ELECTIONS FOUGHT: None
- CONSTITUENCY: Greenwich
- DATE OF FIRST ELECTION: 26 February 1987
- DATE LEFT PARLIAMENT: 9 April 1992
- PARTY ROLES: SDP spokesman on Health and SDP spokesman on Education
- MINISTERIAL POSITIONS & DATES: None
- MOST FAMOUS QUOTATION: 'I am not the motherhood, apple pie and furry rabbit party.'

When Rosie Barnes stepped up to the lectern as the newly elected Social Democratic Party MP for Greenwich on 26 February 1987, she was the embodiment of that party's aspirations to 'break the mould of British politics'. Like many of its supporters, she had never previously been active in any party, but shared the SDP founders' dismay at Labour's leftward drift. That night her by-election victory deprived Labour, the party she had previously supported, of a seat it had held for decades.

David Owen, the breakaway party's leader, wrote afterwards that in the attractive figure presented by Barnes 'we had at last absolutely the right image for the SDP'.

Down-to-earth, plain-speaking, and retaining the accent of her native Nottingham, she was hailed as a breath of fresh air among all the RP-voiced, suited male politicians of the 1980s against whom she seemed such an unstuffy contrast. Hugo Young of *The Guardian* summed up her appeal: 'a classless, strong-minded political ingénue of no previous fixed allegiance'. Other commentators made much of her dimples and curls while the National Portrait Gallery commissioned an informal photographic portrait. Barnes herself described winning her seat as 'being part of a process of trying to pioneer a different kind of politician, from a less political apparatchik kind of background ... I think that ordinary people, particularly women with children, have got a contribution to make that is being overlooked.'

In her maiden speech, she launched an attack on Margaret Thatcher's government over its social policies, raising eyebrows for defying the convention that such introductions to the House of Commons should consist of uncontroversial bromides about the predecessor MP and the constituency.

These outsider qualities ('fluffy but not frivolous' in the words of Alan Watkins) made her an ideal candidate to run against a Labour Party that twice chose a left-winger to fight the Greenwich seat (it was recaptured at the 1992 general election by Nick Raynsford, a Kinnockite reformer). But Barnes's image became, over time, something to use against the SDP. After starring in a soft-focus, soft-sell election broadcast, she was roundly ridiculed for being filmed giving one of her three children an extensive lesson in stroking the pet rabbit. The 'non-partisan appeal' had edged over into an appearance of naivety and middle-class cosiness. On polling day in June 1987, her by-election majority of 6,611 was cut to 2,141.

By the time of the next national run-off in 1992, with Barnes one of a tiny rump of MPs still loyal to Owen after the bulk of the SDP had merged with the Liberals to form the Liberal Democrats, she was fighting a doomed battle to hold on in Greenwich as an independent social democrat. Stung by personal criticism from her challenger Raynsford (and to modern ears his words do sound, as she said, 'arrogant and condescending'), Barnes was forced to insist: 'I am not the motherhood, apple pie and furry rabbit party.'

The constant jibes about being mumsy must have riled – particularly while she was using her own personal experiences to campaign on women's reproductive health in Parliament at a time when such subjects were more likely to be taboo, ignored, or both.

Barnes argued for early stillborn babies and miscarried foetuses to be given a burial. During the debates to defeat Liberal MP David Alton's bill to limit the right to abortion, which she helped talk out, she described her own intimate dilemmas. When she had her first child at twenty-six, he was born with only partial hearing because she had been infected with the rubella virus while pregnant. She went ahead with the birth after being warned there was a chance that her baby would not be fully able: she later said, 'It was the right decision but only just.' Opting to have a test during her third pregnancy, she had intended to choose a termination if the news was bad.

She took a rational, cross-party approach to education policy too, where she had some experience as a member of the Inner London Education Authority appeals panel and (briefly) as a teacher: she urged the SDP to support Kenneth Baker's landmark school reforms.

Although she spent her career before becoming an MP in market research, she later concentrated on maternal and child health campaigning.

After losing Greenwich, she took over the mother and baby charity Birthrights, applying for the job the morning after the count. Her experiences of the male-dominated Commons chamber barracking female MPs when they raised these issues made her more determined to continue in the same vein once she had been ejected: 'I want men to stop sniggering,' she told *The Times*. Later she became chief executive of the Cystic Fibrosis Trust. Her idea of what should be valued in public life became increasingly clear: when asked in an interview who she would choose as president of the UK, she nominated Claire Rayner, the health service campaigner, for being 'practical and compassionate and not motivated by ideology'.

But the non-partisan, non-ideological dream of the SDP had by then long faded. And Barnes, as one of those most fervently opposed to the merger with the Liberals (she called them 'dotty') was at the heart of the bitter feuding that marked the end of the Alliance, which had once seemed such a happy political home for voters attracted by neither right nor left.

In 1989 she was put in charge of devising a survival strategy for the post-merger refuseniks, and recommended concentrating on only ten constituencies at the following generation election – 'If we spread ourselves too thinly we face extinction,' she warned, to the dismay of members, who called it defeatist. But Owen decided to wind up the SDP in 1990 after a disastrous by-election result in Bootle. And Barnes agreed with her erstwhile leader when he decided to endorse John Major in 1992: 'If forced to make a choice I would reluctantly come down on the same side,' she admitted. Being a non-tribal politician, Rosie Barnes had been the perfect poster girl for the SDP's bold experiment in attracting a moderate majority of voters. But for her political career this lack of ideology and shared history was also its weakness in terms of endurance; the charity sector became a better vehicle for Barnes's attempts to influence health policy.

DIANE ABBOTT

KATE OSAMOR

- FULL NAME: Diane Julie Abbott
- DATE OF BIRTH: 27 September 1953
- PLACE OF BIRTH: Paddington, London
- DATE OF DEATH: –
- MARRIED TO: David Ayensu-Thompson (m. 1991; div. 1993)
- CHILDREN: James
- UNSUCESSFUL ELECTIONS FOUGHT: None
- CONSTITUENCY: Hackney North & Stoke Newington
- DATE OF FIRST ELECTION: 11 June 1987
- PARTY ROLES: Member of the Labour Party National Executive Committee 1994–97
- MINISTERIAL POSITIONS & DATES: Shadow Public Health minister 2010–13; shadow Secretary of State for International Development 2015–16; shadow Secretary of State for Health 2016; shadow Home Secretary 2016–present
- MOST FAMOUS QUOTATION: 'Outsiders often have an insight that an insider doesn't quite have.'

In 1987, Diane Abbott made history by becoming the first black woman to ever be elected to the House of Commons. Diane recalled recently in an interview what an unlikely aspiration it was at the time. After the 1983 general election, there were no BAME MPs and only twenty-three women as opposed to 627 men. I was only nineteen at the time but that same year, I watched as my mother became a councillor in Haringey. For me, it was a time of hope; it seemed that black people, and black women in particular, would make it, that they would crack the system and tackle discrimination head-on. Yet Diane remained the only black woman in Parliament for a decade. This fact alone says a lot about the strength and resilience she must have required in order to make it.

The 2017 general election returned twenty-six ethnic-minority female

MPs, 4 per cent of all MPs. It is still a pretty low number, but the twenty-six of us could not have made it to Parliament without pioneering figures like Diane Abbott, paving the way and fighting on our behalf. She has continued to be a vocal advocate for ethnic-minority women MPs, constantly pushing for more to enter Parliament.

Diane was born in Paddington, London, in 1953 to Jamaican parents. Her father was a welder and her mother a nurse. They divorced when Diane was sixteen and her mother moved to Yorkshire, leaving her daughter to effectively run the household in London. Nonetheless, Diane attended the Harrow County Grammar School and was admitted to Newnham College, Cambridge, where she was tutored by historian Simon Schama and obtained a Master's degree in history. Although she was never particularly encouraged by her teachers at school, she was known for her essay-writing skills and, following a school trip to Cambridge, Abbott set her sights on attending the university. Her experience of Cambridge, while life-changing, also threw into sharp contrast the extent of white privilege. Even in 2015, only twenty-three black women were accepted to Cambridge out of an intake of 2,573 students, so you can only imagine how lonely it must have felt in the 1970s.

After graduating from Cambridge, Diane joined the government as a Home Office civil servant, a position she maintained from 1976 to 1978, before becoming a race relations officer for the lobby group National Council for Civil Liberties. Diane also worked extensively as a freelancer and became a researcher and reporter at Thames Television in 1980, and remained in the position for three years. She followed this up with a two-year stint as a researcher and reporter at the breakfast television company TV-am in 1983.

Diane remains an experienced public speaker and broadcaster. She has spoken at colleges and universities all over the United States, including Ivy League university Harvard. She also appears regularly on radio and television and, from 2002 to 2010, made weekly appearances on BBC One's *This Week*, presented by Andrew Neil and featuring Michael Portillo. She has known the latter since their school days, with Portillo attending the affiliated boys' grammar school, and some have noted that the pair's easy rapport was a contributing factor to the show's success. A few of Diane's interventions on the show remain memorable today – such as the time she argued that Mao 'on balance did more good than harm'. She enjoyed questioning common knowledge and beliefs.

A Labour Party member since 1971, she was elected as a councillor for the Westminster City Council in 1982. She became involved in the Black

Sections, a movement for Labour's African Caribbean and Asian supporters. At the 1983 Labour Party conference, Black Sections tabled a motion describing their goal as the 'right for black people to organise within the party'. While the force of character of the four BAME MPs – Diane Abbott, Paul Boateng, Bernie Grant and Keith Vaz – who were elected to Parliament in 1987 played a big part in their achievement, so did the protests organised by Black Sections activists across the country who had to fight indifference, complacency and racism when it came to political representation. In her speech following her election, Diane Abbott rightly acknowledged that: 'This campaign and result has been a victory for faith, a victory for principle and a victory for socialism.'

Before being elected MP for Hackney North & Stoke Newington, Diane had stood against Ken Livingstone for the Labour nomination in the northwest London constituency of Brent East in 1985, but was unsuccessful. In 1985, she became a press officer at the Greater London Council under Ken Livingstone and was head of press and public relations at Lambeth Council from 1986 to 1987.

In 1987, she was selected as the candidate for Hackney North & Stoke Newington and subsequently became the first-ever black woman MP. Her election sparked much comment, ranging from enthusiasm to doubt regarding whether she was up to the job. Some wondered that her 'outspoken views' did not lose her votes. She said that while no one explicitly referred to her race, it was an underlying issue during the campaign. She was fearless in using her position to call out racism, starting with her first speech in Parliament, before later becoming president of Stand Up To Racism. She came under fire in 1988 for claiming that the 'British invented racism' – referring to the British Empire.

In her early years as an MP, Diane had a reputation of being a 'hard-lefter' and featured alongside Jeremy Corbyn in a Conservative campaign advert that attempted to scare away moderate Labour voters. From the beginning, Diane made it clear that she saw her role as defending 'the poor, the sick, the elderly' and the people of Hackney North from damaging cuts made by the Thatcher government.

In 1992, she gave birth to a son with her then husband, Ghanaian architect David Ayensu-Thompson, to whom she was married from 1991 to 1993. She later talked about the struggle of juggling the demands of being an MP, which meant long hours and late nights, with family time. For decades, women MPs have not been entitled to maternity leave; it is only this year that MPs were able to vote on a system of baby leave, backed by Harriet Harman, which should offer improvements to young parents.

Diane was elected to the National Executive Committee of the Labour Party in 1994 and served on the Treasury committee from 1989 to 1997 and the Foreign Affairs committee from 1997 to 2001.

As a member of the Treasury committee, Diane travelled frequently to Washington DC, New York, Frankfurt and other financial centres. She met with senior politicians, bankers and financial regulators, and helped to author a series of official reports on issues such as Britain adopting the euro.

She went on to serve on the Foreign Affairs Select Committee, which involved trips to Kenya, Uganda, China, Hong Kong and many European countries. She held a particular interest in human rights and always believed at its core, foreign policy should take into account human rights. It is still one of her main interests in her current role.

In 2008 Diane was awarded *The Spectator* Parliamentarian Award for Best Speech of the Year, as well as a special prize at the Human Rights Award for her '42 days' speech in which she opposed proposals to increase the amount of time terrorism suspects can be detained without charge. But for me, this is only one of the many times when Diane's speeches in the chamber have left me in awe. I remember her giving a voice to the women refugees in the Yarl's Wood Immigration Removal Centre and beyond, arguing in favour of family planning clinics, and promoting a more human immigration policy – and that is just to mention some of the speeches made during my own time as an MP. What Diane achieved in the twenty-eight years before I joined the Commons then is incredible. In May 2010, Diane was re-elected to Hackney North & Stoke Newington, with her majority doubled on an increased turnout. In June 2010, she made the ballot for the Labour leadership contest against four white male ex-Cabinet ministers, gaining thirty-three nominations after the withdrawal of her now shadow Cabinet colleague John McDonnell. Critics said she was a token candidate, to which David Miliband, one of her nominators, rightly replied, 'It is not tokenistic. She has twenty years of experience and commitment. It is right she is on the ballot.' She was eliminated after the first round, gaining a total of 7.4 per cent of the vote.

Following Ed Miliband's election as Labour Leader, Diane was appointed shadow Minister for Public Health and was named 'one of Labour's best frontbench performers' by the *Daily Telegraph* in September 2011. Working with shadow Secretary of State for Health Andy Burnham, she was particularly active on the issues of the sexualisation of women and girls and sexual health.

Whether on the front bench or on the back bench, Diane has always been very vocal on the issues that she cares about and has broken party discipline on a number of occasions. She voted against the Iraq War, the renewal of Trident and the implementation of ID cards. She was one of sixteen MPs who sent an open letter to Ed Miliband against austerity cuts in January 2015.

Diane is the founder of the London Schools and the Black Child initiative, which aims to raise educational achievement levels among black children. She hosts an annual conference for educators, children and their parents and an annual academic awards ceremony.

She has also discussed her own role as a mother, as well as poor GCSE results for black boys in Hackney and the need for better financing of schools in her constituency. In May 2015, she was re-elected again in Hackney North & Stoke Newington with an improved majority and 62 per cent of the vote. Diane joined the front benches after the election of her long-term friend and political ally Jeremy Corbyn as Labour Party leader. Their friendship dates back to their days spent campaigning together in the 1970s. Diane was appointed the shadow Secretary of State for International Development in September 2015, shadow Secretary of State for Health in June 2016 and shadow Home Secretary in October 2016.

As shadow Secretary of State for International Development, she spoke up on the lack of leadership of the government on climate change and on the refugee crisis, visiting refugee camps on the Greek island of Lesbos. She also spoke about the risks of the Transatlantic Trade and Investment Partnership on the Sustainable Development Goals and was early to argue that it was wrong to sell arms to Saudi Arabia. She criticised the fact that the Department for International Development was not consulted on the arms sales to Saudi Arabia, even though it has a major aid programme in Yemen.

In her short time as shadow Secretary of Health, she spoke up on NHS spending and on NHS staff from outside the UK, as well as on issues such as the Sustainability and Transformation Plans and Alcohol Consumption.

Her role as shadow Home Secretary has offered her a platform to speak up on some of the issues that she has campaigned on for decades. Redefining Labour's policy on immigration, she called for a humane approach to immigration and for an end to artificial targets. She said that immigration should be based on human rights, including the right to a family life, on economic needs for the country and not on politically driven numbers. She also called for children to be allowed to stay in the UK when they turn eighteen if their parents have the right to remain, and to put an end to indefinite detention in immigration removal centres.

She is a strong critic of the government's immigration policy and criticised the infamous 'go home' vans and the anti-immigration rhetoric adopted during the EU referendum campaign. On security, she has championed an increase in police numbers and the fight against cybercrime and has set up a special parliamentary committee investigating gun crime.

During the 2017 general election campaign, she revealed that she was suffering from type 2 diabetes and that her condition had spiralled 'out of control', affecting her performance and public appearances. Diane was largely criticised, even after disclosing her medical troubles and stepping away from the campaign trail for a short time.

In fact, an Amnesty International survey estimated that 45 per cent of all online abuse in the weeks leading up to the 2017 general election was directed at Diane Abbott. While there were those who criticised her before being made aware of her condition, it is fair to say that there are plenty of other politicians who should come to mind first when it comes to gaffes. And yet, despite her obvious competency as shadow Home Secretary, Diane was doubted and labelled stupid – and called other names that were much worse. It was shocking to witness the misogyny and racism that underpinned some of the attacks.

Diane Abbott spoke up bravely in Parliament, and later in the media, about the abuse that she was subjected to, and about how it might deter young people, particularly young women from minority backgrounds, who are the main targets of those abuses, from entering politics. She called on the government to address the issue of online abuse on social media. She spoke about the relationship between online abuse and mainstream media commentary.

Despite being subjected to vicious and highly personal attacks for most of the campaign, Diane was re-elected with an astonishing 75 per cent of the vote in 2017.

Diane Abbott possesses many admirable qualities, but if I were to pick one I would say I admire her most for her ability to raise big issues and foster national change while still staying very close to her constituents. She has always put the people of Hackney & Stoke Newington first and has spent three decades campaigning on local issues alongside national issues and speaking up for people who wouldn't otherwise have had a voice in the public debate.

When asked what I believed Diane Abbott's most memorable quote to be, I picked the phrase, 'Outsiders often have an insight that an insider doesn't quite have.' It is so simple, yet rings so undoubtedly true. Diane was an outsider at university, an outsider in a media industry that was still predominantly male and white, and an outsider in Parliament with its 'club-like atmosphere'. And yet her intelligence and fine sense of analysis have allowed her to reach a position where she can effect change from the inside.

Politics is a closed world. We need to bring outsider perspectives in order to make our democracy more representative and fair. It is time we all paid tribute to Diane Abbott for being a true pioneer in that change.

HILARY ARMSTRONG

JULIE ELLIOTT

- FULL NAME: Hilary Jane Armstrong, Baroness Armstrong of Hill Top
- DATE OF BIRTH: 30 November 1945
- PLACE OF BIRTH: Sunderland
- DATE OF DEATH: –
- MARRIED TO: Paul David Corrigan
- CHILDREN: None
- UNSUCCESSFUL ELECTIONS FOUGHT: None
- CONSTITUENCY: North West Durham
- DATE OF FIRST ELECTION: June 1987
- DATE LEFT PARLIAMENT: 6 May 2010
- PARTY ROLES: Member of the Labour NEC 1992–94 and 1996–2006
- MINISTERIAL POSITIONS & DATES: Parliamentary private secretary to John Smith 1992–94; Minister for Local Government 1997–2001; Chief Whip and Parliamentary Secretary to the Treasury 2001–06; Minister for Social Exclusion 2006–07; Minister for the Cabinet Office and Chancellor of the Duchy of Lancaster 2006–07

Hilary Armstrong was born in Sunderland shortly after the end of the Second World War, the second of two children. Both of Armstrong's parents were teachers and her father, the future Labour MP Ernest Armstrong, was also a Methodist lay preacher and a local councillor. The family shared a house with the parents of Hilary's mother. The chapel, politics and teaching were all strong influences on the young Hilary.

Ernest Armstrong was chair of the local authority's education committee when comprehensive education was introduced, which did not make Hilary popular with some teachers at her grammar school – one teacher claimed her dad was 'bringing clots into the cream'. Ernest Armstrong twice stood unsuccessfully for Parliament in Sunderland, before becoming the MP for North West Durham in October 1964. Hilary and her brother were both involved in their father's campaigns, leafleting and attending meetings.

Hilary left Sunderland in 1964 to study sociology at West Ham Technical Institute (now the University of East London). She had not yet decided what career path she wanted to follow, but knew she didn't want to be a teacher. Partly this was because both her parents were teachers, but it also owed to the fact that another teacher had told her teaching was a job for girls. After completing her sociology course, Hilary won a place at the University of Birmingham to train as a social worker. But she deferred this for two years in order to work in Kenya, ironically as a teacher in a girls' school!

During those two years in Africa, Hilary honed her views on the importance of leadership and the choices that education gives to young people. She often invited girls from the school to her house, to listen to BBC World Service, and to discuss things like population growth. She loved her years in Kenya and kept up an active interest in the region after she had left Africa. On her return to the UK, she knew that she wanted to be involved in politics.

After qualifying as a social worker, Hilary worked with children in Newcastle and ran groups for adolescent girls. She then moved to Sunderland and became a youth worker in the Southwick area, where she set up advice services for young people and play schemes for children, and worked with tenants to get them organised. One of the youth projects that she established in Southwick is still going strong today, playing the same vital role in young people's lives as it did some forty years ago.

Hilary then worked at Sunderland Polytechnic, where she established a groundbreaking training course for mature students without traditional qualifications. This was a forerunner to today's access courses, but back then it was truly visionary. The course gained an excellent reputation nationally and got people back into work. Aware that students needed to broaden their experiences and knowledge in order to work effectively in the community, Hilary invited speakers from gay and lesbian groups. She and her colleagues believed that exposure to the realities of life, rather than to the perceived norms of the day, was required if students were to become successful community workers. She also worked with local charities, including the Rape Crisis Centre, which at that time were very much on the fringes and not readily welcomed by the establishment.

The women's organisation of the Labour Party in the north-east in the late 1970s and early 1980s was strong, active and supportive. In 1982, it became clear that women needed to put themselves forward for selection and not just talk about inequality in representation. Joyce Quin had recently become an MEP, but no woman had yet broken through into Westminster.

In 1982 Hilary decided to seek selection in Sunderland North, where she lived and was constituency secretary; Sunderland North forms part of the constituency that I represent today. It was a bruising selection process. Militant were very active in the Labour Party, meaning Hilary faced a battle on two fronts: she was a woman and her politics were far removed from the hard-left stance of Militant. In those days candidates were selected by the general management committee, not by all party members; Hilary lost to the Militant candidate by one vote. She then tried to be selected for Sedgefield, but was beaten by a certain Tony Blair! She was finally chosen to contest North West Durham, the seat previously held by her father, and was elected an MP in 1987. I'm sure that Hilary's experience of the general management committee selection process increased her determination to push through Labour's 'one member, one vote' rule change some years later.

In the Labour governments after 1997, Hilary excelled in several different positions. As Minister of State in the 'super' Department of Environment, Transport and the Regions, she developed the regional policy which had a hugely positive impact on the north-east. She also introduced the elected mayoral system into local government. The changes she initiated improved the lives of working-class people. Hilary became Chief Whip in 2001, a role she excelled at. She is a people person and loves to chat, so she established good relationships with Labour MPs.

Finally, I would like to expand on her role in the women's movement of the Labour Party and on what she has done to help more women get elected as councillors or MPs. For many years she was a member of the party's National Executive Committee and chaired the Women's Committee. I was an organiser for the party in the 1990s and worked closely with Hilary in developing women's membership of the party in the north-east. I was also one of the national representatives for the GMB trade union and attended the NEC Women's Committee as part of my role. It was an exciting time to be a woman involved in Labour politics. We introduced all-women shortlists for the 1997 general election. Although in some ways this was a very blunt instrument, in numerical terms it facilitated a breakthrough of women being elected to Parliament.

The derogatory term 'Blair's Babes' could not mask the enormous changes not just in Labour politics but in British politics. Hilary Armstrong played an enormous role in bringing about these changes. She spoke at training events, talked to women, and did anything and everything she could do to support women at a local level. At a national level, she championed all-women shortlists; when they were temporarily halted by a tribunal, she played a key role in changing the law to bring them back.

For me personally, having known Hilary for more than thirty years, I believe that the role she played in getting more women elected at all levels is her greatest achievement. Women in the Labour Party now have far more opportunities than I could ever have imagined when I joined the party in 1984. People in working-class communities, not only in Sunderland but across the whole of the UK, now have greater opportunities because of women like Hilary Armstrong.

MARIA FYFE

HELENA KENNEDY

- FULL NAME: Maria Fyfe (née O'Neill)
- DATE OF BIRTH: 25 November 1938
- PLACE OF BIRTH: Glasgow
- DATE OF DEATH: –
- MARRIED TO: James Joseph Fyfe
- CHILDREN: Two sons
- UNSUCCESSFUL ELECTIONS FOUGHT: NONE
- CONSTITUENCY: Glasgow Maryhill
- DATE OF FIRST ELECTION: 11 June 1987
- DATE LEFT PARLIAMENT: 7 June 2001
- PARTY ROLES: Convenor of the Scottish Group of Labour MPs 1991–92
- MINISTERIAL POSITIONS & DATES: Deputy shadow Minister for Women 1988–91 and spokesperson on Scotland 1992–95
- MOST FAMOUS QUOTATION: 'I recall many an all-male shortlist. Party members had a choice: they could pick any bloke they wanted.'

A photograph appeared in the Scottish press when Maria Fyfe was elected to the safe Labour seat of Maryhill in Glasgow in the 1987 general election. It was of the Labour contingent of MPs heading off to Westminster – a sea of men, all standing on the steps of Keir Hardie House; it is hard to find the one small woman among their number. It said everything about politics at the time. Only 6.3 per cent of MPs were women and in Scotland the percentage was even lower, 4.1. There were only three women out of the total of seventy-two Scottish MPs, one was SNP politician Winnie Ewing and the other was Ray Michie of the Alliance (Lib Dem). Many of the men in the photo were familiar big beasts in Scottish politics: John Smith who became leader of the Labour Party; Donald Dewar who became First Minister when a Scottish Parliament came into being; Henry McLeish who followed Dewar in that role; and Gordon Brown, who became a formidable Chancellor of the Exchequer and then Prime Minister. George Robertson who became the head of NATO is also present, as is that other George, Mr Galloway, who became the scourge of New Labour.

The Scottish Labour Party was never without its activist women. From the suffrage movement, the female-led rent strikes during the First World War, the organising during the depression to the opposition to Mrs Thatcher, Scottish women battled against social injustice as committedly as their menfolk, but there was a swaggering machismo in Scottish Labour Party politics which meant that even doughty women had to fight very hard to get ahead. Too often decisions were made in smoke-filled rooms above pubs. As one wag put it, 'Scottish Labour likes having women MPs, but one at a time.'

Maria Fyfe is the sort of person who is nowadays in short supply in Parliament. She is a down-to-earth daughter of the working class who left school, got a job, married young and had two children before returning to education in her mid-thirties. She received a degree in economic history from Strathclyde and became a further education teacher, a sector close to my own heart because it gives so many people second chances. She had joined the Labour Party young and politics was in her veins, as it is for most of us brought up in Glasgow. She stood for the district council and learned the hard stuff of local government, convening committees that dealt with the tough lives led by her local people in Govan.

It was her fierce opposition to the poll tax, which was initially introduced in Scotland, that really spurred her to stand for Westminster. It was such a disgraceful piece of unjust legislation, which allowed a rich man living alone in his castle to pay half as much tax as his cleaner, who lived with a husband and children in a tiny cottage or council flat. The idea that this had been spawned by a Parliament so many miles away with no understanding of its impact on ordinary people was shameful. Scots resisted, were brought before courts for non-payment and threatened with imprisonment.

The fire in Maria's heart that won her a seat and her campaigning leaflet addressed to women spoke to another passion – justice for women. It advocated genuine equal pay, elimination of low-paid jobs, nurseries for all under-fives, separate tax for married women, regular cervical and breast screening, and more help for carers of disabled, sick or elderly family members. Her majority was especially huge because women turned out in droves to vote for her.

The House of Commons was a shock to Marie Fyfe's system but she made many friends on all sides, including Conservatives Nicholas Soames and

James Douglas Hamilton, because of her sunny nature and the sincerity of her political convictions. She joined forces with another great feminist, Jo Richardson, and wrote a Charter for Women, before helping to form the Labour Women's Caucus for both the Commons and the Lords which exists to this day, but is now called a committee. Eventually she became Labour shadow Minister for Women – this was when there was no Minister for Women at all and I do not imagine she foresaw the day when David Cameron would embrace the idea and create the role.

Maria then became convenor of the Scottish Labour Group for a year, before being appointed by John Smith, then leader of the Labour Party, front bench spokesperson for Scotland from 1992 to 1995, something which came as a surprise. She had opposed the first Gulf War when Neil Kinnock was Leader and had been somewhat out of favour thereafter.

Playing this crucial spokesperson role for her home country meant she became increasingly engaged with constitutional reform issues. She spent a good part of the '90s championing devolution in Scotland, which she had initially opposed, but had come to realise was the only way that domestic policy would develop coherently, as they got little time in the Westminster debates when a Conservative government was in power. She realised domestic decisions had to be made closer to the people affected by them.

Throughout her time in Parliament, she championed women's causes and was at the forefront of the campaign for all-women shortlists throughout the UK, though it went down like a lead balloon in Scotland. Reform had started with 'A woman on every shortlist' but it got nowhere. Party smart Alecs worked out how to game the system – you just had to have a woman on the list and then vote as usual for the favourite son. It was John Smith who swung it at the Labour Party conference, deciding that 50 per cent of constituency shortlists should have all-women lists. The newspaper columnist George Warner wrote that forty-nine Maria Fyfes would turn Scotland into a Tory heartland in five years. Little did he know that it would be ten years of New Labour's embrace of market-driven policies and the Iraq War that turned Scotland into a Scottish Nationalist heartland.

On the shortlist issue, Maria, as ever, told it like it was,

> I recall many an all-male shortlist. Party members had a choice: they could pick any bloke they wanted, a left-winger or right-winger, old or young, fat or thin, with or without a trade union card, with a nice grey suit or a woolly jumper, a moderniser of a traditionalist. Varied as they were, I do not recall one

ever complaining that he felt patronised at being on an all-male shortlist. Of course not. And why? Because the job was seen as a man's job.

When John Smith had his first heart attack, Maria organised a get-well card, which one of the Scots MPs said was a 'wifey' thing to do. Cultural change comes slowly!

Maria's record as an MP tells you everything you need to know about her. Her cause was social justice at home and abroad, and when New Labour came to power she found herself increasingly at odds with 'The Project', as it was called. Tony Blair's decision to embrace so many policies that had been forged by Mrs Thatcher appalled her, especially the assault upon trade unionism. She supported liberation movements against dictators in Latin America, championed the cause of justice for the Palestinians and support-ed peace in Ireland. She opposed the privatisation of many things that she believed should remain in public hands. She was and is an Attlee-style demo-cratic socialist, who believes with all her heart in the NHS and the welfare state. She is not a member of the loony left or any extreme group and she speaks for many who lost heart, even while Labour was winning elections. 'Is this Labour?' they asked. This was particularly true in Scotland.

Marie Fyfe had a bout of illness at the end of 2000, which forced her to appraise her situation and the competing demands of her constituents whom she loved, her new granddaughter, whom she barely saw, and her health. She had always said she would leave Parliament before she was sixty-five. She decided that she would not stand again in 2001.

To me, Marie Fyfe is the embodiment of a principled MP whose primary purpose was always to represent the best interests of her constituency and to follow her conscience. I might even hazard a guess that her viral illness and its attack on her immune system was the product of the deep feelings of conflict she felt about having to disagree too often with her party. It is not easy to rebel and to feel the disapproval of party colleagues who accuse you of disloyalty, when in fact you are being loyal to the very things which made you support the Labour Party in the first place. I have been there and I know the pain. Many of New Labour's achievements in government had her full support and mine, especially devolution in Scotland and Wales, the Good Friday Agreement, the minimum wage, Sure Start, the reductions in unemployment and the work she passionately supported to reduce world poverty; however, she could make no sense of Tony Blair's failure to tackle the fundamentals of wealth and power, or his failure to tackle the shackles put on trade unions. She was shocked by his boast that Britain's labour laws were the most restrictive in Europe.

Marie Fyfe was a great MP. The salt of the earth. And a heroine. Perhaps if Tony Blair had listened better to what she and MPs like her were saying, we may not have suffered such losses in Scotland and perhaps the vote for Brexit would not have been supported in so many Labour constituencies. Who knows?

MILDRED GORDON

RUSHANARA ALI

- FULL NAME: Mildred Gordon (née Fellerman)
- DATE OF BIRTH: 24 August 1923
- PLACE OF BIRTH: Stepney, London
- DATE OF DEATH: 8 April 2016
- MARRIED TO: Sam Gordon (m. 1948; d. 1982); Nils Kaare Dahl (m. 1985; d. 1996)
- CHILDREN: One son
- UNSUCCESSFUL ELECTIONS FOUGHT: None
- CONSTITUENCY: Bow & Poplar
- DATE OF FIRST ELECTION: 11 June 1987
- DATE LEFT PARLIAMENT: 1 May 1997
- PARTY ROLES: Member of the Education, Science and Arts Select Committee and vice-chair of Labour's Parliamentary Education and Social Services Committee
- MINISTERIAL POSITIONS & DATES: None

Mildred Gordon was Labour Member of Parliament for Bow & Poplar from 1987 until 1997, when the constituency boundaries were re-drawn. She was sixty-four when she became an MP, having been a teacher and activist for forty years in the East End. Her late entry to Parliament belied her long involvement in left-wing politics. Her father was a Labour councillor in Stepney. Mildred Gordon was governor of Hackney College and an adviser on older women's issues to the GLC women's committee. In 1983, she was elected to the London Labour Party executive.

She was passionate about decent housing, education, healthcare and social security for her fellow East Enders. In her maiden speech in 1987, she told the House that 'The mark of a civilised society is that it is one in which people can expect to be decently housed and clothed, to have enough to eat and to have access to healthcare and to education for their children.' She was a strong anti-fascist and anti-racism campaigner, working alongside the new immigrant communities who had arrived in London after the war.

She was born in 1923, as Mildred Fellerman, into a large East End Jewish family, and as a teenager took part in the Battle of Cable Street. She served as an air-raid warden during the Blitz. She later joked that working all day in an office and all night during air raids was perfect training for life as an MP.

In 1948, she married Sam Gordon in Reno, Arizona. They remained married until his death in 1982. Sam Gordon was a lifelong Trotskyist, serving as secretary to the Fourth International, and playing a leading role in American Trotskyist politics alongside James P. Cannon and Max Shachtman. In 1985, she married her second husband Nils Kaare Dahl, a Norwegian revolutionary. He, too, knew Leon Trotsky, and reputedly saved his life during a blizzard in the 1930s. When Dahl died in 1996, Gordon discovered a cache of rifles and a machine gun at his home, hidden there in case the revolution required the workers to take up arms.

Gordon was one of the first MPs to open a constituency office with a full-time caseworker, during a period when many MPs lived near Westminster and 'visited' their constituencies a few times a year. She campaigned in Parliament for the rights of carers and for regulation of nuisance phone calls. She worked hard to commemorate the civilians killed in the bombing of the East End.

She was also effective at holding the Thatcher and Major governments to account, and once dragged a Tory Housing minister to Poplar to stand in a tower block lift 'full of piss' (her phrase) to demonstrate what some of her constituents had to contend with daily.

In 1987, when Gordon was first elected there were just forty-one female MPs, just 6.3 per cent of the total, and just twenty-one Labour women MPs (the same number as in 1945). Like other Labour women, she fought tirelessly to improve the position of women across the country in a male-dominated Parliament and in the face of appalling misogyny. She died where she was born, in the East End, in 2016, aged ninety-two.

TERESA GORMAN

NICKY MORGAN

- FULL NAME: Teresa Ellen Gorman (née Moore)
- DATE OF BIRTH: 30 September 1931
- PLACE OF BIRTH: Putney, London
- DATE OF DEATH: 28 August 2015
- MARRIED TO: James (Jim) Gorman (m. 1952; d. 2007); Peter Clarke (m. 2010)
- CHILDREN: None
- UNSUCCESSFUL ELECTIONS FOUGHT: Streatham October 1974. She stood as an 'Anti-Heath' independent.
- CONSTITUENCY: Billericay, Essex
- DATE OF FIRST ELECTION: 11 June 1987
- DATE LEFT PARLIAMENT: 7 June 2001
- PARTY ROLES: Conservative councillor for Westminster City Council 1982–86 and member of the Conservative Women's National Committee
- MINISTERIAL POSITIONS & DATES: None
- MOST FAMOUS QUOTATION: 'I am Florence Nightingale to the middle-aged woman; St Teresa of the menopause.'

I joined the Conservative Party in 1989, two years after Teresa Gorman was first elected as the MP for Billericay. I do remember that, as a newly active young female Conservative member, she was one of several strong female MPs who were very visible in the late 1980s and 1990s.

I never stopped to think about the hurdles they must have overcome to be in Parliament nor how outnumbered they were on the green benches. And, because of these phenomenal women and the trails they blazed, I took it for granted that the Conservative Party was ready to select more women MPs, when I put my name forward for the candidates list in 1998.

Teresa Gorman was the 134th female MP ever elected to the UK House of Commons and served between 1987 and 2001. Her successor, John Baron MP, said in his 2001 maiden speech,

> Essex is known for the independence and entrepreneurial character of its people, and Teresa earned the respect of many by not being afraid to make up her own mind on things and speaking out on what she thought was right ... Teresa was never afraid to stand alone and challenge conventional wisdom.

Teresa Gorman's views on Europe as well as hormone replacement therapy (HRT) and the menopause are well known. Perhaps less obvious is her feminist streak, although she probably wouldn't have called it that. She is also remembered for having championed the cause of small businesses.

Teresa Gorman was born Teresa Ellen Moore in Putney to a self-made demolition contractor father, who had started out as a builder's labourer. Her mother was a waitress in a tea room. After leaving Fulham County, a grammar school in London, at sixteen, she went on to qualify as a teacher at Brighton College of Education in 1951. Around the same time, she married Jim Gorman, a former major in the Royal Marines. Jim died in 2007 and she remarried Peter Clarke in 2010. Peter died in February 2017.

In 1961, she gained a First in Biology from London University and became a science teacher. From 1965 to '66 she spent an exchange year in New York at the Convent of the Sacred Heart School, despite not being a Catholic. One of her charges was a Kennedy. Her time in the USA inspired her to set up her own business, Banta Ltd, with her husband, exporting biological and nursing teaching aids to developing countries. This was a great success and reportedly had a turnover of more than £30 million by the 1980s.

Her interest in politics was piqued in 1973, with the introduction of VAT, and she subsequently organised a demonstration following the suicide of a businessman who was being pursued by the VAT man. In 1974, she founded and became chair of the Alliance of Small Firms and Self-Employed People.

She first stood for election under her maiden name, Teresa Moore, in October 1974, when she contested the Conservative seat of Streatham as an anti-Heath independent (she won 210 votes). After the 1979 election, she joined the Conservatives and was elected to Westminster Council in 1982, which she served on until 1986, and the Conservative Women's National Committee the following year. In 1987, she was selected as the candidate for Billericay, the ninth seat she had tried to be adopted for.

When she first sought to be the Billericay candidate, she claimed to have been born in 1941 rather than 1931. She believed that this would improve her selection chances. This was, however, later criticised as it didn't seem to fit with her views on HRT.

Her support and extensive campaigning for HRT is well known, and Gorman claimed that it had helped her to retain her 'youthful vigour'. She insisted that 'if men's testicles packed up at sixty you can bet your boots there'd be a treatment available' and wanted 'to see a centre in every town, to which mature women can go without embarrassment to talk to qualified nurses, chat about all their symptoms, be given screening and generally undergo a check-up in a friendly, happy atmosphere'.

As a feminist, she strongly opposed the Liberal and Catholic MP David Alton's anti-abortion stance. Her April 1990 speech opposing his Bill to curb abortions is worth reading today with its passionate advocacy for a woman's right to control her own body.

She is remembered best, though, for her dedication to fighting the EU integration envisaged in the Maastricht Treaty and being a leading critic during John Major's negotiation of the treaty and the battle for its ratification in 1992. The leadership's patience eventually ran out when Eurosceptics endangered the government's majority by voting against the European Communities (Finance) Bill on 28 November 1994.

The whip was subsequently withdrawn from her, Nick Budgen, Michael Carttiss, Christopher Gill, Tony Marlow, Richard Shepherd, Teddy Taylor and John Wilkinson, with Sir Richard Body resigning it too.

Although the 'Whipless Nine' were threatened with deselection, they were readmitted to the party due to the government's slim majority. However, their rebellion did pave the way for John Redwood's challenge for the leadership, which Gorman supported, in 1995.

When Major refused to cooperate with the EU over its rejection of British beef during the BSE scare, she was delighted: 'I don't know whether the Prime Minister is on Ecstasy or had oysters for lunch, but he was terrific.'

Her successor, John Baron, remembers her having a very good sense of humour and also being very supportive of him when he opposed the Conservative Party's position on the Iraq War in 2003. Teresa Gorman surprised him with a call to express her understanding and to counsel that politics was about 'choosing a course'. His office remember many former MPs and constituents calling to express their condolences when she died, including former Scottish Labour MP Tam Dalyell.

Teresa Gorman was considered a talented but maverick politician, and delighted in being referred to by *Guardian* columnist Polly Toynbee as the 'most right-wing member of Parliament'. She certainly saw herself as 'the enemy of the old, wet Tories who think they were born to rule' and was conscious that she must be thought of as 'that ghastly vulgar woman' by many colleagues. The main conclusion, though, is that she didn't waste the platform she had been given, which makes her a very Honourable Lady.

MAUREEN HICKS

LUCY FISHER

- FULL NAME: Maureen Patricia Hicks (née Cutler)
- DATE OF BIRTH: 23 February 1948
- PLACE OF BIRTH: Hordle, Hampshire
- DATE OF DEATH: –
- MARRIED TO: Keith Hicks (m. 1973; divorced)
- CHILDREN: Marcus and Lydia Hicks
- UNSUCCESSFUL ELECTIONS FOUGHT: None
- CONSTITUENCY: Wolverhampton North East
- DATE OF FIRST ELECTION: 11 June 1987
- DATE LEFT PARLIAMENT: 8 April 1992
- PARTY ROLES: PPS to the Earl of Caithness and Mark Lennox-Boyd
- MINISTERIAL POSITIONS & DATES: None
- MOST FAMOUS QUOTATION: 'There are only seventeen Tory ladies and we'd like the world to know, of course we'd like to see women promoted, but only when they are ready for it.' – On criticism that John Major's Cabinet contained no women.

Maureen Hicks brooked no fuss about the challenges faced by women in Parliament at the end of the 1980s. She had enjoyed 'no silver spoon' in her youth and boasted 'no contacts, no network', but armed solely with tenacity had arrived in Parliament to represent Wolverhampton North East in 1987. Inspirations along the way had been her father, a 'self-starter' who had built a small construction business, and Margaret Thatcher.

Arriving in the Commons as part of a cohort of seventeen women, the group took the number of female MPs in the House to forty-one, and the number of women ever elected in the UK to 140.

Any sense of special pleading did not impress Hicks, who at the time dismissed claims of rampant male chauvinism in Parliament, telling the *Sunday*

Times in 1989, 'If you build up respect for one another as people there is no problem. Women can be a bit oversensitive.'

Reflecting on the culture two and half decades on, she conceded that there had been 'a lot of yah boo', but added, 'The women gave as good as the men. I didn't take any of it sensitively.'

Born Maureen Patricia Cutler, she was one of four siblings raised by her English father and Northern Irish mother. On the borderline at 11-plus, she went to a local secondary before transferring to grammar school at sixteen. Nicknamed 'four-eyes' by fellow pupils, a pair of large, round, heavy-rimmed spectacles became central to her look long into adulthood.

After A Levels, Hicks went to teacher training college in London. She had initially wanted to be an actress and joked later in life, 'I starred in the longest-running Whitehall farce in Westminster.'

A two-year stint as an English and drama teacher was followed by a place on Marks & Spencer's management graduate scheme. A later stint as an education officer in Surrey, where she gained her first glimpse of local politics, was followed by a move into the tourism industry.

After calling off her first engagement, she met Keith Hicks, a British Airways pilot, at twenty-one and the couple went on to marry a couple of years later. When his job moved to Birmingham, the couple relocated. 'Even though I knew then I was a career woman, it was a bit "where my husband goes, I do follow",' she reflected. They had a son and then a daughter.

Another move followed, this time to Stratford-upon-Avon, and there she started working in tourism. In a bid to influence local policy on the sector, she ran – successfully – to become a Conservative councillor. Soon bigger ambitions began to emerge and, encouraged by colleagues and friends, she sought to join the Tories' parliamentary candidates list.

Vetting took place over a weekend in Maidenhead and comprised a debate on NATO, showing off social skills during a cocktail party and being interviewed by incumbent Tory MP Nicholas Soames – 'an ordeal'.

As a young working mother of two, Hicks had little more capacity for preparation than reading *The Economist* and *Financial Times* in the three-month run-up. Most of the fellow interviewees were men, and many were barristers. However, to her surprise, she was accepted.

It took chivvying from party officials, who noticed eighteen months later that she had made no applications, for her to start looking for a seat. She applied for the Leicester West nomination, coming in the top three. Then she won the nomination for Wolverhampton North East, a predominantly working-class seat that had been Labour for almost forty years. 'It was a tough constituency, there were no airs or graces,' she said.

Hicks did not expect to win a seat on her first attempt, but against the national trend she was swept into the Commons with a 204-vote majority. The shock result threw her family into turmoil and, she believed, ultimately led to the breakdown of her marriage. The couple went on to separate, but remained friends. Keith was 'such a modern husband and so supportive, but the reality [of being an MP] was a bit different', she said, noting that she gained a lot of attention for her high-profile job.

She rented a one-bed flat in London to use on weekdays spent at Westminster, another flat in Wolverhampton to sleep in on a Thursday and Friday night, then returned to her husband and children on a Saturday and Sunday.

In the Commons her focus was primarily on education, manufacturing and mental health, including the effects of drugs – with crack being a major problem in Wolverhampton – and prostitution. Her maiden speech was made during the Education Reform Bill and she sat on the Education, Science and Arts Select Committee as well as the Tory backbench Tourism committee.

Hicks had met Thatcher several times before 1987, but winning an inner-city seat in the West Midlands firmly seized the Prime Minister's attention.

'As soon as I got in, within days she'd call me over and say, "How is Mrs Wolverhampton?",' recalled Hicks. 'I'd say, "Prime Minister" and she'd respond, "You must call me Margaret." It was a very personal relationship.'

On one occasion she persuaded Thatcher to visit her seat for a ceremonial tree planting. With 'a twinkle in her eye', the PM flicked a spadeful of soil at Hicks, who was wearing a cream jacket, delighting the gathered press.

Hicks also relied on the cross-party camaraderie among female MPs, counting Mo Mowlam, the Labour MP for Redcar with whom she was paired, a good friend.

Although 'heartbroken' when Thatcher went, Hicks switched loyalties to John Major and worked on his leadership campaign. His wife, Norma, once sent a note from the Commons Gallery admiring Hicks's green dress and enquiring as to its origin. She was embarrassed to respond that it was from the good-value department store Principles.

She was widely tipped to be on the fast track to becoming a minister when she was ousted in the 1992 general election. Her seat swung back to Labour and remained red in the succeeding decades.

In 1995 she put herself up for the Tory nomination in another seat but was unsuccessful. She continued to work in tourism, then education and the hospice sector. Roles as a governor of The Kingsley School in Stratford-upon-Avon and a director of Earl Mountbatten Hospice in the Isle of Wight followed.

Looking back at her parliamentary career decades on, Hicks said, 'Representing an inner-city area, a marginal, while being a young woman and mother, that was a breakthrough.'

ALICE MAHON

CAROLINE LUCAS

- FULL NAME: Alice Mahon
- DATE OF BIRTH: 28 September 1937
- PLACE OF BIRTH: Halifax
- DATE OF DEATH: –
- MARRIED TO: John Gledhill (divorced); Tony Mahon
- CHILDREN: Kris Gledhill and Kurt Gledhill
- UNSUCCESSFUL ELECTIONS FOUGHT: None
- CONSTITUENCY: Halifax
- DATE OF FIRST ELECTION: 12 June 1987
- DATE LEFT PARLIAMENT: 11 April 2005
- PARTY ROLES: None
- MINISTERIAL POSITIONS & DATES: None

Alice Mahon, a left-wing working-class peace campaigner, sat in the House of Commons from 1987 to 2005. While politics in Britain narrowed significantly during her tenure as an MP, Mahon avoided a drift to the centre and remained a politician of principle throughout.

Mahon was born in 1937. Her father was a 'big Labour Man', a bus driver, and had served in the Royal Artillery during the Second World War. Her mother, from a family of eleven, grew up 'very poor' and worked in a mill and in a pub during the war. Politics was central to her family life – and hard to avoid in poverty-stricken Halifax. Like so many people of their class, her parents supported the post-war Labour government and their programme of nationalisation. Mahon's anti-war politics, which would come to define her place in Parliament in later years, was forged in the shadow of a conflict that saw her father and uncles sent abroad to fight – they were lucky to survive.

Mahon's political education came from a wide variety of sources, not least the landmark book *The Ragged Trousered Philanthropists*, which her father owned. Her working life and education were crucial too. She worked as an auxiliary nurse and became involved with the National Union of Public Employees. In 1979, she gained a BA in social policy from the University of Bradford and taught trade union studies at Bradford College from 1980 to 1987.

She was originally persuaded to stand for Parliament at a regional Labour Party meeting in 1980, urged on by many members including Tony Benn. She was first elected as a councillor to Calderdale Council, where she managed to abolish the rent arrears sub-committee after just two years, before setting up the Equality committee. She was then selected as a Labour candidate in 1985 – and wouldn't have considered standing anywhere else but her home town of Halifax.

Alice Mahon does not sound like most MPs. Her accent, which sounds like those of the people she represented, was so out of place in Parliament that – shockingly – it affected her ability to be called to speak. During a debate about the first Iraq War, Mahon recalls Bernard Weatherill, the Speaker of the House, comment on the accents of Maria Fyfe and herself when they tried to get his attention: 'If the honourable ladies spoke the Queen's English then they might get called more often.'

It wasn't just her accent that felt different. Indeed, she felt the class divide, and the way that women were treated in the Commons hit her 'smack in the face'. When in debates, she spent her time trying to describe to MPs what life was like for miners, weavers and working-class people whom the majority of her parliamentary colleagues simply hadn't come into contact with.

I first came across Alice Mahon in her work as a foreign policy campaigner. She sat on the Parliamentary NATO committee and travelled widely as part of her work, including the monitoring of elections in Russia and Ukraine where she exposed US influence in the country's democratic process.

In the run-up to, and aftermath of, the Iraq War in 2003, Alice Mahon was a persistent and effective critic of government policy. Her speeches read back as damning indictments of a shared US–UK foreign policy that had utterly lost its way, and abandoned its moral compass. Speaking at the end of 2004, she summed up the state of play in Iraq, just as Tony Blair was making a self-congratulatory visit to the country:

> To go to Basra and the green zone, as the Prime Minister has done today, in relative safety, is not to visit Iraq. I would like to have seen the Prime Minister talk to some of the refugees. Where are the estimates for the number of dead in Falluja? The battle in Falluja is the battle that we have not been allowed to see

– the hidden battle. It is the battle that was going to bring democracy to Iraq, so I have a few questions. What is happening there? Where are the 200,000 or 300,000 refugees who have left the city? Why are there no pictures of the people still living in Falluja, some in extremely bad conditions? What kind of weapons were used in Falluja? The Americans admitted using a substance similar to napalm when the invasion began and we have heard stories from certain people and bodies, including Reuters, who have been in the city, that such dreadful weapons have been deployed there. I have tried to get answers here, but to no avail.

In 2009, Mahon resigned from the Labour Party, after seeing Gordon Brown continue with New Labour-style politics, and amid continued anger at what happened in Iraq. Her letter to her local party was damning, saying, 'This Labour Government should hang its head in shame for inflicting [the Welfare Reform Bill] on the British public just as we face the most severe recession any of us have experienced in a lifetime.'

In recent times, Alice Mahon has turned her fire on the behaviour of Labour centrists – labelling their attacks on Jeremy Corbyn as 'disgraceful'. Her commitment to the people she used to represent in Halifax is hardwired into her politics. She dismisses cast members of the New Labour elite like Tony Blair, Jack Straw and Peter Mandelson – and recalls Labour's best traditions: 'The Labour Party as I know is one that looks after the people who are working, who are struggling, who are trying to make their lives better.'

RAY MICHIE

ALISON SUTTIE

- FULL NAME: Janet Ray Michie (née Bannerman), the Baroness Michie of Gallanach
- DATE OF BIRTH: 4 February 1934
- PLACE OF BIRTH: Balmaha, Scotland
- DATE OF DEATH: 6 May 2008
- MARRIED TO: Iain Michie
- CHILDREN: Three daughters
- UNSUCCESSFUL ELECTIONS FOUGHT: Argyll & Bute 1979 and 1983
- CONSTITUENCY: Argyll & Bute
- DATE OF FIRST ELECTION: 11 June 1987
- DATE LEFT PARLIAMENT: 7 June 2001. In 2001, she was elevated to the Lords, where she sat as Baroness Michie of Gallanach.
- PARTY ROLES: Spokesperson on Transport and Rural Development 1987–88; spokesperson on Women's Issues 1988–94; spokesperson on Scotland 1988–97; vice-chair of the Scottish Liberal Party 1977–79; chair of the Scottish Liberal Democrats 1992–93
- MINISTERIAL POSITIONS & DATES: None

Born in Balmaha by Loch Lomond in 1934, Janet Ray Michie had two very notable firsts during her political career. She was the first Liberal woman MP to be elected in Scotland and, in the 1987 general election, was the only woman Liberal MP to be elected to the House of Commons. Her second political first occurred on 31 October 2001, when she became the first peer ever to use Gaelic to take the oath of allegiance in the House of Lords. The Gaelic language was something that Ray remained deeply committed to throughout her time in Parliament.

I met Ray Michie on my first day working in the House of Commons, as a young Scottish research assistant, in May 1991, at a meeting of Highlands & Islands Liberal Democrat MPs. From that initial exchange, I was struck by her warmth, her humour and her deeply familiar Scottish no-nonsense approach to life – all of which led me to refer to Ray as 'my mum in Westminster'. But, whereas I come from a mostly apolitical family, Ray was steeped in a Scottish Liberal tradition from a young age.

Her father, John Bannerman, was chairman of the Scottish Liberal Party from 1954 to 1964 and stood unsuccessfully for Parliament several times, including in Argyll in 1945. Although never elected an MP, he became Lord Bannerman of Kildonan in 1967 and made much of his maiden speech in Gaelic. When her father was the Liberal candidate in Inverness, Ray sometimes acted as his introductory speaker before he arrived at political meetings, which gave her her first taste of what it would be like to stand for Parliament.

Ray was educated at Aberdeen High School for Girls and then at Landsdowne House in Edinburgh. After school, she studied at the Edinburgh School of Speech Therapy and it was in Edinburgh that she met her future husband, Iain Michie. A physician originally from Skye and a native Gaelic speaker, who went on to serve in the Royal Army Medical Corps, Iain had several postings abroad. The family settled in Oban where he became a consultant at the county hospital in order that their three daughters, Dinny, Jo and Deirdre, would benefit from a 'good Scottish education'. Ray became area speech therapist for the Argyll & Clyde Health Board in 1977.

In Oban, Ray renewed her interest in politics and set about building up the Liberal Association in the constituency. During this time, she also became active in Scottish Liberal Party politics, serving on the party's executive and becoming its vice-chair. She first stood for Parliament in 1979, in Argyll, and held her deposit, which was in itself a significant achievement given the strength of the Conservative and SNP vote at the time. She stood again in 1983, coming a good second. On her third attempt in June 1987, Ray beat the sitting.Conservative MP and became the first woman MP for Argyll & Bute.

As the only woman MP elected for the Liberal Party in Parliament, in 1987, Ray took on the role of speaking on equality and women's rights, but her real passion was always speaking up for the people in her constituency of Argyll & Bute.

As her former colleague Jim Wallace said of Ray, 'she spoke about "her people" and "her islands", not in a feudal, paternalistic way, but because she felt honoured and privileged that they had voted for her, and she wanted to do her best for them'.

Ray described herself as being

> driven by the need to do something about the shameful neglect of the High-
> lands and Islands and halt the sorry trail of its people, scattered to the four
> corners of the earth in search of jobs and self-respect denied them at home.
> It seemed to me that Liberal policies, particularly on Home Rule and land
> reform, offered the area some hope.

During her fourteen years in the House of Commons, Ray served on the
Scottish Affairs Select Committee and was chosen to chair the Public Bill
committee and other general committees. She used the platform of Parliament to promote the many causes that she was passionate about – and
became vice-president of the College of Speech and Language Therapists.

Ray never particularly sought the limelight; however, when the fatal Chi-
nook crash took place on the Mull of Kintyre and the fishing trawler *Antares*
sank after snagging its nets on a nuclear submarine, resulting in the loss of all
four crew members, all of whom were from her constituency, her empathy
with those who had lost their lives, as well as her dogged determination to
pursue the necessary changes to avoid repetition of these tragic accidents,
was clear for all to see.

Outside politics, Ray shared her father's passion for rugby. Her father,
John Bannerman, had thirty-seven caps for Scotland and Ray recalled that
'my brothers and I used to practise scrumming down with him'. Ray was
equally proud when her nephew, Shade Munro, also went on to play for
Scotland.

If she had been born a couple of decades later, there can be little doubt
that Ray would have wanted to stand for election to the Parliament at Holyrood. She had spent so much of her political career campaigning for home
rule and a Scottish Parliament. It would also have allowed her to be closer to
the people and communities that she loved. Family life and spending time
with her loved ones were always of prime importance to Ray, especially when
her husband, Iain, became ill.

Throughout her political career, Ray Michie remained true to herself. She
was not somebody to be swayed by fads or fashion. I will always remember
her kindness, her humour and above all her dedication to the communities
and causes she championed.

Ray died at home in Oban, after fighting cancer, in May 2008, aged
seventy-four.

MO MOWLAM

JULIA LANGDON

- FULL NAME: Marjorie Mowlam
- DATE OF BIRTH: 18 September 1949
- PLACE OF BIRTH: Watford
- DATE OF DEATH: 19 August 2005
- MARRIED TO: Jonathan Norton
- CHILDREN: Henrietta and Freddie Norton (stepchildren)
- UNSUCCESSFUL ELECTIONS: None
- CONSTITUENCY: Redcar
- DATE OF FIRST ELECTION: 11 June 1987
- DATE LEFT PARLIAMENT: 7 June 2001
- PARTY ROLES: None
- MINISTERIAL POSITIONS & DATES: Shadow spokeswoman Northern Ireland 1988; shadow Minister for Women and Equalities 1992–93; shadow Secretary of State for National Heritage 1992–94; shadow Secretary of State for Northern Ireland 1994–97; Secretary of State for Northern Ireland 1997–99; Minister for the Cabinet Office and Chancellor of the Duchy of Lancaster 1999–2001
- MOST FAMOUS QUOTATION: 'Bloody well get on and do it, otherwise I'll headbutt you.' – To Gerry Adams, during talks on the Belfast Good Friday Agreement.

The life of Mo Mowlam was, in so many ways, haunted by tragedy. While she was alive, even before she became famous, there was always a sense that because she lived so dangerously, so close to the edge, she was somehow hurtling towards some impending, unspecified doom. After she died, she never really secured sufficient recognition for the extraordinary achievements of her last years and then, all too swiftly, it was almost as if she had been completely forgotten. Yet it is fair to assert that the Good Friday Agreement (officially known as the Belfast Agreement), which gave written form to a peace process in Northern Ireland that has held in place for twenty years at the time of publication of this book, might never have been signed without the extraordinary personal contribution she made towards it.

It was her personality that was so vital. The reason why her personality came to matter so much to the wider world was because of the singular impact she made upon the political chaos of Northern Ireland, through simply being the person that she was. She was pushy, determined, tough and prepared to do anything that was needed. But that much could be said about many people, politicians in particular. What made Mo exceptional was that she could talk to anyone – and she did. She talked to anyone and everyone and she always gave the impression, at least, that whoever it was, the Prime Minister or the postman, she would address them in the same way. She didn't, of course. She knew exactly what she was doing, and she was very careful indeed about the message she conveyed, but her significant skill was to make everyone believe that she was behaving naturally, that they were looking at the real Mo.

Her natural affability helped her win over her constituency in the northeast, worked wonders in Parliament and in Northern Ireland, when she became the first woman appointed to the role of Northern Ireland Secretary. And the press loved her. She would walk into a working men's club in her constituency, go up to the bar and pick up someone's pint and take a swig out of it. A man who did that might get floored for such sacrilege; another woman wouldn't dare go in to the bar in the first place. Mo just made everyone love her all the more.

On another occasion, she went to comfort a Belfast woman whose husband was in jail for terrorist offences and she put her arm about the distraught woman, stroked the crying child that the woman was holding and then bent down to take a bite out of the child's sandwich. The surprised child stopped crying and everybody around laughed. At Westminster she would go into Annie's Bar, full of her fellow MPs and journalists, and wail plaintively, 'Oh, get me a gin and tonic someone! My period pains are terrible.' Nobody had ever spoken of menstruation in Annie's Bar before. Not even quietly. But nobody minded because Mo was Mo.

We know now that these actions may have been examples of disinhibited behaviour, a symptom consistent with the brain tumour from which Mo Mowlam was suffering, which was diagnosed in the first days of 1997 and which would ultimately kill her. It didn't matter, though, that she behaved in such an unusual way because it was her remarkable ability to communicate with other people that would prove to be her unique gift to the people of Northern Ireland and to its peace process. She brought Sinn Féin to the negotiating table and, despite the reservations of the buttoned-up Unionist political leaders, her popularity meant that she brought the people with her. They used to say, when she first went to Belfast, that if you hadn't been kissed by Mo then you must have been running very fast in the other direction. She would even kiss journalists. She would pick her prey, go straight up and kiss the startled target full on the lips, before swiftly swerving past and away. Then she would turn and call, laughing over her shoulder, as she disappeared, 'Oh, by the way, I've got flu!'

It was the brain tumour that was, of course, the ultimate tragedy, but it was not until five years after she died that it became evident just how much of a tragedy it really was. Mo was a terrific liar. She had always been careless with the truth, about things that didn't matter much. In interviews she would tell one person that she was born in Watford and in another that she was born in Southall, where the family moved when she was small. It was quite simple: she was easily bored by minor details and who cared anyway? In her personal and political life she had learned similarly to dissemble when the facts were inconvenient. When she was told by her consultant that she had a malignant brain tumour and probably three years to live, just six months before she might confidently expect to be a Cabinet minister, what else was there to do but lie about it? She told everybody, except possibly her husband, that the tumour was benign.

I am the author of a biography of Mo Mowlam, published in the autumn of 2000, shortly after her decision to stand down at the coming 2001 general election was prematurely disclosed. It was not an authorised book, nor based on interviews with her, although I did know her passably well before I started researching it. I had no privileged information about her state of health, but I did not use the word benign to describe her cancer in the book, because I suspected it wasn't the case.

When her consultant revealed in 2010 that she had lied, that she had been living with a death sentence, all the pieces fell into place. Knowing as she did that she had limited time, that her chance to make a difference was going to be strictly curtailed, she determined that she would do everything that she could to make a difference in politics in the time that she had available because she wasn't going to get another chance. This was it. As the consultant, Mark Glaser, would say later, 'She was racing against time.'

It was a difficult time for Glaser, a professional nightmare as he said, because anything could have happened. As Northern Ireland Secretary her judgement and her behaviour would be critical. She was, after all, operating in a war zone and lives were at risk. Glaser ordered Mo to be honest with the Prime Minister about her tumour. Instead, Mo lied to Glaser, telling him that she had. But, perhaps, it was precisely because she was running out of time that she made so much progress on the peace process.

There is an irony here. Mo Mowlam never wanted to be Northern Ireland Secretary. She didn't even want to be the shadow minister, when Tony Blair first sent her to Belfast, after he became Labour leader in 1994. She saw it as political exile and she wanted instead to be close to the heart of the New Labour project. In 1997, having convinced Blair that her benign tumour had been treated, Mo once again argued to be appointed to a major domestic portfolio. Although she lost that argument, she went on to win on every other front: the Northern Ireland appointment made her name and she was recognised for courage and charisma – she even became, arguably, more popular than Tony Blair was himself at the time.

It must have been a very strange time for her. Although Mo was used to being well liked, she recognised that her newfound popularity was different and correctly sensed the danger in it.

Mo had always been outgoing, rebellious and an extrovert, but she was demonstrably kind and caring, too, and that was why people liked her. Her father had been an alcoholic and the strain within the family had turned Mo, the middle child of three, into an incredibly caring and understanding woman. All her life, she wanted to help people who had never had a chance, in particular the disabled, and she would always look out for disabled children. It was an instinct which would, in time, lead her to Labour politics. As a girl she was good at things and, although she wasn't clever, Mo worked hard and did well at school; she was athletic on the sports field; took the lead in the school play; and was elected head girl under a system which gave votes to both staff and pupils. Importantly, she had time for anyone and a startling ability, which she inherited from her father, to remember everyone's name. This would prove invaluable when she became a college politics lecturer and even more so when she got into politics.

There was something else about her that was significant. She was also remarkably pretty. It is hard now, given the familiarity of her looks in the years when she was famous, to imagine how difficult it must have been for her to lose the glowing radiance of that youthful beauty. She never spoke of it, but those who understood her knew how much it must have affected her.

And then, a few weeks after the radiotherapy and steroid treatment for her cancer, she was unkindly described in a newspaper as resembling 'an only slightly effeminate Geordie trucker'. She dismissed the jibe by saying that she had always been very fond of Geordie truckers and got on with the job, but who could not have been hurt by that?

She was able to carry on, seemingly regardless, because criticism had led Mo to develop a tough skin. The self-confidence she exuded had always masked a desperately vulnerable woman and the knowledge that she did not have much time left must have further hardened her already steely exterior. When I was writing her biography, I was struck by the frequency with which those I interviewed would comment cheerfully that, with Mo 'what you saw was what you got'. It wasn't – what you saw was what she wanted you to see. She was always a profoundly secretive person and now she had the secret of her own mortality to conceal.

The disinhibitions of her behaviour in office were often remarked at this time. She would whisk off her wig to disconcert visitors. She used coarse language, made crude jokes and would behave inappropriately. She sat with her legs apart, apparently on purpose, and she followed people into the lavatory. Just before an interview with Iain Dale, the co-editor of this book, she nonchalantly walked into the radio studio, lifted her leg and farted. When asked to say a few words into the microphone for a sound check, she burped. Loudly. All this was labelled and excused as idiosyncratic, all part of her eccentricity. In reality, of course, it was her illness, but the problem was that because her behaviour was accepted, as 'Mo being Mo', and because she knew how popular she was with the people on the streets, she began to believe in her own political invincibility. It was this which would bring about her public downfall.

She had recognised the danger her popularity could spell. Blair didn't much care for the fact that she had received a standing ovation in the middle of his big speech to the party conference in 1998. She had been very successful in the negotiations in the run-up to the Belfast Agreement, but Tony Blair and his Downing Street team had understandably moved in towards the end because, if there was to be a triumphant outcome, it was his government that was going to take the credit, not his Secretary of State. When Bill Clinton arrived to stamp his seal of approval on the peace negotiations, Mo Mowlam poured the tea. 'Don't you know?' she commented sarcastically, when Clinton asked why she was making the tea, 'I'm the new tea girl around here.'

The New Labour establishment moved against her. There was a whispering campaign about her behaviour and her shortcomings. There was an unsuccessful attempt to try to get her to run for the post of London Mayor, as the one candidate who would be sufficiently popular to challenge her friend Ken Livingstone, who was suspended from the Labour Party at the time. Rumours spread that Peter Mandelson, who could use a bit of popularity himself, wanted to take over from her in Belfast. She ignored all of this and used her personal standing to stay in Northern Ireland, when she had, in reality, outlived her usefulness. She had by this time alienated the Unionists and thus created a stalemate. By the autumn of 1999, she had also exhausted the goodwill of most of the rest of the government.

She was obliged to take another job but by now she was convinced, perhaps by the effects of her illness, and certainly by her close circle of friends, that she could choose to do what she liked. She wanted to be Foreign Secretary and she had begun to believe that she could become Prime Minister in succession to Blair. She had, after all, been tipped as the first woman Prime Minister as a student at Durham University. She had lost the first woman race already, but there was no reason why she couldn't be the second. This self-delusion was a source of great alarm to her consultant. He was profoundly relieved when she left Belfast and, having refused an offer of the post of Health Secretary, was appointed to the Cabinet as Chancellor of the Duchy of Lancaster with responsibility for parliamentary reform. She was, in reality, made the equivalent of Minister for Paperclips. Somewhat to the alarm of No. 10, she did also have responsibility for drugs policy – it was meant to have been removed from her portfolio – but she was so disaffected by her evident demotion that it became irrelevant.

She left Parliament and died four years later. I saw her occasionally and she was a sad figure during that time. She was drinking a lot and clearly very ill, although she refused to acknowledge it. What I didn't know until five years after her death, however, was that she had then only latterly come to understand that her brain tumour had possibly been growing and affecting her behaviour for as long as twenty years. And that it had left her wondering who she really was. She had constructed a persona to hide the real Mo Mowlam, but now she didn't know what was real, after all. It must have been an irredeemably sad discovery for someone who had always believed in herself.

EMMA NICHOLSON

ELINOR GOODMAN

- FULL NAME: Emma Harriet Nicholson, Baroness Nicholson of Winterbourne
- DATE OF BIRTH: 16 October 1941
- PLACE OF BIRTH: Farnham
- DATE OF DEATH: –
- MARRIED TO: Sir Michael Caine (m. 1987; d. 1999)
- CHILDREN: Fostered one son in 1991
- UNSUCCESSFUL ELECTIONS: Blyth 1979
- CONSTITUENCY: Torridge & West Devon
- MEP: South East England 1999–2009
- DATE OF FIRST ELECTION: 11 June 1987
- DATE LEFT PARLIAMENT: 1 May 1997. She has since sat in the Lords as Baroness Nicholson of Winterbourne.
- PARTY ROLES: Conservative Party vice-chair 1983–87
- MINISTERIAL POSITIONS & DATES: None

Emma Nicholson is one of a rare breed of politician to have defected from one party to another, only to defect back again to the nascent party. Like Winston Churchill, Nicholson was brought up in a patrician Conservative household, became a Conservative MP, quit to become a Liberal Democrat and then rejoined the Tories. Unlike Churchill, though, she never became a minister, let alone Prime Minister. Arguably, though, she has affected far more lives crusading from the back benches than she would have done as a junior minister.

Nicholson's family possessed a strong public service ethic, which had produced generations of Conservative MPs, including her father, Sir Geoffrey Nicholson. But she didn't accept his brand of high conservatism. After several years of working in Africa, and then fundraising for Save the Children, Nicholson knew she wanted to change things. 'Parliament was the place to get things changed, but I knew my views were very different to anyone else in the family.'

Nevertheless, she didn't like the centralism of the Labour Party, and at that point the Liberals barely registered on her horizon, so she applied to Conservative Central Office to become a parliamentary candidate. Baroness Young, about the only female politician Mrs Thatcher rated, told her she was wasting her time: 'They don't want women.' But having overcome deafness as a child to get into the Royal School of Music, Nicholson has always been fiercely determined. Indeed, determination is the rod of iron that runs through her career, taking her on hopeless trips to Conservative committee rooms in every part of the UK in the 1970s, to the swamps of Iraq and the desert of Yemen in her various parliamentary roles.

Eventually, she was selected in 1979 for a rock-solid Labour mining seat. She didn't win it, but she did slash Labour's majority, so she asked Mrs Thatcher for the job of recruiting more prospective female candidates. She got rid of the thirteen on the list and trained 300 new ones, although only seventeen were elected in 1987, when she herself won Torridge & West Devon.

Chauvinism was rife when she entered Parliament. She backed Labour MP Clare Short's attempt to ban page-3 girls in *The Sun*. Mathew Parris, a former Tory MP turned sketchwriter, described 'her nipples sticking out when she spoke in the Commons'. Despite being a birthright Conservative, Nicholson wasn't tribal and was seen by the whips as too independent for her own good. She says that being deaf made her a loner. She was beautiful and well dressed, but because she lip-read, she looked very intense and spoke with a booming, cut-glass voice which could make her seem bossy. Determination, one of her greatest strengths, was also a potential weakness in that she could be very difficult to work with.

At first she concentrated on constituency issues, which, because she represented a rural seat, made her realise how important Brussels was becoming. She joined the European committee and, in 1991, went as part of a delegation to Romania where she witnessed the horrific conditions orphans were living in. This prompted her to campaign to end foreign adoptions from Romania, which she saw as a form of human trafficking.

That same year she went on a life-changing trip to Kuwait and Iraq, where she saw 'the unspeakable trail of damage' left by Saddam Hussein. In Parliament, she started a highly effective campaign to shine a light on the plight of the Marsh Arabs. Outside of Westminster she started a foundation, AMAR, named after a very badly disfigured boy she had fostered in Iraq. In its first twenty-five years of existence it has spent £15 million and helped, she says, ten million patients and five million people, including Yazidis, Romanians, Marsh Arabs, Nigerians and Kurds.

Chairing it would have been a career in itself, but Nicholson kept her seat at Westminster, even though she was becomingly increasingly disenchanted with Mrs Thatcher, who she had once regarded as a friend. Her father had told her that she should only break a three-line whip once, but she became a serial rebel, openly challenging Mrs Thatcher on the poll tax. When Michael Heseltine wrestled for the leadership, she backed him. 'Her local party disagreed with her stance on the premiership and tried to deselect her.

Even though Mrs Thatcher's successor, John Major, shared Emma Nicholson's opposition to the poll tax, she didn't think highly of him. So, after much courting by the Liberal Democrats, she joined them in 1995, reducing his parliamentary majority to three.

Although Nicholson had defected to the Lib Dems in 1995, she was unable to contest Torridge & West Devon, as another candidate had already been selected by the party. Instead, Nicholson joined the Lords as a peer and expanded her charitable interests. In 1999, her husband, Sir Michael Caine, whom she had married when she was forty-five, died. His death left Nicholson bereft and she decided to embark on a new life as an MEP: 'I wrapped up my old life in Devon and put it in a drawer where I could treasure it, and tried to focus on the future.'

She found the European Parliament in some ways easier than Westminster, because everybody, like her, used headphones to listen to debates, and the translators were very helpful. She always kept busy, and rapidly became vice-president of the Foreign Affairs committee. She seemed to be continually flying from one Middle Eastern danger spot to another, highlighting oppression among minority groups and setting up projects to enable local people to help themselves. After seven years, she moved to become a member of the European Council in Strasbourg to concentrate on human rights. She became increasingly detached from the Liberal Democrats, even voting against their holy grail of proportional representation, and felt more at home among European social democrats. Nicholson recalls Angela Merkel once telling her to join her party.

But she wouldn't have been happy as a European social democrat either, because she didn't like the way power was being accreted from member states to Brussels. Her decision to vote remain at the 2016 referendum was made at the very last moment. And when the Liberal Democrat leader Tim Farron said he wanted another referendum to reverse the result, she formally quit the party to return to the Conservatives.

Nicholson had been appointed Britain's envoy to Iraq by David Cameron and was kept on by Theresa May, who she describes as a 'very sensible, resilient woman'. Now in her mid-seventies, Nicholson's lifestyle is slightly more settled, but she still exudes determination – and glamour. She attends the Lords, where Tory peers welcomed her back to the fold, but her real legacy is not as a legislator but as a campaigner and charity executive who has given practical help to millions of people around the world.

DAWN PRIMAROLO

KARIN SMYTH

- FULL NAME: Dame Dawn Primarolo DBE, Baroness Primarolo
- DATE OF BIRTH: 2 May 1954
- PLACE OF BIRTH: London
- DATE OF DEATH: –
- MARRIED TO: Ian Ducat (m. 1990)
- CHILDREN: One son
- UNSUCCESSFUL ELECTIONS FOUGHT: None
- CONSTITUENCY: Bristol South
- DATE OF FIRST ELECTION: 11 June 1987
- DATE LEFT PARLIAMENT: 30 March 2015. She joined the Lords as Baroness Primarolo on 26 October 2015.
- PARTY ROLES: None
- MINISTERIAL POSITIONS & DATES: Shadow spokesperson for Health 1992–94; shadow spokesperson for the Treasury 1994–97; Financial Secretary to the Treasury 1997–99; Paymaster General 1999–2007; Minister for Public Health 2007–09; Minister for Children, Young People and Families 2009–10; shadow Minister for Children, Young People and Families 2010; Deputy Speaker 2010–15

For twenty-eight years, former MP Dawn Primarolo served the people of Bristol South before becoming a life peer. A key player in the Labour Party and a close ally of former Prime Minister Gordon Brown, Dawn took on several frontbench roles in the '90s and '00s before stepping down in 2015. She was a great advocate for women's rights and was committed to tackling child poverty.

Dawn was first elected to Parliament at a difficult time, both for her constituents and the local Labour Party. A member of the National Women's Committee, she first put her name forward for the Bristol East constituency selection to ensure that there was a woman on the shortlist - a key demand of the women's committee at the time. A newly elected local councillor, Dawn had also recently started a PhD and had expected to pursue a career as a university lecturer, but in 1985 she was adopted as the Labour candidate for Bristol South after a long and acrimonious battle to replace the then Labour Chief Whip, Michael Cocks. She defeated Cocks by seventy-one votes to fifty-six, after an exhaustive ballot of five candidates. She went on to win the seat in the 1987 election, although the Labour majority was slashed to just 1,400.

In her maiden speech in 1987, Dawn described Bristol South as a community where industry had been devastated and long-term unemployment was a fact of life for many, particularly the young. She highlighted the lack of opportunities for sixteen- to seventeen-year-olds, many forced into the Youth Training Scheme which, she believed, exploited school leavers for cheap labour and provided little genuine training. The child poverty and health inequalities resulting from the lack of decent work opportunities became the focus of Dawn's work locally and nationally.

At the age of thirty-three, Dawn became the youngest woman Member of Parliament in an institution that was over 90 per cent male. She was also a single mother, isolated at Westminster not just through her age and gender, but by being the only Labour MP in the south-west and by the actions of her predecessor's friends in Parliament. Undaunted, she wrote at the time of 'challenging the gentlemen's club' in Westminster. A review of the Parliamentary Labour Party in 1990 suggested increasing the number of women elected to the shadow Cabinet to just three out of eighteen positions – Dawn's response was to demand 40 per cent of places be reserved for women.

In Westminster, Dawn became close to stalwart left-wing Labour women such as Audrey Wise and Alice Mahon, both members of the Campaign Group, which she joined.

The bitterness surrounding the selection process did not subside, an (unsuccessful) appeal being immediately submitted to Labour's National Executive Committee.

Frequently described as a 'hard-left Bennite', Dawn was regularly attacked in the media, including over the anti-pornography 'Off the Shelf' campaign, which she launched with Clare Short MP, and presenting the Location of Pornographic Materials Bill to Parliament. Prior to becoming an MP, she had successfully sued a local Bristol newspaper for libel, which resulted in a rare printed apology.

In 1989, she posed a question to Margaret Thatcher on behalf of Ann Clwyd, MP for Cynon Valley, who was ill at the time, asking the then Prime

Minister if the only hope for low-paid women was 'to follow her example and find herself a wealthy husband'.

In Parliament, Dawn described that within hours of her question tabloid journalists were at her home in Bristol, harassing friends and family and re-sulting in the police being called. She was also questioned about her sexuality by the media – she refused to answer – purely because of her support for gay rights and the equalising of the age of consent.

In not paying her poll tax, visiting Nicaragua and Latin America, voting against the Prevention of Terrorism Bill and opposing the 1991 Gulf War, Dawn certainly fitted the profile of the left-winger in her first parliament. But she followed through with her beliefs – using her position to push for action and change. Focusing on her low-paid constituents, Dawn introduced a Ten Minute Rule Bill on a statutory minimum wage in October 1990.

Dawn supported Bryan Gould in the 1992 leadership election but was in-vited by the winner, John Smith, to join David Blunkett's frontbench Health team. She received mixed advice from fellow members of the Campaign Group before accepting the position. Her decision to join the front bench was motivated by the desire to make changes for her constituents. Dawn saw little point in opposition.

The tragic death of John Smith led to another leadership contest in which Dawn supported Margaret Beckett, but was asked by Gordon Brown to join his shadow Treasury team, and she stayed with Brown until he became leader in 2007.

Dawn took ministerial office for the first time in 1997, and was one of a handful of ministers to remain a member of the government for the thirteen years of Labour rule. She served as Financial Secretary to the Treasury and Paymaster General. In 2000, she announced the reduction in VAT on tam-pons and sanitary towels from 17.5 per cent to 5 per cent, arguing that these were necessities and not luxuries. Shocked by the inexperience of some civil servants about the impact of policy in areas like Bristol South, Dawn sent some to visit her constituency, so they could see at first hand the challenges faced by the people she represented.

Throughout the 1990s, following tragedies from drug misuse among young people, high health inequality and continued poor employment opportu-nities, Bristol community groups, and particularly women, developed their own responses and built employment hubs, centres to aid children and family development, as well as and drug and alcohol support. In opposition, and then in government, Dawn supported and kept closely in touch with these communities and brought the experience to Westminster and the Labour front bench.

Tax credits were the greatest challenge and the greatest legacy of Dawn's time at the Treasury. Millions of families benefited from one of the most re-distributive policies of any government. The aim was to dramatically reduce child poverty – and that was the outcome.

Child poverty fell from 26 per cent in 1997 to 18 per cent in 2010. In-dependent studies suggest that if the old benefit system inherited from the Conservatives in 1997 had remained in place, child poverty would have risen to over 30 per cent. Without Labour's tax credits, 1.8 million addi-tional children would have been in poverty in 2010. However, for a time this achievement was completely overshadowed by significant problems with overpayments, which led to some very difficult encounters in the House of Commons and the media.

Following Tony Blair's resignation in 2007, Dawn moved firstly to the Department of Health as Minister for Public Health and then to the De-partment for Children, Schools and Families. At the Department of Health her focus was on sexual health and the prevention of teenage pregnancy. She was also able to continue work on health inequalities, women and families with overseeing the development of children's centres. Dawn also took the Human Fertilisation and Embryology Act through Parliament, which updat-ed the regulations for medical research and also recognised same-sex couples as legal parents of children. It also removed in law the need for a father and replaced it with the much more inclusive supportive parenting, a move that was welcomed by many campaigners for equal rights for same-sex partners.

Dawn was encouraged by women in the Parliamentary Labour Party to seek election as the Deputy Speaker in 2010, and became popular on social media for her correcting of ministers and backbenchers alike when they failed to respect the rules of Parliament. Dawn contributed her long experience and understanding of parliamentary process to cross-party efforts to change the House of Commons in order to make it more accommodating of women and those with caring responsibilities. She also made sure new MPs were welcomed and encouraged to play their full part in proceedings, in stark contrast to her own experience.

After a quarter of a century as an MP, Dawn revealed her plans to retire in 2012; this gave the local party plenty of time to select her successor as Labour candidate before the 2015 general election.

Looking back on her career, Dawn herself cited the work on the tampon tax and sexual health as having effected positive change. Locally, the South Bristol Community Hospital had been promised for decades but had yet to be delivered. With a Labour government and relentless campaigning by Dawn, the construction of the hospital was finally agreed in the final days of the Brown administration. Without Dawn's persistence the hospital simply would not exist today.

The left-winger who became a Baroness, her career was summed up at the awarding of an honorary degree at the University of Bristol thus:

> Her ministerial positions reflected her concern for education, housing, social security, health, and – running throughout all of these – equal opportunities. In particular, Dawn's advocacy of tax credits and Sure Start Centres, which addressed babies and children, parents and parenting, employment and housing, epitomise her politics.

JOYCE QUIN

SHARON HODGSON

- FULL NAME: Joyce Gwendolen Quin, Baroness Quin of Gateshead
- DATE OF BIRTH: 26 November 1944
- PLACE OF BIRTH: Tynemouth
- DATE OF DEATH: –
- MARRIED TO: (Francis) Guy MacMullen
- CHILDREN: None
- UNSUCCESSFUL ELECTION FOUGHT: None
- CONSTITUENCY: Gateshead East 1987–97 and Gateshead East & Washington West 1997–2005
- DATE OF FIRST ELECTION: 12 June 1987
- DATE LEFT PARLIAMENT: 11 April 2005. She joined the House of Lords on 30 May 2006.
- MEP: Tyne South & Wear 1979–89
- PARTY ROLES: Joyce worked for the Labour Party as a researcher in the International Department. Joyce was the first woman to chair the Northern Group of Labour MPs.
- MINISTERIAL POSITIONS & DATES: Minister of State in the Home Office 1997–98; Minister for Europe 1998–99; Minister for Agriculture, Fisheries and Food 1999–2001; shadow spokesperson for Environment, Food and Rural Affairs 2010–11 (Lords)
- MOST FAMOUS QUOTATION: 'When one grows up in the north-east, one is aware that the region is a long way from the English seat of power in London.'

Throughout her career, Joyce Quin has been a vocal campaigner and passionate advocate for many issues, including issues affecting her constituency in the north-east of England, but also those which she worked on within her other roles, including in academia and politics at national and international levels.

Joyce's education stood her in good stead for her later career. She graduated from Newcastle University with First-class honours in French in 1967, and then went on to gain an MSc in International Relations from the London School of Economics in 1969.

Upon graduating, Joyce worked as a research officer for the International Department at Labour Party HQ, before becoming a French lecturer at Bath University. She then returned to the north-east, where she took up a post as lecturer in French and politics at the University of Durham.

Joyce's combined expertise in linguistics and politics gave her invaluable knowledge upon her election as the first Member of the European Parliament for the then Tyne South & Wear constituency in 1979, and during her time as a MEP she sat on several committees, including Agriculture (1979–84); Women's Rights (1984–85), and Economic and Monetary Affairs and Industrial Policy (1984–89).

When Joyce was elected in 1979 to the European Parliament, she was the only woman in the north-east in either the European Parliament or Westminster.

After nearly a decade as a Member of the European Parliament, Joyce stood successfully to become the first woman to represent the seat of Gateshead East in 1987 in the UK Parliament, and then the seat of Gateshead East & Washington West in 1997 following boundary changes.

When Labour was swept into government following the landslide victory in 1997, Joyce was appointed as a Minister at the Home Office (1997–98) and served for the duration of the parliament in various other ministerial positions, including Minister for Europe (1998–99) and as a minister in the Ministry of Agriculture, Fisheries and Food (1999–2001) before returning to the back benches. Joyce was appointed to the Privy Council in 1998.

During her Westminster parliamentary career, Joyce was a well-known local constituency MP who raised issues on behalf of residents alongside issues she was passionate about. But, at times, her passions and local constituency work came together in various campaigns she worked on.

This was seen on 6 December 1991, when Joyce secured a parliamentary debate on the need for regional government in England – one of the first instances of debate around this topical question. In this debate, Joyce set out her belief that England's regions should be able to have a say over how money was spent regionally and was a long-time advocate and campaigner for the establishment of a north-east regional assembly.

As part of her campaigning on this issue, Joyce was successful in contributing to a commitment in Labour's 1997 manifesto to address the West Lothian question and the issue of regional assemblies in England. This is an issue she returned to following the end of her ministerial career in 2001, when she spoke from the back benches on this topic, most notably in 2003, during the passage of the Regional Assemblies (Preparations) Act which paved the way for a referendum on introducing a regional assembly in the north-east. Joyce strongly campaigned for the North East Regional Assembly, but this was rejected by the majority in a regional referendum in late 2004.

Despite the rejection of a new constitutional settlement in the north-east, Joyce continued to champion constitutional issues until she stepped down as a Member of Parliament in 2005 – but continued this work upon her appointment to the House of Lords in May 2006. Joyce's recent book, published in 2010, *The British Constitution, Continuity and Change – an inside view*, shows her passion for constitutionalism and her continued interest in this area.

Joyce's legacy on north-east issues did not stop at devolution, but reached to cultural and transport issues too. Firstly, Joyce campaigned in both Houses of Parliament for the return of the Lindisfarne Gospels to the region after decades of being homed at the British Library in London. After being the one to table an Early Day Motion in 1997 for the very first time on this issue, I know how proud Joyce would have been to visit the Gospels in Durham when they were eventually returned on a short-term loan sixteen years later, in 2013. Secondly, she was a tireless campaigner for the reopening of the Leamside Line alongside Fraser Kemp, the former MP for Houghton and Washington East, which would have brought this major rail route back into use and benefited the town of Washington and the wider north-east.

Both of these issues were ones that I took up when I succeeded Joyce as the Member of Parliament for Gateshead East & Washington West in 2005, specifically the Leamside Line, which has evolved into my campaign to extend the Tyne and Wear Metro to Washington.

Joyce also campaigned for bus passes to be available throughout the country, as previously they had been restricted to certain cities or areas. Joyce worked with Age Concern on this and also introduced a Ten Minute Rule Bill. Joyce also lobbied Gordon Brown directly as Chancellor with costings and detailed information. Gordon subsequently brought in the country-wide scheme via the Budget. Joyce is proud to have recognition from Gordon on this, and has a letter from him saying that it was her campaigning that had persuaded him.

On an international level, Joyce has always tried to promote closer relations with our European neighbours and worked for a positive European policy. In 2010, Joyce was made an Officier of the Légion d'honneur by the French government for her work promoting Franco-British relations as chair of the Franco-British council and of the All Party Parliamentary Group on relations with France.

Joyce has been a city guide in Newcastle since the 1970s, and currently serves as the vice-president of the Association of City Guides. Joyce is the President of the Northumbrian Pipers Society and chair of the Strategic Board of Tyne and Wear Museums.

Throughout her career, it is clear that Joyce has remained passionate and dedicated to the issues that she cares about deeply, including promoting the north-east; as her successor, I am honoured to continue this work.

DAME JOAN RUDDOCK

VICKY FOXCROFT

- FULL NAME: Rt Hon. Dame Joan Mary Ruddock DBE (née Anthony)
- DATE OF BIRTH: 28 December 1943
- PLACE OF BIRTH: Pontypool, Monmouthshire
- DATE OF DEATH: –
- MARRIED TO: Keith Ruddock (m. 1963; d. 1996); Frank Doran (m. 2010; d. 2017)
- CHILDREN: None
- UNSUCCESSFUL ELECTIONS FOUGHT: Newbury 1979
- CONSTITUENCY: Lewisham Deptford
- DATE OF FIRST ELECTION: 11 June 1987
- DATE LEFT PARLIAMENT: 30 March 2015
- PARTY ROLES: None
- MINISTERIAL POSITIONS & DATES: Parliamentary Under-Secretary of State for Women 1997–98; Parliamentary Under-Secretary of State for Climate Change, Biodiversity and Waste 2007–08; Parliamentary Under-Secretary of State at the Department of Energy and Climate Change 2008–09; Minister for Energy and Climate Change 2009–10; shadow Minister for Energy and Climate Change 2010
- MOST FAMOUS QUOTATION: 'Adapting to climate change: It really is time for action … we are on a never-ending road; this is with us for the rest of our natural lives.' – Joan Ruddock MP, Minister for Climate Change Adaptation, addressing Environment Agency climate change adaptation conference, London, 31 March 2008.

Many a freshly selected prospective parliamentary candidate will tell you that the words they most dread hearing are, 'You have big shoes to fill.' I was no exception. When I was selected as the Labour candidate to contest Lewisham Deptford in the 2015 general election, I braced myself for the inevitable reproval from constituents – and I wasn't disappointed. In fact, I was even accused of standing against Joan Ruddock, as constituents refused to believe that she would ever retire. Around this time, I discovered that she had started working on an autobiography titled *Going Nowhere*, and I thought to myself, surely not?! In this short essay, I will do my best to show her just how wrong the title was.

From humble beginnings in the Welsh valleys, Joan was an influential political figure before she even began her parliamentary career. Like many of us, her campaigning days began in earnest at university (she attended Imperial College). Joan, along with her first husband, Keith, joined the Labour Party and took a particular interest in international politics and the anti-Apartheid movement.

Her first 'real' job was at the then fledgling charity Shelter, which was already making its mark as a strong advocate for homeless people and housing rights. Joan quickly rose through the ranks and was instrumental in producing Shelter's 'Grief Report', a seminal work which eventually fed into the preparation of the Housing (Homeless Persons) Act 1977. The Act provided the first statutory definition of homelessness and placed a clear duty on local councils to assist families.

The first big event in Joan's prospective parliamentary career came in 1979, when she stood as the Labour Party candidate for Newbury, where she was now living. She was persuaded to stand by friends who saw the need for a local candidate to raise visibility and work hard. Despite coming third, in her own words, 'I lost my deposit but I'd got the bug. I knew I would want to stand again.'

After the 1979 election, Joan began working as manager of the Reading Citizens Advice Bureau, but a 1980 newspaper headline announcing, 'US MISSILES FOR GREENHAM COMMON' provided the catalyst for her next calling. In conjunction with the secretary of her Constituency Labour Party (CLP), she set up the Newbury Campaign Against Cruise Missiles which, although a non-partisan organisation, agreed to work with the Campaign for Nuclear Disarmament (CND). It was through this campaign that Joan came to be elected as chair of CND in 1981, an unpaid position she held until 1984.

Joan took another step on the road to Parliament in the mid-1980s, when she stood for selection as Leo Abse's replacement in her home constituency of Torfaen. However, she was now an outsider and – perhaps even more shockingly to some – a woman, so she lost out to the CLP secretary Paul Murphy. Following this disappointment, she was persuaded by Harriet Harman (who was to become a great friend and colleague) and encouraged by local members to put her name forward for Lewisham Deptford when incumbent John Silkin announced his decision to stand down in 1987. The selection process was tough, but Joan found her working-class upbringing, anti-racism activism and leadership within the peace movement stood her in good stead. She also promised to move into the constituency and to prioritise advice surgeries in the most deprived areas – both things which are expected of 21st-century MPs, but which were not a priority for many in the 1980s.

Joan won the election comfortably with a majority of 6,771. She has many tales of her early days in Parliament and, although things had vastly improved by the time I was elected in 2015, I can certainly identify with the feeling of being thrown in at the deep end. In her first report to the CLP she wrote,

> Everything seems designed to make life difficult. There is no induction pro-gramme, no comprehensive handbook and no training in how to be an effec-tive backbencher. Protocol and language ensure that the newcomer gets lost, breaks rules, cannot work out the business of the day and is thus unlikely to disturb the establishment.

From the very start of her parliamentary career, she fought to make Parlia-ment more accessible to people from any background and was twice instru-mental in effecting changes to the sitting hours of the House, something for which newer Members are very grateful.

In her early years in the House, Labour were in opposition, but that didn't stop Joan from exerting her influence over policy and legislation. Her ex-perience made her a suitable candidate for shadow frontbench positions in transport, environmental protection and home affairs. She was clearly on the up and was virtually guaranteed a job when Labour finally made it back into power. During this period, she also successfully piloted a Private Members' Bill through Parliament, which became the Control of Pollution (Amend-ment) Act 1989. The Bill introduced new fly-tipping regulations and was born out of the dangerous situation that had developed on the Silwood estate in her constituency; people were regularly being threatened for confronting those who were dumping huge amounts of waste and building material.

It seemed as if Joan would be a shoo-in for a Cabinet position, but her ambitions were not to be realised. In the first few days after Tony Blair's historic landslide victory in 1997, Joan watched as her colleagues were called into Downing Street and offered ministerial posts. She was devastated not to receive a call herself, having worked closely with Tony in opposition. A call from the Chief Whip to apologise was not enough to placate her – she felt betrayed. The press picked up on her exclusion from the Cabinet and she has evidently never forgotten an article which proclaimed that she was 'going nowhere', despite having previously been rumoured for a top job.

A month later, Tony agreed that Joan could work alongside Harriet Harman (who had now been appointed Minister for Women, as well as Secretary of State for Social Security) as her junior minister. At the 1997 election the number of women MPs had doubled to 120, but there was clearly still a huge amount of work to be done by the women the press nicknamed 'Blair's Babes'.

Tony delivered another blow by sacking Joan and Harriet in July 1998, giving the women's brief to Margaret Jay, Leader of the Lords, with Tessa Jowell as her part-time minister in the Commons. Joan could not disguise her anger following a second snub and I don't think she was ever able to forgive Tony.

In the early 2000s, Joan threw her efforts into finding other ways of exerting her influence. She set up the UK Women's Link with Afghan Women, an organisation to provide support for Afghan women coming to the UK. Their work helped the government to understand the particular issues encountered by women fleeing the oppressive Taliban regime and led to the Department for International Development setting up a project to educate girls in Afghanistan. She also had success with a second Private Members' Bill, introducing the compulsory doorstep collection of recycled waste with the Household Waste Recycling Act 2003.

Joan's years of hard graft eventually paid off when Gordon Brown appointed her a minister in the Department for Environment, Food and Rural Affairs in 2007. In 2008, she moved to the newly formed Department for Energy and Climate Change. Her work focused on delivering a low-carbon economy and ensuring a secure and affordable energy supply. She once again found herself negotiating on the world stage and is especially proud to have been part of the team at the Copenhagen Climate Change Conference in 2009.

After Labour was defeated in 2010, Joan returned to the back benches – but she did not give up the fight. She campaigned once again for changes to the sitting hours of the Commons in the knowledge that it would be future Members who would benefit the most. She was appointed to the Privy Council and, in 2012, she received a DBE for her public and political service. Any thoughts of turning down the latter were banished when she considered how proud her mum would be.

The story of Joan's career is one of considerable success on the national stage, but I know that she will always be remembered by the people of Lewisham Deptford as a fierce campaigner and champion of their rights. She fought hard for the families of the victims of the New Cross fire (which killed thirteen young black people in 1981), assisting them in pushing for a second inquest. She campaigned against the downgrading of A&E and maternity services at Lewisham Hospital and made a nuisance of herself in the eyes of many a planner and developer, most notably criticising the Convoys Wharf development in Deptford for its lack of affordable housing in a deprived area and for its failure to be sympathetic to the site's rich history. Above all, Joan always made sure she ran regular advice surgeries and placed a huge amount of importance on assisting constituents in their hour of need.

Despite being an inspirational feminist and role model for younger women, it is telling that Joan maintains a distinct air of modesty about her achievements. The Rt Hon. Dame Joan Ruddock DBE certainly did not go 'nowhere'. She may not be quite as much of a household name as some of her contemporaries, but she blazed a trail through Parliament and I for one am proud to be following in her footsteps.

GILLIAN SHEPHARD

ELIZABETH TRUSS

- FULL NAME: Gillian Patricia Shephard (née Watt) PC, DL, Baroness Shephard of Northwold
- DATE OF BIRTH: 22 January 1940
- PLACE OF BIRTH: Cromer, Norfolk
- DATE OF DEATH: –
- MARRIED TO: Thomas Shephard (m. 1975)
- CHILDREN: Two stepsons
- UNSUCCESSFUL ELECTIONS FOUGHT: None
- CONSTITUENCY: South West Norfolk
- DATE OF FIRST ELECTION: 11 June 1987
- DATE LEFT PARLIAMENT: 11 April 2005
- PARTY ROLES: None
- MINISTERIAL POSITIONS & DATES: Parliamentary Under-Secretary at the Department of Social Security 1989–90; Minister for the Treasury 1990–92; Secretary of State for Employment 1992–93; Secretary of State for Agriculture, Fisheries and Food 1993–94; Secretary of State for Education and Science 1994–95; Secretary of State for Education and Employment 1995–97; shadow Leader of the House of Commons 1997–98; shadow Secretary of State for the Environmen, Transport and the Regions 1998–99

Gillian Shephard was a Tory moderniser long before the open-necked shirts, the brownies and smoothies and the Notting Hill Set. She recognised that the party had to move with the times – and she presented a modern, practical and classless brand in the 1990s. She has always been prepared to fight for what is right and to take on the vested interests. She succeeded through a mixture of guile and charm at achieving significant reforms at both agriculture and education, while also providing John Major with important counsel through one of the most difficult periods of Conservative government. Like him, she was very much an outsider to the Tory elite in Westminster, coming from a humble background in Norfolk and making her way through teaching and local government. Her influence continues, through her work in the House of Lords and her stable of protégées whom she continues to coach in the ways of politics. And I personally owe her a huge amount; she helped me get through the most testing time of my political career.

I first met Gillian Shephard under rather fraught circumstances. It was on the Saturday afternoon after my selection for South West Norfolk in 2009 that I got an ominous call from a Sunday paper – I was to be splashed on the next day's edition. I was immediately summoned for a meeting with Gillian – the grandee of the Association – at the House of Lords. She was clearly checking me out and this would be make or break.

At first I couldn't concentrate, as the Peers' Tea Room was infested with what I thought were mice, but were later confirmed to be rats. We retreated to her upstairs study where I was grilled. She was hugely impressive – someone who understood Norfolk to the core and who had her fingertips on the pulse of the party. She wanted to make sure that I was committed to doing a good job. I think I passed because she invited me to stay at her house in Swaffham for the Extraordinary Executive Meeting, where the Association were to decide what to do with me.

There was now a lot of interest in the saga from the media. After leaving the Reform think tank, where I was working at the time, via the fire escape to evade the cameras stationed outside, I hotfooted it to Kings Cross to get the train to Norfolk. There I was met by Gillian's fantastic husband, Tom, who drove me from Downham Market station to the star chamber for judgement. Tom, long practised in decoy and wile, understands the unusual life of a politician, which tends to oscillate between the sublime and the absurd. I hear he once turned up to the Treasury to collect Gillian – then a Minister of State – only to be told by officials that they had never heard of her.

After the rather torrid meeting, Tom was my getaway driver. He valiantly attempted to combat the paps by shining a torch in cameras from the car but I am sorry to say the tactic did not work. The meeting hadn't gone according to plan. Rather than endorsing my candidacy the Executive Council had referred the matter to a meeting of all the members of the Association. It was devastating and I was unsure how to proceed. Gillian had no such doubts. As I arrived back at her house, I was handed a big glass of red wine and told on no account to resign.

My resolve stiffened, I prepared myself for weeks of media scrutiny and the hard business of winning over the electorate of South West Norfolk. It was great to have someone who would help me through the process and who understood what it feels like to be under siege. Over twenty years earlier, Gillian saw three members publicly resign as they 'could not go home and say to people in their village that the next MP would be a woman'. Times had changed since then and despite the stereotypes perpetrated in the press, I found local party members very reasonable and decent.

I soldiered on with Gillian's constant encouragement, touring the constituency and meeting members. Described as 'a pawn in a proxy war for the soul of the party', it was a baptism of fire for which I had not volunteered. Thankfully, there was a big turnout at the members meeting and I was confirmed as the candidate.

She didn't just help me retain the nomination during the tumultuous events of my selection. She also gave me a huge amount of practical assistance to get settled in – including bringing round sandwiches when we moved into our house. Our children were very little at the time, aged one and four. Tom made my daughter a cot for her dolls. Ever since that moment, I have always had a hotline to Gillian to ask for help and advice. As a former Food Secretary, Education Secretary and Treasury minister, she has worked in almost every department I have been appointed to. One Norfolk wag described Gillian Shephard as my 'fairy godmother' and I think that's just about right.

One thing that everybody says about Gillian is that she is a people person and a particularly good judge of character. She puts this down to being the daughter of a cattle dealer. From the age of eight she would accompany her father to the cattle market, watching the organised chaos and studying the characters who came and went. You were either a 'good man', 'good woman' or a 'wrong 'un'. To this day a number of people are dismissed on the basis that they wouldn't have been trusted at the cattle market. There is a 'certain shiftiness of look'.

Gillian carried this insight into her political career. She told me she once mentioned to the whips that an obscure backbencher by the name of Ann Widdecombe might be a good choice for promotion as she could see her competence and ability. The whip admonished Gillian for telling him how to do his job. Sure enough, a few months later, Widdecombe had a government job.

Of course, the leading lady when Gillian entered the House of Commons in 1987 was Mrs Thatcher. So annoyed was Gillian by the portrayal of Margaret Thatcher in the film *The Iron Lady*, which she complained recycled 'all the old clichés', that she decided to set the record straight with a book of her own: *The Real Iron Lady: Working with Margaret Thatcher.*

You won't hear any complaining from Gillian, despite having a harder time than the much larger group of women that are in today's House of Commons – she is clear that she didn't let her gender define her as a parliamentarian, and if people talked behind her back, so what. She also says that John Major was very much an equal opportunities boss.

You can't understand Gillian Shephard without understanding Norfolk. Born in Cromer, she was educated at North Walsham Girls' High School, before winning a scholarship to study French at St Hilda's College, Oxford. (She is a committed Francophile and has been awarded the French Légion d'Honneur.) Before entering the political fray, Gillian had worked in education as a teacher, school inspector and senior administrator.

After her marriage to Tom Shephard, a head teacher, she put her career on hold for ten years to bring up her two young stepchildren. Gillian entered local politics through Norfolk County Council, where she was senior county councillor in 1977, chair of the Norfolk Health Authority in 1985 and deputy leader thereafter. She played a vital role in transforming the county into one with more industrial jobs and modern housing.

As I discovered on the campaign trail, Gillian's tentacles spread very wide and many people have been helped by her work. She knows all the local characters and her contact book seems never-ending. Once, when Jeffrey Archer was on day release from prison (Gillian sticks by her friends), he arrived at her house in Northwold for lunch. The media had decided to bring satellite trucks for the occasion. One of Gillian's friends has an earth-moving business, so, at her request, he arrived driving an immense grabber and the media fled.

Gillian still lives in Norfolk and attends events across the county. One of her favourite haunts is the Ceres Bookshop in Swaffham where she has launched several books including one on Norfolk country life and also her autobiography *Shephard's Watch.* As she says, 'If I was taken away from the land I don't think I could survive.'

Although she entered Parliament relatively late – she was forty-seven when she was elected – she quickly climbed the ladder. Like now, it was a period of great upheaval, which made it a hugely exciting time to be involved in politics. The Conservative Party was experiencing great success, but a number of critical events from the BSE crisis to the Maastricht debate also took place. After her election as Member of Parliament for South West Norfolk in 1987, Gillian spent a year as a backbencher before she became

PPS to Peter Lilley MP, then Economic Secretary to the Treasury. Gillian was then appointed Parliamentary Under-Secretary of State at the Department for Social Security. On her appointment in the summer of 1989, Margaret Thatcher, who started in the same post, imparted the following advice: 'It's important to work on the detail.' Gillian was then promoted to Minister of State at the Treasury.

After her time at the Treasury, John Major put her in the Cabinet as Secretary of State for Employment and as the first ever Minister for Women. Gillian went on to serve in key roles on the front bench for the entirety of his premiership and was a loyal friend that he could absolutely rely on. Her next role after Employment was Agriculture. Having grown up and lived in a farming county, Gillian knows the brief back to front – in fact, she can still quote the price of sugar beet or comment on the likelihood of a good harvest.

She was a reformer in the role, seeking to make British agriculture more competitive and encouraging the adopting of modern techniques. One of her most important changes was abolishing the Milk Marketing Board and advocating the end of milk quotas that prevented farmers from increasing the amount of milk they produced.

As a minister she was required – as Ministers still are – to vote in divisions in the House of Commons. These were often tight as the Major government had a very small majority. This was before the House of Commons was changed to be more 'family friendly', so they would often be voting until well after 10 p.m. every night of the week. Labour stalwarts Dennis Skinner and Bob Cryer kept debates going even on a Thursday, so Gillian would often end up arriving back at her constituency at 1. 30 a.m. All of this was in addition to her family duties, which included looking after elderly parents, helping with cooking and washing and taking them to the doctors and dentist. And, of course, the red boxes, which would often come four at a time, had to be done. She told me that some days she would lie on the floor when she arrived home, with her coat and gloves still on, and promptly fall asleep. Although as ministers we now have to deal with the perils of 24-hour news and social media, I think the sheer exhaustion of the late nights in the 1990s must have been horrendous.

In government, Gillian developed a reputation for being formidable but fair-minded, even as an opponent. Her charm and way with people made her popular on all benches, and she could easily establish trust even with the most hostile political foe. She is astute, quick to spot things, doesn't panic under pressure and has widely recognised political nous and judgement

– indeed, both Margaret Thatcher and John Major would repeatedly come to her for private counsel. She was important in ways that the outside observer may not have known. As Lord Waldegrave put it, 'In any government there are some absolutely crucial, core people who are more important behind the scenes necessarily than they are in outward-facing roles.' In every department she was able to steady the ship and get things done. After there had been a stormy spell for Education, with the vital introduction of testing and league tables, her appointment marked an improvement in relations with teachers and she faced down a proposed strike. She took strong action on failing schools and developed new policies such as vouchers for training.

Another trait people often associate with Gillian is her wicked sense of humour, described by many as 'waspish'. Though serious when called for, she can be mischievous in the most delightful way. This 'very Norfolk' sense of humour, as described by one constituent, has served her well and helped her to bamboozle people in a helpful way. She is also a very amusing mimic. She doesn't like pomposity and pricks it wherever she can – with the target often not realising that the sharp word is directed at them.

The 1990s were a time of great change for the country. The bitter Conservative battle over Europe emerged. The party found itself looking tired and outdated compared to a fresh, youthful appeal from Tony Blair and Labour. During this time, Gillian was a voice for reason and progress, and she held things together on a day-to-day basis. There are many in the party and in Norfolk who felt that she would have made a very good leader.

Her career in government did not end through her own personal action or that of the Prime Minister, but by the whole party being swept from office. She served for two further terms as the MP for South West Norfolk before standing down in 2005. The genial Christopher Fraser took over in 2005 and she was elevated to the House of Lords as Baroness Shephard of Northwold.

One of only a handful of women in government, she carried Margaret Thatcher's torch and encouraged a new generation to get involved in politics. I know without her personal support I would have struggled to get to where I am today. I know that Norwich North MP Chloe Smith also benefits hugely from her counsel. Recently the three of us met to celebrate 100 years of women's suffrage and Gillian was off organising and conducting interviews with the press. She is a politician, the best sort of politician, to her bones and I don't see her giving politics up any time soon.

JOAN WALLEY

MARY HONEYBALL

- FULL NAME: Joan Lorraine Walley
- DATE OF BIRTH: 23 January 1949
- PLACE OF BIRTH: Stoke-on-Trent
- DATE OF DEATH: –
- MARRIED TO: John Ostrowski
- CHILDREN: Two sons
- UNSUCCESSFUL ELECTIONS FOUGHT: None
- CONSTITUENCY: Stoke-on-Trent North
- DATE OF FIRST ELECTION: 11 June 1987
- DATE LEFT PARLIAMENT: 30 March 2015
- PARTY ROLES: London Borough of Lambeth councillor 1982–86 and chair of the Lambeth Social Services Committee 1982–85
- MINISTERIAL POSITIONS & DATES: Shadow spokesperson for Environment, Food and Rural Affairs 1988–90 and shadow spokesperson for Transport 1990–95
- MOST FAMOUS QUOTATION: 'I ended up being selected [to be a Labour parliamentary candidate] because I was a councillor in Lambeth at the time and basically was removed from office for standing up for local services. It was the height of the Thatcher government and I was invited to stand in my home area of Stoke-on-Trent.' – Interview with the *Daily Telegraph*, 27 February 2015.

Joan Walley won the selection for the safe parliamentary seat of Stoke-on-Trent North ahead of Valerie Wise, who at the time was the chair of the Greater London Council Women's Committee and was also the daughter of Labour Party NEC member and former MP Audrey Wise. Elected in June 1987, Joan went on to have a solid, if unremarkable, career, finally standing down from Parliament in 2015.

Walley gained some national prominence in 1985, as a member of Lambeth Council, which was led by Ted Knight, the infamous 'Red Ted'. That same year, Prime Minister Margaret Thatcher introduced strict limits on local government spending – this came to be known as rate-capping. Along with other councils, including some led by Conservatives, Lambeth opposed rate-capping. However, unlike most dissenting local authorities, Lambeth's opposition was both radical and illegal.

The leaders of Lambeth, Sheffield, Liverpool, Islington and Haringey councils decided to confront the Thatcher government by not setting a rate, hoping to generate mass opposition. The road to extra-parliamentary illegality ultimately proved to be too much, and all the councils who attempted not to set a rate eventually backed down. Nevertheless, a number of councillors from Lambeth and Liverpool were surcharged and disqualified from being councillors, as a result of the financial losses incurred by their authorities. Joan Walley was one of them.

According to Walley, the national publicity she gained from the rate-capping saga resulted in an offer from the Stoke-on-Trent North Labour Party, the area where she grew up, to stand for selection as their MP. Once Walley's surcharge was paid from a national fighting fund, she was on her way to the House of Commons, returned in 1987 as one of only forty-one women MPs, 6.3 per cent of the total number of Members.

Life in the House of Commons appears to have been hard for Joan Walley. In an interview with the *Daily Telegraph* in 2015, she freely admits that she missed her husband and two children and did not immediately adjust to her new surroundings. 'It was a case of feeling your way in the place, which [had] much more of a public school aura than it does today.' She also found working in two places – Westminster and her constituency – difficult. She was, she freely admits, encouraged by the idea that she could affect decision-making and help improve life for her constituents.

Walley, a supporter of the then Labour Leader Neil Kinnock, was soon promoted to the front bench as Transport spokesperson in June 1988. Having begun her Commons career feeling left out and disorientated, she appears to have settled in well as a frontbencher and even began to enjoy the night sittings that were very much part of parliamentary life at the time. There were, in fact, times when she was the only Labour MP covering the late debates on transport and environment issues. Reading her account of these 'long, long weeks', you sense the exhaustion she felt during Labour's many years in opposition. She did, however, enjoy the camaraderie she enjoyed with other MPs, describing how, since most of them were based in small offices, they would spend time together in the Commons itself or in the tea room, where there was more of a sense of unity.

Having established herself under Neil Kinnock, she remained on the front bench when John Smith took over as Labour Leader. The years following the 1997 Labour landslide, which she referred to as 'a new era in terms of the Labour Party', were, however, a different matter. Walley did not become a minister. Having supported John Prescott, now Lord Prescott, in the deputy leadership race in 1992, Walley was pleased when Prime Minister Tony Blair appointed Prescott Deputy Prime Minister. In her eyes, this meant that New Labour had not completely lost touch with the party's working-class roots. Prior to the Iraq War, Walley was never an outspoken critic of New Labour and Tony Blair. She felt the government had achieved a great deal and that having Labour in power was more important than anything else.

Iraq, of course, changed all that. Walley voted against the invasion of Iraq, despite intense pressure from the Labour whips. Although she claims she did not want to vote against a Labour government, she knew that there was no way she could vote for the war. She simply felt that Tony Blair was wrong. When she was interviewed by the *Daily Telegraph* in 2015, Walley said that she felt vindicated by the ensuing events.

Throughout her time in Parliament, Walley specialised in environmental and transport issues. In 2010, she was elected chair of the House of Commons Environmental Audit Select Committee whose task was to scrutinise all aspects on government policy to ensure due regard to the environment. A little-known committee, it nonetheless had an important role to play in examining all aspects of government work and assessing how they were impacting the environment. The committee could therefore ensure that environmental concerns could be embedded into policy across government at the early stages of legislation. Walley chaired the committee until 2015.

Joan Walley was above all else a constituency MP. She always felt that her most important work was in Stoke-on-Trent North. She was elected to the House of Commons before the Labour Party adopted all-women shortlists for parliamentary selections – an achievement that should not be underestimated. She retired from Parliament in 2015, at the age of sixty-six, noting that, were the Parliament elected in 2015 to continue for a full five-year term, she would be seventy-one when it was dissolved. Her constituency was inherited by another woman.

ANN WIDDECOMBE

DAME CHERYL GILLAN

- FULL NAME: Ann Noreen Widdecombe
- DATE OF BIRTH: 4 October 1947
- PLACE OF BIRTH: Bath, Somerset
- MARRIED TO: Unmarried
- CHILDREN: None
- DATE OF DEATH: –
- UNSUCCESSFUL ELECTIONS FOUGHT: Burnley 1979 and Plymouth Devonport 1983
- CONSTITUENCY: Maidstone 1987–97 and Maidstone and the Weald 1997–2010
- DATE OF FIRST ELECTION: 12 June 1987
- DATE LEFT PARLIAMENT: 12 April 2010
- PARTY ROLES: None
- MINISTERIAL POSITIONS & DATES: Parliamentary Under-Secretary of State at the Department of Social Security 1990–93; Parliamentary Under-Secretary of State at the Department of Employment 1993–94; Minister of State at the Department of Employment 1994–95; Minister for Prisons 1995–97; shadow Secretary of State for Health 1998–99; shadow Home Secretary 1999–2001
- MOST FAMOUS QUOTATION: 'Something of the night.'

How do I view Ann Widdecombe? Self-contained. Plain-speaking. Competent. True to her principles. An individual who stands out because she steadfastly refused to compromise her own principles. Often stubborn, unyielding and oblivious to other people's opinions of her. A curious mixture of someone who does not suffer fools gladly, but who has a kind, caring side to her character, often concealed by a no-nonsense attitude.

Ann is certainly tenacious. From trying as a child to convince her parents to buy her a pet to her determination to study at Oxford. From her eagerness to be adopted as a parliamentary candidate to doing what she believed to be right as a minister – and to then enjoy her well-earned retirement to the utmost, writing, dancing, hosting quizzes and even becoming a surprisingly willing participant in reality TV shows.

A fervent religious faith underpins her life. Being true to that innate faith is immensely important to her and, while her views may differ from others on issues such as abortion (an issue that she has engaged with from the outset of her parliamentary career), Ann has always acknowledged that everyone has a right to their own opinion.

If people find this position difficult to reconcile, then I can explain how I came to see Ann in this light. I first met her through the Bow Group; since the group had no corporate view, it was a place where differing opinions could be aired and issues explored with the intellectual rigour that Ann relished then and clearly values to this day. In those days, her practicality – allied to her kindness and consideration – was very evident. She was not one to court popularity, but she always commanded attention for her logical and considered arguments, and her determination.

Securing and then winning a seat was no easy feat for Conservative candidates like us, when the default was still to select a male candidate – especially as there was an unspoken assumption that the man would be married and his wife would carry out duties in the constituency.

Undaunted by this, Ann knew she needed to prove her political credentials and did not shrink from the fray of fighting an unsafe seat. Selected for Burnley in 1977, she not only visited a working coalmine, but also tracked down and was photographed with a dairy cow – unusual in those days! Maidstone, where she was ultimately elected, acquired a highly competitive and experienced campaigner who was to be a tireless advocate for her constituency. Ann's maiden speech followed shortly after the great hurricane of October 1987. Ann referred to the storm and the destruction of apple orchards in the constituency, but she also drew on her earlier experiences as a candidate in Devonport, in 1983, and her experience with Women and Families for Defence (a Conservative campaign group) to talk about Trident and the nuclear deterrent. A force of nature had definitely entered the House of Commons and was not going to be restricted to so-called women's issues!

Ministerial rank followed in the Department of Social Security, Department of Employment and the Home Office and with it a degree of controversy over situations like the policy on whether pregnant prisoners in hospital should be handcuffed. She suffered the strictures of the press that sought to present her in a continuing unflattering light. She certainly pulled no punches even in dealing with colleagues. Her differences with the then Home Secretary, Michael Howard, about his treatment of the former leader of the Prison Service, Derek Lewis, became very public. Her description of her erstwhile boss as having 'something of the night about him' certainly stuck, as did her famous speech against foxhunting, when she said that hunting should be confined to the scenes on her dining room curtains. (Her affection for and advocacy of animals extends from cats to donkeys – she is a patron of a donkey sanctuary.)

Labour's general election victory in 1997 saw Ann consigned to the opposition front benches. She remained a prominent, straight-talking politician and was always full of common sense. In a milieu which famously 'did not do God', she might have been considered an aberration, but the public acknowledges and often applauds the vigour of an independent voice. However, on rare occasions, she could change her mind. After being seen in the company of Father Michael Seed on numerous occasions, she converted to Catholicism (the ordination of women priests having been the last straw that caused the rift with Anglicanism). This religious turn in her life resulted in her being offered the post of UK ambassador to the Holy See, which she decided to turn down. Despite this, Pope Benedict XVI hounoured Ann by naming her a Dame of the Order of St Gregory the Great for her services to politics and public life.

She was not one for reading out speeches and long before David Cameron made his 'without notes' addresses, Ann was striding around the party conference stage in 1998, administering a much-needed tonic to a party still coming to terms with election defeat. But, strangely, she could never command enough support to either mount a leadership challenge or run for office.

Is Ann the cat who walks alone? By her own witness, yes. But she is also someone who values her family and friends hugely. I identify strongly, having grown up in my maternal grandmother's home, with her statement that a family that includes a resident grandmother is very special. She does not seem to be a 'clubbable' character, yet when the membership of the Carlton Club was opened to women, she made the decision to be the first woman to enter. She certainly can make more than a debating point.

Similarly, Ann took part in clubs and societies, political and otherwise, while at university. It was there that she had her one and only acknowledged relationship; she has remained a bachelorette since. Ann is of the generation that, if they did not themselves break any specific glass ceilings as individuals, were part of a group who were often present, lending their support to other women and congratulating them warmly, as they helped to brush the glass fragments off their sisters' shoulders. When I became the second woman chair of the Bow Group she was one of the first to congratulate me and, when elected in 1992, to welcome me to the House of Commons. But then we both knew how tough it was for women in those days to establish a place in politics, a fact she acknowledged but like me would not accept.

As Pensions Under-Secretary, Ann must have pondered the pros and cons of retirement many times as part of her brief. Her own retirement took place formally in 2010, but she has not only been active in her post-Parliament years – she has become a national treasure. Ann's decision to take part in *Strictly Come Dancing*, and the fact that she was able to remain a participant despite raillery from critics, endeared her to the public. She had clearly decided after politics that she was going into show business. I remember her telling my husband, who was driving her to speak in my constituency, that she woke up every morning and would ring journalists to see if they needed a quote from her. Her acting credits – which now include pantomime and a non-singing role in a comic opera – would do justice to any actor. Ann has also made appearances on *Celebrity Fit Club*, *Have I Got News For You*, *Countdown* and other game shows, alongside her work as an agony aunt and journalist (she has a regular newspaper column that reflects her forthright view on life).

In January 2018, Ann took up residence in the *Celebrity Big Brother* house and laid bare her personal beliefs, preferences and prejudices that won her if not the respect, then the grudging admiration of a generation and audience that without the show could not have imagined engaging with someone like Ann. An undiluted Ann came second to drag queen Shane Jenek, but even fellow housemate glamour model Jess noted the twinkle in Ann's eye and said that this experience with Ann had shown that opposites can attract. Maybe this was Ann becoming a 'resident grandmother' at her best, and that depth of character and a wicked sense of humour could at last be seen behind the apparent intolerant and plain-speaking exterior.

What Ann shows is that, despite what spin doctors and advisers may say, the public does respond to someone who allies hard work on their behalf with an independence of mind. And at this time, when we celebrate 100 years since women first received the vote, Ann is certainly a woman to admire for her capability, consideration, versatility and steadfastness.

KATE HOEY

LINDA MCDOUGALL

- FULL NAME: Catharine Letitia Hoey
- DATE OF BIRTH: 21 June 1946
- PLACE OF BIRTH: Mallusk, County Antrim
- DATE OF DEATH: –
- MARRIED TO: Unmarried
- CHILDREN: None
- UNSUCCESSFUL ELECTIONS FOUGHT: Dulwich 1983 and 1987
- CONSTITUENCY: Vauxhall
- DATE OF FIRST ELECTION: 15 June 1989
- DATE LEFT PARLIAMENT: Incumbent
- PARTY ROLES: None
- MINISTERIAL POSITIONS & DATES: Parliamentary Under-Secretary at the Home Office 1998–99 and Parliamentary Under-Secretary for Sport 1999–2001
- MOST FAMOUS QUOTATION: 'I have been clear since the day I came into this House that I want us to get out of the European Union, and I am delighted that I have lived long enough to see it happen.'

Kate Hoey is a rebel, an outsider and an enigma. She is also the Labour MP for Vauxhall. During her twenty-nine years in the seat, Hoey and her party have moved further from each other on a number of issues. She is part of the small rump of Labour Brexiteers who voted to leave the European Union. Yet her Inner London constituency is one of the most pro-European in the country.

Hoey is far from being a one-issue rebel. She opposed Labour's ban on foxhunting and became chair of the Countryside Alliance in 2005. She also disagreed with her party's stance on handguns. She approves of grammar schools, wants to renationalise the railways and believes that all cyclists should be registered on a national database. She is warm, friendly and easy to talk to. She's seventy-one years old and says cheerfully that this will be her last term in Parliament.

> I was born on a very small farm in Northern Ireland, outside Belfast. I had an elder sister and later on I had a little brother sixteen years younger than me. My mum and dad were not formally educated but they were very well read and my father was very interested in politics. But they weren't involved in what you would call Northern Ireland politics, Orange Order, or anything like that. We went to church. I went to Sunday school every Sunday afternoon, obviously Protestant.

The Hoey girls were clever, and both won grammar school places at Belfast Royal Academy. Kate loved it there. She also loved sport. She went on to the Ulster College of Physical Education to train as a teacher, and in 1966, she became Northern Ireland's high jump champion. Hoey also became interested in politics; she attended political debates at nearby Queen's University, and in her final year of teacher training represented her physical education college at the National Union of Students conference in Margate.

Hoey moved to London to take a degree in economics, and became vice-president of the National Union of Students under Jack Straw's leadership.

> I was a bit of a rebel even then I remember, and I joined the Labour Party in Islington around 1975. My first Labour Party conference was in '79 and I kept meeting all these MPs. When you look back at it now, they were all chatting me up or whatever. I had this vision of an MP as being really important and really clever. You know I couldn't possibly think of being an MP, and then you realised that some of them were absolutely ghastly.

Kate bought her first home in Hackney and served as a councillor in the borough for four years. She became chair of the Leisure committee; sport was still her first love.

Her first attempt to enter Parliament came in 1983, when she was chosen to contest Dulwich for Labour. She did well and reduced the Conservative majority to 1,800, so she tried again in 1987. This time Hoey lost by 150 votes.

In 1989, following the resignation of the sitting MP Stuart Holland, a by-election was announced in Vauxhall. Labour had lost three London by-elections in a row. Neil Kinnock's chief of staff, Charles Clarke, called Kate and suggested that she put her name forward as a candidate for Vauxhall. But the left-wing Vauxhall party wanted black activist Martha Osamor, who had been involved in battles with the police in north London, to contest the seat. The local party rejected the shortlist of candidates that included Kate.

The National Executive then hustled everyone off to a fresh selection meeting run by Roy Hattersley, Tom Sawyer and Joan Lester. Hoey became the candidate.

'Peter Mandelson was working for them. He was PR at the time and I remember he took me out onto the Green at about half eleven at night to do an interview with somebody for the next morning. All they were interested in was that I was an imposed candidate.'

Kate won more than 50 per cent of the vote in Vauxhall and increased Labour's majority. She is proud of what she has achieved for her constituents over the years.

> I have helped to stop some pretty ridiculous things in Lambeth council. I think I have given people in my constituency the belief that their MP is really genuinely speaking for them. I am aware that Lambeth is a very different kind of council. I am always meeting colleagues who are always hand in glove with their local council. I know when there have been cutbacks and so on, they can't do all the things they want to, but it is the way they have been so willing to just ignore people and use consultation just as a mechanism.

The then Labour Party leader, John Smith, appointed Kate to a job at the Home Office where she found herself working with her old friend from the NUS, Jack Straw.

> I have always been anti-EU, but I was in the Home Office for a year and I did Europe with Jack. We would be against something because it was the wrong thing and all these other countries would say, 'We like this and we are going to go along with it.' Then Jack would usually have to try and block it. To be fair, he was quite anti-EU then. And then we would get a call saying Downing Street had said we must skip this because we want something over in Health or something. I found the whole thing shocking. So then I voted against the Maastricht Treaty in 1992. We spent months and months on it and then, in the end, John Smith ordered us all to abstain. I was on Mo Mowlam's frontbench shadow team on Citizens Charter, and I sat there and I thought I am not abstaining on this. Mo said John Smith will probably not be happy.

Mowlam was right. Smith phoned Kate when she got home and told her she should resign.

'I said, "If you want me to resign, why don't you sack me?" And he said, "Well, I am sacking you then."'

Kate got her chance as a minister in Tony Blair's government.

'I became Sports minister when Tony Blair was obsessed with football. At that time he and Alastair Campbell wanted the electorate to believe that Labour was the party of football.'

Kate's lifetime interest in sport, and the fact that she had worked for Arsenal football club before becoming an MP, made her the ideal candidate.

> We were still in that era where Tony Blair and Downing Street actually ran things a lot more, and on a Friday I would get rung up by [Stalybridge & Hyde MP] James Purnell. 'Kate, Downing Street want a story for the Sunday paper, is there some sport thing they could use?' And they would come up with a daft idea like, 'We are going to introduce skipping for every child', and then I would be the one on the Sunday who had to answer all the questions ... The public would be saying, 'Have we really agreed to that?'

It has taken great bravery and toughness for Kate Hoey to hold so firmly to her beliefs, both in government and in opposition.

> I am disappointed in the Labour Party over the EU. I know Jeremy [Corbyn] has been with us in most votes over the years, and John McDonnell. I take a hard line on it. I don't agree with staying in the single market or the customs union during any transition. In fact, I don't think we need a transition period. I just take a hard line on it. I am disappointed. We took so long. I did all these rallies up in the north-east and the north-west, and I remember all those lovely, lovely people.
>
> Yes, of course a lot of them came out because Nigel Farage was speaking. They weren't racist. They would come up to you at the end of the rally and say that they were so pleased that a Labour person came. We can't let them down. While we are here in this little bubble everybody is talking out there. Most people haven't really changed their minds, and they see the BBC being just as biased as they have always been. If we won despite all that, I still think we can do it.
>
> Brexit will happen. They would have to now find a way of taking back Article 50. Some within the EU may be pleased we are going, because it is going to allow them to carry on. But I do get depressed about it.

On 17 July 2018, Kate Hoey and three other Brexiteers voted with the government to defeat a pro-EU customs amendment. They saved Theresa May's government.

SYLVIA HEAL

SUE HAYMAN

- FULL NAME: Sylvia Heal (née Lloyd Fox)
- DATE OF BIRTH: 20 July 1942
- PLACE OF BIRTH: Hawarden, Flintshire
- DATE OF DEATH: –
- MARRIED TO: Keith Heal
- CHILDREN: One son and one daughter
- UNSUCCESSFUL ELECTIONS FOUGHT: None
- CONSTITUENCY: Mid Staffordshire 1990–92 and Halesowen & Rowley Regis 1997–2010
- DATE OF FIRST ELECTION: 22 March 1990
- DATE LEFT PARLIAMENT: 12 April 2010
- PARTY ROLES: Member of the Young Socialists National Council 1960–64 and youngest constituency secretary for East Flintshire (aged fifteen)
- MINISTERIAL POSITIONS & DATES: Spokesperson for Health and Women 1991; PPS to George Robertson, Secretary of State for Defence 1997–99; PPS to Geoff Hoon, Secretary of State for Defence 1999–2000; Deputy Speaker of the House of Commons 2000–10
- MOST FAMOUS QUOTATION: 'I get angry when people spend a lot of time telling me what they can't do to help, instead of finding some way they can.'

Sylvia Heal was brought up in a very political family. Her parents were both members of the Labour Party and her father, John Lloyd Fox, served as a councillor on Hawarden District Council, as did one of her brothers. Heal's sister, Ann Keen, was MP for Brentford and Isleworth, and her brother-in-law, Alan Keen, became MP for Feltham and Heston.

In such an environment, perhaps it was inevitable that Heal would be motivated to enter politics. But she cites her biggest influence and inspiration as Eirene White, then the MP for East Flintshire, the area where Sylvia grew up.

Sylvia failed her 11-plus exam and left school aged fifteen, but Eirene encouraged her to resume her studies. Heeding this advice, Sylvia attended Swansea University. She still talks about Eirene today. As a young Welsh woman, Sylvia's political thinking was also heavily influenced by Aneurin Bevan and by the campaign to end apartheid in South Africa, a campaign that triggered a life-long interest in the African continent.

As a child, Heal wanted to be a police officer but was never tall enough! Instead, she worked for many years as a social worker, and then for the National Carers Association during her parliamentary interregnum. She has always been interested and involved in women's issues and in disability, health, and the pressures on young carers. She says that one of her proudest parliamentary achievements was supporting new legislation for carers.

Sylvia has always struck me as someone who is extremely pragmatic and who just wants to get things done; she has never been frightened to put herself forward to achieve her aims. So it should come as no surprise to learn, then, that in the early 1970s, aged thirty, she became one of Britain's youngest Justices of the Peace. In the 1980s, she joined the Campaign for Nuclear Disarmament (CND); she travelled to Berkshire with CND chair Joan Ruddock and other campaigners to visit the Greenham Common women.

Heal's keen interest in Africa has seen her visit numerous African countries over the years, sometimes through her work as Deputy Speaker, and sometimes as a patron of the charity Hands at Work in Africa. She says it is the social justice side of this charitable organisation that really appeals to her, including its enabling work on health, education, and supporting children.

Heal's parliamentary career began in 1990, following the suicide of the sitting MP, when she unexpectedly won the Mid Staffordshire by-election. Her talent and passion were obvious, and she soon became a spokesperson for health and women. An early claim to fame came in 1992 when she was appointed, together with future Tory leader William Hague, as an official observer to the Kenyan elections. Sylvia and Hague then appeared together on *Wogan*!

But after two years as an MP Heal was defeated at the 1992 general election by her Conservative opponent, Michael Fabricant. Undeterred, she contested the seat of Halesowen & Rowley Regis in 1997; she won the seat and then held it until she retired from Parliament in 2010.

Back again in the House of Commons, she was appointed parliamentary private secretary to the Secretary of State for Defence. During this time, while holidaying in Cyprus with her husband, Keith, the MoD contacted her to ask if she would like to take part in a helicopter training exercise. An excited Sylvia agreed. On the day of the exercise, she learned that she would be lowered by a winch from the helicopter to a ship. The worst that could happen, crew members assured her, was that she missed the ship and ended up in the water. She would then need to swim to a small boat. Sylvia decided not to mention the fact that she couldn't swim! Fortunately, all went well and she landed safely on the ship.

I got to know Sylvia when I was selected as the candidate for Halesowen & Rowley Regis in 2010, after she had taken the decision to stand down. She welcomed me warmly and was a wonderful support during the campaign, as were her family. I always found her to be very pragmatic, and this was demonstrated one evening following a 'Churches Together' hustings. I came out to discover that Gordon Brown had phoned Sylvia, to ask if she could arrange for him to visit the constituency the next morning – this was the day of the 'bigoted woman' news story. It had clearly been decided that a safe pair of hands were required; Gordon's visit needed to be properly organised, with no pitfalls. Sylvia, of course, was utterly calm and reliable.

In 2000, Sylvia was made Deputy Speaker of the House of Commons. It was a controversial appointment. Due to her inexperience – some members pointed out that she'd never chaired a Commons committee and was the first person to become Deputy Speaker without being on the Speaker's Panel – many Tory MPs were astonished. However, she quickly proved her competence and also showed her steel. She remained in the post until retiring from politics ten years later. Anyone interested in finding out how good she was at managing the often unruly chamber should watch videos of her on YouTube, including 'Sylvia Heal calms the House' and 'Sylvia Heal vs Alex Salmond'.

But she will probably go down in history for being in the Speaker's chair when pro-hunt protestors, including rock star Bryan Ferry's son, Otis, managed to invade the floor of the Commons, apparently the first time this had happened for 400 years. Sylvia kept her cool, suspended the sitting for twenty minutes, and then returned to the business of chairing the debate. Given that her maiden name was Fox, it amused her that the media never picked up on this, even when she turned up at Bow Street Magistrates Court to give evidence in the Otis Ferry trial.

She has said she would like to be remembered as someone who tried to get things done, and I'm sure she will be. But she will also be remembered for so much more. Always calm, always professional, always striving to make a difference, Sylvia Heal will be remembered with great admiration and affection.

IRENE ADAMS

FIONA MILLAR

- FULL NAME: Katherine Patricia Irene Adams (Baroness Adams of Craigielea
- DATE OF BIRTH: 27 December 1947
- PLACE OF BIRTH: Paisley, Scotland
- DATE OF DEATH: –
- MARRIED TO: Allen Adams (m. 1968; d. 1990)
- CHILDREN: Barbara, Kirsty and Allen
- UNSUCCESSFUL ELECTIONS FOUGHT: None
- CONSTITUENCY: Paisley North
- DATE OF FIRST ELECTION: 9 November 1990
- DATE LEFT PARLIAMENT: 11 April 2005
- PARTY ROLES: None
- MINISTERIAL POSITIONS & DATES: None

Irene Adams's career in Parliament began with a family tragedy – the sudden death at forty-four of her husband Allen, who had been MP for Paisley, and then Paisley North, from 1983 to 1990. Some reports at the time described her as 'inheriting' his seat and it is true she had also succeeded him on Strathclyde Regional Council when he went to Westminster. But a quick glance through her biographical details reveals a more solid Paisley heritage than her husband's, and possibly an even more tenacious political ambition.

Born in the town and educated at its Stanley Green High School, Irene Adams was a member of Paisley Town Council by the time she was twenty-three, and became one of the youngest Justices of the Peace in the country aged twenty-five. She was then elected to Renfrew District Council before becoming a Strathclyde regional councillor in 1979, a position she held while raising three children and also working in her husband's office.

In an interview given shortly after being elevated to the House of Lords, Adams attributed her determination to the formidable female role models in family, and her strong political instincts to being brought up by her grand-parents because, as one of eight children, her own family home was too overcrowded. Her grandfather, who had fought at the Battle of the Somme in the First World War, instilled powerful socialist instincts in the young Irene and political debate was encouraged around the kitchen table. Both she and her husband were later seen as being loyalists, but on the left of the Labour Party.

As it happens my own father was born and brought up in Paisley, and though he emigrated down south after the First World War, which meant I was brought up English, I still remember my paternal grandparents' strong-ly socialist home, my grandfather's First World War stories and the town's proud local traditions and culture.

Famous for its textile industry for much of the last 150 years, Paisley was one of the fastest growing towns in the UK in the late nineteenth century and gave its name to the famous Paisley pattern. The J. & P. Coats thread factories dominated employment in the town for much of the twentieth century, but by 1993 all the textile mills had gone. Parts of Paisley are now among the most deprived areas in Scotland.

Inevitably, Adams's political career coincided with the ensuing social and economic difficulties that followed deindustrialisation, in particular the rapid growth of the drugs trade in the town, feeding off a ready supply of black-market sedatives like Temazepam, and the burgeoning criminal under-world that accompanied it.

When Adams decided to challenge the weak regulation of the Temazepam supply chain and the criminal activities of some prominent local businesses in the mid-1990s – some of her constituents were risking amputation by injecting the drugs known as 'jellies' – she put herself and her family at considerable personal risk.

After a period of menacing threats her daughter's car was blown up and she came under the protection of the police. Adams suffered a minor stroke while on holiday in New York with her two daughters. In what was a dark coincidence, this happened on the anniversary of the day her husband, while holidaying in Spain, had contracted a fatal virus that later killed him.

If all this sounds a bit more like *The Sopranos* than SW1, Adams's career appears to have taken a more tranquil turn following the death of one par-ticular local mobster. A boundary change in the run-up to the 2005 general election coincided with the offer of a seat in the House of Lords and she was created a life peer as Baroness Adams of Craigielea later that year.

As with so many parliamentary colleagues of that vintage, Adams's political career became entwined with allegations and counter-allegations about parliamentary expenses, second homes, mortgage payments and attendance allowances in the House of Lords. In the course of the expenses scandal, she threatened to take the parliamentary authorities to court over a long-standing request for repayment of over £4,000. The claim was subsequently dropped. In recent years Adams has spoken rarely in the House of Lords, and mostly on business affecting Scotland.

JANET ANDERSON

CAROLYN QUINN

- FULL NAME: Janet Anderson
- DATE OF BIRTH: 6 December 1949
- PLACE OF BIRTH: Newcastle upon Tyne
- DATE OF DEATH: –
- MARRIED TO: Vincent Humphreys (m. 1972; div. 1988); Jim Dowd
- CHILDREN: Three children
- UNSUCCESSFUL ELECTIONS FOUGHT: Rossendale & Darwen 1987
- CONSTITUENCY: Rossendale & Darwen
- DATE OF FIRST ELECTION: 9 April 1992
- DATE LEFT PARLIAMENT: 12 April 2010
- PARTY ROLES: Member of the Labour Parliamentary Committee and member of the Labour NEC
- MINISTERIAL POSITIONS & DATES: Opposition whip; shadow Minister for Women 1996–97
- MOST FAMOUS QUOTATION: 'Women will become more promiscuous under Labour.'

An early and loyal Blairite, Janet Anderson had her share of ministerial roles and legislative achievements. She was responsible for bringing in free television licences for the over seventy-fives. But Janet Anderson, who entered Parliament in 1992, knows she will be remembered for one thing above all else – her assertion that under Labour there would be more sex!

She was in fact joking. She made the comment during an interview in October 1996, when she was shadow Minister for Women, claiming that 'under Labour women will become more promiscuous – that's an election promise'. Today she winces when it's mentioned, explaining that she was trying to say that women are entitled to the same chances as men; that they should have the same freedom of choice. But still the myth lives on – and she can laugh about it now, just about.

Her reputation as one of the saucier MPs was enhanced when new Prime Minister Tony Blair gave her a role in the Whips' Office. She became Vice Chamberlain of the Household – a grand title and a job which entails being taken hostage at the palace when the monarch heads to Parliament for the State Opening. Another key task is to write a daily report to the Queen concerning the business in Parliament. Janet Anderson took to the job with gusto, deciding to spice up the normally deadly dull reports with a bit of Westminster gossip. She peppered her missives – which opened each time with the words: 'With Humble Duty' – with frank assessments of colleagues on both sides of the House. She told the Queen that John Bercow, now Commons Speaker, was 'a rather odious little MP from Buckingham' and that he was 'one of the regular troublemakers' or 'such a tiresome little man – constantly bores us with his attempts to be more clever than anyone else'.

Mentions of the Transport minister Glenda Jackson were often prefaced by 'poor Glenda' – and the suggestion that she was condemned to 'never-ending adjournment debates'. The Ulster Unionists were a 'sour bunch'. Labour's Diane Abbott 'sank to the occasion'. And former Tory leader Michael Howard was just 'loathsome'. She enlightened Her Majesty on some of the whips' 'tactics' – like the careful timing of votes during the 1998 World Cup to ensure they did not clash with crucial matches involving the England team (and allowing Labour MPs to watch behind their hands as David Beckham was sent off during the Argentina game).

When she was promoted to a new ministerial job, Janet went to Buckingham Palace to hand over her whip regalia including the so-called wand of office. She confessed to Her Majesty that the whips had called it 'the snooker cue' and that they'd used it to change channels on the TV in their House of Commons office. Presumably the Queen was amused.

Janet Anderson later published all her letters in a book entitled *Dear Queen*. It was not blocked by the palace. And the word on the grapevine was that the monarch had rather enjoyed these daily insights.

Janet Anderson was elected Member of Parliament for Rossendale and Darwen in 1992 – the first woman to represent the constituency – and remained its MP until 2010. A miner's granddaughter and former secretary to the MP for Blackburn Barbara Castle and Castle's successor, Jack Straw, she was encouraged by friends to stand for Parliament. She made it on her second attempt in 1992. After entering the Commons she quickly became parliamentary private secretary to the then Deputy Leader of the Opposition,

Margaret Beckett. Under Tony Blair as Labour leader she became shadow Minister for Women.

She introduced two Private Members' Bills which subsequently influenced government policy – one to make stalking a criminal offence, the other to establish a national register of paedophiles.

Once in government, she followed her Vice-Chamberlain Whip job with a promotion to what had formerly been dubbed the 'Ministry of Fun', as Minister of State for Tourism, Film and Broadcasting – a role she relished – though her tenure as Tourism minister coincided with the foot and mouth crisis and she returned to the backbenches after the 2001 election. Never a fan of Gordon Brown, when he became Prime Minister she proved to be one of his forthright critics from the backbenches, and in 2008 was among those asking for a debate on whether he should continue as party leader.

Janet Anderson's parliamentary career had its highs – including the satisfaction of piloting through Parliament a Private Members' Bill to make it an offence to use a handheld mobile phone while driving a motor vehicle. But it also had its lows, for instance a marriage break-up and the ignominy, shared with many other MPs, of seeing her expenses claims splashed across the front of the *Daily Telegraph* in 2009.

She served on the Culture, Media and Sport committee, seizing the opportunity during a visit to Washington to meet one of her heroes – *Washington Post* editor Ben Bradlee – and to quiz him about the Watergate scandal. In 2010 she lost her Rossendale & Darwen seat to the Conservative Jake Berry. These days she works as a freelance consultant.

ANGELA BROWNING

SUZANNE EVANS

- FULL NAME: Angela Francis Browning (née Pearson), Baroness Browning
- DATE OF BIRTH: 4 December 1946
- PLACE OF BIRTH: Reading, Berkshire
- DATE OF DEATH: –
- MARRIED TO: David Browning (m. 1968)
- CHILDREN: Two sons
- UNSUCCESSFUL ELECTIONS FOUGHT: Crewe & Nantwich 1987
- CONSTITUENCY: Tiverton 1992–97, Tiverton & Honiton 1997–2010
- DATE OF FIRST ELECTION: 10 April 1992
- DATE LEFT PARLIAMENT: 12 April 2010. Browning became a life peer in the House of Lords on 13 July 2010.
- PARTY ROLES: Deputy chair of the Conservative Party 2005–07 and vice-chair of the Conservative Party 2001–05
- MINISTERIAL POSITIONS & DATES: Parliamentary private secretary to Education minister Michael Forsyth 1993; Parliamentary Secretary at the Ministry of Agriculture, Fisheries and Food 1994–97; shadow spokesperson on Education and Employment 1997–98; shadow Secretary of State for Trade and Industry 1999–2000; shadow Leader of the House of Commons 2000–2001; Minister for Crime Prevention and Antisocial Behaviour Reduction 2011 (Lords)
- MOST FAMOUS QUOTATION: 'I certainly believe in the promotion of fish. It contains healthy proteins, and I recommend it to hon. Members. I am told that it is good for the brain, and I particularly recommend it to my hon. Friend [Christopher Gill].'

During her maiden speech, the newly elected Conservative MP for Tiverton, Angela Browning, voiced her concerns for people suffering from physical disabilities and learning difficulties. Browning said she hoped that there would be legislation leading to 'an improvement in the quality of life enjoyed by that group of people and a clearer understanding of their needs and the difficulties that they face'. By the time she left Parliament, her hopes had been fulfilled.

Browning's interest in this subject is personal, as one of her sons has Asperger's Syndrome. 'Things have really improved for him, there's been huge progress,' she tells me, 'but back in the days when I was first elected, nobody had even heard of Asperger's.'

After her son was diagnosed with Asperger's, Browning resigned from William Hague's shadow Cabinet. The media assumed there had been a falling out with her party leader, and Browning had to explain that she and her husband were dealing with a family crisis. She says this was probably 'a good thing', because it raised awareness for autism and Asperger's. 'I had correspondence from people who have said, "we have this in our family but we don't like to talk about it", so I hope it helped "normalise" those with Asperger's in our society,' Browning says. Although Browning introduced the first parliamentary debate on Asperger's Syndrome, it is the role she played in the 2009 Autism Act that she is most proud of. Having tried and failed to top the annual ballot for Private Members' Bills herself, Angela was delighted when her close friend Cheryl Gillan (who came first in the ballot) offered to debate an Autism Bill. 'Eighteen years, and just before I left Parliament, we got autism on the statute book,' Browning says. 'That has to be my political highlight.'

However, it was not autism but the raging debate over nuclear defence that influenced her decision to go into politics. In the mid-1980s the Campaign for Nuclear Disarmament (CND) was extremely active; tens of thousands of women had gathered at Greenham Common in Berkshire to protest against nuclear weapons being sited at the RAF base there. Angela became a spokesperson for Peace in NATO, and Women and Families for Defence, regularly debating with CND and articulating the opposite point of view. The experience encouraged her to set her sights on Westminster, and with steely determination, she gave herself ten years to become an MP.

She stood against veteran Labour MP Gwyneth Dunwoody in Crewe & Nantwich at the 1987 general election. Local Tories had not welcomed Browning initially; when she arrived for the selection hustings, she encountered people holding placards demanding that a local man be selected to contest the seat. But gradually Browning charmed the local Tories, and became the candidate. She made sure to post her election leaflets through the letter box of her formidable Labour opponent, whom Browning believes reciprocated by placing a red rose on her campaign car. Dunwoody won their contest by 1,092 votes.

Having fared so well against a high-profile rival, Browning was a shoo-in for her home constituency of Tiverton when the sitting MP Robin Maxwell-Hyslop retired (although she still had to fend off 400 other applicants). She won the seat at the 1992 election with a majority of over 10,000.

Browning quickly names the BSE crisis when asked about the biggest issues she faced during her time in Parliament.

> As an Agriculture minister in John Major's government, it was a challenging time, and getting the policies right to deal with the BSE crisis meant the lights burned very long into the night in the Ministry and at No. 10. I was subject to a public inquiry afterwards. Every decision you make, every meeting you attend, is open to public scrutiny. Making sure I read my papers stood me in good stead when I came under the spotlight.

If Browning worked well with John Major during the BSE crisis, she was far less well disposed towards him when it came to Major's views on the European Union. The first minister to break ranks with the 'wait and see' party line, Browning went public with her view that Britain should not join the euro. Her statement triggered a huge row in the middle of the 1997 general election campaign but, having always voted consistently against more integration into the European Union, this was a war she knew had to be won. 'Like a lot of other people at the time, I was called a lot of names, but I feel we have all been vindicated,' she says. 'If we were in the euro, we would be in great difficulty in this country now.'

Meanwhile, she was also busy battling officials at the Ministry of Agriculture, who tried to dissuade her from saying, 'British Beef is Best' at the party conference. Browning tells me she thought, 'Blow, it, I'm going to say it anyway.'

She fought the EU's attempts to ban Cadbury's from referring to their chocolate as 'chocolate', arguing that because it contained vegetable fat and had a high milk content it was a different product. 'I like Belgian chocolate as much as anyone else, but don't tell me Cadbury's isn't chocolate – it is.' Then Browning went into battle over 'the most ridiculous thing', soya milk not being called milk.

> I can't tell you how frustrating that was. The real reason is that European companies didn't like the competition so they ganged up against us, introducing

legislation limiting the impact of the British marketplace. I took it to the point where they threatened infraction proceedings, meaning the British government could have been fined if we refused to back down.

As shadow Leader of the House of Commons from 2000 to 2001, she found herself at the despatch box for PMQs, up against Labour's John Prescott whenever William Hague was away. 'I certainly trounced him on one occasion,' she recalls. 'In December 2000 ... Blair was desperate for Brown to give approval to joining the euro, but Brown was taking his time. I asked Prescott a simple question about the government's five economic tests for joining the euro, and he was unable to name them!'

Aside from perfectly justified political rows over the EU, Browning seems to have avoided controversy. In 2007, complaints that she spent too much money on her website were, she admits, her fault. 'I never got around to going through material I could have put on my website, so it looked a bit thin.' However, she was given a clean bill of health after the expenses scandal.

A need to slow down because of a heart condition meant that Browning left the Commons in 2010. But she was then named in David Cameron's dissolution honours list, so she went almost straight from the Commons to the Lords. She got stuck in when offered the job of Minister for Crime Prevention and Antisocial Behaviour Reduction, and enjoyed working at the Home Office with Theresa May (whom she names as her 'best boss'). But she stood down when her heart problems reached a crisis point. She says she is now 'sorted out' after extensive treatment.

Although enjoying her time in the Lords, and satisfied with her ministerial career, Browning says that being an MP is the best job because 'you can make such a difference to people's lives'. When she left Parliament, a constituent contacted her to say: 'You probably don't realise when I came to see you all those years ago that I was so at my wits' end; I thought I would have to have my children fostered. Thanks for being there.' Browning says she thought: 'You can forget ministerial office, just doing that for that one person was worth doing.'

ANNE CAMPBELL

AMBER DE BOTTON

- FULL NAME: Anne Campbell
- DATE OF BIRTH: 6 April 1940
- PLACE OF BIRTH: Dewsbury, Yorkshire
- DATE OF DEATH: –
- MARRIED TO: Archibald (Archie) Campbell (m. 1963)
- CHILDREN: Frances, Emily and Diarmid
- UNSUCCESSFUL ELECTIONS FOUGHT: None
- CONSTITUENCY: Cambridge
- DATE OF FIRST ELECTION: 9 April 1992
- DATE LEFT PARLIAMENT: 5 May 2005
- PARTY ROLES: None
- MINISTERIAL POSITIONS & DATES: PPS to John Battle at the Department of Trade and Industry 1997–99 and PPS to Patricia Hewitt at the Department of Trade and Industry 1999–2003
- MOST FAMOUS QUOTATION: 'I am sure that my right honourable friend is aware of the grave anxieties that many people have about an impending war in Iraq, but does he think that this is a good time to make the US President aware of his wider social and environmental responsibilities towards the rest of the world?' – Addressing Tony Blair in 2003.

Anne Campbell was a loyal Blairite, the first MP with her own website and a mother who crusaded for better childcare. She also became a footnote to a huge moment in Labour history when she resigned as a parliamentary private secretary over Iraq.

Born in Yorkshire in 1940, Campbell studied maths at Newnham College, Cambridge. From 1985 to '89 she was a councillor for Cambridge County Council and, later, lectured in statistics at Cambridge College of Arts and Technology. For nine years until her election, she was head of statistics and data processing at the National Institute of Agricultural Botany.

She came to national politics late in life, at the age of fifty-two. In 1992, she was elected as the first-ever female MP for Cambridge (before all-women shortlists existed) and the third Labour politician to represent the seat. Her maiden speech set the tone for her parliamentary career, 'Many [MPs] will recall hazy memories of their student lives in Cambridge: rolling lawns, high tables, garden parties… I make no apology for bias towards the underprivileged. Cambridge elected a Labour MP because we recognised the other side of the city.'

For a time, she shared an office with Harriet Harman and they bonded over how to improve women's lives. Campbell helped found Childcare Links, a free internet service to provide childcare information and get lone parents back into work. When Margaret Hodge became Children minister, it was rolled out to every county council. 'The internet was not just there for industry and selling widgets, it was for social change,' says Campbell.

She is credited with being the first British MP to have their own website. The *New Statesman* reported,

> In the summer of 1994, Dick Robinson, who worked as a researcher for Anne Campbell MP, received a call asking whether she would be interested in having a website. 'What's a website?' asked Robinson … The person who made the call was Bill Thompson, employed by internet company Pipex, tasked with making the web seem exciting to as many people as possible … He built Campbell's website in two weeks.

Campbell remembers, 'We used to hold internet surgeries. People would email and I would answer them within minutes.'

She was instrumental in changing MPs' working hours, first raising the subject with Tony Blair at the post-election PLP meeting in May 1997. A modernisation committee followed, but progress was slow. By 1999 Campbell was 'walking around like a zombie', so she drafted a petition that urged the committee to look again at sitting times. Then she headed for the members' tea room, seeking signatures. 'People were practically snatching it out of my hands,' she recalls. In the end, 215 MPs signed her petition.

Campbell was among a small number of vegetarians in the House (Jeremy Corbyn was another) and says, 'It was quite difficult to find food at times.' A cycling enthusiast, she campaigned for a bicycle allowance for MPs; expenses were ultimately set at 6.2 pence per mile to rise with inflation in 1998. She also fought for more science spending, which trebled during her time in

Parliament. 'Gordon Brown acknowledged that I made the most noise about science funding,' she recalls.

The Iraq War had a huge bearing on Campbell's position in the party and her constituency. She voted to support the government's policy on the war on 26 February 2003. But, just a month later, facing a threat of deselection and in the absence of a second United Nations resolution, she resigned from her post as parliamentary private secretary to long-time friend Patricia Hewitt. Up until this point, Campbell had never voted against the government. *The Guardian* described it as a 'harrowing' moment for her. 'I had about 6,000 emails and letters about it,' Campbell recalls. 'The person who was really supportive was Robin Cook ... I remember having a conversation with him about whether to abstain or vote against, and he said, "Nobody remembers abstainers, Anne."'

Indecision haunted her during another rebellion. In 2004, Tony Blair faced massive backbench opposition over university top-up fees. At the time, Campbell was bullish about her position, telling *The Times*, 'It is no longer satisfactory for government to come with a proposal like top-up fees and MPs to vote for it meekly ... We have passed the point of no return.' She abstained on the bill's second reading but then voted with the government at third reading, despite publicly having promised to oppose the scheme. 'A group of us did a deal with [Education Secretary] Charles Clarke that if he would introduce maintenance grants for low-income families, we would support it.'

At the general election a year later, she lost her seat to Liberal Democrat David Howarth. 'People wanted to protest against the Iraq War,' she explains, 'and the Lib Dems were a convenient protest party.' Cambridge was also a constituency with 20,000-odd students in it. 'It was a pretty difficult loss,' Campbell admits.

JUDITH CHAPLIN

JULIE KIRKBRIDE

- **FULL NAME:** Sybil Judith Schofield Chaplin OBE
- **DATE OF BIRTH:** 19 August 1939
- **PLACE OF BIRTH:** Harpenden, Hertfordshire
- **DATE OF DEATH:** 19 February 1993
- **MARRIED TO:** Robert Walpole (future 10th Baron Walpole; m. 1962; d. 1979); Michael Chaplin (m. 1984)
- **CHILDREN:** Alice, Emma, Jonathan and Benedict
- **UNSUCCESSFUL ELECTIONS FOUGHT:** None
- **CONSTITUENCY:** Newbury
- **DATE OF FIRST ELECTION:** 9 April 1992
- **DATE LEFT PARLIAMENT:** 19 February 1993
- **PARTY ROLES:** None
- **MINISTERIAL POSITIONS & DATES:** None

If Judith Chaplin had not died a tragic 316 days after being elected to the House of Commons, she might well have become the UK's first female Chancellor of the Exchequer.

She was superbly qualified for the job – a Cambridge-educated economist who had worked as a special adviser to two Chancellors with significantly different economic outlooks: Nigel Lawson (1988–89) and John Major (1989–90). Chaplin was clever, politically astute, experienced, likeable and one of a tiny band of just twenty women on the Conservative benches when she won the safe seat of Newbury at the 1992 general election.

Born in 1939, the daughter of a hospital surgeon, she was educated at Wycombe Abbey girls' boarding school, then went to Girton College, Cambridge, and took a postgraduate qualification at the University of East Anglia. She worked at the J. Walter Thompson advertising agency, but quit her job when she married the future 10th Baron Walpole in 1962.

The couple had four children together. Unable to find a suitable nursery for them in rural North Norfolk, Chaplin took over one herself and ran it for a decade until all her brood had moved to a primary school.

She and her first husband were both active in local politics in Norfolk, serving as county councillors; Judith became chair of the county's education committee and vice-chair of the Association of County Councils' Education Committee. She sat on the Burnham Committee, which set the rates for teachers' pay, until the committee was abolished in 1987.

In the mid-'70s, Chaplin found herself looking for a seat in Parliament as a separated, and then divorced woman (her first marriage ended in 1979) with young children. Her daughter, Alice, recalls that Chaplin did not find life easy, but was extremely tenacious. Chaplin's privileged background had endowed her with a strong sense of public service, and the belief that she needed to make a political contribution.

She kept applying for seats, but when called for interview she was patronised and asked about childcare arrangements. More shockingly, she was turned down at one interview for being inappropriately dressed – Chaplin turned up wearing high-heeled leather boots! The experience rankled. Not so much because she had been rejected, but because she considered herself a stylish dresser!

In 1986 she became head of the policy unit at the Institute of Directors, which brought her to the attention of the Treasury and later to her mentor, John Major. She was finally selected (by a clear majority) as the Conservative candidate for Newbury in November 1990, the same month that Major was catapulted into No. 10. Special dispensation was sought for her to become his political secretary while still a Tory candidate.

Elected to the Commons in 1992, she sat on the prestigious Treasury Select Committee and further demonstrated her economic interests with calls to equalise the state retirement age at sixty-five and amend the law to deregulate Sunday trading.

But with little time to make a name for herself in the Commons, it is probably for the diary Chaplin kept while in Downing Street that she will be most remembered by historians. The diary offers an insider's view of the Major premiership and reveals the relationship he had with his predecessor, Margaret Thatcher. It includes the observation that Major thought Thatcher was 'finished' four days before the first ballot on her leadership in 1990, and that the relationship between them had so soured a year into his premiership that he wanted her 'isolated, I want her destroyed'.

As a political journalist during this period, I briefly came across Judith and was struck by how normal and approachable she seemed as a Tory politician – quite an inspiration for someone who had political ambitions herself. Like many others in the Westminster village, I was shocked and saddened when, on 19 February 1993, she died suddenly from cancer after undergoing hospital surgery.

ANN COFFEY

ANN CLWYD

- FULL NAME: Margaret Ann Coffey (née Brown)
- DATE OF BIRTH: 31 August 1946
- DATE OF DEATH: –
- PLACE OF BIRTH: Inverness
- MARRIED TO: Thomas Coffey (m. 1973; div. 1989); Peter Saraga (m. 1998)
- CHILDREN: One daughter
- UNSUCCESSFUL ELECTIONS FOUGHT: Cheadle 1987
- CONSTITUENCY: Stockport
- DATE OF FIRST ELECTION: 9 April 1992
- DATE LEFT PARLIAMENT: incumbent
- PARTY ROLES: None
- MINISTERIAL POSITIONS & DATES: Opposition whip, shadow spokesperson for Health 1996–97, parliamentary private secretary to the Chancellor of the Exchequer 2007–10

Ann Coffey is a woman whose background and career runs against the historic grain of a large number of MPs; her achievements and endeavour marking her out as one of the few women to have broken the barrier into the most elite and male-dominated institution in Britain. 'Strong, stable, and able' is an apt description of Ann!

Ann was brought up in Inverness, attending local grammar schools before studying sociology at the Borough Polytechnic Institute in London, followed by a PGCE in teaching at Walsall College. It was in Walsall that she embarked on her career in social work, which provided her with valuable insight into people and their concerns that was to become vital during her time as a councillor. She agrees that her work gave her perspective, but also notes that it helped give her the hunger to want to help those people that she could not while a social worker.

In both the 1987 and 1992 general elections, Ann stood as a Labour

candidate. Although unsuccessful on her first attempt, she secured the Stockport seat in her second. She had adopted a bullish attitude in the run-up to
the elections – as an elected woman MP, I know what women candidates
have to go through – but naturally the reality of the situation soon hit her.
When she arrived in Parliament, Ann found the place unaccommodating
and unsympathetic. The fact that the Whips' Office was unmoved by her
need to look after her fourteen-year-old daughter and other practical issues
she was facing, made for a very unwelcome environment.

'It did very much feel like a club to which you'd been let in, but it wasn't
really your place,' she admitted. Not only was she a woman, but she was
a woman who had been brought up in Scotland, far away from the heart
of power in London. She had attended local state schools and her father
was 'a working-class Tory', who had imprinted upon Ann his belief in the
importance of education. This experience was atypical of a large proportion
of MPs at the time; often London-centric, privately educated, with a degree
from Oxbridge and, notably, male. Ann is the embodiment of someone who
broke the trend.

She does not try to hide the fact that she felt overwhelmed, freely admitting to having been intimidated by Parliament. The perception on the
outside was that the place was so out of touch. 'Journalists kept ringing
up, asking if we had enough toilets,' she tells me. And the truth is that it
was out of touch – but Ann fears Parliament lacks the capacity to change.
Representation is important to her and, quite neatly, she states, 'I think it's
important that the place is representative because it's supposed to be a representative body.' It is a simple statement that highlights her drive for social
justice and welfare.

Ann's twenty-five years of experience in social work acted as a catalyst
for her determination to run for parliament. While she has been appointed
to high-profile positions, such as Alistair Darling's PPS, her focus over the
years has been on child welfare. She wants to see a fundamental change in
attitudes towards children, so that we regard their protection as a societal
issue rather than a private issue. She continues to fight against child abuse,
admonishing recent failures in the ability to identify trauma. 'I think it's
rewarding to be persistent because the more you persist, the more you find
out. The more knowledge you have the more ability you have to change and
challenge.'

Ann regularly displays a self-deprecating attitude and is not prepared to
rest on her laurels. I asked her what she would like her epitaph to say. 'I wish

I'd tried harder,' she replied. Yet it is never about her. She is quick to stress that any progress made is not down to the efforts of one individual: 'It's not just one individual ... we have a tendency to forget how much progress we've all made.'

The conversation drifted towards retirement and I asked her about her future plans and whether she had any interest in joining the House of Lords. She was very clear, 'No, I have not.'

'I can't envisage you not wanting to be part of the action,' I said. 'Yes, but the action may be at the residents' meetings,' she responded.

Once again, this brief exchange points to Ann's desire to help on a more personal level; she is brilliant at understanding what people's problems are and how to deal with them. She observes that 'people get very obsessed about whether they're ministers or on the shadow front bench'.

'But,' she continues, 'over the years I've known MPs who have made a fantastic difference by being backbenchers, fighting for the issues they have taken up, and that has made a difference.'

JEAN CORSTON

THANGAM DEBBONAIRE

- FULL NAME: Jean Ann Corston (née Parkin)
- DATE OF BIRTH: 5 May 1942
- DATE OF DEATH: –
- PLACE OF BIRTH: Hull
- MARRIED TO: Christopher Corston (m. 1961); Peter Townsend (m. 1985)
- CHILDREN: Sarah (b. 1963) and David (b. 1965)
- UNSUCCESSFUL ELECTIONS FOUGHT: None
- CONSTITUENCY: Bristol East
- DATE OF FIRST ELECTION: 9 April 1992
- DATE LEFT PARLIAMENT: 11 April 2005. She joined the Lords later that year.
- PARTY ROLES: Organiser of Labour South West; chair of the Parliamentary Labour Party 2001–05; co-chair of the Women's Parliamentary Labour Party 1992–97
- MINISTERIAL POSITIONS & DATES: None

Jean Corston cites the experience of 'feeling like the council house kid' at her state grammar school as helping to shape her as an MP. Probably all Members of Parliament say they want to help other people, but when I met Jean in the House of Commons recently, all her favourite memories were of helping constituents.

After bringing up her children, gaining an Open University degree, spending time in the 1980s as South West Regional Organiser for the Labour Party, and marrying Peter Townsend (co-founder of the Child Poverty Action Group), a 47-year-old Jean completed a law degree at the London School of Economics. She was then selected as the Labour Party's candidate for Bristol East at the 1992 election, and duly triumphed, unseating the incumbent Tory MP and securing a majority of 2,692 votes.

I first met Jean in 1996, when I was working at the Women's Aid national office in Bristol. Jean was on the committee of the Family Law Bill, which was seeking to reform laws relating to protection against domestic violence. My colleague and I met Jean in her constituency office. With her political and legal acumen, and dedication to improving the lives of abused women, Jean pierced our arguments, honed a legislative strategy and resolved our concerns about the Bill. All in thirty minutes!

I've never forgotten that meeting.

The experience of seeing what a single MP could achieve, as she turned our ideas into workable amendments and then argued them through the committee stage, is a huge reason why I myself am an MP now, two decades later.

My colleague and I later watched in the public gallery of the House of Commons as the Bill underwent a third reading. We were thrilled to see the various amendments become law; amendments that we both knew would never have been made without the help of sympathetic legislators.

When we meet up in the House of Commons smoking room in January 2018, between votes, Jean cannot recall our initial encounter. But I certainly do. It made me realise the impact that one MP can have on a piece of legislation.

Countless more women's lives were improved by Jean's work in the House of Lords in the years after she stepped down from the House of Commons in 2005. Yet most of these women never even knew of her existence. The 'Corston Report' into women in the criminal justice system created a powerful legacy of a model of work to keep women out of prison, help them to recover from abusive relationships, and help them to maintain a relationship with their children.

Suicides in women's prisons had provoked Jean's interest. A decade on, when I visited a project in Bristol East still known as a 'Corston Project' by some people, it became clear to me just what an impact the report had made. It resulted in more investment in these centres which provide residential space, childcare, training and much more. In my first year as an MP for a neighbouring constituency, I visited the project again. It saddened me to discover that funding for it had been cut drastically, resulting in a detrimental impact on the lives of the women and children who need it.

In 2001, Jean was elected as the first female chair of the Parliamentary Labour Party, the central body for debate and discussion in Parliament for Labour MPs. Her election came eighty years after the first Labour women were elected to Parliament. She successfully steered this often challenging body and gave backbenchers a voice.

Jean had previously chaired the women's PLP, a body established informally by pioneering Labour women. In May 1992 she approached Labour's Chief Whip, Derek Foster, and told him that we wanted a formal PLP women's group. He said that we could not have one, because there was not a PLP men's group. Jean replied: 'But Derek, the PLP is a men's group!'

Jean is proud of the achievements of the women's PLP, which include getting more women into shadow Cabinet and Cabinet, and establishing childcare facilities in Parliament. She describes a time when she and Mo Mowlam took tape measures to the parliamentary shooting range, to measure it up for a possible conversion. Amid worried looks from male MPs, the two Labour women exclaimed how 'you could fit two cribs in here'. I am still reeling from the news that there actually used to be a shooting range in Parliament. Eventually, as a result of hard campaigning by Jean and the women's PLP, a parliamentary bar was converted to a nursery.

Jean's time as chair of the PLP, her role in establishing the Joint Committee on Human Rights and the ways in which she challenged the House to introduce better childcare facilities, show she was a dedicated campaigner. She always used, and continues to use, her political position to further the position of women and strengthen the cause of women's rights. She used her background as a Labour Party organiser to good effect in Parliament, recognising how to identify and build support within the party and beyond for the causes she espoused.

Jean said to me: 'Parliaments which don't have women's voices don't speak for the country. Young women should never allow themselves to be corralled into thinking that women are second-class citizens, but should have the confidence to take the reality of their lives wherever they go.'

As we are packing up to leave the smoking room, which has become full of noisy Tory men (we started off in there because it was quiet), Jean tells me how she had once remarked to Val Davey, my Labour predecessor as MP for Bristol West (1997–2005), that 'it's a far cry for both of us from Yeovil Girls' High, Val!' From Yeovil Girls' to the House of Lords, Jean has taken a Labour route. And she has helped countless women along the way.

ANGELA EAGLE

JACQUI SMITH

- FULL NAME: Angela Eagle
- DATE OF BIRTH: 17 February 1961
- PLACE OF BIRTH: Bridlington, Yorkshire
- DATE OF DEATH: –
- MARRIED TO: Maria Exall (m. 2008)
- CHILDREN: None
- UNSUCCESSFUL ELECTIONS FOUGHT: None
- CONSTITUENCY: Wallasey
- DATE OF FIRST ELECTION: 9 April 1992
- DATE LEFT PARLIAMENT: Incumbent
- PARTY ROLES: Chair of the Labour National Policy Forum 2012 and chair of the Labour National Executive Committee 2013–14
- MINISTERIAL POSITIONS & DATES: Opposition whip 1996–97; Under-Secretary of State at the Department of the Environment, Transport and the Regions 1997–98; Under-Secretary of State at the Department of Social Security 1998–2001; Under-Secretary of State at the Home Office 2001–02; Exchequer Secretary to the Treasury 2007–09; Minister for Pensions and Ageing 2009–10; shadow Chief Secretary to the Treasury 2010–11; shadow Leader of the House 2011–15; shadow Secretary of State for Business, Innovation and Skills and shadow First Secretary of State 2015–16
- MOST FAMOUS QUOTATION: 'I'm not a Blairite. I'm not a Brownite. And I'm not a Corbynite. I am my own woman.'

Angela Eagle is the type of talented, clever, serious politician who should be at the very top in British Labour politics. This was clear to me on the very first occasion that I came across her, at one of my first Oxford University Labour Club meetings, where I watched as she argued forcefully and cogently. This felt like grown-up, 'proper' politics, not the grandstanding and game-playing of students. Angela has never been one for the theatrics or tribalism of politics and this may well explain her failure to make it to the very top – an indictment of our politics, not of her.

Oxford was clearly not her first foray into politics. She came from a family which valued Labour ideology and debate. Her first political education came from reading the forerunner of the *Daily Mail*, the *Daily Sketch*, from the age of six, which her Labour-supporting father bought because it had the Peanuts cartoon in. 'It is possible to grow up reading the *Daily Mail* and then turn out to be a Labour MP,' she told me.

With her twin sister, Maria, she was the first from her extended family to go to university, but her parents' experiences, standards and values drove this ambition. Her mum passed the 11-plus, but with her family unable to afford the uniform and feeling very alone at the grammar school, she left school at fourteen to work in a biscuit factory. Her father had a successful job as a printer, also playing a key role in the trade union. It was her mother's regret at not being able to 'stick it out' at the grammar school that drove a family ethos of work, learning and aspiration. Standing as a Labour candidate in the school mock election when she was nine, Angela's hustings speech was about comprehensive education. Her family was to continue inspiring her politically.

But she was also learning about the Labour Party. She told me that she was a fan of Harold Wilson and particularly of Barbara Castle, who she described as 'fiery, opinionated, glamorous and in control of everything … I thought'. Having joined the Labour Party at sixteen, her early experiences in Merseyside introduced her to the entryism of Militant and the tactics of the hard left. She recalls her first ever Young Socialists meeting, when she had to listen to Militant members complaining about the then Labour government. She bravely stood up to defend the government, but nevertheless decided not to go back to the Young Socialists. She lived through the viciousness that would rear its head again during her campaign against Jeremy Corbyn. 'They followed you home and threatened your pets,' she said about that time.

She enjoyed Oxford, although it came as a shock to the system, particularly attending a rich and complacent college, St John's. She's proud to be their first female honorary fellow.

Work and employment rights are a theme of her political life – perhaps inspired by her father's trade unionism. After a short period at the Confederation of British Industry, she went to work at the Confederation of Health Service Employees. She spent seven years in the research and political department and mocks the accusation that 'she never had a real job' by pointing out that in writing the nurses and midwives pay claim and immersing herself in research about the pay and conditions of public sector workers, she certainly did.

She was elected to Parliament at her first attempt, but the selection process for the Wallasey seat in early 1992 plunged her back into the nasty, hard-left sectarianism of Merseyside politics. Lol Duffy, closely associated with the Socialist Organiser grouping, had fought the seat in 1987, but was excluded from the shortlist for 1992. In a controversial process run by Labour's National Executive Committee, Angela was only confirmed as a candidate about a month before the election was called. Despite never having been Labour, Wallasey was Labour's top target. Angela won with a majority of 3,809. It's now 24,000.

While Angela credits demographic changes and the loyalty of her constituents to those they elect for increasing her majority, she must take credit for the work she has put in to build her support and profile. She still holds four advice surgeries a month and can point to many people who have been directly helped by her strong constituency work. It is clear that this is central to her view of herself as a politician. She speaks passionately about public service and is emotional in remembering those whom she has helped directly. She remembers going into a pub opposite her office where the publican introduced her to a woman who had fled her home. She managed to get help for the woman. Recently, she met her again and she said, 'You saved me – now I've got a family and my own kids.' Angela was visibly moved when she recounted it to me.

Labour locally were delighted to finally win the Wallasey seat, but the nature of the Constituency Labour Party meant that even while people were hugging her and congratulating her on her victory, they were threatening her with deselection.

Angela arrived in Parliament in 1992 with a personal triumph, but at a time of massive disappointment for a Labour Party who had expected to win. She pursued her interest in employment issues, gaining a place on the Employment Select Committee. She also wisely worked hard to learn her 'craft' in the Chamber. This undoubtedly set her in good stead for her long stint as shadow Leader of the House from 2011 to 2015.

In 1996, she was appointed as an opposition whip and then gained her first ministerial role with John Prescott as one of his junior ministers at the Department for Environment, Transport and the Regions. Subsequent roles at Social Security and then at the Home Office saw her doing some of the most technical, but low-profile work in government. In 2002, she was not reappointed in the reshuffle. This surprised many on both sides of the chamber who saw her as a clever minister who could combine difficult technical roles with a good strategic political grip.

It is possible to trace this lack of support from Tony Blair back to 1994, when Angela supported Margaret Beckett in the leadership election. Showing her usual integrity and unwillingness to consider personal positioning in her political choices, she explains that 'If you think a woman should be leader, to be consistent you need to support them if they're good enough.' She laughs wryly at the irony that her local and national opponents have often dubbed her a 'Blairite'.

She sums up her political approach perceptively: 'I wasn't in a tribe. I'm not a follower. I've always had my own intellectual confidence. I don't fit easily into tribes. I didn't realise how tribal male politics was … I missed chances to ingratiate myself with this or that tribe.'

She is clever, imaginative and hard-working. She's in the broad mainstream of the party. Many who are less talented have been ministers longer and at more senior levels. Is this the reason? She describes her view as a 'working-class meritocracy' and then adds 'pile of bollocks'. This humour and self-awareness goes a long way to avoiding the bitterness which she could legitimately feel and demonstrate.

Given her intellectual confidence, she also wishes that she had been in Parliament and government at a time when there was more latitude allowed for different opinions to develop and be expressed. Referencing her early Labour hero, she says, 'I think Harold did that much better.' His Cabinet was a collection of views from right to left. She wonders whether John Smith would have promoted this type of culture more effectively, although she's also clear that his shadow Budget was a key reason why she was elected into opposition in 1992, rather than into government.

On returning to the back benches, Angela put into action her view that there needed to be some challenge to the prevalent thinking. She had already successfully campaigned to get proposals for an Equality Act accepted by Labour's National Policy Forum; she took a seat on the Treasury select committee and she was elected top of the ballot onto Labour's parliamentary committee, representing backbenchers directly to the party leadership.

In 2007, Gordon Brown appointed her to her favourite ministerial role as the Exchequer Secretary. In the run-up to the 2010 election, she returned to the Work and Pensions Department with a role as Minister for Pensions and Ageing. While this played to her strengths of intellectual rigour and technical proficiency, she saw the Treasury as the 'place to be'. She is completely candid that the role she would really have relished is Chancellor, and she argues, with justification, that she would have been a better minister higher up in government being strategic, political and totally loyal to the Labour Party.

Between 2010 and 2015, Angela served as shadow Chief Secretary to the Treasury and then as shadow Leader of the House. The election of Jeremy Corbyn as leader following Labour's defeat in 2015 brought very mixed fortunes for her. There was dismay and concern about Jeremy Corbyn's first shadow Cabinet. There were no women in the most senior positions and late in the evening of the reshuffle, to see off the brewing row, Angela became shadow First Secretary of State alongside the Business, Innovation and Skills portfolio.

She explains the difficulties of working in the Corbyn team: 'When you're in the shadow Cabinet, there's only so much you can do if they won't work with you. I had the second most-important economic role, but although there were weekly meetings scheduled with John McDonnell, shadow Chancellor, all but one was cancelled.'

Angela's anger at the direction in which Jeremy Corbyn was leading the Labour Party crystallised around the EU referendum in 2016, where she felt that the Labour leadership undermined the Remain campaign.

Furthermore, she was shocked to arrive the day after the referendum to find out that Jeremy Corbyn had called for the immediate triggering of Article 50 without having consulted her, even though she was the most senior woman in the shadow Cabinet. At a later shadow Cabinet meeting that day, she describes those around Jeremy Corbyn as 'grinning all over their faces'.

These experiences, and her view that Jeremy Corbyn was leading the Labour Party she'd devoted her life to 'into oblivion', led to her decision to stand for the Labour leadership. She was subsequently forced to stand down to 'make way' for Owen Smith as a sole challenger. Many of us felt angry that she was effectively forced out of the election, given that she had the necessary nominations. She is magnanimous and, once again, displays no personal bitterness, despite recognising that others chose Owen for personal calculation rather than strategic political benefit.

Her decision to publicly challenge the Labour leadership was not without considerable personal cost. She faced attacks on her constituency office and personal vitriol. Her strength comes from intellectual confidence, but also from a stable and happy home life. Coming out as gay while an MP was a liberating thing for her and a positive influence for others. Having been active in politics during the years of Section 28 and what she calls the political weaponising of the debate, she had some trepidation. Her only example had been Maureen Colquhoun, who had faced deselection and subsequently lost her seat.

She told Chris Smith, Labour's first openly gay MP, over dinner. She jokes that the dinner took a long time to organise due to his diary as a serving Cabinet minister. It then took her until dessert to raise it and he was surprised to hear her news. John Prescott, however, said in his blunt style, 'Tell me something I didn't know, love.' All were supportive and following Labour's civil partnership legislation, she married Maria Exall in 2008.

Having built a big majority in her constituency and with a continuing passion for politics and thirst for intellectual stimulation, it is difficult to imagine Angela stepping back from political life. She has recently published a book, *The New Serfdom*, arguing for a new approach to building a competitive and productive economy alongside a fulfilled and happy citizenry. Angela feels strongly that there has been a disconnect between policy thinking and practical application. With her experience, intellect and constituency focus, she is well qualified to help overcome this gap. Let's hope that there is still time for her to put this into action in high public office.

DAME CHERYL GILLAN

SARAH NEWTON

- FULL NAME: Dame Cheryl Elise Kendall Gillan DBE
- DATE OF BIRTH: 21 April 1952
- PLACE OF BIRTH: Cardiff
- DATE OF DEATH: –
- MARRIED TO: John Coates 'Jack' Leeming
- CHILDREN: Two stepsons
- UNSUCCESSFUL ELECTIONS FOUGHT: None
- CONSTITUENCY: Chesham & Amersham
- DATE OF FIRST ELECTION: 9 April 1992
- DATE LEFT PARLIAMENT: Incumbent
- PARTY ROLES: Board member of the Conservative Party
- MINISTERIAL POSITIONS & DATES: Parliamentary Under-Secretary for Education and Employment 1995–97; shadow Minister for Trade and Industry 1997–98; shadow Minister for International Development 1998–2001; shadow Minister for Foreign and Commonwealth Affairs 1998–2001; opposition whip 2001–03; shadow Minister of State for the Home Office; shadow Secretary of State for Wales 2005–10; Secretary of State for Wales 2010–12

The Rt Hon. Dame Cheryl Gillan, MP for Chesham and Amersham for more than twenty-five years, is arguably the first female Conservative Foreign Secretary that Britain never had.

From the moment she made her witty and self-confident maiden speech on climate change in 1992, it was clear that Gillan was destined to play a prominent role on the front benches. She became a member of the NATO parliamentary assembly and was shadow Foreign and Commonwealth Minister from 1998 to 2001; represented the British Islands and the Mediterranean on the executive committee of the Commonwealth Parliamentary Association from 2000 until 2003 (later becoming its first female elected treasurer); and has consistently displayed a keen interest in Britain's role in the world.

Timing is everything, however, and despite her valuable knowledge and experience in foreign policy, William Hague was the obvious front runner for King Charles Street when David Cameron formed a new Conservative and Liberal Democrat coalition government in 2010.

That said, Gillan's many achievements in a long and varied career make her one of the most impressive and energetic female parliamentarians of her generation.

She was well prepared for life in a male-dominated House of Commons thanks to a happy childhood (something she herself feels gave her resilience), an early interest in politics and an impressive business CV. She was born in Wales where her mother was a Wren and her father served as an army officer in the Royal Engineers, and subsequently as a director of a steel company. The family moved to Norfolk when Cheryl was eleven, and she attended Cheltenham Ladies' College and then the College (now University) of Law. Cheltenham Ladies' College had – and still has – a reputation for preparing girls for leadership roles and they must be proud that Cheryl was the first of their alumna to make it into the Cabinet (though she would not be the last).

Gillan joined the Young Conservatives aged fifteen, attending regular meetings in the Plough Inn at Hathersage, Derbyshire, before transferring to Kensington & Chelsea YC as her career took her to London. While she enjoyed the social side of membership, she preferred the YC's political debates; she joined the Bow Group and was elected the second only woman chair in 1987. In those days the Bow Group met at the (men-only) Carlton Club, so Gillan's appointment caused some consternation. It was ultimately decided that the Bow Group could continue to meet at the club – providing the new chair arrived via the back stairs. Even now, this grand old London club can find no room to display portraits of our two female Prime Ministers alongside those of the male Tory politicians that adorn its walls.

Before parliamentary politics came to dominate her life Gillan had enjoyed a varied business career. She joined the International Management Group in 1977 and became a director with the British Film Year in 1984, was appointed senior marketing consultant at Ernst & Young in 1986, and became marketing director of the accounting firm Kidsons Impey from 1991 to 1993. She became a Freeman of the City of London in 1991 and remains a member of the Livery of the Worshipful Company of Marketors and President of the Debating Society, an institution supported by the marketing and advertising professions.

The final preparation for a successful life, of course, is to find a good partner and it was during her time at the British Film Year that she met her husband of thirty years Jack Leeming. She jokes that she turned down the Egyptian actor Omar Sharif for Jack.

In her first election campaign in 1989 Gillan fought – but lost – the Greater Manchester Central seat for the European Parliament. Over the next few years she applied for various Westminster seats and was finally selected to contest the Buckinghamshire constituency of Chesham and Amersham at the 1992 general election. She won with a majority of 22,220 and has remained the local MP ever since, achieving a remarkably consistent share of the vote.

Gillan quickly made her mark as a politician who was friendly, approachable and genuinely interested in people. She has friends across the political divide in both Chambers of the Palace of Westminster. Labour peer David Puttnam, for example, with whom she worked closely at the British Film Year, was the first person to take her to lunch to congratulate her on becoming an MP. A formidable opponent in debate, Gillan's natural political style is to find common ground and build a consensus for change.

Cheryl was an active committee member in her early years in Parliament, serving on select committees. Her first real taste of government came in 1994 when she was appointed parliamentary private secretary to the leader of the House of Lords and Lord Privy Seal, Viscount Cranborne. In July 1995 she became a Parliamentary Under-Secretary of State in the Department for Education and Employment, a role she used to expand the specialist schools programme to include arts and sports colleges. She considers this to be one of her proudest achievements in politics.

With the Conservatives in opposition after the 1997 general election, Gillan became a shadow minister for Trade and Industry as well as for Education (there were so few experienced Conservative MPs that several held more than one shadow post). In June 1998 she became shadow minister for Foreign and Commonwealth Affairs and International Development, and then served in the Whips' Office from 2001 to 2003. Further opportunity beckoned in December 2003 when she was appointed shadow minister for Home, Constitutional and Legal Affairs.

In December 2005 she joined the shadow Cabinet as the shadow Secretary of State for Wales. Gillan had initially opposed the creation of the National Assembly for Wales, arguing that there had not been a large enough majority in favour of it in the devolution referendum of 1997. But as shadow Welsh

Secretary Gillan accepted the settlement, and indicated that the Conservatives might in future support the devolution of further powers. She nevertheless acknowledged that the party was divided on the issue and criticised devolution in Wales as being 'complex and cumbersome'.

Time spent in the Whips' Office, and in a variety of shadow or actual ministerial roles, is traditionally the route to advancement. So it was no surprise when David Cameron chose Cheryl to become the first female Secretary of State for Wales in 2010, and made it a full Cabinet position. That year she was also appointed as a Privy Counsellor.

Notwithstanding her Welsh roots, being Welsh Secretary when MP for a non-Welsh constituency is always challenging and she faced constant agitation from all sides. But her shadow in the Labour Party and Carwyn Jones, the First Minister of Wales, both said they got on well with her in private, despite the public spats, and they respected her achievements in government.

Perhaps Gillan's most significant achievements were holding a referendum on further powers for the Assembly, and securing the government's commitment to electrify the Valley Lines rail network as well as the rail line from London to Swansea.

New rail infrastructure has also been a theme of her work in Chesham and Amersham, as the proposed route for the High Speed 2 rail line runs through her constituency. In a parliamentary debate before the 2010 election, she agreed with neighbouring MP David Lidington who described the planned route as an 'outrage'. During the campaign Gillan said High Speed 2 would be 'a lot more than just the blight on the properties nearby ... the implications for the area will be absolutely phenomenal'. She branded it a project that would 'threaten the quality of our lives – not just now but for generations to come', adding that she 'would defy the party whip – be very, very sure of that'.

Justine Greening, Secretary of State for Transport, confirmed in January 2012 that High Speed 2 would go ahead. While Gillan helped secure significant changes to the original route of Phase One with two tunnel extensions, she remains opposed to Phase Two (covering the West Midlands to Crewe).

In a Cabinet reshuffle in September 2012 Cheryl was replaced as Welsh Secretary by the Parliamentary Under-Secretary of State in the Wales Office, David Jones. Since then her wider interests in foreign and domestic politics have come to the fore, with roles including UK representative to the Council of Europe.

Gillan is now the longest serving female Conservative MP in the House, and has been as energetic on the back benches as she was in government.

She achieved something that few parliamentarians ever do when her Private Members' Bill became the Autism Act 2009, and she remains chair of the All-Party Parliamentary Group on Autism. She also finds time to chair the APPG on Electric Cars and Autonomous Vehicles and to be vice-chair of the APPG on Ancient Woodland; Environment; Trade and Investment; Gardening and Horticulture; Epilepsy; Dermatology; and Timber. She not only sings in the Parliament Choir but has been a trustee and treasurer of it since 2012.

She is still active in the Conservative Party at the highest levels, serving on the board of the party as well as being vice-chair of the 1922 Committee of Conservative backbench MPs.

Cheryl is a reminder of the importance for our democracy of having long-serving MPs to perpetuate Westminster's 'corporate memory', and to mentor the new intake. Her own baptism in the Commons should put our current challenges into perspective. In the early 1990s she was catapulted into frequent and acrimonious late-night debates on the Maastricht Treaty, each debate described as a one, two or three bacon sandwich affair depending on its likely duration. Notwithstanding some ferocious disagreements she recalls the camaraderie on all sides with affection.

Her current concern is the lack of engagement many constituents have with the democratic process. When she was first elected, Gillan says, public meetings were a popular way for discussing and debating issues. Now constituents take a cursory look at a campaign email before pressing the 'send' button on their computer keyboard, or quickly tick and sign a prepaid campaign post card. With fake news polarising opinion and promoting populism over active participation in representative democracy, this passionate and committed Conservative politician is well aware that her work is not yet done.

GLENDA JACKSON

TULIP SIDDIQ

- FULL NAME: Glenda May Jackson CBE
- DATE OF BIRTH: 9 May 1936
- PLACE OF BIRTH: Birkenhead, Cheshire
- DATE OF DEATH: –
- MARRIED TO: Roy Hodges (m. 1958; div. 1976)
- CHILDREN: Daniel Pearce Jackson Hodges
- UNSUCCESSFUL ELECTIONS FOUGHT: None
- CONSTITUENCY: Hampstead & Highgate and Hampstead & Kilburn
- DATE OF FIRST ELECTION: 9 April 1992
- DATE LEFT PARLIAMENT: 6 May 2015
- PARTY ROLES: None
- MINISTERIAL POSITIONS & DATES: Shadow spokesperson for Transport 1996–97 and Parliamentary Under-Secretary of State for Environment 1997–99
- MOST FAMOUS QUOTATION: 'If I'm too strong for some people that's their problem.'

Everyone on my street and the surrounding area knew our local MP Glenda Jackson. People differed in their opinions of her and whether she was an effective local MP, but the one thing no one ever said was, 'Who is Glenda Jackson?'

Not only had Glenda won a seat that had been blue for twenty-two years, she had won the seat in 1992 against all odds. And, of course, she was the only politician in the world who had won two Oscars.

I don't think there's any point in describing Glenda as a friendly, affectionate, warm personality. She was curt, she was blunt and she wasn't one for hugs – or any physical contact at all for that matter. But she had no pretensions.

My younger, more innocent, self was also shocked at the amount Glenda swore. The topic of our conversation turned to education and she reminisced about when she took and passed the 11-plus, punctuated with expletives at every corner. She was not a supporter of the grammar school system.

It was the start of a theme that spanned my experience with Glenda. She had nothing but contempt for labels or formal recognition; indeed, I've been told she's the only actress not to turn up to accept either of her two Oscars.

I had often wondered why Glenda became a socialist. She said it had everything to do with the working-class environment in which she grew up. But as we spoke more, this felt like only half the story, for books had dominated Glenda's childhood.

Glenda's eyes lit up when she described how she read constantly and was a regular fixture at her public library. She adopted a more textbook tone when talking about the day-to-day improvements that were brought into her life by the election of a Labour government in 1945. Even talking to her in 2018, it still felt like Glenda hadn't recovered from the incredulity of having the NHS and a professional doctor. Until the Labour government, she laughingly said, she just went to her 'grans, ma, aunties and people' to be treated if ill.

It was clear that Glenda had never followed the so-called traditional route into Parliament. She was unacquainted with any MPs when she first visited Parliament in the early 1990s with a group of people from the Arts World for a meeting in the House of Lords about funding for the arts. In Glenda's words, 'God, it was obviously a Conservative government and they were all very parsimonious. I suddenly felt so ashamed that I had never set foot in the Houses of Parliament before. I needed to do something.'

Even then, Glenda didn't immediately decide to put herself forward as a candidate and stand as an MP. She describes the moment she got asked to stand as an MP: 'Oh, that lovely old lady … Well, she rang me out of the blue and asked me to stand.' Although she refused to acknowledge it, she was popular on the campaign trail and appeared on programmes like *Any Questions?* as what she described as the 'token lefty woman'.

Glenda also differs from almost every British politician in her apathy to her constituency, Hampstead & Highgate (and later Hampstead & Kilburn). When I tried to emphasise the fact that she had lived in Hampstead in her early married life, she was quite blunt, rubbishing any geographical loyalty she might have had to the constituency. She repeated, 'I didn't really have any territorial association, I just couldn't bloody stand Margaret Thatcher!'

Yet, she still won five elections and was the MP for twenty-three years in a seat which she never moved to. My constituents still grumble and complain that Glenda never moved to the area and compliment me on the fact that I live here. But did that stop them voting for her? I guess it didn't.

Another defiance of the image of a conventional politician was Glenda's unwillingness to engage with the press. She rolled her eyes when I mentioned the media. She discussed the local newspaper and said, 'the *Ham and High* were wanting me to fall flat on my face. Everything that you did, they were waiting for you to absolutely blow it. I mean they long for people to shout and scream at you.'

I remember once asking her about her contacts in the press lobby in Westminster and she practically laughed in my face – her time was better spent elsewhere.

When I asked Glenda what she was most proud to have achieved, she launched into a long monologue about two of her constituents. One had been mistreated in prison and another had been abducted. She said that twice in her life, constituents had come up to her and said, 'You saved my life.' As she recounted those instances of having saved someone's life, it felt like she treasures those cases more than any Cabinet committee meeting she attended or any legislation she was involved in passing.

Glenda never felt the need to behave like a typical MP. When she talked about her first day in Parliament, she said sneeringly that in 1992, all political parties produced a handbook for all new MPs, which she characterised as 'utterly useless'. But I don't think she would have used it even if it had been useful.

Although she conceded she had shared an office with six other MPs, including Tessa Jowell, she wouldn't be drawn on whether she got on with any of them. Gently mocking Tessa's famous commitment to her constituents, Glenda recounted, 'She used to visit the elderly people's homes on Christmas Day! I was never near my constituents on Christmas Day; I was in bed on Christmas Day!'

Despite this, whenever I visit an old people's home in my constituency, I face the inevitable sigh of admiration from the residents while they express their love for the beautiful Glenda, or rather, the role she played as Queen Elizabeth. One old people's home in West Hampstead still has a photo up of Glenda smiling like a movie star in their entrance.

As Glenda talked about life in Parliament, there was no wistful air of bygone glories. Was it because Glenda was one of the few MPs who was better known for what she achieved before becoming an MP? Or was it simply because Glenda isn't a wistful, nostalgic person?

Glenda was made a minister for the first two years of Tony Blair's government. However, she generally claimed to have had little contact with the Labour leadership. She spoke regretfully about the moment she found out that John Smith had died overnight, but generally Glenda felt that her interactions with most of the leaders had been few and far between.

Glenda's views of Jeremy Corbyn were trenchant. While they worked together on some constituency issues, her own summary of his current role as leader of the party needs no paraphrasing,

> He was absolutely marvellous if ... there was something to do with trade unions, and the legal background to workers' rights. He always knew who I needed to talk to, and for local constituency things – he always had time for you. But he's got no more ability to lead a bloody party than to fly to the moon!

Even after knowing Glenda for twenty years as my local MP and even while interviewing her, there is a sense that no one has any insight into her soul. However, I felt confident that Glenda had been in politics for the right reasons. Her passionate arguments against the Iraq War were commendably persuasive – she explained that it was hard to vote against your party, let alone your government, but that it had been the right move for her. Despite spending a lifetime learning to play other people on stage, she was never Tony Blair's ventriloquist dummy. She was threatened with deselection if she didn't stop criticising the government, to which she replied, 'Good, I'd like to see them try.'

The famously divisive politician Enoch Powell said all political lives end in failure. Yet again, he was wrong. If you're Glenda Jackson, your political life comes to an end but a starring role as the first female King Lear in the history of London theatre beckons.

HELEN JACKSON

ANGELA SMITH

- FULL NAME: Helen Margaret Jackson (née Price)
- DATE OF BIRTH: 19 May 1939
- PLACE OF BIRTH: Leeds
- DATE OF DEATH: –
- MARRIED TO: Keith Jackson (m. 1960; div. 1998)
- CHILDREN: Two boys and a girl
- UNSUCCESSFUL ELECTIONS FOUGHT: None
- CONSTITUENCY: Sheffield Hillsborough
- DATE OF FIRST ELECTION: 10 April 1992
- DATE LEFT PARLIAMENT: 11 April 2005
- PARTY ROLES: Member of the Labour NEC 1999–2005
- MINISTERIAL POSITIONS & DATES: Parliamentary private secretary to Mo Mowlam and Peter Mandelson 1997–2001
- MOST FAMOUS QUOTATION: 'The very deep religious and cultural differences there meant that the Equality Commission for Northern Ireland played a crucial role in the Good Friday agreement' – Second reading of the Equality Bill, 5 April 2005.

Helen Jackson was one of those Members of Parliament who was always ahead of her time. Whether she was campaigning to transform the shooting gallery in the Commons into a crèche or standing up for the principle of family-friendly hours, there was always a sense that Jackson was at the forefront of changes we now take for granted.

It was the stand on family-friendly hours that led to her resignation from the Commons in 2005. Irate at the decision of the House to revert to longer hours for two days a week, she shocked everybody by announcing her retirement from politics. Her constituency party paid the best tribute possible to Jackson's record by insisting her successor should be a woman. It was with some sense of ironic pride, therefore, that I voted in 2012 to reinstate those reforms of sitting hours that meant so much to my predecessor.

Helen Jackson was elected to Parliament in April 1992. She succeeded Martin Flannery to Sheffield Hillsborough, a seat that she knew well from living in the area and having spent a long period previous to this serving as a councillor on Sheffield City Council. I hesitate to use the term 'apprenticeship' to describe this phase in Jackson's political career; it denigrates the role, and in particular it overlooks the heady and intensely dramatic nature of the politics of that period.

Sheffield, a city hit hard by a traumatic and short-sighted rationalisation of the steel industry, lost somewhere in the region of 50,000 steel jobs in the early to mid-1980s. Under the leadership of David Blunkett and subsequently Clive Betts, the Labour Group on the council set about responding to the new economic realities. Jackson, never one to avoid a challenge, made a significant contribution to the task. The Department of Employment and Economic Development (DEED), the first such department in local government in the UK, was the consequence. It was a body that played a key part in shaping the city's response to the challenges it faced.

Politics in Sheffield, exciting and vibrant, must have equipped Jackson well for her role at Westminster, where she continued to support unfashionable causes. She championed the rights of consumers by instigating an inquiry into what was perceived to be poor-quality service from her local water company, and she worked on international development, with a focus on Africa. Strategically, she immersed herself in the work of tackling the inequities related to women's pensions. It's thanks to women like Jackson that my generation can look forward to a more secure right to a full state pension. Her work on this was recognised when she was honoured by the Queen with a CBE in 2010.

She will, perhaps, be mainly remembered as the woman who stood with Mo Mowlam and supported her, as a parliamentary private secretary, during Mowlam's time as Northern Ireland Secretary. To this day, the Good Friday Agreement stands as one of the most important legacies of that first Blair government. Jackson took the role in her stride, and we know that Mowlam appreciated her support and her contributions.

Teaching was Jackson's profession and she retains to this day a strong interest in education in her home city. She also remains engaged with the issues that underpinned her local work as an MP; public transport to the rural far north of Sheffield remains imperfect to put it mildly, and Jackson is always there, ready to make the case for bus services in our villages.

What is probably little known outside of Sheffield is Jackson's intense interest in local history. Her village is blessed with activist groups, always campaigning to preserve and extend the knowledge of important local buildings and institutions, and she immerses herself in this work. And of course she remains an active rambler, something which really marks her out as a true Sheffielder.

Nothing typifies the generosity or thoughtfulness of Jackson more than the way she maintains her relationships with the people she has known for years. She continues to retain an interest not just in the area in which she lives, but also its people, her friends and of course her family. It's that warmth that endears everyone to this remarkable woman.

I conclude with this final thought. In 2005, when I won the privileged right to stand as Helen Jackson's successor in the general election, I celebrated with a meal at a local restaurant. The owners were effusive in their welcome. They were originally refugees from Pinochet's regime in Chile and Jackson, they told me, opened her doors and gave a home to as many Chileans as she possibly could. That's Helen Jackson – someone who puts other people before herself and who has never forgotten what it means to have a heart.

LYNNE JONES

CAROLINE LUCAS

- FULL NAME: Dr Lynne Mary Jones
- DATE OF BIRTH: 26 April 1951
- PLACE OF BIRTH: Birmingham
- DATE OF DEATH: —
- MARRIED TO: Christopher Kirk
- CHILDREN: Tom and Jack
- UNSUCCESSFUL ELECTIONS FOUGHT: None
- CONSTITUENCY: Birmingham Selly Oak
- DATE OF FIRST ELECTION: 10 April 1992
- DATE LEFT PARLIAMENT: 12 April 2010
- PARTY ROLES: None
- MINISTERIAL POSITIONS & DATES: None

Lynne Jones was a tenacious MP who started her political career fighting for decent homes, and left Parliament after opposing the rightward drift of the Labour Party under Tony Blair and Gordon Brown. She was fired by anger from a young age after growing up poor and witnessing her dad's struggle with schizophrenia. Her own understanding of injustice deepened after reading Trevor Huddleston's *Naught For Your Comfort*, which details the appalling situation in apartheid South Africa.

Jones never wanted to be an MP, and had the unusual dream in the 1980s of becoming the chair of Birmingham City Council's Housing committee. She succeeded when Labour took control of the council in 1984. Sadly for Jones, and typically for the time, she was on the sharp end of a culture of sexism in her own group on the council; she recalls that they tried to get rid of her and others from positions of power after 'women were given too prominent a role'. From that moment on, Jones considered herself a feminist.

Jones was persuaded to become an MP by people in her local party, and only just won the selection, beating MEP Christine Crawley by 0.01 per cent of the vote. Jones had a doctorate in biochemistry, and certainly had a scientific brain too, but she had by this time realised that her passion was politics. After winning the marginal Tory seat of Birmingham Selly Oak in 1992, she quit her job as a housing association manager and went on to sit in the House of Commons until 2010.

Her scientific brain came in handy, and her own convictions overrode her party loyalties because Jones's ultimate priority was seeking the truth. Indeed, her commitment to voting the right way, 'according to the facts rather than the party line', meant that the whips quickly gave up on her and, as she recalls, 'didn't really bother trying to bully me because I just would not be bullied'.

Her rebellions started early. In 1997, in opposition to cuts in benefits to lone parents pushed through by Harriet Harman, Jones and Audrey Wise led the first major rebellion against the Blair government. In her autobiography, Harman recalls the incident with great regret. Jones's feminism was always rooted in the everyday lived experiences of working people – meaning she was motivated far more by changes to social security and wages than she was by 'family-friendly hours' in Parliament and the like.

By 2003, along with many dissenters in the party no doubt, Jones was beginning to tire of hitting her head against the brick wall of New Labour's machine. Iraq, however, changed everything – it gave backbench Labour MPs a crucial role in trying to hold their leaders to account for what would prove to be the biggest foreign policy mistake of a generation. Jones opposed the invasion and – alongside MPs such as Robin Cook, Jeremy Corbyn and John McDonnell – she made it her role to 'ask the awkward questions', to which there were no decent answers. In 2005, the website Public Whip credited her persistent written questions in the run-up to the Iraq war as one of the major motivations for getting their software written.

Jones was an early pioneer of trans rights, taking up the case of a constituent who was worried that they could be sacked for being transgender. She pushed for changes which allowed trans people to legally stay with their original partners – and was a tireless advocate for a community which few others would champion.

When I spoke to Lynne Jones, asking for her own assessment of her greatest achievement, she was typically humble, saying that 'all political careers end in failure, and I'm just a footnote'. But I don't believe that this is an accurate description of Jones – indeed such a view is symptomatic of a political culture in which women tend to underplay their achievements.

The truth is that Jones's forensic role in the anti-war movement in Parliament, her pioneering work on trans rights and her clear-sighted warnings on private finance initiatives, housing and NHS privatisation had a deeply meaningful impact. Not only are MPs less blind to the perils of following party leaders into war, but the Labour Party is now led by the righteous rebels whom Lynne Jones worked alongside for over a decade. Towards the end of her time in Parliament, Jones stated that her number one policy priority was climate change. That is where the science took her.

What makes Jones stand out is that she was neither scared of saying something unpopular, nor afraid of being cracked down on by the party machinery. She was hard-working and focused on doing what was right. Indeed, when I asked her what advice she would give rebels in Parliament today she said, 'I never wanted to be a rebel; I looked for reasons not to rebel. Just look at the facts – that's it.'

TESSA JOWELL

HELEN HAYES

- FULL NAME: Dame Tessa Jane Helen Douglas Jowell (née Palmer) DBE
- DATE OF BIRTH: 17 September 1947
- PLACE OF BIRTH: Marylebone, London
- DATE OF DEATH: 12 May 2018
- MARRIED TO: Roger Jowell (m. 1970; div. 1977); David Mills (m. 1979)
- CHILDREN: Jessica Mills Vine and Matthew Mills; step-children: Eleanor Mills Lock, Luke Mills and Annie Pesskin
- UNSUCCESSFUL ELECTIONS FOUGHT: Ilford North 1978 (by-election) and Ilford North 1979
- CONSTITUENCY: Dulwich 1992–97 and Dulwich & West Norwood 1997–2015
- DATE OF FIRST ELECTION: 9 April 1992
- DATE LEFT PARLIAMENT: 30 March 2015
- PARTY ROLES: Campaign chair, London Labour Mayoral campaign 2012
- MINISTERIAL POSITIONS & DATES: Shadow Minister for Women 1995–96; Parliamentary Under-Secretary of State for Health 1997–99; Parliamentary Under-Secretary of State for Education and Employment 1999–2001; Secretary of State for Culture, Media and Sport 2001–07; Minister for Women 2005–06; Minister for the Olympics 2005–10; Paymaster General 2007–10; Minister for London 2009–10; shadow Minister for the Olympics 2010–12; Minister for the Cabinet Office 2009–10; shadow Minister for London 2010–13; shadow Minister for the Cabinet Office 2010 and 2011
- MOST FAMOUS QUOTATION: 'In the end, what gives a life meaning is not only how it is lived, but how it draws to a close. I hope that this debate will give hope to other cancer patients like me, so that we can live well together with cancer – not just dying of it – all of us, for longer.' – 25 January 2018, House of Lords.

Tessa Jowell was the Member of Parliament for Dulwich from 1992 to 1997 and for Dulwich & West Norwood from 1997 until 2015. She will be remembered as a courageous, effective politician but also as one who listened and was always ready with a kind word or deed to make people feel better and valued.

Jowell was born in London in 1947, to Kenneth Palmer, a doctor, and Rosemary, a radiographer. She was educated at St Margaret's School for Girls in Aberdeen and at the University of Aberdeen, where she studied arts, psychology and sociology; and at the University of Edinburgh where she received an MA in Social Administration.

Jowell became a social worker, initially in Edinburgh and later in Lambeth. A former colleague in Lambeth said of that time, 'We had such a sense of purpose and commitment to the families we were working with – Tessa was always bustling, determined to make a difference.' Later, she trained as a psychiatric social worker at Goldsmiths College and worked as a family therapist at the Maudsley Hospital – which she would later represent in Parliament.

In 1971, when Tessa was twenty-four, the Labour Party in Camden was struggling to find candidates to stand in 'unwinnable' council wards. Jowell agreed to stand, strictly on the basis that there was no possibility of being elected, but she then took six weeks off work and won the election. She served on Camden Council for sixteen years until 1987, during one of the most turbulent times in the borough's political history. As chair of the Social Services committee, Jowell saw the urgency of the need for the council to set a legal budget despite the Thatcher government's devastating cuts, and she recalled a council meeting during which protestors threw frozen chicken livers and balls of paper with stones concealed in them. Jowell served on Camden Council alongside Roger Jowell, to whom she was married from 1970 to 1977, and David Mills, whom she married in 1979 and with whom she had two children, Jessica and Matthew.

It was in these early roles that the themes were established which would characterise Jowell's politics throughout her career – intervening early to help babies and children born into poverty; working with young mothers in Lambeth empowering women to provide a better future for themselves and their children; creating spaces and places to bring people together; and always looking for the practical difference that could be made.

At Camden, Jowell was involved in setting up the first ever children's centre – where young mothers could come together to be supported as parents and to learn skills to get a job. She said of that time, and of working as a social worker in Lambeth, 'we were focused on babies and how we could alter their future'. At the Maudsley Hospital, she spoke about working with psychiatrist Douglas Bennett to set up a community day centre, explaining that

> we worked with people whose lives were tiny fragments of what they might become and saw their days become better. We spent Friday evenings with patients at the day centre, not as work, but because we wanted to be there. It was a different way of working with people who might otherwise be locked up.

Jowell was chosen as Labour's candidate in the Ilford North parliamentary by-election in 1978. The contest was triggered by the death of Millie Miller MP in 1977. Ilford North was regained by the Conservative candidate Vivian Bendall, who increased her majority a year later at the 1979 general election in a landslide for the Conservatives led by Margaret Thatcher, when Jowell stood unsuccessfully for a second time.

In 1990, Dulwich Constituency Labour Party embarked on the selection of its candidate for the following general election. The seat had been held by Conservative MP Gerald Bowden since 1983 but he had only a slim majority of 180. Local party members who took part in that selection recall that Barbara Follett was the clear favourite to win the nomination, but Jowell delivered an exceptional speech at the meeting and won over members in the room.

Jowell's campaign in Dulwich for the 1992 general election centred on the state of the NHS locally, with a particular focus on the crisis situation at King's College Hospital in the constituency. Patients were facing very long waits in the A&E department.

Jowell won the 1992 election with a majority of just over 2,000 votes – the seat had been number two on Labour's list of target seats, and it was a welcome win for Labour on an election night that was otherwise bitterly disappointing. Upon her election, Jowell ran a campaign called 'Casualty Watch'. She would visit the A&E department at all times of the day and night and count the number of patients waiting on trolleys. This information was used to lobby the then Secretary of State for Health, Virginia Bottomley, relentlessly, and made a key contribution to turning around King's and eventually other hospitals in London.

Jowell's maiden speech in the House of Commons focused on social care, revealing the compassionate and empathetic approach which would come to characterise her politics:

The delivery of health and community care should be measured against a simple question: hon. Members, as they take decisions about the care of vulnerable elderly people, should ask themselves whether what they are deciding is what they would want for themselves or for their families. If the answer is that it is not, the policy is unacceptable. That simple test should set our standards for the judgment of effective community care.

Those who worked closely with Jowell after she was first elected, including the current Mayor of Greater Manchester, Andy Burnham, who worked for her from 1993 until 1997, describe Jowell as the hardest-working person that they had ever come across, with an exceptional interest in people. Burnham says, 'She campaigned in a human way, telling stories and not just trading statistics – no one had ever seen that style of campaigning before.' Burnham also describes a real attention to detail, 'every single letter was the one that might lose the election'. Jowell quickly became known as a campaigning MP, engaging in depth with the local community she represented on issues that really mattered to people.

A key challenge came in 1993, when the Boundary Commission announced plans to abolish the Dulwich constituency. Jowell again sought to engage the local community in order to fight to retain Bellenden ward within the new constituency. She ran a community-based campaign, going door to door and engaging local amenity societies. Contrary to all expectations, the Boundary Commission made unprecedented 'further modified recommendations' after a second round of consultation – the campaign was a success. Burnham says, 'The community rallied for Tessa because of the hours she had put in.' At the time, Jowell's children, Jessica and Matthew, were still very young, and the family home remained in north London. Former colleagues describe how she would sometimes work through the night in order to free up time to be with her children during the evening, or travel home from Parliament for bedtime, before heading out to an evening meeting in her constituency.

In the run-up to the 1997 general election, the Labour Party had to select a candidate for the newly formed seat of Dulwich & West Norwood. Jowell contested the selection against John Fraser who had been the MP for the Norwood constituency – which was also being abolished by the Boundary Commission – for more than thirty years. Despite John Fraser's huge popularity as a local MP, Jowell was selected. It is testimony to the decency of both Fraser and Jowell that, following the selection, a bitter blow for Fraser, they worked together locally for the benefit of the Labour Party for the next twenty-four years.

Many people in Dulwich & West Norwood recall Jowell with enormous affection, speaking of small unseen acts of kindness and generosity, as well as her public-facing work. Jowell championed an enormous range of community activities, from local advice centres in Brixton and West Norwood, to the Ebony Horse Club in Brixton, and from Dulwich Helpline (later Link Age Southwark) to Brixton Soup Kitchen. Jowell worked collaboratively to empower people who wanted to make a positive difference. She worked to secure the delivery of five new schools in the constituency, including working with local parents to establish the first ever parent-promoted local authority school, The Elmgreen School, and transforming wholesale the quality of secondary education for children in Dulwich & West Norwood. And Jowell continued her campaigning work on the NHS, working to secure much-needed investment in King's College Hospital, and establishing an annual tradition of donating a Christmas tree to the paediatric A&E department.

Following the 1997 election, which saw the Labour Party elected to government with a landslide victory, Jowell was appointed as the first ever Public Health minister in the Department of Health, serving under Frank Dobson, the Secretary of State for Health, and with whom she had previously worked during her first term as a councillor in Camden, when Frank was leader of the Council. At the Department for Health, Jowell continued to progress her passion for early years support, masterminding the development of the flagship Labour policy Sure Start, delivering Sure Start centres across the country which brought together public health, classes for parents and early years education to provide intensive support for families and to address disadvantage early in a child's life. David Blunkett, who was then Secretary of State for Education and Employment, and with whom she later continued to work as a junior Employment minister, was also a key ally in the development of Sure Start, helping to secure the support of the Chancellor of the Exchequer, Gordon Brown. Sure Start became a key plank of a Labour government programme that lifted a million children out of poverty.

In 2001, after Labour's second landslide election victory, Tony Blair appointed Jowell to the Cabinet as Secretary of State for Culture, Media and Sport. In this role she led a review of the BBC's charter which led to the establishment of the BBC Trust, separating the governance and regulation of the BBC from its day-to-day executive functions and increasing transparency.

Jowell also established OFCOM, the first comprehensive regulator for the communications industry, which would later replace the BBC Trust as the regulator of the BBC. She was to become the longest-serving Culture Secretary to date and as Simon Tait of *Arts Industry* magazine points out, it is often overlooked that she presided over 'what, in March 2007, Tony Blair was to declare was "a golden age for the arts" in which cultural funding had been doubled'.

Jowell's compassionate and empathetic approach and her ability to forge connections with people became evident again after sixty-seven British citizens were killed in the Al-Qaeda attacks on the World Trade Center towers in New York in 2001. Tony Blair gave her special responsibility for co-ordinating the response of the government to support the families of the British victims.

More controversially, while at the Department for Culture, Jowell introduced the 2005 Gambling Act which liberalised gambling. The act was intended to enable the development of 'super casinos', which it was hoped would bring jobs and investment to declining industrial cities. In reality, no super casinos emerged, but the Act did lead to a huge expansion in the availability of high street gambling, including fixed-odds betting terminals. She wryly observed during this period that 'I seem to have gone from "the nation's nanny-in-chief" to a "gambling gangster's moll" in a few weeks.' Years later, as a Labour peer, Jowell acknowledged that more regulation of this form of gambling was needed, but also suggested that the gambling commission had not utilised the regulatory powers it had been given effectively enough.

The achievement for which Jowell is most remembered while Secretary of State for Culture, Media and Sport is the London 2012 Olympics. The then Prime Minister, Tony Blair, recalls Jowell visiting 10 Downing Street to try and persuade him that the UK should bid for the 2012 Olympics – Blair was highly sceptical of the idea. Seb Coe, who led the successful Olympic bid, says, 'She went straight to Downing Street and basically said to Tony Blair, "What are you? A man or a mouse?"' This encounter was similarly described by Peter Kyle MP, shortly after Jowell's death, 'That, for me, was Tessa. She had learned to weaponise the male ego, and woe betide any big beast that stood between her and one of her political objectives.' Seb Coe had another memorable view of her combination of warmth and steely determination: 'I call her Mary Poppins with a stiletto.'

There were understandable reasons for Blair's reluctance to bid. The UK did not have a great reputation for delivering large infrastructure projects and there was a history of Olympic parks lacking any useful purpose after the event, becoming derelict sites in need of regeneration. Jowell's vision was for an Olympics that would act as the catalyst for the regeneration of east London, delivering a world-class park and sporting facilities, new homes and jobs; and which would also be an authentic and glorious celebration of London and Londoners in all their diversity.

Jowell used her personal and political skills to convince the Prime Minister and the Cabinet that London should bid, and helped to mastermind the winning submission. She kept the vision for London 2012 – from the delivery of a park which was designed as a public space from the outset, the commissioning of Danny Boyle to direct the spectacular opening ceremony, which celebrated UK culture comprehensively, including the contribution of the Windrush generation to building the NHS, and the unprecedented involvement of volunteers from London's diverse communities in helping to host the Olympics.

As part of the Olympic legacy, Jowell also supported the International Inspiration programme to spread the transformative power of sport to communities across the world. Through this she became a regular volunteer for Magic Bus, working with children in poor communities in India. The founder Matthew Spacie commented, 'I remember on her first trip to India I was immediately struck by her intense concern for almost every child we met and her desire to hear every story. This part of her personality was to define much of our future relationship, her innate desire to understand a situation thoroughly, apply thought and understand where she could add value.' Jowell's ability to work pragmatically across political divides and to win support for the causes she chose to champion ensured that, even after Labour lost power in 2010, she retained her role on the London 2012 Olympic Board to see her vision through.

The day after London won the bid to host the Olympics in 2012, on 7 July 2005, London was struck by the most devastating terrorist attack in its history, as four suicide bombers detonated bombs on three tube trains and a bus during the morning rush hour, killing fifty-two people and injuring more than 700. As she had done after the 9/11 attacks, Jowell played a key role in supporting the families of the victims and those who were injured in the aftermath of the bombings, forging a close relationship with many of them, which became a lasting commitment. Jowell played a key role in establishing a permanent memorial to the victims in Hyde Park, and kept the memory of those who were killed alive by tweeting their names on the anniversary of the attacks each year.

It was also while Jowell was Culture Secretary that the controversial decision was taken to send British forces into armed combat in Iraq. There was significant opposition to the Iraq War in Jowell's Dulwich & West Norwood constituency, but as a member of the Cabinet, she chose to support the decision to go to war in Iraq. It is testament to her style of politics and her commitment always to listen and engage that she invited all her constituents who had written to her to express opposition to the Iraq War to attend a public meeting. By the time the day came, it was the eve of the war. So many people came to the Methodist Church Hall on Half Moon Lane in Dulwich that the meeting had to be held in two sittings. The atmosphere was extremely tense and angry. Jowell did not leave the meeting until everyone who wanted to speak had been able to – she had a steely commitment never to duck difficult issues, and she listened with grace and dignity. The issue certainly dented the Labour Party's relationship with the electorate in Dulwich & West Norwood, felt most keenly in the 2005 general and 2006 local elections, but Jowell's wider record meant that she retained the support of many constituents, despite their opposition to the Iraq War.

Jowell possessed a determined, positive and tenacious approach to her work, which won her support across the political divide. In 2006, scandal threatened to engulf her career as her husband, David Mills, faced corruption charges in Italy. He was initially convicted, but was exonerated on appeal. The extent of Jowell's popularity across the political divide was evident as she took to the despatch box on the Monday after the story broke in the press, on 6 March 2006, as members from across the House rallied in support of her. Conservative MP Mark Lancaster set the tone, saying that it was 'a special pleasure to see her here today'; Labour's Kitty Ussher made reference to her continuing 'to lead her Department into the future' and Conservative Sir Henry Bellingham received a resounding reaction from members when he spoke of when he 'next expects to meet' Jowell. Jowell's subsequent temporary marital separation from David Mills was a source of deep sorrow to her.

Jowell's ability to make connections across the political spectrum meant that, while Conservative colleagues were expressing their support for her in Parliament, she was appointed by the Labour Party to run Ken Livingstone's ultimately unsuccessful campaign to be re-elected as Mayor of London in 2012. Jowell was hugely supportive of other people, and mentored many Labour Party members to become candidates and stand for election, particularly women and BAME members. In the competitive environment of politics, she possessed a strong belief that women should work together to support and build each other up, because if that happened, everyone would benefit. She often said, 'There is enough success for everyone.'

In 2013, Jowell announced that she would stand down from the House of Commons at the 2015 election. In her valedictory speech as an MP in 2015, she spoke of her pride in progress that had been made in her constituency in healthcare and education, remarking that, 'I hope we will never forget the optimism and ambition of the Olympic Games, which, in the words of Abraham Lincoln, showed us the better angels of our nature.' She also noted, however, that, 'I am very sad that Sure Start, which was set up as an early nurturing programme by the government of which I was a member, has been hollowed out.'

On the back of her work as a London MP for twenty-three years, a Cabinet member who delivered the Olympics and her involvement with the aftermath of the 7/7 bombings, Jowell ran for selection to be Labour's candidate for the London mayoral election in 2016. She ran a vigorous campaign which engaged many members and through which she developed many ideas, but she ultimately lost out to Sadiq Khan.

Tessa Jowell entered the House of Lords on 27 October 2015, as Baroness Jowell of Brixton, a title of which she was extremely proud. In her maiden speech in the Lords on 23 May 2016, shortly before the EU referendum, Jowell championed the cause of the UK remaining in the European Union:

> I devoutly hope that we will remain in it as fully engaged partners, but with the self-confidence to continue to negotiate change. So a vote to remain is not a vote for the status quo. Amid the daily salvos from warring economists and the claims and counterclaims of the partisans, it is too easy to forget that the European Union is a union of twenty-eight nations, in a continent that saw the deaths of 70 million from wars in the last century, that have bound themselves together by common commitments to standards of human rights, rights at work, democracy, the rule of law and peaceful coexistence. We should never take that for granted.

Just a year later, in May 2017, Jowell suffered a seizure in a taxi while travelling to east London to speak about Sure Start, and shortly afterwards was diagnosed with a brain tumour. It was no surprise to those who knew Jowell that she would use the remaining months of her life to campaign on behalf of other people with brain tumours for better research, diagnosis and treatment. No surprise, but it was remarkable and immensely brave. In January 2018, she led a debate on cancer treatment in the House of Lords, and after a powerful and moving speech in which she called for better access to innovative treatments, data sharing and patient involvement in the development of new therapies, she received a long, standing ovation. In closing her speech, she said,

> In the end, what gives a life meaning is not only how it is lived, but how it draws to a close. I hope that this debate will give hope to other cancer patients like me, so that we can live well together with cancer – not just dying of it – all of us, for longer.

Jowell passed away from her illness on 12 May 2018. Her legacy nationally is in the transformation of children's lives through Sure Start, the 2012 Olympics and the compassionate and sympathetic way in which she engaged with so many people to work for positive change. She remarked, 'You don't talk about love in government, or in public policy. That has got to change, because so many of the mothers who use Sure Start and most other public services are looking for just that. Love, validation, nurture and support.'

She will now also be remembered for the delivery of a step change in the focus on brain tumour research and treatments. As her husband, David Mills, said after her death, 'She had an extraordinarily successful career in politics. Then somehow after this disease struck she added 25 per cent to it.' In her constituency, Jowell is remembered for her natural empathy, the transformation of the quality of local secondary education, the turnaround of King's College Hospital and the countless community groups she championed and empowered to change things for the better.

JANE KENNEDY

LUCIANA BERGER

- FULL NAME: Jane Kennedy (née Hodgson)
- DATE OF BIRTH: 4 May 1958
- PLACE OF BIRTH: Whitehaven, Cumbria
- DATE OF DEATH: –
- MARRIED TO: Malcolm Kennedy (m. 1977; div. 1998); Peter Dowling (partner)
- CHILDREN: Two sons
- UNSUCCESSFUL ELECTIONS FOUGHT: None
- CONSTITUENCY: Liverpool Broadgreen 1992–97 and Liverpool Wavertree 1997–2010
- DATE OF FIRST ELECTION: 10 April 1992
- DATE LEFT PARLIAMENT: 12 April 2010
- PARTY ROLES: None
- MINISTERIAL POSITIONS & DATES: Opposition whip 1995–97; assistant whip 1997–99; Parliamentary Secretary to the Lord Chancellor's Department 1999–2001; Minister of State, Northern Ireland Office 2001–04; Minister for Work and Pensions 2004–05; Minister for Health 2005–06; Financial Secretary to the Treasury 2007–08; Minister for Environment, Food and Rural Affairs 2008–09

Jane Kennedy learned her politics the hard way – as a trade union representative for the National Union of Public Employees in Liverpool during the 1980s. At the time, the Liverpool Labour Party was controlled by Militant Tendency, a revolutionary organisation which aimed to infiltrate Labour.

Kennedy, by contrast, was a supporter of Neil Kinnock's modernising leadership and a steadfast democratic socialist. As such, she was a target for terrible bullying and abuse from the revolutionary left. In this period, Kennedy developed an iron will, and she lived out the creed of staying true to her own beliefs, despite the prevailing winds blowing in the opposite direction. She also displayed the quiet resilience and no-nonsense approach that would later come to characterise her time as a government minister and elected Police and Crime Commissioner.

An early event in her career brought her steely determination to the fore. Working in Liverpool City Council's social services department, she blew the whistle on the abuse of children on council premises. A children's home was closed, and abusive and negligent staff were removed from their posts. She has never been afraid to speak out, regardless of how it might adversely affect her own career. Kennedy resigned not once, but twice, as a government minister, and under two different Labour Prime Ministers.

In September 1985, she became one of many Liverpool Council workers to be handed a redundancy notice by the Militant-led city council. The mass sacking of council staff was an act of political brinkmanship, designed to demonstrate the effects of Thatcher's cuts to local government budgets. The stunt backfired, and gave Neil Kinnock the perfect anecdote for his conference speech a few days later, in which he lashed out verbally, admonishing Militant and its divisive role within the Labour Party. Kinnock famously railed against 'the grotesque chaos of a Labour council – *a Labour council* – hiring taxis to scuttle around the city handing out redundancy notices to its own workers'. Jane Kennedy was in the conference hall, on her feet applauding, amid the cacophony of cheers, boos, cries of 'liar' and walk-outs.

By helping to defeat the Militant entryists on Merseyside, Kennedy was part of a generation that paved the way for Labour's landslide victory in 1997, and thirteen years of Labour majority government.

After a fiercely fought selection process, Kennedy was chosen to be the Labour candidate in Liverpool Broadgreen at the 1992 general election. She beat not only the sitting MP Terry Fields, who had been expelled from Labour due to his affiliation with Militant and was standing as an independent, but also the Liberal Democrat candidate Rosie Cooper, who later became a Labour MP.

The 34-year-old newly elected Kennedy set about her constituency duties with a quiet determination, running regular surgeries and local campaigns. Five years later, with the old Broadgreen constituency abolished after a boundary review, Kennedy was elected as MP for the newly devised Liverpool Wavertree constituency. Her majority at the 1997 election was almost 20,000. She served as MP until I stepped into her shoes at the 2010 general election.

Tony Blair recognised Kennedy's talents and was aware of her reputation.

As Leader of the Opposition, Blair had placed her in the opposition whips' Office, and after Labour's 1997 landslide he appointed her as a government whip. With a Labour majority of 179 in the House of Commons, securing the government's programme did not present a particularly challenging task. Backbench rebellions were confined to a tiny number who consistently voted with the Tories. As a whip in the first two years of the Labour government, Kennedy saw a whirlwind of legislation through to the statute book, including the ban on handguns, referendums on a Parliament for Scotland and an Assembly for Wales, and the national minimum wage.

In 1999, Blair promoted her again, to the Lord Chancellor's Department under Derry Irvine. For the next six years, through Labour's election successes in 2001 and 2005, Kennedy served as a minister at the Northern Ireland Office, the Department of Work and Pensions and the Department of Health. At Northern Ireland, she guided the early, fragile stages of the Good Friday Agreement and was responsible for the justice system and security. As a minister she was diligent, hard-working and considered a 'safe pair of hands' for tricky ministerial briefs.

In 2006, she resigned as Health minister, without any great drama, because of her disquiet at aspects of the Blair government's health reforms. This perhaps shows her personal politics to be more 'Kinnockite' than 'Blairite', or in other words more 'soft-left' than where New Labour ended up after a decade in office.

During her year on the back benches, Kennedy served as chair of Labour Friends of Israel, visiting Israel and the Palestinian Territories.

After Blair's resignation and Gordon Brown's arrival at No. 10, Kennedy secured a second chance to serve in a Labour government. Brown appointed her to the Treasury, as Financial Secretary, just as the financial crash engulfed the world's economy. After a tumultuous two years, Kennedy resigned from the position in 2009, alongside other ministerial colleagues, in protest against Brown's continuing leadership. She stood down at the 2010 general election.

It is a mark of Jane Kennedy's fortitude and commitment to public service that, in 2012, she was elected as Merseyside's new police and crime commissioner – one of only five women out of forty-one elected to the role. A lesser woman might have favoured a quiet retirement. She was re-elected in 2016. In this role, her experiences of the criminal justice system in Northern Ireland, in the Lord Chancellor's Department, and as an assiduous constituency MP have come together to help deliver her crime and policing plan for the whole of Merseyside.

ANGELA KNIGHT

MAGGIE THROUP

- FULL NAME: Angela Ann Knight (née Cook) CBE
- DATE OF BIRTH: 31 October 1950
- PLACE OF BIRTH: Sheffield
- DATE OF DEATH: –
- MARRIED TO: David Knight (divorced)
- CHILDREN: Alex and Robin
- UNSUCCESSFUL ELECTIONS FOUGHT: None
- CONSTITUENCY: Erewash
- DATE OF FIRST ELECTION: 9 April 1992
- DATE LEFT PARLIAMENT: 1 May 1997
- PARTY ROLES: None
- MINISTERIAL POSITIONS & DATES: Parliamentary private secretary to the Minister for Industry, Sir Tim Sainsbury 1993–94; parliamentary private secretary to the Chancellor, Ken Clarke 1994–95; Economic Secretary to the Treasury 1995–97
- MOST FAMOUS QUOTATION: 'I am who I am – if there is a fight to be had, I'm not going to run away from it.'

Described by many as having enjoyed a meteoric rise during her parliamentary career, it's worth considering whether Labour's landslide of 1997 denied Angela Knight an appointment as the UK's first female Chancellor?

Still a formidable operator, Angela doesn't shy away from controversy. Her decision to read chemistry at university, despite it being seen as a traditionally 'masculine' subject, typifies her approach to her life and politics.

Her first foray into politics saw her join Labour stronghold Sheffield City Council as a Conservative councillor, later becoming chief whip – signalling that she was up for a fight. Elected Member of Parliament for Erewash in 1992, upon the retirement of Conservative Peter Rost, Angela was now a player in national politics. However, with unfavourable boundary changes and the rise of New Labour, she lost her seat in 1997. Erewash remained Labour throughout the Blair and Brown years, but since 2010 has been represented by Conservative MPs. It is interesting to note that the constituency has had a woman at its helm since 1992.

As a parliamentary candidate during the run-up to the 1992 election, Angela was thrust into the limelight – something she had never feared. A BBC2 programme titled 'A Safer Sex for a Safe Seat', which featured Angela, was commissioned. I know of current MPs who recall watching the programme and being inspired by Angela and her approach; her sheer force of character has encouraged others to make the move into Parliament.

Trying to stand out in the House of Commons Chamber can be challenging, but Angela's presence was noted by political commentator Matthew Parris, after he witnessed Norman Lamont, who had recently been sacked from his role as Chancellor, vying for a seat on the green benches. Angela was sat where Lamont wanted to be seated and instead of choosing to sit elsewhere, he endeavoured to squeeze himself onto the bench, on which there was really no space, resulting in him perching precariously on Angela's knee.

Angela was appointed PPS to the Minister for Industry just a year after her election to Parliament; two years later, in 1994, she became PPS to the Chancellor before being named Economic Secretary to the Treasury in 1995. This track record is impressive, yet Angela would have expected nothing less.

Kenneth Clarke makes reference to Angela in his autobiography, *Kind of Blue*. Renowned for his penchant for a glass of whisky during Budget speeches, Clarke explained that he would leave it to his PPS to fix one up. Angela made Ken's whisky very strong, perhaps not adding any water at all – a reflection of her strength of character.

One of Angela's most memorable contributions, during her time as Economic Secretary to the Treasury, is the introduction of the £2 coin – which, upon its launch, polarised public opinion.

Angela's life after Parliament has not been without controversy. Taking on the role of chief executive of the British Bankers' Association in 2007, just as the financial crash was beginning to rear its ugly head, was a bold move. Many people felt that she was defending the indefensible. She then took on the role of chief executive at Energy UK, when energy became the political football during the 2015 general election.

During an interview in 2015, Angela advised those starting out in politics to 'always say yes'; a philosophy that she has clearly adhered to throughout her career and which she has passed on to many other aspiring politicians.

JACQUI LAIT

AMBER DE BOTTON

- FULL NAME: Jacqueline Anne Harkness Lait
- DATE OF BIRTH: 16 December 1947
- PLACE OF BIRTH: Giffnock, Glasgow
- DATE OF DEATH: –
- CHILDREN: None
- MARRIED TO: Peter Jones (m. 1974)
- UNSUCCESSFUL ELECTIONS FOUGHT: Tyne Bridge 1985
- CONSTITUENCY: Hastings & Rye 1992–97 and Beckenham 1997–2010
- DATE OF FIRST ELECTION: 9 April 1992
- DATE LEFT PARLIAMENT: 12 April 2010
- PARTY ROLES: Chair of the European Union of Women 1990–91
- MINISTERIAL POSITIONS & DATES: Shadow Secretary of State
  for Scotland 2001–03 and shadow Business, Skills and Innovation
  minister 2003–09
- MOST FAMOUS QUOTATION: 'The most powerful woman in the world
  has to ask her husband to sign her tax form.' – Lait pointing to Margaret
  Thatcher while campaigning for independent taxation for married women
  at the 1986 Conservative Party conference.

Jacqui Lait was known around Westminster as a 'decent kind of Tory woman', confident on the front benches and loyal through some difficult years for her party.

She is also part of Commons history as the first female Conservative whip. Gyles Brandreth recalls in his Westminster diaries:

The office is run entirely like a gentleman's club (that's part of its charm) and, nominally, potential whips come up for election. The Chief certainly goes through the motions of leading a discussion ... but slips into the chat that the PM rather feels it's time for a woman whip – and he rather agrees – and Jacqui seems 'a decent sort of chap' (ho ho) – and immediately we all murmur our assent.

Lait remembers, 'Sir David Lightbown was the last of the resisters to women. He sadly died and caused a by-election. After that, I was invited to join the Whips' Office. The day I was picked, there was a huge summer storm. We joked it was David's last word.' Lait, however, never felt intimidated. 'Politics is not the business for shrinking violets. My husband jokes that I speak two languages: English and aggressive.'

Lait grew up near Glasgow and attended Strathclyde University, where she studied business management. Her early career included a stint as a public relations executive for the jute industry, a spell at the television news agency Visnews, and roles at the Government Information Service and the Department of Employment. In 1980, she became a parliamentary adviser to the Chemical Industries Association.

A lifelong Tory, she was taken to Parliament aged eight by her godmother, Pat Hornsby-Smith, the Conservative MP for Chislehurst. Lait recalls, 'I remember thinking, "I would really like to work here."' She joined the Conservative Party aged sixteen and 'the whole thing became inevitable, really'.

She married Peter Jones, former leader of East Sussex County Council, in 1974 – between the February and October general elections. He won his county council seat in 1997 on the day she lost at Hastings & Rye.

Her first taste of electoral politics came when she stood in Strathclyde West for the 1985 European elections, and she went on to contest the parliamentary seat of Tyne Bridge, finishing third behind Labour and the SDP.

Victory did not come until seven years later, when she won Hastings & Rye. 'There were three elections in my lifetime when you knew you were going to win, and 1992 was one.'

She was one of just sixty female MPs elected that year. Only twenty of them were Conservatives. It wasn't always easy in the seaside seat. In the early 1990s, fishermen hung her effigy from the mast of a trawler. An ardent pro-European, Lait did not take the hard line against the Common Fisheries Policy that the fishing community demanded she take. She also struggled against the Blairite tide and lost her seat to Labour's Michael Foster in 1997.

A few months later, she returned to Parliament in the Beckenham by-election, sparked by Piers Merchant's resignation over a sex scandal. She remembers speaking to a voter who said, 'I hope you're not going to get yourself into the kind of trouble of your predecessor.' Lait looked at her flat shoes and sensible coat, and replied, 'I think not, somehow.' Tony Blair's New Labour was still riding high in the polls but Lait held the seat, though her majority was cut to 1,227.

An article in *The Scotsman* about who might succeed Iain Duncan Smith as Tory leader gave Lait a loyalty rating of eight out of ten, but just a three for ambition. It surmised that Lait was 'one of the few who chooses to sit beside Mr Duncan Smith at question time and laugh at his jokes' but 'not a heavy hitter, and she knows it. Her loyalty has brought her status in the party.'

One of her most high-profile roles was shadow Secretary of State for Scotland; despite being MP for a Kent seat, Lait was tasked with trying to reverse Tory fortunes north of the border. She was eventually sacked by Michael Howard in 2003, in favour of Peter Duncan, the party's sole Scottish MP at the time.

A declared feminist, Lait was on the party's progressive wing. 'I am not a left-winger but on the more liberal wing. I have always been more attuned to change.' One of her proudest achievements was convincing Chancellor Nigel Lawson to change the personal tax system as part of his 1988 Budget, so that a married woman's income was no longer treated as belonging to her husband. 'It was an absurdity,' she said. 'The most powerful woman in the world [Margaret Thatcher] has to ask her husband to sign her tax form.'

When she was shadow Social Security minister in 2000, Lait became the first top Tory woman to admit to smoking marijuana. 'I tried smoking a cigarette when I was ten or eleven and gave up because it spoiled the taste of my food. I tried cannabis ten years later. It had the same unpleasant effect.'

When the Conservative Party held its first 'gay summit' in 2004 , an event that was intended to mark 'a sea change in the party's thinking on gay rights', Lait was the only Conservative MP (apart from event organiser and deputy Tory chairman Charles Hendry and the summit's three frontbench speakers) who attended.

Her later years saw her lead a campaign to defend the 24-week limit for abortions and a controversial bid to allow early medical abortions at GP surgeries or in the home.

Matthew Parris once wrote, 'Mrs Lait is one of those sensible, genial women – decisively moderate, resolutely mild – who make you hesitate to despair of the Tory Party quite yet.'

In January 2009, Lait resigned as shadow Planning minister after a decade on the front bench. In September of the same year, she wrote to her local association: 'With the prospect of a Conservative government after the next election, I have for some months been considering whether it might be time to move over for a younger person.' She was sixty-two and had a majority of over 14,000.

At the next election, sixty-year-old Colonel Bob Stewart won the seat.

Lait's twilight years were overshadowed by the expenses scandal. She was criticised for overclaiming £7,000 in mortgage interest before repaying it. She described it as 'an honest mistake' between her and the Fees Office. 'It dragged down what would have been a feeling of achievement and a job done well,' she says.

LIZ LYNNE

CAROLINE PIDGEON

- FULL NAME: Elizabeth Lynne
- DATE OF BIRTH: 22 January 1948
- PLACE OF BIRTH: Woking
- DATE OF DEATH: –
- MARRIED TO: Unmarried
- CHILDREN: None
- UNSUCCESSFUL ELECTIONS FOUGHT: Harwich 1987
- CONSTITUENCY: Rochdale
- DATE OF FIRST ELECTION: 9 April 1992
- DATE LEFT PARLIAMENT: 1 May 1997
- MEP: West Midlands 1999–2012
- PARTY ROLES: Liberal Democrats spokesperson on Health and Community Care 1992–94 and spokesperson on Social Security and Disability 1994–97
- MINISTERIAL POSITIONS & DATES: None

A champion for the underdog sums up Liz Lynne, MP for Rochdale in the 1990s.

Liz had a tough childhood, growing up in a single-parent family with her mother and older brother. By the age of eleven she had attended ten schools, been homeless and seen her mother take whatever work she could, mainly nursing jobs, to support her family.

It was her mother's job when Liz was only eleven years old that most influenced her passion for championing people with disabilities. Her mother became a warden at Dorincourt in Leatherhead, a sheltered home with a cutting-edge approach to disability. The family lived at the home with forty-three disabled residents who also worked on the site. This experience transformed Liz's views of society and made her understand the challenges that those with disabilities face. She became a great champion of disabled people throughout her UK and European parliamentary career.

Liz left school at sixteen and headed for London. She modelled for a year before becoming an actress. Her ambition was to act in plays with a clear message about equality in society. Living in bedsits and in and out of work, Liz would, on occasion, live a hand-to-mouth existence, surviving with no parental support. From bar work and waitressing to selling central heating door to door, Liz did whatever she could to pay the bills while in between acting jobs. At times, she was on the dole, experiencing at first hand the reality of living in poverty.

As an actress, she mainly worked in theatres around the country, but she also appeared on screen in television and films such as *The Hiding Place*. At the age of nineteen, she appeared in a West End production of *Tom Paine* at the Vaudeville Theatre. Her last stage performance was in another West End play, Agatha Christie's *The Mousetrap*. While still acting, she stood as the Liberal–SDP Alliance candidate for Harwich during the 1987 election, but lost to the Conservative candidate. Liz's interest in politics had developed as a child. She attended her first Liberal meeting in Leatherhead, when she was eleven years old, and immediately felt a special affinity with the Liberal Party.

Outside of party politics, Liz set up Amnesty International's Indonesian Coordination Group and was chair of the Citizens Advice Bureau in Paddington as well as on the management committee of a boxing club that helped young black men turn their lives around. After juggling standing for Parliament and performing in the West End, Liz left acting and became a speech consultant, helping people with presentation skills, including the then new leader of the Liberal Democrats, Paddy Ashdown.

In 1989, Cyril Smith, Liberal MP for Rochdale, was threatening to step down and cause a by-election. Liz decided to apply for the seat but was warned that she did not stand a hope in hell of being selected. The assumption at the time was that a woman, from outside Rochdale, stood no chance against Cyril Smith's chosen successor.

However, sheer determination and hard work paid off. Liz spent day after day meeting as many Liberal members as she could, lodging with a local activist. And against all the odds, she won against Cyril Smith's candidate. After the selection, Cyril did not speak to Liz for a year and a half. With no support from the incumbent MP, Liz used every friend and contact she could to help produce her own literature and deliver it in the constituency.

She moved to Rochdale and, alongside some speech consultancy work, threw herself into every local community group and campaign. Her efforts paid off. Liz was elected in the 1992 general election. When the results were announced, Liz did not immediately celebrate as she was concerned about one of her key activists, Diane, who had lost part of her finger to a dog while out delivering leaflets. Instead of going to hospital, Diane had continued posting leaflets to get Liz elected.

Liz's determination to stand up for vulnerable and disabled people saw her lead for the Liberal Democrats first on Health and then Social Security, before turning to the Disabled People's Rights brief. She was also an active member of the All-Party Parliamentary Group on Disability.

However, Liz soon became the thorn in the side of Leader Paddy Ashdown. In 1994, Paddy made his famous Chard speech, where he proposed getting rid of the party's equidistant position between the two main parties. Liz knew this meant that Paddy wanted to move the party into a deal with Labour. She felt strongly that this would be the end of the party and she would not stand by and let that happen. In Liz's mind, there was a world of difference between collaborating on specific issues and in allowing the Liberal Democrats to be submerged into the Labour Party. She moved motions against this at party conference and continued to fight Paddy's increasingly friendly relationship with Tony Blair and Peter Mandelson. Liz resigned as a frontbench spokesperson over the matter, but was eventually persuaded back to leading on Social Security and Disability.

Looking at Liz's record in Parliament it should be stressed that she never hesitated to work alongside MPs and peers from other parties. Indeed, far from being hostile to individual Labour MPs, she had a good working relationship with many, especially those worried about the direction Tony Blair was taking the Labour Party. A particular footnote of history is that in her five years in Parliament, her Norman Shaw office was adjacent to Jeremy Corbyn's. Their views on some social and foreign affairs issues, and their opinion of Tony Blair, were sometimes as close as the location of their offices.

When Liz was in Parliament, the momentum was growing for comprehensive disability discrimination legislation. Private Members' Bill after Private Members' Bill came up on disabled people's issues and mass lobbies of Parliament were a frequent occurrence. One of Liz's first successes was to persuade William Hague, then Minister of State for Social Security and Disabled People, to improve disabled access for new buildings by changing building regulations.

Liz sat on the Disability Discrimination Bill committee, spending hour after hour painstakingly going through every line and detail of the legislation. However, she felt frustrated about the pace of change and, like most disability campaigners and members of the All-Party Parliamentary Disability Group, felt that the 1995 Disability Discrimination Act did not go far enough, especially as its powers were not enforced by a commission and it failed to address education provision.

Due to Rochdale having a large Kashmiri population, Liz was active in ensuring their voice was heard and she worked hard to try and achieve a just and lasting solution for the people of Kashmir. She was the first female MP to visit the refugee camps in Azad Kashmir in the early 1990s.

In 1994, Rochdale saw one of the first privatised prisons in the UK open, HMP Buckley Hall. The prison was continually plagued with problems, including prisoners not returning from authorised leave and escaping. This was dramatically illustrated when a Channel 4 television crew, already filming outside the prison for a documentary, caught live footage of a prisoner successfully escaping, leaving Group 4 prison officers chasing desperately behind.

Her numerous written parliamentary questions and an adjournment debate clearly provoked the then Home Office Prison minister, Ann Widdecombe, not least when the Speaker of the House of Commons censured the Home Office for permitting Group 4 employees access to the House of Commons Chamber during Liz's parliamentary debate.

In 1997, Tony Blair's New Labour took seats across the UK, one of which was Liz Lynne's Rochdale. However, in 1999, Liz was elected to the European Parliament, where her championing of the disabled and vulnerable continued. She was vice-president of the Employment and Social Affairs committee and was a rapporteur on disabled people's employment rights across the EU. She stood down in 2012.

Determined and outspoken, Liz was the first female MP for Rochdale and a strong voice for people with disabilities.

LADY OLGA MAITLAND

ANN WIDDECOMBE

- FULL NAME: Helen Olga Hay (née Maitland)
- DATE OF BIRTH: 23 May 1944
- PLACE OF BIRTH: –
- DATE OF THE DEATH: –
- MARRIED TO: Robin Hay (m. 1969)
- CHILDREN: Alastair, Fergus and Camilla
- UNSUCCESSFUL ELECTIONS FOUGHT: Bethnal Green 1987, Sutton & Cheam 2001
- CONSTITUENCY: Sutton & Cheam
- DATE OF FIRST ELECTION: 8 May 1992
- DATE LEFT PARLIAMENT: 1 May 1997
- PARTY ROLES: None
- MINISTERIAL POSITIONS & DATES: Parliamentary private secretary to John Wheeler and Northern Ireland minister 1996–97
- MOST FAMOUS QUOTATION: 'I would not put my trust in Denis Healey. Going over to Moscow, rolling on his tummy like a great big puppy and having it tickled by Gorbachev, and to go back to Britain waving a piece of paper saying "We will not attack Britain" – what naiveté!'

Allied forces were beginning a new offensive on the Anzio beachhead as Lady Olga Maitland was born to the Earl and Countess of Lauderdale in May 1944, and it is tempting to conclude that the sound of gunfire was in her very blood as she burst on to the political scene nearly forty years later.

Until then her reputation was that merely of a privileged aristocrat who milked her connections for the gossip column she wrote for the *Sunday Express*, but suddenly the steel began to show.

Ever since the Cuban Missile Crisis of 1962, which demonstrated to any who doubted it the value of matching the then Soviet Union's arsenal of nuclear weapons, the Campaign for Nuclear Disarmament (CND) had been in the shadows, licking its wounds. Gone were the days of the huge Aldermaston marches. Then a proposal to replace Polaris by Trident, and another to site US cruise missiles on UK soil, revitalised the cause.

A group of women began to protest at the Greenham Common RAF base and their peace camp grew in numbers, in media coverage and in activity. Their message seemed to imply that if you were a woman you must oppose nuclear weapons. Therefore a counter-message was needed: if you were a woman then you and your children would be kept safe only by strong and resolute defence.

Olga Maitland was chosen by the powers that then were to spearhead the campaign and form the group which became known as Women and Families for Defence (WFFD). Committees? Collective decisions? The lady could not be bothered with them; she simply did whatever she thought best as and when she thought it – and it made an impact. The group I joined as vice-chair was actually called the Defence Is Safer Campaign, as we believed it would be more appealing to young people as DISC. When it was formally launched, its name had morphed into WFFD and Olga could not understand why we thought we might have been consulted.

Olga simply steamrollered on. She took over Trafalgar Square on the day it was annually booked by CND; the group launched 'A Layman's Guide to Defence', which set out to explain the often confusing nuclear terms; and it visited Mrs Thatcher at No. 10, in each case to a fanfare of press coverage. The Maitland energy was boundless.

Maitland's visit to the United States in 1986 spawned a long article in the *Washington Post*. Despite having no real status to do so, she met the Defense Secretary and Reagan's senior arms control adviser, not to mention various senators. Responding to the tendency of the British press to mock Maitland, one former senator remarked that the British were too reserved but that Lady Olga would go down much better in America.

She did not actually make it to the White House and meet the President, but on her return she tried to meet the Pope in the hope that His Holiness might come out with a defence of nuclear arms. Nobody could have called her a pessimist.

It was therefore no surprise, when Olga Maitland arrived in Parliament in 1992, that she focused on defence issues or that she should become parliamentary private secretary to John Wheeler in Northern Ireland, working closely with Patrick Mayhew and Michael Ancram.

Olga says she was told by a particularly stuffy Member of Parliament that she should stick to women's issues, but instead she moved Private Members' Bills on such issues as knife crime and was elected to the Select Committee on Defence and Foreign Affairs. With her usual energy, and being no stranger to controversy, she tabled a large number of amendments to the Civil Rights (Disabled Persons) Bill. The fallout from the collapse of the proposed measure caused her some brief damage, which she met with her usual fearless defiance.

Alas, her tenure of Sutton and Cheam was limited to a single parliamentary term as her seat fell in the electoral carnage of 1997, and she failed to regain it in the general election four years later, when the British public was still in love with Blair. Had she joined Parliament at a different stage in the electoral cycle, she would eventually have probably joined the circle of grand dames – long-serving older women with strong personalities such as Dames Joan Vickers, Pat Hornsby-Smith, Elaine Kellett-Bowman and Janet Fookes.

CND was eventually to fade once more into the background: Michael Foot's 1983 manifesto promising to scrap Britain's nuclear deterrent ended in a record majority for Thatcher – Trident did replace Polaris and the Greenham Common peace camp was abandoned. WFFD had played its part.

In all her activities, Olga Maitland was well supported by her husband, the barrister Robin Hay, whom she married in 1969 and by whom she has three children. They would escape from their London townhouse to their Norfolk cottage when the fray became too tiresome.

Today, Maitland is prominent in the British Algeria Business Conference, which she launched in 2005. When I last saw her she told me Trump was wrong to take on Kim Jong-un, who was busy firing rockets over Japan. I suppose old age mellows us all.

ESTELLE MORRIS

JESS PHILLIPS

- FULL NAME: Estelle Morris, Baroness Morris of Yardley
- DATE OF BIRTH: 17 June 1952
- PLACE OF BIRTH: Manchester
- DATE OF DEATH: –
- MARRIED TO: Unmarried
- CHILDREN: None
- UNSUCCESSFUL ELECTIONS FOUGHT: None
- CONSTITUENCY: Birmingham Yardley
- DATE OF FIRST ELECTION: 10 April 1992
- DATE LEFT PARLIAMENT: 11 April 2005. In 2005, she was made a life peer, and she now sits in the Lords as Baroness Morris.
- PARTY ROLES: Labour councillor, Warwick District Council 1979–91; Labour Group leader, Warwick District Council, 1981–92
- MINISTERIAL POSITIONS & DATES: Parliamentary Under-Secretary for Education and Employment 1997–98; Minister for School Standards 1998–2001; Secretary of State for Education and Skills 2001–02; Minister for the Arts 2003–05

'I knew Estelle Morris well when she was the MP' is a common phrase that people say to me when I am out door-knocking in the Yardley constituency. It is a sure sign of a well-loved Member of Parliament, when constituents remember them as a friend. It was over a decade ago that Estelle stepped down as MP and, knowing how well liked she is by many of my voters, I still feel a bit like I am borrowing her constituency. It is most certainly ours, not mine.

The Baroness of Yardley is fresh from a visit to the area when we meet. She explains that she has been to a ceremony to name the great-great-granddaughter of a cow that was named after her when she was first elected. There are not many MPs, let alone ex-MPs, who would travel for hours to see

Willow the calf. She tells me of the people she popped in to see on her visit – our shared friends and stalwarts of the local Labour Party. Despite growing up in Manchester and no longer living in the area, she is definitely still considered one of us.

Estelle Morris was elected for the first time in 1992, with a tiny majority of only 162. 'Politics is about luck,' she exclaims, as she talks about how she doesn't think she would have been selected to contest the seat if anyone had believed that there had been a real chance of her taking it from the Tories. This is typical of Estelle's understated style. She is, after all, the daughter of the MP Alfred Morris, who sat in the house for thirty-three years. She has also been a Labour leader on Warwick District Council. Prior to her election in Birmingham, Estelle also taught in a comprehensive school in neighbouring Coventry. She had political grounding in the party and what would be much lauded today, real world experience. I wouldn't call her election luck, I'd call it inevitable.

Managing a marginal constituency, where, in 1992, she was the only Labour voice with nine Liberal Democrat councillors, was a challenge. She relished it and says that getting herself known and established in the area was the hardest but most rewarding part of her job. Some twenty-six years later, her continuing popularity is a testament to her people skills.

She described her first five years in the House of Commons as an opposition MP as being serendipitous. Unlike so many of the women elected later in 1997, whom Estelle worked alongside in government, she felt that those initial five years gave her a chance to learn the ropes.

> We were very lucky those of us that came in at the time. I came in with Richard Burden, Peter Mandelson, Stephen Byers and Barbara Roche, and there was a sense that we were supportive of each other. It felt like a time of opportunity in a time that was buzzing with ideas, as if we were on a bus that was gathering pace.

When the bus arrived at its destination, Estelle was very much one of those in the driving seats, rather than a hapless passenger. Immediately after Labour came to power, Estelle, who had put in her time on the shadow front bench, was appointed a junior minister in the Department for Education and Employment; she was then promoted to Minister of State in the team, working under David Blunkett.

It is this job that makes Estelle's eyes light up while we are chatting. She describes the years in the Education team as her happiest, and stresses how well she and her colleagues worked together as a team. In an era where the slogan was 'education, education, education', she excelled in an environment that she describes as tough, rapid and innovative. 'David let us get on with it and so we could really get stuck in.' When I ask her about her proudest achievement, she tells me that it is the department's work on reforming the teaching profession during these years. She waxes lyrical about changing the structures of school staff and making pathways to leadership for good teachers. She talks about the advent of teaching assistants, and I am suddenly struck by the fact that when I was at school in Birmingham in the 1980s, there was only ever one teacher in a class of around thirty-five pupils, but my children, attending the same school some twenty years later, had at least three adults supporting only thirty children. This was down to Estelle, but now we take such staffing for granted. She has every reason to feel proud, and I thank her as a mother of a child who needed that bit extra.

Following the 2001 election – the last election Estelle would ever stand in – she was promoted to Secretary of State for Education and Skills. She was the first former comprehensive school teacher to hold the position, and her first-hand experience meant that many teachers (I remember my own teacher father commenting on it) saw her as someone they could trust. However, her tenure as Education Secretary was short-lived, with Estelle suddenly resigning from the post in October 2002, citing that she did not feel up to the job. I can think of many Education Secretaries who should have felt underqualified, but I am not sure I can square this with the woman who earned her stripes in both the profession and the government department. When I ask her about this, she says that being in charge of the department with the pull and push of negotiating with No. 10 hadn't afforded her the same freedom as her junior ministerial role. Estelle Morris is a thoughtful woman – diligent and kind is how I would describe her. In the much satirised male, macho environment of Blair's government, I am not surprised that Estelle Morris felt she was more a worker bee rather than the queen.

'The job I loved best was that of a junior minister,' she tells me. I ask her about her regrets she has from that time. She doesn't mention her decision to stand down from one of the biggest jobs in politics. She answers with characteristic caution and says, 'I think sometimes the department made a virtue of making an enemy of teachers.' She thinks for a little while longer and then says, 'Also, I think further education never got enough attention.'

Dutiful to the end, Estelle Morris is not concerned with personal regrets, but instead remains concerned for the education of the nation.

Estelle returned to the backbenches after her resignation, but found the transition difficult. She was appointed Minister for the Arts in the Department for Culture, Media and Sport in 2003, and stayed in the role until she resigned her seat prior to the 2005 election – the seat was then lost to the Liberal Democrats.

I still think that, had Estelle stood, Labour would have held the seat in 2005, although when I put this to her, she is not so sure. 'I was tired; I'd been in Parliament for thirteen years and fighting a marginal constituency for that long is tough.'

In a reflection of the esteem in which she was held by Tony Blair, Estelle was elevated to the House of Lords. In the last thirteen years, she has been a hard-working peer and has never given up her commitment to both Birmingham and education. Between 2005 and 2009, she was pro vice-chancellor of the University of Sunderland. In May 2005, she was appointed chair of the Children's Workforce Development Council. In September 2005, she was appointed president of the National Children's Bureau. Since 2007, she has been chair of the executive group of the Institute for Effective Education at the University of York. In 2015, local newspapers in Birmingham described her as 'respected former education secretary', when it was announced that Estelle Morris would take charge of improving performance at city schools in her new role as the head of Birmingham Education Partnership.

While out door-knocking with me on the campaign trail in 2015, the year Labour won the seat back from the Lib Dems, Estelle Morris was approached by a woman on the street. The woman had seen us as she drove past and had pulled over her and leapt out of her car. She strode confidently over to Estelle and me, exclaiming how, as a teacher, she was thrilled that Estelle had been given a leading role in improving Birmingham schools. She said, 'We teachers were relieved that it's you, because you get it.'

She might not have felt she was up to the role of Secretary of State for Education, and I cannot put this down to anything other than female imposter syndrome in a macho environment, because Estelle Morris is remembered with respect and warmth. For someone who was not a native to my city, who always felt that she was hanging on by a thread, she has a pretty sound reputation. If I said this to her, she would shrug it off, because Estelle Morris is nothing if not humble. You see, she's one of us.

BRIDGET PRENTICE

HEIDI ALEXANDER

- **FULL NAME:** Bridget Theresa Prentice (née Corr)
- **DATE OF BIRTH:** 28 December 1952
- **PLACE OF BIRTH:** Glasgow
- **DATE OF DEATH:** –
- **MARRIED TO:** Gordon Prentice (m. 1975; div. 2000); Kevin Foley (partner)
- **CHILDREN:** None
- **UNSUCCESSFUL ELECTIONS FOUGHT:** Croydon Central 1987
- **CONSTITUENCY:** Lewisham East
- **DATE OF FIRST ELECTION:** 9 April 1992
- **DATE LEFT PARLIAMENT:** 12 April 2010
- **PARTY ROLES:** None
- **MINISTERIAL POSITIONS & DATES:** Government whip 1995–98; parliamentary private secretary to the Minister for Trade 1998–99; parliamentary private secretary to the Lord Chancellor 1999–2001; government whip 2003–05; Parliamentary Under-Secretary at the Department for Constitutional Affairs/Ministry of Justice 2005–10
- **MOST FAMOUS QUOTATION:** I am not sure this is particularly well known, but I think she would like me to repeat what she once told me: 'If you think of me like a stick of rock, you'd cut me down the middle and it would say Tony Blair.'

If the qualities required of a successful politician are resilience and patience, as well as good communication and classroom-management skills, then teacher Bridget Prentice's switch to a career as a Member of Parliament, minister and government whip is perhaps not surprising. However, Bridget's place on the green benches was far from preordained. Educated at Charlotte Street Secondary School and brought up in Glasgow's East End, it was the virtues instilled in Bridget from an early age – self-discipline, high standards and a desire to be involved in the major issues of the day – that would prove most useful in her journey to Parliament.

At Glasgow University she was a lively contributor to the Student Representative Council and the Catholic Society, whose Jesuit chaplain Father Gerard Hughes made a big impression on her. Another major influence was Bridget's older brother, Jim, who worked for both Harold Wilson and Jim Callaghan, and then for the World Bank and IMF. Bridget taught history and English at The London Oratory School for twelve years before taking her first steps towards elected politics at Hammersmith & Fulham Council, where she served from 1986 to 1992.

Labour veterans now, of course, look back at the general election of 1992 with dismay. But having secured selection as the Labour candidate for Lewisham East – seen as something of a bellwether seat at the time – Bridget would have had every reason to believe she was on the threshold of entering Parliament, and that Labour was destined for government. She duly won her own contest at Lewisham East, after a tough battle with the incumbent Conservative MP and former Olympian, Colin Moynihan (her majority was 1,095), but Labour lost the general election.

Bridget inherited a seat that had once been represented by Herbert Morrison (a plaque bearing his name is in Downham Leisure Centre) and was Lewisham East's first female MP. Hansard reveals that she focused on constituency matters, especially trains (Lewisham boasts a large commuter population and was the scene of two of Britain's worst rail disasters), and school standards. She once clashed with a local headteacher who believed that you couldn't expect too much from 'Lewisham kids'.

Parallel to Bridget's local concerns were some far-sighted enquiries in Parliament on the writing-off of Third World debt – an ambition later realised by the Labour government some twelve years later – and a question to the Prime Minister about tax loopholes and non-domiciled status; an early shot in a debate that would rumble on for another twenty years.

An enthusiastic supporter of Labour's new leader, Tony Blair, Bridget was appointed an opposition whip in 1995 and then became a government whip in 1997. Roles as a parliamentary private secretary, first to Brian Wilson and then to Lord Irvine, followed. Perhaps unfulfilled by these appointments, Bridget left the front bench to devote herself to constituency work and her membership of the Home Affairs Select Committee. A supporter of ID cards, anti-social behaviour orders and other New Labour initiatives, she found herself a committee colleague of a young David Cameron, whose approach to illegal drugs she somewhat disapproved of. Another spell in the Whips' Office followed before she was appointed as Parliamentary Under-Secretary at the Department for Constitutional Affairs in 2005.

In her five years at the DCA (later renamed the Ministry of Justice) under Jack Straw and Lord Falconer respectively, Bridget was able to pursue changes to the law that benefited women and young people. The introduction of specialist Domestic Violence Courts and the Forced Marriage Act made women in Britain safer and freer. Meanwhile, the Electoral Administration Act ironed out the anomaly that eighteen-year-olds could vote in elections but not contest them. Important changes were also introduced to legal services and the coroners' system. The idiosyncrasies of her departmental responsibilities meant that she became more knowledgeable on the topple testing of gravestones than she would ever have thought possible.

Well regarded in the constituency, and blessed with a dedicated local party, Lewisham East evolved into a Labour stronghold under Bridget's stewardship. She was assiduous in dealing with constituency casework, and whether it was evenings spent at the Blackheath Joint Working Party, top-table lunches at Bonus Pastor School, or meetings of the Grove Park Community Association, her reputation as a hard-working, well-liked and well-respected representative preceded her.

As one of her constituents in 2009, I was as stunned as anyone when she announced she planned to stand down from Parliament at the next election. But Bridget arguably judged it right, and has enjoyed a rewarding career since leaving the Commons. Her dedication to improving life-chances for young people saw her appointed as chair of governors at Trinity School in Lewisham, and her experience as a government minister was put to good use when she became a commissioner for the Electoral Commission.

Few of us can remain entirely immune to the charms and allure of the Palace of Westminster, but unlike some colleagues, Bridget never forgot that our place in it is temporary and that Parliament will endure without us. In the Gothic splendour of the Commons, she never lost her Glaswegian common sense, her down-to-earth attitude or fundamental desire to help others. Lewisham will also endure without us but, perhaps because she loves it a little more than the refinements of Westminster, Bridget remains a positive and encouraging presence in the community and the local Labour Party. As her successor in Lewisham East, I can say with authority that she is not only an exemplary ex-Member of Parliament; she is a trusted confidante, an inspiration to many and a friend I could not do without.

BARBARA ROCHE

CATHERINE WEST

- FULL NAME: Barbara Maureen Roche (née Margolis)
- DATE OF BIRTH: 13 April 1954
- PLACE OF BIRTH: London, England
- DATE OF DEATH: —
- MARRIED TO: Patrick Roche
- CHILDREN: One daughter
- UNSUCCESSFUL ELECTIONS FOUGHT: Surrey South-West 1984 (by-election) and Hornsey & Wood Green 1987
- CONSTITUENCY: Hornsey & Wood Green
- DATE OF FIRST ELECTION: 9 April 1992
- DATE LEFT PARLIAMENT: 11 April 2005
- PARTY ROLES: None
- MINISTERIAL POSITIONS & DATES: Parliamentary Under-Secretary for Small Firms, Trade and Industry 1997–99; Financial Secretary to the Treasury 1999; Minister for Asylum and Immigration 1999–2001; Minister of State, Cabinet Office 2001–02; Minister for Women and Equalities 2001–03; Minister of State, Office of the Deputy Prime Minister 2002–03
- MOST FAMOUS QUOTATION: 'We had a brief tussle and I disarmed him.'

It was a Friday in September 2003, and 49-year-old MP Barbara Roche was urging her assistant to summon the police, while at the same time wrestling a constituent to the floor – the said constituent having just threatened to set himself ablaze after pulling out a plastic bag full of petrol and a bottle of barbecue lighter fuel.

Roche's response to the incident, 'I believe it is vital for constituents to have easy access to their MPs and I'm not going to overact. I'm fine and nobody in my office was harmed.'

It is not surprising that 'tenacious', 'popular in the constituency' and 'positive' are just some of the words and phrases people who have worked with

Roche use to describe her. To this day, I am regularly stopped by numerous constituents who like and ask after Barbara.

She was a modern politician, selected to contest Hornsey & Wood Green at a time when Neil Kinnock was moving Labour towards the centre-left. Although she reduced the long-standing Conservative MP Sir Hugh Rossi's majority to less than 2,000 at the 1987 general election, her hard work during the campaign was not rewarded with a parliamentary seat.

But she was overwhelmingly endorsed as Labour's candidate for Hornsey & Wood Green in the 1992 election, and went into the count feeling that while she might not have triumphed locally Labour would win nationally. The reverse happened. Barbara won her seat with a majority of 5,177 – one of the largest in London – but John Major's Conservatives formed the next government. Five years later, though, a wave of optimism swept Tony Blair and Labour to power. In Hornsey & Wood Green, Barbara easily retained her seat, securing an overwhelming majority of more than 20,000 votes.

Invariably loyal, she rebelled against the Labour government in only four out of 1,570 votes and held a number of ministerial offices, from Parliamentary Under-Secretary of State in the Department of Trade and Industry, to Financial Secretary to the Treasury. She also served in the Cabinet Office and in the office of the Deputy Prime Minister.

But in no area was Barbara's approach to politics and influence more important than in immigration. Serving as Minister for Asylum and Immigration between 1999 and 2001, she introduced policies that changed the UK.

Key to this was making the positive case for immigration, and introducing a fairer, more transparent system for migrants coming to the UK. During a speech at the Institute for Public Policy Research in September 2000, she announced that asylum seekers would be dispersed from Kent with 'no choice' of where they were sent. At the time this was considered controversial, as most newly arrived communities were based in London and other big cities. Roche defended her stance on asylum seekers, stating that the issue should not be conflated with economic migration and concerns of racism. Immigration would be separated from asylum cases, she said. Granting asylum would depend on whether a person met the 1951 UN Convention relating to refugees.

Growing up in east London, Roche's Jewish family had bequeathed to her a strong sense of social justice and human rights. She had always fought hard against racism, xenophobia and anti-Semitism, and on her appointment as Immigration minister she set about combatting these issues directly. Not just highly skilled migrants would now be welcomed to the UK, but also people who could work for the NHS, and in hospitality and agriculture.

Leaving her Immigration brief, Barbara went on to champion women's rights. As Minister for Women and Equalities, she urged the promotion of family-oriented policies and gender equality. Her new team was tasked with implementing EU directives that protected workers from being discriminated against on the grounds of sexual orientation and religious belief. She also helped to usher in UK civil partnerships, which paved the way for equal marriage. Her instinct for equality was evident in her push for LGBT rights.

Despite huge opposition in Hornsey & Wood Green to both the Iraq War and the introduction of tuition fees, Roche supported both. She voted the former through on the basis of stopping human rights abuses, and backed tuition fees after government amendments to the original bill.

Two years after stopping a constituent from setting himself ablaze, Barbara Roche lost her seat at the 2005 general election. But she left behind her a solid parliamentary record. She battled hard to help those who do not have a voice. As a lawyer at the North Lewisham Law Centre, she worked on human rights and the criminal justice system, and championed the rights of local people. She now chairs the Migration Matters Trust as well as the Migration Museum Project. Once again she is promoting the progressive argument for immigration.

RACHEL SQUIRE

OONAGH GAY

- FULL NAME: Rachel Squire (formerly Binder)
- DATE OF BIRTH: 13 July 1954
- PLACE OF BIRTH: Carshalton, Surrey
- DATE OF DEATH: 5 January 2006
- MARRIED TO: Allan Lee Mason (m. 1984)
- CHILDREN: None
- UNSUCCESSFUL ELECTIONS FOUGHT: None
- CONSTITUENCY: Dunfermline West and Dunfermline & West Fife
- DATE OF FIRST ELECTION: 9 April 1992
- DATE LEFT PARLIAMENT: 5 January 2006
- PARTY ROLES: None
- MINISTERIAL POSITIONS & DATES: parliamentary private secretary to Stephen Byers and, later, Estelle Morris 1997–2001
- MOST FAMOUS QUOTATION: 'There is compelling evidence of the disadvantage caused by copyright barriers to blind and partially sighted learners in particular. The largest ever survey of blind and partially sighted young people … revealed that nearly half – 47 per cent of students – in university or higher education do not usually get books in their preferred formats and that 33 per cent of visually impaired children do not always get their textbooks in an accessible format when they need them' – On introducing her successful Private Members' Bill in 2002.

Rachel Squire was born on 13 July 1954. Her mother, Louise Binder, was a waitress. No father was registered on the baby's birth certificate but Rachel later took the surname of her stepfather, Percy Garfield Squire. She went to Durham University, where she studied archaeology and anthropology, and then trained as a social worker at Birmingham University from 1975 to 1978.

Squire worked as a full-time union official for NUPE, the public service union that later became part of Unison, initially on Merseyside and then in

Scotland, where as the education officer Squire's commitment to helping low-paid workers, mainly women, acquire skills they had missed out on in formal education won her much praise. In 1984 she married an American naval petty officer, Allan Lee Mason, who later served as her constituency caseworker.

Squire became the only woman trade unionist on Labour's Scottish executive. When the sitting MP for Dunfermline West, Dick Douglas, defected from Labour to the SNP in 1990, Squire beat four men to be selected to contest the seat for Labour. She then won the seat by 7,484 votes at the general election in 1992. A female MP in Scotland was a rarity in those days; Squire had just Maria Fyfe and Irene Adams to keep her company in Westminster. Even rarer was Squire's English background in a tough Scottish east coast seat, where her predecessors had all been Scots working-class men.

The electoral boundaries were redrawn in 2005 and the name of the constituency was changed to Dunfermline and West Fife.

Squire was seen as a loyal Labour MP, as well as an outstanding constituency worker, which inevitably led to her taking an interest in defence, due to the proximity of the Rosyth dockyards and naval base. In 1993 she joined forces with Gordon Brown, the MP for the neighbouring constituency of Dunfermline East, and battled to keep Trident submarine work at Rosyth. But the government ultimately transferred the work of refitting the nuclear submarines to Devonport that year. Squire also lobbied unsuccessfully to preserve Fife's last deep coal mine, Longannet, and then fought to secure compensation and retraining for miners when Longannet finally closed in 2002.

In 1993 she underwent surgery to remove a non-malignant brain tumour. Despite this she immediately travelled to Westminster on 22 July for crucial votes on the Maastricht Treaty debates – a trip which illustrates the tight parliamentary arithmetic of the early 1990s. When Labour took power in May 1997, Squire became a parliamentary private secretary to the Minister for Schools Stephen Byers and, later, to Estelle Morris. She never achieved ministerial office herself and returned to the back benches where her pro-NATO support for defence spending, and her backing of the US and UK's military interventions in Kosovo in 1999 and Iraq in 2003, helped her become the first woman chair of the Parliamentary Labour Party's backbench defence group in 2001.

Squire served on the Procedure committee and the Modernisation committee from 1992 to 1999. Her final select committee was Defence, from

2001. She chaired the Select Committee on the Armed Forces Bill in 2001. Her interest in disability support led Squire to promote a Private Members' Bill in March 2002, which became the Copyright (Visually Impaired Persons) Act 2002.

Aware that a recurrence of her tumour was always a possibility, she took a leading role in the Brain Tumour Action cancer charity. An operation to remove a second brain tumour left her with partial facial paralysis. Despite this, Squire fought the 2005 general election in May, but then suffered a stroke in June.

She died from cancer six months later on 5 January 2006.

At her memorial service at Dunfermline Abbey on 3 February 2006 Gordon Brown, then Chancellor of the Exchequer, read from a letter that Squire had allowed to be made public after her death. 'It is for you to decide whether or not I have been a successful MP,' she wrote. 'All I can say is that I have given the job my undivided attention and my very best efforts.'

Liberal Democrat Willie Rennie captured Squire's old seat in a by-election on 9 February 2006, defeating Labour's Catherine Stihler.

DIANA MADDOCK

OLLY GRENDER

- FULL NAME: Diana Margaret Maddock, Baroness Maddock, Lady Beith
- DATE OF BIRTH: 19 May 1945
- PLACE OF BIRTH: –
- DATE OF DEATH: –
- MARRIED TO: Robert 'Bob' Maddock (divorced); Lord (Alan) Beith (m. 2001)
- CHILDREN: Two daughters
- UNSUCCESSFUL ELECTIONS FOUGHT: Southampton Test 1992
- CONSTITUENCY: Christchurch
- DATE OF FIRST ELECTION: 29 July 1993
- DATE LEFT PARLIAMENT: 1 May 1997. She was made a life peer in 1997 and has sat in the Lords since.
- PARTY ROLES: President of Liberal Democrats 1999–2000
- MINISTERIAL POSITIONS & DATES: Government whip 2010–15
- MOST FAMOUS QUOTATION: On election to Christchurch with a stunning swing of 35 per cent she urged Prime Minister John Major to 'change your policies or change your job'.

The House of Commons nearly didn't happen for Diana Maddock. At the last minute she was persuaded by her friend, Andrew Stunell MP, and her daughters to put her name forward as a by-election candidate. On 29 July 1993, Diana overturned a Conservative majority of 23,000 in Christchurch with a stunning swing of 35 per cent – the largest ever achieved by a woman candidate in any English by-election. Her strong beliefs, background in local government and organisational know-how made her the perfect candidate in an era when by-elections commanded significant daily media attention, and were often like mini general elections.

By-election victors can sometimes fall for the hype of believing that their triumph was all down to them. Not so Diana. Her feet have always been planted firmly on the ground, which is why she is particularly loved in the Liberal Democrats – a party that holds a special affection for someone who has worked their way up from the grassroots.

Diana trained as a teacher at Shenstone Training College, now Portsmouth University. She married her first husband, Bob Maddock, in 1966 and moved to Stockholm for his career in 1969. It was here that she started to become more politically aware; she also formed several lasting friendships and learned Swedish.

After returning to the UK, Diana taught English as a foreign language, but she quit the job in 1976 to concentrate on raising her two daughters. She joined the Liberal Party at this time, motivated by local issues.

As a councillor on Southampton City Council she was leader of the Liberal Democrat group through a difficult 'hung authority' period. She then advised the Liberal Democrat group on Hampshire County Council, which was another local authority where no political party had overall control. She is widely acknowledged to have established the foundations that enabled the Liberal Democrats to win several parliamentary seats in the region.

In the House of Commons Diana represented the party on her particular interests of housing, homelessness and education. She had developed an awareness of energy conservation while living in Sweden, and having worked in her own community here in the UK, she had witnessed at first hand the results of fuel poverty and unfit housing. She secured a slot for a Private Members' Bill and piloted the Home Energy Conservation Act (the 'Warmer Homes Bill') through Parliament – a considerable feat for a new MP. It was exciting for me to be there advising her.

In the 1997 general election, Christchurch went back to the Conservatives, but the Liberal Democrats were determined to keep Diana on the national stage. She went to the Lords in November 1997, and was elected President of the Liberal Democrats in July 1998. As president she proved popular with the local parties and was in great demand.

Her marriage to Liberal Democrat grandee Alan Beith, in 2001, made them one of the few Swedish-speaking couples in the House of Lords.

Meet with Diana without a ready plan at your peril. She is hard-working, highly organised and expects the same from others. She places a high value on communication with the media. She can be plain-speaking, and will challenge your thinking behind the scenes. But when she is seated next to you on the benches in the Lords her support for colleagues, advocacy for the party, and encouragement of other women has all the command and dedication of a lioness.

JUDITH CHURCH

LINDA GILROY

- FULL NAME: Judith Church
- DATE OF BIRTH: 19 September 1953
- DATE OF DEATH: –
- PLACE OF BIRTH: –
- MARRIED TO: Separated
- CHILDREN: Two sons
- UNSUCCESSFUL ELECTIONS FOUGHT: Stevenage 1992
- CONSTITUENCY: Dagenham
- DATE OF FIRST ELECTION: 9 June 1994 (by-election)
- DATE LEFT PARLIAMENT: 7 June 2001
- PARTY ROLES: Member of the Labour NEC 1992–94
- MINISTERIAL POSITIONS & DATES: None
- MOST FAMOUS QUOTATION: 'Only those companies, large and small, that invest in people by providing high-quality training and good working conditions can compete and win in today's global markets.' – During her maiden speech, 12 July 1994.

Judith Church was born in 1953 and attended St Bernard's Convent School in Slough, before studying at the University of Leeds, where she gained a BA in mathematics and philosophy in 1975. She also studied at Huddersfield Polytechnic, Aston University and Thames Valley College. She became a trade union official and gained a reputation as a keen moderniser when she sat on Labour's ruling National Executive Committee from 1992 to 1994.

In the 1992 general election, she stood unsuccessfully for Labour in Stevenage. Then, in 1994, she was selected to contest a by-election in Dagenham after the sitting Labour MP, Bryan Gould, quit to return to his native New Zealand.

Judith became the third MP to serve Dagenham, increasing Labour's share of the vote from 52 per cent to 72 per cent.

In her maiden speech she described how Dagenham had the largest man-ufacturing workforce in London, as well as being a home for major compa-nies like Ford, GPT Telephone and Rhone Poulenc Rorer. 'Those companies have not succeeded through paying low wages and having poor working conditions and low health and safety standards. I know that because, before coming to the House, I worked in industry, including seven years as one of Her Majesty's inspectors of factories.'

That experience of industrial and factory life formed the basis of many of her contributions to debates during her seven years as an MP. She also took an interest in promoting the role of women in science and engineering, and introduced a Ten Minute Rule Bill outlining measures to increase the number of girls and women studying information technology. The other key strand of her work reflected her passion for modernising the House of Com-mons, which she thought would enable more people with young families to serve as MPs. She made a conscious decision not to seek office or any major position on a select committee.

When Judith was elected as an MP she had two young children, and she often spoke of the importance of being a part of their lives. She normally travelled to and from Parliament twice a day, so that she could be at home with her children in the evening and – as was often the case during this period – be present at the Commons for a 10 p.m. vote.

In 1999, she announced that she would not be seeking re-election. Friends were quoted as saying that she had been in poor health, and that she also found it difficult to meet the challenges of being a lone parent; her mar-riage had collapsed shortly before the 1997 election. Frustration at a lack of facilities and consideration for mothers in Parliament was also believed to have played a part in her decision. In the years after she stood down, Judith devoted most of her time and energy to her family.

DAME MARGARET HODGE

MEG HILLIER

- NAME: Margaret Eve Hodge (formerly Watson, née Oppenheimer)
- DATE OF BIRTH: 8 September 1944
- PLACE OF BIRTH: Cairo, Egypt
- DATE OF DEATH: –
- MARRIED TO: Andrew Watson (m. 1968; div. 1978); Henry Hodge (m. 1978; d. 2009)
- CHILDREN: One son and three daughters
- UNSUCCESSFUL ELECTIONS FOUGHT: None
- CONSTITUENCY: Barking
- DATE OF FIRST ELECTION: June 1994
- DATE LEFT PARLIAMENT: Incumbent
- PARTY ROLES: None
- MINISTERIAL POSITIONS & DATES: Parliamentary Under-Secretary for Employment and Equal Opportunities 1998–2001; Minister for Lifelong Learning, Further and Higher Education 2001–03; Minister for Children 2003–05; Minister for Work 2005–06; Minister for Industry and the Regions 2006–07; Minister for Culture, Creative Industries and Tourism 2007–08; Minister for Culture and Tourism 2009–10; shadow Minister for Culture and Tourism 2010

If Margaret Hodge had retired at sixty, her career would have been up there with some of the most eventful and colourful in British politics. Anyone writing her political obituary would also have acknowledged that she fiercely divided opinion. When I took over her Islington Council seat in 1994, constituents either loved her or loathed her. All had a story to tell. Margaret does not provoke ambivalence.

But that early career – elected to Islington Council in 1973, visionary chair of the Housing committee, leader for ten years during the bitter battles be-tween the Thatcher government and local government – has been eclipsed by her international achievements over the last eight years.

Ever the mistress of opportunity, Margaret surprised even herself when she transformed into a formidable tax campaigner at age sixty-seven – she has received rock-star standing ovations at international tax gatherings.

It would have been understandable if she had stepped away from politics after the death of her beloved second husband, Henry Hodge, in 2009. But the threat of the BNP, which had its eye on her east London Barking seat, spurred her back into the political fray. The challenge reignited a fire in her.

One long-standing friend to whom she turned when she considered running for Mayor of London described her as having more energy than most forty-year-olds. As someone a generation younger whose career has intertwined with hers, I have seen that energy first-hand. When you work with Margaret, or in her orbit, life is fast-paced, never dull and punctuated with sharp-tongued judgements.

Margaret can be quick to judge and does not hold back, as witnesses at Public Accounts committee hearings can testify. But in private, while she can still be harsh on people who have failed in their responsibilities, she's ready and willing to provide wise counsel.

Margaret was elected an MP for the first time aged fifty, but her political skills had been honed on Islington Council – the so-called socialist republic of Islington. She was spurred on to stand by changes in Islington, which were forcing out long-standing residents. Compared with neighbouring Finsbury, the pre-1964 Islington had had a woeful record on housing, with the Labour government of the day threatening to take it over. This meant that when Margaret became chair of the Housing committee, she inherited Georgian and Victorian private-sector housing stock. The plan was that a steamroller would roll down Archway hill to flatten this poor-quality street housing. Margaret led the battle to save Charteris Road in Finsbury Park and bought up the street properties for council housing. She wanted to provide quality homes for local people. The mantra among council officers acting on her orders was, 'If it doesn't move, buy it.' Since the 1990s, house prices have risen and made it practically impossible for a tenant to exercise their right to buy, meaning that the Hodge legacy lives on in the streetscape of Islington where council tenants live in listed Georgian properties. Margaret also led a huge building campaign of new council housing.

For a woman who courts publicity in the political sphere, her private life is just that – private. Her divorce from first husband Andrew Watson (she was eight months pregnant when she married lawyer Henry Hodge) is well documented. His death and the death of her daughter-in-law in 2017 in a road accident are also public knowledge. But for Margaret, family is central and private and she is a hands-on grandmother.

Her early years have shaped her outlook. Born Margaret Oppenheimer in Cairo in 1944 to Jewish refugee parents, German father and Austrian mother, her family then fled again, this time ending up in Orpington, south London, in 1950. Margaret has always described herself as feeling like an outsider and is very aware of her Jewishness – although she was baptised a Christian by her father to ease her entry into Britain. Her mother died when she was ten, but no one told the young Margaret and she did not even attend the funeral.

The rebellious teenager that emerged from this childhood experience can be seen in the local housing campaigner, the council leader who led a rate-capping rebellion and in the doughty tax campaigner. Margaret has no fear of authority and despite being firmly part of the establishment these days, she is still never afraid to take it on.

The Oppenheimer family interest in steel and its tax arrangements have also hit the headlines. However, as a tax campaigner and in her robust fashion, she went out and argued her corner head on.

I first met Margaret in 1994. I had just been elected to her former council seat in Islington North and she to Parliament. A year later I became chair of the Neighbourhood Services committee, which oversaw housing and social services delivered through the controversial decentralisation experiment that she had pioneered with councillor Maurice Barnes. The idea was that all services would be within pram-pushing distance (this before the days of the internet). She pioneered a customer-led, service delivery model and this consumer focus has been a feature of her political career.

Margaret may have left Islington Council, but she was still very present. Faced with huge housing challenges and a paltry £7 million housing capital budget, I pressed officers about how we could secure enough funding to meet local need, only to find that the most frequent answer to any suggestion was, 'Well, Mrs Hodge tried that…'

This may explain why she pursued the controversial Satman loans, borrowing at very high, 1980s interest rates that improved housing but saddled Islington with debt for years to come. In many ways, this was a forerunner to private finance initiatives under national governments. Now she would acknowledge she has come almost full circle in her concerns about saddling future generations with debt. For all that, the council tenants of Islington, who benefited from Satman, understood the difference it made.

One of her fellow councillors at the time says that she gambled on a Kinnock victory in 1992. It didn't happen and, as a result, the funds dried up and even as late as the late 1990s the unimproved council blocks that Satman had not reached were still awaiting refurbishment – a stark reminder of what Margaret sees as the power of municipal government for making change against the poor-quality housing that tenants are forced to live in if public investment is not available.

She was adept at handling the diverse Labour Group, which included a broad church of talent and political views. Her embrace of equalities issues, which saw her repeatedly making *Daily Mail* headlines about the Loony Left, are now mainstream – paid maternity leave, domestic violence support and support for gay rights among them.

A former council colleague highlights her skills as a political operator: 'Despite the numerous factions, she held us all together without the need for suspensions.' And Henry Hodge used to recall how Sunday nights were spent on the phone speaking to group members to make sure everyone was on board.

A low point in Margaret's career came when, in 1990, Liz Davies, a senior social worker in Islington, approached the *Evening Standard* with allegations of abuse in the borough's children's homes. When contacted by the paper, Margaret called her officers in, who assured her that there was no problem and dismissed the *Standard*'s reports as gutter journalism. She was later proved wrong and has thereafter always been sceptical, if not critical, of the answers given by officials.

Margaret stood down as leader of the council in 1992 and went to work at Pricewaterhouse Coopers. But when the Barking MP Jo Richardson died in 1994, the opportunity to enter parliamentary politics was too tempting. The selection campaign was one of the first under the Labour Party's new one member, one vote rules. She was elected in the subsequent by-election and joined former Islington councillors Jack Straw (who had been her deputy on the Housing committee) and Chris Smith in Parliament.

Margaret backed Tony Blair, her close neighbour in Islington, as leader on the death of John Smith in 1994. She became a minister in 1998 and held a number of ministerial posts, but never made it into the Cabinet. She once told me that she enjoyed being a minister of state, because it gave her the space to really get things done without having to ride the same level of public scrutiny that Cabinet ministers face.

She was the first minister to take compassionate leave – an unpaid year out as Arts minister so that she could care for Henry who had cancer. Barbara Follett covered her ministerial role in her absence.

Henry's death in 2009 was a shock. They had been a formidable political team since first meeting on Islington Council and publicly leaving their respective spouses for each other. Margaret brought a son and daughter to their family home from her first marriage and Margaret and Henry had two daughters of their own. In one interview, she describes walking through an airport on a family holiday with Henry and the children (the youngest then only one) and thinking *this is the best of times.* Commenting on this years later, she says poignantly, 'I wish I could have stopped the clock.'

Margaret has never been afraid to speak the truth as she sees it, even if it makes her unpopular. When she spoke about the challenges of immigration in communities like Barking, she was criticised by many. But when British National Party leader Nick Griffin declared he was going to fight her Barking seat, people were more willing to listen. The world's press descended on east London for that 2010 election and she roundly beat him.

The newly reinvigorated Margaret arrived in Parliament to plaudits from MPs of all parties. Under the Wright reforms, the 2010 parliament saw the first election of select committee chairs by fellow MPs of all parties. Margaret stood for the Public Accounts committee. In a tough race, she just won through on the final of five rounds.

It was in 2011 that she and the committee first uncovered concerns about tax settlements between HMRC and large corporate companies. I remember that in one of those very heated meetings she demanded an HMRC lawyer be made to swear on the Bible.

Thereafter, as well as the bread and butter of the Public Accounts committee work, she became the scourge of HMRC and big business. She got tax on the agenda by calling out practices that were a million miles from the experience of the average taxpayer or small business. I was with her for the ride and it was thrilling and breathless at times. We knew we were part of a historic shift, and the atmosphere in the committee room was sometimes electric. One Conservative member of the committee even used her picture on his 2015 election leaflets rather than David Cameron's.

As a result, the OECD took up the baton and international tax reporting rules changed in a two-year period. This would not have happened without the storm of publicity she generated.

After toying with the idea of running for Mayor of London, Margaret backed down, saying London needed a different sort of mayor. She has not retired gracefully – taking on a range of roles and writing a book. She still campaigns on tax transparency and in tax circles her name is recognisable the world over.

Professor Dame Margaret Hodge MBE MP has come a long way since arriving as a child in London in 1950. But the little German-speaking Jewish girl is still in there – still dreaming in German. Her strength is that she retains an outside perspective and continues to challenge the establishment.

HELEN LIDDELL

JULIA LANGDON

- FULL NAME: Helen Lawrie Liddell (née Reilly) PC, Baroness Liddell of Coatdyke
- DATE OF BIRTH: 6 December 1950
- PLACE OF BIRTH: Coatbridge
- DATE OF DEATH: –
- MARRIED TO: Alistair Liddell (m. 1972)
- CHILDREN: One son and one daughter
- UNSUCCESSFUL ELECTIONS FOUGHT: East Fife October 1974
- CONSTITUENCY: Monklands East 1994–97 and Airdrie & Shotts 1997–2005
- DATE OF FIRST ELECTION: 30 June 1994
- DATE LEFT PARLIAMENT: 11 April 2005
- PARTY ROLES: General secretary of the Labour Party in Scotland 1975–86
- MINISTERIAL POSITIONS & DATES: Economic Secretary to the Treasury 1997–98; Minister for Education and Industry 1998–99; Minister for Environment, Transport and the Regions 1999; Minister for Energy and Competitiveness in Europe 1999–2001; Secretary of State for Scotland 2001–03

The recurring factor that distinguished the career of Helen Liddell and in many ways defined it, was being the right woman in the right place at precisely the right time. To a certain extent she was lucky, but she was also streetwise, tough and – as the Scots would put it – doughty. Most of all, she was pragmatic. Like many politicians of her generation, she was the first member of her family to go to university, but she was also the first woman to run the Labour Party in Scotland, the first to be Secretary of State for Scotland and the first appointed British High Commissioner to Australia. Not bad for a bus driver's daughter – and when she went to Canberra, she took her old dad along too.

It was, after all, his influence as a shop steward that got her going in politics. She joined the Young Socialists as a schoolgirl at fifteen and, after receiving her economics degree from the University of Strathclyde, she took her new-found knowledge to the Scottish TUC, where she worked for five years. Then she spent what would prove to be a very useful year learning about journalism, as economics correspondent for BBC Scotland. In 1977, when rampant Scottish nationalism was threatening Labour's historic hold on the country's politics, it was a canny idea to appoint a woman as general secretary in Keir Hardie House. Helen Liddell was twenty-six when she was appointed and ran the place for eleven years.

She was in favour of devolution and had already starred in a TV commercial promoting Labour's plans for an assembly. In the run-up to the crucial 1979 devolution referendum, which helped to bring down the Labour government and put Margaret Thatcher in office, Liddell became a familiar figure to the Scottish electorate. More importantly for her, she got to know everyone who mattered, not just north of the border but in Westminster as well. They didn't like Thatcherism in Scotland and it was Liddell – or 'Little Nell' as they called her then – who was credited for Labour's continued dominance in Scotland through the 1980s. Emboldened by this, in 1985, Liddell stood as the right-wing candidate to be the party's general secretary in London but lost to Larry Whitty, Neil Kinnock's man on the soft left.

Liddell's next career move was a mistake, but only in retrospect. Her connections brought her the highly paid post of public affairs director for the *Daily Record* and the *Sunday Mail* in Scotland. At a time when the Mirror Group Newspapers mattered very much in Scotland, the position should have brought her power and influence, but the Scots didn't like that she was working for Robert Maxwell. She was said to be his eyes and ears in Scotland, and she was once filmed even following him into the gents – it turned out the ladies was behind the same door, but the damage was already done. During the four years that Liddell held the job, until Maxwell went off the boat, she didn't help her reputation by writing a novel about an auburn-haired Glaswegian politician on the make – the book featured lines like, 'Goddess or bitch? Both – and often at once' – which proclaimed itself to be the most exciting novel about women in politics and in the vein of Jeffrey Archer. Her own helmet of hair has always been a topic of debate in Scotland and the whole thing was meant to be a sort of joke, but if so, the Scots didn't get it. When she was done with helping to pick up the floating debris of the pensions scandal, it seemed as if it was her career that would need salvaging.

It didn't take long. Liddell kept her head down for a couple of years as a chief executive in a meaningful business venture programme, when news arrived that John Smith had passed away. Helen Liddell had already had one crack at Westminster, back in October 1974, when she contested the rock-solid Tory seat of East Fife; coming in a poor third and declaring that her parliamentary ambitions were over. Twenty years later, when the constituency in which she was born seemed up for the taking, things looked different. It was, by general consent, one of the ugliest by-elections in modern times; Monklands East was meant to be a safe seat, but there were issues of local corruption featuring the age-old west of Scotland religious divide between Catholics and Protestants, and the appeal of the Scottish Nationalists in the face of Labour complacency was compelling. Liddell, raised a Catholic and now caught in the maelstrom, wondered how she would live with herself if she lost John Smith's seat. It was a close call.

A new life beckoned. In 1997, she comfortably won a redistributed constituency; Labour held all its seats in Scotland and Tony Blair was triumphantly in office. The likes of Liddell, trusty, experienced apparatchiks whose loyalty would never be questioned, were bound to prosper. There was a bit of jostling for place among the Scottish ranks of aspirant ministers, but that was ever thus. She had been shadow Scotland Office minister when first elected and went into government in the junior job at the Treasury (economics: tick; pensions: tick) and was then bumped up to Minister of State at the Scottish Office with the important unwritten responsibilities of deputy to Scottish Secretary Donald Dewar and heading the first elections campaign for the new Scottish Parliament. She hit the nationalists hard, which wasn't popular with Gordon Brown and wouldn't play well for her later.

Once in every generation, one woman politician gets to be known as 'Stalin's granny' and now it was Liddell's turn. Her upward progress through the ministerial ranks continued, but when she made it to the Cabinet as Scottish Secretary in 2001, with the new Parliament up and running in Holyrood, the Scottish press started asking awkward questions such as: what is the point of Helen Liddell? It turned out she had time for French lessons in her comfortable ministerial schedule, and she was then mercilessly mocked as 'Helen Do-Little' and 'Minister for Monarch of the Glen' because she had visited the set of the TV programme. Two days after a defiant rearguard action – 'I've still got a career in front of me,' she insisted – the government announced that her job was being rolled into the Department of Constitutional Affairs. The Scottish press rejoiced that her departure was the only palatable bit in a constitutional dog's breakfast.

And it looked as if that was that. Liddell announced that she would stand down at the next election, in 2005, to spend more time with her family – this was before she realised that she would be in Australia, thanks to a valuable consolation prize for unswerving loyalty to Tony Blair. She returned after a surprisingly successful four years – they liked her Glaswegian street-fighting style down under – to the further compensations of the House of Lords. She makes herself useful on official inquiries, trying to help withstand the nationalist tide, speaking on Brexit and practising a little light journalism. In a *Prospect* article as this book went to press in 2018, she opined on the prospects of trade with, for example, Australia. 'The future will not be secured by trading Irn Bru for Sauvignon Blanc,' she wrote. That's Helen Liddell. Down to earth. Ever the pragmatist.

ROSEANNA CUNNINGHAM

ELAINE GIBB

- FULL NAME: Roseanna Cunningham
- DATE OF BIRTH: 27 July 1951
- PLACE OF BIRTH: Glasgow
- DATE OF DEATH: –
- MARRIED TO: Unmarried
- CHILDREN: None
- UNSUCCESSFUL ELECTIONS FOUGHT: Perth and Kinross 1992
- CONSTITUENCY: Perth & Kinross 1995–97 and Perth 1997–2001
- DATE OF FIRST ELECTION: 25 May 1995
- DATE LEFT PARLIAMENT: 7 June 2001
- MSP: Perth 1999–2011 and Perthsire South & Kinross-shire 2011–present
- PARTY ROLES: Depute leader of the SNP 2000–04
- MINISTERIAL POSITIONS & DATES: None in the UK government. In Scottish government: Minister for Environment 2009–11; Minister for Environment and Climate Change 2010–11; Minister for Community Safety and Legal Affairs 2011–14; Secretary for Fair Work, Skills and Training 2014–16 and Secretary for Environment, Climate Change and Land Reform since May 2016
- MOST FAMOUS QUOTATION: 'I don't believe the monarchy should have any role in Scottish politics, or indeed in British politics, and I have long believed that we should have an elected head of state.'

Roseanna Cunningham's main battle in the 1995 Perth and Kinross by-election was not persuading the traditionally Tory Perthshire to elect a left-wing feminist nationalist, it was securing her own party's nomination to fight the seat. A furore around a former love affair led Cunningham to initially withdraw her name from the race. Luckily, she was persuaded to reconsider and went on to win the nomination – and eventually the seat.

Cunningham grew up far from Scotland, near another place called Perth.

When Roseanna was nine years old, the Cunningham family emigrated to Australia, settling in Fremantle, where Roseanna attended school. In 1976, she graduated from the University of Western Australia with a degree in politics. Then she did what she'd always vowed she would – packed up and came home.

Within a few months of returning to Scotland, Cunningham was working as a researcher for the SNP, which she had joined in 1969 while still in Australia. She worked for the party for two years before returning to her studies, gaining a law degree from the University of Edinburgh then a diploma in legal practice from the University of Aberdeen. Stints as a solicitor in local government and private practice followed, before she joined the Faculty of Advocates in 1990. A career in Parliament must have seemed like a natural next step. When Cunningham arrived at the House of Commons in 1995, she swelled the SNP's parliamentary ranks to four and was only the seventh Scottish woman MP. Despite picking up some portfolios from colleagues eager to share them out, she kept a fairly low profile as an MP, concentrating on constituency work. Cunningham held her seat at the general election two years later, the first ever SNP by-election victor to do so.

Cunningham is nicknamed 'Republican Rose' for her long-held anti-monarchy stance. When sworn in at Westminster in 1997, she took the oath of allegiance to the Queen, only to add 'she lied' under her breath. In later years, whenever Her Majesty has addressed the Scottish Parliament, Cunningham has found business to attend to elsewhere. On this issue, her stance is at odds with SNP policy: the party wants the Queen and her successors to be head of state in an independent Scotland.

Cunningham must have begun her second term at Westminster with an inkling that it was likely to be her last. Labour's general election victory set the wheels in motion for a devolved Scottish Parliament. Despite regarding devolution as 'half a loaf', Cunningham stood for the new Parliament. She was elected in 1999 as the constituency MSP for Perth. Initially, she held a dual mandate, continuing to sit in the UK Parliament, too, until standing down at the 2001 general election. She has been an MSP ever since, and since 2009 has held various ministerial posts in the Scottish government. Cunningham has been Cabinet Secretary for Environment, Climate Change and Land Reform since May 2016, and has said she 'couldn't have asked for a post that would have been a better fit for me'.

Cunningham's appointment to Nicola Sturgeon's first Cabinet came as a surprise to some, given that the 2004 SNP leadership contest drove a wedge between these two formerly close friends. Cunningham, then depute leader, was quick to announce her bid to succeed John Swinney. She immediately became the odds-on favourite, but she didn't bet on Sturgeon standing against her, nor on the party's former leader Alex Salmond, the 'King over the Water', returning to reclaim his throne. Sturgeon made a pact with Salmond to run as his depute and stood aside. When the votes were counted, Cunningham came a distant second. She has not stood for office in the party since.

Away from politics, Cunningham enjoys reading and goes on walking holidays, at home and abroad, whenever she can find the time. She is also a sci-fi addict and a Trekkie who, at least when she was first elected, shared her small flat with a life-size cardboard cut-out of Mr Spock.

Roseanna Cunningham's by-election win gave her a fast pass to the SNP's top ranks at an important time for the party. Soon after, the Scottish Parliament was established, and the SNP began its slow transformation into the party of government it is today. This is a woman who's been a 'senior nationalist' for more than twenty years, through two Parliaments, three leaders, and five ministerial jobs. She has lived long and prospered.

CONTRIBUTORS

HEIDI ALEXANDER was the Labour MP for Lewisham East from 2010 to 2018.

RUSHANARA ALI is the Labour MP for Bethnal Green & Bow.

SHAZIA AWAN-SCULLY is a broadcaster and former Conservative candidate.

KEMI BADENOCH is the Conservative MP for Saffron Walden.

LIZ BARKER is a Liberal Democrat peer.

MARY BEARD is a professor of classics at the University of Cambridge.

MARGARET BECKETT is the Labour MP for Derby South.

ANNE BEGG was the Labour MP for Aberdeen South from 1997 to 2015.

NATALIE BENNETT is a former leader of the Green Party.

LUCIANA BERGER is the Labour MP for Liverpool Wavertree.

POLLY BILLINGTON is a former Labour candidate and adviser.

VIRGINIA BOTTOMLEY is a Conservative peer.

AMBER DE BOTTON is a political journalist.

LYN BROWN is the Labour MP for West Ham.

ANGELA BROWNING is a Conservative peer.

JOANNA CHERRY is the SNP MP for Edinburgh South West.

PAM CHESTERS is a former Conservative candidate.

SARAH CHILDS is a professor of politics at Birkbeck, University of London.

ANN CLWYD is the Labour MP for Cynon Valley.

THERESE COFFEY is the Conservative MP for Suffolk Coastal.

YVETTE COOPER is the Labour MP for Normanton, Pontefract & Castleford.

CHRISTINE CRAWLEY is a Labour peer.

TRACEY CROUCH is the Conservative MP for Chatham & Aylesford.

EDWINA CURRIE was Conservative MP for South Derbyshire from 1983 to 1997.

JAGRUTI DAVE is a broadcast journalist.

RUTH DAVIDSON is leader of the Scottish Conservative Party.

THANGAM DEBBONAIRE is the Labour MP for Bristol West.

ANNABELLE DICKSON is a political journalist.

NADINE DORRIES is the Conservative MP for Mid Bedfordhire.

MARIA EAGLE is the Labour MP for Liverpool Garston & Halewood.

JULIE ELLIOTT is the Labour MP for Sunderland Central.

SUZANNE EVANS is a former UKIP deputy chairwoman.

LYNNE FEATHERSTONE is a Liberal Democrat peer.

LUCY FISHER is a political journalist.

COLLEEN FLETCHER is the Labour MP for Coventry North East.

JANET FOOKES is a Conservative peer.

VICKY FOXCROFT is the Labour MP for Lewisham Deptford.

OONAGH GAY is a political historian.

NUSRAT GHANI is the Conservative MP for Wealden.

ELAINE GIBB is a communications professional and former political journalist.

DAME CHERYL GILLAN is the Conservative MP for Chesham & Amersham.

LINDA GILROY was the Labour MP for Plymouth Sutton from 1997 to 2010.

ANNABEL GOLDIE is a Conservative peer.

JULIA GOLDSWORTHY was the Liberal Democrat MP for Falmouth & Cambourne from 2005 to 2010.

ELINOR GOODMAN is a political journalist.

JOYCE GOULD is a Labour peer.

MIRANDA GREEN is a political journalist.

OLLY GRENDER is a Liberal Democrat peer.

LOUISE HAIGH is the Labour MP for Sheffield Heeley from 2001 to 2015.

HELEN HAYES is the Labour MP for Dulwich & West Norwood.

SUE HAYMAN is the Labour MP for Workington.

SARAH HAYWARD is a former Labour leader of Camden Council.

AYESHA HAZARIKA is a political commentator and broadcaster.

MEG HILLIER is the Labour MP for Hackney South & Shoreditch.

SHARON HODGSON is the Labour MP for Washington & Sunderland West.

MARY HONEYBALL is Labour MEP for London.

ANNE JENKIN is a Conservative peer.

SALLY KEEBLE was the Labour MP for Northampton North from 1997 to 2010.

HELENA KENNEDY is a Labour peer and barrister.

JULIE KIRKBRIDE was the Conservative MP for Bromsgrove from 1997 to 2010.

SUSAN KRAMER is a Liberal Democrat peer.

ELEANOR LAING is the Conservative MP for Epping Forest.

JUSTINE LANCASTER is a political adviser.

JULIA LANGDON is a political journalist and biographer.

CAROLINE LUCAS is the Green Party MP for Brighton Pavilion.

HOLLY LYNCH is the Labour MP for Halifax.

SARAH MACKINLAY is a political journalist.

FIONA MACTAGGART was the Labour MP for Slough from 1997 to 2017.

DEBORAH MATTINSON is a political pollster.

SCARLETT MCCGWIRE is a political adviser.

LINDA MCDOUGALL is a political journalist and author.

ANNE MCGUIRE was the Labour MP for Stirling from 1997 to 2015.

ANN MCKECHIN was the Labour MP for Glasgow Maryhill from 2001 to 2005 and Glasgow North from 2005 to 2015.

ESTHER MCVEY is the Conservative MP for Tatton.

JANE MERRICK is a political journalist.

GILLIAN MERRON was the Labour MP for Lincoln from 1997 to 2010.

FIONA MILLAR is a journalist and educationalist.

JULIE MORGAN was the Labour MP for Cardiff North from 1997 to 2010.

NICKY MORGAN is the Conservative MP for Loughborough.

ESTELLE MORRIS was the Labour MP for Birmingham Erdington from 1992 to 2005.

MEG MUNN was the Labour MP for Sheffield Heeley from 2001 to 2015.

JO-ANNE NADLER is a political journalist and biographer.

SARAH NEWTON is the Conservative MP for Truro & Falmouth.

KATE OSAMOR is the Labour MP for Edmonton.

ELIZABETH PEACOCK was the Conservative MP for Batley & Spen from 1983 to 1997.

BRIDIE PEARSON-JONES is a journalist and writer.

KATHRYN PERERA is a barrister and NHS innovator.

LINDA PERHAM was the Labour MP for Ilford North from 1997 to 2005.

ANNE PERKINS is a political journalist.

CLAIRE PERRY is the Conservative MP for Devizes.

JESS PHILLIPS is the Labour MP for Birmingham Yardley.

CAROLINE PIDGEON is a Liberal Democrat member of the London Assembly.

CAROLYN QUINN is a political journalist and broadcaster.

MARY READER is a political researcher.

RACHEL REEVES is the Labour MP for Leeds West.

EMMA REYNOLDS is the Labour MP for Wolverhampton North East.

LAURA SANDYS was the Conservative MP for South Thanet from 2010 to 2015.

JANET SEATON is a political historian.

TULIP SIDDIQ is the Labour MP for Hampstead & Kilburn.

NAN SLOANE is director of the Centre for Women and Democracy.

RUTH SMEETH is the Labour MP for Stoke-on-Trent North.

ANGELA SMITH is the Labour MP for Penistone & Stocksbridge.

CAT SMITH is the Labour MP for Lancaster & Fleetwood.

JACQUI SMITH was the Labour MP for Redditch from 1997 to 2010.

KARIN SMYTH is the Labour MP for Bristol South.

KATHRYN STANCZYSZYN is a broadcast journalist.

GISELA STUART was the Labour MP for Birmingham Edgbaston from 1997 to 2017.

ALISON SUTTIE is a Liberal Democrat peer.

JO SWINSON is the Liberal Democrat MP for East Dunbartonshire.

EMILY THORNBERRY is the Labour MP for Islington South & Finsbury.

MAGGIE THROUP is the Conservative MP for Erewash.

ANNE-MARIE TREVELYAN is the Conservative MP for Berwick-upon-Tweed.

ELIZABETH TRUSS is the Conservative MP for South West Norfolk.

KITTY USSHER was the Labour MP for Burnley from 2005 to 2010.

ELIZABETH VALLANCE is a political academic and writer.

CAROLE WALKER is a political journalist and broadcaster.

CATHERINE WEST is the Labour MP for Hornsey & Wood Green.

ANN WIDDECOMBE was the Conservative MP for Maidstone & The Weald from 1987 to 2010.

KIRSTY WILLIAMS is a Liberal Democrat member of the Welsh Assembly.

ZOE WILLIAMS is a political journalist.

FEMALE MPS INDEX

560PP HARDBACK, £30

The 1997 general election resulted in a landslide victory for female representation in Parliament. Nearly eighty years on from the historic Act that afforded women the right to stand for election to the Commons, a record-breaking 120 of them were elected. This was double the number of women elected in 1992 – indicating that the tide was turning in Westminster. Today, 491 women have taken their seats on the famed green benches of the Commons.

The second, hotly anticipated volume of *The Honourable Ladies* will include profiles of every female MP elected between 1997 and 2019, shining a light on the stories of more pioneering women who continue to fight for their constituents, campaign for reform and instigate change in the Commons. Women to have joined the Chamber since 1997 include Prime Minister Theresa May, Labour Party stalwart Yvette Cooper, former Home Secretary Amber Rudd and leader of the Green Party Caroline Lucas.

384PP HARDBACK, £20

As a young civil servant, Caroline Slocock became the first ever female private secretary to any British Prime Minister, and was at Margaret Thatcher's side for the final eighteen months of her premiership. A left-wing feminist, Slocock was no natural ally – and yet she became fascinated by the woman behind the 'Iron Lady' façade and by how she dealt with a world dominated by men.

As events inexorably led to Margaret Thatcher's downfall, Slocock observed the vulnerabilities and contradictions of the woman considered by many to be the ultimate anti-feminist. When Thatcher eventually resigned, brought down by her closest political allies, Slocock was the only woman present to witness the astonishing scenes in the Cabinet Room. Had Thatcher been a man, it would have ended very differently, Slocock feels.

Now, in this vivid first-hand account, based on her diaries from the time and interviews with other key Downing Street personnel, Slocock paints a nuanced portrait of a woman who to this day is routinely demonised in sexist ways. Reflecting on the challenges women still face in public life, Slocock concludes it's time to rewrite how we portray powerful women and for women to set aside politics and accept that Margaret Thatcher was 'one of us'.

496PP HARDBACK, £25

As the party that has won wars, reversed recessions and held prime ministerial power more times than any other, the Conservatives have played an undoubtedly crucial role in the shaping of contemporary British society. And yet, the leaders who have stood at its helm — from Sir Robert Peel to David Cameron, via Benjamin Disraeli, Winston Churchill and Margaret Thatcher — have steered the party vessel with enormously varying degrees of success.

With the widening of the franchise, revolutionary changes to social values and the growing ubiquity of the media, the requirements, techniques and goals of Conservative leadership since the party's nineteenth-century factional breakaway have been forced to evolve almost beyond recognition — and not all its leaders have managed to keep up.

This comprehensive and enlightening book considers the attributes and achievements of each leader in the context of their respective time and diplomatic landscape, offering a compelling analytical framework by which they may be judged, detailed personal biographies from some of the country's foremost political critics, and exclusive interviews with former leaders themselves.

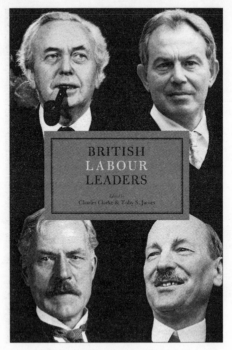

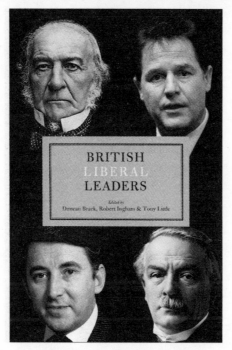